STREET ATLAS

Norfolk

www.philips-maps.co.uk

First published in 2003 by
Philip's, a division of
Octopus Publishing Group Ltd
www.octopusbooks.co.uk
Carmelite House
50 Victoria Embankment
London EC4Y 0DZ
An Hachette UK Company
www.hachette.co.uk

Fourth edition with interim revision 2016
First impression 2016
NORDA

ISBN 978-1-84907-428-5 (spiral)

© Philip's 2016

Map data
This product includes mapping data licensed from Ordnance Survey® with the permission of the Controller of Her Majesty's Stationery Office.
© Crown copyright 2016. All rights reserved. Licence number 100011710.

Contents

III	**Key to map symbols**
IV	**Key to map pages**
VI	**Route planning**
X	Major administrative and Postcode boundaries

1	**Street maps** at 1¾ inches to 1 mile
132	**Street maps** at 3½ inches to 1 mile
178	**Street map of Norwich city centre** at 7 inches to 1 mile

| 179 | **Index** of towns and villages, streets, hospitals, industrial estates, railway stations, schools, shopping centres, universities and places of interest |

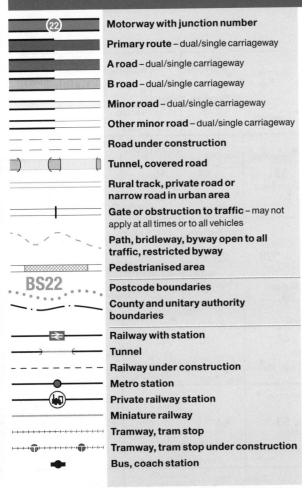

Key to map symbols

Motorway with junction number	
Primary route – dual/single carriageway	
A road – dual/single carriageway	
B road – dual/single carriageway	
Minor road – dual/single carriageway	
Other minor road – dual/single carriageway	
Road under construction	
Tunnel, covered road	
Rural track, private road or narrow road in urban area	
Gate or obstruction to traffic – may not apply at all times or to all vehicles	
Path, bridleway, byway open to all traffic, restricted byway	
Pedestrianised area	
Postcode boundaries	
County and unitary authority boundaries	
Railway with station	
Tunnel	
Railway under construction	
Metro station	
Private railway station	
Miniature railway	
Tramway, tram stop	
Tramway, tram stop under construction	
Bus, coach station	

BS22

Ambulance station
Coastguard station
Fire station
Police station
Accident and Emergency entrance to hospital
H Hospital
+ Place of worship
i Information centre – open all year
Shopping centre, parking
Park and Ride, Post Office
Camping site, caravan site
Golf course, picnic site
Non-Roman antiquity, Roman antiquity

Church   ROMAN FORT

Univ   Important buildings, schools, colleges, universities and hospitals

Woods, built-up area

River Medway   Water name
River, weir
Stream
Canal, lock, tunnel
Water
Tidal water

58 87
246

Adjoining page indicators and overlap bands – the colour of the arrow and band indicates the scale of the adjoining or overlapping page (see scales below)

The dark grey border on the inside edge of some pages indicates that the mapping does not continue onto the adjacent page

The small numbers around the edges of the maps identify the 1-kilometre National Grid lines

Abbreviations

Acad	Academy	Meml	Memorial
Allot Gdns	Allotments	Mon	Monument
Cemy	Cemetery	Mus	Museum
C Ctr	Civic centre	Obsy	Observatory
CH	Club house	Pal	Royal palace
Coll	College	PH	Public house
Crem	Crematorium	Recn Gd	Recreation ground
Ent	Enterprise		
Ex H	Exhibition hall	Resr	Reservoir
Ind Est	Industrial Estate	Ret Pk	Retail park
IRB Sta	Inshore rescue boat station	Sch	School
		Sh Ctr	Shopping centre
Inst	Institute	TH	Town hall / house
Ct	Law court	Trad Est	Trading estate
L Ctr	Leisure centre	Univ	University
LC	Level crossing	W Twr	Water tower
Liby	Library	Wks	Works
Mkt	Market	YH	Youth hostel

Enlarged maps only

Railway or bus station building

Place of interest

Parkland

The map scale on the pages numbered in green is 1¾ inches to 1 mile
2.76 cm to 1 km • 1:36206

0	½ mile	1 mile	1½ miles	2 miles
0	500m 1 km	1½ km	2km	

The map scale on the pages numbered in blue is 3½ inches to 1 mile
5.52 cm to 1 km • 1:18103

0	¼ mile	½ mile	¾ mile	1 mile
0	250m 500m	750m	1km	

The map scale on the pages numbered in red is 7 inches to 1 mile
11.04 cm to 1 km • 1:9051

0	220yds	440yds	660yds	½ mile
0	125m 250m	375m	500m	

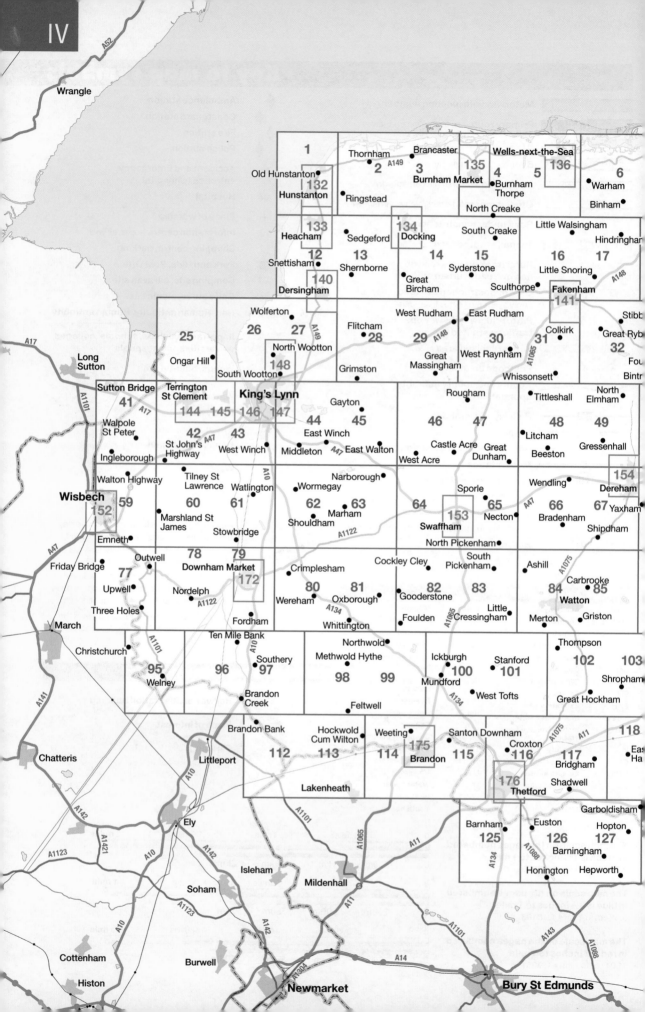

Wrangle

Old Hunstanton

1

Thornham

Brancaster

2 A149

3

135

Wells-next-the-Sea

4

Burnham Thorpe

5

136

6

Warham

Binham

Burnham Market

North Creake

Hunstanton

132

Ringstead

Heacham

133

Sedgeford

134

Docking

South Creake

Little Walsingham

Hindringha

12

13

14

15

16

17

Snettisham

Shernborne

Syderstone

Little Snoring

Dersingham

140

Great Bircham

Sculthorpe

Fakenham

141

Wolferton

West Rudham

East Rudham

Stibb

Great Ryb

25

26

27

Flitcham

28

29 A148

30

31

Colkirk

32

Fou

Bintr

Ongar Hill

North Wootton

148

Grimston

Great Massingham

West Raynham

Whissonsett

Long Sutton

South Wootton

Rougham

Tittleshall

North Elmham

Sutton Bridge

Terrington St Clement

King's Lynn

Gayton

144 **145**

146 **147**

44

45

46

47

48

49

41

Walpole St Peter

42

St John's Highway

43

West Winch

East Winch

Middleton

East Walton

West Acre

Castle Acre

Great Dunham

Litcham

Beeston

Gressenhall

Ingleborough

Walton Highway

Tilney St Lawrence

Watlington

Narborough

Wormegay

Sporle

Wendling

154

Dereham

Yaxham

59

60

61

62

63

64

153

65

66

67

Wisbech

152

Marshland St James

Stowbridge

Shouldham

Marham

Swaffham

Necton

Bradenham

Shipdham

Emneth

North Pickenham

Friday Bridge

Upwell

77

Outwell

78

Downham Market

79

172

Crimplesham

Cockley Cley

South Pickenham

Ashill

Carbrooke

80

81

82

83

84

85

Nordelph

Wereham

Oxborough

Gooderstone

Watton

Three Holes

A1122

Fordham

Whittington

Foulden

Little Cressingham

Merton

Griston

March

Christchurch

Ten Mile Bank

Northwold

Thompson

95

96

97

98

99

100

101

102

103

Welney

Southery

Methwold Hythe

Ickburgh

Stanford

Shropha

Chatteris

Brandon Creek

Mundford

West Tofts

Great Hockham

Feltwell

Brandon Bank

Hockwold Cum Wilton

Weeting

Santon Downham

Croxton

118

Eas

Ha

112

113

114

175

Brandon

115

116

117

Bridgham

Littleport

Lakenheath

176

Thetford

Shadwell

Garboldisham

Ely

Barnham

Euston

Hopton

125

126

127

Mildenhall

Barningham

Isleham

Honington

Hepworth

Soham

Cottenham

Burwell

Newmarket

Bury St Edmunds

Histon

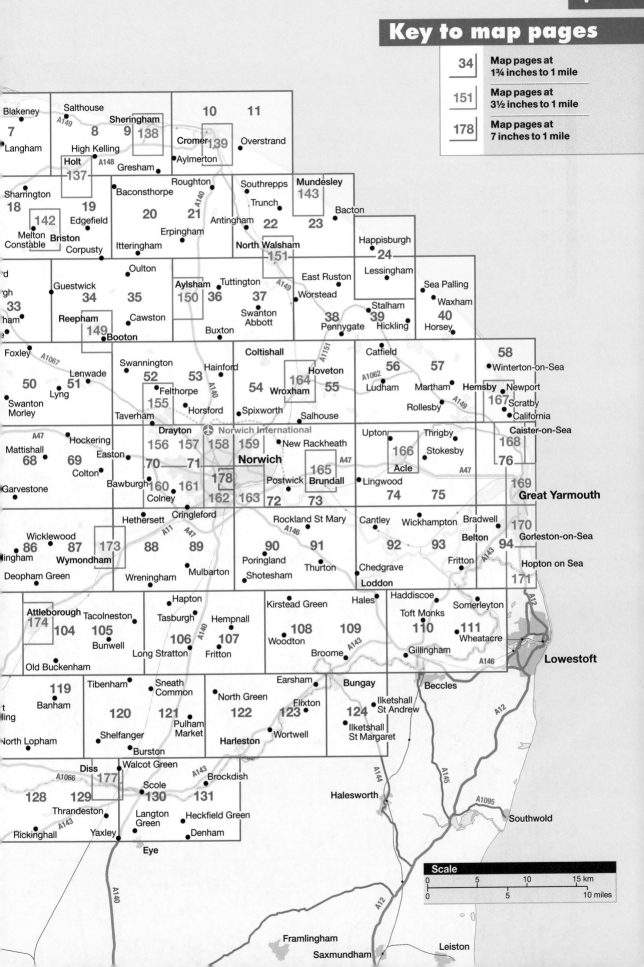

Key to map pages

34	**Map pages at** 1¾ inches to 1 mile
151	**Map pages at** 3½ inches to 1 mile
178	**Map pages at** 7 inches to 1 mile

Blakeney **7** Langham

Salthouse **8** A149

Sheringham **9** **138** Cromer **139** High Kelling **Holt 137** A148 Gresham Aylmerton Overstrand

10 **11**

Sharrington **18** Edgefield **19** **142** Melton Constable **Briston** Corpusty

Baconsthorpe Roughton **20** **21** Erpingham Antingham Itteringham **North Walsham 151**

Southrepps Trunch **22** **Mundesley 143** **23** Bacton

Happisburgh **24** Lessingham

'd 'gh 'ham **33** Guestwick **34** **35** Oulton Cawston **Reepham 149** **Booton** Tuttington **Aylsham 150** **36** **37** Swanton Abbott Buxton

East Ruston Worstead **38** Pennygate Stalham **39** Hickling Sea Palling Waxham **40** Horsey

Foxley A1067 Lenwade **50** **51** Lyng Swanton Morley

Swannington **52** **53** Hainford Felthorpe **155** Horsford Taverham

Coltishall **54** **Hoveton 164** **Wroxham** **55** A1151 A1062 Ludham Catfield **56** **57** Martham Rollesby **58** Winterton-on-Sea **Hemsby** **167** Newport Scratby California

Spixworth Salhouse

Hockering **68** Mattishall A47 **69** Easton Colton **156** **157** **158** **159** Drayton Norwich International **70** **71** **Norwich** New Rackheath **160** **161** **178** **162** **163** **72** Colney Postwick **73** Bawburgh

Upton **166** Thrigby Stokesby **Acle** A47 Lingwood **74** **75** A47 Caister-on-Sea **168** **76** **169** **Great Yarmouth**

Garvestone

Cringleford Hethersett **88** **89** Wicklewood **86** **87** **173** **Wymondham** Wreningham Mulbarton Deopham Green

Rockland St Mary A146 **90** **91** Poringland Thurton Shotesham

Cantley Wickhampton **92** **93** Chedgrave **Loddon** Bradwell **Belton** **94** Fritton A143 Gorleston-on-Sea **170** Hopton on Sea **171**

Hapton **Attleborough 174** **104** Tacolneston **105** Bunwell Tasburgh **106** **107** Fritton Hempnall Long Stratton Old Buckenham

Kirstead Green **108** **109** Woodton Broome A143 Hales Haddiscoe Toft Monks **110** Gillingham **111** Wheatacre Somerleyton A12 **Lowestoft**

119 Banham North Lopham Tibenham Sneath Common **120** **121** Shelfanger Pulham Market Burston

North Green **122** **Harleston** Earsham Flixton **123** Wortwell **Bungay** Ilketshall St Andrew **124** Ilketshall St Margaret Beccles A145

128 **129** Thrandeston A143 Rickinghall Yaxley **Diss** **177** Walcot Green Scole **130** Langton Green **131** Heckfield Green Denham **Eye** A1066 Brockdish A143 Halesworth A1095 Southwold

Framlingham Saxmundham Leiston

A140 A144 A12

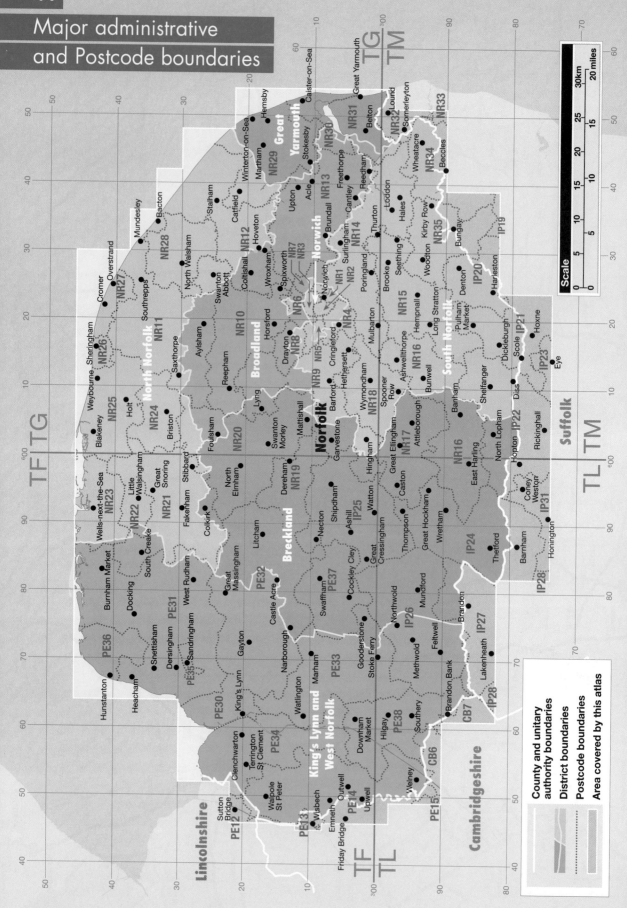

Scale: 1¾ inches to 1 mile
¼ ½ mile
250m 500m 750m 1 km

A B C D E F

8

45

7

BROADWATER RD

44

6

BEACH RD

Peddars Way & Norfolk Coast Path

WESTGATE RD

43

A149

132

CH Hotel

Old Hunstanton

GOLF COURSE ROAD

WODEHOUSE RD

WATSON'S RD

Motel

5

St Edmund's Point

HAMILTON RD

OLD HUNSTANTON RD

PO

CHURCH RD

Chalkpit Wood

Birthday Wood

42

LIGHTHOUSE CL

St Edmund's Chapel

CLIFF PARADE B1161

BELGRAVE AVE

BERNARD CRESCENT

PEDDARS DR

CLAREN CE RD

CHAPEL BANK

Hunstanton Hall

Deodara Wood

CROMER ROAD

Kimberley Plantation

Ilex Wood

4

VICTORIA AVE

Glebe House Sch

PE36

Ada Grove

Heart Plantation

Sensory Park

HUNSTANTON

Hunstanton Park Earthwork

132

Cross

HARTLEY CL

NURS ERY DR

DOWNS RD

Lodge Farm

Oak Grove

Half Moon Plantation

41

3

GREEVEGATE

WESTGATE

Liby

CRESCENT LA

SANDRINGHAM RD

KING'S LYNN RD

Smithdon High Sch

Hunstanton Sea Life Sanctuary

MELTON DR

Cemy

Old Bank Wood

SEAGATE RD

WA

South Hill Wood

Larch Plantation

40

SOUTHEND ROAD

SOUTH BEACH RD

B1161 OASIS WAY

St Andrew's Chapel (remains of)

Downs Farm

Hill Wood

Ringstead Downs Nature Reserve

BISHOP'S RD

MANOR RD

WINDSOR RISE

PRINCESS DR

REDGATE HILL

SOUTH BEACH ROAD

2

The Firs

Redgate Hill

Ringstead Downs

CH

39

Searles Golf Course

Pit

NORTH BEACH

PE31

Manor Farm

MANOR RD

HALL CL

HUNSTANTON RD

Long Wood

RINGSTEAD ROAD

133

Whin Covert

1

ROBIN HILL

Ind Est

Little Wood

GARDENERS CT

Heacham Park

A149

CHURCH FARM RD

Church Farm

38

64 A 65 B 66 C 67 D 68 E 69 F

132

132

133

133

12

133

2

For full street detail of the highlighted area see page 132

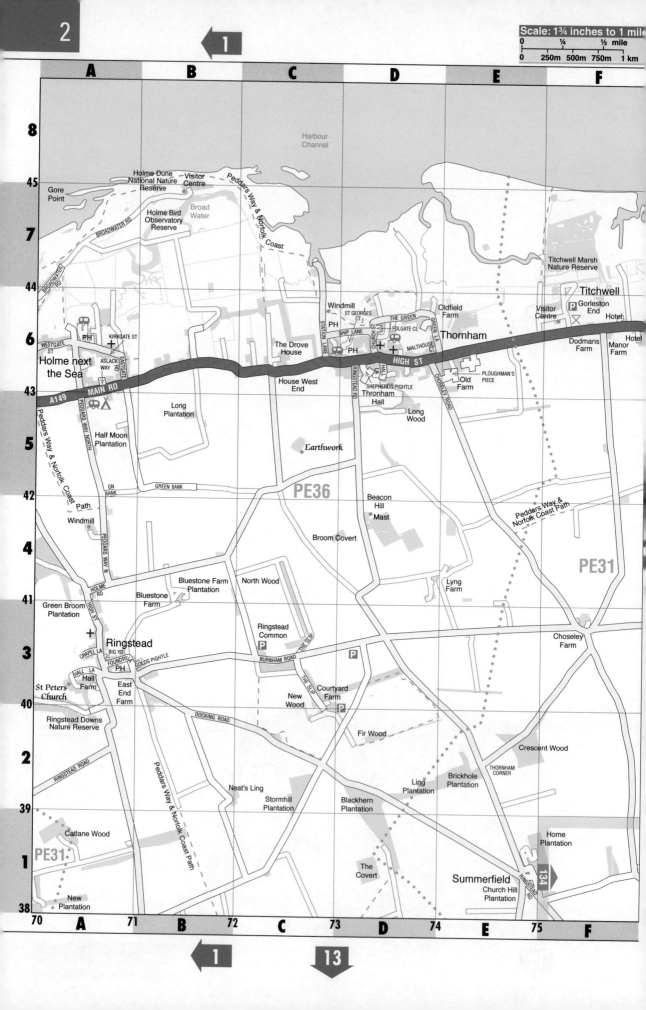

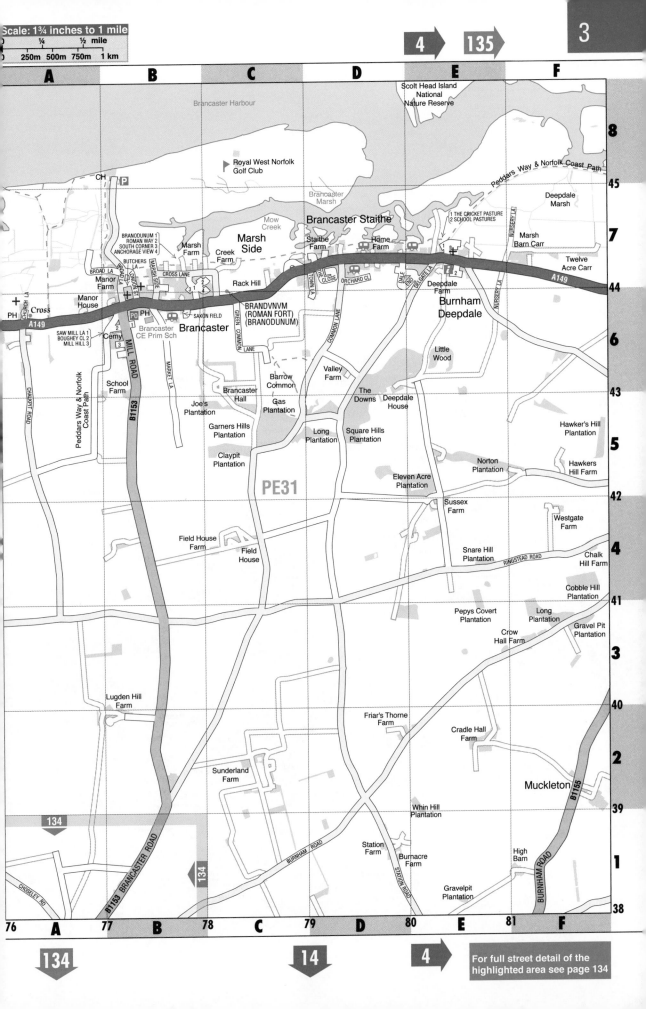

A   B   C   D   E   F

Brancaster Harbour

Scolt Head Island
National
Nature Reserve

8

Royal West Norfolk
Golf Club

Peddars Way & Norfolk Coast Path

45

CH P

Brancaster
Marsh

Deepdale
Marsh

7

Mow
Creek

Brancaster Staithe

1 THE CRICKET PASTURE
2 SCHOOL PASTURES

Marsh
Barn Carr

Marsh
Side

Marsh
Farm

Staithe
Farm

Home
Farm

Twelve
Acre Carr

BRANODUNUM 1
ROMAN WAY 2
SOUTH CORNER 3
ANCHORAGE VIEW 4

Creek
Farm

BROAD LA

BUTCHERS
LA

CROSS ST

CROSS LANE

MARSH SIDE

Manor
Farm

THE CLOSE

TOWN LA

ORCHARD CL

DALE
END

THE GATE LA

Deepdale
Farm

A149

44

CH

+

+

Manor
House

Rack Hill

Burnham
Deepdale

PH + Cross

A149

BRANDVNVM
(ROMAN FORT)
(BRANODUNUM)

SAXON FIELD

GREEN COMMON

COMMON LANE

NURSERY LA

6

SAW MILL LA 1
BOUGHEY CL 2
MILL HILL 3

PO PH

Cemy

1

Brancaster
CE Prim Sch

Brancaster

Little
Wood

CHALKPIT ROAD

MILL ROAD

MARKET LA

2
3

School
Farm

Valley
Farm

Barrow
Common

Peddars Way & Norfolk Coast Path

B1153

Brancaster
Hall

Gas
Plantation

The
Downs

Deepdale
House

43

Joe's
Plantation

Long
Plantation

Square Hills
Plantation

Hawker's Hill
Plantation

5

Garners Hills
Plantation

Hawkers
Hill Farm

Claypit
Plantation

Eleven Acre
Plantation

Norton
Plantation

PE31

42

Sussex
Farm

Westgate
Farm

Field House
Farm

Field
House

Snare Hill
Plantation

Ringstead Road

Chalk
Hill Farm

4

Cobble Hill
Plantation

41

Pepys Covert
Plantation

Long
Plantation

Gravel Pit
Plantation

Crow
Hall Farm

3

Lugden Hill
Farm

40

Friar's Thorne
Farm

Cradle Hall
Farm

2

Muckleton

B1155

Sunderland
Farm

39

134

BRANCASTER ROAD

Whin Hill
Plantation

BURNHAM ROAD

134

Station
Farm

High
Barn

BURNHAM ROAD

1

B1153

Burnacre
Farm

STATION ROAD

CHOSELEY RD

Gravelpit
Plantation

38

76   A   77   B   78   C   79   D   80   E   81   F

◀ 3

Scale: 1¾ inches to 1 mile

0   ¼   ½   mile
0   250m 500m 750m 1 km

A   B   C   D   E   F

8

Norton
Creek

Scolt Head Island
National Nature Reserve

Gun Hill

Trowland Creek

Burrow Gap

Meals House

45

Peddars Way & Norfolk Coast Walk

135

Fort

7

Overy Marsh

Burnham Overy Staithe

Overy Marshes

Decoy Wood

BONE'S DRIVE

Gun Hill Farm

Marsh Farm

Hotel

WELLS ROAD

Marsh House Farm

Dale Hole

44

Dairy Farm

TOWER ROAD

A149

A149

GONG LA

GLEBE LA

OVERY MILL RD

NEW ROAD

B1156

Church Wood

Bone's Belt

6

Burnham Norton

Burnham Overy Mill

LUCAS LANE

GONG LANE

Burnham Overy Town

Peterstone Farm

Model Farm

Howe Hill

River Burn

HERRING'S LA

BELLAMY'S LA

B1355

FRIARS LA

MILL RD

OVERY RD

Cross (remains of)

Church Farm

B1155

135

Sandpit Plantation

Garden Cottage

43

PE31

Cemy

Sch

Friary

Leath House

5

Mill Wood

WHITEWAY ROAD

Hall Farm

Mill Farm

Osier Carr

Tumulus

NR23

Lucas Hill Wood

Whiteway Farm

Westgate

NORTH ST

PH THE GN

FRONT ST

PO

Sewage Works

42

Mound

Chalk Hill

CHURCH WK

STATION RD

Manor House Moat

RINGSTEAD ROAD

CREAKE RD

Church

CAMBERS LA

Burnham Market

WALSINGHAM RD

LOWE'S LA

BACK LA

MILL LA

Burnham Thorpe

4

Pagets Farm

Cottage End

BEACON HILL RD

East End Farm

Croft's Wood

Beacon Hill

PH

Ivy House Farm

Whitehall Farm

Gallow Hill Farm

Gravelpit Hill

41

135

Hillock Wood

CREAKE ROAD

GREEN LANE

Scarboro' Wood

Herongound Plantation

3

B1155

Gallow Hill

Rectory Wood

Gallow Hill Wood

Mast

Cottage Glebe

Coldham's Cross Wood

B1355

Longlands Farm

40

Field Barn

Open Meadow Plantation

2

Neil's Plantation

Crossways Farm

St Mary's Abbey

Deepdale Wood

39

NR21

Abbey Farm

Fox Covert

BURNHAM RD B1355

WELLS ROAD

Crowdale Wood

1

Glebe Farm

NORMANS LA

Larch Wood

Chantry Hills

Mill Hill Plantation

Long Plantation

DUNNS LA

North Creake

Plateau Plantation

Ringate Wood

WEST STREET

PH

38

82 A 83 B 84 C 85 D 86 E 87 F

◀ 3

For full street detail of the highlighted area see page 135

15 ▼

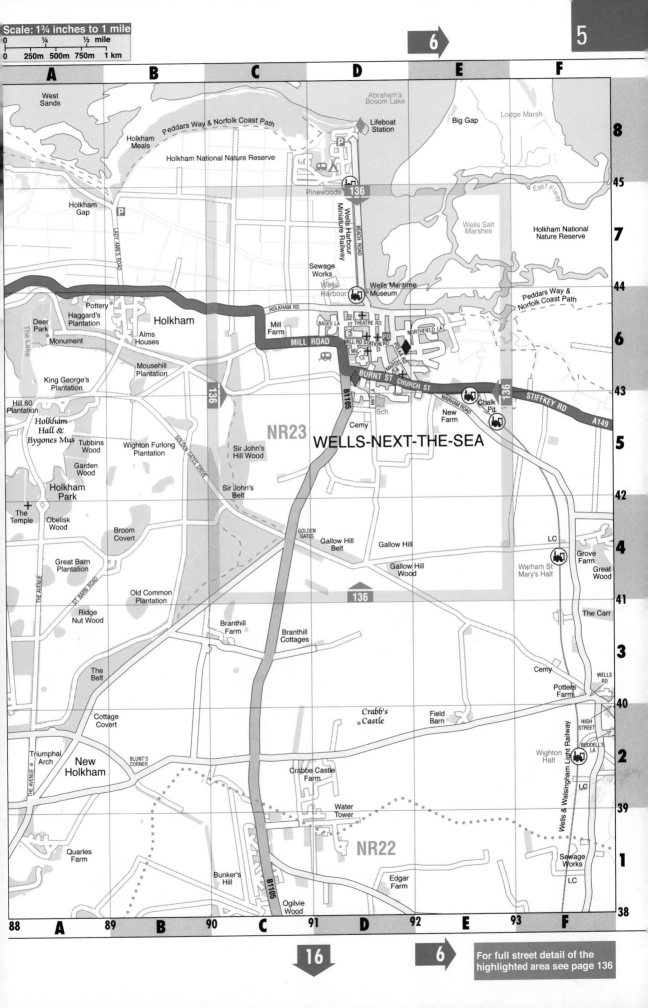

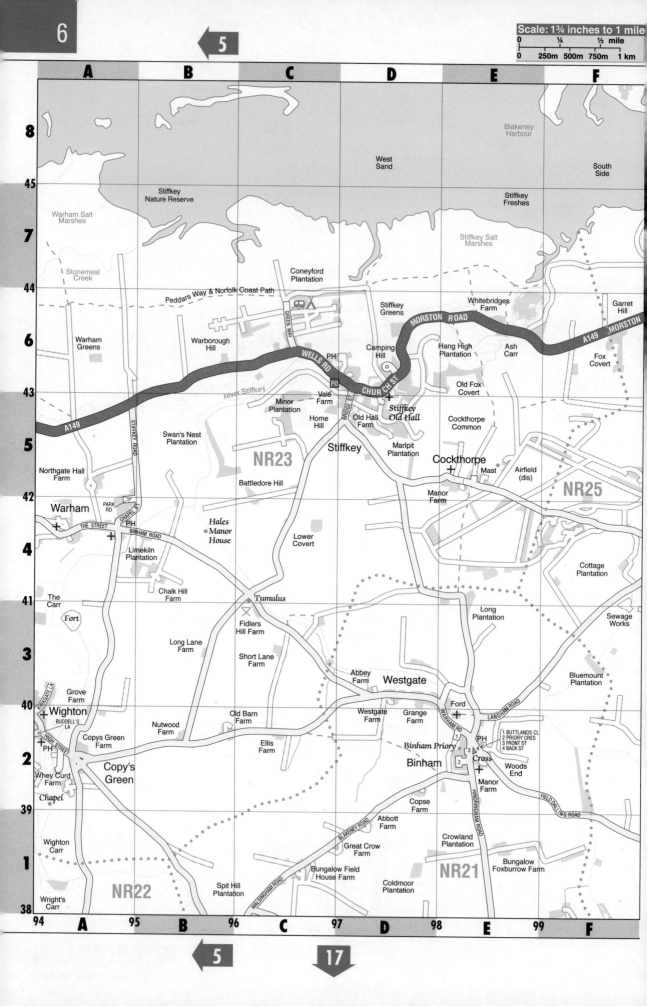

Scale: 1¾ inches to 1 mile

0   ¼   ½ mile
0 250m 500m 750m 1 km

A   B   C   D   E   F

8

45

Blakeney
Harbour

West
Sand

South
Side

Stiffkey
Nature Reserve

Stiffkey
Freshes

7

Warham Salt
Marshes

Stiffkey Salt
Marshes

Stonemeal
Creek

44

Coneyford
Plantation

Peddars Way & Norfolk Coast Path

Stiffkey
Greens

Whitebridges
Farm

Garret
Hill

MORSTON ROAD

6

Warham
Greens

Warborough
Hill

GREEN WAY

Camping
Hill

Hang High
Plantation

Ash
Carr

A149 MORSTON

Fox
Covert

WELLS RD

PH

43

A149

River Stiffkey

Minor
Plantation

Vale
Farm

PO

BRIDGE ST

CHURCH ST

Old Hall
Farm

Stiffkey
Old Hall

Old Fox
Covert

Cockthorpe
Common

5

STIFFKEY ROAD

Swan's Nest
Plantation

Home
Hill

Stiffkey

Marlpit
Plantation

Cockthorpe

Mast

Airfield
(dis)

NR25

NR23

Northgate Hall
Farm

Battledore Hill

Manor
Farm

42

Warham

PARK
RD

Hales
Manor
House

Lower
Covert

4

THE STREET

PH

BINHAM ROAD

Limekiln
Plantation

Cottage
Plantation

41

The
Carr

Fort

Chalk Hill
Farm

Tumulus

Fidlers
Hill Farm

Long
Plantation

Sewage
Works

3

Long Lane
Farm

Short Lane
Farm

Abbey
Farm

Westgate

Bluemount
Plantation

40

MYRGATE LA

Grove
Farm

Wighton

BUDDELL'S
LA

Nutwood
Farm

Old Barn
Farm

Westgate
Farm

Grange
Farm

Ford

WARHAM RD

LANGHAM ROAD

1 BUTTLANDS CL
2 PRIORY CRES
3 FRONT ST
4 BACK ST

2

HIGH STREET

PH

Copys Green
Farm

Ellis
Farm

Binham Priory

Binham

PH

Cross

Woods
End

Whey Curd
Farm

Copy's
Green

Manor
Farm

FIELD DALLING ROAD

39

Chapel

Copse
Farm

Abbott
Farm

Crowland
Plantation

BLAKENEY ROAD

HINDRINGHAM ROAD

Wighton
Carr

Great Crow
Farm

Bungalow
Foxburrow Farm

1

Bungalow Field
House Farm

Coldmoor
Plantation

NR21

WALSINGHAM ROAD

Spit Hill
Plantation

Wright's
Carr

NR22

38

94   A   95   B   96   C   97   D   98   E   99   F

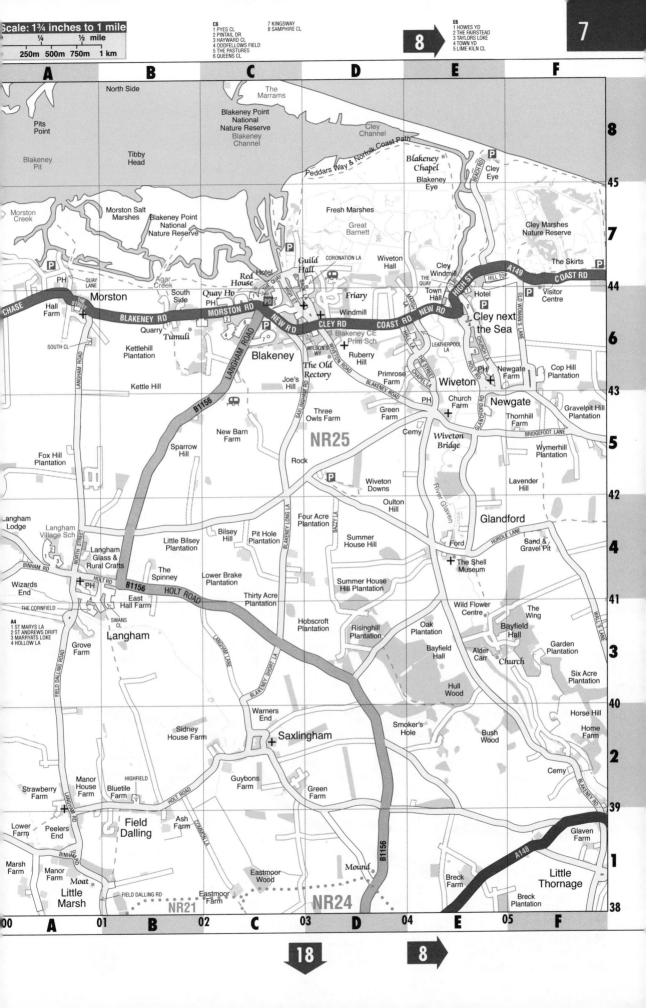

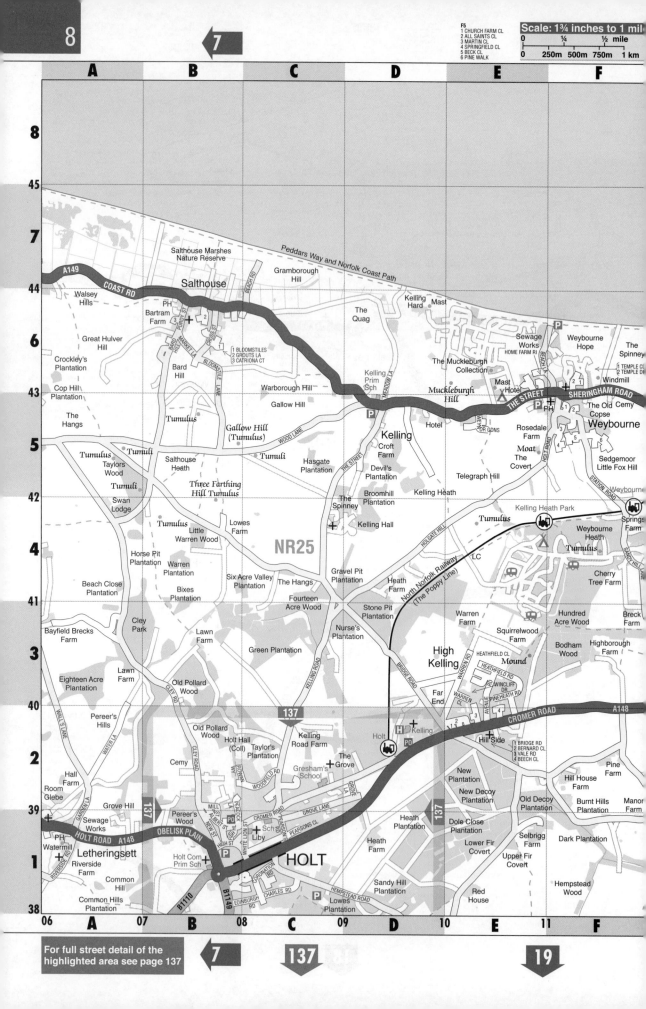

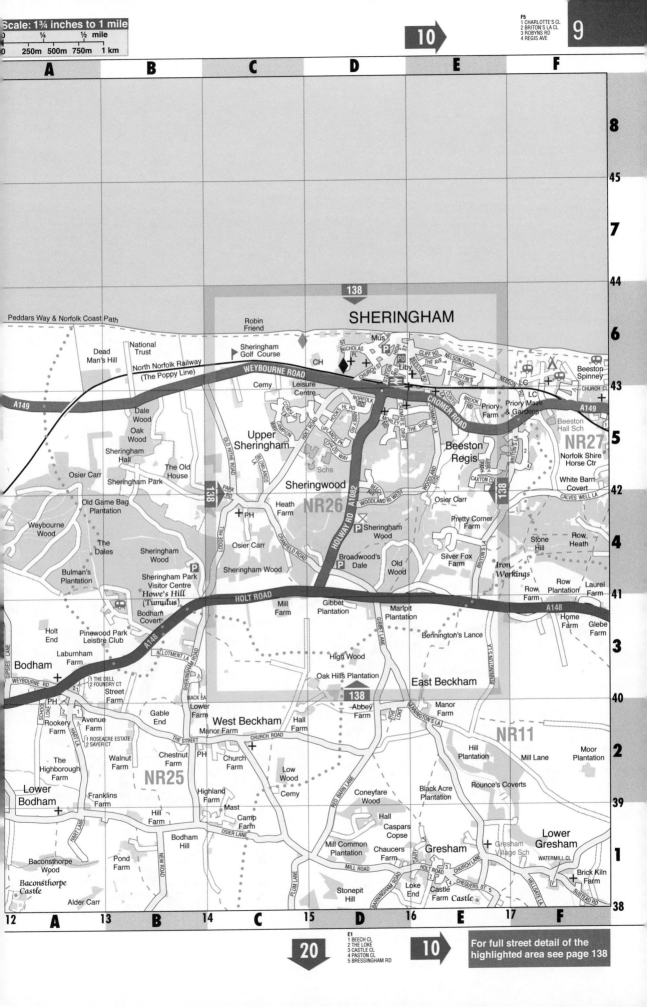

Scale: 1¾ inches to 1 mile

0   ¼   ½   mile
0   250m 500m 750m 1 km

10

F5
1 CHARLOTTE'S CL
2 BRITON'S LA CL
3 ROBYNS RD
4 REGIS AVE

9

A   B   C   D   E   F

8

45

7

44

138

SHERINGHAM

6

Peddars Way & Norfolk Coast Path

Robin
Friend

Dead
Man's Hill

National
Trust

Sheringham
Golf Course

ST
NICHOLAS
PL

Mus
P
High St

PO
Libry

Nelson Road

Cliff Rd

THE AVE

Beeston
Spinney

North Norfolk Railway
(The Poppy Line)

WEYBOURNE ROAD

CH

CH

Church
St

Station Rd

St Austin's
Gr

LC

LC

CHURCH CL

43

A149

Cemy

Leisure
Centre

CAMPION
WAY

NORFOLK
RD

HOOKS
HL RD

ABBEY RD

CRAMER'S DRIFT

CROMER ROAD

BROOK
RD

Priory
Farm

Priory Maze
& Gardens

A149

NR27

Dale
Wood

Oak
Wood

Sheringham
Hall

The Old
House

Upper
Sheringham

HOLT ROAD

UPLANDS PK

CHU'S WAY

MORLEY'S RD

THE RISE

COMMON LA

WOODLAND RISE

Beeston
Regis

ABBEY
PARK

BRITON'S LA

CAXTON CU

Norfolk Shire
Horse Ctr

White Barn
Covert

5

Sheringham Park

OLD HITHE ROAD

BLOWLANDS
LA

Sheringwood

NR26

A1082

WOODLAND RI WEST

BEECH
AVE

Osier Carr

CALVES WELL LA

42

Osier Carr

Old Game Bag
Plantation

138

PARK
RD

+ PH

Heath
Farm

CRANFIELD ROAD

HOLWAY RD

X

P

Sheringham
Wood

Pretty Corner
Farm

Stone
Hill

Row
Heath

4

Weybourne
Wood

The
Dales

Sheringham
Wood

Osier Carr

Sheringham Wood

P

Broadwood's
Dale

Old
Wood

Silver Fox
Farm

Iron
Workings

Row
Farm

Row
Plantation

Laurel
Farm

Bulman's
Plantation

Sheringham Park
Visitor Centre
Howe's Hill
(Tumulus)

P

HOLT ROAD

Mill
Farm

Gibbet
Plantation

Marlpit
Plantation

A148

41

Bodham Covert

Pinewood Park
Leisure Club

A148

ALLOTMENT LA

SHERINGHAM ROAD

GIBBET LANE

High Wood

Bennington's Lance

BENNINGTON'S LA

Home
Farm

Glebe
Farm

3

Holt
End

Laburnham
Farm

Bodham

GIPSIES LANE

WEYBOURNE RD

Street
Farm

1 THE DELL
2 FOUNDRY CT

BACK LA

Lower
Farm

Oak Hills Plantation

138

Abbey
Farm

THE LOKE

East Beckham

Manor
Farm

40

PH

SCHOOL LOKE

HART LA

Rookery
Farm

Avenue
Farm

Gable
End

THE STREET

Manor Farm

West Beckham

CHURCH ROAD

Hall
Farm

BENNINGTON'S LA

NR11

2

1 ROSEACRE ESTATE
2 SAYER CT

Walnut
Farm

NR25

Chestnut
Farm

PH

Church
Farm

Low
Wood

Hill
Plantation

Mill Lane

Moor
Plantation

The Highborough
Farm

Franklins
Farm

Highland
Farm

Mast

Cemy

RED BARN LANE

Coneyfare
Wood

Black Acre
Plantation

Rounce's Coverts

39

Lower
Bodham

Hill Farm

Camp
Farm

OSIER LANE

PLUM LANE

Hall
Caspars Copse

DAIRY LA

Gresham

HOLT RD

Gresham
Village Sch

Lower
Gresham

WATERMILL CL

1

Baconsthorpe
Wood

Baconsthorpe
Castle

Pond
Farm

NEW ROAD

Bodham
Hill

Mill Common
Plantation

MILL ROAD

Chaucers
Farm

BARRINGHAM ROAD

Stonepit
Hill

Loke
End

CHEQUERS ST

Castle
Farm

Castle

HELLGATE LA

SUSTEAD RD

Brick Kiln
Farm

Alder Carr

38

12   A   13   B   14   C   15   D   16   E   17   F

For full street detail of the
highlighted area see page 138

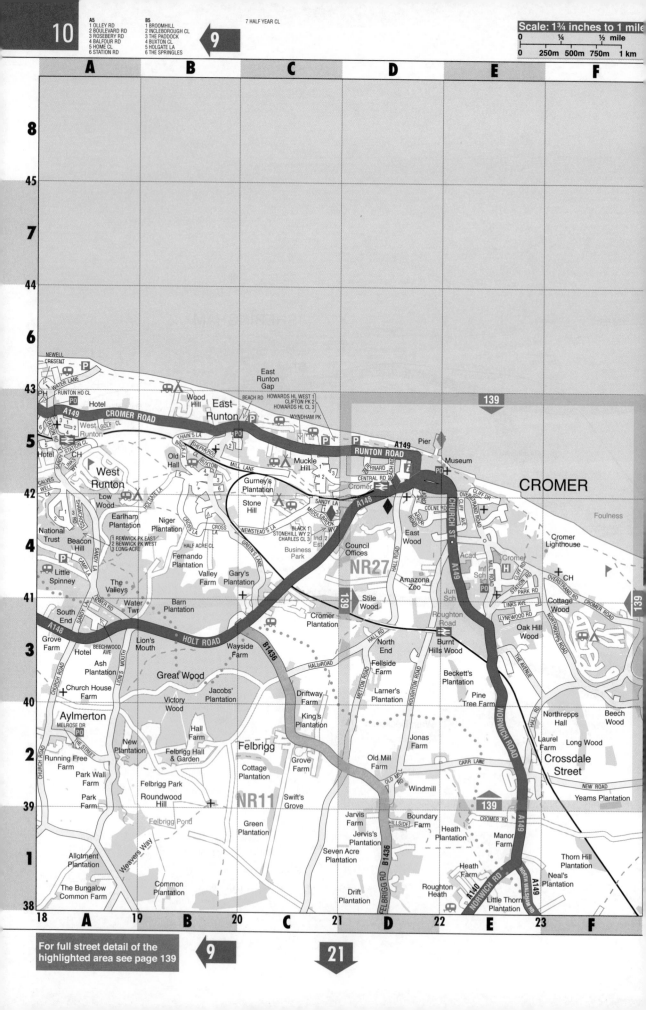

Scale: 1¾ inches to 1 mile

¼   ½ mile
250m 500m 750m 1 km

A   B   C   D   E   F

8

45

7

44

6

43

5

42

4

DANISH HOUSE GDS   Overstrand
HILLINGDON PK
BEACH CL   PAUL'S LA   PROMENADE
THE LONGS   THURST
HARBOR   RD   CLIFF RD   RD
ARDEN CL   HIGH STREET
BRACKEN AV   Belfry CE   CLIFTON WAY
VA Prim Sch   PO
CABLE LA   MUNDESLEY ROAD   GRANGE AV
1 CHURCH CL
2 THE GLADE

41

3

Toll's Hill
Wood
Manor
Farm
TOWER LANE

Long Broom
Covert
Mast

40

Hungry
Hill
Sidestrand
Hall Sch
Sidestrand

Northrepps
Shrublands
Farm
STARLING RISE
HUNGRY HILL
Osier
Carr
Ivy
Farm
Pond
Plantation

2

Football
Gd
SCHOOL CL
Northrepps
Prim Sch
PH
CHURCH
ST
BULL'S ROW
NUT LANE
1 BROADGATE CL
2 SILVER CT
3 FOUNDRY CL
4 GALLUS CL
5 STOREY'S LOKE
6 EMERYS CL
Shrieking Pits
Plantation
NR27
Bizewell
Farm
Rome
Plantation
NR11
Trimingham
CROMER ROAD
WHITE GATE LANE
Hall
Farm
CHURCH ST
BROADWOOD CL

39

PIT RD
RECTORY RD
CRAFT LANE
Furyhill
Plantation
India
Wood
Fox
Hills
BUCK'S HEATH LA
STAGEN PK
LOOP RD
TAYLOR'S LA
Beacon
Hill
Marl Point

1

Lower
Plantation
Frogshall
Hill
Covert
The
Carr
Osier
Carr
BLACKBERRY HALL LA
Ballast
Plantation
HEATH LA
MIDDLE STREET
Water Tower
Farm
MUNDESLEY ROAD
TRIMINGHAM RD
BEACON RD
Mast
Little Marl
Point

38

24   A   25   B   26   C   27   D   28   E   29   F

1

133

E5
1 KENSIDE RD
2 KENHILL CL
3 TEAL CL
4 GOOSANDER CL
5 BEWICK CL
6 CANADA CL
7 SHELDUCK DR
8 MALTHOUSE CT
9 HALL RD
10 SCHOOL RD
11 LANCASTER PL
12 FISHERS END CL
13 ROOSTERS CL

Scale: 1¾ inches to 1 mile

0 ¼ ½ mile
0 250m 500m 750m 1 km

A · B · C · D · E · F

Heacham

Stubborn Sand

North Beach

Norfolk Lavender Visitor Centre

Ford

B1454

Heacham River

PE36

Swimming Pool

South Beach Road

Staithe Farm

Folgate Road

Marea Farm

133

Sewage Works

Fenway

Summerhill

PE31

South Moor

Lamsey Lane

Mount Pleasant Farm

Pit

Sedgeford Carr

Heacham Bottom Farm

Dunston Drove

Hovel Wood

Heacham Harbour

Ken Hill Wood

133

Half Moon Plantation

Limekiln Plantation

Beech Wood

Ken Hill

Carrstone Pit

Hall Farm

Snettisham

Snettisham Prim Sch

Lodge Hill Farm

Frogpits Wood

Manor Farm

Lodge Hill Plantation

Allotment Plantation

Common Road

Snettisham Park

ROMAN VILLA

Snettisham Scalp

Beach Road

Locke Hill Farm

Wood's Corner Plantation

The Cedars

Shepherd's Port

Snettisham House

Anchor Pk

Snettisham House

Limekiln Plantation

Wolferton Creek

The Ingol

Snettisham Beach

Paper Hall Farm

The Old Coal Yard

Beach Rd

140

Old Hall

The Drift

Rec Gd

Ingoldisthorpe Hall

Ingoldisthorpe

Prim Sch

Sewage Works

Hall Farm

Shernborne Road

Chalk Pit Road

Snettisham Nature Reserve

The Ingol

Ingoldisthorpe Common

Brickley Lane

Brickley Wood

High Farm

The Decoy

140

PE31

Life Wood

Hunstanton Road

Woodside Dr

Dersingham

Mill House

140

Hill House Farm

Jubilee Rise

Glebe Rd

Station Road

Inf Sch

Liby

Boathouse Creek

Steer Road

Chapel Rd

Caudle Carr

B1440

PH

Doddshill

Doddshill Road

64 · 65 · 66 · 67 · 68 · 69
A · B · C · D · E · F

D4
1 SPRING VIEW
2 THE MEWS
3 FORGET-ME-NOT RD
4 CAMERON CRES

140

E4
1 MALLARD CL
2 DAWES LA
3 PINE CL
4 LONGVIEW CL
5 CHESTNUT RD
6 BIRCH CL
7 JUBILEE GDNS
8 STRICKLAND CL
9 STRICKLAND AVE
10 GRANGE CL
11 STILEMAN WY
12 ST MARY'S CL
13 LODGE LA
14 CREMER CL

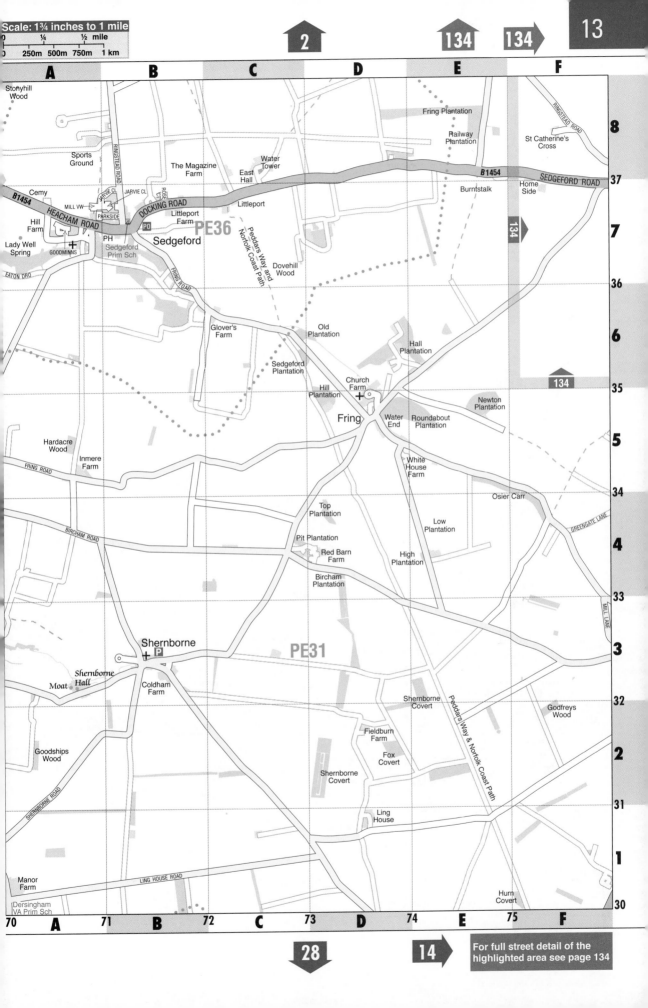

Scale: 1¾ inches to 1 mile

0   ¼   ½   mile
0 250m 500m 750m 1 km

2
134   134

A   B   C   D   E   F

8

Stonyhill Wood

Fring Plantation

Railway Plantation

St Catherine's Cross

RINSTEAD ROAD

37

Sports Ground

The Magazine Farm

East Hall

Water Tower

B1454   SEDGEFORD ROAD

Burntstalk

Home Side

RINGSTEAD ROAD

JARVIE CL   JARVIE CL

ROSE CT

Cemy

MILL VW

PARKSIDE

DOCKING ROAD

Littleport

7

134

Hill Farm

PH

PO

Littleport Farm

PE36

B1454

HEACHAM ROAD

GOODMINNS

Sedgeford Prim Sch

Sedgeford

Lady Well Spring

EATON DRO

FRING ROAD

Peddars Way and Norfolk Coast Path

Dovehill Wood

36

Glover's Farm

Old Plantation

Hall Plantation

6

Sedgeford Plantation

Hill Plantation

Church Farm

Fring

Water End

Roundabout Plantation

Newton Plantation

134

35

Hardacre Wood

Inmere Farm

FRING ROAD

White House Farm

5

Osier Carr

34

GREENGATE LANE

Top Plantation

Low Plantation

BIRCHAM ROAD

Pit Plantation

Red Barn Farm

High Plantation

4

Bircham Plantation

MILL LANE

33

Shernborne

P

PE31

3

Shernborne Hall

Moat

Coldham Farm

Shernborne Covert

Godfreys Wood

32

Fieldburn Farm

Fox Covert

Peddars Way & Norfolk Coast Path

Goodships Wood

Shernborne Covert

2

SHERNBORNE ROAD

Ling House

31

1

Manor Farm

LING HOUSE ROAD

Hurn Covert

Dersingham VA Prim Sch

30

28   14

For full street detail of the highlighted area see page 134

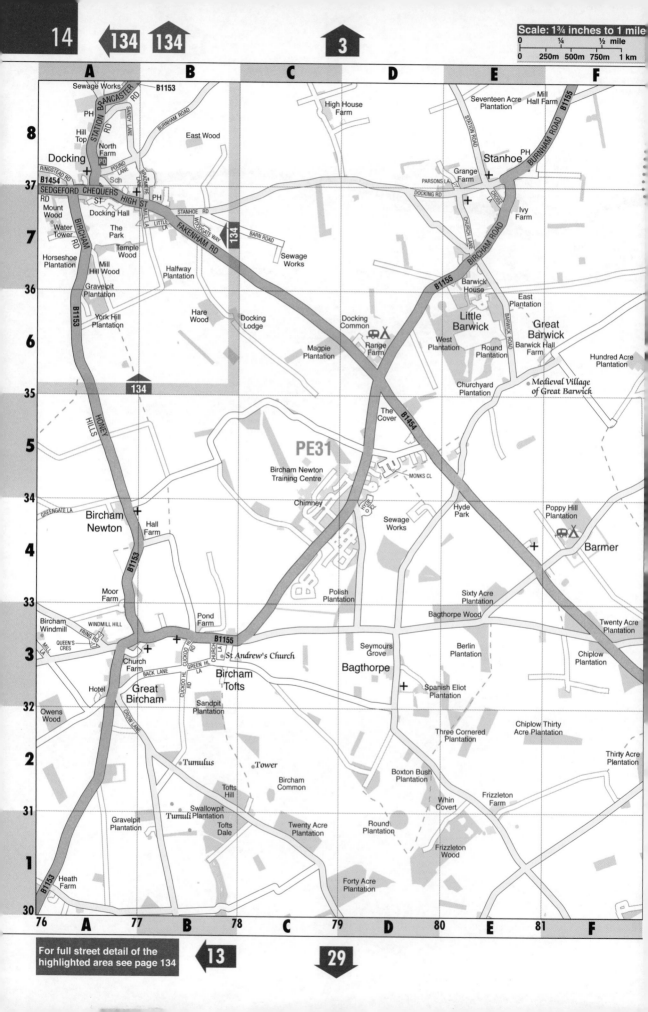

A **B** **C** **D** **E** **F**

Sewage Works
B1153
PH
Hill Top
STATION BRANCASTER RD
SANDY LANE
BURNHAM ROAD
East Wood
High House Farm
Seventeen Acre Plantation
Mill Hall Farm
BURNHAM ROAD B1155

8

Docking
North Farm
PO
POUND LANE
Stanhoe
PH

37
RINGSTEAD RD
B1454
SEDGEFORD RD
CHEQUERS
HIGH ST
BRAEMERE LANE
LITTLE LA
Sch
Docking Hall
PH
STANHOE RD
FAKENHAM RD
WALSINGATE WAY
134
BARN ROAD
PARSONS LA
Grange Farm
DOCKING RD
CHURCH LANE
BIRCHAM ROAD
CROSS
Ivy Farm

7
Mount Wood
Water Tower
BIRCHAM RD
The Park
ST
Temple Wood
Mill Hill Wood
Halfway Plantation
Sewage Works

36
Horseshoe Plantation
B1153
Gravelpit Plantation
York Hill Plantation
Hare Wood
Docking Lodge
B1155
Barwick House
East Plantation
Great Barwick

6
Magpie Plantation
Docking Common
Range Farm
Little Barwick
West Plantation
Round Plantation
Barwick Hall Farm
Hundred Acre Plantation

35
134
Churchyard Plantation
Medieval Village of Great Barwick

5
HONEY HILLS
The Cover
B1454
PE31
Bircham Newton Training Centre
MONKS CL

34
GREENGATE LA
Bircham Newton
Hall Farm
Chimney
HYDE CL
Hyde Park
Poppy Hill Plantation

4
B1153
Moor Farm
Sewage Works
Barmer

33
Bircham Windmill
WINDMILL HILL
FRING RD
Pond Farm
Bagthorpe Wood
Sixty Acre Plantation
Twenty Acre Plantation

3
QUEEN'S CRES
MILL LA
CUCKOO HL RD
BACK LANE
GREEN HL LA
CHURCH LA
B1155
St Andrew's Church
Seymours Grove
Bagthorpe
Berlin Plantation
Chiplow Plantation

Church Farm
Hotel
Great Bircham
Bircham Tofts
Spanish Eliot Plantation

32
Owens Wood
CROW LANE
Sandpit Plantation
Three Cornered Plantation
Chiplow Thirty Acre Plantation

2
Tumulus
Tower
Bircham Common
Boxton Bush Plantation
Frizzleton Farm
Thirty Acre Plantation

Tofts Hill
Swallowpit Plantation
Tofts Dale
Whin Covert

31
Gravelpit Plantation
Tumuli
Twenty Acre Plantation
Round Plantation
Frizzleton Wood

1
B1153
Heath Farm
Forty Acre Plantation

30

A 76 **A** 77 **B** 78 **C** 79 **D** 80 **E** 81 **F**

For full street detail of the highlighted area see page 134

← 13

↓ 29

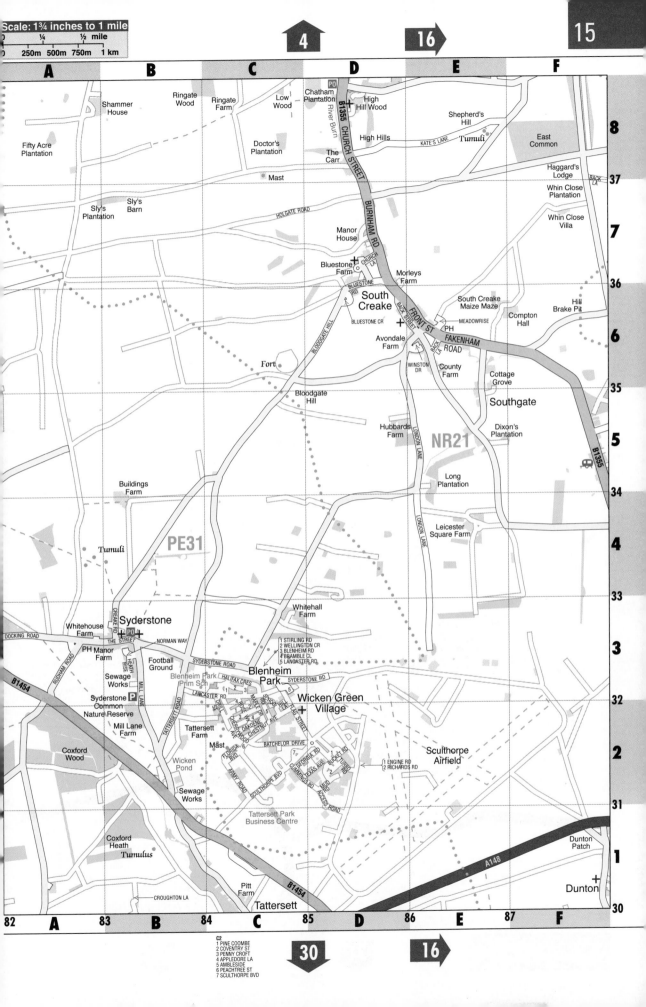

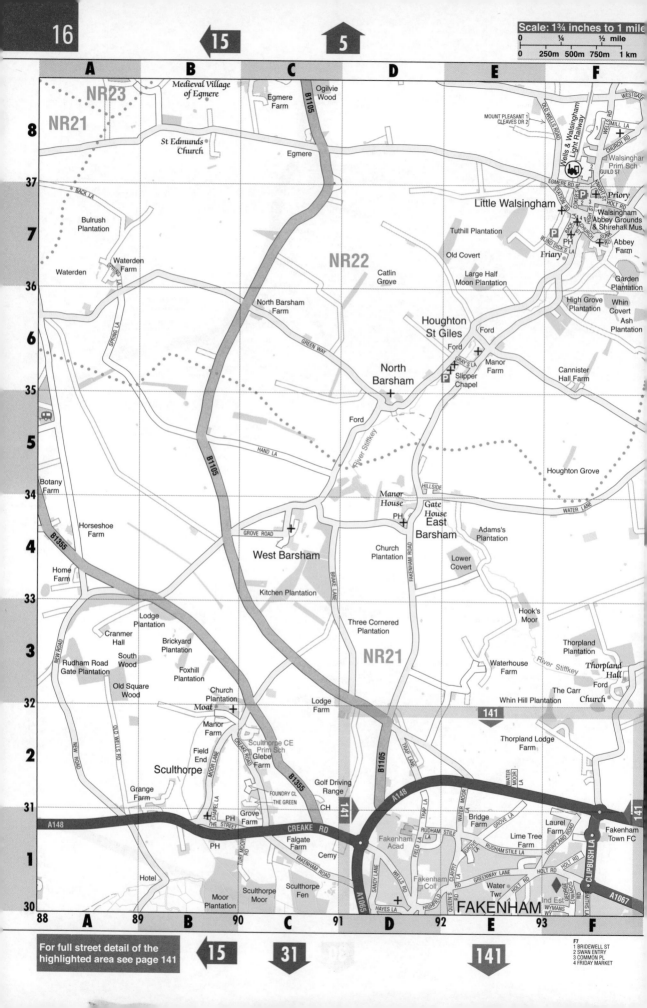

15
5

Scale: 1¾ inches to 1 mile

0   ¼   ½ mile
0 250m 500m 750m 1 km

A **B** **C** **D** **E** **F**

NR23

NR21

Medieval Village
of Egmere

Egmere
Farm

Ogilvie
Wood

MOUNT PLEASANT 1
CLEAVES DR 2

Wells & Walsingham
Light Railway

WESTGATE

WELLS MILL LA

OLD WELLS ROAD

CHURCH RD

8

St Edmunds
Church

Egmere

Walsingham
Prim Sch

GUILD ST

37

BACK LA

EGMERE RD

STATION RD

COKER'S HILL

KNIGHT ST

RICHARDS

HIGH ST

HOLT RD

P
1 2
3

Little Walsingham

Priory

Walsingham
Abbey Grounds
& Shirehall Mus.

7

Bulrush
Plantation

NR22

Tuthill Plantation

Old Covert

P

BACK LA

BLIND DICK'S LA

CHURCH

SUNK
RD

PH

Friary

Abbey
Farm

Waterden

Waterden
Farm

SPRING LA

Catlin
Grove

Large Half
Moon Plantation

High Grove
Plantation

Garden
Plantation

Whin
Covert
Ash
Plantation

36

North Barsham
Farm

Houghton
St Giles

Ford

6

GREEN WAY

North
Barsham

Ford

GRAY'S LA

P

Slipper
Chapel

Manor
Farm

Cannister
Hall Farm

35

HAND LA

B1105

Ford

River Stiffkey

Houghton Grove

WATER LANE

5

Botany
Farm

HILLSIDE

Manor
House

PH

Gate
House
East
Barsham

Adams's
Plantation

34

Horseshoe
Farm

B1355

GROVE ROAD

West Barsham

Church
Plantation

Lower
Covert

Hook's
Moor

Thorpland
Plantation

River Stiffkey

Thorpland
Hall

4

Home
Farm

Kitchen Plantation

BRAKE LANE

FAKENHAM ROAD

Three Cornered
Plantation

NR21

Waterhouse
Farm

Ford
The Carr Church

33

Lodge
Plantation

Cranmer
Hall

Brickyard
Plantation

Whin Hill Plantation

3

NEW ROAD

OLD WELLS RD

Rudham Road
Gate Plantation

South
Wood

Foxhill
Plantation

Church
Plantation

Lodge
Farm

141

Thorpland Lodge
Farm

32

Old Square
Wood

Moat

Manor
Farm

SCULTHORPE CE
Prim Sch
Glebe
Farm

B1105

TRAP LANE

WATER
MOOR
LA

2

CHAPEL LA

MOOR LANE

CREAKE ROAD

Field
End

Sculthorpe

B1355

Golf Driving
Range

A148

141

WATER MOOR
LA

Laurel
Farm

Fakenham
Town FC

31

Grange
Farm

TURF MOOR RD

PH
THE STREET

Grove
Farm

FOUNDRY CL
THE GREEN

CH

141

Bridge
Farm

GROVE LA

Lime Tree
Farm

HOLT RD

CLIPBUSH LA

A1067

A148

PH

Falgate
Farm

CREAKE RD

Cemy

A148

RUDHAM
STILE
LA

FIELD LA

CLAYPIT
RD

GROVE LN

RUDHAM STILE LA

THORPLAND ROAD

1

Hotel

Moor
Plantation

Sculthorpe
Moor

Sculthorpe
Fen

FAKENHAM ROAD

A1065

Fakenham
Acad

SANDY LANE

WELLS RD

Fakenham
Coll

QUEEN'S

Water
Twr

GREENWAY LANE

Water
Moor
HIGHFIELD

HAYES LA

FAKENHAM

Ind Est
WYMANS
WY

GEORGE
EDWARDS
RD

HOLT RD

30

A **B** **C** **D** **E** **F**

88   89   90   91   92   93

For full street detail of the
highlighted area see page 141

15
31
141

F7
1 BRIDEWELL ST
2 SWAN ENTRY
3 COMMON PL
4 FRIDAY MARKET

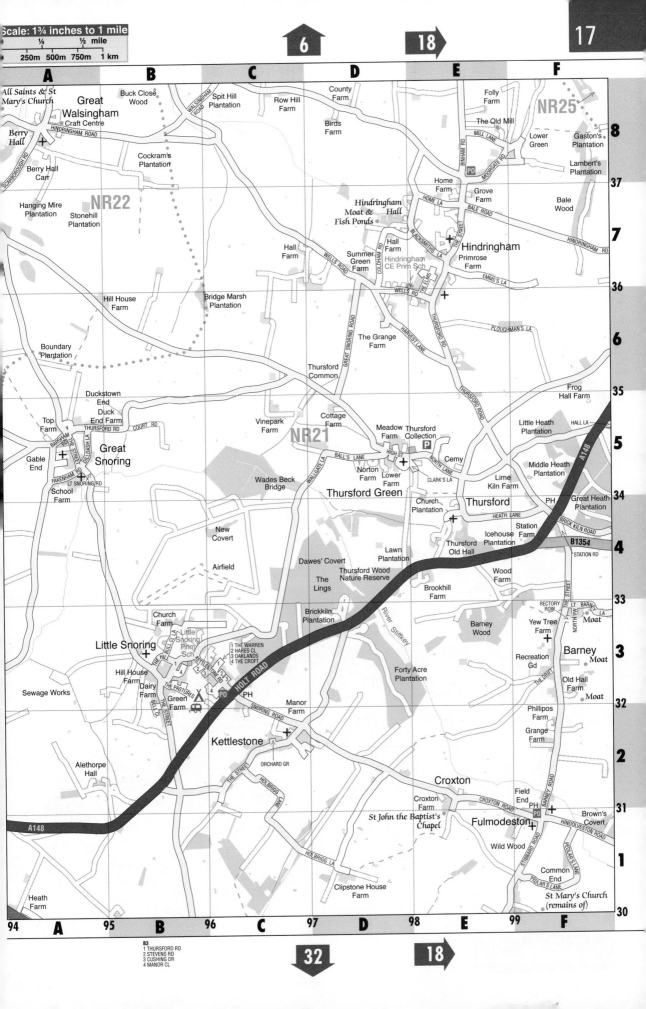

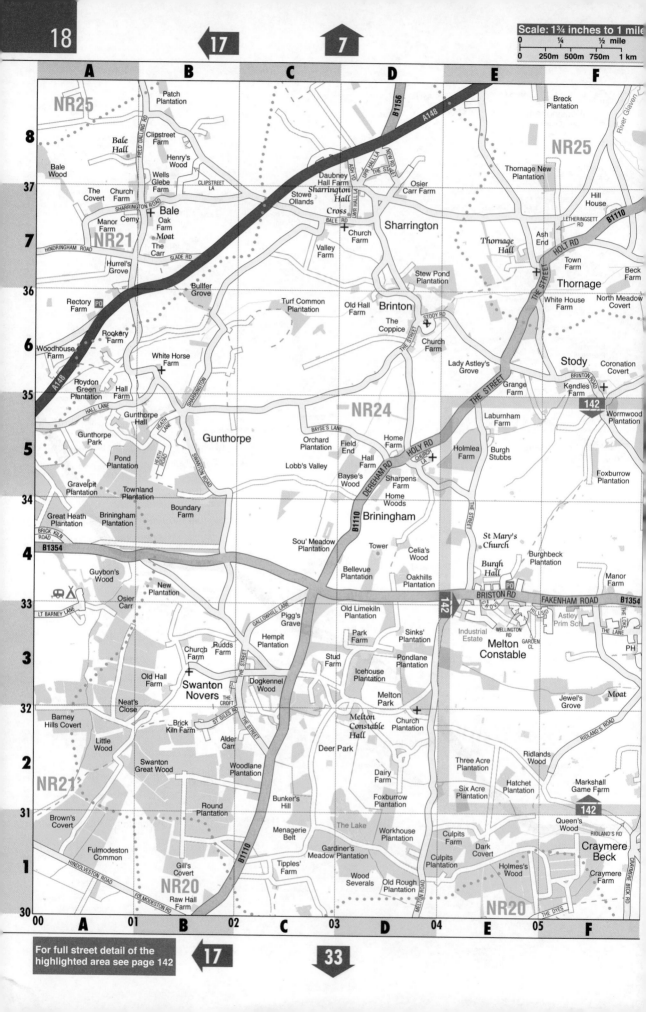

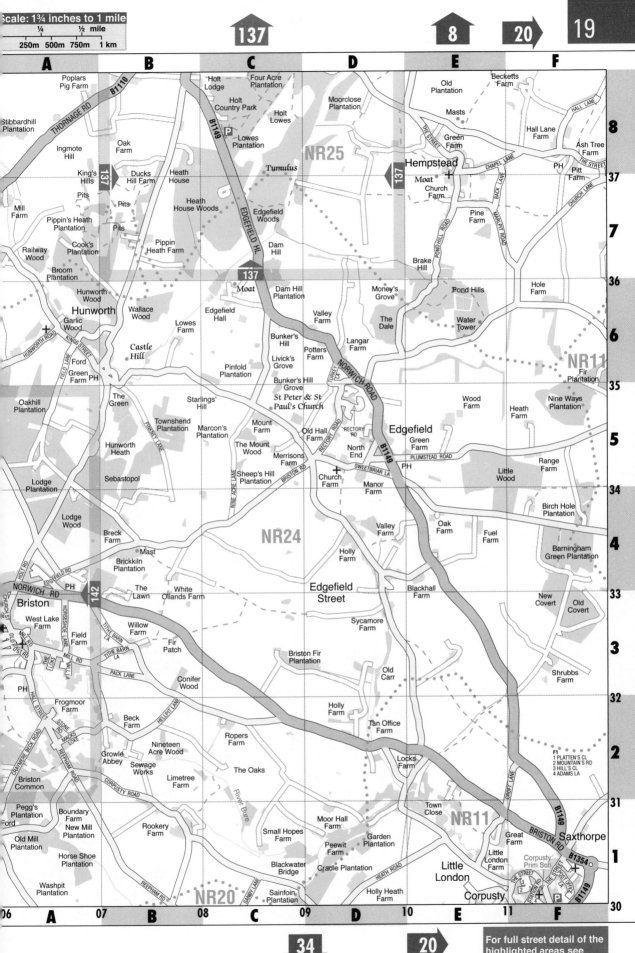

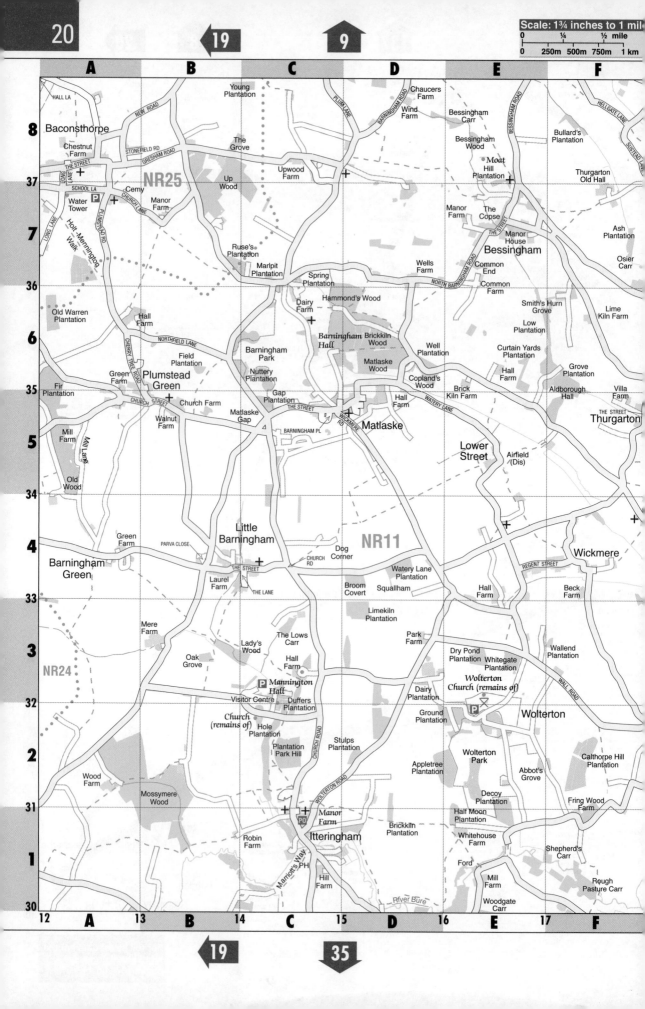

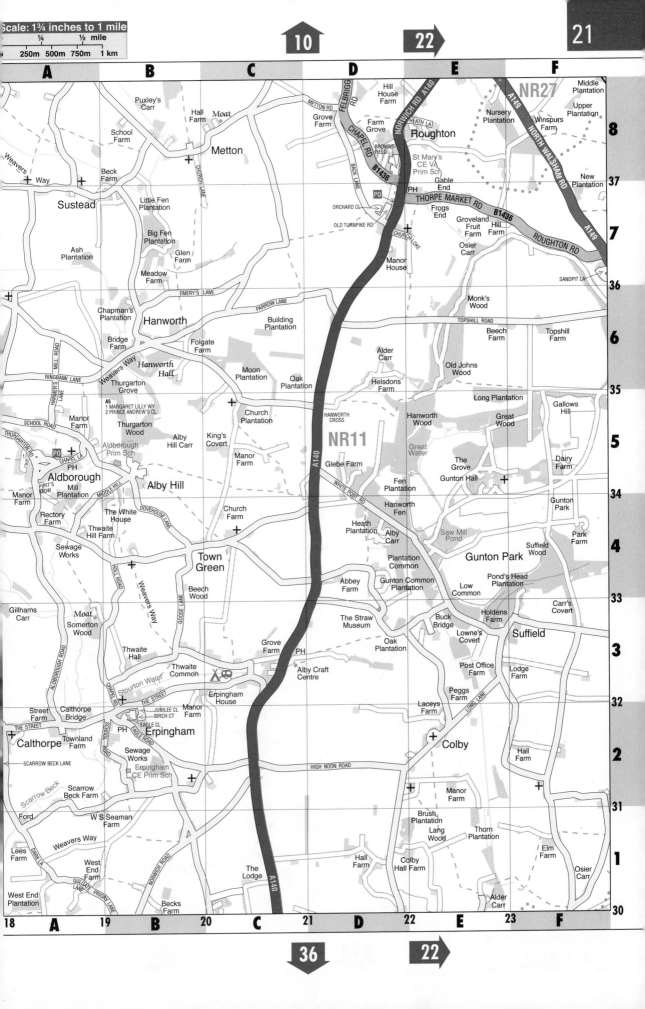

Scale: 1¾ inches to 1 mil

0 ¼ ½ mile
0 250m 500m 750m 1 km

A B C D E F

8

Bridge Farm
NR27
Glover's Plantation
Clapham Dams
Lodge Farm
The Grove
Ashtree Farm
Paston Way
Grove Farm
Bungalow Farm
Hill Farm
White House Farm
Hotel
Brake Hill Plantation
Home Farm
Bridge Farm
LIVINGSTONE RISE 1
COLLINGWOOD DR 2
ALEXANDER RISE 3
TASMAN DR 4
NELSON WAY 5
WELLINGTON CLOSE
LANCASTER RISE
Southrepps Hall

37
Pond Farm
Cook's Hill
Beechlands Farm
CHURCH STREET
Stump Cross
Gimingham Hall Farm
HARVEY EST
Gimingham
Church Farm
Mundesley

7
Thorpe Road
Upper Street
PH
P.O.
BEECHLANDS PK
ORCHARD LOKE
Rec Gd
Southrepps
GIMINGHAM ROAD
NR11
HALL ROAD
Royal Farm
MILL STREET
SCHOOL LA
Mundesley Beck
H

36
THE LOKE
Hotel
Thorpe Market
COMMON LA
Manor Farm
SOUTHREPPS RD
MUNDESLEY ROAD
John of Gaunts House

6
NORTH WALSHAM ROAD
Nursery Farm
Church Farm
CHURCH ROAD
Loke End
CHAPEL RD
Hill House
PIT STREET
Lower Street
Oak Tree Farm
Hollies Farm
Ash Plantation
The Stables
Manor Farm
White House Farm
Hall Farm
Millers Farm

35
A1149
STATION RD
PH
Wild Wood
WARREN RD
Gunton
Antingham & Southrepps Com Prim Sch
BRADFIELD ROAD
Mill Farm
Southrepps Common
Brickkiln Wood
Trunch Plantation
Long Plantation
Warren Farm
Gorrel Hill Farm
BREWERY ROAD
WRIGHT'S LOKE
BACK STREET
FRONT ST
PH
Cemy
KNAPTON ROAD
Brick Kiln Farm
Hall Farm

5
Beechcroft Farm
Hall Farm
Elderton Lane Farm
Antingham Wood
ELDERTON LANE
PASTON WAY
Goldens Farm
Warren Farm
Alder Carr
ALBION RD
Warren Farm
BLOOMS TURN
CORNISH AVE
Sewage Works
1 PRIMROSE CL
2 KINGSLEIGH CL
3 CARL CR
4 ROBERT CL
Park Farm
Knapton Green

34
Hotel
Mast
Bells Farm
Bridge Farm
Poplars Farm LC
Bradfield Hall
Bradfield
Green End
The Covert
Swafield House
NORTHWAL SHAM ROAD
Hill Fruit Farm
Straithern Farm
Knapton House
The Grove

4
White Lodge Farm
Antingham
SOUTHREPPS RD
POND RD
Chapel Farm
CHURCH ROAD
Baythorn End
COMMON ROAD
HALL ROAD
Swafield House
TRUNCH RD
Beeches Farm
Nature Reserve
HALL LANE

33
Church Farm
CHURCH LA
Oakcroft Farm
CHURCH CL
Glebe Farm
Pond Farm
Thackley End
SOUTHREPPS RD
Brookmeadows Farm
Spriggate Farm
Red House Farm
Tavistock Farm
ANTINGHAM HILL

3
Moat Farm
Antingham Ponds
Barge Farm
NR28
Bridge Farm
KNAPTON ROAD
Swafield
Pigrey's Wood
Antingham Hall
CROMER ROAD
LYNGATE ROAD
CHAPEL ROAD
Bradfield Bridge

32
Antingham Hall
Wilds Farm
Lyngate Farm
151
Paston Way
LITTLE LONDON ROAD
BACTON ROAD

2
NR11
Meadow Side
Lyngate
Brick Kiln Farm
Rookery Farm
CORNISH WAY
Swafield Rd
MAYFIELD RD
Little London
Alder Carr
151
Brick Kiln Farm
Boundary Farm
BRICKYARD ROAD
FOLGATE ROAD
B1145
CROW LOKE
MUNDESLEY RD
MELBOURNE RD
BLUEBELL RD
MARSHGATE
Sewage Works
Bacton Mill Wood

31
East Side
GREENS RD
KINGSWAY
BRADFIELD ROAD
NORTHFIELD RD
LAUNDRY LOKE
MARKET ST
ACORN RD
Orchard Farm
BRICKKILN ROAD
MANOR RD
ANCHOR RD
Alder End

1
Vernon Wood
Ruggs Hall Farm
Rugg's Hall
Bradmoor Farm
AYLSHAM RD
B1145
AYLSHAM ROAD
Football Gd
NORTH WALSHAM
A1149
MARKET PL
Libry
Golf
Cemy
HALL LANE
PARK AVE
SADLERS WY
NEW RD
NTA CL

30
Neach's Farm

A B C D E F
24 25 26 27 28 29

For full street detail of the highlighted area see page 151

Scale: 1¾ inches to 1 mile
¼ ½ mile
250m 500m 750m 1 km

A B C D E F

8
37
7
36
6
35
34
4
33
3
32
2
31
30

Cliftonville
Liby
Mundesley Maritime Museum
Mundesley
SEA VW RD
CROMER ROAD
LINKS ROAD
Water Tower
WARREN DR
CHURCH LA
HIGH ST
BEACH RD
MEADOW WY
PASTON RD
Hotel
HEATH LANE
BECKMEAD WY
WATER LANE
Sch
TRUNCH ROAD
Stow Mill
Stow Hill Farm
Stow Hill
Holiday Centre
Paston Way
143
143
NR11
B1145 KNAPTON RD
MUNDESLEY ROAD
POND LANE
Paston
The Spinney
Knapton
Church Farm
143
VICARAGE RD
BEARS CHAPEL RD
BACTON RD
Great Barn
Hall Farm
Mast
Mast
Gas Distribution Station
Rookery Plantation
B1159 BACTON ROAD
Bacton Green
COAST ROAD
BEACH RD
PH
Bacton
WODEHOUSE RD
Watch House Gap
Bromholm Field End
WATCH HO LA
Keswick
Anne Stannard Way
KESWICK RD
Water Tower
Sewage Works
Paston Green
Old Hall Street
Paston Way
Parrs Farm
Lowlands Farm
Church Farm
Hall Farm
NR12
CHURCH ROAD
MILL LANE
Bacton Prim Sch
Abbey Farm
ABBEY STREET
WALCOTT RD (COAST RD)
PH
PH
Rudram's Gap
B1159
THE PADDOCKS
EDEN
PRIORY RD
Gap End
ST HELENS RD
HELENA RD
THE CEDARS
POPLAR DR
COAST RD
Croft Farm
Church Farm
RECTORY ROAD
CHURCH LANE
SCHOOL ROAD
Pollard Street
Grange Farm
SANDY LANE
BLOODSLAT LANE
Broomholm
Stories Farm
The Grange
Rookery Farm
Dead Man's Grave
Barchams Farm
Honeytop Farm
The Grove
BOUNDARY LANE
CLAY LANE
Clay Lane Farm
Edingthorpe
NR28
NORTH WALSHAM ROAD
Ash Tree Farm
Park Farm
WELL STREET
North Plantation
Odessa Farm
Mill Common
ROOKERY FARM ROAD
PH
Barrington Farm
BACK LANE
Heath Farm
HENNESSEY'S LOKE
THE STREET
Edingthorpe Green
Cooper's Covert
Green Farm
BRIAR LANE
Witton Hall
Church Plantation
Common Farm
Stonebridge Cottage Selfs Carr
MILL COMMON ROAD
STONEBRIDGE ROAD
BACHELOR'S LANE
NORTH WALSHAM RD
Edingthorpe Heath
MILL ROAD
Bacton Wood
Philip's Grove
Road Plantation
Verona Plantation
BACTON ROAD
Manor Farm
Ivy Farm
MARSH LOKE
Witton Bridge
HAPPISBURGH ROAD
Church Farm
Ridlington
South Side
THE STREET
NASH'S LANE
Nashs Farm
OLD LANE
NR12
Spa Common
Muckle Hill Farm
Witton Heath
Tumulus
OLD HALL RD
Old Hall
HALL ROAD
NORTH WALSHAM ROAD
Hoole House
Primrose Farm
Ridlington Street
Bransmeadow Carr
Heath Farm
TEN'S RD
Ridlington Plantation
A B C D E F
30 31 32 33 34 35

38 24

For full street detail of the highlighted area see page 143

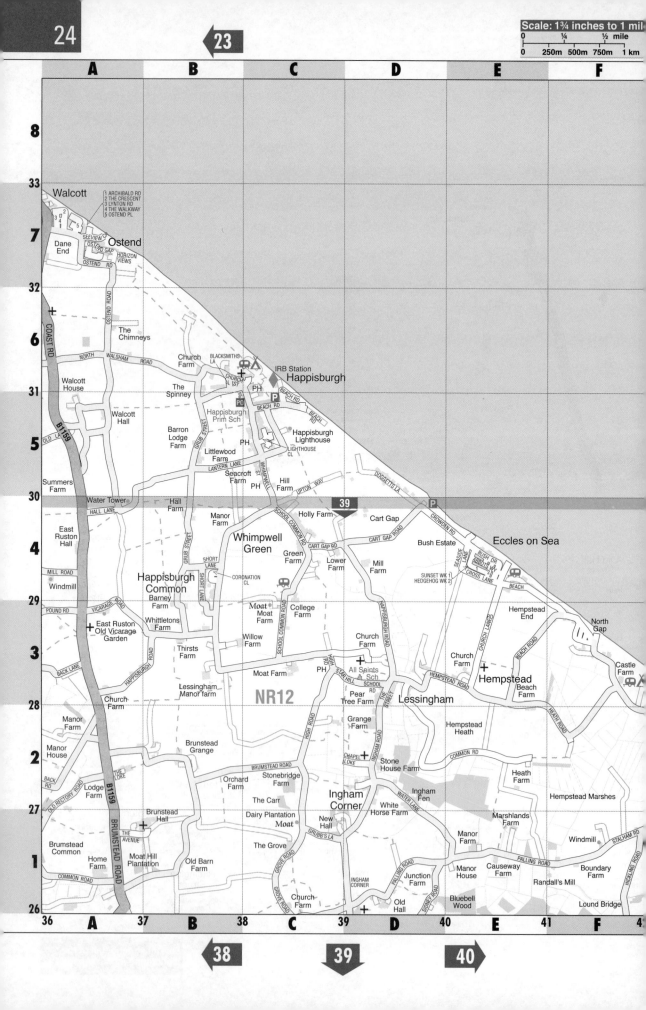

A   B   C   D   E   F

8

33

Walcott

1 ARCHIBALD RD
2 THE CRESCENT
3 LYNTON RD
4 THE WALKWAY
5 OSTEND PL

Dane End

7

Ostend

SEEVIEW CR
OSTEND GAP
HORIZON VIEWS

OSTEND RD

32

The Chimneys

6

COAST RD

NORTH   WALSHAM   ROAD

OSTEND ROAD

BLACKSMITHS LA

Church Farm

CHURCH LA

IRB Station

Happisburgh

Walcott House

31

The Spinney

PH

PO
P

BEACH RD

Walcott Hall

Barron Lodge Farm

GRUB STREET

Happisburgh Prim Sch

BEACH RD

5

B1159

OLD LA

Littlewood Farm

PH

Happisburgh Lighthouse

LIGHTHOUSE CL

LANTERN LANE

Seacroft Farm

WHIMPWELL ST

Hill Farm

UPTON WAY

DOGGETTS LA

PH

Summers Farm

30

Water Tower

HALL LANE

Hall Farm

Manor Farm

Holly Farm

39

Cart Gap

P

4

East Ruston Hall

GRUB STREET

Whimpwell Green

SCHOOL COMMON RD

CART GAP RD

Green Farm

CART GAP ROAD

Lower Farm

CART GAP ROAD

Bush Estate

CROWDEN RD

Eccles on Sea

SEASIDE LANE

BUSH DR
ABBOTS WK

Mill Farm

SUNSET WK 1
HEDGEHOG WK 2

BEACH

MILL ROAD

Windmill

POUND RD

29

VICARAGE ROAD

SHORT LANE

CORONATION CL

Moat
Moat Farm

College Farm

Happisburgh Common

Barney Farm

SHORT LANE

SCHOOL COMMON RD

HAPPISBURGH ROAD

Hempstead End

BEACH ROAD

North Gap

East Ruston Old Vicarage Garden

Whittletons Farm

Willow Farm

Church Farm

Church Farm

CHURCH LANE

Hempstead

Castle Farm

3

BACK LANE

HAPPISBURGH ROAD

Thirsts Farm

Moat Farm

PH

HIGH STAR HILL

All Saints Sch

SCHOOL RD

Church Farm

HEMPSTEAD ROAD

Beach Farm

HEATH ROAD

Lessingham Manor farm

NR12

THE STREET

Pear Tree Farm

Lessingham

28

Manor Farm

Church Farm

Brunstead Grange

Grange Farm

INGHAM ROAD

Hempstead Heath

2

Manor House

BRUMSTEAD ROAD

Stonebridge Farm

CHAPEL CLOKE

Stone House Farm

COMMON RD

Heath Farm

Hempstead Marshes

BACK RD

THE LOKE

Orchard Farm

The Carr

Ingham Fen

WATER LANE

Ingham Corner

White Horse Farm

Manor Farm

Windmill

STALHAM RD

OLD RECTORY LANE

B1159

Brunstead Hall

Dairy Plantation

Moat

New Hall

PALLING ROAD

Marshlands Farm

27

Lodge Farm

THE AVENUE

Ingham Corner

Manor House

Causeway Farm

Boundary Farm

HICKLING RD

Brumstead Common

Home Farm

Moat Hill Plantation

BRUMSTEAD ROAD

Old Barn Farm

The Grove

GRUBB'S LA

GROVE ROAD

Junction Farm

PALLING ROAD

SIDNEY ROAD

Bluebell Wood

Randall's Mill

Lound Bridge

1

COMMON ROAD

Church Farm

INGHAM CORNER

Old Hall

26

36   A   37   B   38   C   39   D   40   E   41   F

A   B   C   D   E   F

8

29

The Wash

7

28

Breast
Sand

6

27

5

Peter Scott Walk

26

Boat Creek

4

Peter Scott Walk

Admiralty
Point

Admiral's
Farm

25

New Inclosed
Marsh

Admiral's
Marsh

Ongar
Hill

PE34

SILT ROAD

3

Wingland Marsh

Horseshoe
Hole Farm

24

Walkers
Marsh

New
Marsh

Pierrepont
Farm

Terrington
Marsh

Balaclava
Farm

2

Bankside
Farm

Burman
Farm

Governor's
Marsh

Sharpes
Bank Farm

The Laurels
Farm

Grove
Farm

Fern House
Farm

23

New Common
Marsh Farm

Myrabella
Farm

Old New
Marsh

Creek
Farm

Green
Marsh

Bentinck
Farm

Weatherall
Farm

LONG ROAD

Marshland
Farm

1

Sycamore
Farm

Bungalow
Farm

RHOON RD

Bentinck
Marsh

Welbeck
Marsh

Tommyshop
Farm

GREEN MARSH RD

22

Lincolnshire STREET ATLAS

25

Scale: 1¾ inches to 1 mile

| 0 | ¼ | ½ | mile |
| 0 | 250m | 500m | 750m | 1 km |

A B C D E F

8

The Wash

PE31

29

7

28

6

Estuary
Farm

27

MARSH ROAD

5

PE30

26

The Wash National
Nature Reserve

Wooton
Marsh

4

Lynn Channel

Marsh
Farm

MARSH ROAD

25

Vinegar Middle

MARSH ROAD

3

Peter Scott Walk

PH

24

148

Orchard
End

Ongarhill
Marsh

NURSERY LA

KILHAM'S WAY

2

PE34

South Outmarsh

RYALL
DRIFT

Mas

23

Bank
Farm

Point
Farm

River Great Ouse

1

East Anglian
Farm

South
Wootton

BIRKBECK
CL

Banklands

Sch

KILHAM'S WAY

EDWARD
BENEFER WAY

A1078

22

58 A 59 B 60 C 61 D 62 E 63 F

Sewage
Works

Scale: 1¾ inches to 1 mil

0   ¼   ½   mile
0   250m 500m 750m 1 km

A B C D E F

8

Slash Wood
Perrys Wood
PE31
Admiral's Dr
Anmer Field Covert
Anmer
Blacksmith's Covert
Tumulus Hurn Covert

29

Home Farm
PE35
Captain's Close
King's Avenue
Blowndown Plantation
East Plantation
Anmer Minque

7

Commodore Wood
West Wood
Fox Covert
Norman Road
Tumulus
Beech Plantation
Westwood Belt
Tumulus

28

Cross Belt
Osier Carr

6

Water Tower
Appleton Farm
Denbeck Wood
Nuns Wood

27

St Mary's Church
Appleton Dro
Earthwork
B1440
Flitcham
Anmer Rd
Sandy's Belt

5

Common Drove
Flitcham CE Prim Sch
Flitcham Hall
Decoy Plantation
Church Road
PE31
Flitcham Barns Ind Units
Abbey Road
Flitcham Abbey
Abbey Farm
Middle Back Wood
Further Back Wood

Common Drove

26

Broom Covert
Oldfen Plantation
Whin Covert
Hilligton Park
Flitcham
The Carr
Hillington Hall
B1153
Field Farm
A148

4

Babingley River
Hotel
Hillington
Buck Farm
Church Farm
Eastgate Dro
Belmont Ring
Bunker's Hill
Warren Farm
Sewage Works
Wheatfields
Pasture Cl

25

A148
Congham Lodge
Southern's Plantation
Chalk Pit
Forty Acre Plantation
Valley Farm
Pithole Plantation

3

Congham Wood
Skate's Wood
Beech Plantation
Moat Wood
Garden Plantation

24

St Andrews Lane
Congham
Beeches Fell
Manor Farm
Pond Farm
Eastgate Drove

2

Pig Farm
PH
Wood Farm
B1153
Avenue Plantation
Stonepit Hills
Roydon
Broadgate Lane
Congham House
Crimea Plantation
Scotch Wood
Congham Heath
Broom Covert

23

Station Rd
Birch Dr
Low Rd
PH
Little La
Lynn Road
Congham Hall
Low Rd
Congham Rd
Mill Farm
Old South Wood
Alexandra Plantation
Massingham Road
Grimston
Chequers Rd
Nursery Way
Lodge Farm
Lynn Road
Gayton Rd
Ivy Farm
Bell Rd
PO
Grimston Carr
Snipe Covert
Long Hills

1

Blake Cl
Back La
Kings Way
Manor House Farm
Hawthorne Ave 1
Hazel Cl 2
Briar Cl 3
The Walnuts 4
PH
PE32
Chapel Road

22

Holly Meadows Sch
Vong Farm
Vong La
Church Farm
Moat
Eastmans La

70 A 71 B 72 C 73 D 74 E 75 F

A1
1 CHEQUERS CL
2 NURSERY CL
3 STEBBINGS CL
4 PHILLIPPO CL

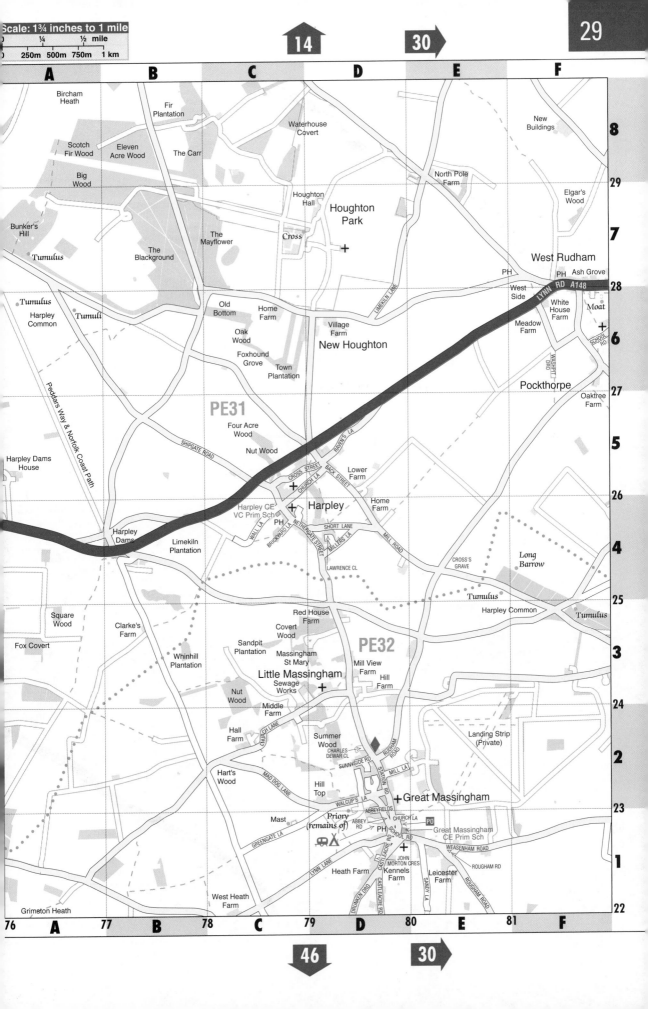

Scale: 1¾ inches to 1 mile

0 ¼ ½ mile
0 250m 500m 750m 1 km

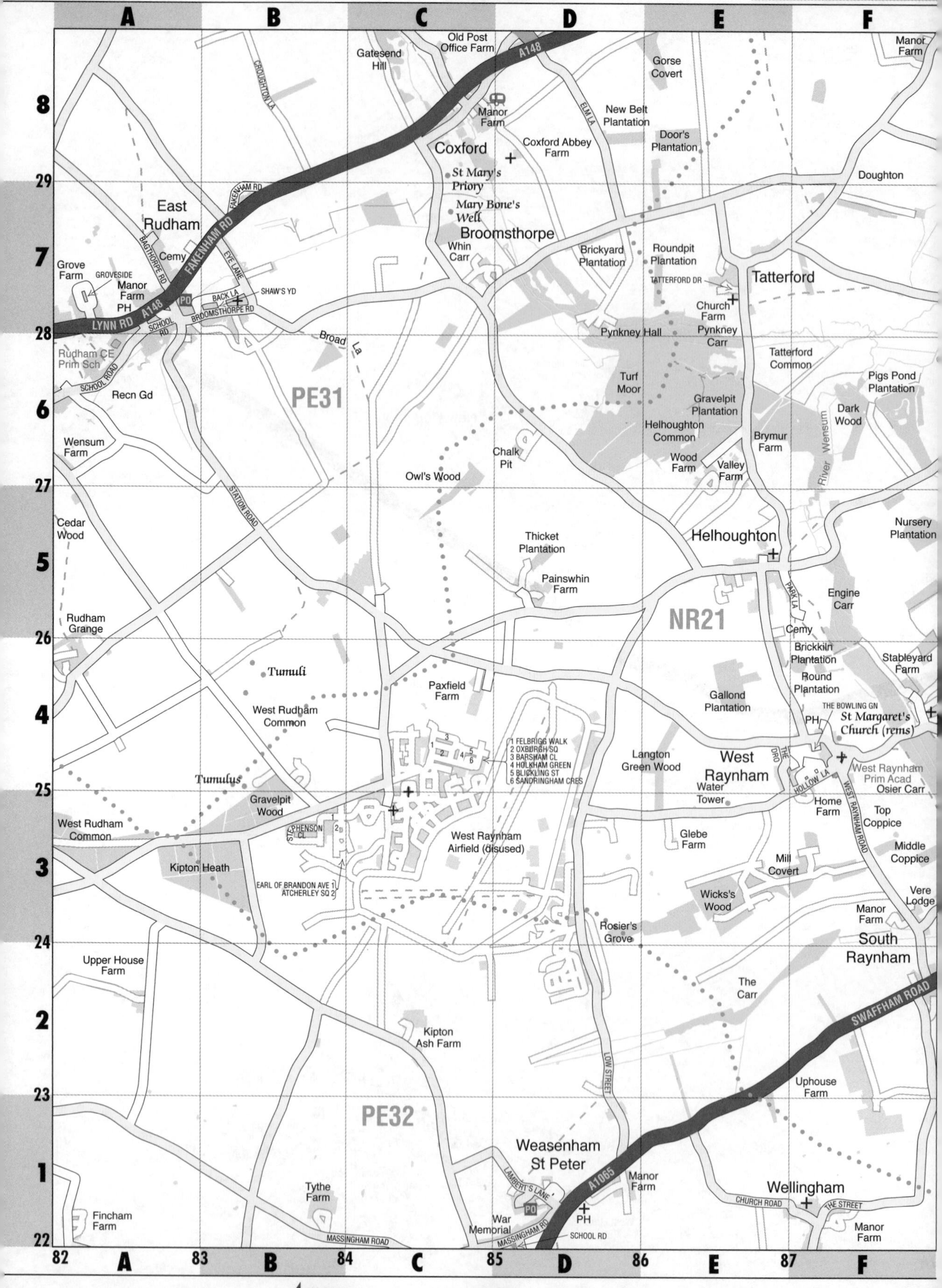

A B C D E F

8

Gatesend Hill
Old Post Office Farm
A148
Gorse Covert
Manor Farm
Manor Farm
New Belt Plantation
Coxford Abbey Farm
Door's Plantation
ELM LA

29

Coxford
St Mary's Priory
Doughton
Mary Bone's Well
Broomsthorpe
Brickyard Plantation
Roundpit Plantation
Tatterford
TATTERFORD DR

7

East Rudham
FAKENHAM RD
Grove Farm
GROVESIDE
Manor Farm PH
Cemy
EYE LANE
BACK LA
SHAW'S YD
Whin Carr
Church Farm
Pynkney Hall
Pynkney Carr
Tatterford Common
Pigs Pond Plantation

28

LYNN RD
A148
PO
SCHOOL RD
BROOMSTHORPE RD
BAGTHORPE RD
Rudham CE Prim Sch
Broad La
Turf Moor
Gravelpit Plantation
Dark Wood

6

PE31
SCHOOL ROAD
Recn Gd
Helhoughton Common
Brymur Farm
Wood Farm
Valley Farm
STATION ROAD

27

Wensum Farm
Owl's Wood
Chalk Pit

5

Cedar Wood
Thicket Plantation
Helhoughton
Nursery Plantation
Painswhin Farm
NR21

26

Rudham Grange
Tumuli
Brickkiln Plantation
Cemy
Round Plantation
Stableyard Farm
PARK LA

4

West Rudham Common
Paxfield Farm
Gallond Plantation
THE BOWLING GN
St Margaret's Church (rems)
PH
1 FELBRIGG WALK
2 OXBBRGH SQ
3 BARSHAM CL
4 HOLKHAM GREEN
5 BLICKLING ST
6 SANDRINGHAM CRES
3 1
2 4 6 5

25

Tumulus
Gravelpit Wood
STEPHENSON CL
West Raynham Airfield (disused)
Langton Green Wood
West Raynham
Water Tower
West Raynham Prim Acad
Osier Carr
Home Farm
Top Coppice
HOLLOW LA
DRO
WEST RAYNHAM ROAD

3

West Rudham Common
Kipton Heath
EARL OF BRANDON AVE 1
ATCHERLEY SQ 2
Glebe Farm
Mill Covert
Middle Coppice
Wicks's Wood
Vere Lodge
Manor Farm
South Raynham

24

Upper House Farm
Rosier's Grove
The Carr

2

Kipton Ash Farm
LOW STREET
SWAFFHAM ROAD
Uphouse Farm

23

PE32

1

Tythe Farm
LAMBERT'S LANE
Weasenham St Peter
A1065
Manor Farm
Wellingham
CHURCH ROAD
THE STREET

22

Fincham Farm
MASSINGHAM ROAD
War Memorial
PO
PH
SCHOOL RD
Manor Farm
River Wensum
Engine Carr
Brandon Ave

82 A 83 B 84 C 85 D 86 E 87 F

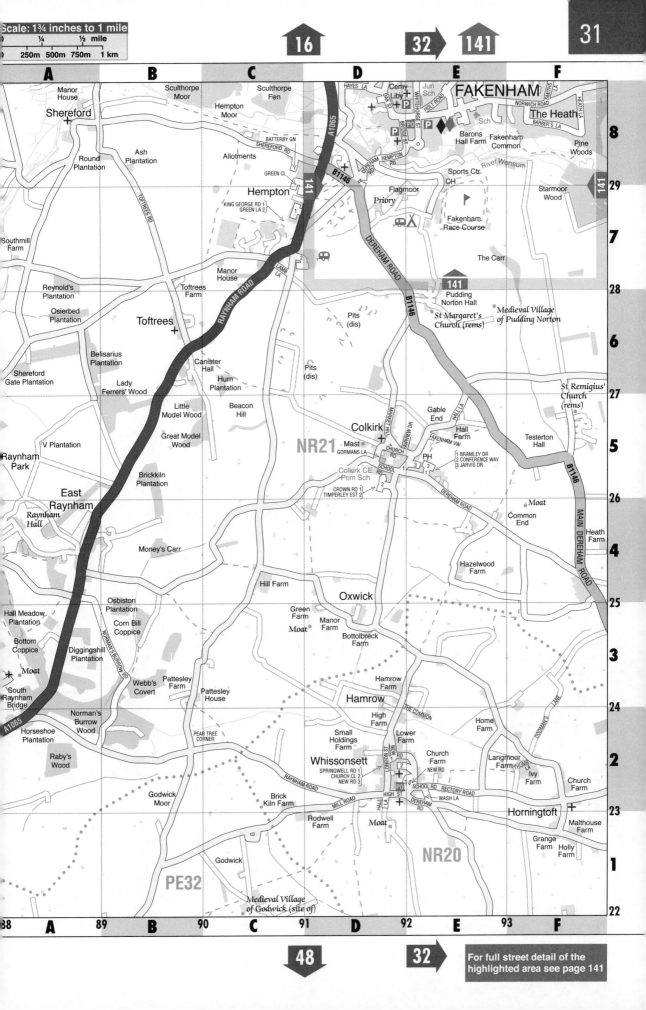

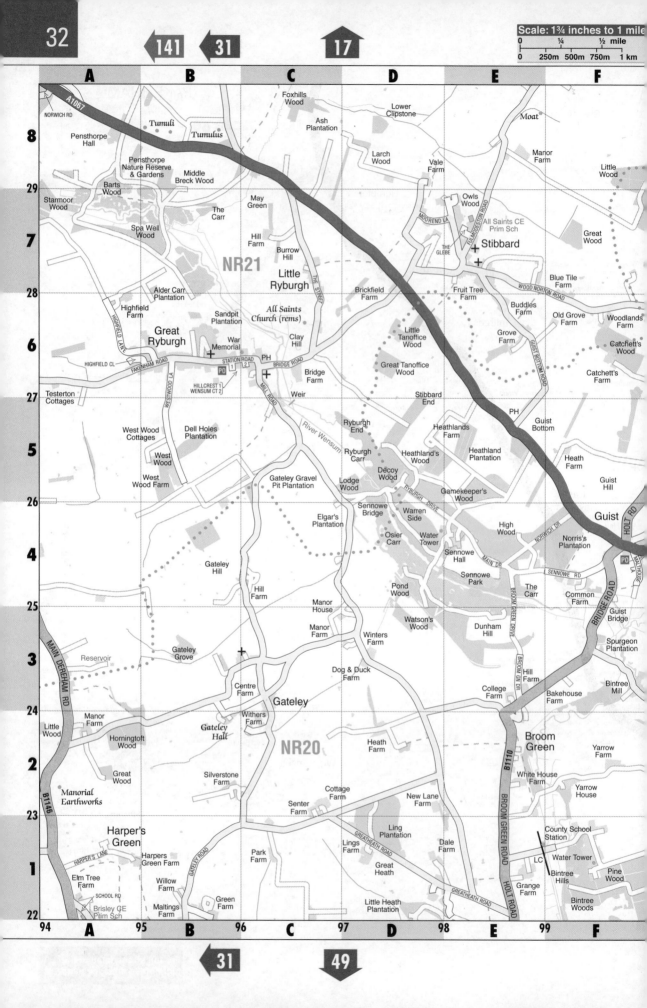

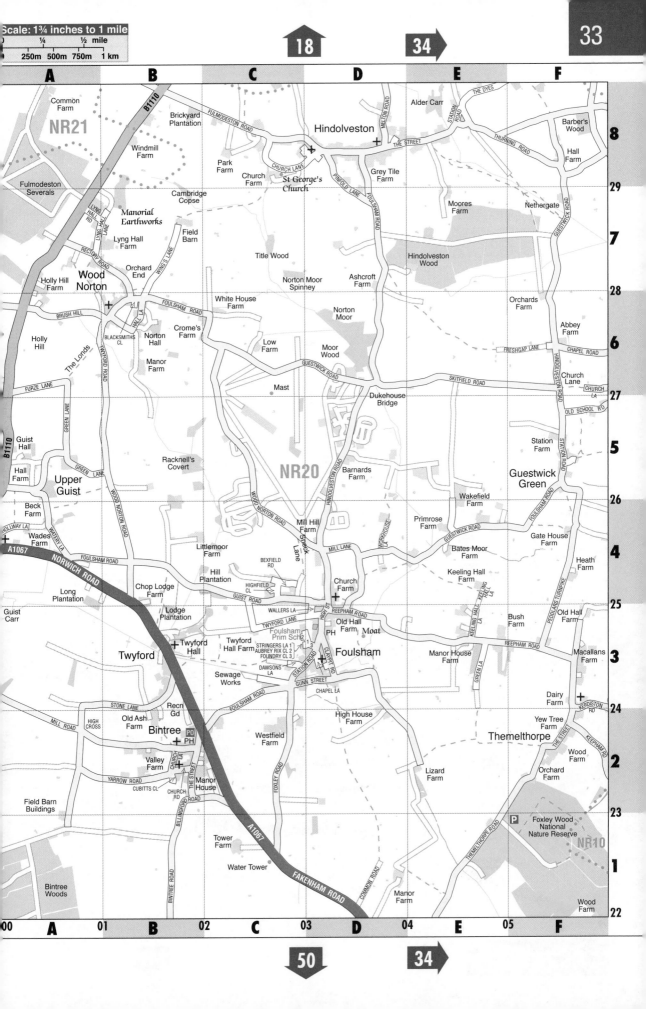

NR24
Burnt House Farm
Thurning Wood
Roundabout Farm
Conifer Plantation
Blackwater Plantation
Coconut Grove
Leechpit Plantation
Valley Farm
MONKS LA
ADAMS LA
B1149
IRMINGLAND RD
Ivy Farm

HINDOLVESTON ROAD
Icehouse Plantation
Gravelpit Plantation
Black Water
Ash Carr
Low Carr
Corpusty Hill
Bullock Shed Plantation

Hall Farm
Wade's Carr
Thurning
Foundry Hill
Victoria Farm
Bell's Grove
Red Pits
Grove Farm
Cropton Hall
Massingham's Grove

NR20
James Wood
Manor Farm
Wiggets Farm
Moat Farm
Oak Grove
Dairy Farm

Page's Farm
Crow Hill
Norton Corner
Moat
Woodhouse Farm
Grove End
Holly Grove
Cross
Icehouse Plantation
Heydon Hall

Moat
Old Hall
Tyby Farm
Glebe Farm
Palm Farm
NR11
Crabtree Farm
Heydon
The Grove

Guestwick
Blue Tile Farm
HEYDON ROAD
Crabgate Farm
Crabgate
THE STREET PH

Church Farm
Wood Dalling Hall
School Farm
Wood Dalling
Hill Farm
Cottages
Harold's Grove
American Plantation

OLD SCHOOL RD
REEPHAM RD
HALL ROAD
CHURCH LANE
Low Farm
Home Farm
Fieldhouse Farm
Brookdish Plantation

Odessa Farm
Church Plantation
Hempskey Wood
Swanhills Plantation
Stinton Hall Farm

Palgrave Farm
GUESTWICK LANE
Seaman's Farm
George Farm
Forest Farm
Potash Wood
Manor Farm
Manor House

Palgrave Wood
Newlands Farm
Gatehouse Farm
THE STREET

Thorney Farm
Primrose Farm
Salle
Water Tower
Salle Park

KERDISTON ROAD
FORWATER ROAD
Kerdiston
Manor Farm
Salle Moor Hall
149
Bath Plantation
B1145

Carr Farm
Blue Tile Farm
Moat
Bottom Wood
NR10
Upper Barn Farm

Marriot's Way
Old Hall Farm
New Plantation
149
Renpark Farm
WOOD DALLING ROAD
CAWSTON ROAD
Manor Farm
Moor Farm

Wood Farm
Brick Kiln Farm
The Grove
Pettywell
STONEY LANE
ORCHARD LA
THE MOOR
Booton Common Nature Reserve

Grange Farm
Reepham
NORWICH RD
Reepham Moor
Booton
Booton Hall

FIR LANE
Oaks Farm
OLD LANE
Vale Farm
MARKET PL
DEREHAM RD
STATION ROAD
NEW ROAD
Beck Farm
Town Farm
THE STREET

Model Cottage Farm
Marriot's Way
Park Farm
Cemy
Rookery Farm
Whitwell Street
FURZE LANE

B1145
Hackford Hall
Sch & Coll
Prim Sch
RUDDS LA
WHITWELL RD
MILL ROAD
THE STREET
Dairy Farm

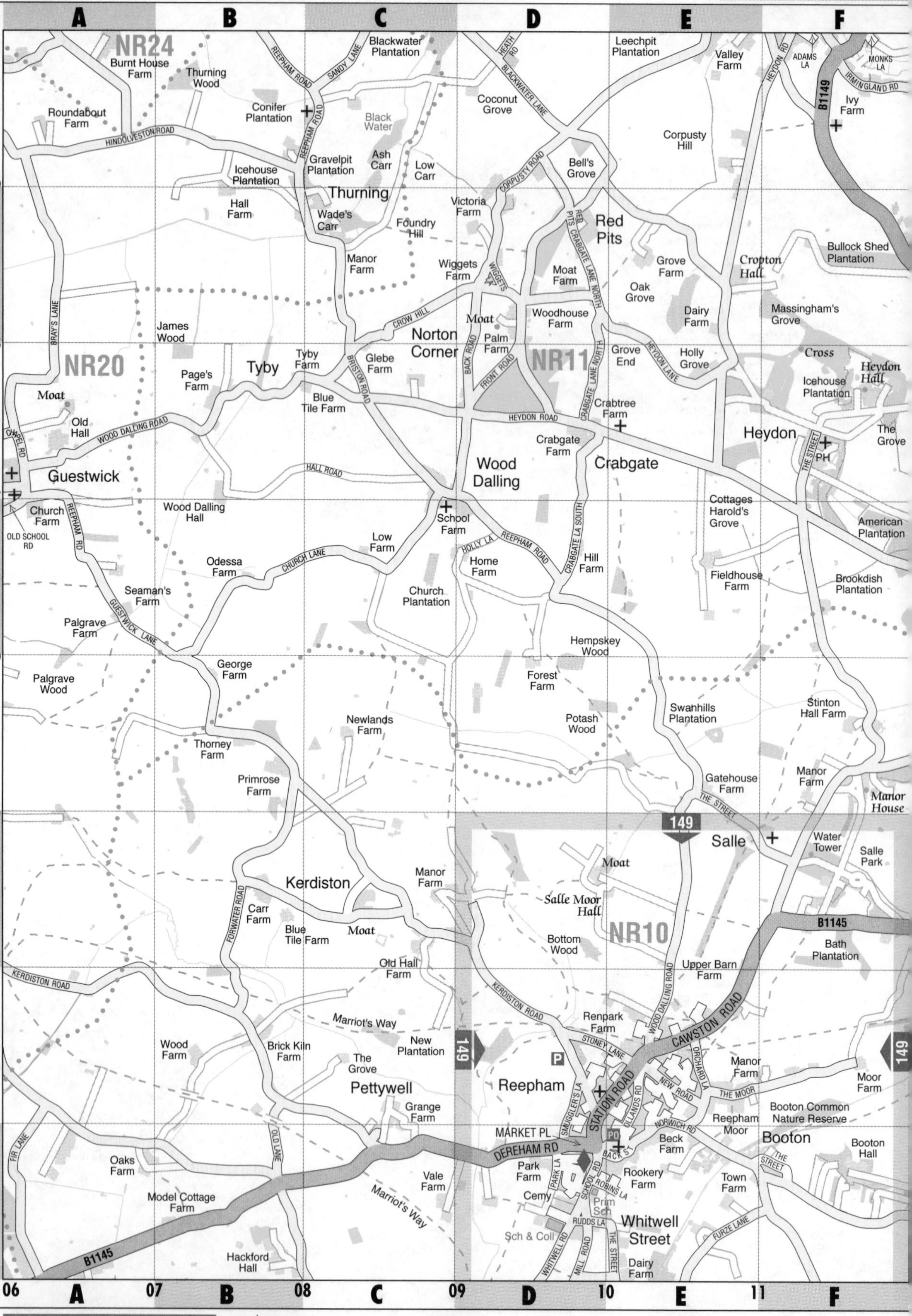

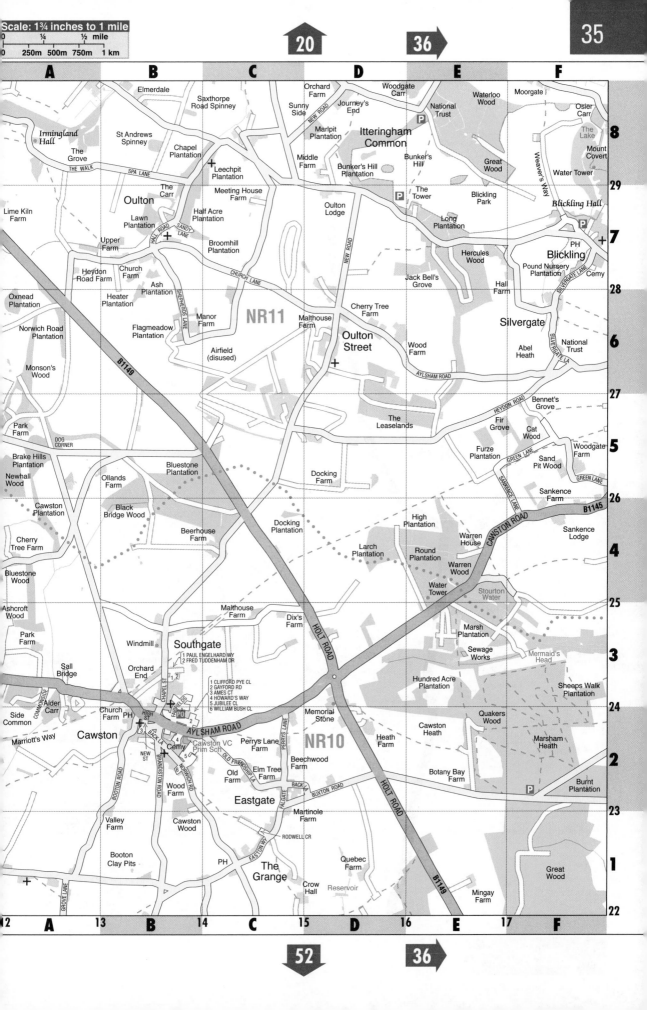

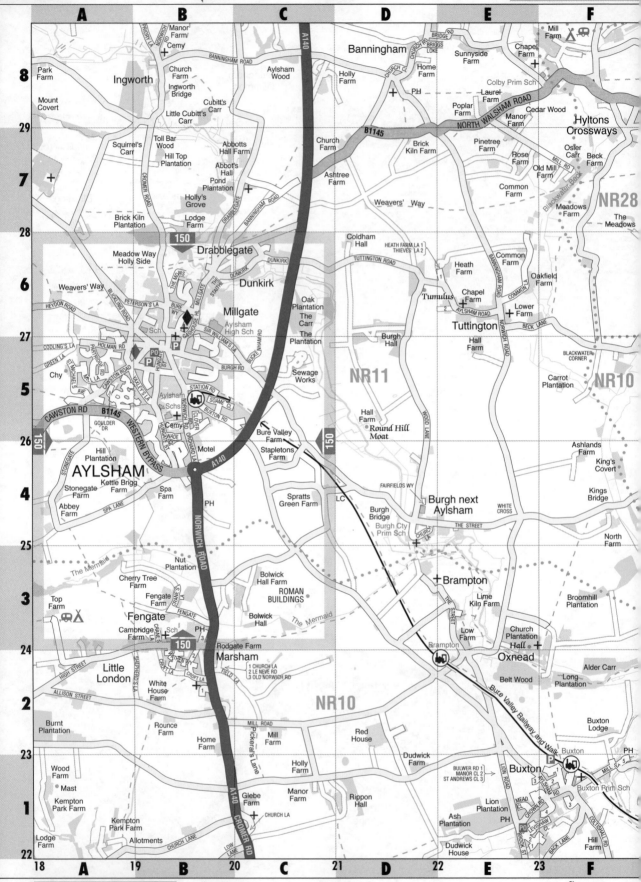

A B C D E F

8
Park Farm
Mount Covert
Ingworth

Manor Farm/ Cemy
Church Farm
Ingworth Bridge
Cubitt's Carr
Little Cubitt's Carr

BANNINGHAM ROAD
Aylsham Wood

Banningham
Holly Farm
Home Farm
PH
Sunnyside Farm
Chapel Farm
Mill Farm

Colby Prim Sch
Hyltons Crossways

29
Squirrel's Carr
Toll Bar Wood
Hill Top Plantation
Abbotts Hall Farm
Abbot's Hall Pond Plantation

B1145
Church Farm
Brick Kiln Farm

NORTH WALSHAM ROAD
Poplar Farm
Laurel Farm
Manor Farm
Cedar Wood
Osier Carr
Old Mill Farm
Beck Farm

7
Brick Kiln Plantation
Holly's Grove
Lodge Farm

Ashtree Farm
Weavers' Way

Pinetree Farm
Rose Farm
Common Farm

Meadows Farm
NR28
The Meadows

28
150
Drabblegate
DUNKIRK

Coldham Hall
HEATH FARM LA 1
THIEVES LA 2
Heath Farm
Common Farm
Oakfield Farm

6
Meadow Way
Holly Side
Weavers' Way
HEYDON ROAD
The Mews
Dunkirk
Millgate
Oak Plantation
The Carr
The Plantation

TUTTINGTON ROAD
Tumulus
Chapel Farm
Lower Farm

BECK LANE

27
Sch
Aylsham High Sch
PETERSON'S LA

Burgh Hall
Hall Farm
Tuttington
AYLSHAM ROAD

BLACKWATER CORNER

5
Chy
GREEN LA
CODLING'S LA
ST MICHAELS AVE
HOLMAN RD
PO
P
BURGH RD
Sewage Works

NR11
Hall Farm
Round Hill Moat

WOOD LANE

Carrot Plantation
NR10

Ashlands Farm
King's Covert

26
150
CAWSTON RD
B1145
GOULDER DR
Aylsham Schs
STATION RD
SOAME CL
BUXTON RD
Bure Valley Farm
Stapletons Farm

150
FAIRFIELDS WY
Burgh Bridge
Burgh next Aylsham
Burgh City Prim Sch
WHITE CROSS

Kings Bridge

4
AYLSHAM
Hill Plantation
Stonegate Farm
Kettle Brigg Farm
Abbey Farm
SPA LANE
Spa Farm
WESTERN BYPASS
STONEGATE
A140
Motel
PH

Spratts Green Farm
LC

CHURCH LA
Brampton
THE STREET
Lime Kiln Farm
Low Farm
Church Plantation Hall
Oxnead

North Farm
Alder Carr
Long Plantation

25
The Mermaid
Nut Plantation

Bolwick Hall Farm
ROMAN BUILDINGS
The Mermaid

Brampton

Broomhill Plantation

3
Top Farm
Cherry Tree Farm
Fengate Farm
CRANE'S
Fengate
FENGATE
Bolwick Hall

Belt Wood
Brampton

Buxton Lodge

24
Cambridge Farm
CROFT LA
Sch
PH
150
Marsham
Rodgate Farm
1 CHURCH LA
2 LE NEVE RD
3 OLD NORWICH RD

Buxton
P
PH
MILL ST

2
Little London
White House Farm
ALLISON STREET
SHEPHERD'S LA

MILL ROAD
Mill Farm
Red House

NR10

Dudwick Farm
BULWER RD 1
MANOR CL 2
ST ANDREWS CL 3
Lion Plantation
PH

Buxton Lodge

23
Wood Farm
Mast
Burnt Plantation
Rounce Farm
Home Farm
Pickeral's Lane
Holly Farm
Manor Farm
Rippon Hall
Dudwick Farm
Buxton
P
Buxton Prim Sch
MILL ST

1
Kempton Park Farm
Kempton Park Farm
Allotments
A140
Glebe Farm
CHURCH LA
CROMER RD
LOW LANE

Ash Plantation
Dudwick House
Hill Farm

22
Lodge Farm

F1
1 STRACEY RD
2 SEWELL RD
3 DRAKES LOKE
4 CHURCH CL
5 MILL REACH

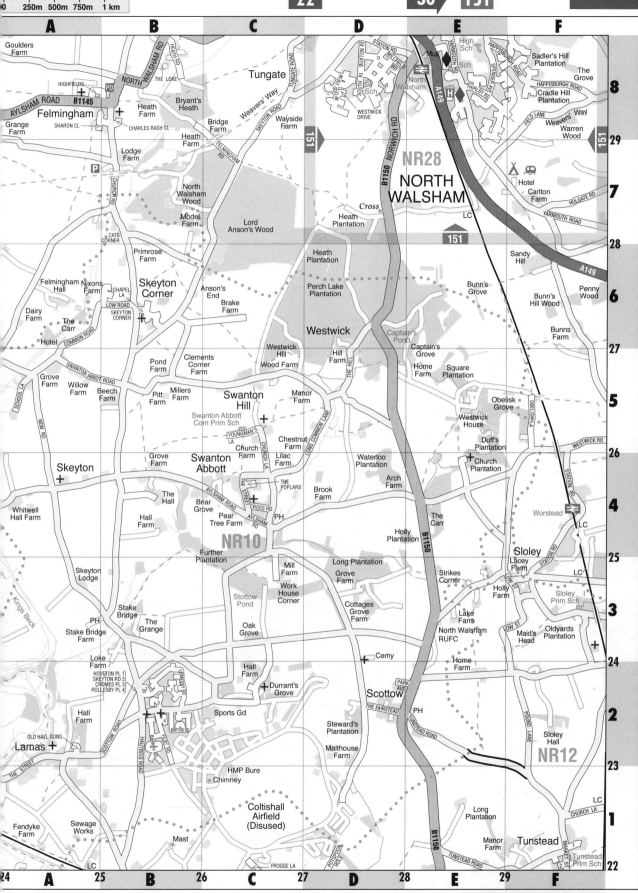

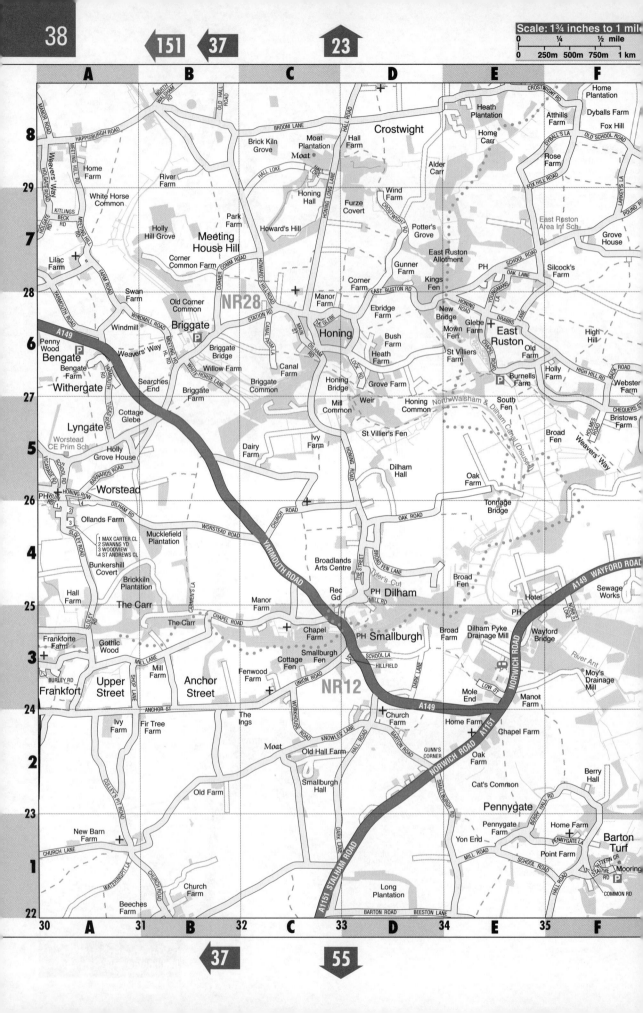

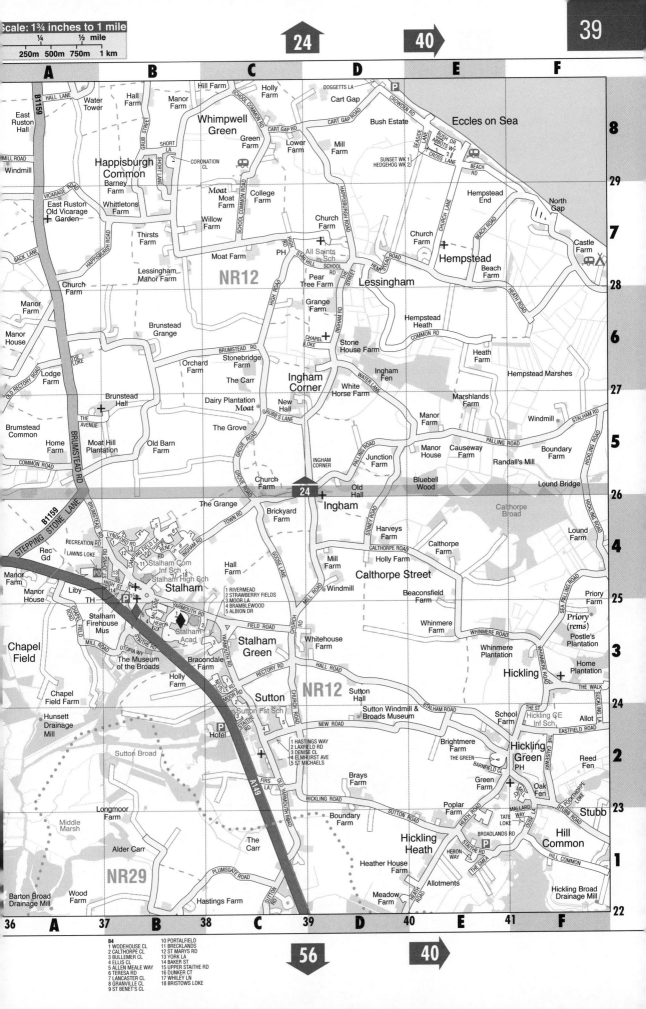

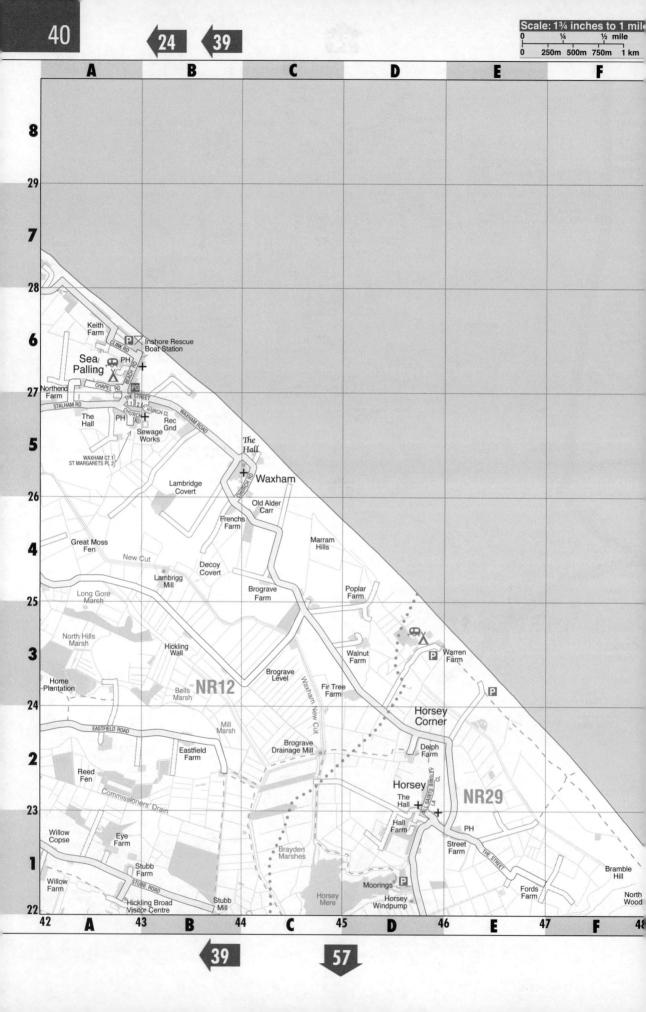

Scale: 1¾ inches to 1 mile

A   B   C   D   E   F

8

29

7

28

6   Keith Farm   Inshore Rescue Boat Station
CLINK RD
PH
Sea Palling
BEACH RD

27   Northend Farm   PO
STALHAM RD   THE STREET   WAXHAM ROAD
CHAPEL RD
The Hall   PH   CHURCH RD   CHURCH CL
Sewage Works   Rec Gnd

5   WAXHAM CT 1
ST MARGARETS PL 2   The Hall

Waxham
Lambridge Covert   Old Alder Carr

26   Frenchs Farm

4   Great Moss Fen   Marram Hills
New Cut   Decoy Covert
Lambrigg Mill   Brograve Farm   Poplar Farm

25   Long Gore Marsh

North Hills Marsh   Walnut Farm   Warren Farm
3   Hickling Wall
Home Plantation   Brograve Level   Fir Tree Farm
Bells Marsh   NR12   Waxham New Cut   Horsey Corner

24   EASTFIELD ROAD   Mill Marsh   Delph Farm
Reed Fen   Eastfield Farm   Brograve Drainage Mill   Horsey
2   The Hall   NR29
ALL SAINTS   BINSLEY CL
Commissioners' Drain   Hall Farm

23   Willow Copse   Eye Farm   PH
Street Farm   THE STREET
Brayden Marshes
1   Stubb Farm   Bramble Hill
Willow Farm   STUBB ROAD   Moorings   P
Horsey Mere   Horsey Windpump   Fords Farm   North Wood
Hickling Broad Visitor Centre   Stubb Mill

22   42   A   43   B   44   C   45   D   46   E   47   F   48

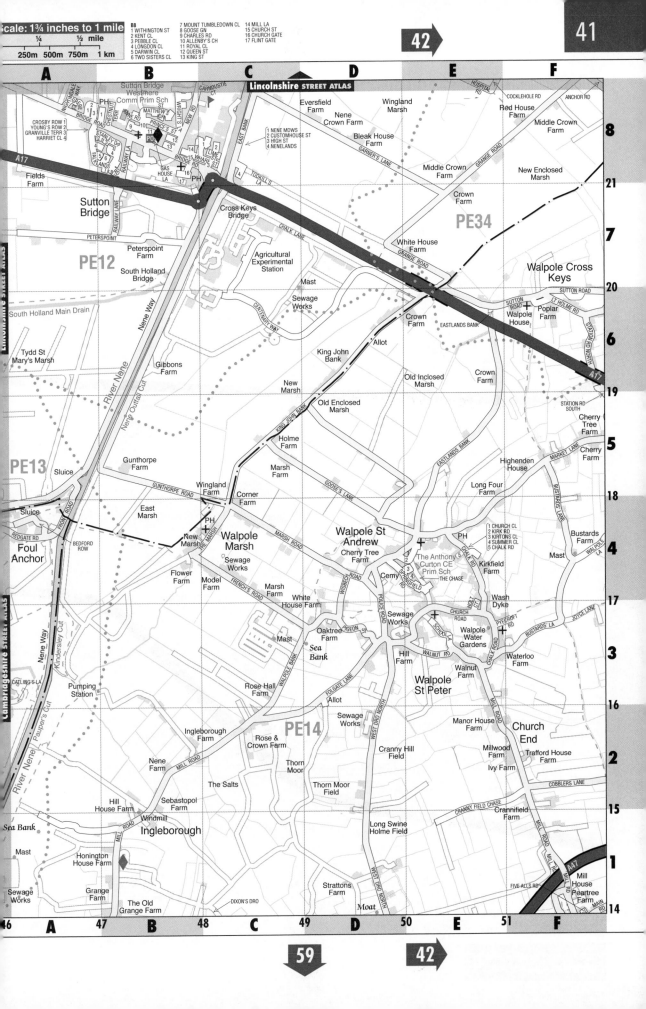

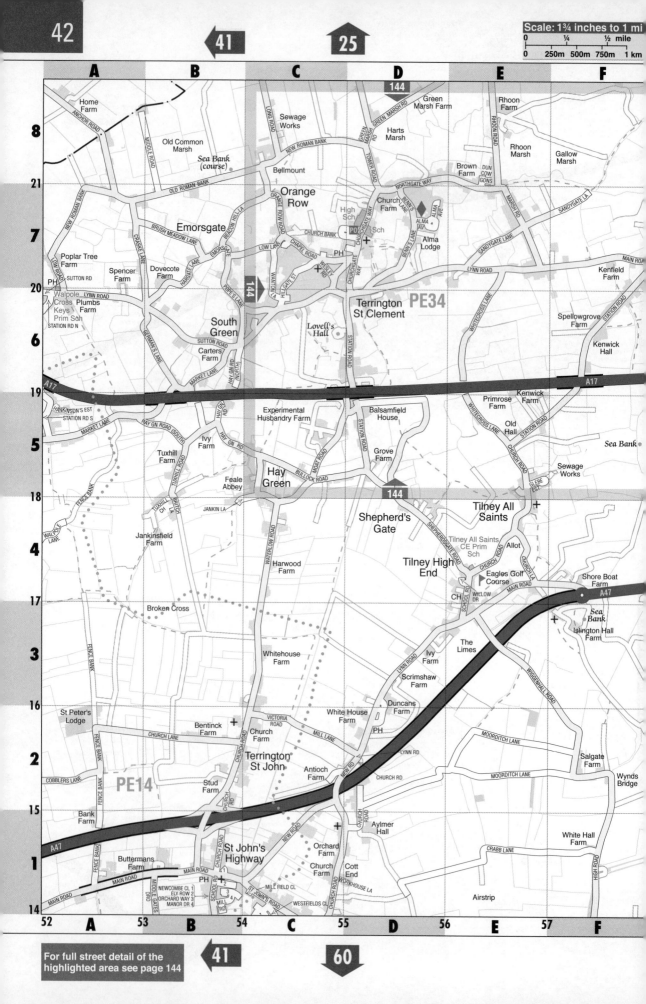

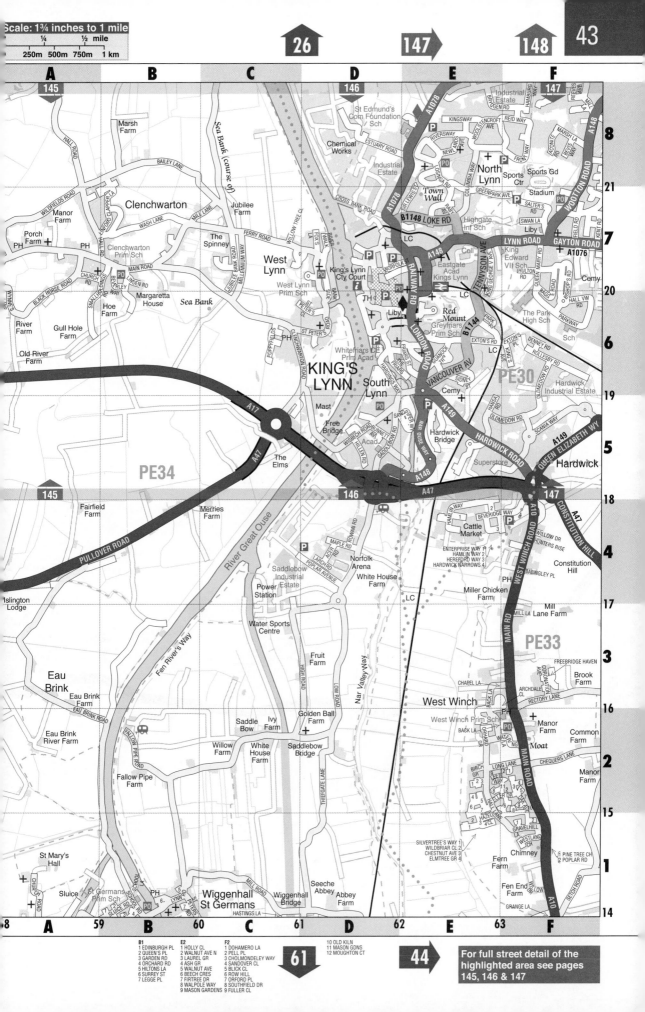

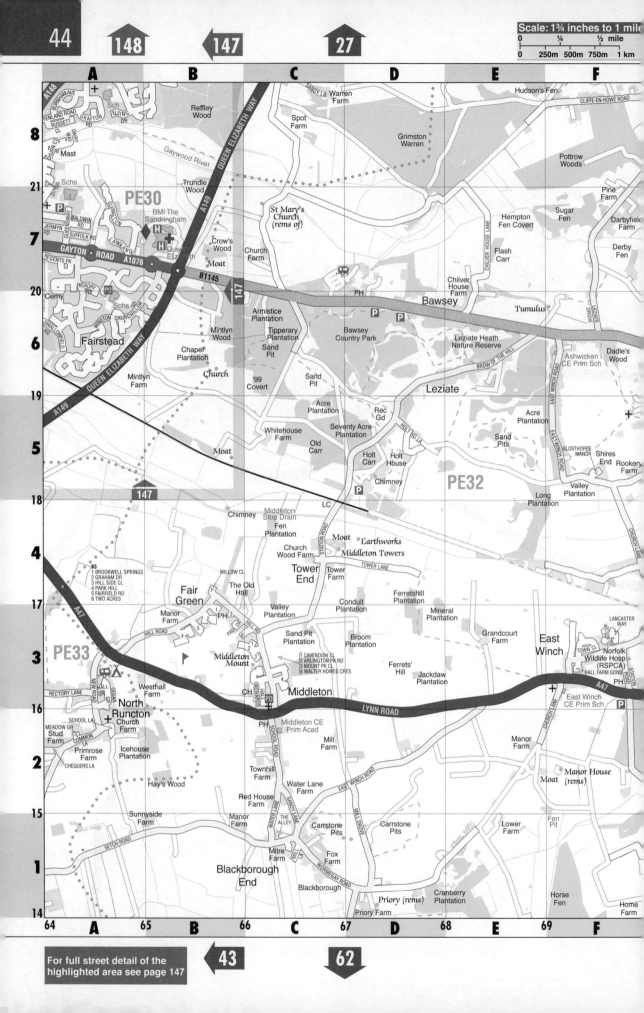

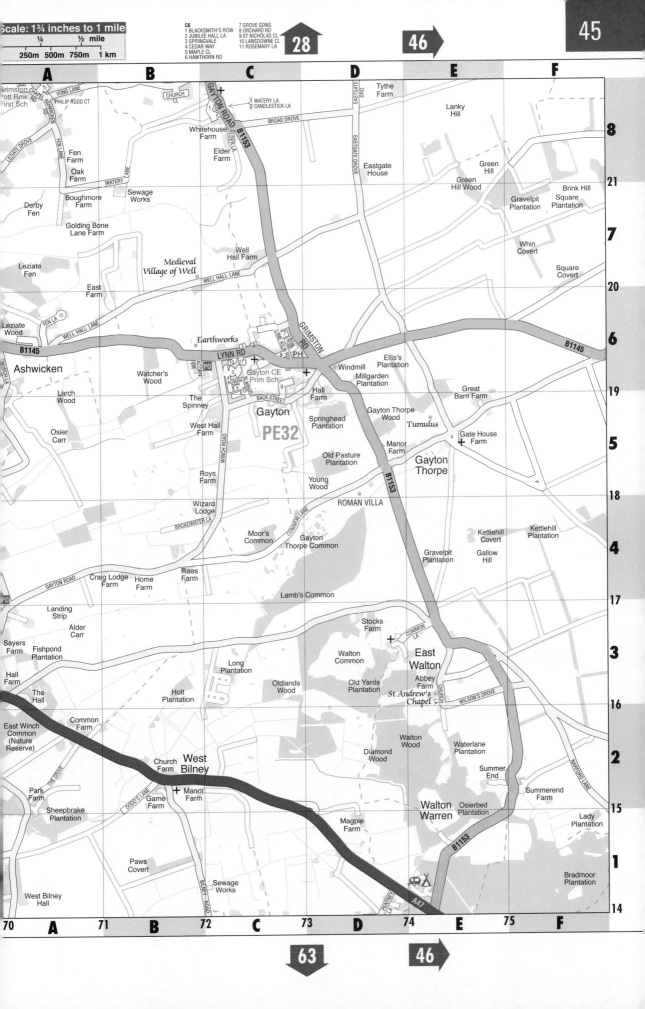

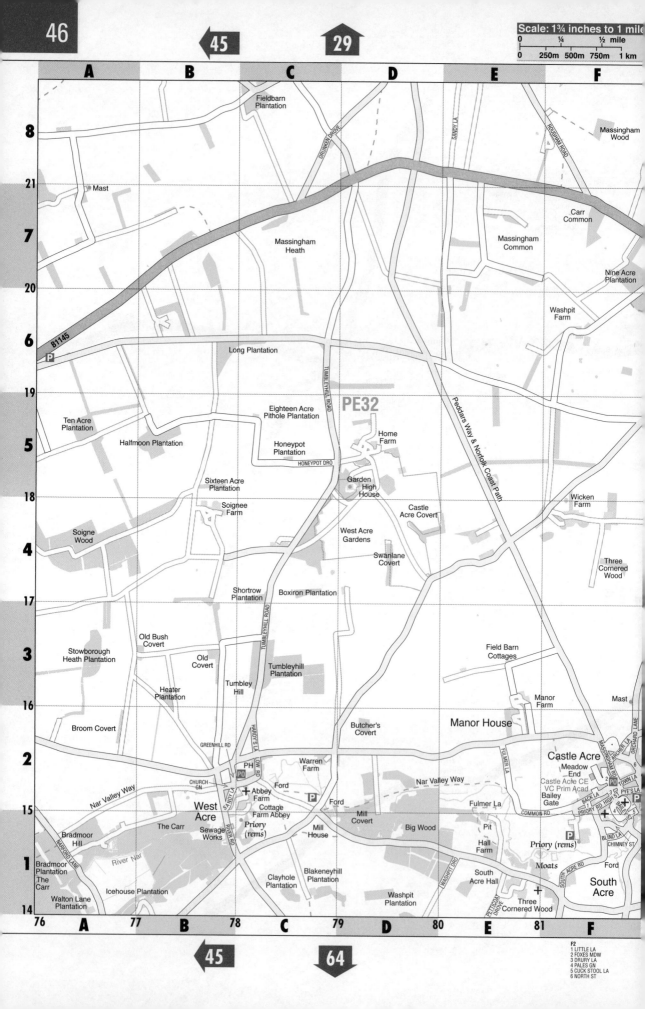

A   B   C   D   E   F

8
Fieldbarn Plantation
DRUNKEN DROVE
SANDY LA
ROUGHAM ROAD
Massingham Wood

21
Mast
Carr Common

7
Massingham Heath
Massingham Common
Nine Acre Plantation

20
B1145
Washpit Farm

6
P
Long Plantation
TUMBLEYHILL ROAD
Peddars Way & Norfolk Coast Path

19
PE32

5
Ten Acre Plantation
Halfmoon Plantation
Eighteen Acre Pithole Plantation
Honeypot Plantation
HONEYPOT DRO
Home Farm
Wicken Farm

18
Sixteen Acre Plantation
Soignee Farm
Garden High House
Castle Acre Covert

4
Soigne Wood
West Acre Gardens
Swanlane Covert
Three Cornered Wood

17
Shortrow Plantation
TUMBLEYHILL ROAD
Boxiron Plantation

3
Stowborough Heath Plantation
Old Bush Covert
Old Covert
Tumbleyhill Plantation
Field Barn Cottages
Manor Farm
Mast

16
Heater Plantation
Tumbley Hill
Butcher's Covert
Manor House

2
Broom Covert
GREENHILL RD
HARDY'S LA
LOW RD
Warren Farm
Nar Valley Way
FULMER LA
Castle Acre
Meadow End
Castle Acre CE VC Prim Acad
MASSINGHAM RD
ARCHER LA
ORCHARD LANE
Nar Valley Way
PH
PO
CHURCH GN
SANDY LA
Ford
Ford
Bailey Gate
BACK LA
PRIORY RD
HIGH ST
TOWN LA
PYE'S LA
P

15
Nar Valley Way
MARFORD LANE
RIVER RD
West Acre
Abbey Farm
Cottage Farm Abbey
P
Ford
Mill Covert
Fulmer La
COMMON RD
BLIND LA
CHIMNEY ST

1
Bradmoor Hill
The Carr
Priory (rems)
Sewage Works
Mill House
Big Wood
Pit
Hall Farm
Moats
Priory (rems)
Ford
P
SOUTH ACRE RD
South Acre

Bradmoor Plantation The Carr
Walton Lane Plantation
Icehouse Plantation
Clayhole Plantation
Blakeneyhill Plantation
WASHPIT DRO
Washpit Plantation
PETTICOAT DROVE
South Acre Hall
Three Cornered Wood

14
River Nar

76 A 77 B 78 C 79 D 80 E 81 F

F2
1 LITTLE LA
2 FOXES MDW
3 DRURY LA
4 PALES GN
5 CUCK STOOL LA
6 NORTH ST

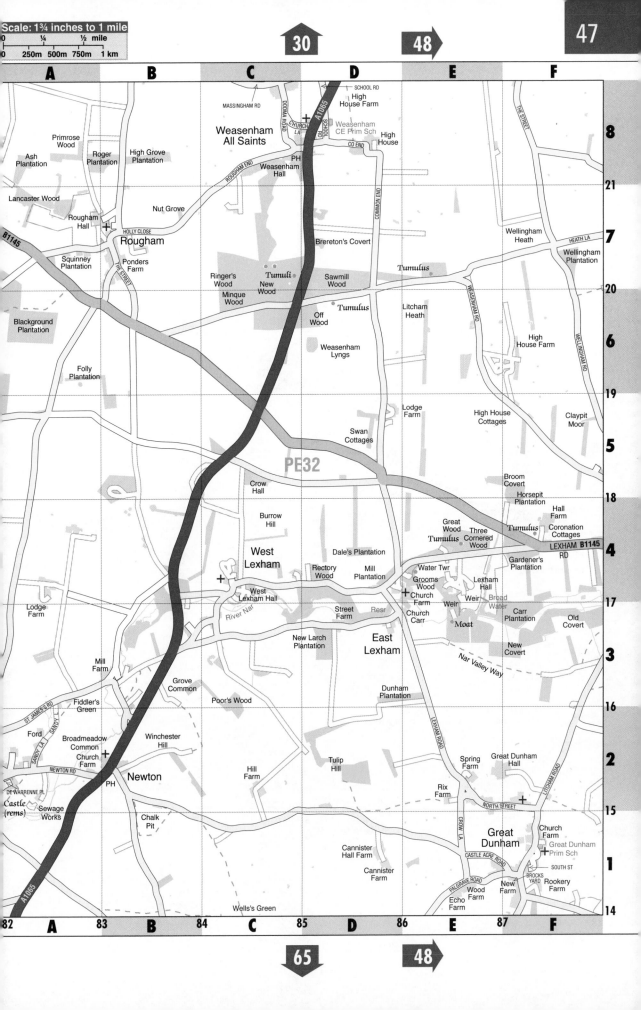

47 31

Scale: 1¾ inches to 1 mile

| 0 | ¼ | ½ | mile |

| 0 | 250m | 500m | 750m | 1 km |

A B C D E F

8

Tittleshall Common

Moat

Manor Farm

1 PEAKHALL RD
2 RENOWOOD CL
3 FOLLY YARD

Church Wood

Eastfield Wood

Fox Covert

Sinclair's Grove

Norman's Wood

Hurdle Wood

Dandy Farm

Tuttle Farm

Water Tower

BACK LANE

21

TITTSHALL RD

BARTON'S LA

High St

Tittleshall

Sandholes Wood

Wicken Farm

TITTLESHALL RD

WHISSONSETT RD

CHURCH LANE

Lyng Farm

High Green Farm

Glebe Farm

Stanfield

WELLINGHAM RD

CLAY HILL

7

War Memorial

HEATH LANE

BLENHEIM CRES

FAKENHAM RD

Model Farm

High House Farm

STANFIELD ROAD

Cokesford Farm

Tittleshall Hill

NEW ROAD

Cherry Tree Farm

Chapel Farm

20

Field Barn

LITCHAM ROAD

MILEHAM ROAD

Grenstein Grove

Nar Valley Way

TITTLESHALL ROAD

Lounds Wood

Moat

BURGHWOOD DR 1
CLAXTON CL 2
CASTLE DRIFT 3

Rookery Plantation

THE PADDOCKS

Mileham Prim Sch

Burwood Hall

Moat

Park Farm

THE STREET

STANFIELD ROAD

NR20

Reed Lane Farm

Willow Grange

6

Grenstein Farm

Meadow Cottages

Wyken Farm

RATTLE ROW

Sunnyside Farm

BACK LANE

Game Farm

Castle (rems)

Rec Gd

PO

Rudd's Drift

Lodge Farm

Home Farm

19

TITTLESHALL ROAD

Mill Farm

LITCHAM ROAD

PE32

White House Farm

BEESTON ROAD

Mileham

Horse Wood

RUDD'S DRIFT

Pheasant Covert

Manor House

5

Grenstein Moor

Oaklands Farm

Newlings Farm

Coronation Farm

B1145

Nar Valley Way

River Nar

COLLEY PL DRIFT

Colley Hill

Colley Hill Farm

Nar Valley Way

Medieval Village of Little Bittering (site of)

WELLINGHAM RD

WEASENHAM RD

Litcham Prim Sch

KEPPEL CL

Litcham Village Museum

MILEHAM ROAD

Hell Pit

Sand & Gravel Pit

Moat

Bittering

18

BUTT LA

DRURS

Litcham High Sch

The Warren

Windmill

Padgetts Farm

Hulver Hill

Launditch

SALTER'S LANE

LITCHAM ROAD

REED LANE

HONEYPOT LANE

Litcham Hall

LEXHAM RD

BACK ST

PO

CHAMBER ST

DEREHAM ROAD

Litcham

Holly Farm

NR19

4

MANOR DR 1
RECTORY MDW 2

Moat PH

Litcham Priory

P

Sewage Works

Bridge Farm

DURHAM RD

Nar Valley Way

Nature Reserve

Punch Farm

Manor Farm

Crossways Farm

Point Farm

Spreadoak Plantation

17

BEESTON ROAD

Sand & Gravel Pit

MILEHAM ROAD

Holmedene Farm

Primrose Farm

Longham Hall

Church Cottages

REED LANE

3

Kempstone Manor Farm

St Pauls Church (rems)

Narrowgate Farm

WATERY LANE

LORD NELSON CL 1
BURRELLS MDW 2
MACE DR 3
TOWN HOUSE DRIFT 4

Dykewood Farm

Moat

NEW ROAD

16

Church Farm

CHURCH ROAD

MILL DRIFT

BACK LANE

High House Farm

THE STREET

CHAPEL LA

PH

STYES L

Beeston Prim Sch

WATER END

Waterend Farm

Race Course Farm

Mast Works

Canister Farm

WENDLING ROAD

Hall Green

PH

Holly Farm

2

Drury Square

Beeston

Rectory Plantation

DEREHAM RD

DAIRY DRIFT

War Memorial

Airfield (dis)

Moat

Park Farm

15

Church Road

Moat

Sewage Works

DRURY FARM BRIDGE SCH

Drury Farm

Herne Hill Farm

HERNE LA

BEESTON ROAD

Honeypot Wood

P

Nursery Farm

Walnut Tree Farm

HERNE LA

Nature Reserve

1

Tuck's Farm

BEESTON LA

New Farm

FRANSHAM RD

Herne Lane Farm

High Green

14

Beeston Road Farm

88 A 89 B 90 C 91 D 92 E 93 F

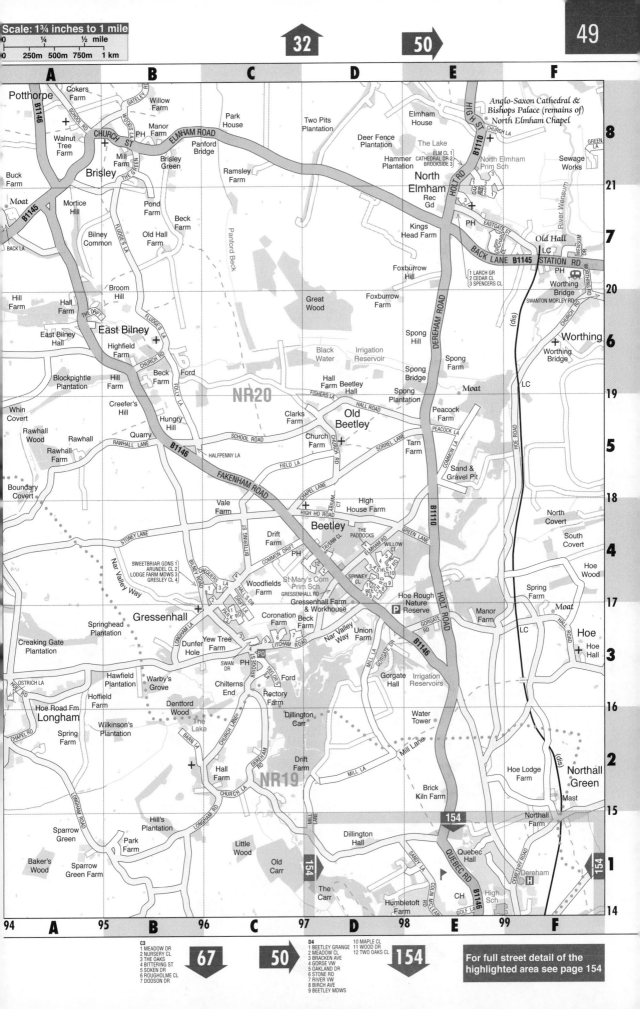

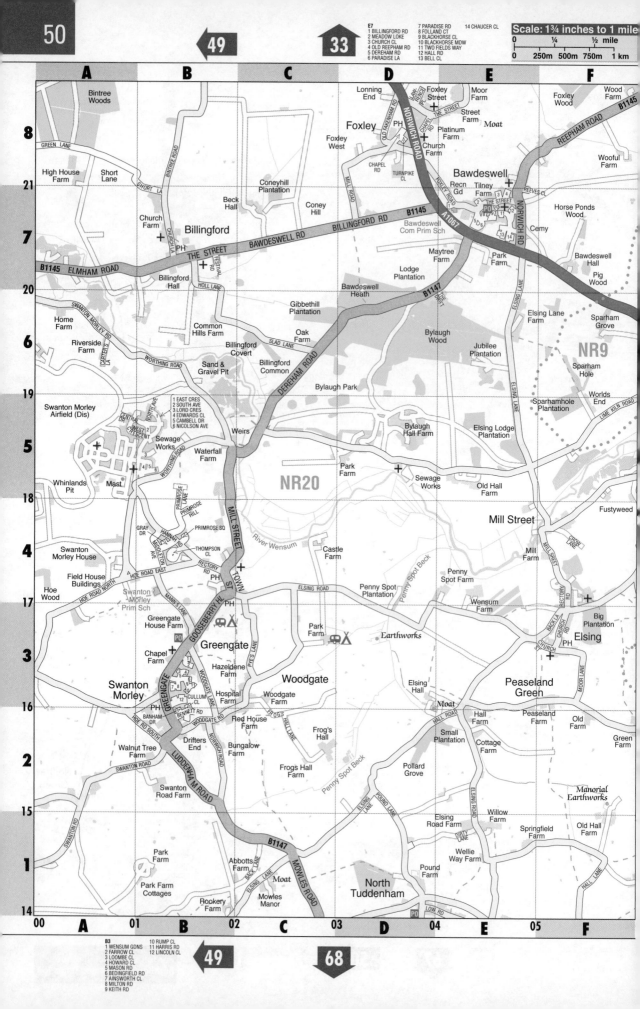

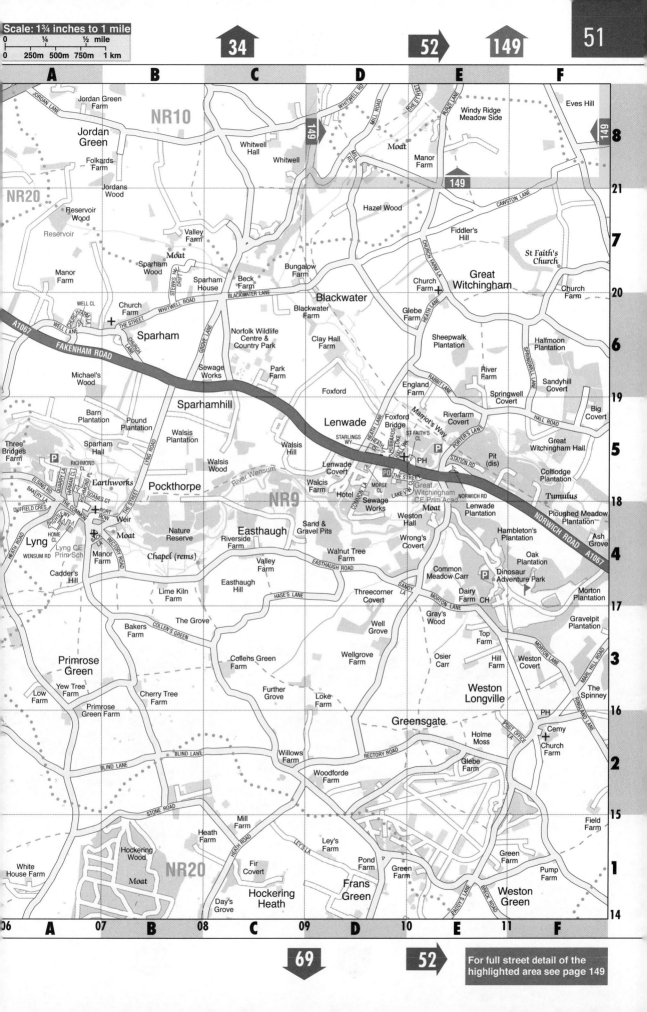

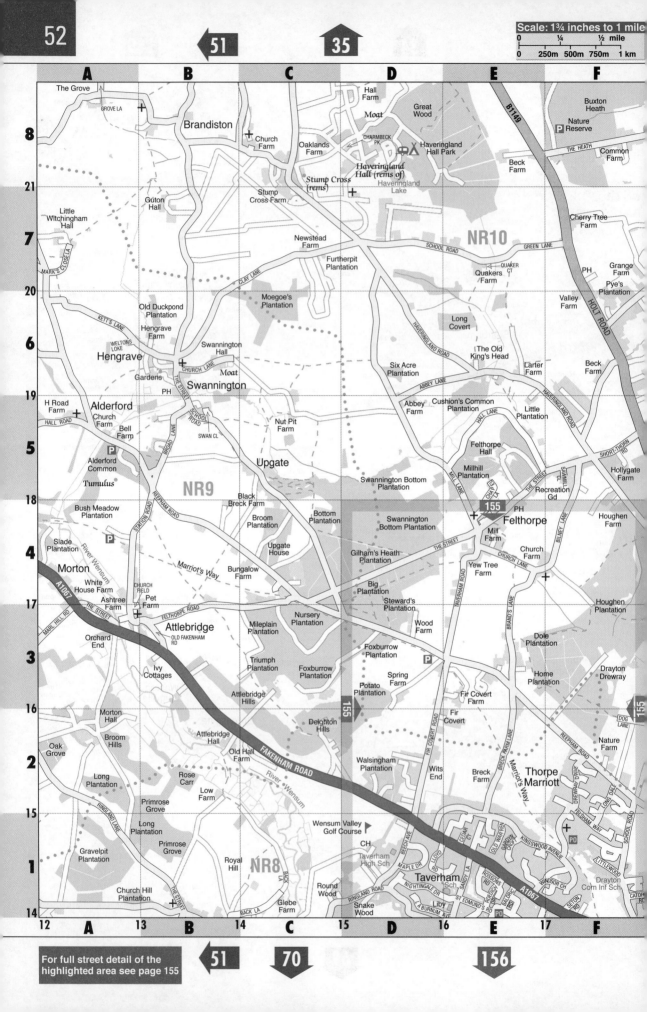

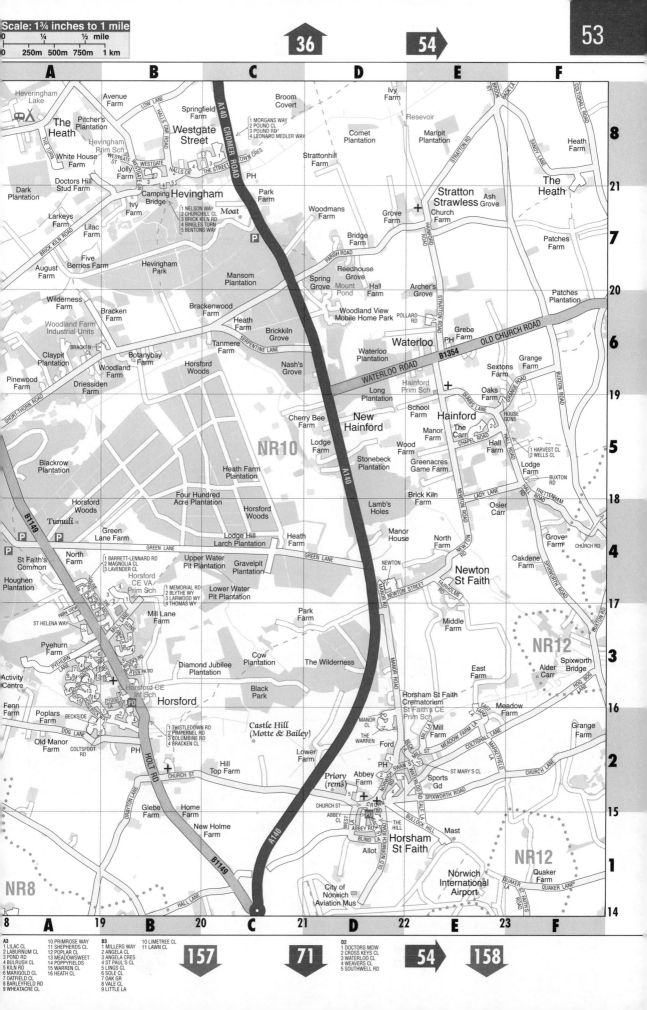

Scale: 1¾ inches to 1 mile
0   ¼   ½   mile
0   250m 500m 750m 1 km

A3
1 LILAC CL
2 LABURNUM CL
3 POND RD
4 BULRUSH CL
5 KILN RD
6 MARIGOLD CL
7 OATFIELD CL
8 BARLEYFIELD RD
9 WHEATACRE CL
10 PRIMROSE WAY
11 SHEPHERDS CL
12 POPLAR CL
13 MEADOWSWEET
14 POPPYFIELDS
15 WARREN CL
16 HEATH CL

B3
1 MILLERS WAY
2 ANGELA CL
3 ANGELA CRES
4 ST PAUL'S CL
5 LINGS CL
6 SOLE CL
7 OAK GR
8 VALE CL
9 LITTLE LA
10 LIMETREE CL
11 LAWN CL

D2
1 DOCTORS MDW
2 CROSS KEYS CL
3 WATERLOO CL
4 WEAVERS CL
5 SOUTHWELL RD

53

C6
1 CHURCH CL
2 RECTORY RD
3 ST MARGARET'S CL
4 CAUSEWAY DR
5 GLEBE WAY
6 TUNGATE WAY

7 HAVERGATE
8 PATRICIA AVE
9 CHURCH CL

C7
1 LING CL
2 ADDISON CL
3 HANCOCK CL
4 HIGHFIELD WAY

37

Scale: 1¾ inches to 1 mile

NR10

Moat
Mayton Wood
Mayton Hall
Bridge Farm
Mayton Bridge
Little Hautbois
Landfill Site
Hernes Farm
Colkes Farm
Grove Farm
Great Hautbois
Ling Common
Sco Ruston
St Michael's Church
B1150
Hall Farm
LC
PH
LC
LC

Grange Farm
Boathouse Carr
Hall Farm
St Theobalds Church (rems)
Stewpond Carr
Castle (site of)
Largate Farm
Church Farm
Ling Wy
Coltishall
P
PH
New Buildings Farm
1 WESTBOURNE RD
2 ST JOHN'S CL
3 RECTORY CL
4 COLLEGE CL
THE HILL
THE STREET
St James
Coltishall Prim Sch
Chapel La
College Cl
LC

Park Farm
BUXTON RD
B1354
Glebe Farm
Cooper's Grove
Church Farm
RECTORY RD
GLEBE WAY
NORWICH RD
PH
HIGH STATION RD
Coltishall
CHURCH ST
THE GROVE
White Lion Rd
Coltishall Hall
PH
PO
Moorings
Anchor St
Anchor Wood
WROXHAM ROAD
Belaugh Green Lane
Belaugh Green

Langmere Farm
CHURCH LANE
Horstead Mill
ROBERT NORGATE CL
Hotel
Dove House Farm
COLTISHALL ROAD
B1354
Mill Farm

Horstead
Green Lane
MILL ROAD
FRETTENHAM RD
Hill Farm
Horstead Lodge
Water Tower
B1150
NORWICH ROAD
Heggatt Road
Heggatt Hall
Proclamation Wood
Grange Farm
THE STREET
Croft House
Mill Farm

NR12
Glebe Farm
Clamp Wood
Heggatt Farm
Blackman's Fen
Belaugh
Moorings
HORSTEAD TOP RD

Church Farm
Windmill
Frettenham
Stanninghall Farm
STANNINGHALL ROAD
Church (rems)
Caius Hill Farm
BURNTWOOD LANE
Burnt Wood
Blake's Wood
High and Low Bridge
Juby's Farm
Old Hall
Old Hall Farm
164
Belaugh Old Hall Drainage Mill
Church Farm
Cemy
A1151

Chisel Hill
COURT HILL
MILL ROAD
BUXTON RD
SCHOOL ROAD
POST OFFICE RD
FRED EDGE CL
Frettenham Prim Sch
FRETTENHAM WY
HALL LANE
Hillside Animal Sanctuary
GRANNY BARD'S LA
Gravelhole Plantation
Belaugh Broad
Hills and Holes Plantation
SKINNERS LA

West View Farm
Willow Farm
Beck Farm
Hill Top Farm
HALL LANE
Hill Farm
Long Plantation
GRANNY BARD'S LANE
Old Hall Farm
Boathouse Carr
Water Plantation
Home Farm
Football Gd
SALHOUSE RD
B1140

NR10
Irrigation Reservoir
PH
DOW LANE
Crostwick
Oak Plantation
Cut Plantation
Garden Plantation
Big Wood
Low Carr
Dobb's Plantation
NORWICH RD

Cemy
Woodland Vw Jun Sch
Spixworth Inf Sch
Spixworth
Spixworth Rec Gd
Trafford Wy
MARGARET DEWING CL
RACKHEATH LANE
NORTH WALSHAM ROAD
PRIMROSE LANE
Manor Farm
WROXHAM ROAD
Normans Farm
Hagg Wood
LC

PH
CROSTWICK LN
BOWLING GN CL
DOBBS LANE
SWASH LANE
BACK LA
PH
STONEHOUSE RD
Redwing Farm

BUXTON ROAD
ARTHURTON RD
PARK RD
ROSA CL
B1150
Beeston Park
Lady's Carr
SLOE LANE
Church Wood
Strip Plantation
The Springs
GREEN LA WEST
A1151
MUCK LANE
NR13
Old Hall Farm
Spixworth Plantation
Salhouse

A1
1 CHRISTINE RD
2 BRAMBLES CL
3 HAWTHORN CL
4 GILES RD
5 CHITTOCK CL
6 FIELDFARE CL
7 REDWING GDNS
8 QUAKER LA

A2
1 CHESTNUT AVE
2 ORCHARD RD
3 IVY RD
4 CEDAR AVE
5 GODFREY RD
6 JULIAN RD
7 WILLIAM PECK RD
8 JENNY RD
9 RUSSELL AVE

10 ELVINA RD
11 SYDNEY RD
12 ST PETER'S WAY
13 MARSHALL CL
14 JAMES GN CL

A4
1 HARBOUR RD
2 MAYTON AVE
3 SHIRLEY CL
4 REDMERE CL
5 MILL FIELD CT

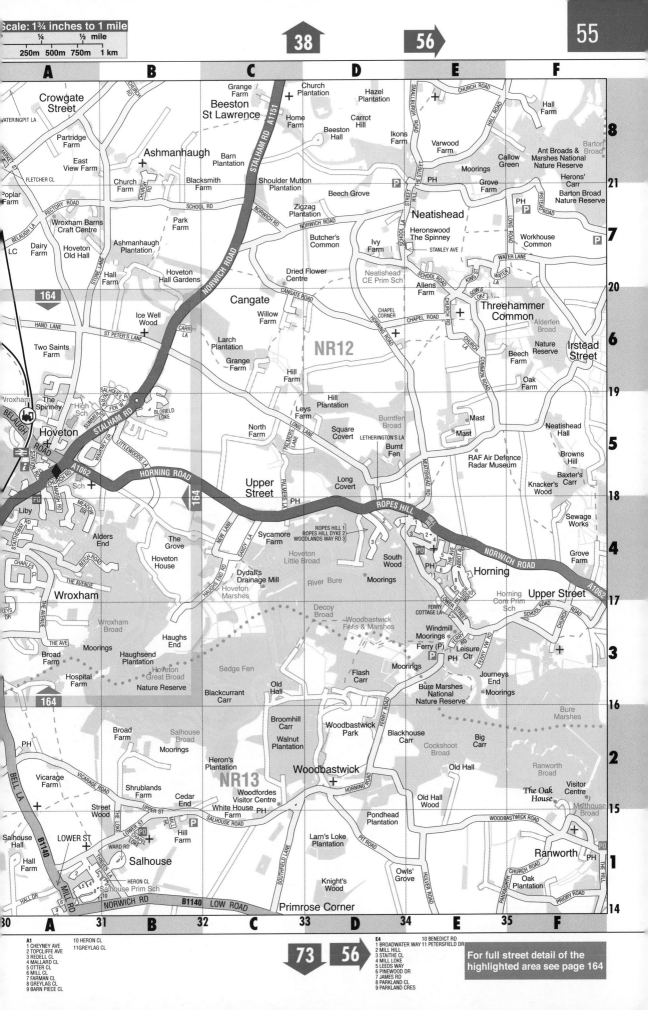

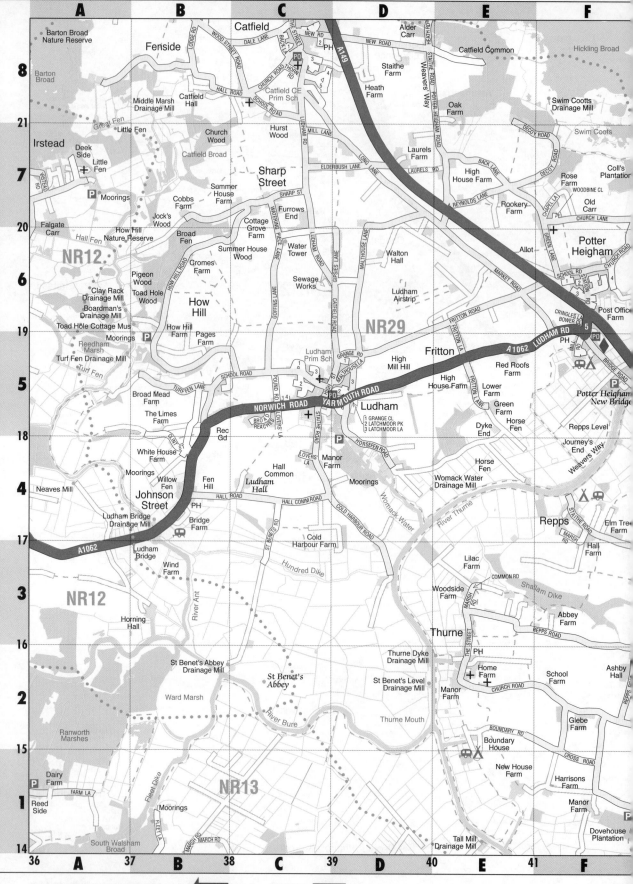

55   39

C5
1 LAURELS CRES
2 WILLOW WAY
3 SCHOOL CL
4 PIKES NURSERY

C8
1 CHAPELFIELD CL
2 LEA RD
3 LIMES RD
4 CANON WAKE CT
5 ST CATHERINE'S AVE

F6
1 VICARAGE CL
2 GLEBE CL
3 ORCHARD DR
4 DOVE HOUSE LA
5 STATION RD

Scale: 1¾ inches to 1 mil
0   ¼   ½   mile
0   250m   500m   750m   1 km

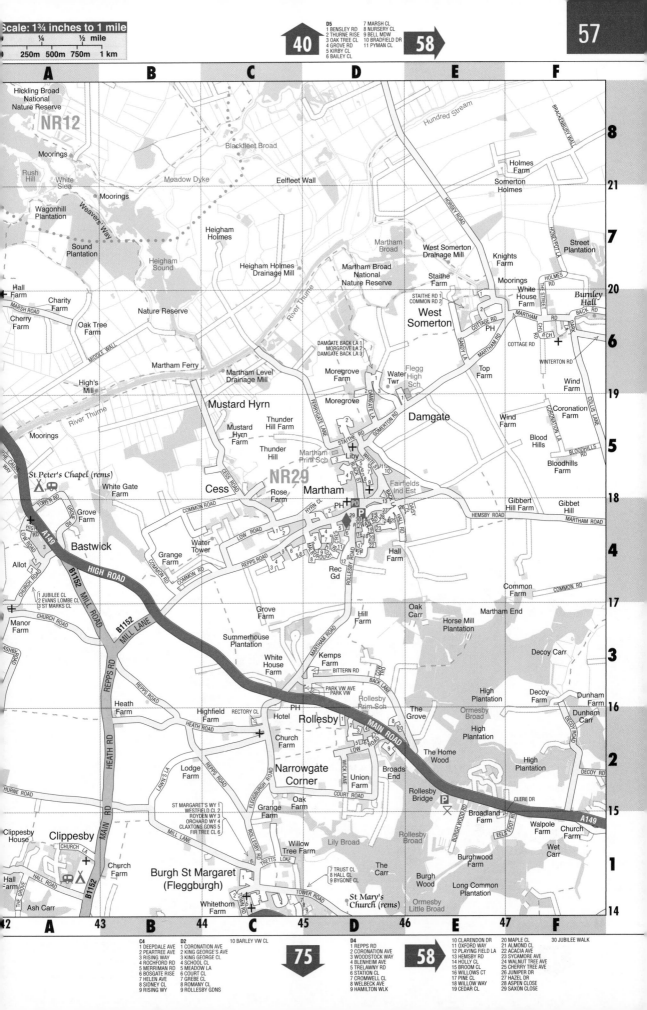

← 40   58 →

D5
1 BENSLEY RD
2 THURNE RISE
3 OAK TREE CL
4 GROVE RD
5 KIRBY CL
6 BAILEY CL
7 MARSH CL
8 NURSERY CL
9 BELL MDW
10 BRADFIELD DR
11 PYMAN CL

58

B6
1 BACK PATH
2 OLD CHAPEL RD
3 BACK RD
4 THE LOKE
5 MARINE CRES
6 WINMER AVE
7 ACKLAND CL
8 GEORGE BECK RD
9 THE COBBLEWAYS
10 GREENCOURTS
11 SPINDRIFT CL
12 LAVENDER CT
13 SANDPIPER CT
14 MARKET PL

57

Scale: 1¾ inches to 1 mile
0   ¼   ½   mile
0   250m 500m 750m   1 km

North Wood
Winterton Ness
South Wood
Decoy Wood
Winterton Dunes National Nature Reserve
Home Covert
Manor Farm
East Somerton
St Mary's Church (rems)
The Spinney
Winterton Prim Sch
Church Farm
BLACK ST
KING ST
Hermanus Leisure Centre
Winterton-on-Sea
WINTERTON RD
SOMERTON RD
BACK RD
PH
THE CRAPE
THE LANE
HILLVIEW DR
HENSBY ROAD
BULMER LA
EDWARD RD
BUSH RD
High Barn Farm
Mill Farm
Rainbows End
COLLIS LANE
NR29
Hemsby
MARTHAM ROAD
Fengate Farm
MILL RD
COMMON
PH
North Rd
Sch
THE PASTURES
THE CLOSE
KINGS LOKE
KINGS LOKE
KINGS LOKE
THE GLEBE
IRB Station
Hemsby Hole
BRIDGECOURT 1
BRIDGE MDW 2
SUMMERFIELD RD 3
SPRINGFIELD CL 4
SPRINGFIELD RD 5
SPRINGFIELD N 6
COMMON RD
HALL ROAD
The Spinney
PO
THE STREET
THE AVENUE
KINGS WAY
YARMOUTH RD
BEACH ROAD
BACK MKT LA
ST THOMAS'S
ST THOMAS'S
PH
Newport
FAKES RD
FAKES RD
Cross (rems)
EASTERLEY WAY
ORMESBY ROAD
NORTH ROAD
YARMOUTH ROAD
NEWPORT ROAD
Swimming Pool
SEAGULL RD
TERN RD
THE ESP
167
Dowe Hill Farm
Dowe Hill
Scratby
BECK AVE
THOROUGHFARE LANE
Scratby Hall
Mill Farm
BEACH DR
Pettingills Farm
DECOY ROAD
Home Farm
Ormesby St Margaret
Gables Farm
HEATHER AVE
BEACH ROAD
PO
THE PROMENADE
ACORNS
ROTTENSTONE LA
Barn Farm
Manships Farm
Manor Farm
ST MICHAEL'S CL
Sch
FIRS LNE
PINE CL
APPLETON DR
NORTH RD WEST
BARTON WAY
FRITTON CL
LADY HAMILTON LA
RANWORTH DR
SCRATBY RD
STATION ROAD
California
CALIFORNIA RD
PH
MAIN RD
A149
CROMER RD
Ormesby St Michael
Manship's Plantation
FILBY LA
PH
Ormesby Hall
NOVA SCOTIA RD
BRACECAMP CL
RPE
Willow Farm
YARMOUTH ROAD
OLD COAST ROAD
ORMESBY RD
PH Hotel
California Farm
CALIFORNIA CR
NR30
MILL LANE
Filby Lane Farm
FILBY LA

For full street detail of the highlighted area see page 167

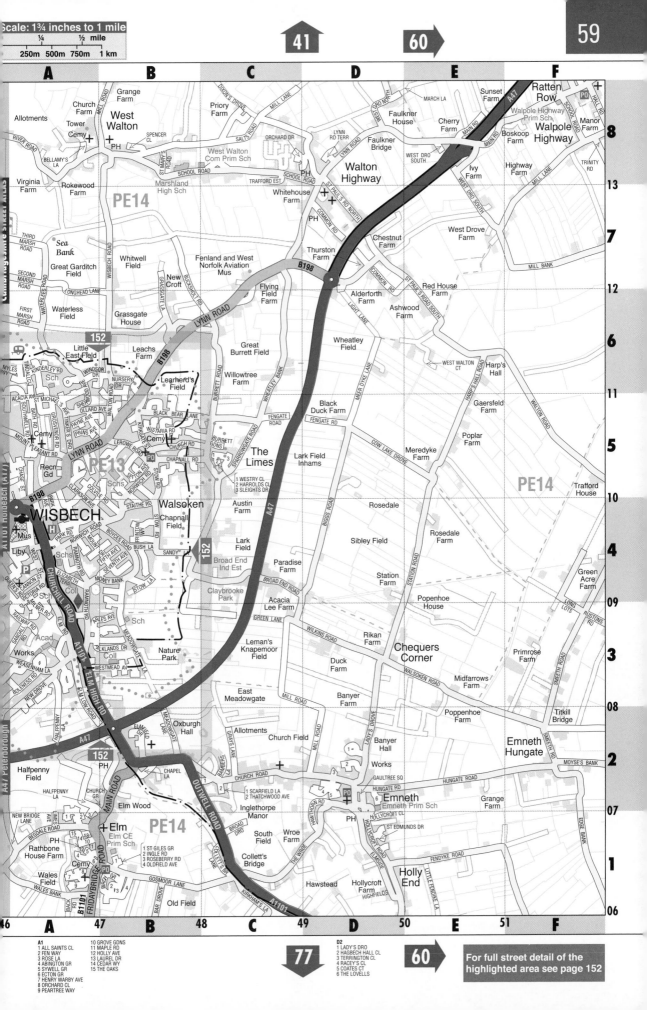

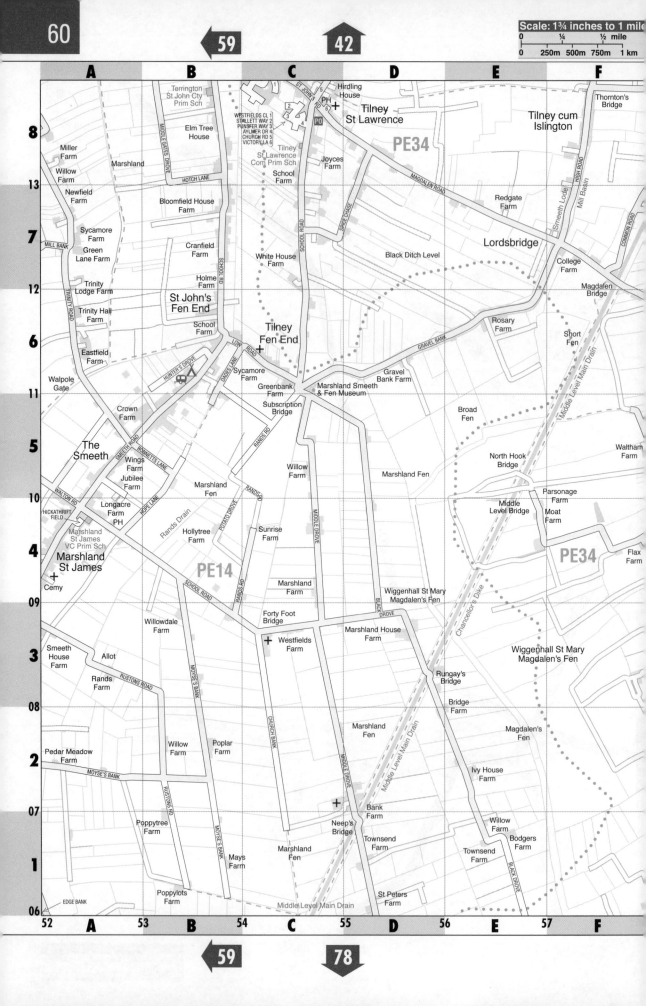

Scale: 1¾ inches to 1 mile

0   ¼   ½ mile
0   250m   500m   750m   1 km

A   **B**   **C**   **D**   **E**   **F**

8
Miller Farm
Willow Farm
Marshland
Terrington St John Cty Prim Sch
Elm Tree House
WESTFIELDS CL 1
STALLETT WAY 2
PUNSFER WAY 3
AYLMER DR 4
CHURCH RD 5
VICTORY LA 6
Tilney St Lawrence Com Prim Sch
Hirdling House
Tilney St Lawrence
PE34
Tilney cum Islington
Thornton's Bridge

13
Newfield Farm
Bloomfield House Farm
School Farm
Joyces Farm
Magdalen Road
Redgate Farm
Smeeth Lodge
High Road
Mill Basin

7
Sycamore Farm
Green Lane Farm
MILL BANK
Cranfield Farm
White House Farm
Black Ditch Level
Lordsbridge
College Farm

12
Trinity Lodge Farm
Trinity Hall Farm
TRINITY ROAD
Holme Farm
St John's Fen End
School Farm
Space Chase
Gravel Bank
Rosary Farm
Magdalen Bridge
Short Fen

6
Eastfield Farm
LOW ROAD
Tilney Fen End
Sycamore Farm
Greenbank Farm
Marshland Smeeth & Fen Museum
Gravel Bank Farm
Middle Level Main Drain

11
Walpole Gate
Crown Farm
HUNTER'S DROVE
DADE'S LANE
Subscription Bridge
Broad Fen
North Hook Bridge
Waltham Farm

5
The Smeeth
Wings Farm
SMEETH ROAD
BONNETT'S LANE
RANDS RD
Willow Farm
Marshland Fen
Parsonage Farm
Moat Farm

10
Jubilee Farm
Longacre Farm PH
HOPE LANE
Marshland Fen
Rands Drain
RANDS RD
POTATO DROVE
Sunrise Farm
MIDDLE DROVE
Middle Level Bridge
PE34
Flax Farm

4
WALTON RD
HICKATHRIFT FIELD
Marshland St James VC Prim Sch
Marshland St James
Cemy
Hollytree Farm
PE14
Marshland Farm
Wiggenhall St Mary Magdalen's Fen
Chancellor's Dike

09
Smeeth House Farm
Allot
Rands Farm
Willowdale Farm
SCHOOL ROAD
Forty Foot Bridge
Westfields Farm
Marshland House Farm
Wiggenhall St Mary Magdalen's Fen

3
RUSTONS ROAD
MOYSE'S BANK
Rungay's Bridge
Bridge Farm
Magdalen's Fen

08
Pedar Meadow Farm
MOYSE'S BANK
Willow Farm
Poplar Farm
CHURCH BANK
Marshland Fen
Marshland Fen
BLACK DROVE
Middle Level Main Drain
Ivy House Farm

2
RUSTONS RD
Poppytree Farm
MOYSE'S BANK
Mays Farm
Marshland Fen
Neep's Bridge
Bank Farm
Townsend Farm
Willow Farm
Townsend Farm
Bodgers Farm

07
EDGE BANK
Poppylots Farm
Middle Level Main Drain
St Peters Farm
BLACK DROVE

06
52   **53**   **54**   **55**   **56**   **57**
A   **B**   **C**   **D**   **E**   **F**

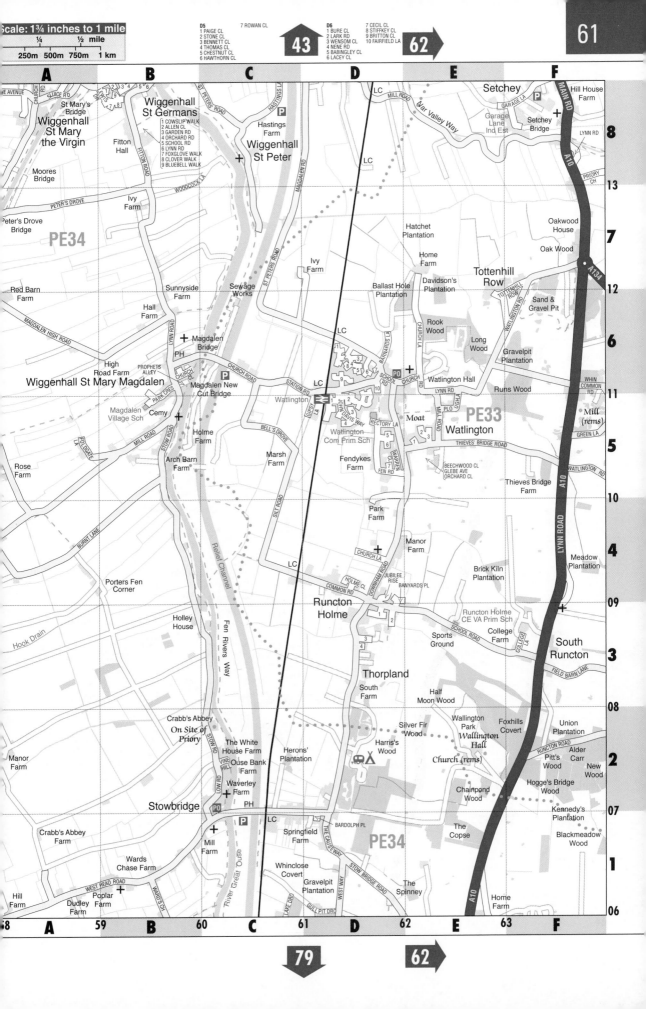

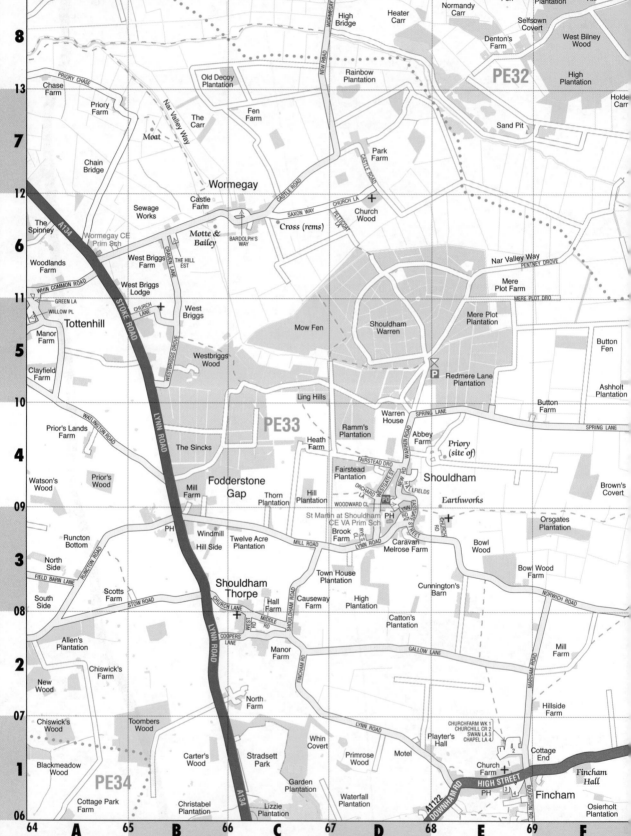

A   B   C   D   E   F

8

13

7

12

6

11

5

10

4

09

3

08

2

07

1

06

64   A   65   B   66   C   67   D   68   E   69   F

PE32

PE33

PE34

Chase Farm
Priory Farm
Priory Chase
The Spinney
Woodlands Farm
Moat
Chain Bridge
Wormegay
Castle Farm
Sewage Works
Motte & Bailey
Bardolph's Way
Cross (rems)
Saxon Way
Church La
Church Wood
Old Decoy Plantation
Fen Farm
The Carr
Rainbow Plantation
High Bridge
Heater Carr
Normandy Carr
Horse Fen
Whinhill Plantation
Fox Hill
Selfsown Covert
Denton's Farm
West Bilney Wood
High Plantation
Holde Carr
Sand Pit
Park Farm
Nar Valley Way
Pentney Drove
Mere Plot Farm
Mere Plot Dro
Mere Plot Plantation
West Briggs Farm
West Briggs Lodge
The Hill Est
Church Lane
West Briggs
Tottenhill
Manor Farm
Clayfield Farm
Whin Common Road
Green La
Willow Pl
Westbriggs Wood
Mow Fen
Shouldham Warren
Button Fen
Ashholt Plantation
Button Farm
Redmere Lane Plantation
Ling Hills
Warren House
Spring Lane
Spring Lane
Prior's Lands Farm
Watlington Road
The Sincks
Heath Farm
Ramm's Plantation
Abbey Farm
Priory (site of)
Shouldham
Brown's Covert
Watson's Wood
Prior's Wood
Mill Farm
Fodderstone Gap
Thorn Plantation
Hill Plantation
Fairstead Plantation
Fairstead Dro
Earthworks
Orsgates Plantation
Runcton Bottom
North Side
Field Barn Lane
South Side
Scotts Farm
Stow Road
PH
Windmill Hill Side
Twelve Acre Plantation
Mill Road
Brook Farm
St Martin at Shouldham CE VA Prim Sch
PH
Caravan
Melrose Farm
Bowl Wood
Bowl Wood Farm
Cunnington's Barn
Norwich Road
Allen's Plantation
Chiswick's Farm
New Wood
North Farm
Shouldham Thorpe
Church Lane
West Rd
Middle Rd
Coopers Lane
Hall Farm
Manor Farm
Town House Plantation
Causeway Farm
High Plantation
Catton's Plantation
Gallow Lane
Mill Farm
Hillside Farm
Chiswick's Wood
Toombers Wood
Carter's Wood
Stradsett Park
Whin Covert
Garden Plantation
Primrose Wood
Lynn Road
Motel
Player's Hall
Churchfarm Wk 1
Churchill Cr 2
Swan La 3
Chapel La 4
Church Farm
Cottage End
Fincham Hall
Blackmeadow Wood
Cottage Park Farm
Christabel Plantation
Lizzie Plantation
Waterfall Plantation
High Street
PH
Fincham
Osierholt Plantation
Downham Rd
Boughton Rd
Marham Road
Fincham Rd
Lynn Road
Stoke Road
Lynn Road
Nar Valley Way
A134
A1122

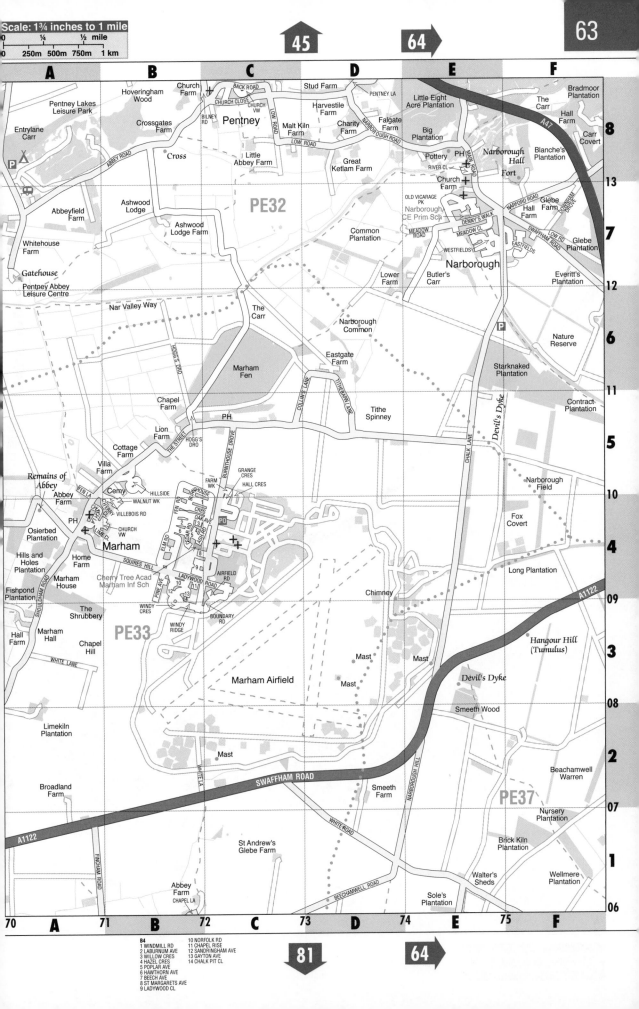

A   B   C   D   E   F

Narford Lake

Narford Hall

Spinner Plantation

Cambrian Plantation

Royal Oak Plantation

New England Plantation

Eight Acre Plantation

Twenty Acre Plantation

Washpit Plantation

Three-cocked-hat Plantation

Petticoat Drove

Wash Pit

Fingerhill Plantation

Herrington's Pit

Bartholomew's Hill Plantation

8

13

Young Heater Plantation

Fourteen Acre Plantation

Hall Farm

PE32

Forty Acre Pit

7

Thirty Acre Plantation

Eyetrap Plantation

12

A47

LOW ROAD

Burntstalk Plantation

Round Covert

6

Stella Farm

Scoot Wood

FINCHAM DROVE

11

Chalk Farm

Brick Kiln Wood

Pithole Plantation

5

Great Thorns Farm

Great Friars' Thornes

Thief's Pit Plantation

Fourteen Acre Plantation

SILVER DRIFT

Silverdrift Plantation

10

FINCHAM DROVE

Little Thorns Farm

Little Friars' Thornes

Lowroad Plantation

Eco Ctr

Fen Pit

Swaffham Plashes Mast

Long Plantation

Broom Covert

P

A1122

SWAFFHAM ROAD

Heath Farm

A47

LOW RD

Bsns Pk   Sch

Bear's La   P

STATION ST

4

Swaffham Heath

Swaffham Raceway

LYNN ROAD

WHITSANDS RD

WEST ACRE ROAD

TURBINE WY

PRINCES ST

PO

09

SHOULDHAM LANE

SHOULDHAM LANE

153

Water Tower

Narford Wood

SHOEMAKERS LANE

Football Ground

3

Town Farm

Stratton Farm

HASPALLS RD

Lodge Farm

Edwards's Plantation

Cemy

SOUTHLANDS

Sch

08

PE37

The Lodge

Fox Covert

Lightland Plantation

BEACHAMWELL RD

Snails Pit Farm

CLEY ROAD

2

New Plantation

Drymere Plantation

Home Wood

07

Warren Farm

P

Swaffham Golf Course

CH

Gravelpit Plantation

Brake Hill Farm

Oakwood Farm

1

Swaffham Heath

Torch Covert

Brake Hill

Larch Wood

Shingham Heath

Drymere

06

76   A   77   B   78   C   79   D   80   E   81   F

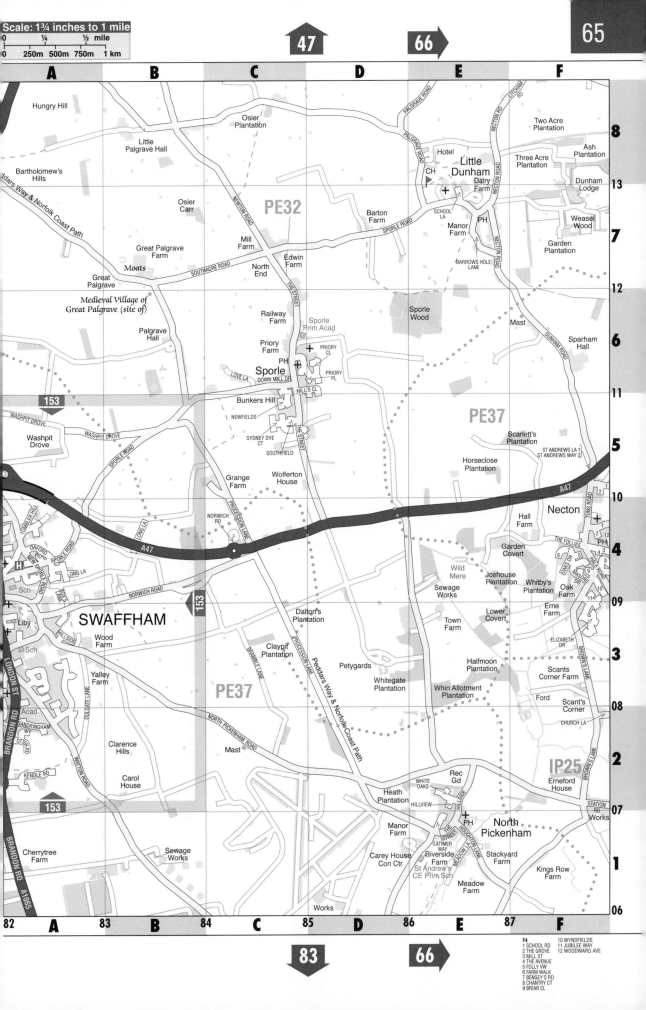

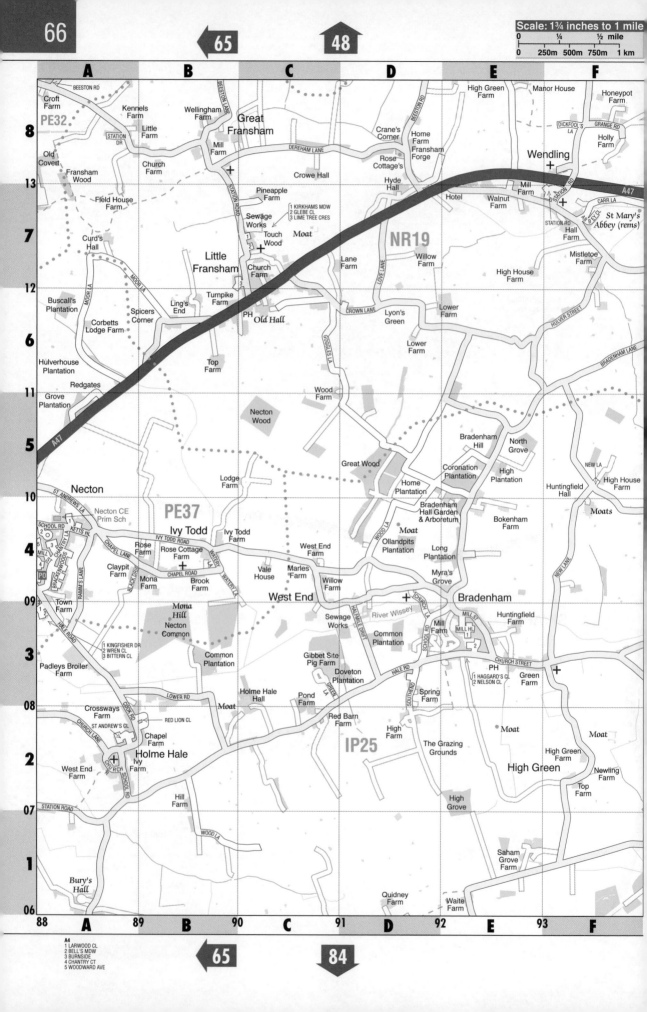

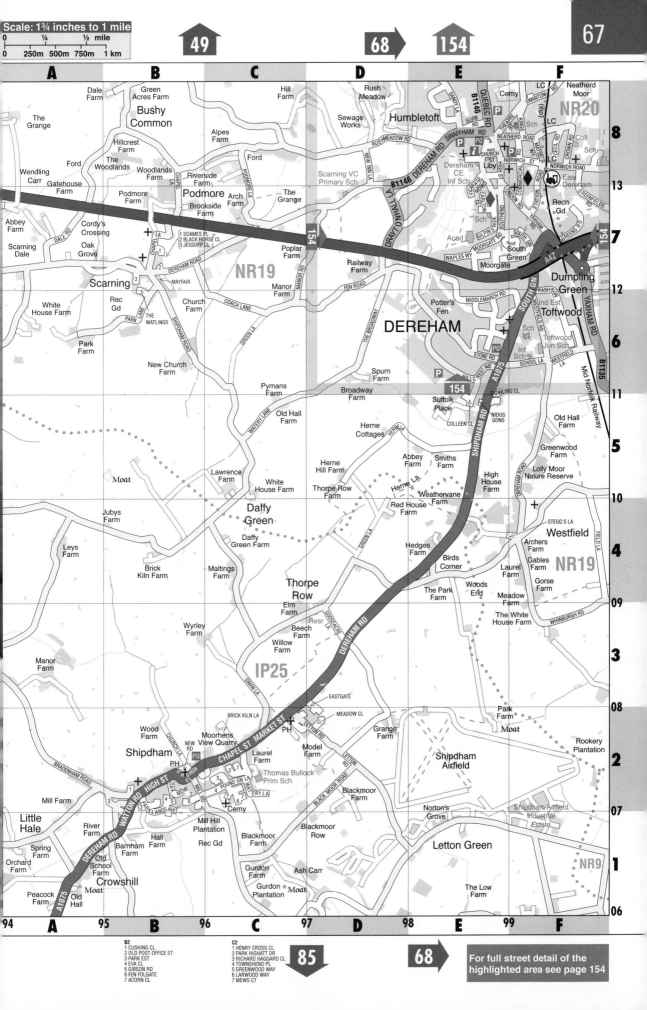

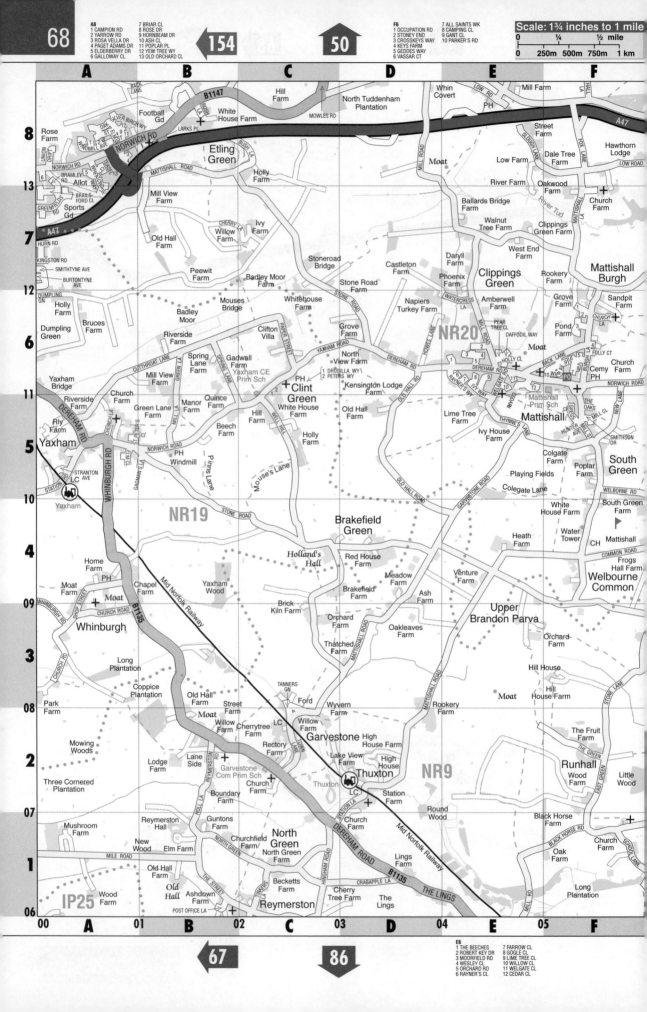

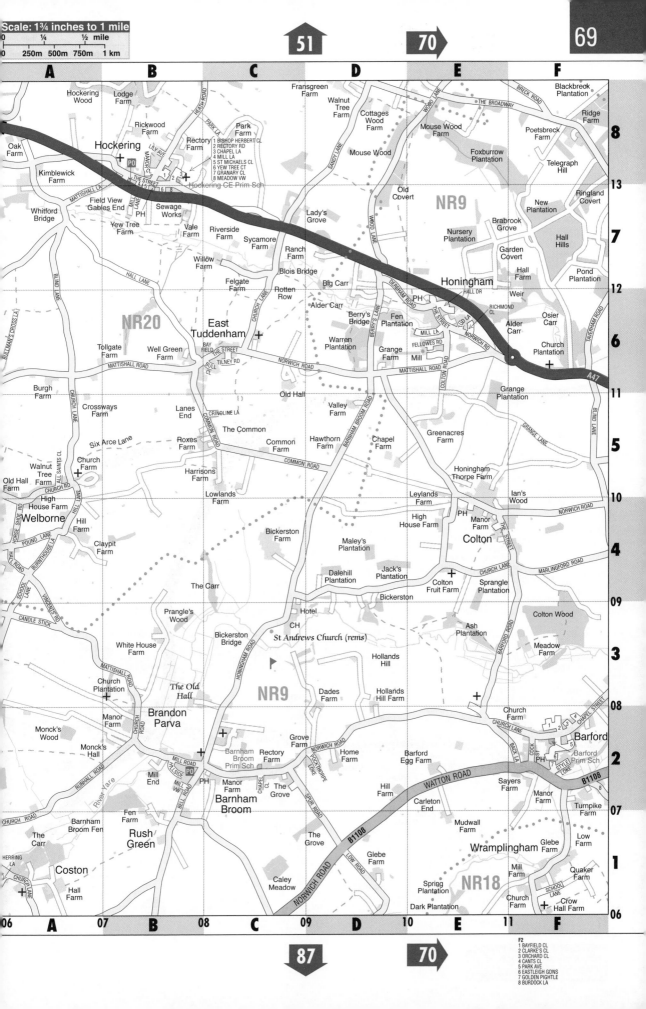

70

← **69**

↑ **52**

C7
1 FOXHOUSE RD
2 STONY GR
3 BLYTH'S WOOD AV
4 WOODCOCK HILL
5 FAIRWAY
6 KNAPPERS WY

7 LORDS HILL
8 MAZE AVE

↑ **155**

Scale: 1¾ inches to 1 mile

0 — ¼ — ½ mile
0 — 250m — 500m — 750m — 1 km

Blackbreck Plantation

Poets Breck Farm

Honingham Lane

Dryhill Plantation

Jennis' Wood

Manor Farm

PH

THE STREET

Low Common

PITT FARM GN

Ringland

Snake Wood

Ringland Road

Taverham Jun Sch

Ghost Hill Inf Sch

A1067 FAKENHAM RD

Church Farm

Taverham Hall Sch

SHAKESPEARE WAY

DR BANK

SYLVAN WAY

STATION RD

Poetbreck Plantation

Slade Hills

Ave's Gap

Field Road

Costessey Lane

Ringland Wood

NR8

Blyth's Wood

Ringland Road

Fleet Road

Ringland Lane

Taverham

Place Farm

MACK'S LANE

Church Farm

Barn Plantation

Weston Road

Ringland Road

Stonyhole Plantation

Spruce Plantation

Ringland Hills

Three Corner Plantation

Costessey Lane

Ringland Hills

Blackhill Wood

Sch

KESTREL AVE

PEACOCK CR

REDPOLL

PEDPOLL

Brickfield Farm

Costessey Pits

Transport Plantation

THE STREET

THE CROFT

Harman's Grove

Ringland Plantation

Snake's Hills

Old Wood

Lord's Hills

156

Queen's Hills

SIR ALFRED MUNNINGS RD

Brickfield

WEST END

LOWE

Snake's Hills

TOWER HL

WEST END AVE

Costessey

Green Hills

Hill Farm

Riverside Farm

Westlodge Hills

Holly Wood

Paddock Plantation

Weir

PUMP HOUSE CL

Bog Wood

Longdell Hills

Reservoir Hill

Sand & Gravel Pit

WEST END

Tower Hill

CH

Costessey Park

Sch

PH PO

LIME TREE AVE

MYRTLE AVE

LAYER

CLEVES WAY

River Tud

River Tud

A47

CHURCH LA

LONG LA

Water Tower

AV

Easton

PO

MARLINGFORD WAY

GARNETT

Dereham Road

Royal Norfolk Showground

A1074 DEREHAM ROAD

Sand & Gravel Pits

NR5

Costessey High Sch

Bunker's Hill

Four Acre Plantation

St Peter's CE Prim Sch

Stafford's Plantation

Hotel

Cemy

LONGWATER LANE

MIDDLETON CRES

GROVE AV

Fir Covert

HALL ROAD

BAWBURGH ROAD

BROOM LA

Sand Pit Dunham's Plantation

P&R

Lodge Farm

Round Well

EAST HILLS ROAD

RICHMOND RD

STAFFORD AVE

PO

Costessey Jun Sch

Model Farm
BUXTON CL 1
EDDINGTON WAY 2
PARKER'S 3
RINGLAND LA 4
ST PETERS DR 5
KENNEDY CL 6
PEGG CL 7
PEACOCK CL 8
CARDINAL CL 9
WHEELER CRES 10

Broom Farm

Playing Fields

A47

LONG LANE

LONG LA

Beech Plantation

BARNARD ROAD

Water Tower

Hotel

Marlingford Sports Club

Easton & Otley Coll

NR9

Three Cornered Plantation

Marlingford Road

The Harrings

BRITANNIA WY

CHAPEL BREAK ROAD

Sch

HARPSFIELD

Sch

Mast

Hill Grove Plantation

Cobb's Grove Plantation

Valley Farm

Glen Lodge Farm

DRAPER

HUDSON

Bowthorpe

Marlingford

The Old Hall

Bawburgh Road

Woods End

HART'S LANE

NEW ROAD

St Michael's Church (rems)

PO

BISHY

Blue Cedar Farm

BARFORD RD

PH

River Yare

St Walston's Well

Bawburgh

Lodge Farm

Sand & Gravel Pits

BARNEBEE WAY

THREE SCORE RD

Morris' Grove

The Common

MILL ROAD

Beech Grove

Algarstthorpe Farm

Bridge

CHURCH ST

PH

NEW ROAD

Clinkhill Plantation

Summer House Plantation

THREE SCORE RD

Home Farm

COTTON ST

Chapel Farm

HOCKERING LA

The Bawburgh Sch

Colney Wood

NR4

Moat

CHURCH ROAD

BOW HILL

Earthworks

Admiral's Wood

Mast

Limekiln Wood

Bungalow Farm

Marlingford Hall

STOCKS HILL

WATTON ROAD B1108

Rybeck Plantation

SCHOOL LANE

Common Farm

River Plantation

160

Bow Hill

BAWBURGH ROAD

Villa Farm

Milestone Plantation

Four Oak Plantation

WATTON ROAD

GREEN LANE

HETHERSETT LANE

Swan's Harbour

B1108

High House Farm

Thorn Pit Plantation

Bawburgh Hill

SCHOOL LANE

Manor Farm

Norfolk & Norwich Univ

Ryehill Plantation

Port Arthur Wood

Gravel Pit Plantation

RECTORY LANE

Sewage Works

MILL RD

Little Melton

Hospital Farm

Oak Pollard

BURDOCK LANE

LANGLOW LANE

School Plantation

Coronation Wood

HALL RD

GIBBS CL

Sch

PH

SCHOOL LA

Coleseed Plantation

Furze Ground

Melton Hall (rems)

Lodge Plantation

Market Lane

Great Melton Road

Elm Farm

BRAYMEADOW LANE

Braymeadow Bottom

Hall Farm

NR18

Great Melton

Church Plantation

Church Farm Plantation

LT MELTON RD

BURHOUSE ROAD

Beckhithe

Walnut Tree Farm

Braymeadow Farm

Pockthorpe

Church (rems)

160

A47

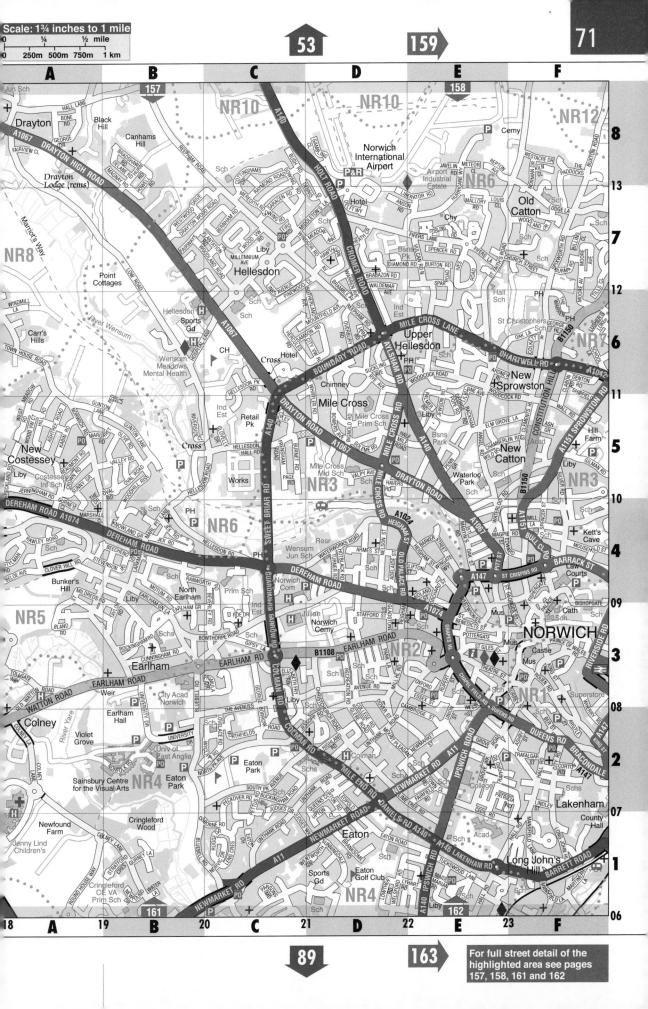

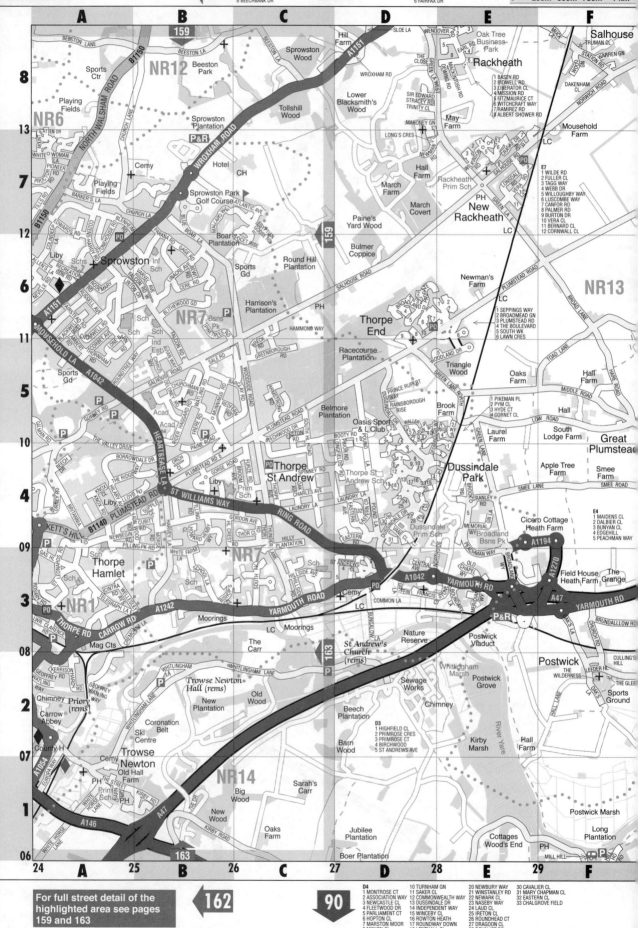

D6
1 ALTONGATE
2 HALLGATE
3 NORTHGATE
4 BROAD VW
5 BARKER WAY
6 BEECHBANK DR

7 HEATHERWOOD CL
8 ST DAVIDS DR
9 HEATH RD
10 PERCY HOWES CL

D5
1 WOODLANDS CRES
2 LUCAS CT
3 GUNNER CL
4 FIENNES RD
5 DOWSING CT
6 FAIRFAX DR

7 LYNN CL
8 LEVEN CL
9 JOYCE WAY
10 MARVELL GN

Scale: 1¾ inches to 1 mile
0   ¼   ½   mile
0   250m 500m 750m   1 km

158   54   159

E7
1 WILDE RD
2 FULLER CL
3 TAGG WAY
4 WEBB DR
5 WILLOUGHBY WAY
6 LUSCOMBE WAY
7 CANFOR RD
8 PALMER RD
9 BURTON DR
10 VERA CL
11 BERNARD CL
12 CORNWALL CL

1 SEPPINGS WAY
2 BROADMEAD GN
3 PLUMSTEAD RD
4 THE BOULEVARD
5 SOUTH WK
6 LAWN CRES

For full street detail of the
highlighted area see pages
159 and 163

162   90

D4
1 MONTROSE CT
2 ASSOCIATION WAY
3 NEWCASTLE CL
4 FLEETWOOD DR
5 PARLIAMENT CT
6 HOPTON CL
7 MARSTON MOOR
8 MINION CL
9 CULVERIN CL

10 TURNHAM GN
11 SAKER CL
12 COMMONWEALTH WAY
13 LUSSINDALE DR
14 INDEPENDENT WAY
15 WINCEBY CL
16 ROWTON HEATH
17 ROUNDWAY DOWN
18 LENTHALL CL
19 HAMPDEN DR

20 NEWBURY WAY
21 WINSTANLEY RD
22 NEWARK CL
23 NASEBY WAY
24 LAUD CL
25 IRETON CL
26 ROUNDHEAD CT
27 DRAGOON CL
28 ROYALIST DR
29 MUSKETEER WAY

30 CAVALIER CL
31 MARY CHAPMAN CL
32 EASTERN CL
33 CHALGROVE FIELD

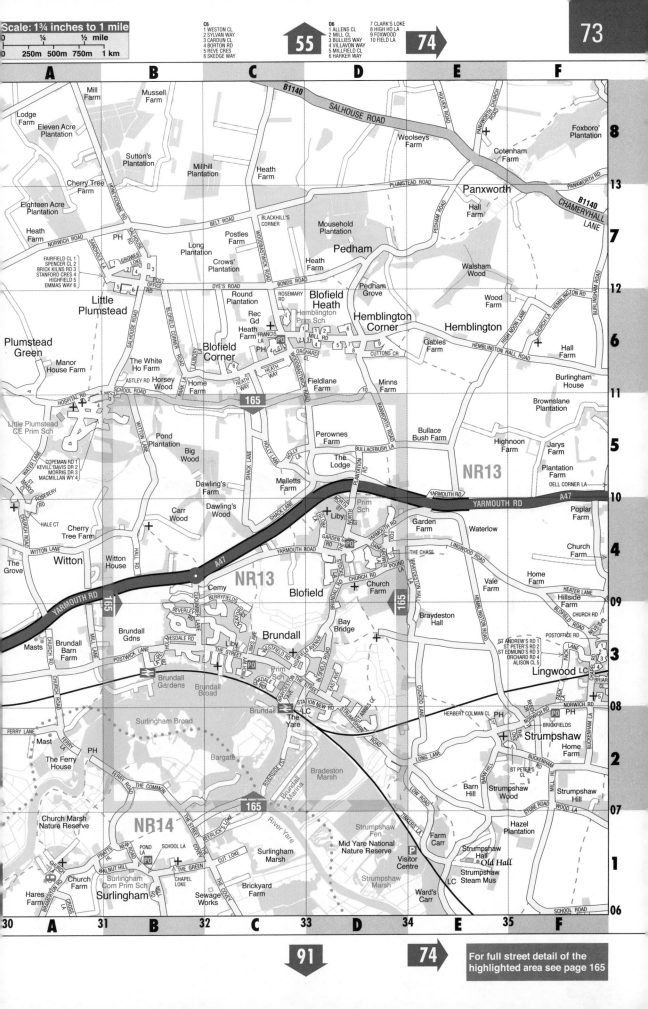

Scale: 1¾ inches to 1 mile

0   ¼   ½ mile
0   250m 500m 750m 1 km

A   B   C   D   E   F

8

Norton Hill
Panxworth Rd
Fairhaven Woodland & Water Garden
Town House Farm
Pilson Green
Low Farm
Ivy Farm
Upton Fen Nature Reserve
The Doles
Upton Marshes
Wisemans' Oby Mill
NR29

Hamilton Cl
PO
St Mary's Cl
PH
Fairhaven CE VA Prim Sch
Rec Gd
Holly Farm
Cargate Green
Upton Broad (Nature Reserve)
Meadow Farm
Clippesby Mill

13

South Walsham
Newport Rd
Town Green
Hare Fen
Field Farm
Mill Hill Farm
Upton North Farm
Sandpit Plantation
Prince of Wales Road
Cargate Lane
PH
Upton Green
Upton Hall Farm
166

7

Old Hall Farm
Highfield Farm
Harefen La
County Farm
Flowerdew's Lane
Grup Farm
Upton Carr
Fishley
Fishley Hall Farm
NR13

12

B1140
Newport Farm
Green Lane
Hamlinghill
Church Road
Cedar Farm
Fishley Barn Farm
Rattlesnake Carr
River Bure
Acle Bridge
PH
Bridge Farm

6

Newport Road
Long Plantation
Watt's Hall Farm
South Walsham Rd
Cemy
Recreation Ctr
Old Road
166
PH

11

Burlingham Green
Kings Close Farm
White's Farm
The Windle
Mast
Acle High Sch
Mill House Farm
Boat Dyke La
Acle Dyke

5

Dell Corner La
Homel Farm
North Burlingham
Belt Plantation
Half Round Plantation
South Walsham Rd
Burlingham Lodge Farm
Windle Farm
Acle
PH
PO
Motel
A1064

Church Farm

10

A47
Main Road
Norwich Road
The Hall
Acle Hall Farm
Hillcrest
Acle
Norwich Rd
Borderland Farm
Damgate La
The Carr
LC
NR29
Sewage Works

4

View Farm
Coxhill Farm
NR13
Beighton Rd
Jolly's Lane
Damgate
Monies Farm
Warren Farm
Decoy Carr
166

Glebe Farm
B1140

09

Church Rd
Oak Farm
Lingwood Lodge
Hillcrest Farm
Lodge Rd
Staithe Farm

3

PO
School Rd
Oak Tree Cl
Elm Rd
Lingwood
LC
Low Farm
White House Farm
Manor Farm
Church Hill
Church Farm
Wood Farm
Tunstall
Manor House

Lingwood Prim Acad
P
Burlingham Rd

08

Norwich Road
Old Hall Farm
Rec Gd
Beighton
Lincoln Hall
Hell Carr
Tunstall Road

2

Buckenham Road
1 WILLOW CL
2 CHRISTINE AVE
3 FARM CL
4 AVONDALE CL
5 WEST VW DR
St Edmunds Farm
Willow Farm
South Burlingham
Dauber's Lane
Morley Road
Sandy Lane
Moulton St Mary
Moat
Hall's Farm
Oaklands La

07

Hill Farm
Buckenham Wood
Hantons Loke
Carin Cl
High Rd
Old Southwood Rd
Cantley Corner
World's End Farm
Well
Cucumber Corner
Ash Tree Rd
Reedham Rd
Moat
Halvergate Road
Halvergate
Church Ave

1

Wood Lane Farm
Wood Lane
School Road
Church Road
B1140
Grove Farm
Southwood Road
Kittles Road
Lyndhurst Farm
Ash Tree Farm
Manor Hall Farm
Moulton Road
The Street
Sandhole Road
Hall Farm La
Freethorpe Rd
Mill Rd

06

Porter's Rd

36   A   37   B   38   C   39   D   40   E   41   F

A3
1 BARN CL
2 LINGWOOD GDNS
3 MANOR GDNS
4 STATION CL
5 ELM CL
6 HILARY CL
7 HOMESTEAD CL
8 POST OFFICE CL
9 GRANARY CL
10 CLARKSON RD
11 SPENCER CL
12 NEW RD
13 HOMELEA CRES
14 BRIAR CL
15 HIGH WAY
16 KINGSDALE
17 MEMORIAL WY
18 POPPY CL

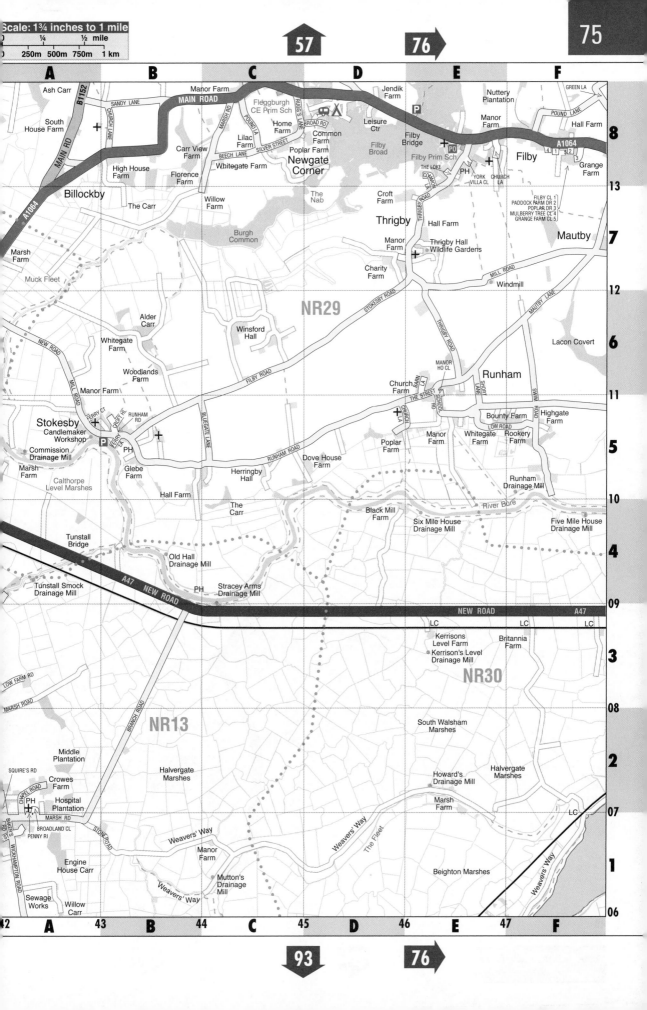

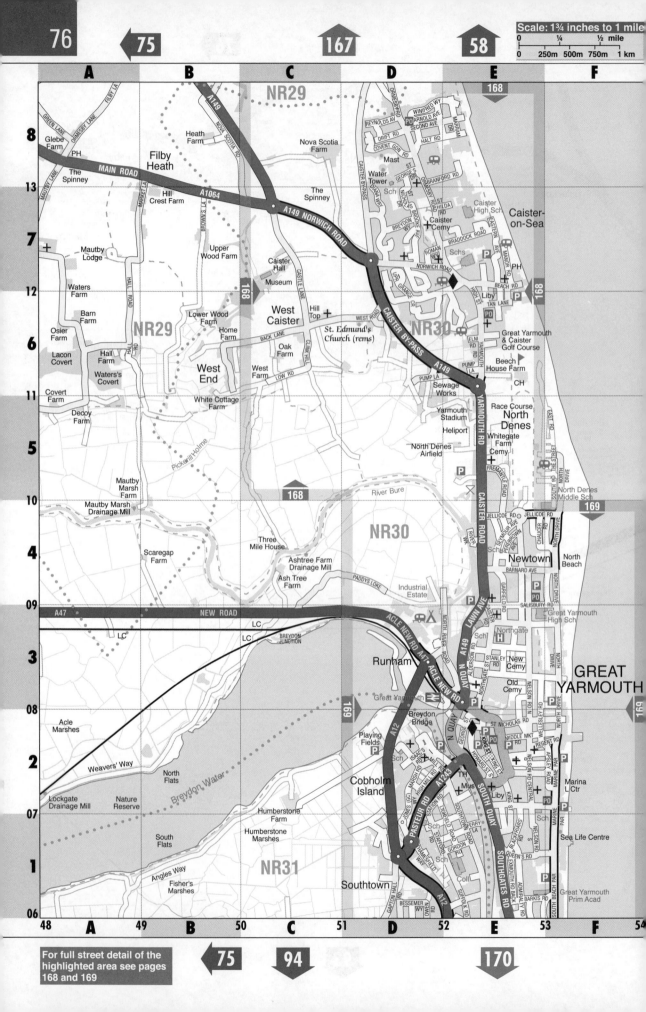

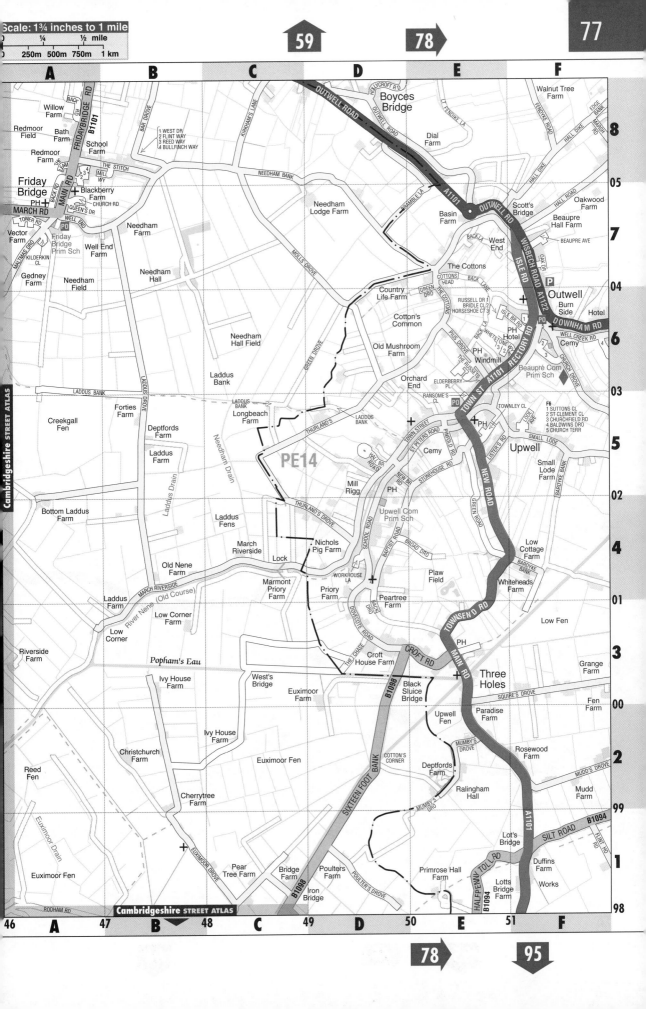

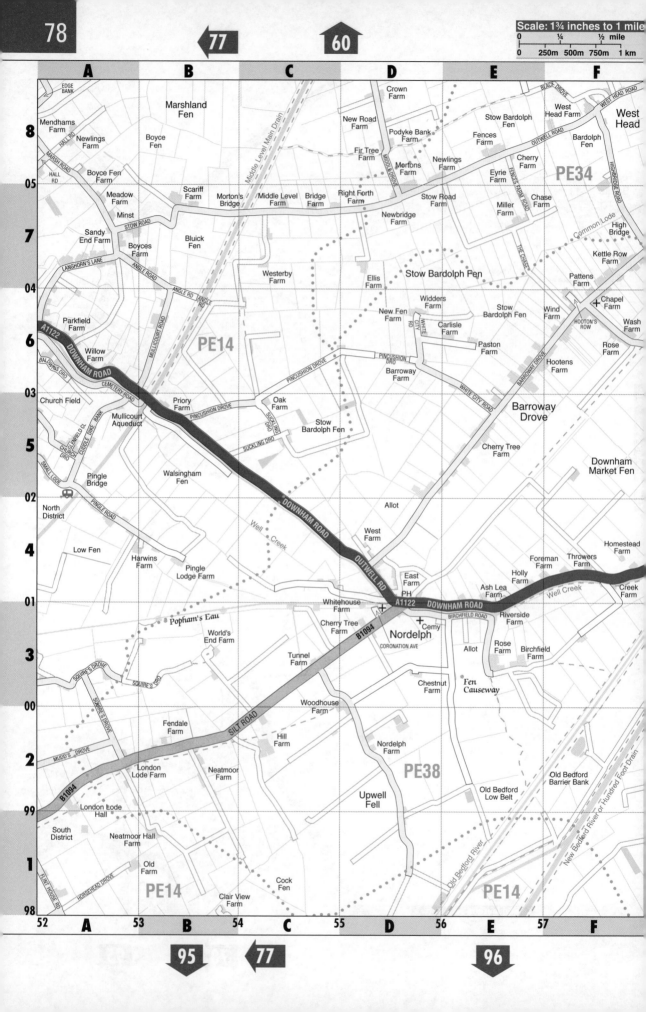

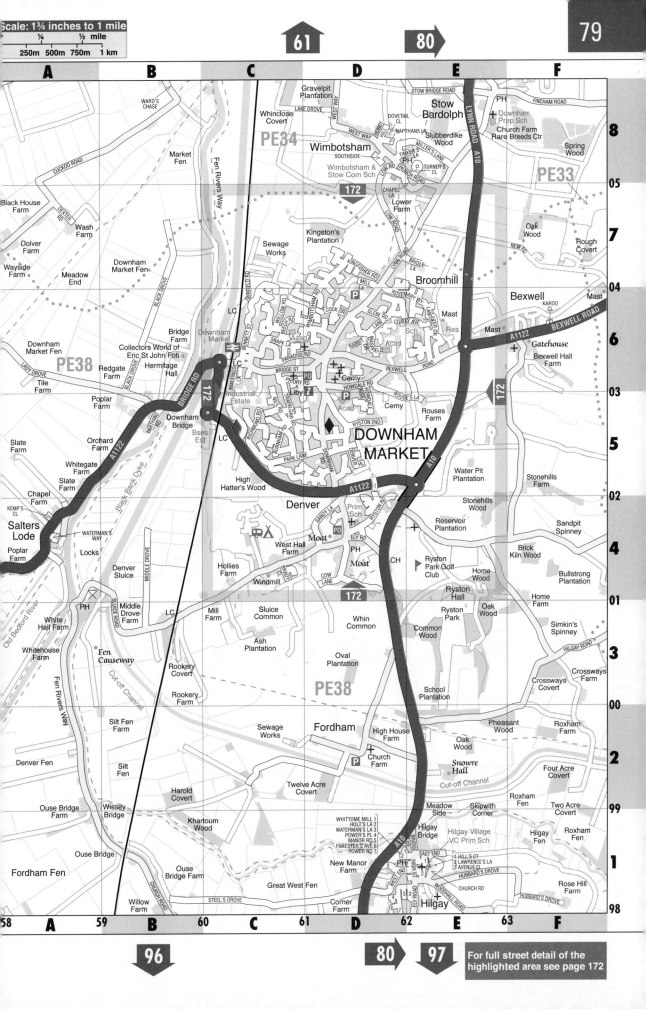

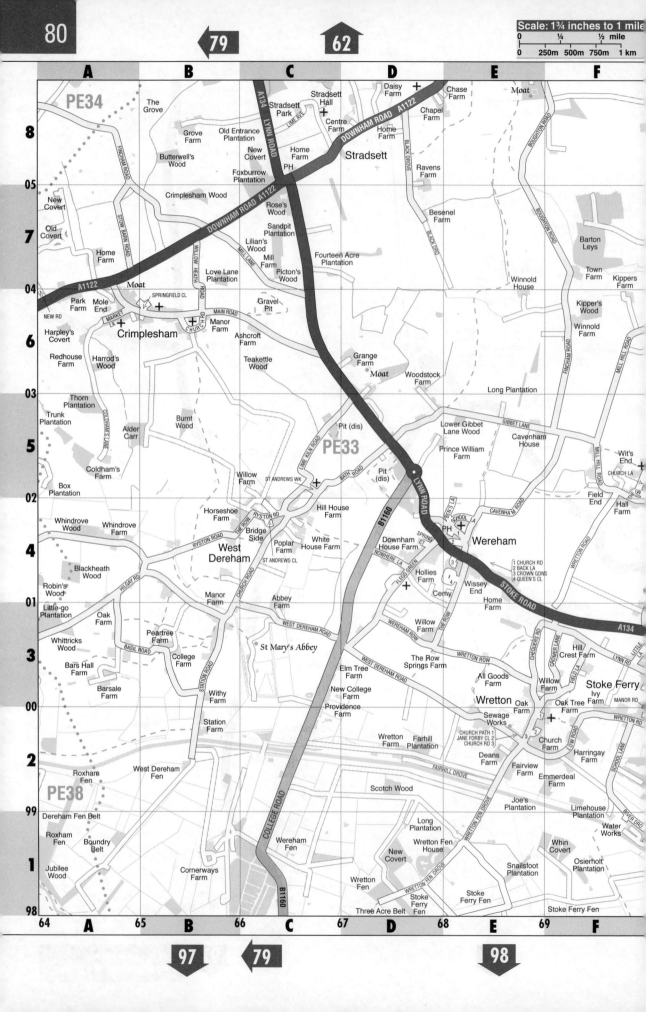

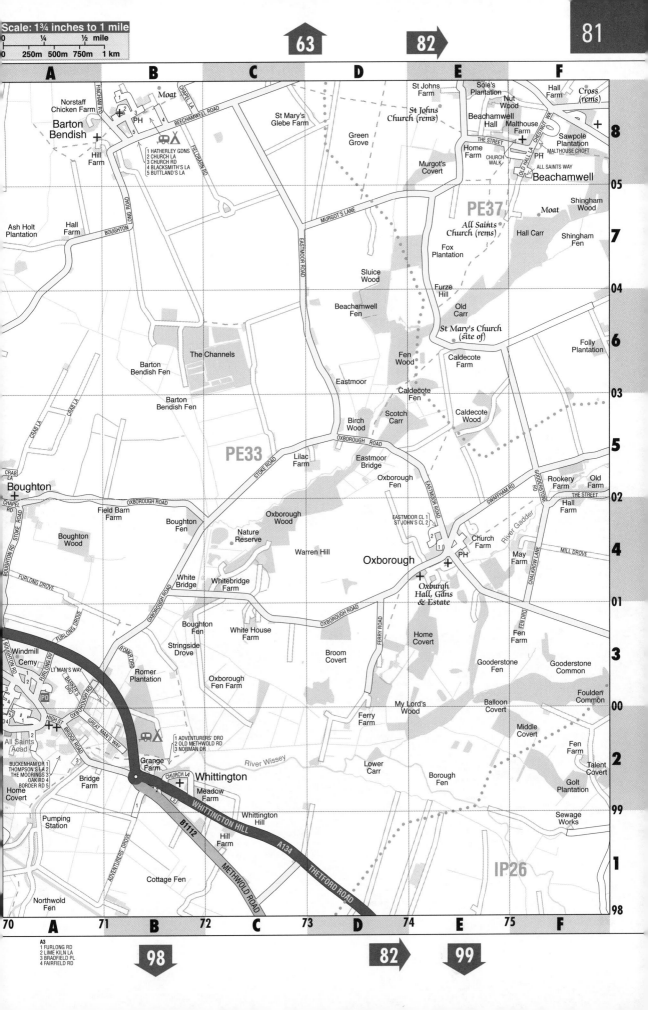

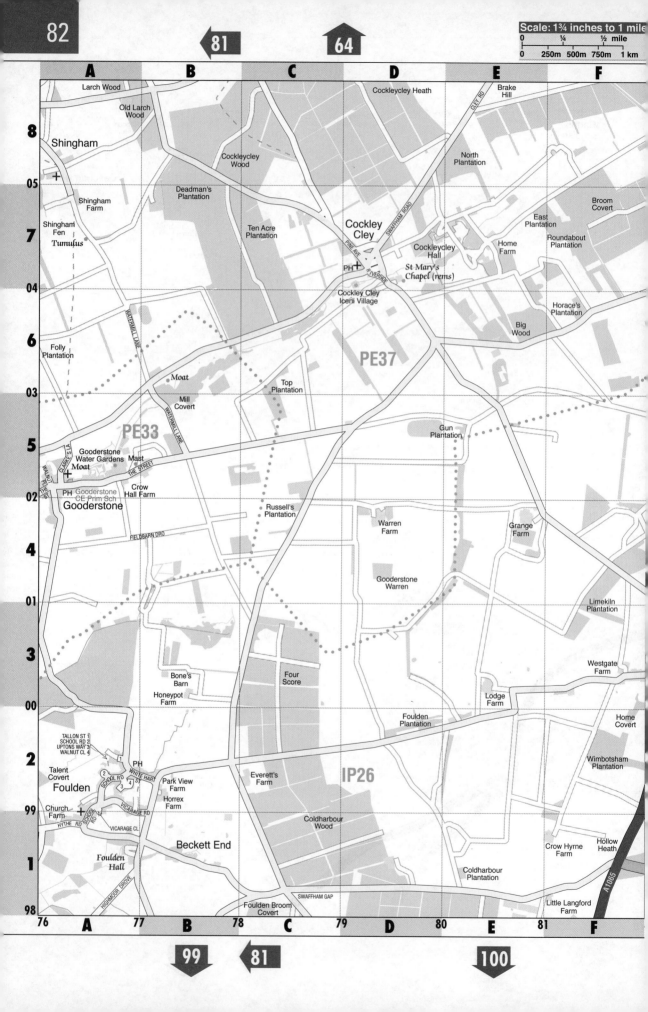

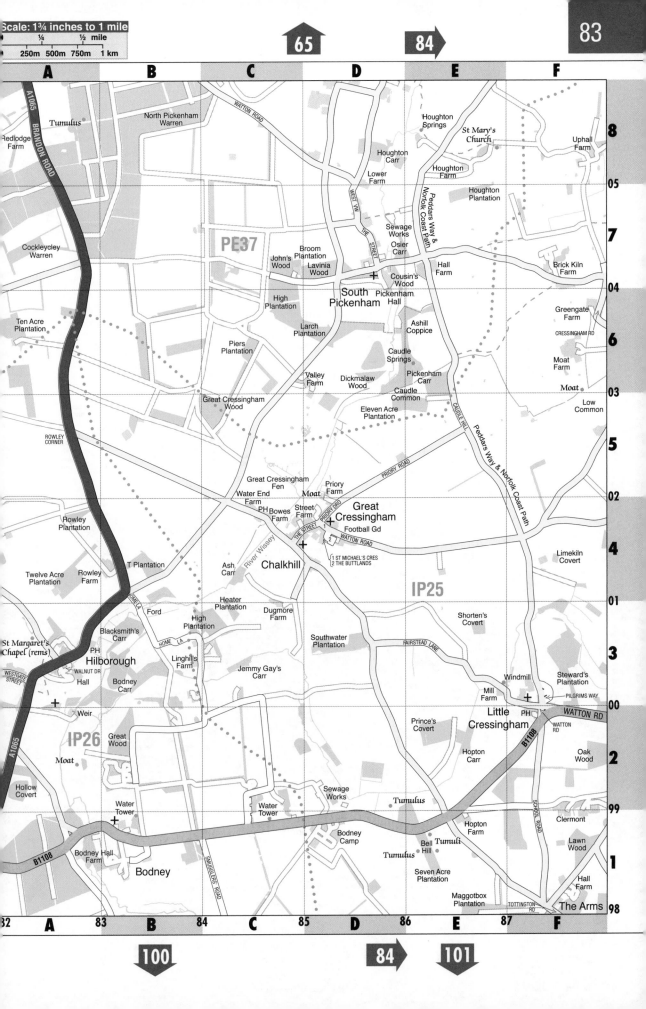

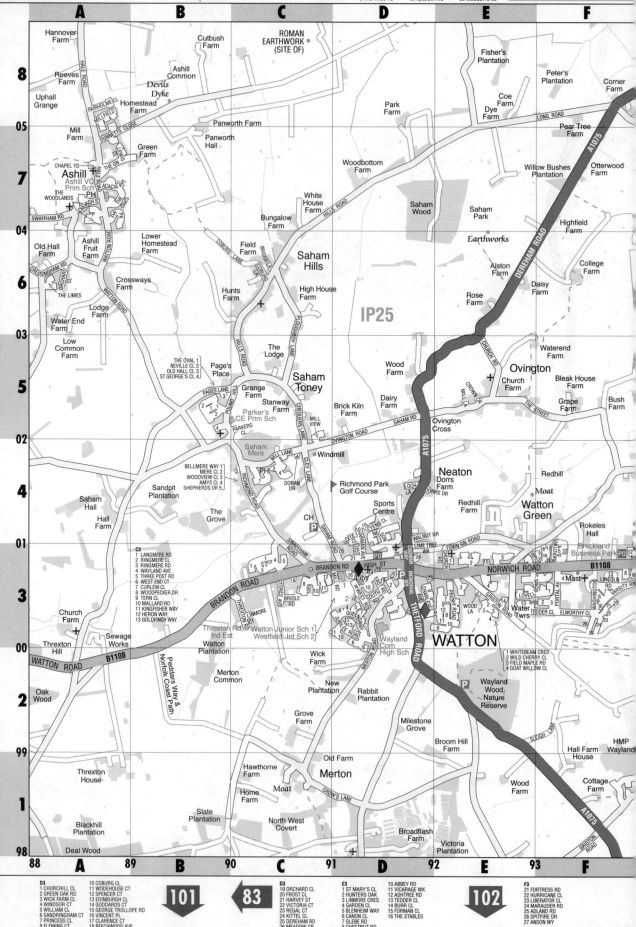

F3
1 HENRY'S CT
2 SLESSOR CL
3 DOWDING RD
4 TRENCHARD CRES
5 CHANGI RD
6 HASTINGS RD

7 COMET RD
8 HALTON RD
9 FARNBOROUGH RD
10 CRANWELL RD
11 SALMOND RD
12 HARRIS RD
13 HENDON AVE

14 PADDOCK CL
15 SHIRE HORSE WY
16 THE GALLOPS
17 HORSE SHOE CL
18 FARRIER RD
19 SADDLERS DR
20 MOSQUITO CL

D3
1 CHURCHILL CL
2 GREEN OAK RD
3 WICK FARM CL
4 WINDSOR CT
5 WILLIAM CL
6 SANDRINGHAM CT
7 PRINCESS CL
8 FLEMING CT
9 MALTHOUSE CL

10 COBURG CL
11 WODEHOUSE CT
12 SPENCER CT
13 EDINBURGH CL
14 GODDARDS CT
15 GEORGE TROLLOPE RD
16 VINCENT PL
17 CLARENCE CT
18 BEECHWOOD AVE
19 ORCHARD CL

D3
19 ORCHARD CL
20 FROST CL
21 HARVEY ST
22 VICTORIA CT
23 REGAL CT
24 KITTEL CL
25 DEREHAM RD
26 MEADOW CT
27 GREGOR SHANKS WAY

E3
1 ST MARY'S CL
2 HUNTERS OAK
3 LINMORE CRES
4 GARDEN CL
5 BLENHEIM WAY
6 CANON CL
7 GLEBE RD
8 CHESTNUT RD
9 MONKHAMS DR

10 ABBEY RD
11 VICARAGE WK
12 ASHTREE RD
13 TEDDER CL
14 BURR CL
15 FORMAN CL
16 THE STABLES

F3
21 FORTRESS RD
22 HURRICANE CL
23 LIBERATOR RD
24 MARAUDER RD
25 ADLAND RD
26 SPITFIRE DR
27 ANSON WY

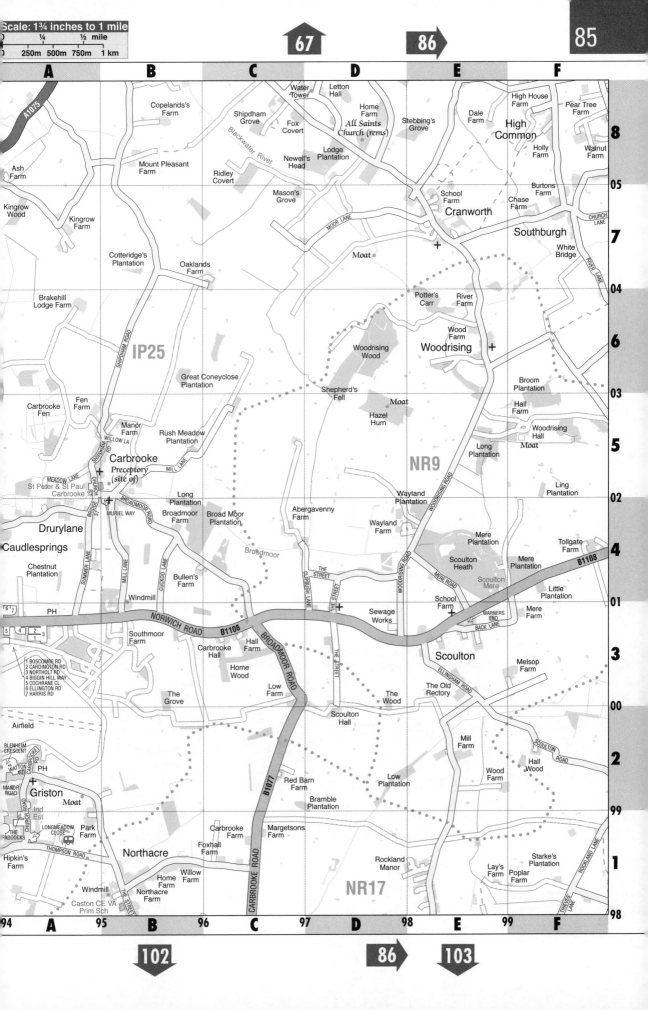

← 85   68 →

C5
1 BELL MDW
2 BAXTER CL
3 FOLLY LA
4 POTTLES ALLEY
5 BOND ST
6 CHAPEL ST
7 ADMIRALS WK
8 COPPER LA
9 DRINKWATER CL

Scale: 1¾ inches to 1 mile
0   ¼   ½   mile
0   250m 500m 750m   1 km

A   B   C   D   E   F

8

Moat

THE LINGS
Long Plantation

Station Farm

Danemoor Green

POST OFFICE LA

SILVER ST
CH
P

The Grove

Low Street Farm

Low Street

LOW ST
NORWICH ROAD
B1135
Mid Norfolk Railway

Danemoor Farm

05

Southburgh
Church Farm
CHURCH LANE
SOUTHBURGH RD

Calveley Hall

Pittwood Farm

Bridge Farm

Blackwater Bridge

DEREHAM ROAD

Old Hall

CHURCH ROAD

WHITE CROSS

White Cross Farm

STATION ROAD

MIDDLE ROAD

7

Blackwater River

IP25

Gresham Farm

Moat

04

Manor Farm

Park Farm

Browns Farm

Manson Green Farm

Nordelph Corner

SANDY LANE

White Farm

BEECHES LA

6

River La

Pond Farm

Willow Farm

Grove Farm

Gibraltar Farm

Manson Green

Manson Green Farm

PLOUGH LA

HINGHAM ROAD

NORDELPH CORNER

HACKFORD ROAD

Hardingham

Boundary Farm

Ash Tree Farm

HARDINGHAM RD

03

PYE LANE

College Farm

Hall Farm

SPRINGFIELD WY

Cutbush Farm

White Lodge

HARDINGHAM ROAD

Hill Farm

B1108

NR9

Brickyard Plantation

SOUTHBURGH LANE
WOOD RISING LN

PRIMROSE RD 1
THE DELL 2
LONSDALE CRES 3
GLEBE CL 4
RECTORY GDNS 5

Hingham

Hingham Prim Sch

THE FIELDS

Mill Farm

LINCOLN AVE

Alexanders Farm

Hill Farm

Church Farm

05

The Willows

GREENACRE RD

BAXTER RD

HARDINGHAM ST

YONGERS LA

IRONSIDE WAY

HINGHAM ROAD

B1108

Watton Road Farm

Rectory Farm

WATTON ROAD

CHURCH ST

Liby
PO

NORWICH ST

BEARS CL

NORWICH ROAD

02

Frost Row

ATTLEBOROUGH ROAD

RECTORY GDNS

HALL LA

MILL

Windmill

SEAMERE ROAD

Pearces Farm

Wades Farm

LOW COMMON

Spring Farm

HALL LANE

Bridge Farm

CHURCH LANE

NORWICH RD

Cemy

The Coppice

PITTS SQ

Moat

Jubilee Plantation

Sea Mere Farm

LOW COMMON

4

Pine Plantation

NR9

Sewage Works

Sea Mere

01

Frostrow Farm

Gurney's Plantation

Gurney's Manor

LOW ROAD

Sycamore Farm

LOW RD

DEOPHAM ROAD

Seamere Plantation

Deopham Plantation

Crown Farm

Hall Farm

Home Farm

Ivy Farm

VICTORIA LA

CHURCH ROAD

Deopham

3

Lyngwhite Farm

CADGE'S LANE

Money Hill

MONEYHILL LANE

NEW ROAD

Oldmans Farm

Sunnyside Farm

Shaws Farm

VICARAGE ROAD

High Elm Farm

LINDEN CL

00

LT ELLINGHAM ROAD

Pond Farm

THE STALLAND

Chestnut Farm

PYE LANE

NR18

2

Hall Farm

Green Farm

Little Ellingham

HINGHAM ROAD

ATTLEBOROUGH LA

Lyngwhite Farm

Warren Farm

Deopham Stalland

Stalland Farm

STALLAND LANE

Ivy Green Farm

Laurel Farm

Morley Manor

MILLHILL LANE

SCOULTON RD

ROCKLAND LANE

OUGH RD

Websters Farm

THE GREEN

Woodrow Farm

Deopham Green

Willow Farm

99

Church Farm

Rookery Farm

CHURCH AVE

ATTLEBOROUGH ROAD

HINGHAM ROAD

Stalland Common

HALFIELD LAN

Half Field Farm

MORLEY ROAD

Chase End

South Hill Farm

Hill Farm

1

NR17

Goose Common

WOOD LANE

BOW ST

Lays Farm

Holly Croft Farm

Stalland Farm

Brick Kiln Farm

Bush Green Farm

Croft Farm

ATTLEBOROUGH RD

Mill Farm

Old Hall

Moat

Morley Wood

98

Anchor Corner

Anchor Farm

GREEN LA

HIGHAM LN

High Elms Farm

Manor Farm

00   A   01   B   02   C   03   D   04   E   05   F

C4
1 ST ANDREWS CL
2 OAK LA
3 HALL CL
4 HARDINGHAM ST
5 STONE LA
6 THE MEADOWS
7 BEARS CL

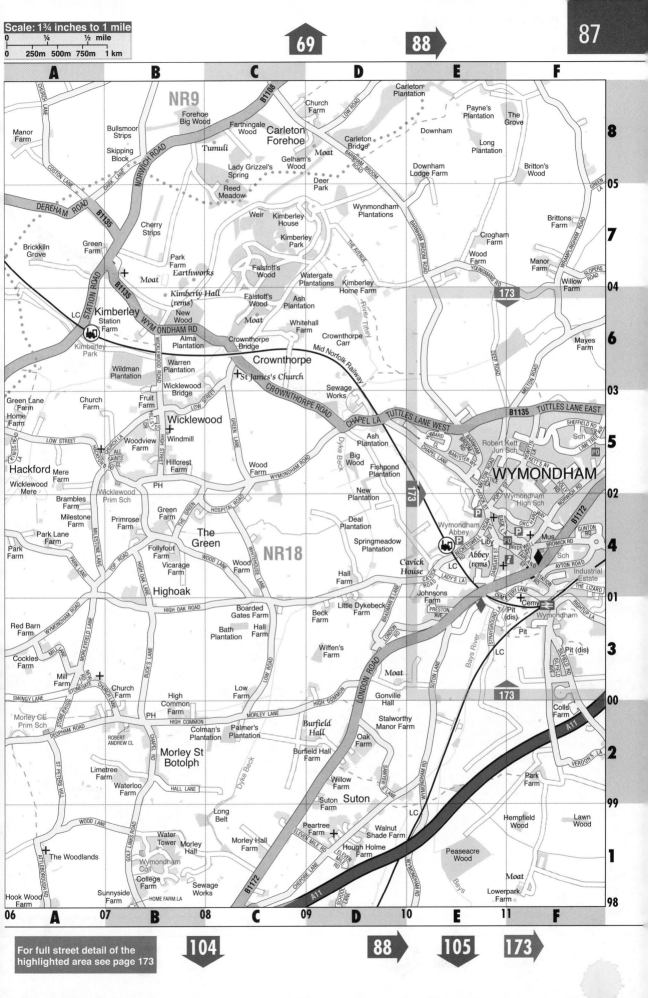

Scale: 1¾ inches to 1 mile

0   ¼   ½ mile
0 250m 500m 750m 1 km

69
88

A | B | C | D | E | F

NR9

B1108

Church Farm
Carleton Plantation
Payne's Plantation
The Grove

Forehoe Big Wood
Farthingale Wood
Carleton Forehoe
Low Road
Downham

Bullsmoor Strips
Skipping Block
Tumuli
Moat
Carleton Bridge
Downham Lodge Farm
Long Plantation

Norwich Road
Park Lane
Lady Grizzel's Spring
Gelham's Wood
Barnham Broom Road
Britton's Wood

Dereham Road
B1135
Reed Meadow
Deer Park
Downham Lodge Farm
Green La

Cherry Strips
Weir
Kimberley House
Wynmondham Plantations
Brittons Farm

Brickkiln Grove
Green Farm
Kimberley Park
Crogham Farm
Wramplingham Road
Youngmans Rd

Park Farm
Earthworks
Falstoff's Wood
Kimberley Home Farm
Wood Farm
Manor Farm
Slopers Road

B1135
Kimberly Hall (rems)
New Wood
Falstoff's Wood
Ash Plantation
River Tiffey
173
Willow Farm

LC
KIMBERLEY
Station Farm
Moat
Whitehall Farm
Crownthorpe Carr
Deep Road
Mayes Farm
Melton Road

Kimberley Park
WYMONDHAM RD
Alma Plantation
Crownthorpe Bridge
Mid Norfolk Railway

Wildman Plantation
Warren Plantation
Crownthorpe
St James's Church
Sewage Works

Green Lane Home Farm
Church Farm
Wicklewood Bridge
Fruit Farm
Low Street
CROWNTHORPE ROAD
Chapel La
Tuttles Lane West
B1135
Tuttles Lane East
Sheffield Rd
Sch

Low Street
Wicklewood
Windmill
Ash Plantation
Big Wood
Fishpond Plantation
Chapel Lane
Robert Kett Jun Sch
Lime Tree Av
PO

Hackford
Mere Farm
Woodview Farm
Hillcrest Farm
Wood Farm
Dyke Beck
WYMONDHAM
Norwich Rd

Wicklewood Mere
All Saints
PH
New Plantation
173
Wymondham High Sch

Brambles Farm
Primrose Farm
Green Farm
Deal Plantation
Wymondham Abbey
P

Milestone Farm
The Green
Wood Farm
Springmeadow Plantation
Abbey (rems)

Park Lane Farm
Folkfoot Farm
Vicarage Farm
Wood Farm
Hall Farm
Cavick House
Johnsons Farm
Industrial Estate

Red Barn Farm
Highoak
High Oak Road
Boarded Gates Farm
Beck Farm
Little Dykebeck Farm
Preston Ave
Pit (dis)
Wymondham

Cockles Farm
Mill Farm
Church Farm
Bath Plantation
Hall Farm
Wiffen's Farm
London Road
Pit

Swingy Lane
High Common Farm
Low Farm
Moat
Gonville Hall
173

Morley CE Prim Sch
PH
High Common
Palmer's Plantation
Burfield Hall
Stalworthy Manor Farm
Colls Farm
A11

Colman's Plantation
Morley St Botolph
Oak Plantation
Suton Lane
Park Farm

Limetree Farm
Dyke Beck
Burfield Hall Farm
Willow Farm
Suton Farm
Suton
Hempfield Wood
Lawn Wood

Waterloo Farm
Long Belt
Morley Hall Farm
Peartree Farm
Walnut Shade Farm
Hough Holme Farm
Peaseacre Wood

The Woodlands
Water Tower
Morley Hall
Eleven Mile Rd
Moat
Lowerpark Farm

Hook Wood Farm
Wymondham Coll
College Farm
Sunnyside Farm
Sewage Works
B1172
A11
Bays

06 | A | 07 | B | 08 | C | 09 | D | 10 | E | 11 | F

104
88
105
173

For full street detail of the highlighted area see page 173

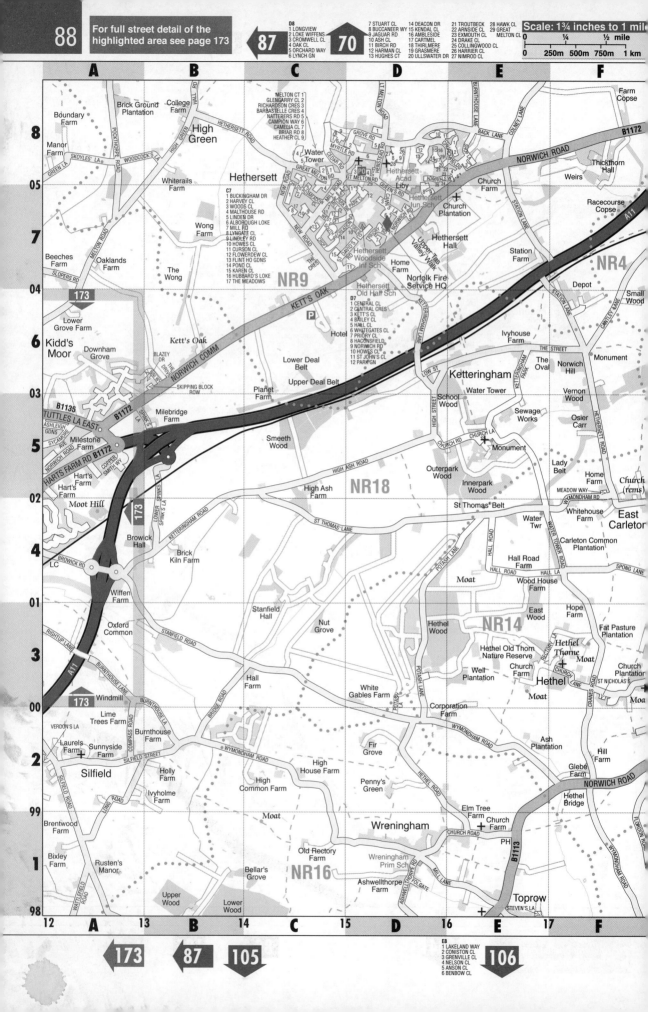

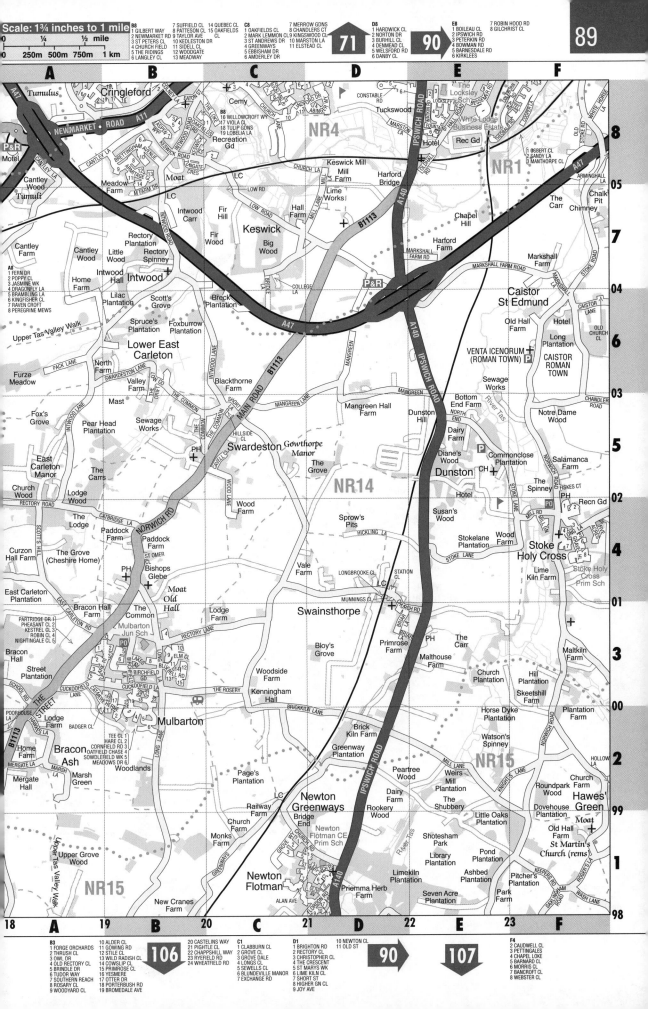

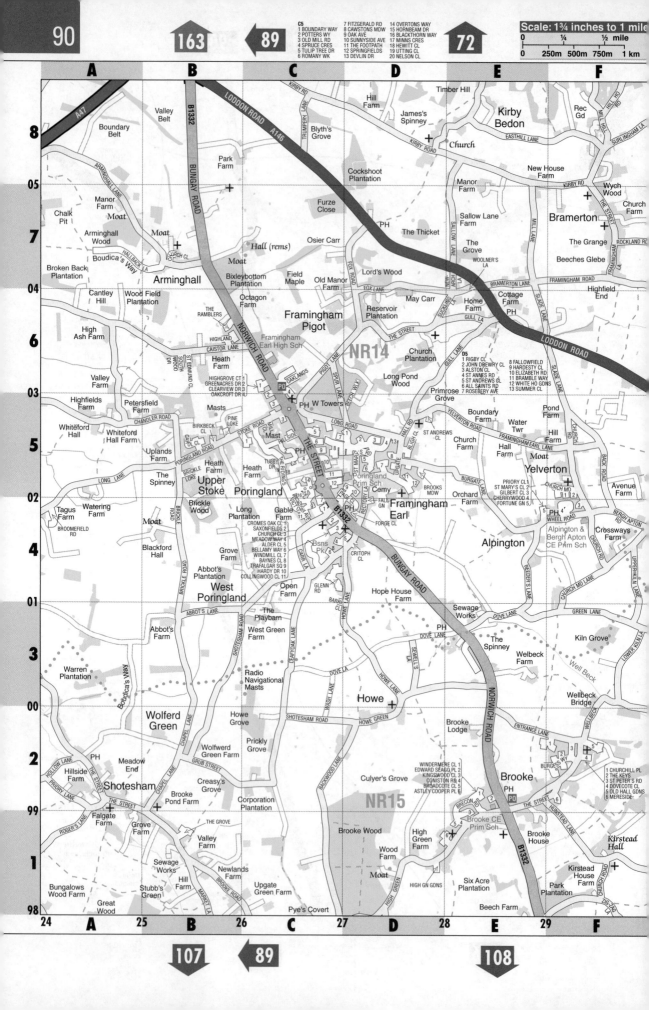

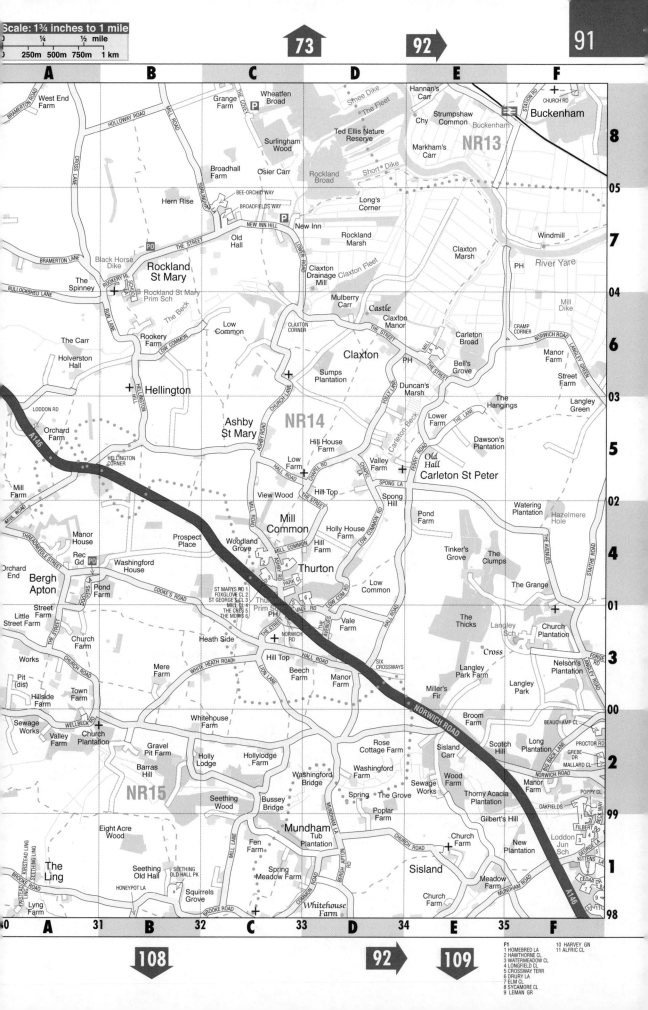

Scale: 1¾ inches to 1 mile

0   ¼   ½ mile
0   250m 500m 750m 1 km

A B C D E F

8

Buckenham Carrs
Hassingham
Broad Farm
Cottage Carr
Earth Wall Carr
Goldie's Carr
Swill's Meadow
Barn End

Thatch Farm
PH
HIGH RD
MANOR RD
Manor Farm
COW MDW ROAD
HALL RD
Church
GRIMMER LANE
B1140
CHURCH CL

Primrose Grove
GROVE ROAD
Hall Farm
SOUTHWOOD RD
Grove Farm
Southwood
Oaks Farm

PORTER'S ROAD
Lower Green Farm
REEDHAM RD
THE LOKE
Lower Green
Windmill
Lower Green Farm
WHEELWRIGHTS CL
PO
PALMER'S LA
SUTTON CRES
CHURCH RD
MILL RD
White House Farm
Freethorpe
Manor House
SCHOOL RD
LOW ROAD

GRANARY CL 1
PEARSONS CL 2
YOUNG'S CRES 3
BOWLERS CL 4
PRESTON CL 5
CRICKETER'S WLK 6
WALPOLE WY 7
PROSPECT CL 8

THE COMMON
PH
THE GREEN
Freethorpe Com Prim Sch

05

7

Cantley Prim Sch
SCHOOL LANE
BURNT HO RD
CHURCH RD
STATION RD
Cantley
LC
Sports Gd
GRANGE RD
MARIE CL 1
STANLEY CL 2
MALTHOUSE LA 3
Cantley
LC
Marsh Farm
Red House
Chimney

LIMPENHOE ROAD
Cantley Grange
Wood Farm
Cantley View Farm
Spong Carr
NORWICH ROAD
SOUTHWOOD RD
OLD CHAPEL LA
DOBBS LA
RICH RD
FREETHORPE RD
Limpenhoe
NR13
Marsh Farm
Factory
Chimney
Chimney
Chimney
WELL RD
MARSH ROAD
Low Farm
REEDHAM ROAD
Hill Farm
SANDY LANE
LIMPENHOE ROAD
Mast
Wood Farm
HALL ROAD
FREETHORPE ROAD

04

6

River Yare
Monks Plantation
Langley Abbey
Moat
PH
The Wherry
LANGLEY GN
Abbey Carr
LANGLEY DIKE
STAITHE ROAD
Staithe Farm
Poplars Farm
Langley Marshes
LANGLEY STREET
Sewage Works
1 LANGLEY RD
2 HIGHLAND CL
3 WINDSOR RD
4 STATION RD
Reservoir
Settling Basins
Round House
Limpenhoe Marshes
LC
Settling Basins
Limpenhoe Hill
John's Carr
Sprowston Wood
Gurney Wood
Reedham
1 STATION DR
2 WITTON CL
3 THE HAVAKER
POTTLE'S LA
WITTON GN
Reedham

03

5

Willow Farm
Langley Street
Hardley Street
Great Yard Farm
Chestnut Farm
White House Farm
Westgate Farm
Rustygate Farm
HARDLEY DIKE
Hardley Drainage Mill
Hardley Marshes
Hardley Cross
Norton Staithe
Norton Drainage Mill
FERRY ROAD
Limpenhoe Drainage Mill
Reedham Ferry (V)
PH
Reedham Drainage Mill
PO
BOYCE'S DYKE
Norton Marshes
YARE VIEW CL 1
CLIFF CL 2
NEW RD 3
MIDDLE HILL 4
RIVERSIDE 5
THE HILLS

02

4

GENTLEMAN'S WALK
HARDLEY ROAD
CROSS STONE ROAD
COCK ROAD
FORGE ROAD
Boundary Farm
Ash Plantation
Avenue Farm
LOWER HARDLEY ROAD
HARDLEY STREET
CHURCH LANE
HARDLEY HALL LA
Church Farm
Broom Hill
River Chet
Hardley Marshes
Norton Marshes
Marshlands Farm
Leys Farm
Nogdam End
MILL DYKE
Firs Farm
Ash Carr
LOW ROAD
Thatched House Farm

01

3

00

Chedgrave Hills
LOWER HARDLEY ROAD
Hardley Wood
Hardley Hall
NR14
Hall Carr
Moat
Old Hall Carr
Hill House
FERRY ROAD

2

RECTORY LA
Chedgrave
COMM LOKE
Chedgrave Carr
River Chet
Hardley Flood Nature Reserve
Loddon Common
Riverside Farm
Valley Farm
Little Church Farm
Church Farm
CHURCH LA
NEW ROAD
Firs Farm
Carr Farm
Walnut Tree Farm
Willow Farm
Low Farm
SOC DYKE
THE BECK

99

Liby
PH
Bsns Ctr
MILTON DR
Hobart High Sch
Hall Green Farm
Beechgrove Farm
HECKINGHAM HOLES
NORTON ROAD
Heckingham
CHURCH LA
Reservoir
LODDON ROAD
Highfield Farm
Beacon Hill
Elm Farm
THE STREET
Church Farm
Church Farm
THURLTON PRIM SCH

1

PO
PH
Loddon
Ind Est
SANDY LANE
SCHOOL LANE
Hill Farm
Hall
BRIAR LANE
FARM RD
High House Farm
BUTTER LA
BOUNDARY RD
Norton Plantation
Norton Subcourse
LODDON ROAD
Thurlton
CROFT RD
BECCLES RD
CHURCH ROAD
MILL RD
PH

98

36   37   38   39   40   41
A   B   C   D   E   F

A1
1 GARDEN CT
2 GEORGE LA
3 OLD MARKET GN
4 MARKET PL
5 SALE CT
6 BEECH CL
7 DAVY PL
8 LEMAN CL
9 LEMAN GR
10 CEDAR DR
11 CANNELL RD
12 FOXES LOKE
13 REEDS WAY
14 BROWNES GR
15 Loddon Inf Sch

A2
1 BIG BACK LA
2 BEAUCHAMP RD
3 PROCTOR AVE
4 PROCTOR CL
5 PROCTOR RD
6 SNOW'S HILL
7 HILLCREST
8 HURST RD
9 MALLARD CL
10 THE RISE
11 FARM CL
12 NORWICH RD
13 CHURCH CL

F1
1 LOW RD
2 TITHEBARN LA
3 HAMPTON AVE
4 LINKS WAY
5 MEADOW CL
6 LINKS CL

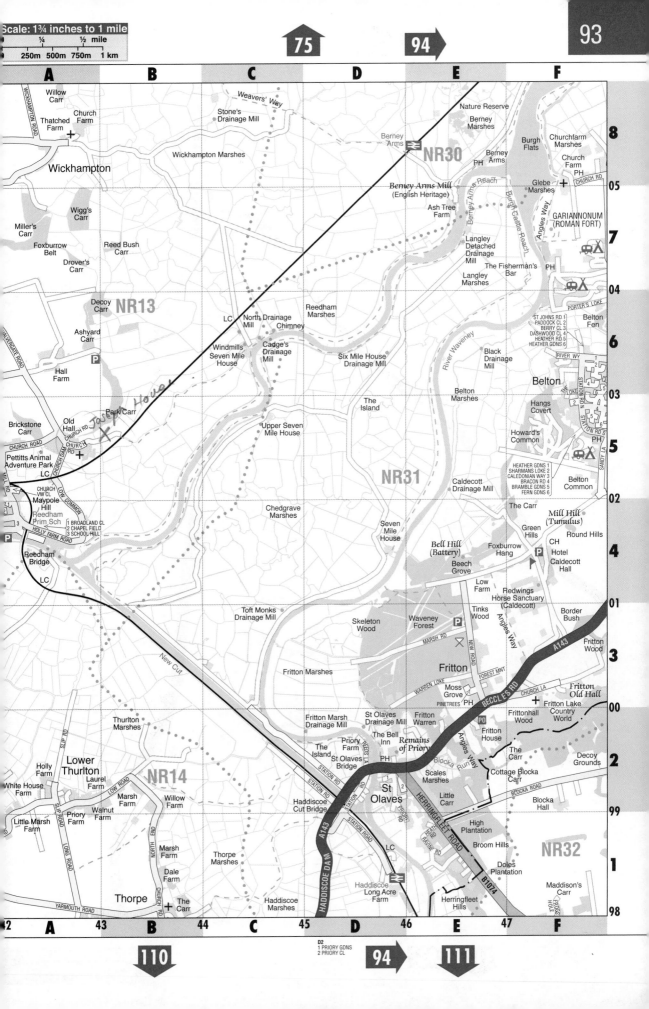

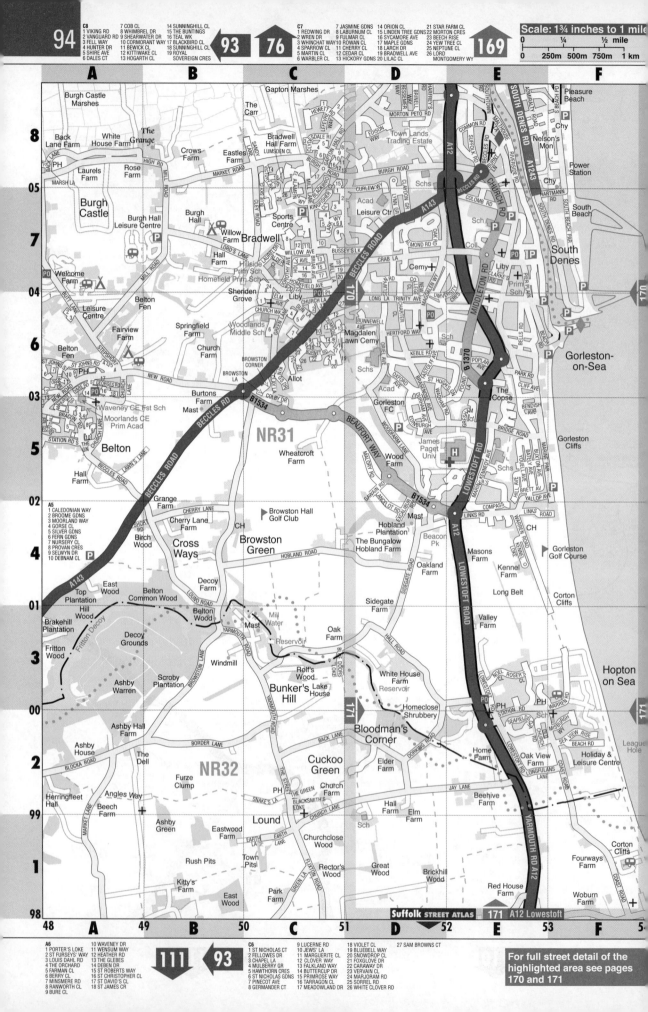

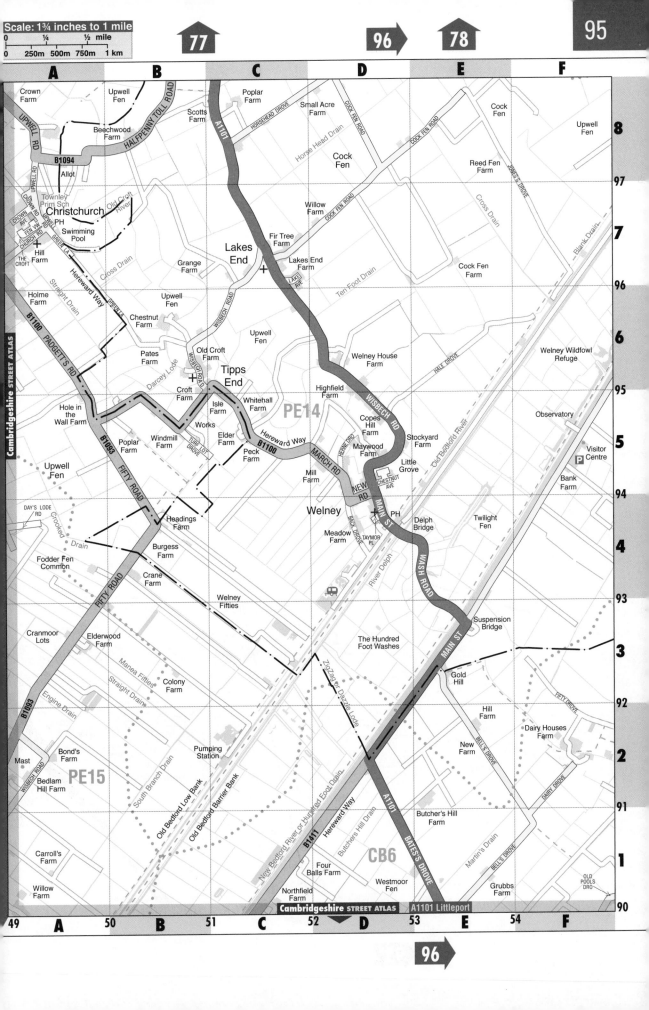

A B C D E F

Crown Farm
Upwell Fen
Beechwood Farm

HALFPENNY TOLL ROAD
B1094
Allot
UPWELL RD
Townley Prim Sch
Christchurch
PH
Swimming Pool
THE CROFT
Hill Farm
GREEN LA
Hereward Way
GREEN LA

Scotts Farm
Poplar Farm
HORSEHEAD DROVE
Small Acre Farm
COCK FEN ROAD
Cock Fen
COCK FEN ROAD
Reed Fen Farm
Cock Fen
Upwell Fen
JONES'S DROVE

8

97

A1101
Horse Head Drain
Willow Farm
COCK FEN ROAD
Blank Drain

7

Lakes End
Fir Tree Farm
Lakes End Farm
LAKE AVE
Ten Foot Drain
Cock Fen Farm

96

Grange Farm
Upwell Fen
WISBECH ROAD
Chestnut Farm
Pates Farm
Darcey Lode
Old Croft Farm
Upwell Fen
Tipps End
Croft Farm
Welney House Farm
HALE DROVE

6

Holme Farm
Straight Drain
B1100
PADGETT'S RD

Isle Farm
Whitehall Farm
Highfield Farm
WISBECH RD
Welney Wildfowl Refuge

95

Hole in the Wall Farm
B1093
Poplar Farm
Windmill Farm
TURF LOT DROVE
Works
Elder Farm
Peck Farm
Hereward Way
B1100
MARCH RD
Mill Farm
HERNE DRO
Copes Hill Farm
Maywood Farm
Stockyard Farm
Little Grove
Old Bedford River
Observatory
P Visitor Centre
Bank Farm

5

Upwell Fen
FIFTY ROAD
DAY'S LODE RD
Crooked Drain
Headings Farm
Welney
CHESTNUT AVE
NEW RD
MAIN ST
PH
Delph Bridge
Twilight Fen

94

Fodder Fen Common
Burgess Farm
Crane Farm
Meadow Farm
BACK DROVE
TAYMOR PL
River Delph
WASH ROAD

4

Welney Fifties
The Hundred Foot Washes
MAIN ST
Suspension Bridge

93

Cranmoor Lots
Elderwood Farm
Manea Fifties
Straight Drain
Colony Farm
ZigZag Dro
Dazzle Lode
Gold Hill
Hill Farm
FIFTY DROVE

3

Mast
Bond's Farm
WISBECH ROAD
PE15
Bedlam Hill Farm
Engine Drain
B1093
South Branch Drain
Pumping Station
Old Bedford Low Bank
Old Bedford Barrier Bank
New Farm
BELL'S DROVE
Dairy Houses Farm
DAIRY DROVE

2

New Bedford River or Hundred Foot Drain
B1411
Hereward Way
Butler's Hill Drain
CB6
Butcher's Hill Farm
Martin's Drain
BELL'S DROVE

91

Carroll's Farm
Willow Farm
Four Balls Farm
Northfield Farm
Westmoor Fen
A1101
BATES'S DROVE
Grubbs Farm
OLD POOLS DRO

1

PE14

78 95 79

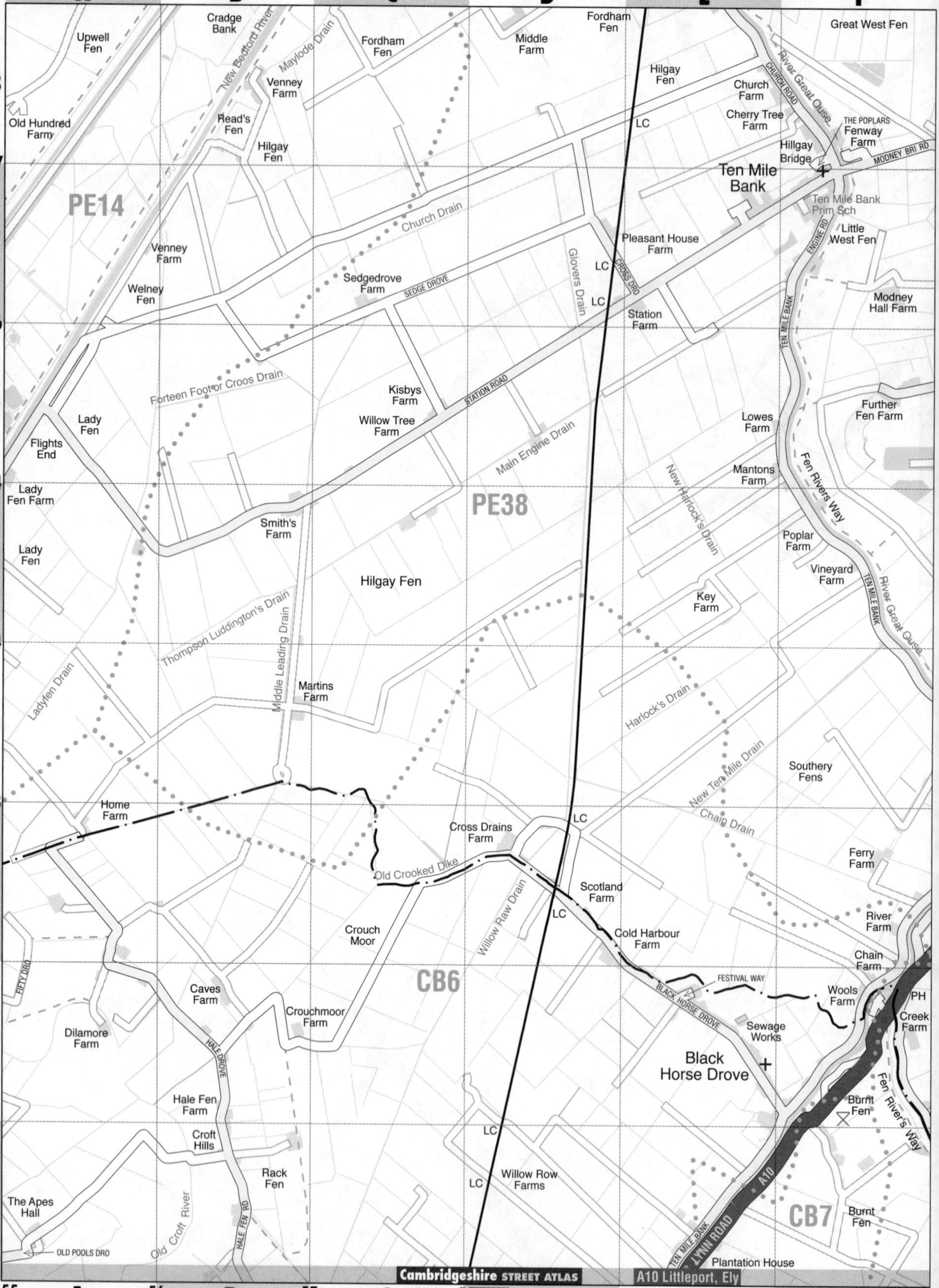

Scale: 1¾ inches to 1 mile
0 ¼ ½ mile
0 250m 500m 750m 1 km
A B C D E F
8 97 7 96 6 94 5 94 4 93 3 92 2 91 1 90
55 56 57 58 59 60
Upwell Fen
Cradge Bank
New Bedford River
Maylode Drain
Fordham Fen
Middle Farm
Fordham Fen
Great West Fen
Venney Farm
Hilgay Fen
Old Hundred Farm
Read's Fen
Hilgay Fen
River Great Ouse
CHURCH ROAD
Church Farm
Cherry Tree Farm
THE POPLARS
Fenway Farm
Hillgay Bridge
MODNEY BRI RD
Ten Mile Bank
Ten Mile Bank Prim Sch
Little West Fen
PE14
Church Drain
Venney Farm
Welney Fen
Sedgedrove Farm
SEDGE DROVE
Glovers Drain
CROSS DRO
Pleasant House Farm
ENGINE RD
TEN MILE BANK
Station Farm
Modney Hall Farm
Forteen Foot or Croos Drain
Kisbys Farm
STATION ROAD
Willow Tree Farm
Lady Fen
Flights End
Main Engine Drain
Lowes Farm
Further Fen Farm
Lady Fen Farm
New Harlock's Drain
Mantons Farm
Fen Rivers Way
PE38
Smith's Farm
Lady Fen
Poplar Farm
Hilgay Fen
Vineyard Farm
TEN MILE BANK
Key Farm
River Great Ouse
Thompson Luddington's Drain
Middle Leading Drain
Ladyfen Drain
Martins Farm
Harlock's Drain
New Ten Mile Drain
Southery Fens
Home Farm
Cross Drains Farm
Chain Drain
Ferry Farm
Old Crooked Dike
Scotland Farm
Willow Raw Drain
Crouch Moor
Cold Harbour Farm
River Farm
FIFTY DRO
CB6
Chain Farm
FESTIVAL WAY
BLACK HORSE DROVE
Wools Farm
PH
Creek Farm
Caves Farm
Crouchmoor Farm
Sewage Works
Dilamore Farm
HALE DROVE
Black Horse Drove
Hale Fen Farm
Burnt Fen
Fen Rivers Way
Croft Hills
Rack Fen
Willow Row Farms
The Apes Hall
Old Croft River
HALE FEN RD
TEN MILE BANK
LYNN ROAD
A10
CB7
Burnt Fen
OLD POOLS DRO
Plantation House
LC

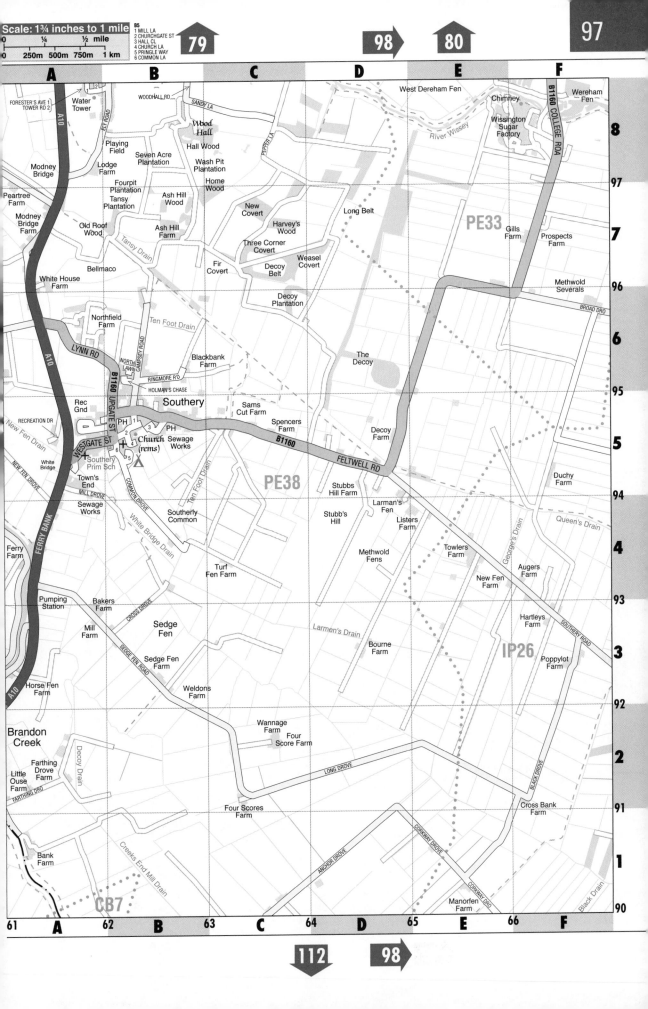

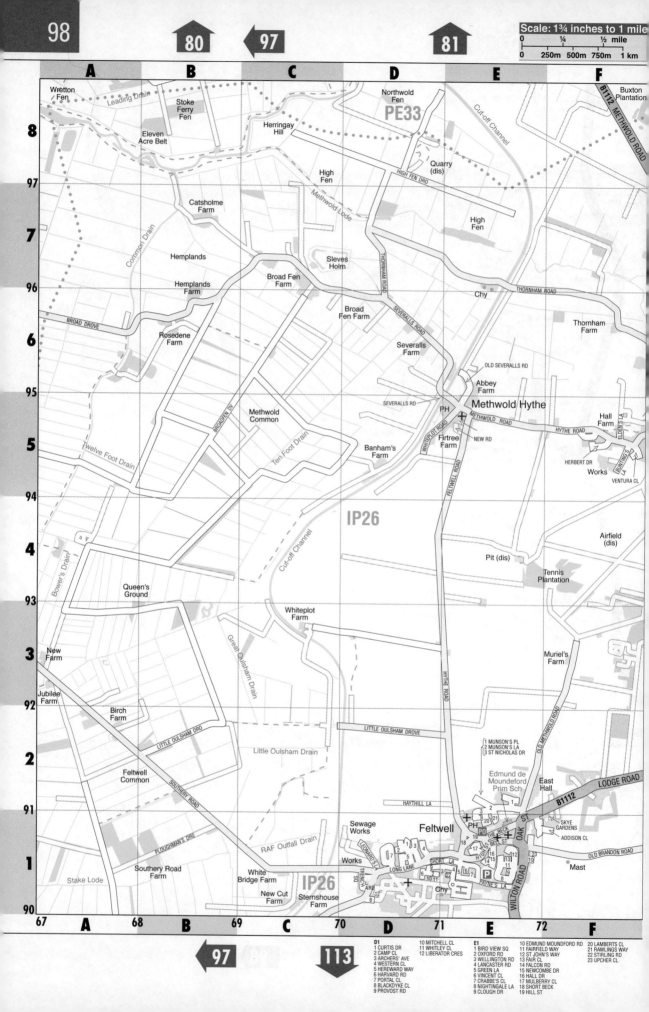

Scale: 1¾ inches to 1 mile
0   ¼   ½ mile
0   250m 500m 750m   1 km

D1
1 CURTIS DR
2 CAMP CL
3 ARCHERS' AVE
4 WESTERN WAY
5 HEREWARD WAY
6 HARVARD RD
7 PORTAL CL
8 BLACKDYKE CL
9 PROVOST RD

10 MITCHELL CL
11 WHITLEY CL
12 LIBERATOR CRES

E1
1 BIRD VIEW SQ
2 OXFORD RD
3 WELLINGTON RD
4 LANCASTER RD
5 GREEN LA
6 VINCENT CL
7 CRABBE'S CL
8 NIGHTINGALE LA
9 CLOUGH DR

10 EDMUND MOUNDFORD RD
11 FAIRFIELD WAY
12 ST JOHN'S WAY
13 FAIR CL
14 FALCON RD
15 NEWCOMBE DR
16 HALL DR
17 MULBERRY CL
18 SHORT BECK
19 HILL ST

20 LAMBERTS CL
21 RAWLINGS WAY
22 STIRLING RD
23 UPCHER CL

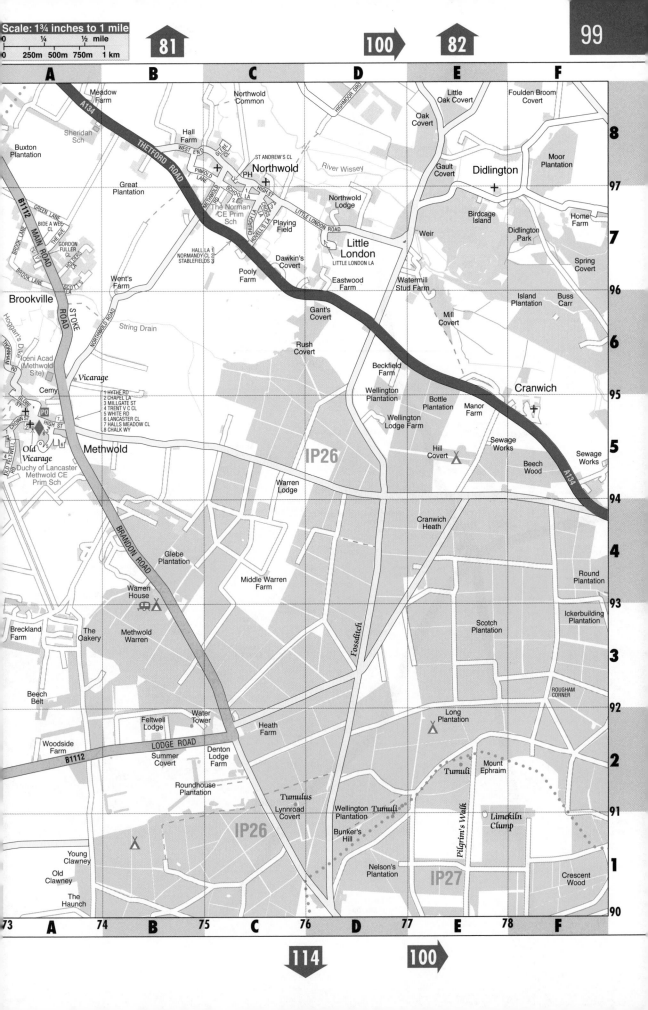

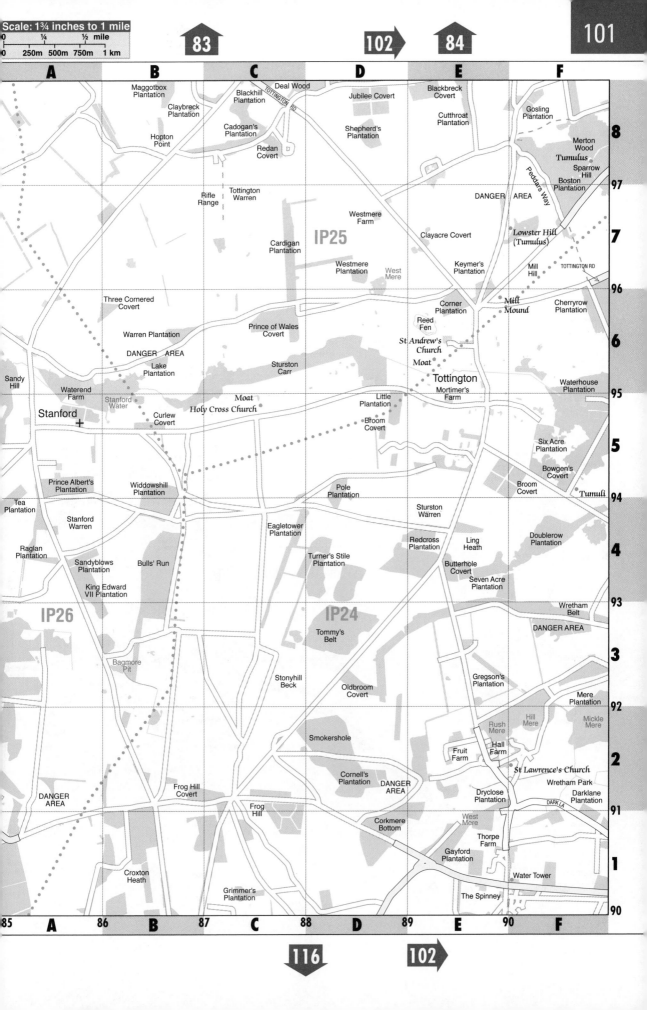

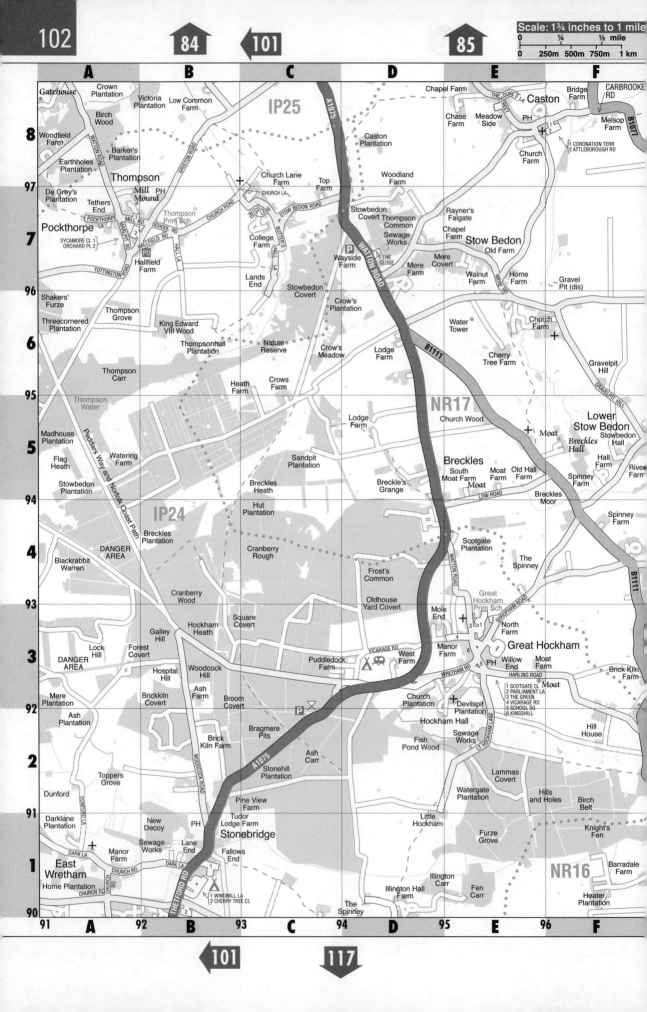

Scale: 1¾ inches to 1 mile

0   ¼   ½ mile
0 250m 500m 750m 1 km

A   B   C   D   E   F

8

Cottage Farm
Cemy
Mere Farm
North End
Thieves Lane
Primrose Farm
Laurel Farm
Wood La
Honeypot Farm
Green La
Cannells Farm
Hingham Rd
Hill House Farm
Broad Way
Park Farm
Flymore La
Bell Road
Chapel St
Model Farm
WATTON RD
Walnut Tree Farm
Bow Street
Sewage Works
Hall Farm
Rockland St Peter
Field Side
Plantation Farm
Home Farm
Rookery Farm
Pond Farm
Curriers Farm
Great Ellingham Prim Sch
Bury Hall
St Peter's Cl
Flymore Farm
Corner Farm
Bray's La
Wayland Rd
Recreation Centre
97
Great Grove
Green La
Cocksmere Farm
B1077
The Street
The Green
Mill La
CHEQUERS LA 1 RECTORY LA 2 HOME CL 3
Chequers La
Orchard End
Windmill
PH
Attleborough Road
Swamp La
Whews Farm
Rocklands Com Prim Sch
PO
PH
Mill La
Mill Lane
Chestnut Grove
Church St
Great Ellingham
B1077
7
The Whews
Rockland All Saints
Rockery Farm
Magpie Lane
The Spinney
Oak End
Norrold's Farm
Penhill Lane
Old Hall Farm Moat
GLEBE MDW
Poplar Farm
Home Farm
The Old Queens Head
Flybarn Farm
Rectory Road
Low Lane
Church Farm
Penhill Farm
Broadmarsh Farm
Long Street
Sewage Works
Wayland
H
96
STOWLAY LANE
Rectory Farm
Fen Street
St Andrew's Church (rems)
Homelea Farm
White House Farm
Cades Hill Farm
Whiting's La
Peels Farm
Sandy Lane
Holly Farm
Low La
Foster's Plantation
Dianas Wood
Home Cottage Farm
Cherry Tree Farm
Lyng Farm
Sewage Works
6
Staffords Farm
Beacon Farm
Rosary Farm
Wylands Farm
Walnut Tree Farm
Hillside Farm
Halfway Farm
Whitehall Farm
Tropical Butterfly World
West Carr Farm
West Carr Rd
95
Finchams Farm
Rocklands Farm
Mount Pleasant
Gravel Pit
Ford Farm
Ford
Swangey Farm
West Carr
Corner Farm
Shackles Farm
Honeypots Plantation
White Bridge
NR17
Swangey Farm
Swangey La
Swangey Lane
Wroo Road
Workhouse Common
94
Longmeadow Plantation
SPONG LANE
Wroo Farm
4
Shropham Hall
Highview Farm
Field End
THE MEADOWS
Manor Farm
Shropham Fen
River Thet
Gravel Pit
Swangey Fen
Willow Farm
Fen Farm
Fen St
A11
Pond Meadow Plantation
WATTON ROAD
Lynwood Farm
Shropham
WESTGATE
Glebe End
Grange Farm
Church Road
North Heath
Barnes Oak Plantation
Fox Covert
Peter Beales Roses
London Road
93
Rond Farm
Mill Farm
Horseshoe Farm
Pit (dis)
Swangey Plantation
Fen Plantation
Hotel
Watering Farm
PH
Duffus' Plantation
Hockham Lodge
Cranberry Rough Farm
Church Farm
Low Road
Hargham Road
White House Farm
Red Bridge
North Farm
NORTH END LANE
Swangey Farm
Old Plantation
Hargham Hall
Tollgate Plantation
Hargham Road
Furze Covert
Poplars Farm
Shropham Grove
Home Farm
Holly Farm
North End
Cross (rems)
92
Linger Hill
Oldhall Plantation
Bradcar Rd
River Thet
Lodge Plantation
Hall Farm
Church Belt
Broad Moor
Lingerhill Plantation
Snetterton
Chalk Lane
NR16
Cross (rems)
Moat
Burnthills Plantation
2
IP24
Grange Farm
Hall Farm
Horse Rescue Centre
ADA COLE AVENUE
Hargham Road
LC
91
Moat
Bradcar Farm
All Saint's Church
Ada Cole Ave
ST MARYS DR 1 ST ANDREWS DR 2
South Farm
Tuzzy Muzzy
Ford
Manor Farm
London Road
Gallows Hill
South Farm Plantation
Batz Farm
Barkers Farm
Larling Fen
Wash Lane
Sallow Lane
Homerton Ind Est
Gallows
Eccles Road
1
B1111
Folly Plantation
Fen Lane Farm
Hassock Fen
Mill Common Farm
Mill Common
LIMEKILN LANE
South End
A11
P
Oakwood Farm
Eccles Road
LC
Eccles Road
Barker's Plantation
Larling Fen
90

97   A   98   B   99   C   00   D   01   E   02   F

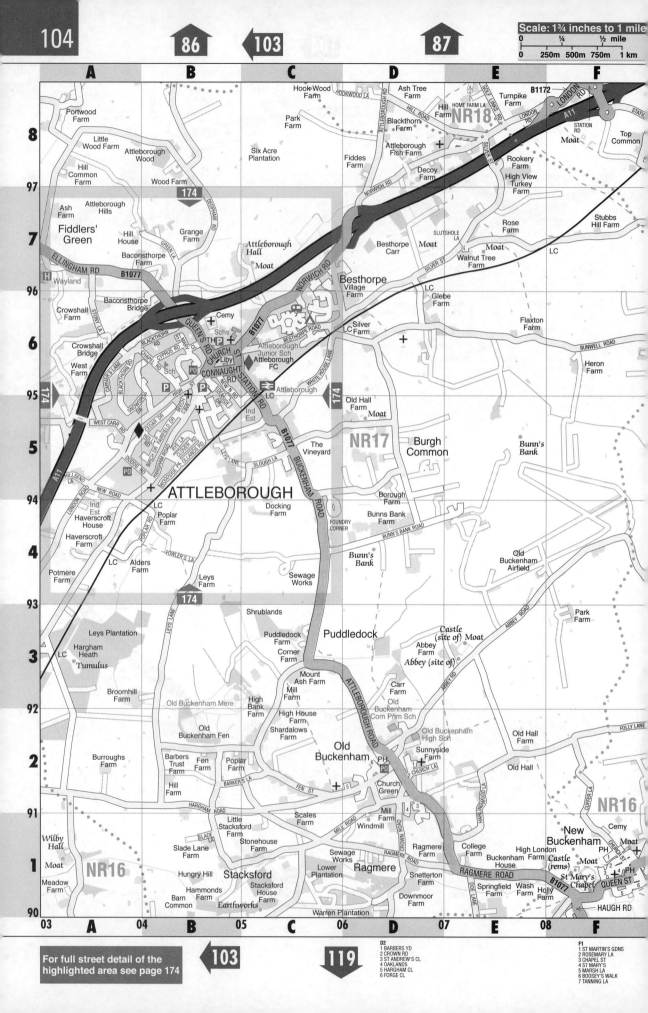

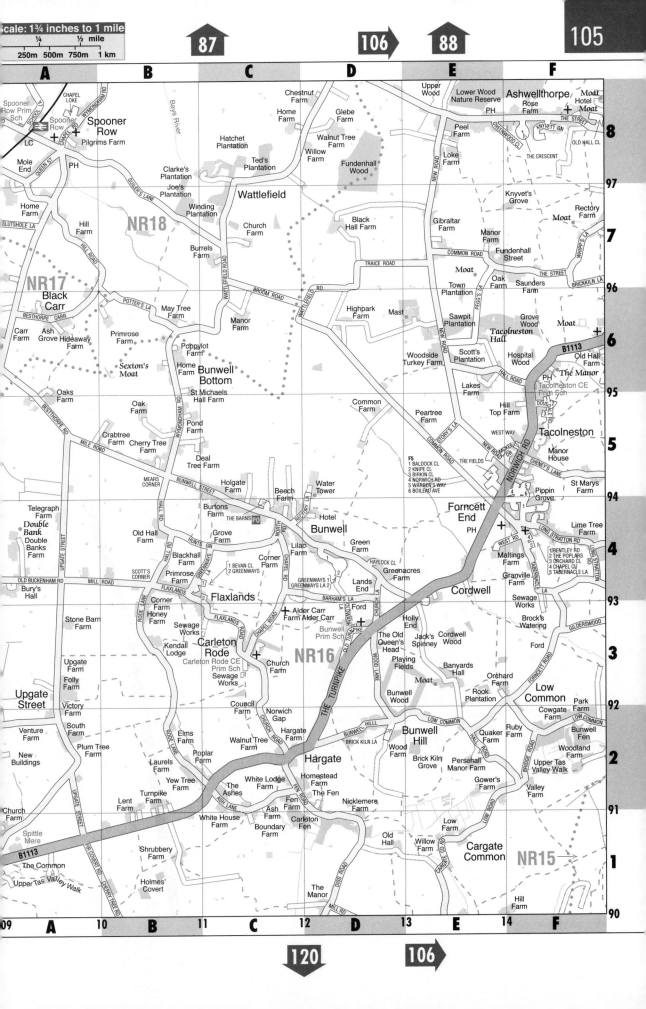

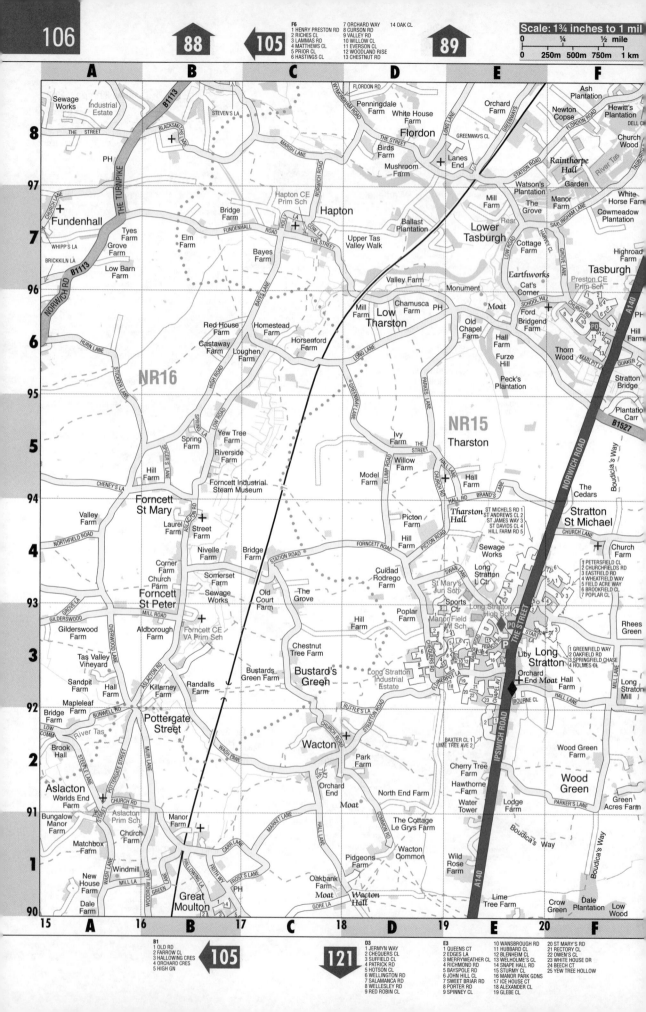

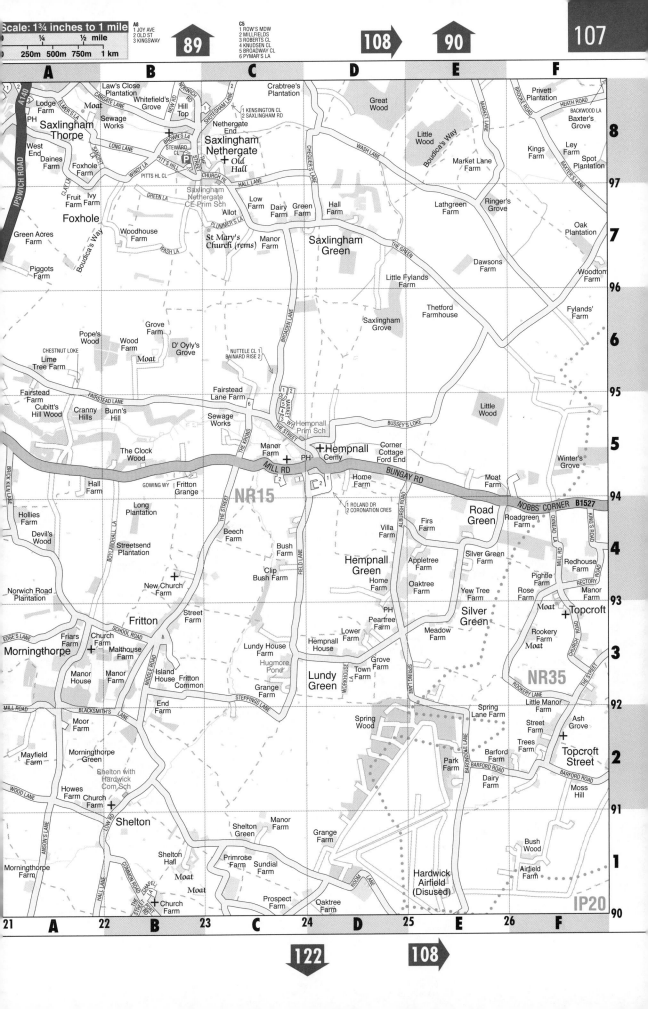

Scale: 1¾ inches to 1 mile

¼   ½   mile
250m 500m 750m 1 km

A8
1 JOY AVE
2 OLD ST
3 KINGSWAY

89

C5
1 ROW'S MDW
2 MILLFIELDS
3 ROBERTS CL
4 KNUDSEN CL
5 BROADWAY CL
6 PYMAR'S LA

108

90

107

A   B   C   D   E   F

Law's Close Plantation
Whitefield's Grove
Hill Top
Crabtree's Plantation
Great Wood

Lodge Farm
PH
Moat
Sewage Works
Nethergate End
1 KENSINGTON CL
2 SAXLINGHAM RD

Little Wood
Boudica's Way
Baxter's Grove
Privett Plantation
HEATH ROAD
BACKWOOD LA

Saxlingham Thorpe
Saxlingham Nethergate
Old Hall

Kings Farm
Ley Farm
Spot Plantation

West End
Daines Farm
Foxhole Farm
Brown's La
Steward Cl
Pitt's Hill
Saxlingham Nethergate CE Prim Sch
Low Farm
Dairy Farm
Green Farm
Hall Farm

Market Lane Farm
Lathgreen Farm
Ringer's Grove

97

Fruit Farm
Ivy Farm
Foxhole
Woodhouse Farm
St Mary's Church (rems)
Manor Farm
Saxlingham Green
THE GREEN

Oak Plantation

Dawsons Farm
Woodton Farm

7

Green Acres Farm
WASH LA
Little Fylands Farm

96

Piggots Farm
Pope's Wood
Wood Farm
Grove Farm
D' Oyly's Grove
Saxlingham Grove
Thetford Farmhouse

Fylands' Farm

6

Lime Tree Farm
Moat
NUTTELE CL 1
BAINARD RISE 2

95

Fairstead Farm
Cubitt's Hill Wood
Cranny Hills
Bunn's Hill
Fairstead Lane Farm
Sewage Works
Hempnall Prim Sch
BUSSEY'S LOKE
Little Wood

The Clock Wood
Manor Farm
PH
Hempnall
Cemy
Corner Cottage Ford End
Winter's Grove

5

Hall Farm
GOWING WY
Fritton Grange
MILL RD
NR15
BUNGAY RD
Moat Farm

94

Hollies Farm
Devil's Wood
Long Plantation
Streetsend Plantation
Beech Farm
Bush Farm
Home Farm
1 ROLAND DR
2 CORONATION CRES
Villa Farm
Firs Farm
Road Green
Roadgreen Farm
NOBBS' CORNER B1527

Silver Green Farm
Pightle Farm
Redhouse Farm

4

New Church Farm
Clip Bush Farm
Hempnall Green
Appletree Farm
Oaktree Farm
Home Farm
Yew Tree Farm
Rose Farm
Moat
Manor Farm

93

Norwich Road Plantation
Street Farm
PH
Peartree Farm
Meadow Farm
Silver Green
Topcroft

Morningthorpe
Friars Farm
Church Farm
Malthouse Farm
Fritton
Lower Farm
Hempnall House
Grove Farm
Rookery Farm Moat

3

Manor House
Manor Farm
Island House
Fritton Common
Lundy House Farm
Hugmore Pond
Lundy Green
Town Farm
Spring Lane Farm
Little Manor Farm
NR35

End Farm
STEPPINGS LANE
Grange Farm
92

MILL ROAD
BLACKSMITH'S
Moor Farm
Spring Wood
Spring Lane Farm
Street Farm
Trees Farm
Ash Grove

Mayfield Farm
Morningthorpe Green
Barford Farm
Topcroft Street

2

Howes Farm
Church Farm
Shelton with Hardwick Com Sch
Park Farm
Barford Road
Dairy Farm
BARFORD ROAD
Moss Hill

Shelton
Manor Farm
Grange Farm
91

Shelton Green
Shelton Hall
Bush Wood

Morningthorpe Farm
Moat
Primrose Farm
Sundial Farm
Hardwick Airfield (Disused)
Airfield Farm

1

Moat
Church Farm
Prospect Farm
Oaktree Farm
IP20
90

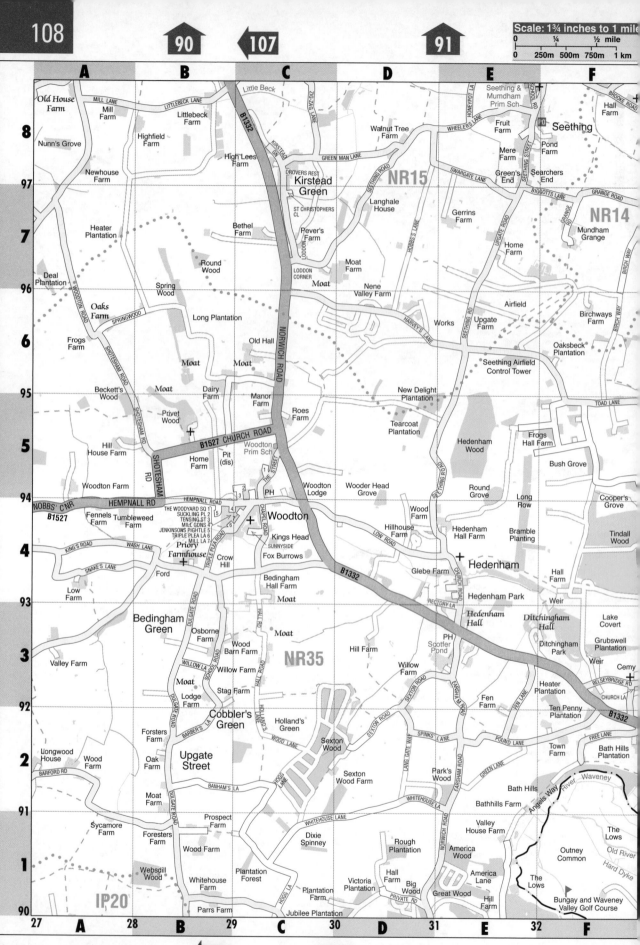

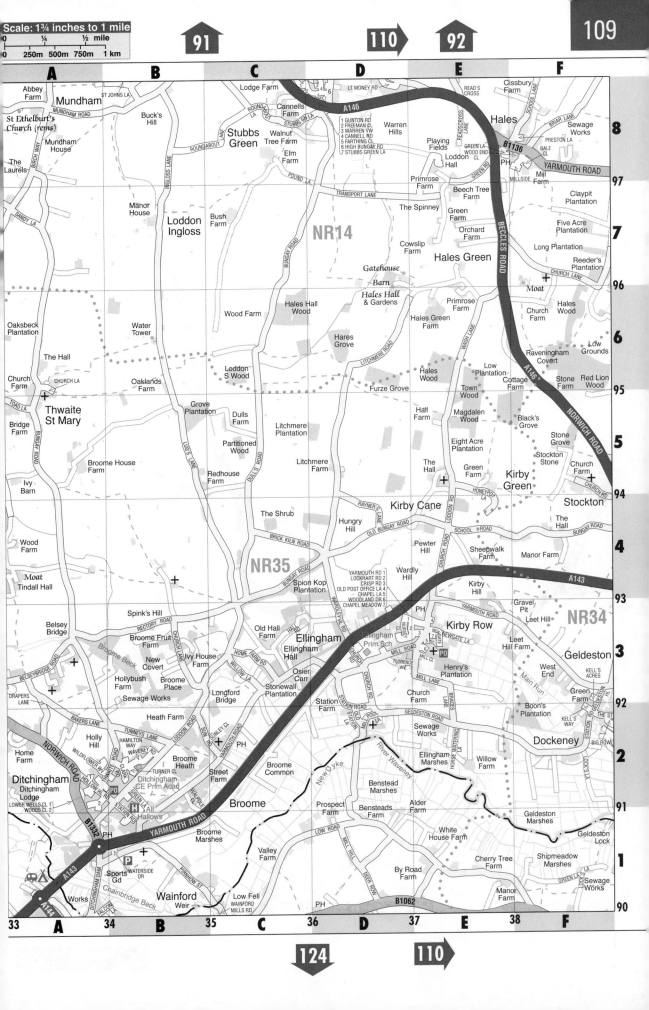

Scale: 1¾ inches to 1 mile

0   ¼   ½ mile
0   250m   500m   750m   1 km

A   B   C   D   E   F

8

BOUNDARY RD
SANDY LANE
North Farm
Redhouse Farm
COLLEGE RD
Hall Farm
The Carr
Craft Plantation
NR14
Hill Farm
Haddiscoe
White House Farm
CRAB APPLE LA
CHURCH ROAD
THORPE ROAD
GRAVEL PIT LANE
LOW ROAD
North Belt
97
B1136   YARMOUTH ROAD   LODDON ROAD   B1136
Manor Farm
A143
PH

Sycamore Farm
MILL ROAD
Crossway Farm
Downings Farm
Hall Farm
CHURCH LA
The Chestnuts
Hill Top
NEW ROAD
WIGGS ROAD
Raveningham
THE SPINNEY
Castell Wood
BECCLES ROAD
RECTORY ROAD
Landspring Beck
7
Hall Farm
THURLTON ROAD
Pockthorpe
Lock Plantation
Orchard Farm
Three Cocked Hat
Glebeland Com Prim Sch
Long Row Wood
Grange Farm
Raveningham Moat Gardens
STONY LA   BILBYS
PEDDARS LA
GREEN LANE
LODDON ROAD
Clinks Farm
NEW ROAD
Eaton Farm
FIELDS ROAD
Middle Row Wood
HADDISCOE ROAD
96
Reservoir
Brundish Wood
Tiled House Farm
Church Farm
Pond Farm
Toft Monks House
Wood Farm
STATION ROAD
Dam Plantation
The Raveningham Ctr
Priory Farm
Maypole Green
PUMP LA
Blyth Wood
6
Brundish
BILLS GN RD
Moat
YARMOUTH ROAD
Church Farm
The Grove
Brundish Farm
Moat
Toft Monks
Moat
Great Wood
Thumpers End
Waterheath Farm
BURROWS GN
Three Corner Plantation
BRUNDIS HD
Daw's Wood
Water Tower
FULLER'S CL
BURNTHOUSE
MARDLE RD
PH
Woodstock Farm
Waterheath
95
Mill Mount
Stockton Old Hall
Grove Farm
College Farm
Bull's Green
Bulls Green Farm
ST BENEDICTS CL
Hill House Farm
BULLS GREEN LANE
POST OFFICE RD
Virginia Farm
Moat
5
Calfpightle Clump
High Grove
Lodge Farm
Old Grove
Windle Hills
The Elms
ELMS LA
WATERHEATH RD
Grove Farm
George's Wood
Long Plantation
Lodge Wood
Black's Grove
Boundary Farm
Waterloo
BECCLES RD
4
A146
NORWICH ROAD
A143
Forge End
Upland Farm
Primrose Grove
Ivy House Farm
NR34
Round Wood
Gillingham Wood
Cottages Woods
Thrower's Grove
Freelands Plantation
HOLLOW WAY HILL
Stanley Hills
THE STREET
CRABTREE LA
Aldeby
3
Hobb's Hill Wood
Winston Game Farm
Rose Farm
Town Wood
RECTORY RD
DOGS LA
Dogs Lane Plantation
Boathouse Hill
Stanley Carrs
Round Hill
Remains of Priory
Moat
A143
William's Wood
Beech Wood
Hall
Hill Farm
Alder Carrs
Angles Way
Winston Hall Farm
2
Kell's Heath
Brick Kiln Plantation
War Memorial Plantation
Church Plantation
1 HEMMANT WAY
2 TODHUNTER AVE
3 ASHFORD CL
4 KENYON ROW
5 FORGE GR
Our Lady's Grove
River Waveney
Gillingham Marshes
Beccles Marshes
Worlingham Wall
STOCKTON RD
YARMOUTH ROAD
HEATH ROAD
GILLINGHAM RD
GELDESTON RD
THE STREET
Dunburgh Farm
Bigod's Hill
Gillingham St Michaels CE Prim Acad
Little Carr
Beccles New Bridge
92
Geldeston
Dunburgh Wood
Dunburgh Hill
KING'S DAM
PH
Motel
A146   NORWICH ROAD
BECCLES
LC
East Fen Carr
Geldeston Dyke
Manor House Farm
Hillside Farm
Gillingham
River VW
NEW RD
Beccles New Bridge
LC
Lotman's Carr
LC
Wild Carr
Marsh Farm
1
PH
Reservoir
GILLINGHAM DAM
BECCLESGATE
Beccles Old Bridge
Ravensmere Inf Sch
Hotel
PLOUGHMOOR
NORTHGATE
FEN LA
GEORGE WESTWOOD WY
Boney's Island
CH
Football Gd Beccles
Beccles Common
Wolsey's Woods
Firhill Covert
Sewage Works
Moat
Barsham Marshes
Printing Mus
DENMARK
CAXTON RD
STATION RD
Football Gd
Woodview Farm
Westhill Covert
Horseshoe Covert
Worlingham Hall
A146
90
Barsham Hall (rems)
Beccles Mus
BALLYGATE
PO
Lib
COMMON LA
Beccles Carr
Lowestoft A146
Suffolk STREET ATLAS
A145 Saxmundham (A12)

39   A   40   B   41   C   42   D   43   E   44   F

D1
1 CLOWES CT
2 COMMON LA NTH
3 DOBSON WAY
4 OLD MILL TERRACE
5 ST BENEDICT'S RD
6 ROOK'S LA
7 MIDMEADOW
8 GOOSE GREEN WEST
9 KINGSTON DR
10 MAPLE WAY

For full street detail of Beccles see Philip's STREET ATLAS of Suffolk

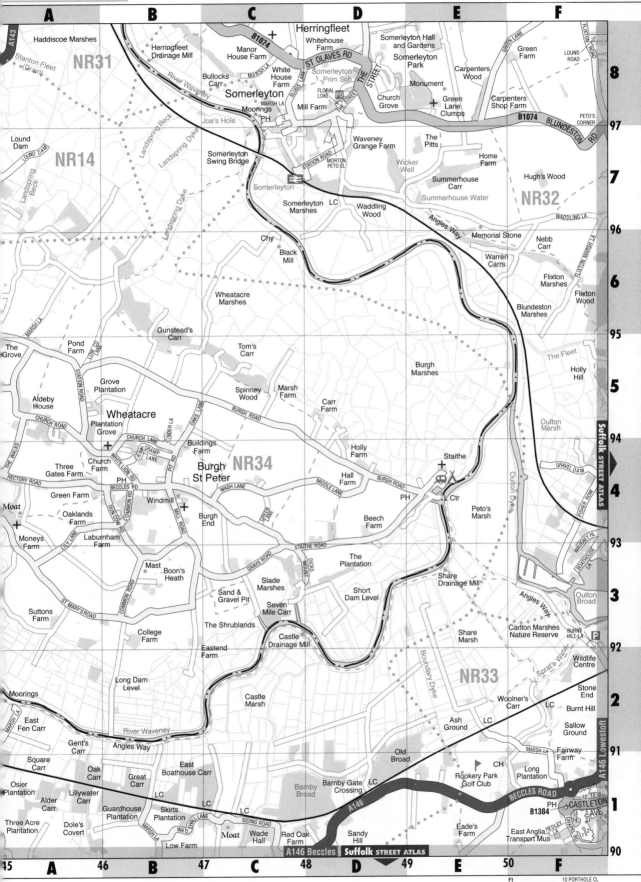

A B C D E F

8 7 97 7 96 6 95 5 94 4 93 92 3 2 91 1 90

45 A 46 B 47 C 48 D 49 E 50 F

Haddiscoe Marshes
Stanton Fleet (Drain)
NR31
Lound Dam
NR14
Landspring Beck
Landspring Dyke
Herringfleet Drainage Mill
River Waveney
Bullocks Carr
White House Farm
Manor House Farm
B1074
Herringfleet
Whitehouse Farm
Somerleyton Hall and Gardens
Somerleyton Park
ST OLAVES RD
Somerleyton Prim Sch.
Carpenters Wood
Green Farm
Green Lane
LOUND ROAD
FLIXTON ROAD
Somerleyton
Moorings
PH
MARSH LA
SLUGS LANE
White House
Mill Farm
FLORAL LOKE
PO
THE STREET
Church Grove
Monument
Green Lane Clumps
Carpenters Shop Farm
B1074 BLUNDESTON RD
PETO'S CORNER
Joe's Hole
Somerleyton Swing Bridge
STATION ROAD
MORTON PETO CL
Waveney Grange Farm
The Pitts
Wicker Well
Home Farm
Hugh's Wood
NR32
Somerleyton
Somerleyton Marshes
LC
Waddling Wood
Summerhouse Carr
Summerhouse Water
WADDLING LA
Memorial Stone
Nebb Carr
FLIXTON MARSH LA
Chy
Black Mill
Angles Way
Warren Carrs
Flixton Marshes
Flixton Wood
Wheatacre Marshes
Gunstead's Carr
Tom's Carr
Burgh Marshes
Blundeston Marshes
The Grove
Pond Farm
LOVEY CO LANE
Grove Plantation
Spinney Wood
Marsh Farm
Carr Farm
The Fleet
Holly Hill
Aldeby House
STATION ROAD
Wheatacre
Plantation Grove
CHURCH LANE
OAKS LANE
CINDER LA
BURGH ROAD
Buildings Farm
Holly Farm
Oulton Marsh
Suffolk STREET ATLAS
GRAVEL DAM
THE WALKS
CHURCH ROAD
Three Gates Farm
Church Farm
WHITE LION RD
CRAMP LANE
PIT RD
Burgh St Peter
NR34
Hall Farm
Staithe
PH
L Ctr
Peto's Marsh
FISHER ROW
RECTORY ROAD
BECCLES RD
Green Farm
Windmill
Burgh End
WASH LANE
MIDDLE LANE
BURGH ROAD
Oulton Dyke
WAVENEY HL
BOATHOUSE LA
Moat
Oaklands Farm
Moneys Farm
DITCHON RD
COMMON RD
Laburnham Farm
Mast
Boon's Heath
GRAYS ROAD
GREEN LANE
STAITHE ROAD
DICK'S MOUNT
Beech Farm
The Plantation
Share Drainage Mill
Angles Way
Oulton Broad
ST MARY'S ROAD
COMMON ROAD
Sand & Gravel Pit
Slade Marshes
Seven Mile Carr
Short Dam Level
Share Marsh
Carlton Marshes Nature Reserve
BURNT HILL LA
P
Suttons Farm
College Farm
The Shrublands
Eastend Farm
Castle Drainage Mill
Boundary Dyke
NR33
Wildlife Centre
Long Dam Level
Castle Marsh
Woolner's Carr
LC
Stone End
Burnt Hill
Moorings
MARSH LA
East Fen Carr
River Waveney
Angles Way
Gent's Carr
East Boathouse Carr
Ash Ground
LC
Sprat's Water
A146 Lowestoft
Sallow Ground
Fairway Farm
MARSH LA
Square Carr
Oak Carr
Great Carr
LC
Old Broad
CH
Rookery Park Golf Club
Long Plantation
BECCLES ROAD
PH
B1384
CASTLETON
Osier Plantation
Alder Carr
Lillywater Carr
Guardhouse Plantation
Skirts Plantation
LC
Barnby Broad
Barnby Gate Crossing
LC
HEDLEY LA
CHAPEL RD
Three Acre Plantation
Dole's Covert
MARSH LA
WAD D
Moat
Wade Hall
Red Oak Farm
SIDING ROAD
A146
Sandy Hill
Eade's Farm
East Anglia Transport Mus
A146 Beccles Suffolk STREET ATLAS
Low Farm
FLXLL LANE
CHY

F1
1 THORNYCROFT GDNS
2 BURLINGHAM DR
3 MILNES WAY
4 WILLOWBROOK CL
5 MONARCH WAY
6 AVELING WAY
7 ANCHOR WAY
8 GALLEY CL
9 CAPSTAN WAY
10 PORTHOLE CL
11 CABIN CL
12 KEEL CL
13 MAST CL
14 APPLEWOOD CL

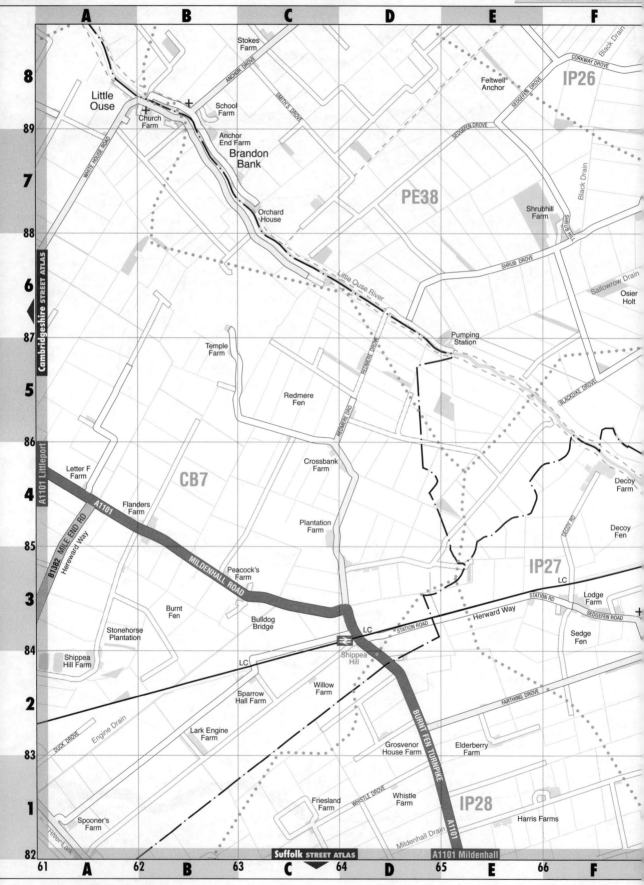

Scale: 1¾ inches to 1 mile

0   ¼   ½ mile
0 250m 500m 750m 1 km

A **B** **C** **D** **E** **F**

Cambridgeshire STREET ATLAS

A1101 Littleport

Little Ouse

Church Farm

Stokes Farm

School Farm

Anchor End Farm

Brandon Bank

ANCHOR DROVE

SMITH'S DROVE

Feltwell Anchor

CORKWAY DROVE

Black Drain

IP26

SEDGEFEN DROVE

PE38

Shrubhill Farm

SHRUB DRIVE

Orchard House

Little Ouse River

Black Drain

Sallowrow Drain

Osier Holt

Temple Farm

REDMERE DROVE

Pumping Station

BLACKDIKE DROVE

Redmere Fen

REDMERE DROVE

Crossbank Farm

CB7

Letter F Farm

Flanders Farm

Decoy Farm

Decoy Fen

WHITE HOUSE ROAD

Plantation Farm

DECOY RD

B1382 MILE END RD

Hereward Way

A1101

MILDENHALL ROAD

Peacock's Farm

Burnt Fen

Bulldog Bridge

LC

STATION RD

Herward Way

IP27

LC

Lodge Farm

SEDGEFEN ROAD

Sedge Fen

Stonehorse Plantation

Shippea Hill Farm

LC

Shippea Hill

STATION ROAD

Sparrow Hall Farm

Willow Farm

FARTHING DROVE

DUCK DROVE

Engine Drain

Lark Engine Farm

Grosvenor House Farm

BURNT FEN TURNPIKE

Elderberry Farm

Spooner's Farm

River Lark

Friesland Farm

WHISTLE DROVE

Whistle Farm

IP28

Harris Farms

Mildenhall Drain

A1101

A1101 Mildenhall

Suffolk STREET ATLAS

A 61 **B** 62 **C** 63 64 **D** 65 **E** 66 **F**

8 89 7 88 6 87 5 86 4 85 3 84 2 83 1 82

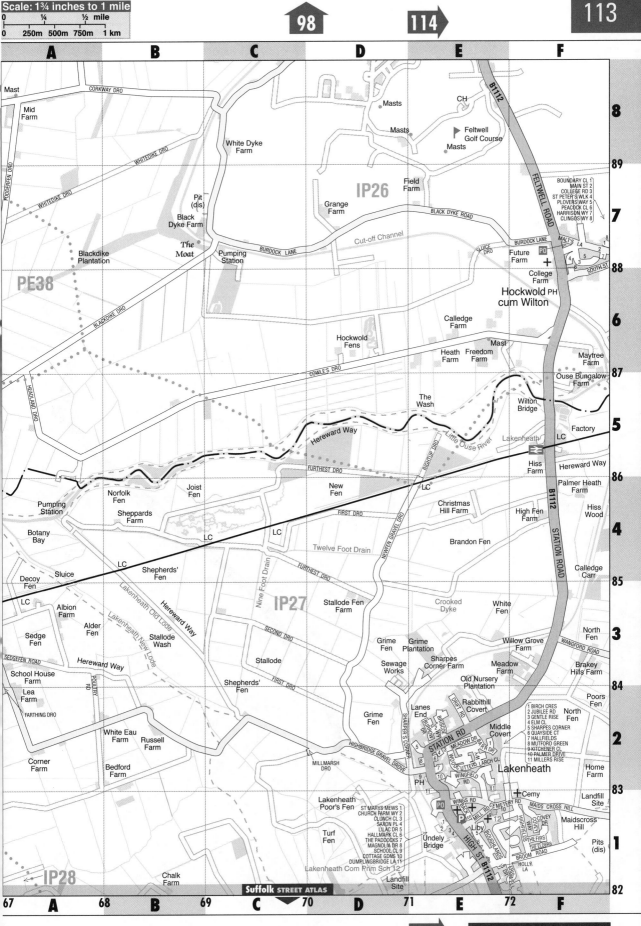

Scale: 1¾ inches to 1 mile
0 ¼ ½ mile
0 250m 500m 750m 1 km

98
114

A B C D E F

8
89
7
88
6
87
5
86
4
85
3
84
2
83
1
82

CORKWAY DRO

Mast
Mid Farm

WHITEDIKE DRO

White Dyke Farm

PODDEREN DRO

WHITEDIKE DRO

Pit (dis)
Black Dyke Farm
The Moat

Blackdike Plantation

PE38

BLACKDIKE DRO

Pumping Station

BURDOCK LANE

IP26

Grange Farm

Field Farm

Masts
Masts

Masts

CH
Feltwell Golf Course

Masts

B1112

FELTWELL ROAD

BOUNDARY CL 1
MAIN ST 2
COLLEGE RD 3
ST PETER'S WLK 4
PLOVERS WAY 5
PEACOCK CL 6
HARRISON WY 7
CLINGOS WY 8

Black Dyke Road

Cut-off Channel

SLUICE DRO

MALT'S LA

BURDOCK LANE
Future Farm
PO
College Farm
Hockwold cum Wilton PH

SOUTH ST

HEADLAND DRO

Hockwold Fens

Calledge Farm

COWLE'S DRO

Heath Farm
Freedom Farm
Mast

Maytree Farm

Ouse Bungalow Farm

The Wash
Hereward Way

Little Ouse River
Wilton Bridge

Lakenheath
LC
Factory

Hiss Farm
Hereward Way

Palmer Heath Farm

FURTHEST DRO

Pumping Station

Norfolk Fen

Sheppards Farm

Joist Fen

New Fen

RIGHTUP DRO

LC

Hiss Wood

Christmas Hill Farm

High Fen Farm

B1112

STATION ROAD

LC
LC

FIRST DRO

Twelve Foot Drain

NEWTEN GRAVEL DRO

Brandon Fen

Botany Bay

Decoy Fen
Sluice
LC

Albion Farm
Alder Fen

LC

Shepherds' Fen

FURTHEST DRO

Crooked Dyke

White Fen

Calledge Carr

North Fen

WANGFORD ROAD

Hereward Way

LAKENHEATH OLD LODE

IP27

Nine Foot Drain

Stallode Fen Farm

Willow Grove Farm

Meadow Farm

Brakey Hills Farm

SEDGEFEN ROAD

School House Farm
Lea Farm

FARTHING DRO

Sedge Fen

LAKENHEATH NEW LODE

Hereward Way
Stallode Wash

POULTRY RD

SECOND DRO

Stallode

Shepherds' Fen

FIRST DRO

Grime Fen

Grime Plantation

Sharpes Corner Farm

Old Nursery Plantation

Sewage Works

1 BIRCH CRES
2 JUBILEE RD
3 GENTLE RISE
4 ELM CL
5 SHARPES CORNER
6 QUAYSIDE CT
7 HALLFIELDS
8 MUTFORD GREEN
9 KITCHENER CL
10 PALMER DRIVE
11 MILLERS RISE

North Fen

Poors Fen

White Eau Farm
Russell Farm

Corner Farm
Bedford Farm

MILLMARSH DRO

HIGHBRIDGE GRAVEL DROVE

Grime Fen

SHARPER'S CORNER

STATION RD

DRIFT RD

Lanes End
Rabbithill Covert

BRIDGOR RD
BARR RD

MEADOW DR
CUTTERS
LARCH CL

Middle Covert

Lakenheath

Home Farm

Landfill Site

Lakenheath Poor's Fen

Turf Fen

ST MARYS MEWS 1
CHURCH FARM WY 2
CLUNCH CL 3
SAXON PL 4
LILAC DR 5
HALLMARK CL 6
THE PADDOCKS 7
MAGNOLIA DR 8
SCHOOL CL 9
COTTAGE GDNS 10
DUMPLINGBRIDGE LA 11
Lakenheath Com Prim Sch 12

Undely Bridge

PH

WINGFIELD RD

PO
P

WINGS RD

MILL RD

CEMETERY RD

Cemy

HIGHFIELD

COVEY CL
COVEY DR

Maidscross Hill

MAIDS CROSS HILL

Libr
The Firs
The Elders

ROUGHLANDS

BROOM ROAD

HOLLY LA

FENFIELD

HIGH ST B1112

Pits (dis)

IP28

Chalk Farm

Suffolk STREET ATLAS

Landfill Site

67 A 68 B 69 C 70 D 71 E 72 F

114

For full street detail of Lakenheath see
Philip's STREET ATLAS of Suffolk

113
99

E8
1 LAMBERT CL
2 OLIVER CT
3 FAIRFAX CT
4 MONTAGU DR
5 VALE CT
6 WENTWORTH CL

Scale: 1¾ inches to 1 mile

113

For full street detail of the highlighted area see page 175

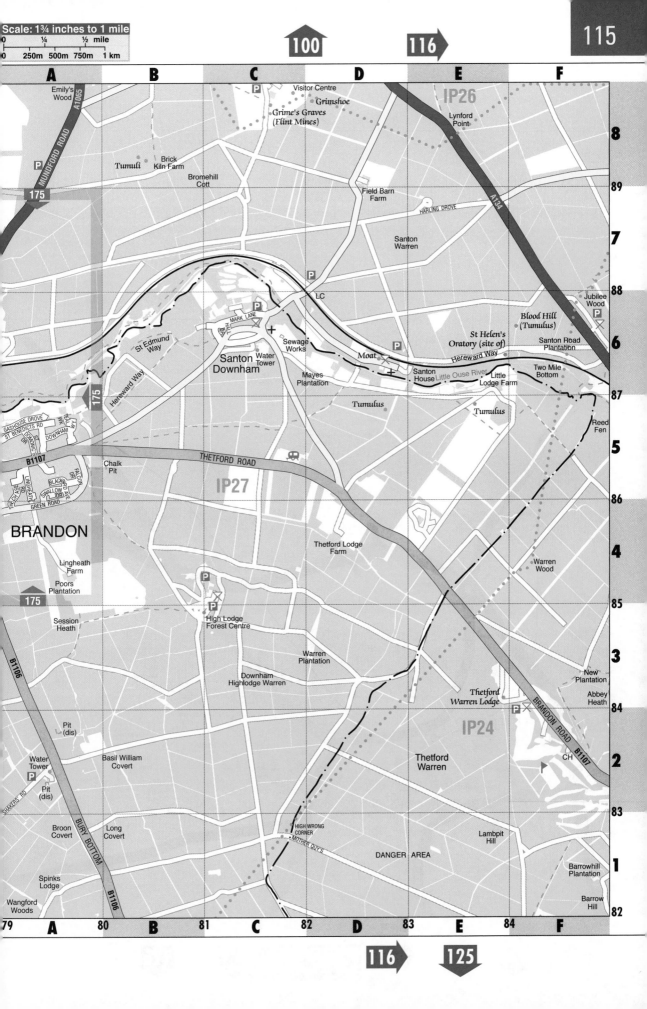

Scale: 1¾ inches to 1 mile

0   ¼   ½ mile
0 250m 500m 750m 1 km

100

116

115

A   B   C   D   E   F

Emily's
Wood

IP26

Grimshoe

Grime's Graves
(Flint Mines)

Visitor Centre

Lynford
Point

8

Tumuli

Brick
Kiln Farm

Bromehill
Cott

Field Barn
Farm

HARLING DROVE

89

Santon
Warren

7

MUNDFORD ROAD

A1065

175

A134

88

LC

Jubilee
Wood

St Edmund
Way

Water
Tower

+

Moat

Sewage
Works

P

Santon
House

St Helen's
Oratory (site of)

Hereward Way

Blood Hill
(Tumulus)

Santon Road
Plantation

6

Santon
Downham

HALL LANE
MARK LANE

Hereward Way

175

Mayes
Plantation

Little Ouse River

Little
Lodge Farm

Two Mile
Bottom

87

Gashouse Drove
St Benedicts Rd

Tumulus

Tumulus

Reed
Fen

5

TEAL WK

DOWNHAM

St Edmonds Dr

B1107

Chalk
Pit

THETFORD ROAD

IP27

86

BLACKBIRD RD

FALCON RD

SWALLOW DR

GREEN ROAD

BRANDON

Thetford Lodge
Farm

Warren
Wood

4

Lingheath
Farm

Poors
Plantation

175

P

P

High Lodge
Forest Centre

85

Session
Heath

Warren
Plantation

New
Plantation

3

B1106

Downham
Highlodge Warren

Thetford
Warren Lodge

P

IP24

Abbey
Heath

84

Pit
(dis)

Basil William
Covert

Thetford
Warren

BRANDON ROAD

B1107

CH

2

Water
Tower

P

Pit
(dis)

83

SHAKERS' RD

BURY BOTTOM

B1106

Broon
Covert

Long
Covert

High Wrong
Corner

Mother Quy's

DANGER AREA

Lambpit
Hill

Barrowhill
Plantation

1

Spinks
Lodge

Wangford
Woods

Barrow
Hill

82

79   A   80   B   81   C   82   D   83   E   84   F

116

115

101

Scale: 1¾ inches to 1 mile
0   ¼   ½   mile
0 250m 500m 750m 1 km

IP27

Home
Mere

New
Bldgs

Thorpe
Great Heath

Park
Heath

P

Devil's
Punchbowl

Little Lang
Plantation

Mickle Hill
(Tumulus)

Fowlmere
Wood

Langmere
Plantation

Hereward Way

Langmere

Fenmere

Croxton
Park

Croxton
Heath

Beauchamp
Plantation

Ringmere
Plantation

Ringmere

Cottage
Wood

Pit
(dis)

IP24

Jubilee
Wood

P

Sugarhill
Covert

Pit
(dis)

A1075

Chapel
Farm

The Street

Kilverstone
Heath

NR16

Chy LC

EARL WARREN

Croxton

PO

Pit
(dis)

LC

Works

Hill
Farm

Hadler's
Hole

Reed
Fen

1
2 3
4
5

A134

Warren
Wood

Broom Covert

1 CHURCH AVE
2 LAWSON RD
3 MELVILLE RD
4 HAREFIELD RD
5 DOUGLAS CL

Pit
(dis)

Chestnut
Plantation

Larch
Plantation

Dreadnought

LC
Ladyship
Wood

Hockham
Belt

A11

Milestone
Plantation

Chisley
Vale

Breck
Plantation

Box
Covert

Pit
(dis)

Landfill
Site

LC

176

A11

Little Ouse River
St Edmund Way

176

A1066

Lodge
Farm

Blakeney
Farm

Jane's
Wood

A1075

Waterloo
Wood

New
Plantation

WYATT WY

LODGE WY

ST HELENS WY

ANNIE BARTHOLOMEW

CROXTON ROAD

The Thetford
Academy
(North Campus)

1 ALDER COVERT
2 SYCAMORE COVERT
3 BIRCH COVERT
4 HAZEL COVERT
5 COMFREY WAY
6 CHERVIL WK
7 PETER DR
8 PENNYCRESS DR
9 LAWRENCE RD
10 VALERIAN RISE

Field Barn
Farm

Abbey Heath
Weir

Abbey
Heath

Mast

FISON WY

HOWLETT WY

BRUNEL WY

Ind
Est

Rec Gd

WOODLANDS DR

THE GLADE

FAIRFIELD

TENNYSON WY

SHELLEY WY

HARWOOD

War
Memorial

Lodge
Farm

Kilverstone
Hall

Burntyard
Carr

A2
1 HUDSON CL
2 STUART DR

THETFORD

Inf
Sch

Acad

CHARLOCK RD

9
8
7
6
5 10
4
3
2
1

River Thet

Snarehill
Hall

Church
(rems)

B1107
BRANDON
RD

CANTERBURY WAY

MONKSGATE

STATION RD

Thetford
Acad

VICARAGE
RD

NORWICH RD

CHURCH RD

MALLOW RD

Square
Covert

CANTERBURY RD

P

Sch

Mus

NORWICH RD

BRIDGE

CASTLE ST

BODGER RD

CORIANDER DR

CARAWAY RD

FOXGLOVE RD

HURTH WY

176

Snarehill
Wood

Thetford
Priory(rems)

Gram
Sch

London RD

Mus
PO
Mus

GROVE LA

Weir

A1066

Limekiln
Plantation

MCKENZIE RD
ST JOHN'S WY

Red
Castle

P

Church
Sch

Liby

RAMPART WAY

Church

CASTLE LA

A1088

BRANDON RD

PO

D WAY

Cemy

Nuns'
Bridges

The
Nunnery
(rems)

A1

Ind
Est

KING ST

BURRELL WAY

LONDON ROAD

QUEENSWAY

FULMERSTON RD

NUNS BRIDGES RD

MILL LA

A134 BURY RD

IP24

The
Slough

Oak
Wood

Superstore

Acad

85   A   86   B   87   C   88   D   89   E   90   F

A1
1 MONTPELIER DR
2 NEW ENGLAND WAY
3 PORTLAND PL
4 MAINE ST
5 NEW HAMPSHIRE WAY
6 BOSTON END

176   125   115

For full street detail of the
highlighted area see page 176

126

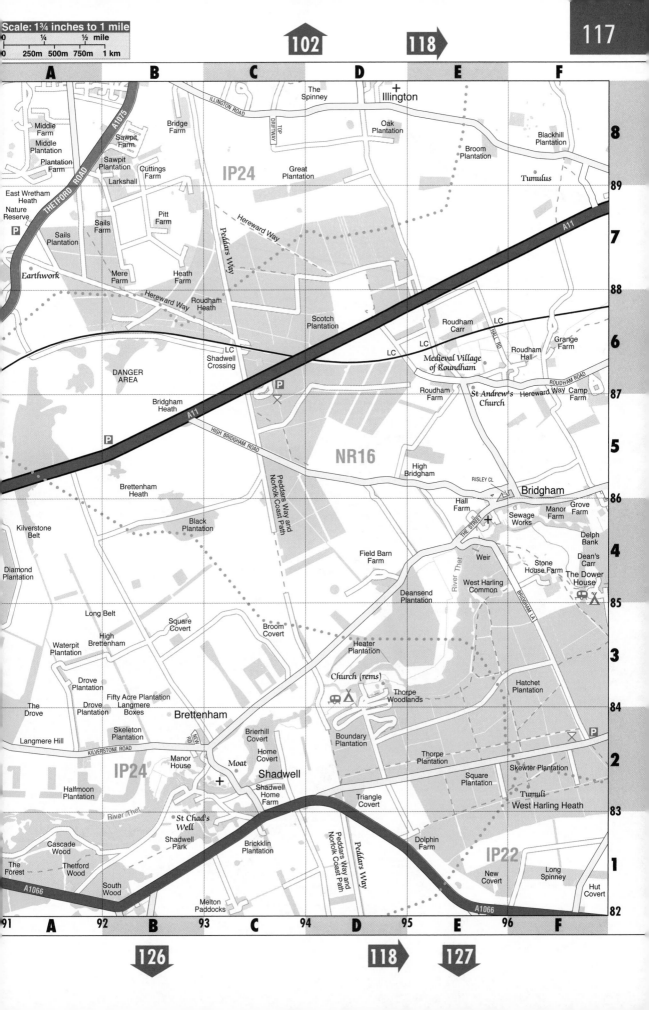

Scale: 1¾ inches to 1 mile

0   250m   500m   750m   1 km

¼   ½ mile

102

118

A   B   C   D   E   F

Middle Farm
Middle Plantation
Plantation Farm

Sawpit Farm
Sawpit Plantation
Larkshall
Cuttings Farm

Bridge Farm

ILLINGTON ROAD

TOP DRIFTWAY

The Spinney

Oak Plantation

Illington

Broom Plantation

Blackhill Plantation

IP24

Great Plantation

Tumulus

8

89

East Wretham Heath Nature Reserve

THETFORD ROAD

A1075

Sails Plantation

Sails Farm

Pitt Farm

Hereward Way

Peddars Way

7

Earthwork

Mere Farm

Heath Farm

Hereward Way

Roudham Heath

Scotch Plantation

A11

Roudham Carr

HALL RD

LC

Roudham Hall

Grange Farm

88

6

DANGER AREA

LC
Shadwell Crossing

LC

LC

Medieval Village of Roundham

ROUDHAM ROAD

Hereward Way
Roudham Farm

Camp Farm

87

Bridgham Heath

A11

P

HIGH BRIDGHAM ROAD

Roudham Farm

St Andrew's Church

High Bridgham

NR16

RISLEY CL

Bridgham

5

Kilverstone Belt

Brettenham Heath

Peddars Way and Norfolk Coast Path

Black Plantation

Field Barn Farm

Hall Farm

THE STREET

Sewage Works

Manor Farm

Grove Farm

86

Diamond Plantation

Deansend Plantation

River Thet

Weir

West Harling Common

Stone House Farm

BRIDGHAM LA

Delph Bank

Dean's Carr
The Dower House

4

Long Belt

Square Covert

Broom Covert

Heater Plantation

85

Waterpit Plantation

High Brettenham

Church (rems)

Thorpe Woodlands

Hatchet Plantation

P

3

Drove Plantation

Fifty Acre Plantation
Langmere Boxes

Drove Plantation

Brettenham

84

The Drove

Langmere Hill

Skeleton Plantation

NEW RD

KILVERSTONE ROAD

Brierhill Covert

Home Covert

Boundary Plantation

Thorpe Plantation

Square Plantation

Skewter Plantation

2

IP24

Manor House

Moat

Shadwell

Shadwell Home Farm

Triangle Covert

Tumuli
West Harling Heath

83

Halfmoon Plantation

River Thet

St Chad's Well

Shadwell Park

Brickklin Plantation

Peddars Way and Norfolk Coast Path

Peddars Way

Dolphin Farm

IP22

New Covert

Long Spinney

1

Cascade Wood

The Forest

Thetford Wood

A1066

South Wood

Melton Paddocks

A1066

Hut Covert

82

91   A   92   B   93   C   94   D   95   E   96   F

126

118

127

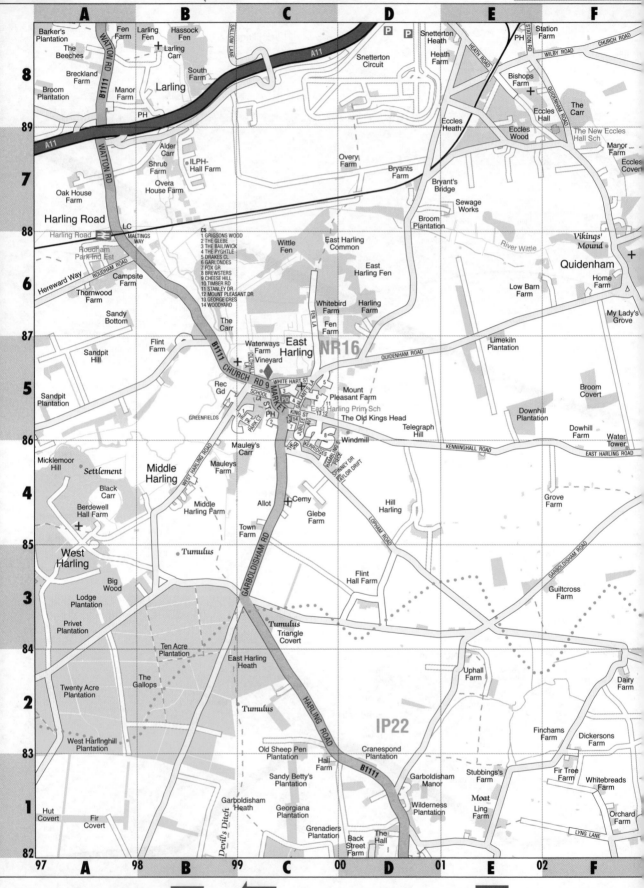

← 117   ↑ 103

Scale: 1¾ inches to 1 mile
0   ¼   ½ mile
0   250m 500m 750m 1 km

8

Barker's Plantation
The Beeches
Breckland Farm
Broom Plantation
Fen Farm
Larling Fen
Hassock Fen
Larling Carr
South Farm
Larling
Manor Farm
PH
WATTON RD
B1111
SALLOW LANE
A11
Snetterton Heath
Heath Farm
Snetterton Circuit
HEATH ROAD
STATION RD
PH
Station Farm
WILBY ROAD
CHURCH ROAD
Bishops Farm
Eccles Hall
The Carr
The New Eccles Hall Sch
QUIDENHAM ROAD

89

Oak House Farm
Alder Carr
Shrub Farm
Overa House Farm
ILPH-Hall Farm
WATTON RD
A11
Overy Farm
Bryants Farm
Bryant's Bridge
Eccles Heath
Eccles Wood
Manor Farm
Eccles Covert

7

88

Harling Road
Harling Road
LC
MALTINGS WAY
Roudham Park Ind Est
Hereward Way
ROUDHAM ROAD
Campsite Farm
Thornwood Farm
Sandy Bottom
Sewage Works
Broom Plantation
River Wittle
Vikings' Mound
Quidenham

C5
1 GRIGSONS WOOD
2 THE GLEBE
3 THE BAILIWICK
4 THE PYGHTLE
5 DRAKES CL
6 GARLONDES
7 FOX GR
8 BREWSTERS
9 CHEESE HILL
10 TIMBER RD
11 STANLEY DR
12 MOUNT PLEASANT DR
13 GEORGE GRES
14 WOODYARD

Wittle Fen
East Harling Common
East Harling Fen
Whitebird Farm
FEN LA
Fen Farm
Harling Farm
Low Barn Farm
Home Farm
My Lady's Grove

6

87

Sandpit Hill
Flint Farm
The Carr
Waterways Farm Vineyard
B1111
CHURCH RD 9
East Harling
NR16
QUIDENHAM ROAD
Limekiln Plantation
Broom Covert

5

Sandpit Plantation
Rec Gd
GREENFIELDS
SCHOOL LA
THE PK
PARK CT
MARKET ST
WHITE HART ST
PO
GALLANTS
KING ST
JUBILEE AVE
White Hart St
Mount Pleasant Farm
East Harling Prim Sch
The Old Kings Head
Telegraph Hill
Windmill
Downhill Plantation
Dowhill Farm
Water Tower
EAST HARLING ROAD

86

Micklemoor Hill
Settlement
Middle Harling
Mauley's Carr
Mauleys Farm
KERRIDGES
NAMBLINGS PIECE
SPINNEY DR
TAYLOR DRIFT
KENNINGHALL ROAD
Grove Farm

4

Black Carr
Berdewell Hall Farm
WEST HARLING ROAD
Middle Harling Farm
Allot
Cemy
Glebe Farm
Hill Harling
GARBOLDISHAM ROAD

85

West Harling
Tumulus
Town Farm
LOPHAM ROAD
Flint Hall Farm
Guiltcross Farm

3

Lodge Plantation
Privet Plantation
Big Wood
GARBOLDISHAM RD
Tumulus
Triangle Covert
GARBOLDISHAM ROAD

84

Ten Acre Plantation
East Harling Heath
Uphall Farm
Dairy Farm

2

Twenty Acre Plantation
The Gallops
Tumulus
HARLING ROAD
IP22
Finchams Farm
Dickersons Farm

83

West Harlinghill Plantation
Old Sheep Pen Plantation
Hall Farm
B1111
Cranespond Plantation
Garboldisham Manor
Stubbings's Farm
Fir Tree Farm
Whitebreads Farm

1

Hut Covert
Fir Covert
Garboldisham Heath
Sandy Betty's Plantation
Georgiana Plantation
Grenadiers Plantation
Back Street Farm
The Hall
Wilderness Plantation
Moat
Ling Farm
Orchard Farm
LYNG LANE

82
Devil's Ditch

A 97 **A** 98 **B** 99 **C** 00 **D** 01 **E** 02 **F**

↓ 127   ← 117   ↓ 128

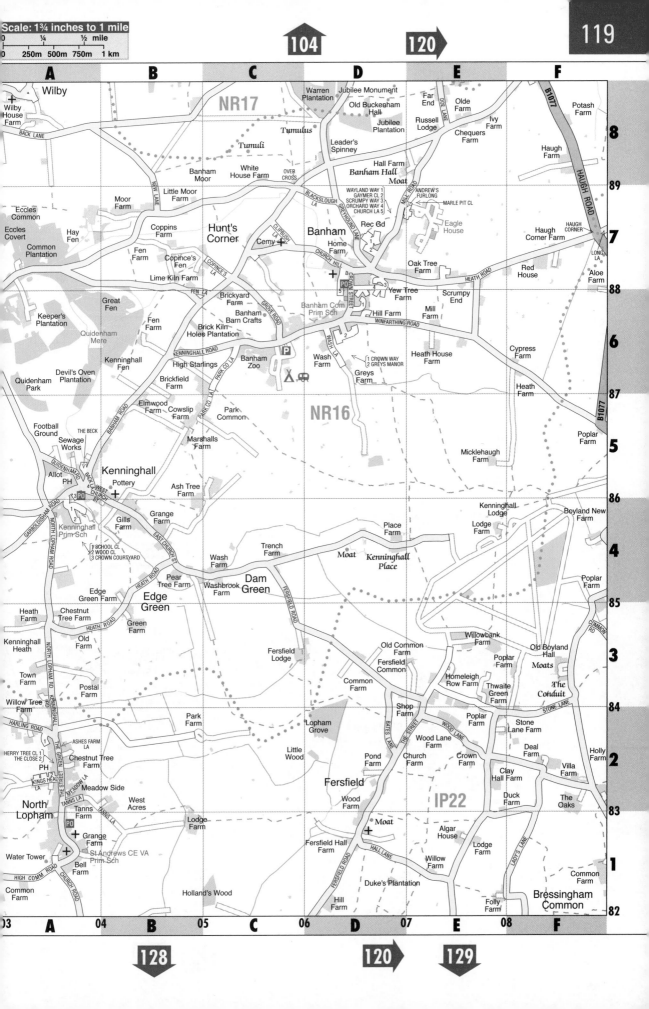

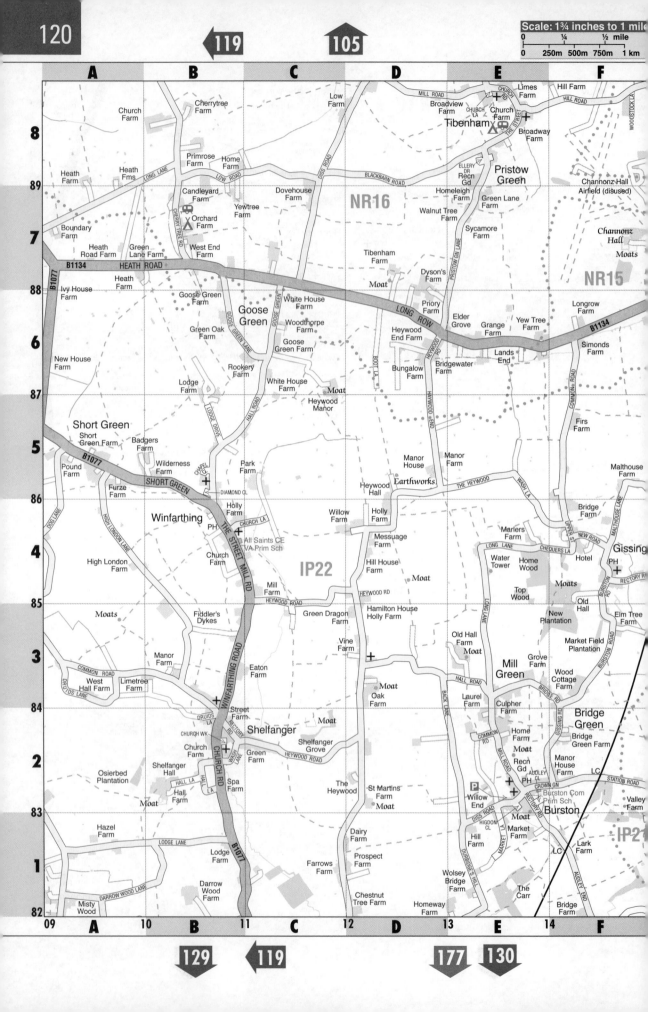

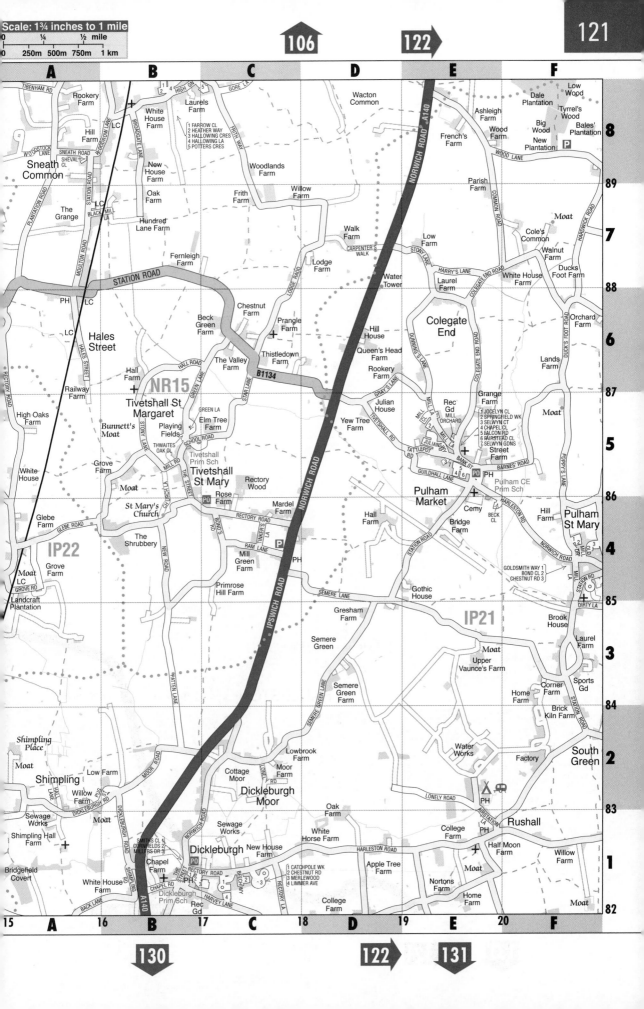

122

← 121

107↑

Scale: 1¾ inches to 1 mile
0   ¼   ½ mile
0   250m 500m 750m 1 km

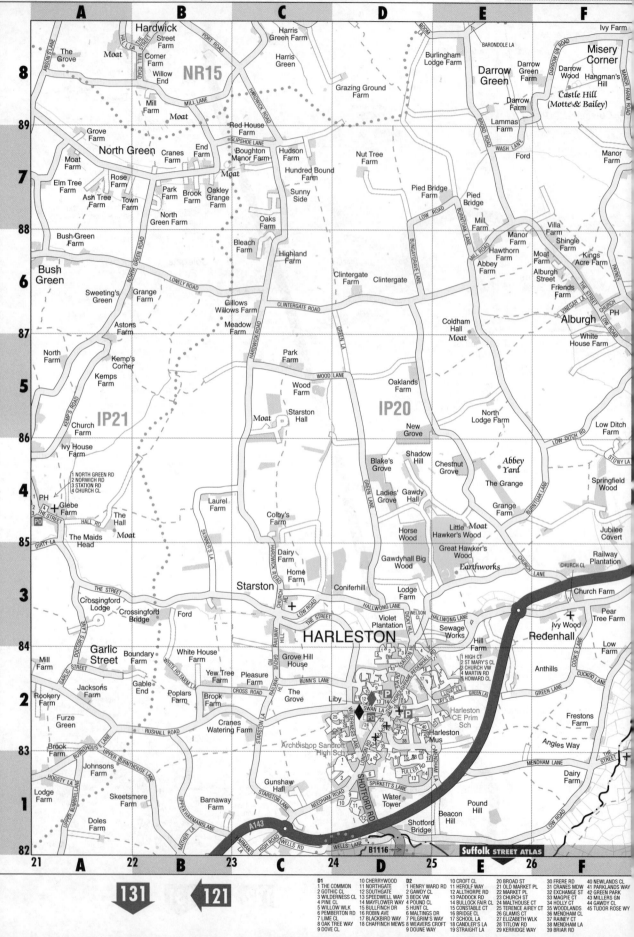

D1
1 THE COMMON
2 GOTHIC CL
3 WILDERNESS CL
4 PINE CL
5 WILLOW WLK
6 PEMBERTON RD
7 LIME CL
8 OAK TREE WAY
9 DOVE CL
10 CHERRYWOOD
11 NORTHGATE
12 SOUTHGATE
13 SPEEDWELL WAY
14 MAYFLOWER WAY
15 BULLFINCH DR
16 ROBIN AVE
17 BLACKBIRD WAY
18 CHAFFINCH MEWS

D2
1 HENRY WARD RD
2 GAWDY CL
3 BECK VW
4 POUND CL
5 HUNT CL
6 MALTINGS DR
7 PILGRIM'S WAY
8 WEAVERS CROFT
9 DOUNE WAY
10 CROFT CL
11 HEROLF WAY
12 ALLTHORPE RD
13 PADDOCK RD
14 BULLOCK FAIR CL
15 CONSTABLE CT
16 BRIDGE CL
17 SCHOOL LA
18 CANDLER'S LA
19 STRAIGHT LA
20 BROAD ST
21 OLD MARKET PL
22 MARKET PL
23 CHURCH ST
24 MALTHOUSE CT
25 TERENCE AIREY CT
26 GLAMIS CT
27 ELIZABETH WLK
28 TITLOW RD
29 KERRIDGE WAY
30 FRERE RD
31 CRANES MDW
32 EXCHANGE ST
33 MAGPIE CT
34 HOLLY CT
35 WOODLANDS
36 MENDHAM CT
37 RAINEY CT
38 MENDHAM LA
39 BRIAR RD
40 NEWLANDS CL
41 PARKLANDS WAY
42 GREEN PARK
43 MILLERS GN
44 GAWDY CL
45 TUDOR ROSE WY

Suffolk STREET ATLAS

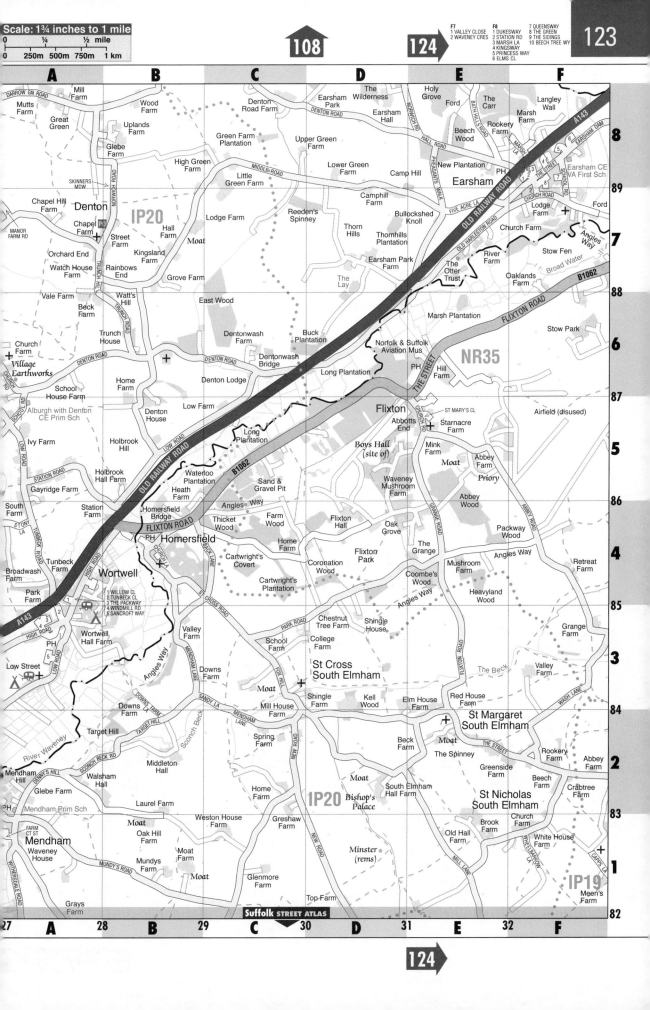

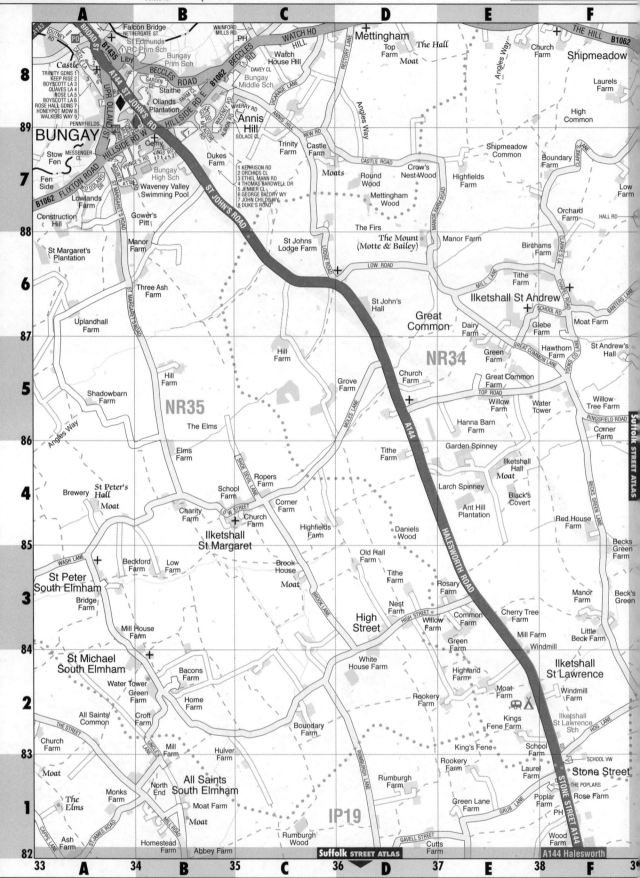

B8
1 ANNIS HILL LA
2 YEOMAN'S CL
3 REEVE'S CL
4 MILLERS CL
5 OLD GRAMMAR LA
6 BIGOD RD

A   B   C   D   E   F

8

89

7

88

6

87

5

86

4

85

3

84

2

83

1

82

33   A   34   B   35   C   36   D   37   E   38   F   3

BUNGAY

Castle
TRINITY GDNS 1
KEEP RISE 2
BOYSCOTT LA 3
QUAVES LA 4
ROSE LA 5
BOYSCOTT LA 6
ROSE HALL GDNS 7
HONEYPOT MDW 8
WALKERS WAY 9

Stow Fen
MESSENGER CL
Fen Side

Lowlands Farm
Construction Hill

St Margaret's Plantation

Uplandhall Farm

Hill Farm

Shadowbarn Farm

NR35

The Elms

Brewery
St Peter's Hall
Moat

St Peter South Elmham
Bridge Farm

Mill House Farm

St Michael South Elmham
Water Tower
Green Farm
Croft Farm
Home Farm

All Saints Common

Church Farm

Moat
The Elms
Ash Farm

Monks Farm
North End

Mill Farm

All Saints South Elmham

Homestead Farm

Abbey Farm

Moat Farm
Moat

Hulver Farm

Rumburgh Wood

IP19

Falcon Bridge
NETHERGATE ST
St Edmunds RC Prim Sch
Bungay Prim Sch
Liby
BECCLES ROAD
Staithe
Ollands Plantation

WATCH HO HILL
Watch House Hill
PH
Bungay Middle Sch
DAVEY CL

Annis Hill
SOLACE CL

Dukes Farm
Gower's Pitt

Manor Farm

Three Ash Farm

Hill Farm

The Elms

Elms Farm
SHOE DEVIL LANE

School Farm
LOW STREET
Charity Farm
Church Farm

Ilketshall St Margaret

Beckford Farm
Low Farm

WASH LANE

Bacons Farm

Mill Farm

Moat Farm
Moat

Waveney Valley Swimming Pool

Bungay High Sch

1 KENRISON RD
2 ORCHIDS CL
3 ETHEL MANN RD
4 THOMAS BARDWELL DR
5 JENNER CL
6 GEORGE BALDRY WY
7 JOHN CHILDS WY
8 DUKE'S ROAD

Trinity Farm

St Johns Lodge Farm

Ropers Farm

Corner Farm

Brook House
Moat

Boundary Farm

Mettingham
Top Farm
Moat

The Hall

Castle Farm

Moats

Round Wood

Mettingham Wood

The Firs
The Mount
(Motte & Bailey)

St John's Hall

Hill Farm

Grove Farm

MOLES LANE

Tithe Farm

Highfields Farm

Old Hall Farm

High Street
Nest Farm

White House Farm

Daniels Wood

Tithe Farm

Rookery Farm

Rumburgh Farm

Rookery Farm

Green Lane Farm

Church Farm

Crow's Nest Wood

Great Common

NR34

Willow Farm

Hanna Barn Farm

Garden Spinney

Larch Spinney

Ant Hill Plantation

Rosary Farm

Willow Farm

Common Farm

Green Farm

Highland Farm

Moat Farm

Kings Fene Farm

King's Fene

Laurel Farm

Green Farm

Shipmeadow

Church Farm

Laurels Farm

High Common

Shipmeadow Common

Highfields Farm

Boundary Farm

Orchard Farm

Birchams Farm

Tithe Farm

Ilketshall St Andrew
Glebe Farm
Moat Farm

St Andrew's Hall

Hawthorn Farm

Great Common Farm
TOP ROAD
Willow Farm
Water Tower

Ilketshall Hall Moat

Black's Covert

Red House Farm

Cherry Tree Farm

Mill Farm
Windmill

Little Beck Farm

Ilketshall St Lawrence
Windmill Farm

Ilketshall St Lawrence Sch

School Farm
SCHOOL VW

Stone Street
THE POPLARS
Rose Farm

Poplar Farm
PH

Wood Farm

Cutts Farm

Low Farm

Boundary Farm

Corner Farm

Becks Green Farm

Manor Farm

Beck's Green

Willow Tree Farm

A144 Halesworth

Suffolk STREET ATLAS

For full street detail of Bungay see
Philip's STREET ATLAS of Suffolk

F6
1 SALMOND DR
2 ELLINGTON RD
3 NEWALL RD
4 PORTAL CL
5 TEDDER CL
6 EDINBURGH CL

7 WINDSOR CL

A   B   C   D   E   F

8
81
7
80
6
79
5
78
4
77
3
76
2
75
1
74

Parson's Slip Wood
A11 Newmarket
Stonepit Wood
Redneck Farm
Elveden
Water Tower
Home Wood
Summerpit Farm
Old Middlegouch Plantation
B1106
Tumulus
SHELTERHOUSE CORNER
Monument
IP28
Warren Covert
Belchamps Plantation
B1106

Water Tower
Millhill Wood
Elveden Hall
Larch Covert
Albemarle Plantation
Furze Hill Plantation
Old Barnham Slip
St Edmund Way
BARROW'S CORNER
Barrow Clump Buildings
Icknield Way Path
Four Corners
Warren New Covert
Tumulus

Olleys Farm
Rifle Range
LONDON ROAD
A11
Milestone Plantation
Sketchfar Wood
Marmansgrave Wood
Glebe Wood
Princess Mary's Plantation
Sewage Works
Sandgault Plantation
Basin Wood
Coronation Covert
West Calthorpe Heath
Breck Plantation
Rubbinghouse Covert
Traveller's Hill (Tumuli)
Traveller's Hill Plantation
CHALK LA

Forest Retail Park
BURRELL WAY
176
Elveden Gap
St Edmund Way
Boundary Belt
Aughton Spinney
Icknield Way
Gorse Industrial Estate
ELVEDEN ROAD
Thetford Heath
Water Tower
North Farm
IP24
Hunwellspring Plantation
Triangle Plantation
Works
Little Heath
Duke's Ride
Bottom Plantation
New Zealand Cotts
Pits (dis)
Lodge Farm
Wordwell Barn
Ash Covert
Ling Covert
Seven Hills House
IP31
Culfordheath

London Rd
176
FIR RD
ELM RD
Playing Field
A134
NUNNERY DR
176
Barnhamcross Common
Nature Reserve
P
BURY ROAD
Barnham Cross (rems)
Barnham Camp
Pig Farm
PH
WATER LA 1
ST MARTIN'S LA 2
MILL LA 3
BLACKSMITH LA 4
St Martin's Church (rems)
CHURCH LA
THE STREET
Barnham
STATION RD
Works Tumulus
A134
Barnham CE Prim Sch
East Farm
Pit (dis)
Blackbird Spinney
Tumulus
Ixworth Spinney
Fox Pin
Icknield Way Path
West Farm
D House
Works
Field Barn
Rymer Farm
A134
Rymer Barn

Great Snare Hill
Little Ouse River

Suffolk STREET ATLAS

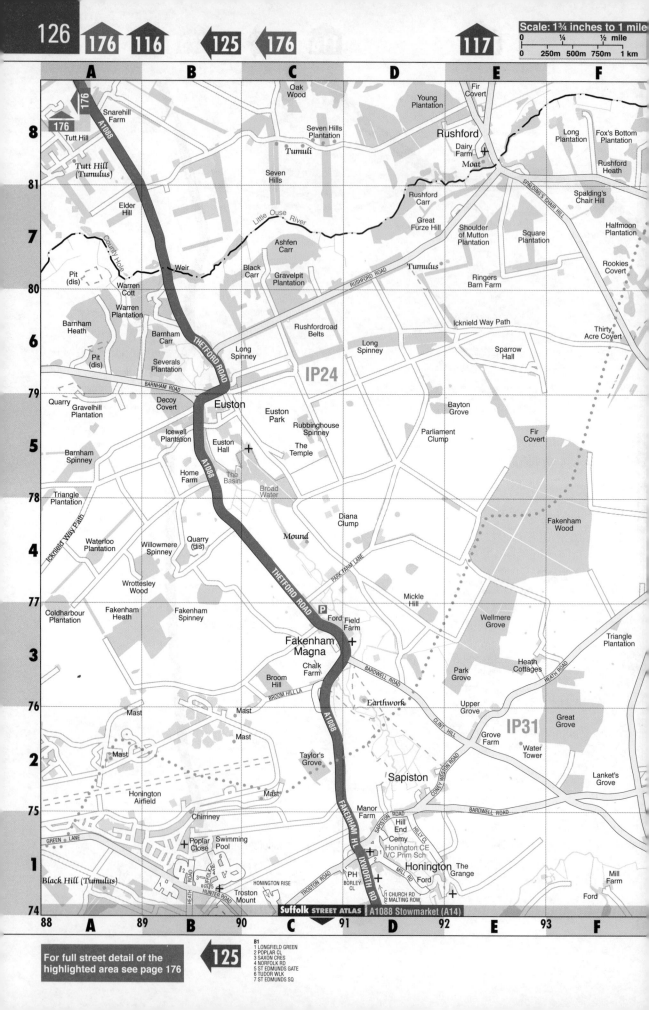

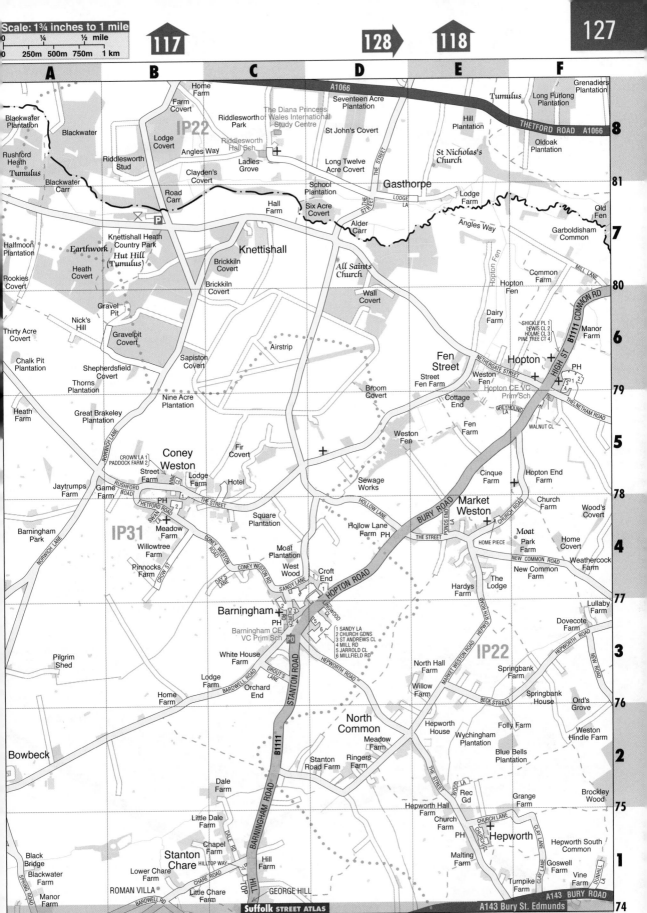

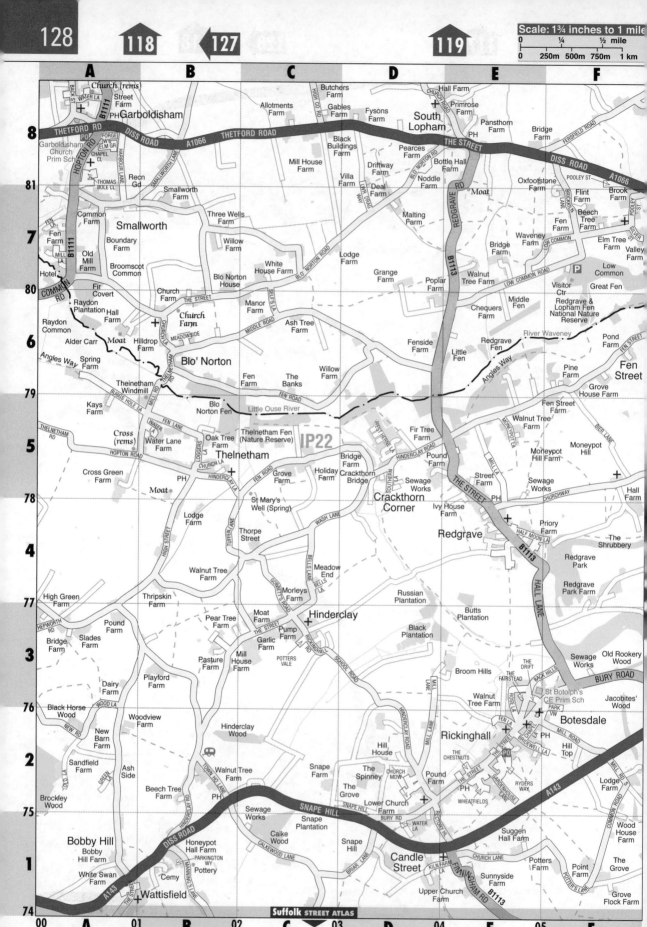

128
118
127
119

Scale: 1¾ inches to 1 mile
0   ¼   ½ mile
0   250m 500m 750m 1 km

A   B   C   D   E   F

8
Church (rems)
Water LA
Street Farm
Garboldisham
BACK ST
B1111
PH
Butchers Farm
Hall Farm
Primrose Farm
Gables Farm
Fysons Farm
Pansthorn Farm
Bridge Farm
FERSFIELD ROAD
South Lopham
THETFORD RD
DISS ROAD
A1066
THETFORD ROAD
THE STREET
PH
DISS ROAD
A1066
Garboldisham Church Prim Sch
HOPTON RD
FORGE
POP
CHAPEL CL
WE GR
Black Buildings Farm
CHURCH RD
Pearces Farm
Bottle Hall Farm
Oxfootstone Farm
POOLEY ST
Brook Farm

81
HARBOUR LANE
THOMAS BOLE CL
Recn Gd
Mill House Farm
Villa Farm
Driftway Farm
Deal Farm
LWR DRAG WAY
Noddle Farm
BLO NORTON RD
REDGRAVE RD
Moat
BRICKKILN LANE
Flint Farm
Beech Tree Farm
POOLEY ST
SILVER ST
Elm Tree Farm

7
SMALLWORTH LANE
Common Farm
Smallworth
Three Wells Farm
Smallworth Farm
Willow Farm
Malting Farm
B1113
Waveney Farm
Bridge Farm
Fen Farm
Low Common Road
Valley Farm
FEN LA
Fen Farm
Boundary Farm
Lodge Farm
Grange Farm
LOW COMMON
Walnut Tree Farm
P
Low Common

80
COMMON RD
Hotel
Old Mill Farm
Broomscot Common
White House Farm
Blo Norton House
SELF'S LA
Poplar Farm
Chequers Farm
Middle Fen
Visitor Ctr
Great Fen
MILL LA
B1111
Fir Covert
Church Farm
THE STREET
Manor Farm
MIDDLE ROAD
Little Fen
Redgrave & Lopham Fen National Nature Reserve

6
Raydon Plantation
Hall Farm
Hilldrop Farm
Moat
MEADOWSIDE
Ash Tree Farm
Fenside Farm
Redgrave Fen
River Waveney
Pine Farm
Fen Street
Raydon Common
Alder Carr
Spring Farm
Blo' Norton
CHURCHILL
THELNETHAM RD
Willow Farm
Little Fen
Angles Way
Pond Farm
Grove House Farm

79
Angles Way
Theinetham Windmill
BUGGS HOLE LA
Fen Farm
The Banks
FEN ROAD
Blo Norton Fen
Little Ouse River
Fen Street Farm
Walnut Tree Farm
BIER LANE
Kays Farm
THELNETHAM RD
MILL RD
Cross (rems)
WATER LA
Water Lane Farm
Oak Tree Farm
FEN LANE
Thelnetham Fen (Nature Reserve)
IP22
WEST HERNE LA
Fir Tree Farm
MONEYPOT LA
Moneypot Hill Farm
Moneypot Hill

5
THELNETHAM RD
HOPTON ROAD
Cross Green Farm
LOGGERS LA
CHURCH LA
Thelnetham
FEN ROAD
Grove Farm
Holiday Farm
Bridge Farm
Crackthorn Bridge
Pound Farm
HINDERCLAY ROAD
Sewage Works
Street Farm
MILL LA
THE STREET
PH
CHURCHWAY
Sewage Works
Hall Farm

78
PH
Moat
HINDERCLAY LA
St Mary's Well (Spring)
TUFFEN LANE
WASH LANE
Crackthorn Corner
SOUTHERN LA
Ivy House Farm
Redgrave
Priory Farm
HALF MOON LA
B1113
The Shrubbery

4
Lodge Farm
Thorpe Street
BELLS LANE
Meadow End
BELLS LA
Russian Plantation
HALL LANE
Redgrave Park
Redgrave Park Farm

77
High Green Farm
HEPWORTH RD
Thripskin Farm
GOBBETT'S ROAD
Walnut Tree Farm
Morleys Farm
Hinderclay
Butts Plantation

3
Bridge Farm
Slades Farm
Pound Farm
Pear Tree Farm
Moat Farm
THE STREET
Garlic Farm
Pump Farm
POTTERS VALE
RICKINGHALL
SCHOOL ROAD
Black Plantation
Broom Hills
THE DRIFT
BACK HILLS
Sewage Works
Old Rookery Wood
BURY ROAD
St Botolph's CE Prim Sch
Jacobites' Wood

76
Black Horse Wood
NEW RD
WOOD LA
Dairy Farm
Playford Farm
Woodview Farm
Hinderclay Wood
Mill House Farm
Pasture Farm
HINDERCLAY ROAD
MILL LANE
ROSE LA
Walnut Tree Farm
PARK
FEN LA
CHAPEL
Rickinghall
BRIDEWELL LA
THE CHESTNUTS
Botesdale
MILL ROAD
Hill Top

2
Sandfield Farm
New Barn Farm
GREEN LA
Ash Side
TOWN HO LANE
Walnut Tree Farm
Beech Tree Farm
PH
Snape Farm
Hill House
The Spinney
CHURCH MDW
Pound Farm
THE STREET
PO
GARDENHOUSE LANE
RYDERS WAY
WHEATFIELDS
Lodge Farm

75
Brockley Wood
DISS ROAD
Honeypot Hall Farm
PARKINGTON WY
Pottery
Sewage Works
Snape Plantation
Calke Wood
SNAPE HILL
The Grove
Lower Church Farm
BURY RD
WATER LA
A143
Wood House Farm
The Grove

1
Bobby Hill
Bobby Hill Farm
CALKEWOOD LANE
Snape Hill
BRIAR LANE
Candle Street
KILN LA
Church Lane
Suggen Hall Farm
Sunnyside Farm
Potters Farm
POTTER'S LANE
Point Farm
The Grove
White Swan Farm
Cemy
A143
Upper Church Farm
FINNINGHAM RD
B1113
Grove Flock Farm

74
THE STREET
Wattisfield

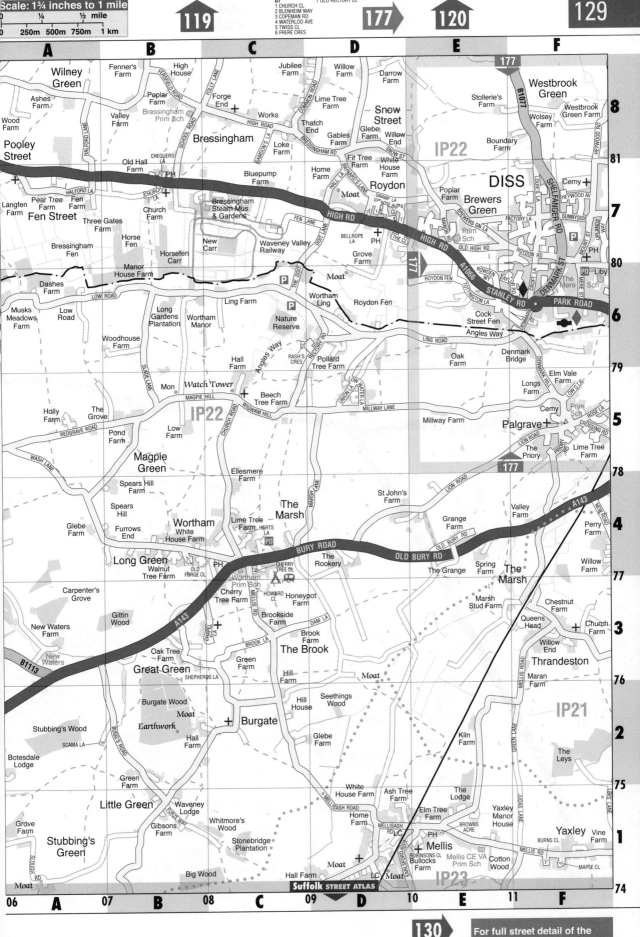

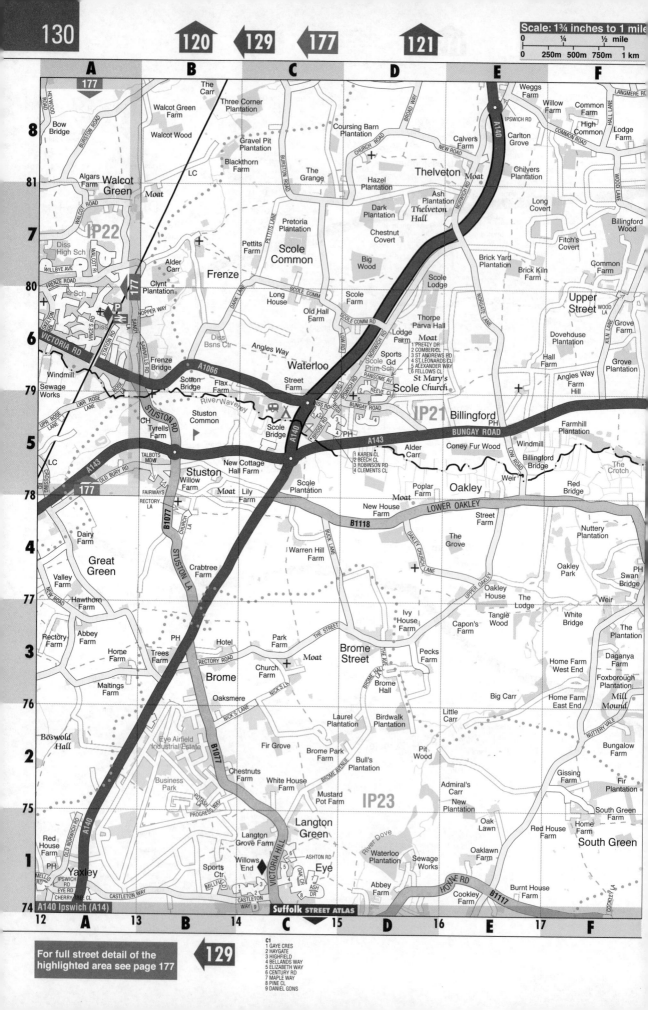

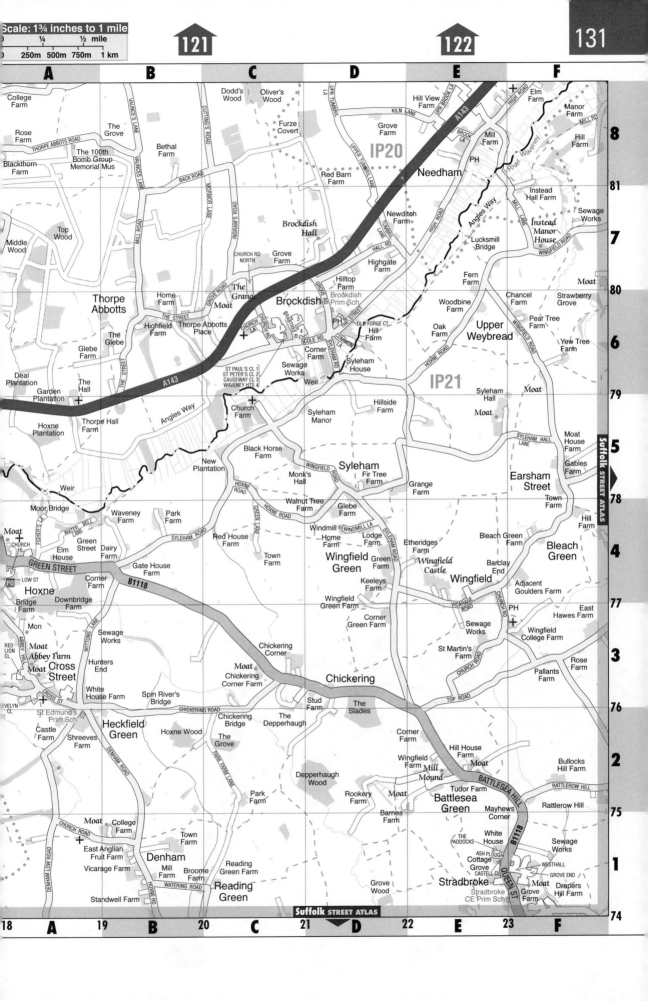

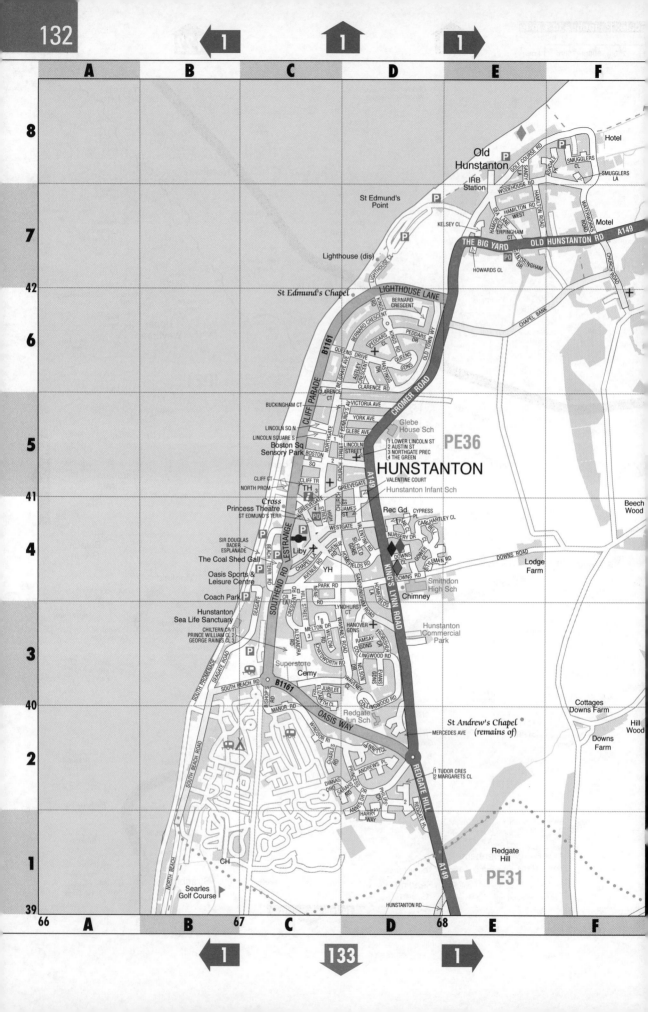

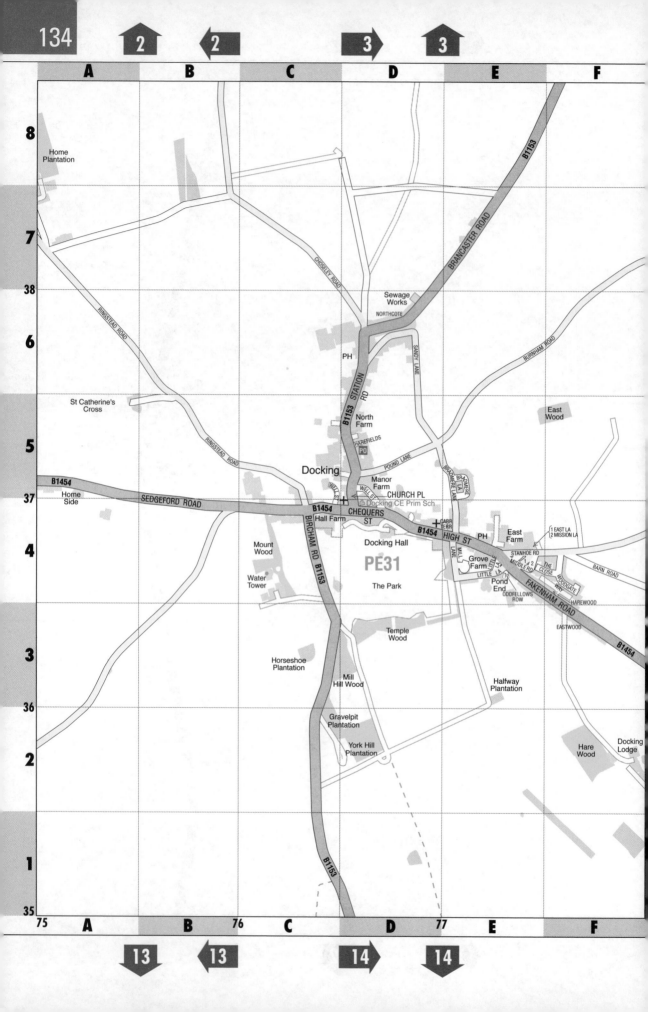

Home
Plantation

RIMSTEAD ROAD

St Catherine's
Cross

RINGSTEAD ROAD

B1454

Home
Side

SEDGEFORD ROAD

Mount
Wood

Water
Tower

Horseshoe
Plantation

Mill
Hill Wood

Gravelpit
Plantation

York Hill
Plantation

BIRCHAM RD B1153

B1153

CHISELEY ROAD

BRANCASTER ROAD

B1153

Sewage
Works

NORTHCOTE

PH

B1153 STATION RD

North
Farm

HAREFIELDS

PO

SANDY LANE

POUND LANE

BURNHAM ROAD

East
Wood

Docking

WELLS RD

WELLS ST

B1454

Hall Farm

Manor
Farm

CHURCH PL

Docking CE Prim Sch

CHEQUERS ST

Docking Hall

PE31

The Park

B1454

CARR
TERR

HIGH ST

PH

BRADMERE LANE

BRADMERE LA

East
Farm

1 EAST LA
2 MISSION LA

STANHOE RD

MILL LANE

LITTLE LA

MIDDLE RD

Grove
Farm

Pond
End

ODDFELLOWS
ROW

THE
CLOSE

WOODGATE WAY

BARN ROAD

HAREWOOD

EASTWOOD

FAKENHAM ROAD

B1454

Temple
Wood

Halfway
Plantation

Hare
Wood

Docking
Lodge

B1153

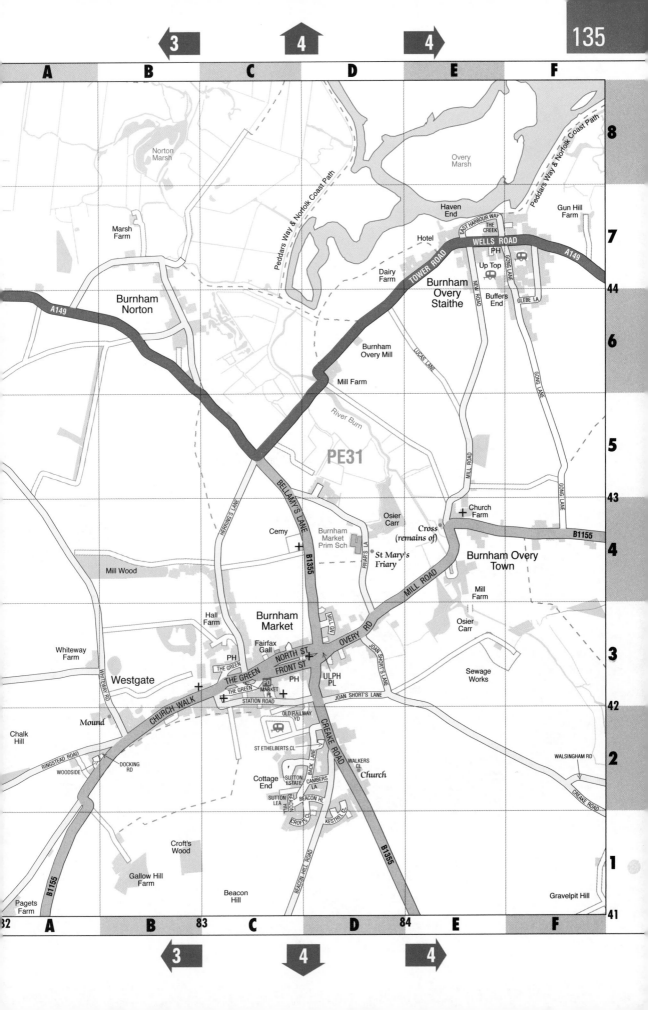

8

7

44

6

5

43

4

3

42

2

1

41

Norton Marsh

Marsh Farm

Burnham Norton

A149

Peddars Way & Norfolk Coast Path

Overy Marsh

Haven End

Peddars Way & Norfolk Coast Path

Gun Hill Farm

EAST HARBOUR WAY

THE CREEK

WELLS ROAD

PH

A149

Hotel

TOWER ROAD

Dairy Farm

Burnham Overy Staithe

Up Top

GONG LANE

Buffers End

NEW ROAD

GLEBE LA

GONG LANE

Lucas Lane

Burnham Overy Mill

Mill Farm

River Burn

PE31

MILL ROAD

Church Farm

B1155

HERRING'S LANE

BELLAMY'S LANE

Cemy

B1355

Burnham Market Prim Sch

Osier Carr

Cross (remains of)

FRIAR'S LA

St Mary's Friary

MILL ROAD

Burnham Overy Town

Mill Farm

Osier Carr

Mill Wood

Hall Farm

Burnham Market

Whiteway Farm

WHITEWAY RD

Westgate

PH

THE GREEN

THE GREEN

Fairfax Gall

NORTH ST

FRONT ST

OVERY RD

MILL GN

PH

ULPH PL

JOAN SHORT'S LANE

Sewage Works

CHURCH WALK

PO

MARKET PL

STATION ROAD

Joan Short's Lane

Chalk Hill

Mound

RINGSTEAD ROAD

DOCKING RD

WOODSIDE

OLD RAILWAY YD

St Ethelberts Cl

CREAKE ROAD

WALSINGHAM RD

CREAKE ROAD

SUTTON ESTATE

CAMBERS LA

BACK LANE

WALKERS CL

Church

Cottage End

SUTTON LEA

BELGRAVE

BEACON HL

HILL

CROFTS CL

KESTREL CL

BEACON HILL ROAD

B1355

Croft's Wood

Gallow Hill Farm

Beacon Hill

Pagets Farm

B1155

Gravelpit Hill

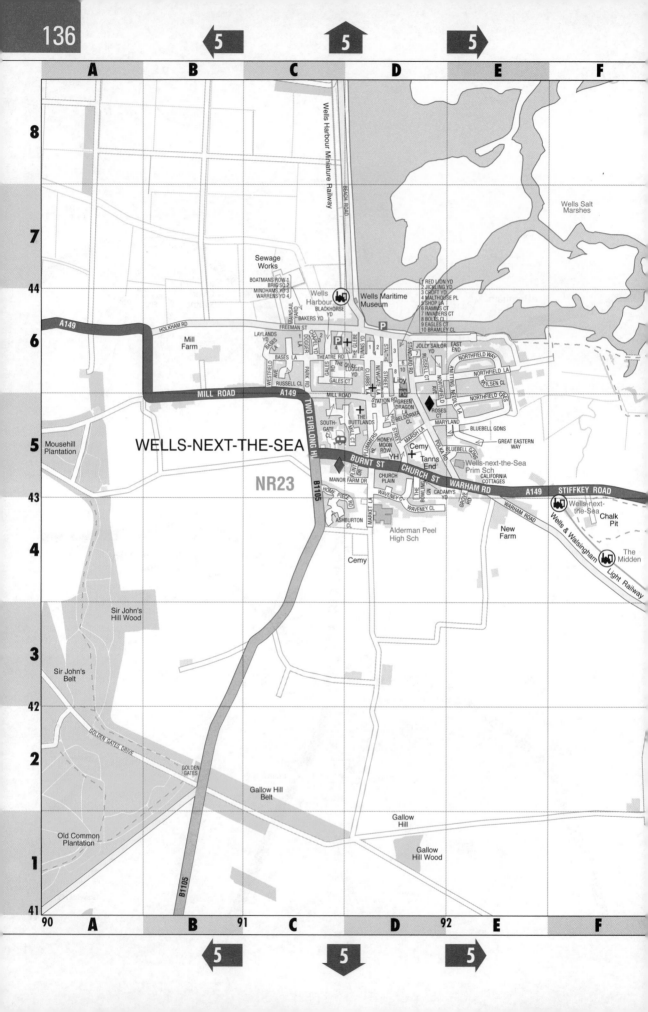

WELLS-NEXT-THE-SEA

NR23

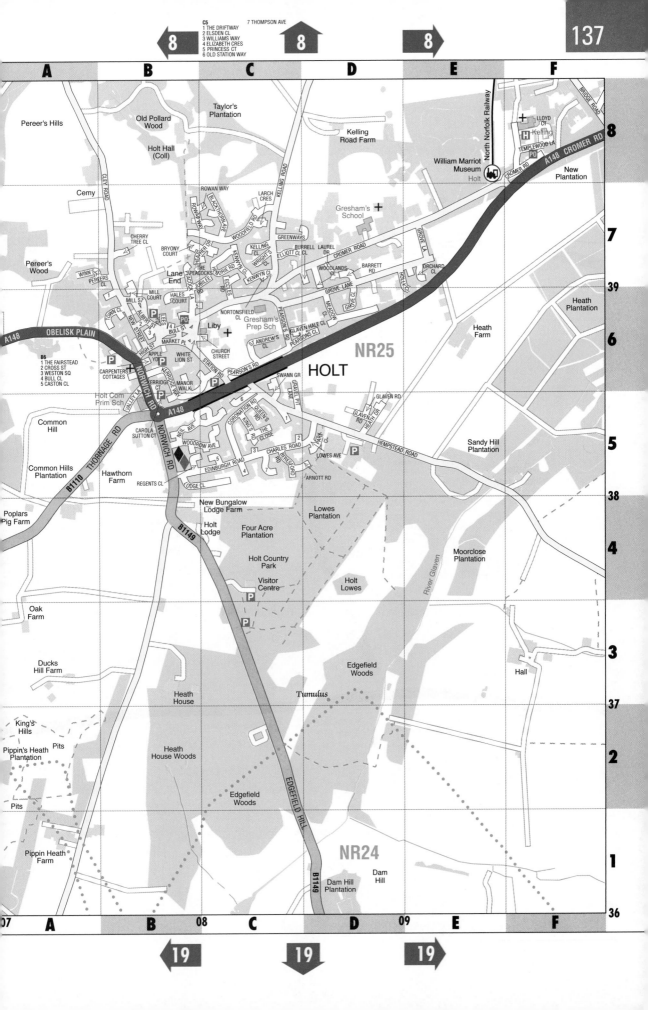

8   **8**   **8**

C5
1 THE DRIFTWAY
2 ELSDEN CL
3 WILLIAMS WAY
4 ELIZABETH CRES
5 PRINCESS CT
6 OLD STATION WAY

7 THOMPSON AVE

A   B   C   D   E   F

Pereer's Hills

Old Pollard Wood

Taylor's Plantation

Kelling Road Farm

North Norfolk Railway

Lloyd CT

Kelling

Holt Hall (Coll)

TEMPLEWOOD LA

A148 CROMER RD

CROMER RD

8

Cemy

William Marriot Museum

Holt

New Plantation

ROWAN WAY

LARCH CRES

Gresham's School

Pereer's Wood

BLACKTHORN AVE

ROWAN WAY

WOODFIELD RD

KELLING ROAD

GREENWAYS

BURRELL

LAUREL

CROMER ROAD

GROVE LA

7

CHERRY TREE CL

BRYONY COURT

THE PEACOCKS

KENWYN

PRIORIE RD

ELLIOTT CL CL

WOODLANDS CL

BARRETT RD

ORCHARD CL

HOLT CL

39

WINN SCH

PEREERS CL

MILL ST

Lane End

HALES COURT

KENWYN CL

ECCLES RD

GROVE LANE

GROVE LANE

Heath Farm

Heath Plantation

MILL COURT

ALBERT ST

LEES

NORTONSFIELD CL

PEARSON'S RD

PEARSONS RD

GLAVEN HALE CL

GROVE CL

MEADOW

6

A148   OBELISK PLAIN

TOWN CL

NEW STREET

BULL ST

PO

Liby

Gresham's Prep Sch

ST ANDREW'S CL

NR25

B6
1 THE FAIRSTEAD
2 CROSS ST
3 WESTON SQ
4 BULL CL
5 CASTON CL

HIGH ST

MARKET PL

APPLE YD

WHITE LION ST

CHURCH STREET

STATION RD

PEARSON'S RD

SWANN GR

HOLT

Carpenters Cottages

NORWICH RD

KERRIDGE CT

MANOR WALK

GRAVEL PIT LANE

GLAVEN RD

Glaven RD

38

Holt Com Prim Sch

A148

CAROLA SUTTON CT

NEIL AVE

WOODROW AVE

CORONATION RD

KING'S RD

QUEEN'S

THE CLOSE

PARK CL

Hempstead Road

GLAVEN DR

HEATH DR

Sandy Hill Plantation

Common Hill

CHARLES ROAD

BERESFORD RD

LOWES AVE

Common Hills Plantation

Hawthorn Farm

REGENTS CL

EDINBURGH ROAD

LODGE CL

ARNOTT RD

5

Poplars Pig Farm

B1110

B1149

New Bungalow Lodge Farm

Lowes Plantation

37

Holt Lodge

Four Acre Plantation

River Glaven

Moorclose Plantation

4

Oak Farm

Holt Country Park

Visitor Centre

Holt Lowes

Hall

Ducks Hill Farm

Heath House

Edgefield Woods

3

King's Hills

Tumulus

Pippin's Heath Plantation

Pits

Heath House Woods

EDGEFIELD HILL

Edgefield Woods

2

Pits

NR24

Pippin Heath Farm

B1149

Dam Hill Plantation

Dam Hill

1

07   A   B   08   C   D   09   E   F   36

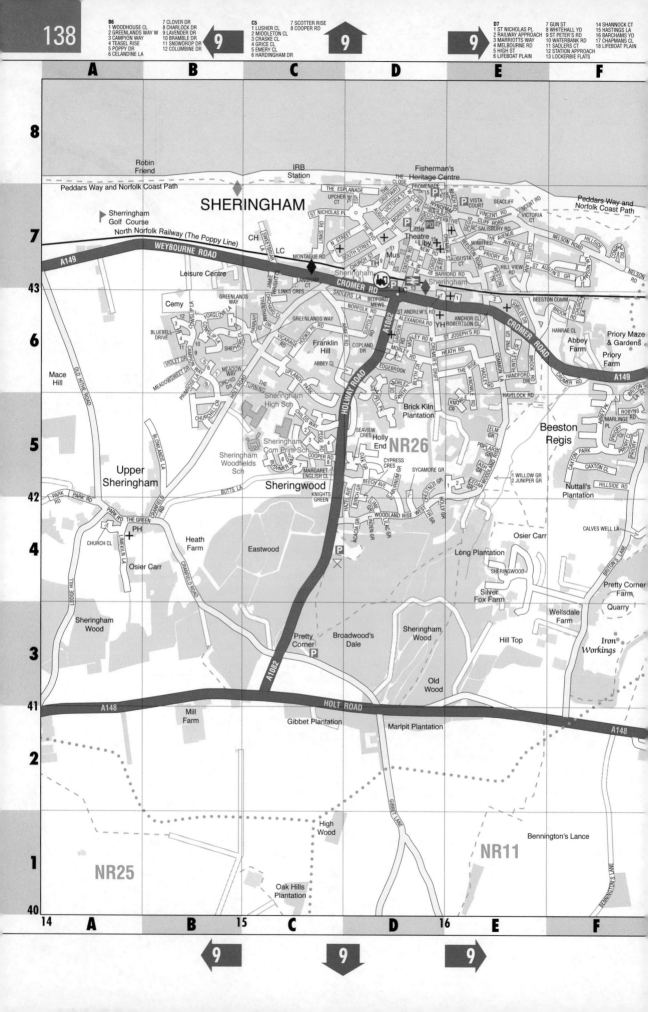

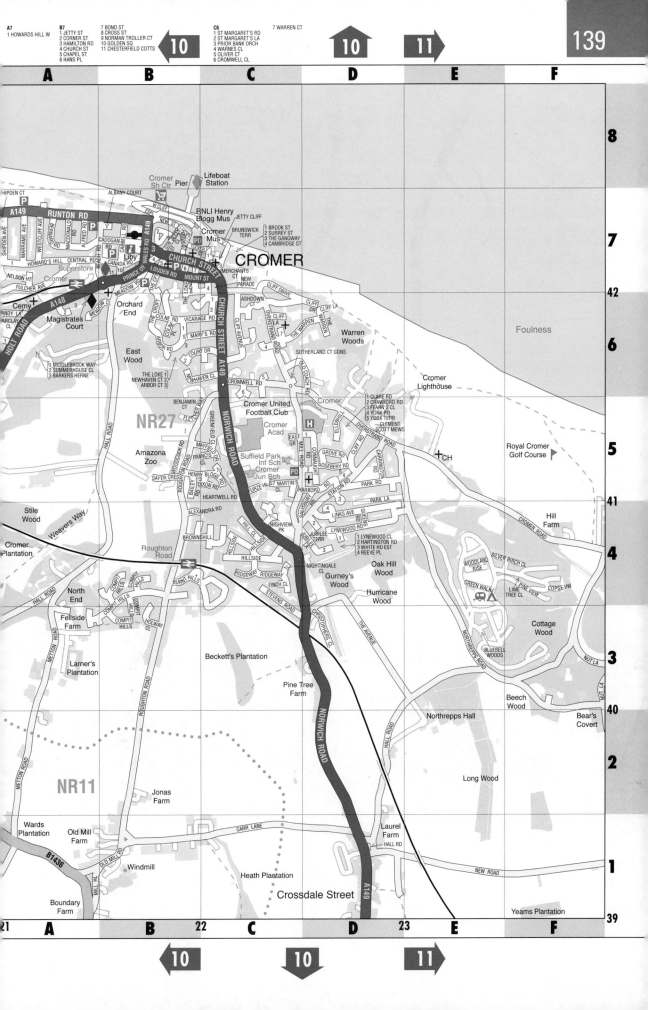

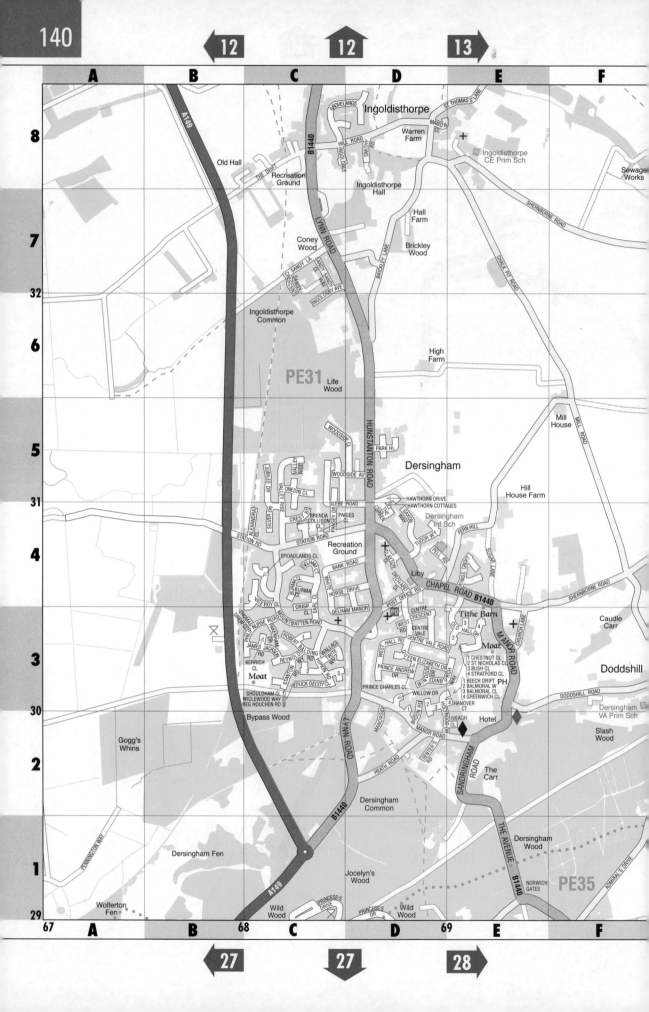

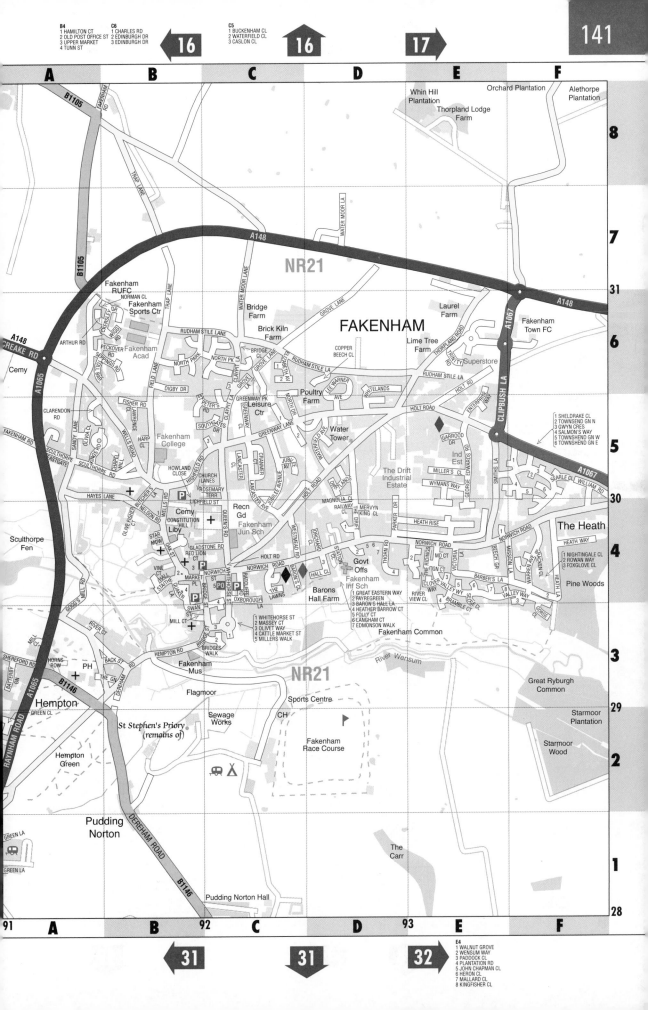

B4
1 HAMILTON CT
2 OLD POST OFFICE ST
3 UPPER MARKET
4 TUNN ST

C6
1 CHARLES RD
2 EDINBURGH DR
3 EDINBURGH DR

C5
1 BUCKENHAM CL
2 WATERFIELD CL
3 CASLON CL

◄ 16

▲ 16

17 ►

141

A B C D E F

8

7

31

6

FAKENHAM

NR21

Whin Hill Plantation
Orchard Plantation
Alethorpe Plantation
Thorpland Lodge Farm

Water Moor La

A148

Laurel Farm

Lime Tree Farm

Fakenham Town FC

A148

B1105

B1105

Fakenham RUFC

NORMAN CL

Fakenham Sports Ctr

Bridge Farm

Brick Kiln Farm

Grove Lane

COPPER BEECH CL

Thorpland Road

TRINITY Superstore

A1067

CLIPBUSH LA

5

RUDHAM STILE LANE

BRIDGE ST

GROVE LANE

RUDHAM STILE LA

Rudham Stile La

Holt Rd

A1067

1 SHELDRAKE CL
2 TOWNSEND GN N
3 GWYN CRES
4 SALMON'S WAY
5 TOWNSHEND GN W
6 TOWNSHEND GN E

CREAKE RD

A148

A1065

ARTHUR RD

PECKOVER RD

SPRINGS RD

Fakenham Acad

NORTH PARK

FIELD LANE

NORTH PK

CLAYPIT CL

ELIZABETH DR

Poultry Farm

LEE WARNER AVE

WHITELANDS

Water Tower

GARROOD DR

Ind Est

ENTERPRISE

GEORGE EDWARDS RD

SMITHS LA

WILLIAM RD

SEARLE CL

A1067

30

The Heath

HEATH WAY

1 NIGHTINGALE CL
2 ROWAN WAY
3 FOXGLOVE CL

Pine Woods

Cemy

CLARENDON RD

FAKENHAM RD

SANDY LANE

OLIVIA CL

KINGS RD

FISHER RD

LAWRENCE

HARP CL

CHAPEL HILL

WELLS ROAD

Fakenham College

DIGBY DR

ST PETER'S RD

SOUTHGATES DR

GREENWAY RD

Greenway Leisure Ctr

GREENWAY LANE

CRAMNER

LANCASTER CL

JUBILEE AVENUE

MAGNOLIA CL

MERVYN KING CL

The Drift Industrial Estate

MILLER'S CL

WYMANS WAY

HEATH RISE

Norwich Road

NORWICH ROAD

MISSION LA

BEECH GN

WARREN AVE

HEATH LA

GORSE

4

SCULTHORPE RD

SCULTHORPE EASTGATE

HOWLAND CLOSE

CHURCH LANES

HIGHFIELD RD

YRDSEMARY TERR

LANCASTER AVE

RAILWAY CL

THE LANTHS

THE DRIFT

THORN RD

PARKER DR

THE RIDINGS

MD CT

GN CT

VICTORIA LA

BARBER'S LA

VALLEY WAY

HAYES LANE

Cemy

CONSTITUTION HILL

Liby

STAR MDW

VINE CT

OLIVE FISHER

BUTCHER'S

NELSON RD

WELLS RD

QUEEN'S RD

Fakenham Jun Sch

Recn Gd

HOLT RD

WESTMEAD RD

ORCHARD

NATIONS

Fakenham Inf Sch

Govt Offs

CLOVER WAY

VALLEY WY

EDGE CL

BRAMBLE CT

3

LICHFIELD ST

P

GLADSTONE RD

Red Lion

P

NORWICH ST

MARKET PL

PO

P

HALL CL

Barons Hall Farm

RIVER VIEW CL

1 GREAT EASTERN WAY
2 FAYREGREEN
3 BARON'S HALL LA
4 HEATHER BARROW CT
5 FOLLY CT
6 LANGHAM CT
7 EDMONSON WALK

Fakenham Common

Sculthorpe Fen

MILL CT

MALL STAITHE

BRIDGE ST

SWAN ST

THE LAWNS

BARON'S CL

1 WHITEHORSE ST
2 MASSEY CT
3 OLIVET WAY
4 CATTLE MARKET ST
5 MILLERS WALK

MILL RD

A1065

RIVER CT

HEMPTON RD

BRIDGES WALK

Fakenham Mus

NR21

River Wensum

Great Ryburgh Common

SHEREFORD RD

HORNS ROW

PH

BACK ST

DEREHAM

THE GN

Flagmoor

Sports Centre

Starmoor Plantation

29

BATTERLY GN

B1146

Hempton

GREEN CL

St Stephen's Priory (remains of)

Sewage Works

CH

Starmoor Wood

Starmoor Wood

2

Hempton Green

Fakenham Race Course

DEREHAM ROAD

RAYNHAM ROAD

A1065

Pudding Norton

B1146

The Carr

1

GREEN LA

GREEN LA

Pudding Norton Hall

28

91 A B 92 C D 93 E F

◄ 31

▲ 31

32 ►

E4
1 WALNUT GROVE
2 WENSUM WAY
3 PADDOCK CL
4 PLANTATION RD
5 JOHN CHAPMAN CL
6 HERON CL
7 MALLARD CL
8 KINGFISHER CL

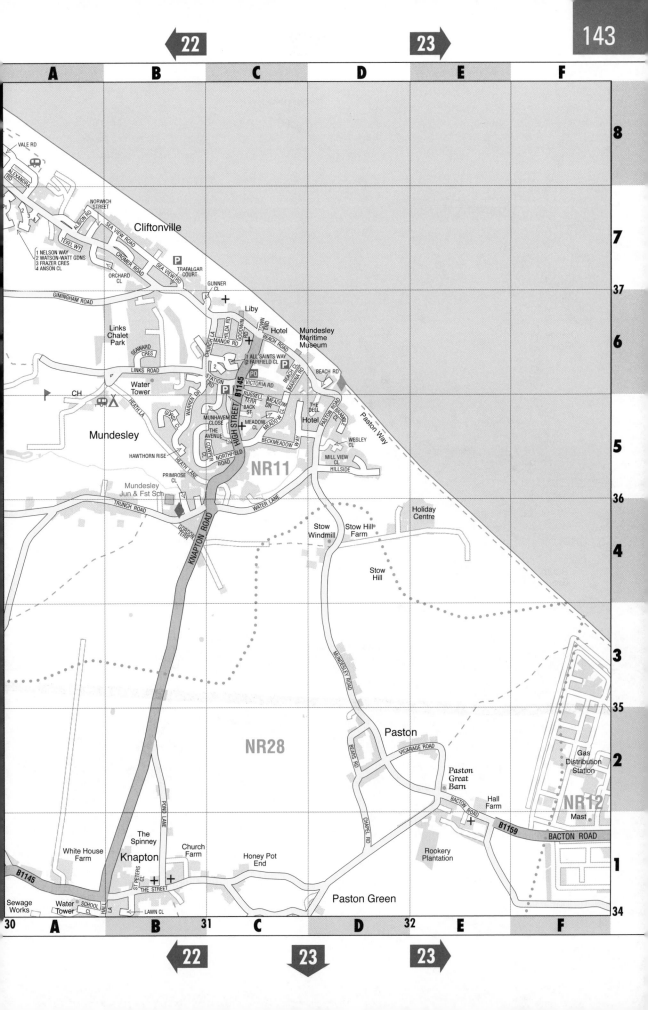

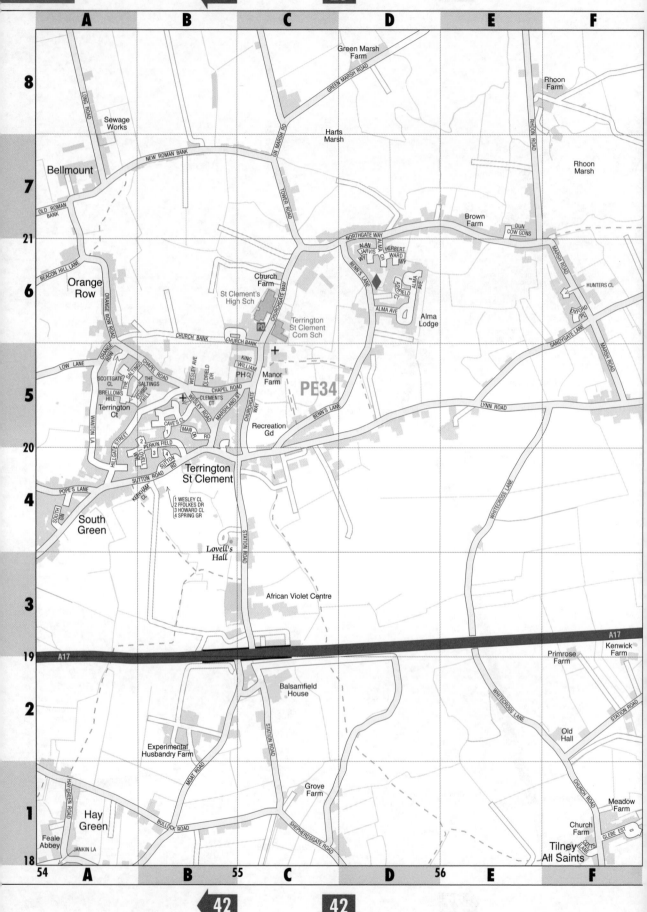

A B C D E F

Green Marsh Farm

Rhoon Farm

GREEN MARSH ROAD

Sewage Works

Harts Marsh

Rhoon Marsh

LONG ROAD

NEW ROMAN BANK

Bellmount

TOWER ROAD

GN MARSH RD

RHOON ROAD

Brown Farm

OLD ROMAN BANK

DUN COW GDNS

21

NORTHGATE WAY

ALAN JARVIS WY HERBERT WARD WY

ALMA CT

MARSH ROAD

BEACON HILL LANE

Orange Row

Church Farm

BENN'S LANE

SEDGEFIELD CT

HUNTERS CL

ORANGE ROW ROAD

St Clement's High Sch

ALMA AVE

OXFORD PL

Terrington St Clement Com Sch

ALMA AVE

Alma Lodge

SANDYGATE LANE

CHURCH BANK

CHURCH BANK

PO

6

LOW LANE

ORANGE ROW

CHURCH BANK

CHURCHGATE WAY

WESLEY AVE

OLDFIELD DR

KING WILLIAM PH CL

Manor Farm

PE34

Scottgate CL THE SALTINGS

CHAPEL ROAD

CHAPEL ROAD

MARSHLAND ST

Brellows Hill DOBBS HILL

WESLEY ROAD

CLEMENTS CT

CHURCHGATE WAY

BENN'S LANE

LYNN ROAD

Terrington Ct

CAVE'S CL

MAN R RD

Recreation Gd

5

HILLGATE STREET

WANTON LA

2

PERKIN FIELD

1

LOVELL WY

3

SUTTON RD

4

WHITECROSS LANE

20

SUTTON ROAD

KERKHAM CL

Terrington St Clement

POPE'S LANE

1 WESLEY CL
2 FFOLKES DR
3 HOWARD CL
4 SPRING GR

4

SOUTH ROW

South Green

STATION ROAD

Lovell's Hall

3

African Violet Centre

A17

Primrose Farm

Kenwick Farm

19

A17

Balsamfield House

WHITECROSS LANE

STATION ROAD

2

Old Hall

MOAT ROAD

Experimental Husbandry Farm

HAY GREEN LANE

Grove Farm

SHEPHERDSGATE ROAD

Hay Green

CHURCH ROAD

Meadow Farm

BULLOCK ROAD

1

GLEBE EST

Feale Abbey

Church Farm

Tilney All Saints

JANKIN LA

18

54 A 55 B C 56 D E F

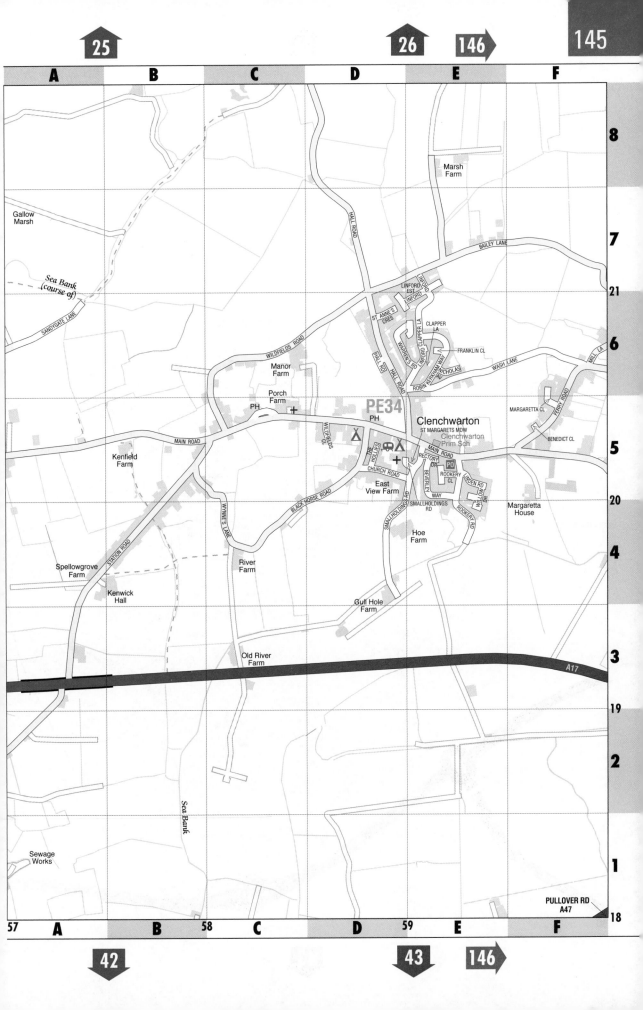

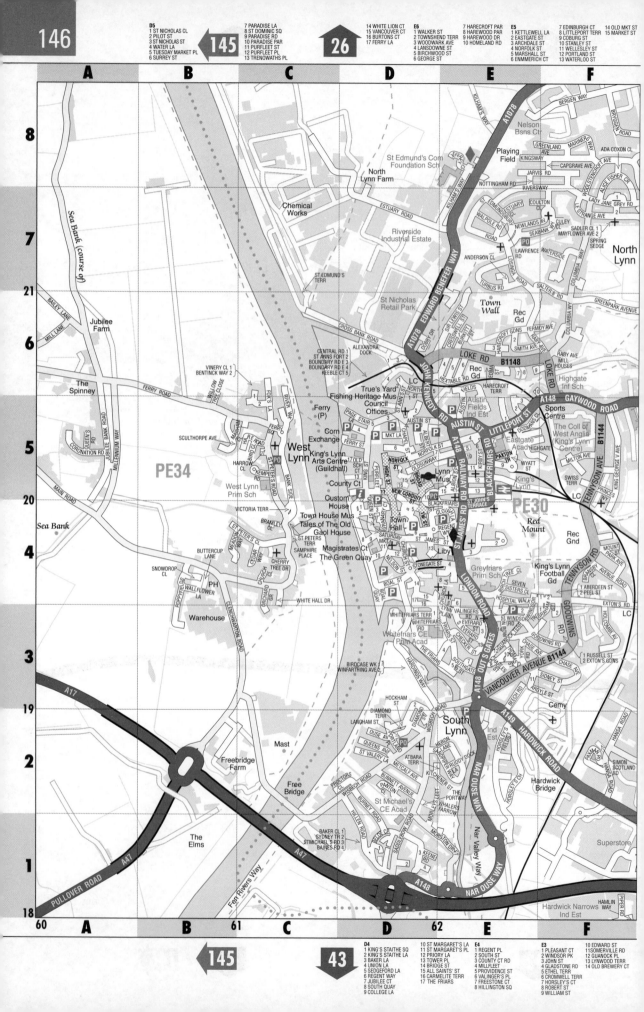

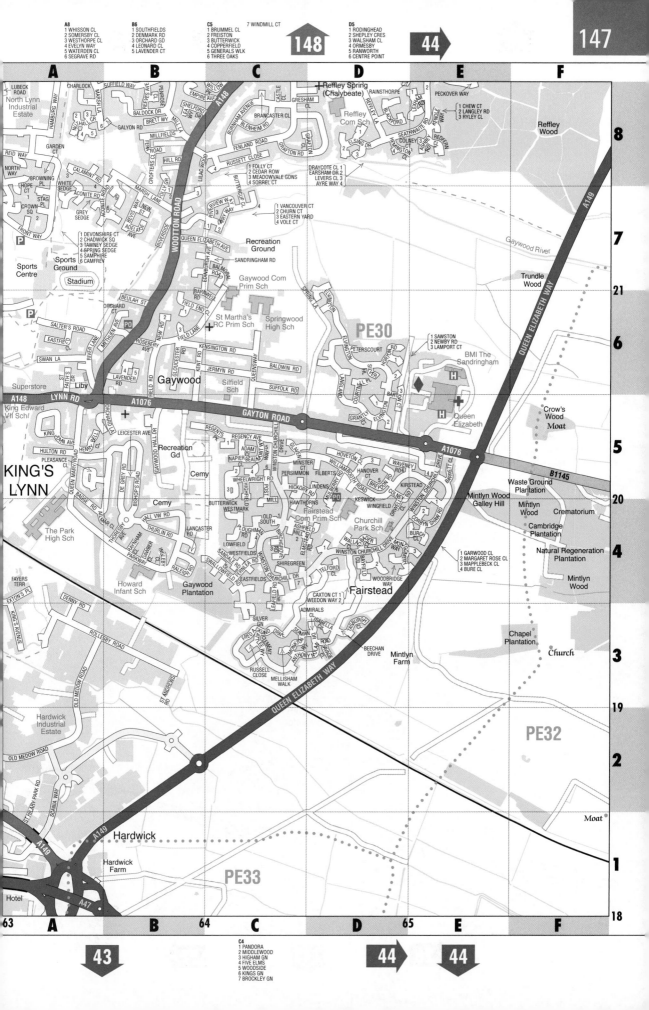

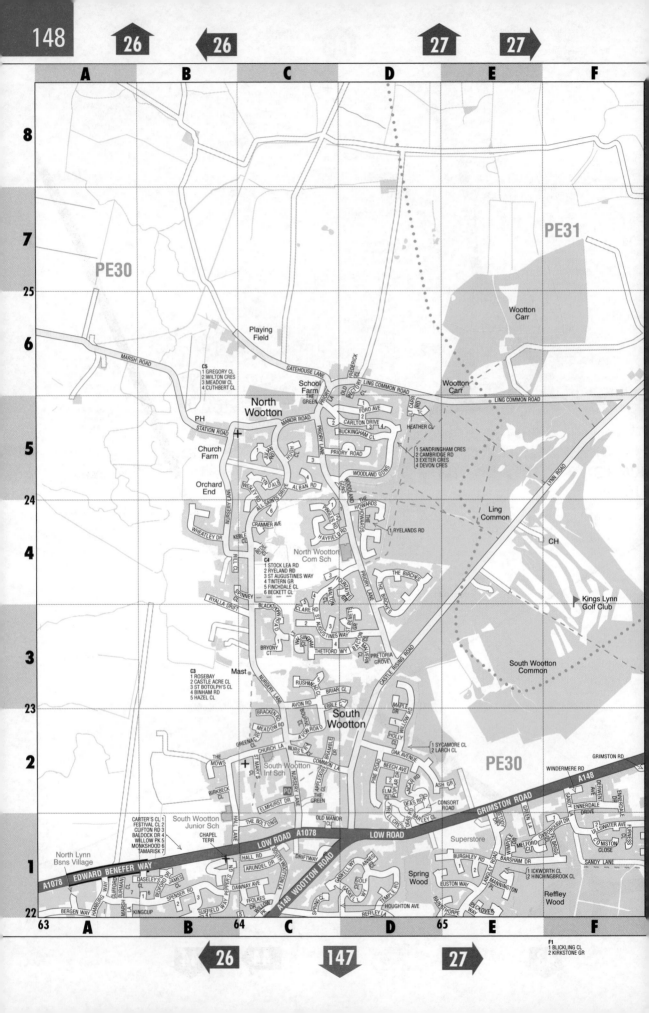

A   B   C   D   E   F

8

PE31

7

PE30

25

Wootton
Carr

6

MARSH ROAD

Playing
Field

GATEHOUSE LANE

C5
1 GREGORY CL
2 WILTON CRES
3 MEADOW CL
4 CUTHBERT CL

School Farm
THE GREEN

Ling Common Road

Wootton
Carr

LING COMMON ROAD

North
Wootton

PH

STATION ROAD

MANOR ROAD

PRIORY LANE

OLD RECTORY LA

FREDERICK

1 Ford Ave

CARLTON DRIVE

BUCKINGHAM CL

LT CARR RD

HEATHER CL

5

Church
Farm

HUGH CL

PRIORY ROAD

1 SANDRINGHAM CRES
2 CAMBRIDGE RD
3 EXETER CRES
4 DEVON CRES

Orchard
End

NURSERY LANE

WESLEY TER

TYNDALE

ALBAN RD

ALL SAINTS DRIVE

WOODLAND GDNS

WOODLAND
GDNS

THE HOWARDS

Ling
Common

CH

24

WHEATLEY DR

KEBLE CL

CRANMER AVE

PINKLES RD

HAYFIELD RD

THE HOWARDS

1 RYELANDS RD

RILL CL

BEN CL

C4
1 STOCK LEA RD
2 RYELAND RD
3 ST AUGUSTINES WAY
4 TINTERN GR
5 FINCHDALE CL
6 BECKETT CL

North Wootton
Com Sch

THE BIRCHES

Kings Lynn
Golf Club

4

SPINNEY CL

RYALLA DRIFT

BLACKTHORN

OLD SINGHAM CL

CLARE RD

WALTON DR

FOUNTAIN DR

ST AUGUSTINES WAY

ST RHETS GR

BACTON CL

MALVERN

PRIORY LANE

THE BIRCHES

South Wootton
Common

BRYONY CT

THETFORD WY

PRETORIA
GROVE

3

C3
1 ROSEBAY
2 CASTLE ACRE CL
3 ST BOTOLPH'S CL
4 BINHAM RD
5 HAZEL CL

Mast

NURSERY LANE

RUSHMEAD

AVON RD

BRIAR CL

CASTLE RISING ROAD

MAPLE DR

WILLOW DR

1 SYCAMORE CL
2 LARCH CL

PE30

GRIMSTON RD

23

BRACKEN CL

MEADOW RD

GREENACRE CL

CHURCH LA

BOURNE RD

AVON ROAD

South
Wootton

HOLLY CL

OAK AVENUE

WINDERMERE RD

A148

2

THE MOWS

ST MARY'S

South Wootton
Inf Sch

NURS RD

COMMON LA

APPLEYARD

BRAMBLE CL

THE GREEN

BEECH AVE

PINE ROAD

ELM CL

POPLAR

VICAR RD

ASH GR

DEAS RD

CONSORT ROAD

GRIMSTON ROAD

GREEN LA

STODY

SANDY LA

ENNERDALE
DRIVE

ENNERDALE DR

BIRKBECK CL

CARTER'S CL 1
FESTIVAL CL 2
CLIFTON RD 3
BALDOCK DR 4
WILLOW PK 5
MONKSHOOD 6
TAMARISK 7

South Wootton
Junior Sch

CHAPEL
TERR

ELMHURST DR

PO

OLD MANOR CL

HALL LANE

THE BOLT ONS

BARLEY CL

CRES

Superstore

WIMPLE RD

MELFORD

OXBOROUGH

FELBRIGG

2 ULLSWATER AVE
CONISTON
CLOSE

FURNESS CL

LOW ROAD A1078

LOW ROAD

BURGHLEY RD

BARSHAM DR

LANGLEY ROAD

MANNINGTON PL

SANDY LANE

North Lynn
Bsns Village

A1078   EDWARD BENEFER WAY

HALL RD

ARUNDEL DR

DAWNAY AVE

DRIFTWAY

A148 WOOTTON ROAD

SOUTH WOOTTON LA

TEMPLE RD

GASKELL WY

ANNES CL

GOLF CL

Spring
Wood

EUSTON WAY

1 ICKWORTH CL
2 HINCHINGBROOK CL

Reffley
Wood

1

HAMBURG WAY

CLIFFORD

BURMAN CL

MARSH LA

BEDFORD RD

JAMES CL

SPENSER RD

FFOLKES DR

DAWNAY AVE

WILTON PK

SUFFIELD WY

PEPPERS GN

SPINK CL

GASKELL

REFFLEY LA

HOUGHTON AVE

RAINSTHORPE

BECKOVER WAY

22

63   BERGEN WAY   DASELEY'S   KINGCUP   64   65

A   B   C   D   E   F

F1
1 BLICKLING CL
2 KIRKSTONE GR

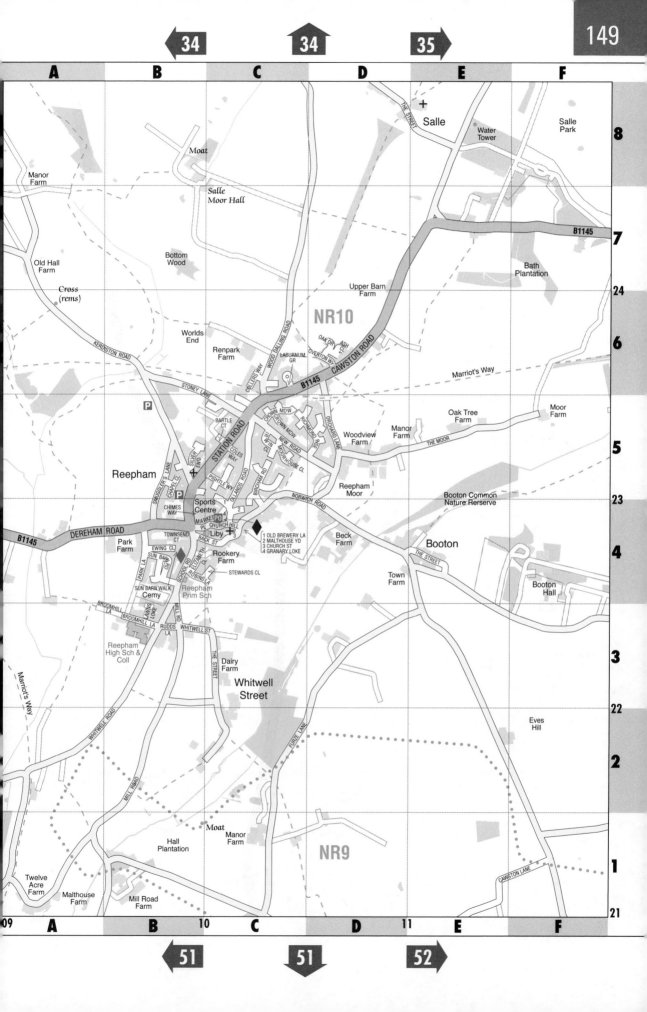

A   B   C   D   E   F

8
7
B1145
24
6
5
23
4
3
22
2
1
21

NR10

NR9

Salle
Water Tower
Salle Park
Bath Plantation

Manor Farm
Moat
Salle Moor Hall

Old Hall Farm
Bottom Wood
Upper Barn Farm

Cross (rems)

Worlds End
Renpark Farm

KERDISTON ROAD
STONEY LANE

Reepham

DEREHAM ROAD
B1145

Park Farm

Sports Centre
Liby

Rookery Farm
STEWARDS CL

Reepham Prim Sch
Cemy

Reepham High Sch & Coll

Whitwell Street

Dairy Farm

Marriot's Way
Twelve Acre Farm
Malthouse Farm
Mill Road Farm

Hall Plantation
Moat
Manor Farm

CAWSTON ROAD
Marriot's Way

Oak Tree Farm
Moor Farm

Manor Farm
THE MOOR

Woodview Farm

Reepham Moor

Booton Common Nature Reserve

Beck Farm
Booton
Booton Hall
Booton Hall

THE STREET
Town Farm

Eves Hill

CAWSTON LANE

1 OLD BREWERY LA
2 MALTHOUSE YD
3 CHURCH ST
4 GRANARY LOKE

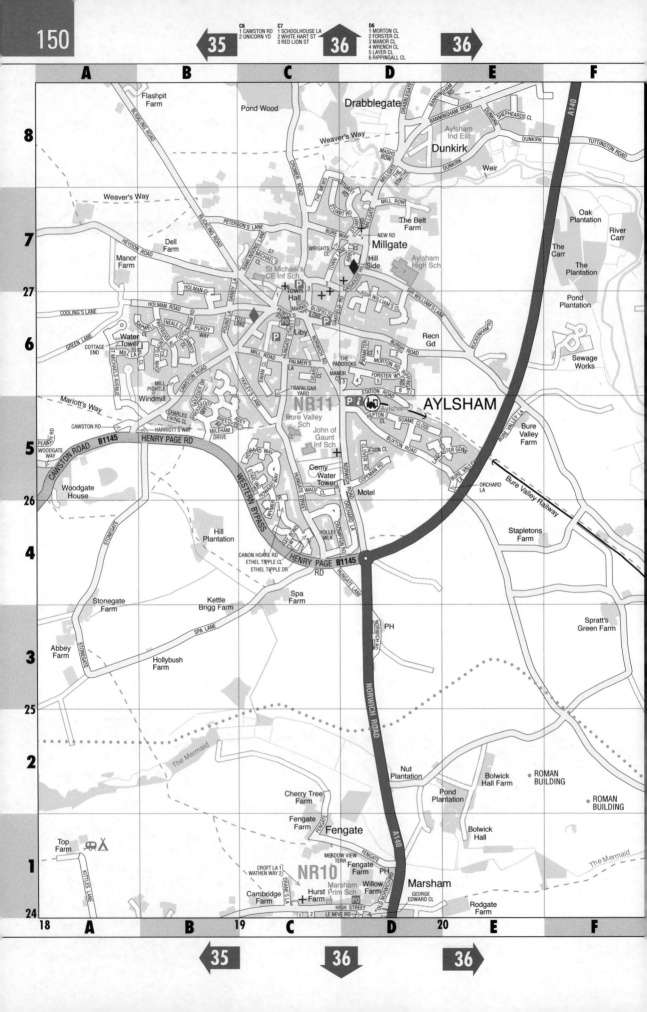

C6
1 CAWSTON RD
2 UNICORN YD

C7
1 SCHOOLHOUSE LA
2 WHITE HART ST
3 RED LION ST

D6
1 MORTON CL
2 FORSTER CL
3 MANOR CL
4 WRENCH CL
5 LAYER CL
6 RIPPINGALL CL

35
36
36

Flashpit Farm
Pond Wood
Drabblegate
Weaver's Way
Dunkirk
Banningham Road
Aylsham Ind Est
Dunkirk
Shepheards Cl
Dunkirk
Weir
A140
Oak Plantation
River Carr

Weaver's Way
Dell Farm
Heydon Road
Blickling Road
Peterson's Lane
The Mews
Stuart Rd
Mill Row
Millgate
Mill Row
The Belt Farm
The Carr
The Plantation

Manor Farm
Rawlinson's Lane
Wrights Cl
Bure Way
New Rd
Millgate
Aylsham High Sch
Pond Plantation

Codling's Lane
St Michael's CE Inf Sch
Holman Cl
Town Hall
Hill Side
Sir William's Cl
Sir William's Lane
Recn Gd
Burgh Road

Green Lane
Cottage End
Water Tower
Holman Road
Neale Cl
Purdy Way
Foxs Luke
Liby
Blofields Loke
The Paddocks
Morton Rd
Forster Wy
Rippingall
Buckenham

Windmill
Mill Pightle
Cawston Road
Mill Road
Swan La
Palmer's La
Sears
Manor Cl
Station Road
Sewage Works

Mariott's Way
Charles Ewing Cl
Cawston Rd
Harriott's Way
Mileham Drive
Yaxley's Lane
Trafalgar Yard
Bure Valley Sch
NR11
Aylsham
AYLSHAM
Bure Valley

Peaby Woodgate Way
Cawston Road
B1145
Henry Page Rd
Howard Way
John of Gaunt Inf Sch
Repton Cl
Soame Close
Bure Valley La
Bure Valley Farm

Woodgate House
Stonegate
Western Bypass
Cerny Water Tower
Norwich
Buxton Road
Lancaster Gdns
Orchard La

Hill Plantation
Wade Cl
Motel
Clover Rd
Copeman Rd
Bure Valley Railway
Stapletons Farm

Stonegate Farm
Kettle Brigg Farm
Canon Hoare Rd
Ethel Tipple Cl
Ethel Tipple Dr
Henry Page
B1145
RD
Hungate Lane
Spratt's Green Farm

Abbey Farm
Stonegate
Spa Lane
Spa Farm
Norwich Rd
PH

Hollybush Farm

The Mermaid
Nut Plantation
Bolwick Hall Farm
ROMAN BUILDING
ROMAN BUILDING

Cherry Tree Farm
Pond Plantation
Bolwick Hall

Fengate Farm
Fengate
A140
The Mermaid

Top Farm
Kittles Lane
Meadow View Terr
Fengate Farm
PH
Marsham

NR10
Croft La
Wathen Way
Crane's La
Hurst Farm
Marsham Prim Sch
Willow Farm
Old Norwich Rd
George Edward Cl
Rodgate Farm

Cambridge Farm
High Street
Le Neve Rd

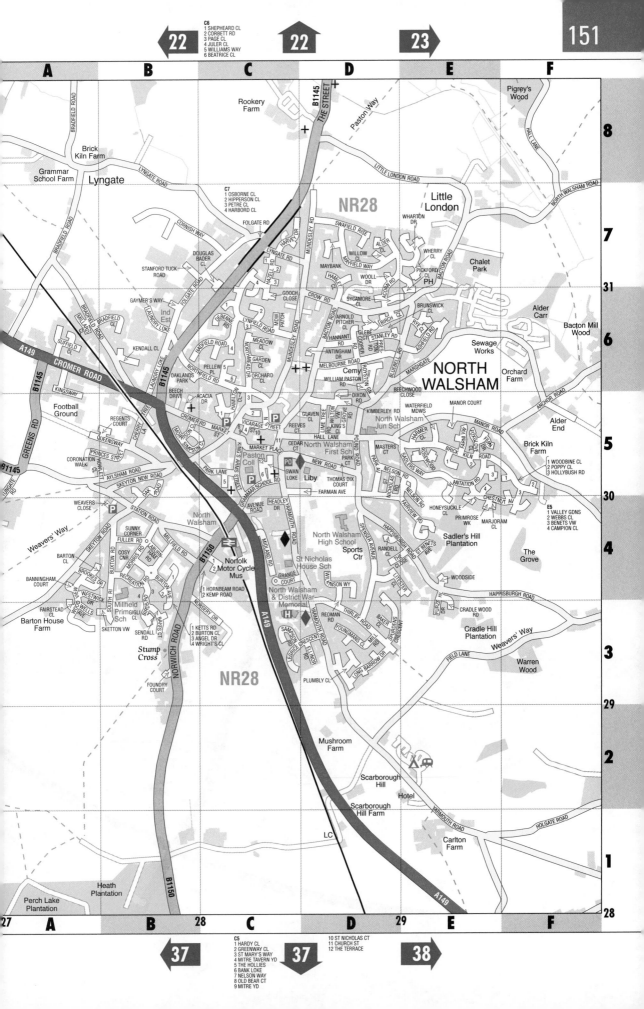

59 **59**

WISBECH

PE13

PE14

PE13

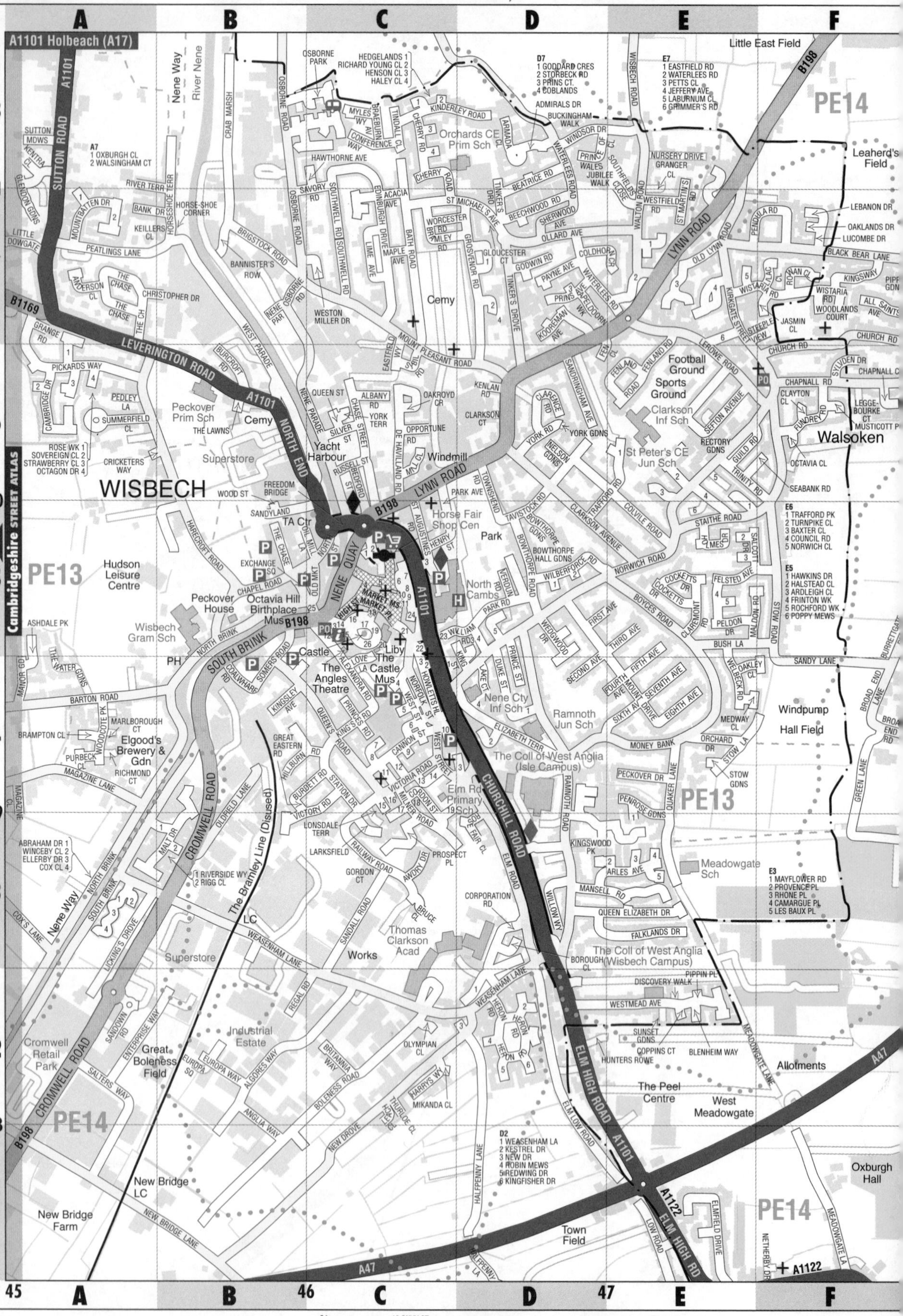

PE14

PE14

59 **59**

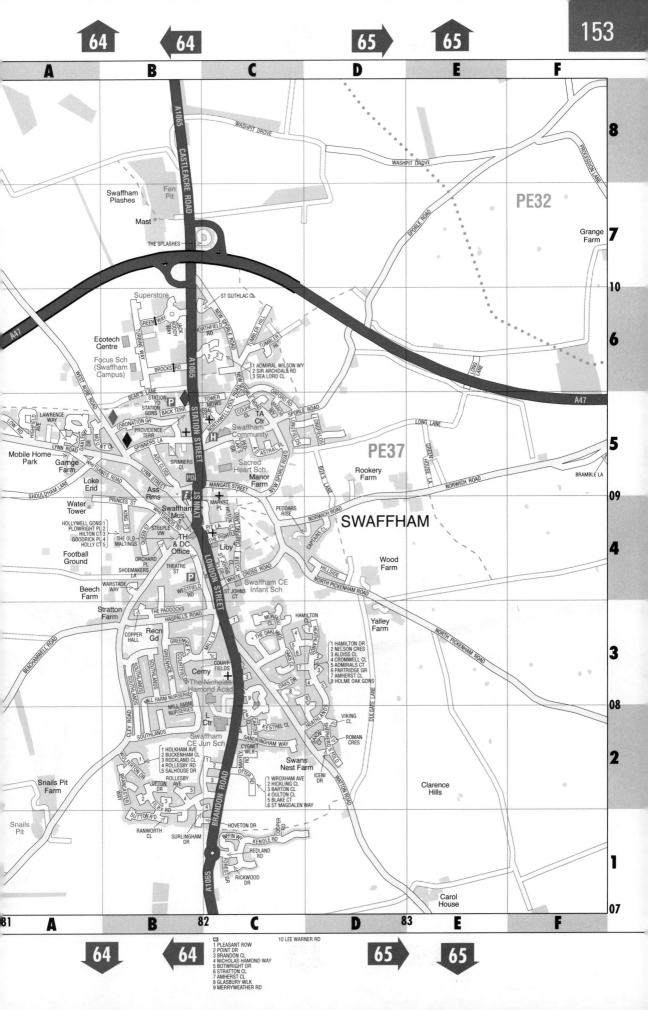

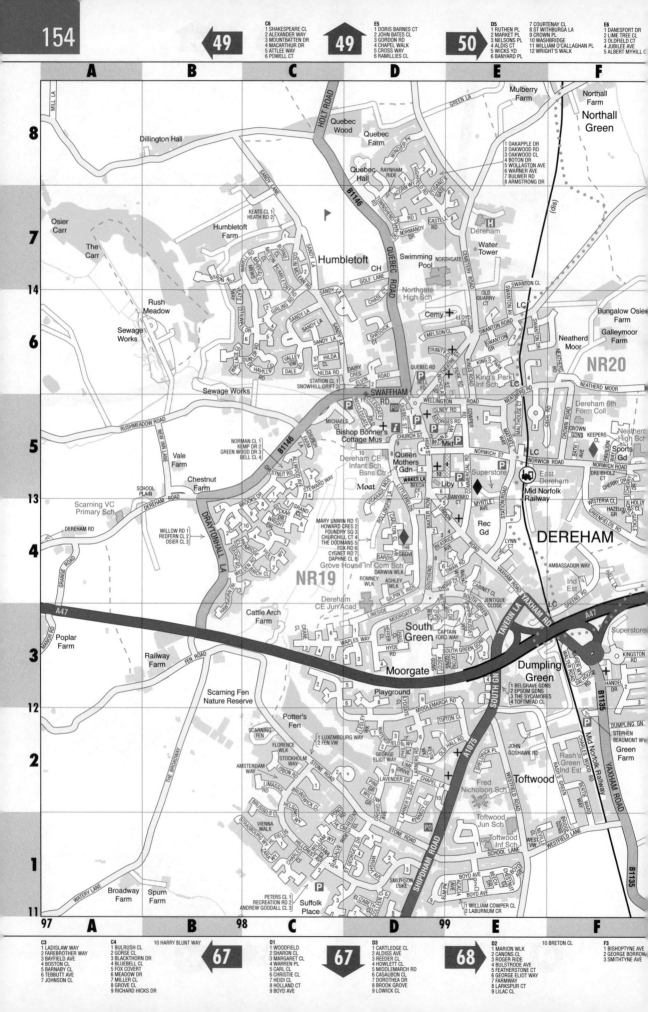

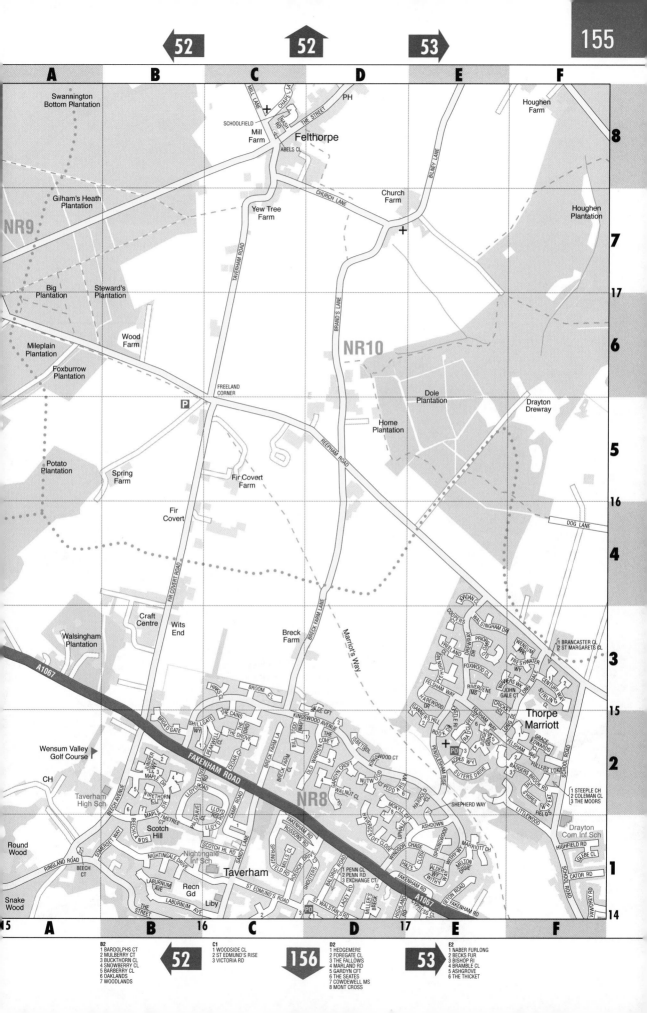

A B C D E F

8
7
17
6
5
16
4
3
15
2
1
14

Swannington Bottom Plantation

Gilham's Heath Plantation

NR9

Big Plantation

Steward's Plantation

Mileplain Plantation

Foxburrow Plantation

Wood Farm

Potato Plantation

Spring Farm

Walsingham Plantation

Craft Centre

Wits End

A1067

Wensum Valley Golf Course

CH

Taverham High Sch

Round Wood

Snake Wood

Ringland Road

BEECH CT

Scotch Hill

Nightingale Inf Sch

Nightingale Drive

Taverham

Recn Gd

Liby

THE STREET

LABURNUM AVE

FAKENHAM ROAD

NR8

FIR COVERT ROAD

TAVERHAM ROAD

Freeland Corner

Fir Covert Farm

Fir Covert

Breck Farm

Marriot's Way

Felthorpe

Mill Farm

SCHOOLFIELD

ABELS CL

Yew Tree Farm

CHURCH LANE

BRAND'S LANE

REEPHAM ROAD

Home Plantation

NR10

Church Farm

BILNEY LANE

Houghen Farm

Houghen Plantation

Dole Plantation

Drayton Drewray

DOG LANE

Thorpe Marriott

1 BRANCASTER CL
2 ST MARGARETS CL

1 STEEPLE CH
2 COLEMAN CL
3 THE MOORS

Drayton Com Inf Sch

HIGHFIELD RD

GLEBE CL

CATOR RD

VAWDREY RD

SCHOOL ROAD

A1067

FAKENHAM RD

SHEPHERD WAY

SUTERS DRIVE

PENDLESHAM RISE

FELSHAM WAY

PO

MALSINGHAM DR

COOPERS CL

FREELAND DREWRAY

PO

B2
1 BARDOLPHS CT
2 MULBERRY CT
3 BUCKTHORN CL
4 SNOWBERRY CL
5 BARBERRY CL
6 OAKLANDS
7 WOODLANDS

C1
1 WOODSIDE CL
2 ST EDMUND'S RISE
3 VICTORIA RD

D2
1 HEDGEMERE
2 FOREGATE CL
3 THE FALLOWS
4 MARLAND RD
5 GARDYN CFT
6 THE SEATES
7 COWDEWELL MS
8 MONT CROSS

E2
1 NABER FURLONG
2 BECKS FUR
3 BISHOP RI
4 BRAMBLE CL
5 ASHGROVE
6 THE THICKET

52 156 53

A B C D E F

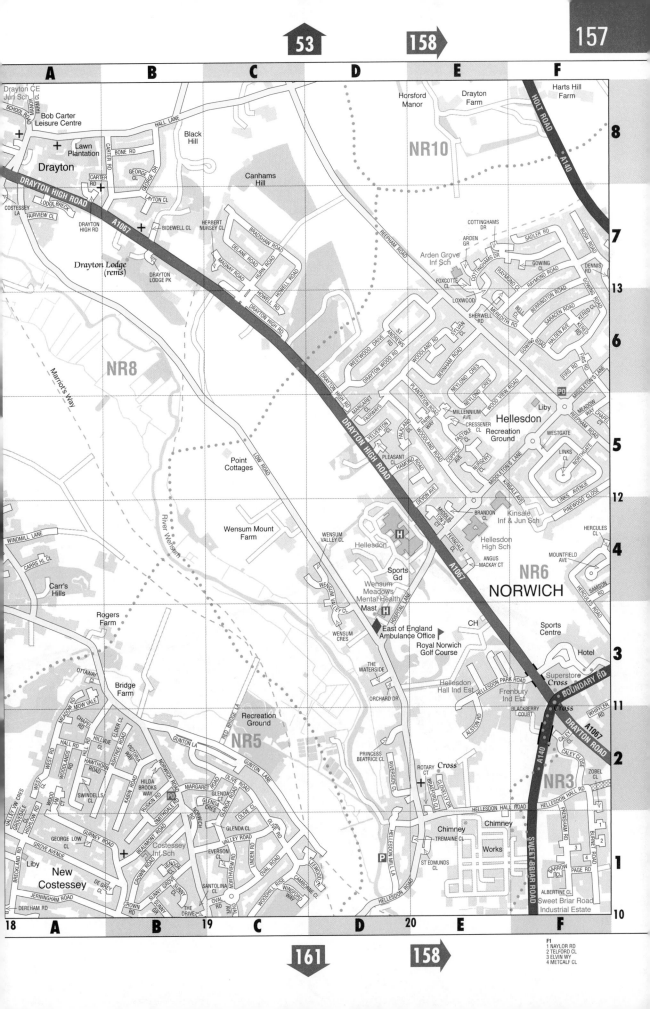

157
53

157
162

D5
1 PENNYROYAL
2 BRYONY CL
3 WOODRUFF CL
4 SOUTHERWOOD
5 ROSEBAY CL
6 WHITETHORN CL

A   B   C   D   E   F

8

7

13

6

5

12

4

3

11

2

1

10

Map labels:

NR10   NR12   NR6   NR3

Norwich International Airport

Airport Industrial Estate

Hurricane Way

Lodge Farm

Cemy

Old Catton

Deer Park

Mile Cross

New Sprowston

New Catton

Waterloo Park

Upper Hellesdon

Fiddle Plantation

St Christophers Sch

Old Catton Hall

Old Catton Hall School

Old Catton CE Jun Sch

Firside Jun Sch

Sports Ground

Rhombus Bsns Park

Heather Ave Inf Sch

Mayfield Avenue

Ashbourne Ind Est

Catton Grove Prim Sch

Garrick Green Inf Sch

Lodge Farm Inf Sch

White Woman La Sch

Brayfield Way

Mill Hill

Sewell Park Acad

Hill Farm

Angel Rd Inf Sch

Angel Road Jun Sch

Mile Cross Mid Sch

Mile Cross Prim Sch

Chimney

Hotel

Holt Rd   Cromer Road   Boundary Road   Drayton Road   Mile Cross Road   Aylsham Road   Mile Cross Lane   Chartwell Road   Constitution Hill   Sprowston Road   Magdalen Rd

A140   A1067   A1024   A1042   A1151   B1150

Blackburn Rd 1
Sunderland Cl 2
Heyford Rd 3
Whitley Cl 4
Embry Cl 5
Embry Cres 6

1 Tansy Cl
2 Blackthorn Cl
3 Dogwood Rd
4 Spindle Rd

Beeches Cl 1
Lucerne Cl 2
Grange Cl 3
St George Loke 4

C1
1 SHORNCLIFFE CL
2 AVONMOUTH RD
3 BYFIELD CT
4 AIREDALE CT
5 ROPEMAKERS ROW
6 WATERLOO PK CL
7 BOOT BINDERS RD
8 FINISHERS RD
9 LIME KILN MEWS

E1
1 NICHOLAS CT
2 MAURICE RAES CL

F1
1 JOHN STEPHENSON CT
2 AMHIRST CL
3 TOLWIN WK

Postle Mews 1
Darlington Mews 2

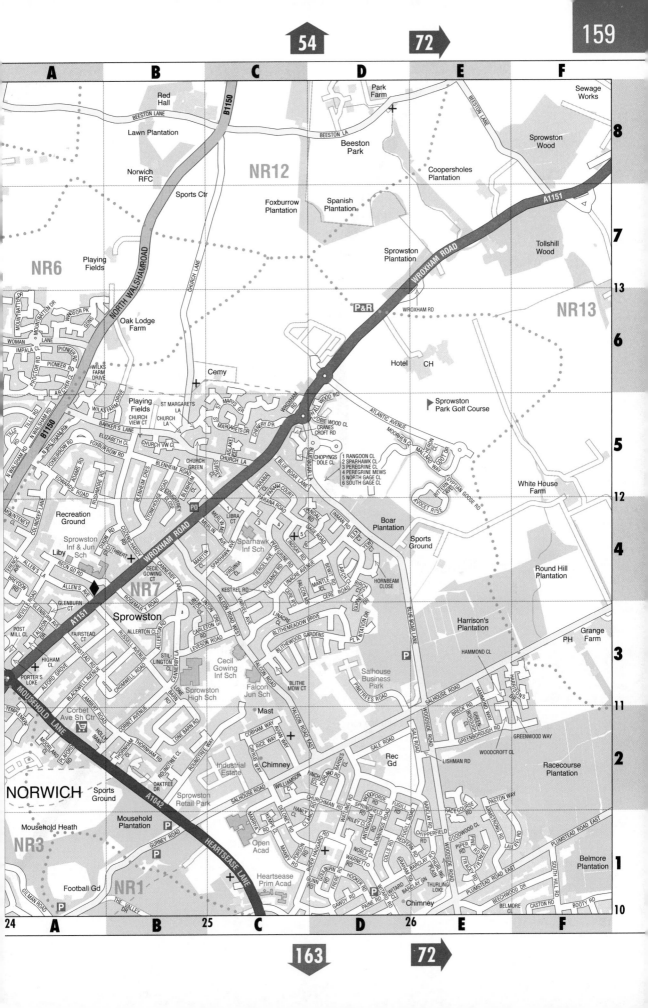

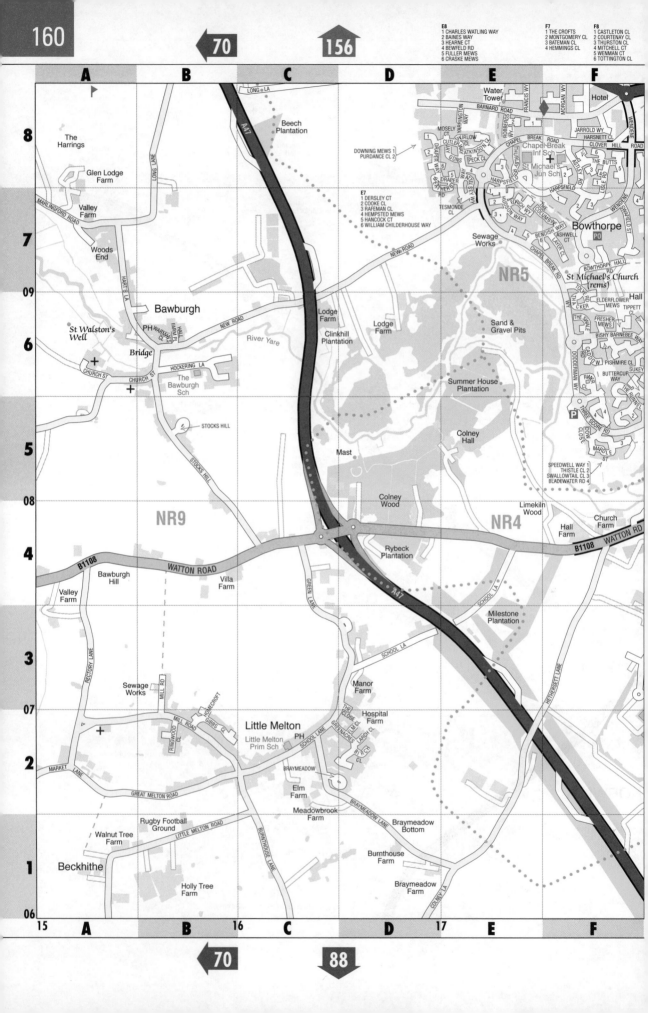

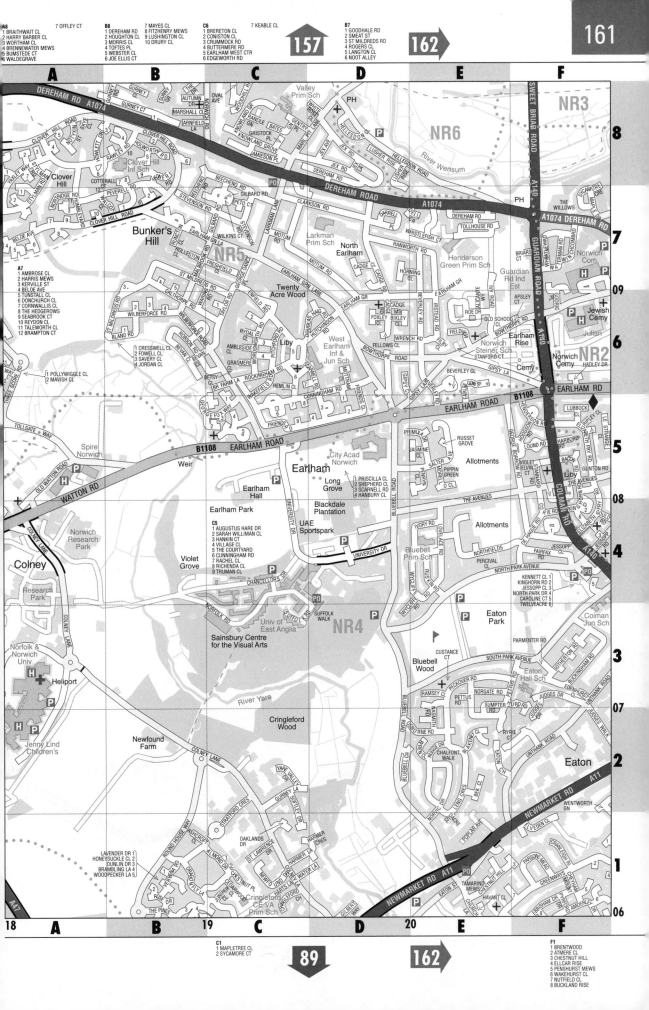

A8
1 BRAITHWAIT CL
2 HARRY BARBER CL
3 WORTHAM CL
4 BRENNEWATER MEWS
5 BUMSTEDE CT
6 WALDEGRAVE
7 OFFLEY CT

B8
1 DEREHAM RD
2 HOUGHTON CL
3 MORRIS CL
4 TOFTES PL
5 WEBSTER CL
6 JOE ELLIS CT
7 MAYES CL
8 FITZHENRY MEWS
9 LUSHINGTON CL
10 DRURY CL

C6
1 BRERETON CL
2 CONISTON CL
3 CRUMMOCK RD
4 BUTTERMERE RD
5 EARLHAM WEST CTR
6 EDGEWORTH RD
7 KEABLE CL

B7
1 GOODHALE RD
2 SMEAT ST
3 ST MILDREDS RD
4 CADGE RD
5 LANGTON CL
6 NOOT ALLEY

A7
1 AMBROSE CL
2 HARRIS MEWS
3 KERVILLE ST
4 BELOE AVE
5 TUNSTALL CL
6 DORNCHURCH CL
7 CORNWALLIS CL
8 THE HEDGEROWS
9 SEABROOK CT
10 REYDON CL
11 TALEWORTH CL
12 BRAMPTON CT

C5
1 AUGUSTUS HARE DR
2 SARAH WILLIMAN CL
3 HANKIN CT
4 VILLAGE CL
5 THE COURTYARD
6 CUNNINGHAM RD
7 RACHEL CL
8 RICHENDA CL
9 TRUMAN CL

C1
1 MAPLETREE CL
2 SYCAMORE CT

F1
1 BRENTWOOD
2 ATMERE CL
3 CHESTNUT HILL
4 ELLCAR RISE
5 PENSHURST MEWS
6 WAKEHURST CL
7 NUTFIELD CL
8 BUCKLAND RISE

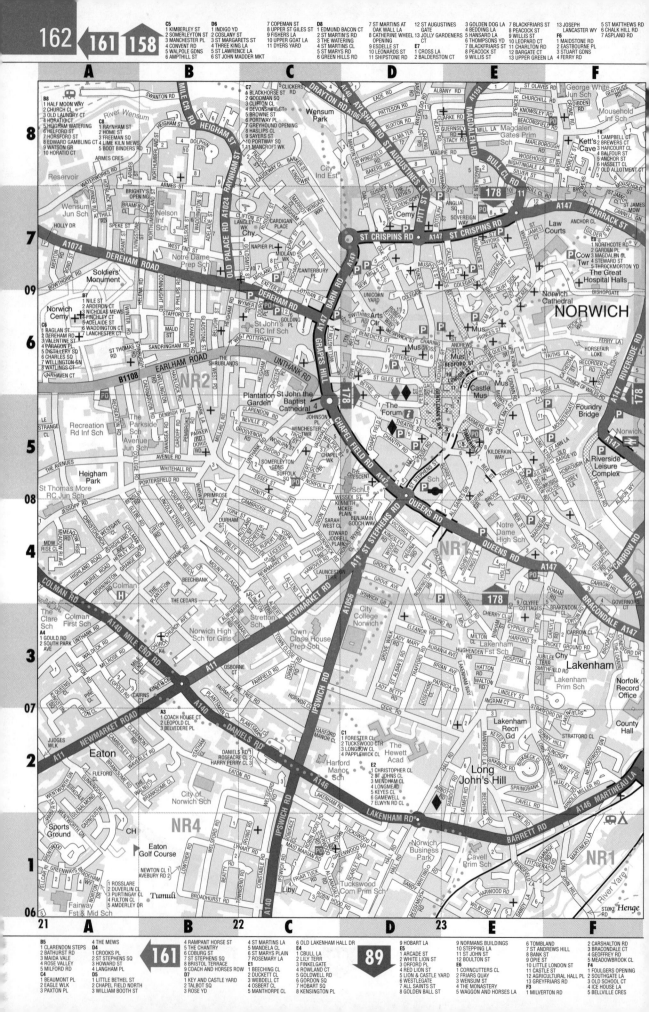

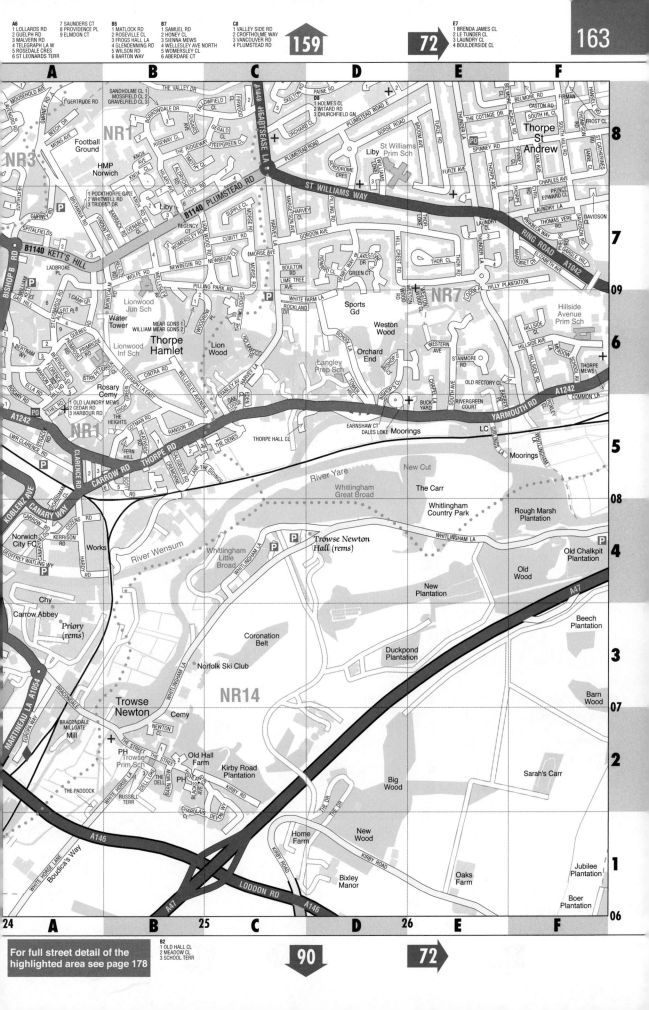

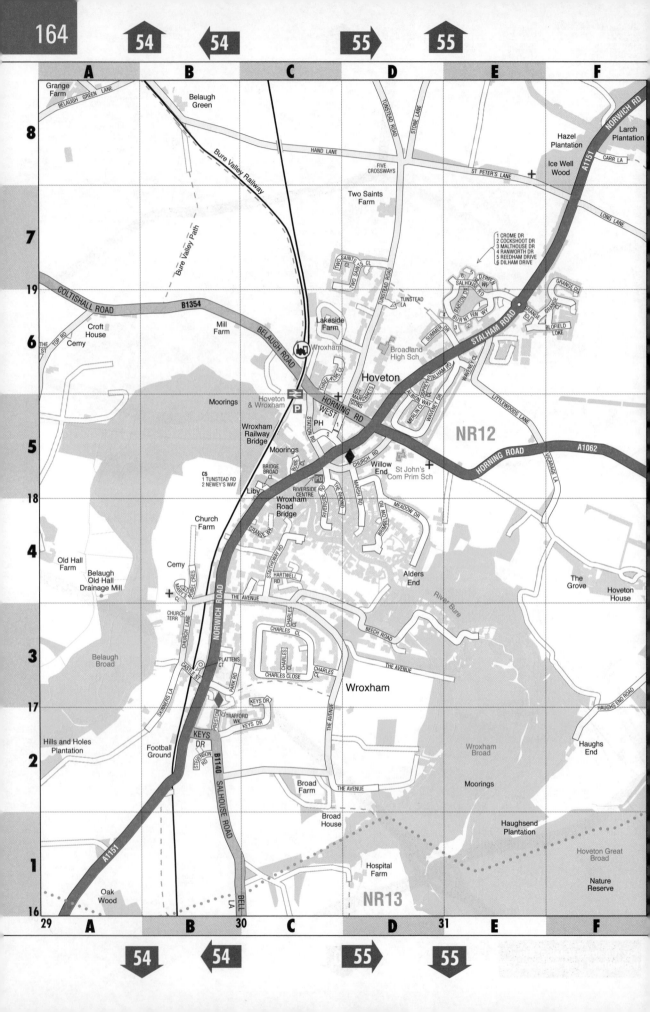

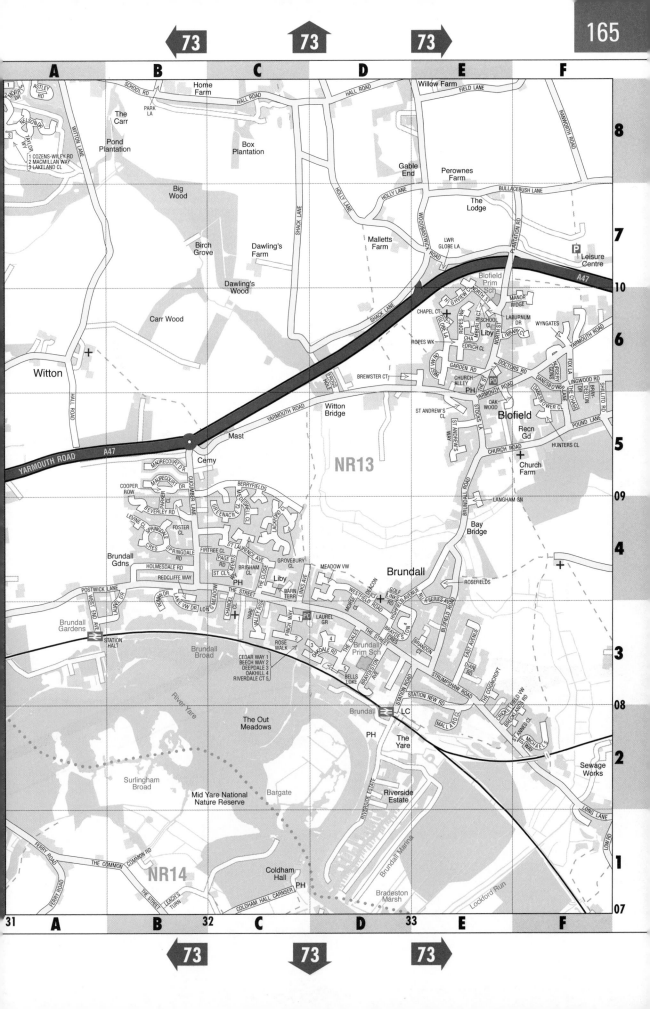

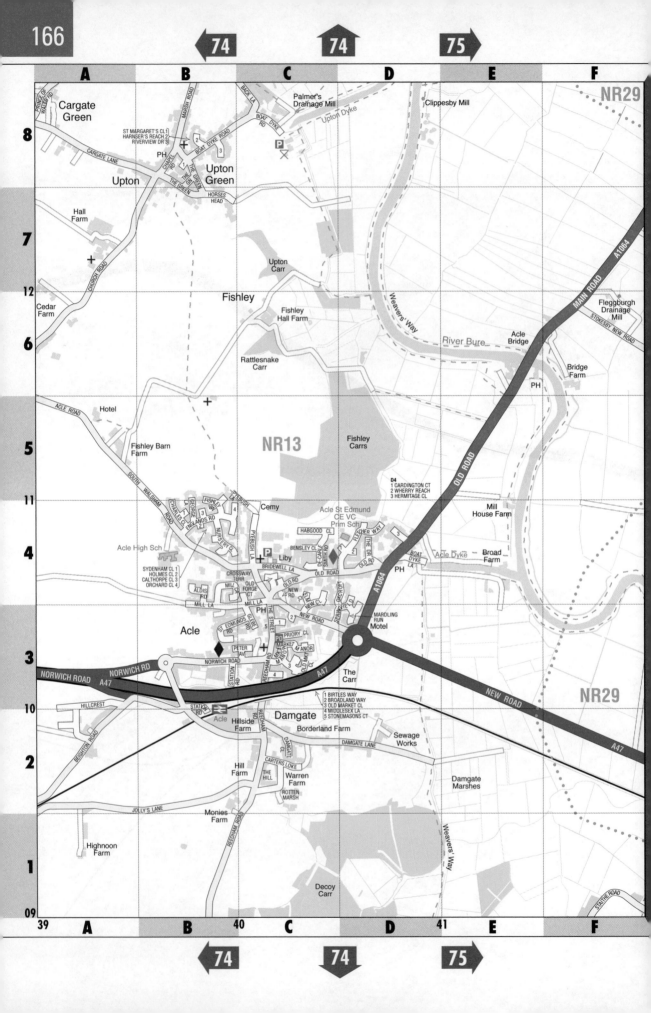

NR29

A   B   C   D   E   F

Cargate Green

Prince of Wales Rd

St Margaret's Cl 1
Harnser's Reach 2
Riverview Dr 3

Palmer's Drainage Mill

Clippesby Mill

8

Boat Dyke Rd   Back La

Upton

PH

Upton Green

Cargate Lane

Chapel Rd   The Grn   The Green

Horses Head

P

Upton Dyke

Hall Farm

7

Church Road

Upton Carr

A1064

Main Road

12

Cedar Farm

Fishley

Fishley Hall Farm

Weavers' Way

River Bure

Acle Bridge

Fleggburgh Drainage Mill

Stokesby New Road

6

Rattlesnake Carr

PH

Bridge Farm

Acle Road

Hotel

NR13

Fishley Carrs

Old Road

5

Fishley Barn Farm

South Walsham Road

Pyebush La

Cemy

Acle St Edmund CE VC Prim Sch

D4
1 CARDINGTON CT
2 WHERRY REACH
3 HERMITAGE CL

Mill House Farm

11

Charles Cl   George La   Fishley Way   Englands Rd

Nursery Cl

Pyebush La

Habgood Cl

Bensley Cl

Fletcher Way   The Dr

Boat Dyke La

Acle Dyke

Broad Farm

4

Acle High Sch

Sydenham Cl 1
Holmes Cl 2
Calthorpe Cl 3
Orchard Cl 4

Crossway Terr

Mill Sch   Old Ct

P   Liby

Bridewell La

De Carle Smith Rd

Old Rd   Old Rd

Old Road

A1064

PH

Aldis Rd   Mill La

New Rd   Old Rd

New Cl

Schoolcroft

Mardling Run Motel

Acle

St Edmunds Rd   Glebe Rd   The Street   PH

Priory Cl

Market   Manor

New Road

3

Norwich Road

Peter Av

Reedham Rd

The Carr

New Road

NR29

Norwich Road   A47

Station Rd

1 BIRTLES WAY
2 BROADLAND WAY
3 OLD MARKET CL
4 MIDDLESEX LA
5 STONEMASONS CT

10

Hillcrest

Station Rd

Acle

Hillside Farm

Damgate

Borderland Farm

Sewage Works

Brighton Road

Hill Farm

Reedham Road

The Hill

Carters Loke

Warren Farm

Rotten Marsh

Damgate Cl

Damgate Lane

Damgate Marshes

2

Jolly's Lane

Monies Farm

Weavers' Way

1

Highnoon Farm

Decoy Carr

A47

Stairie Road

09

39   A   40   B   C   41   D   E   F

58
58
58

B7
1 BUTTERMERE
2 MEDESWELL
3 HAYCROFT
4 FALLOWFIELD
5 RYELANDS
6 CLOVERLAND DR

7 SWEETACRES

A8
1 TAYLORS LOKE
2 PEDLARS CFT
3 MEADOW CL
4 HALL CL

A **B** **C** **D** **E** **F**

LONG BEACH
ESTATE

KINGS LOKE

FOUR ACRES
ESTATE
Dunes
End

THE GLEBE

8

Holiday
Village

IRB
Station

SEA VW RD

7

Hemsby

THE PADDOCK
THE PASTURES
PARKLAND
BEECHWOOD
MEADOW RI 3
EST
NORTH ROAD

Hemsby
Prim
Sch

CLYDESDALE DR

WINTERTON RD

KINGS LOKE

WATERS LANE

HALL ROAD

LEXINGTON CL
THE AVENUE

ST MARY'S
CL
THE STREET
SCHOOL RD
NORTH RD

VINE
CL
THE CLOSE
THE CLOSE
HOLMESTEAD GDNS

Holiday
Village

Chalet
Park

BEACH ROAD

THE CRESCENT
ST THOMAS S

GARDEN
RD
SOUTH RD
ST MARY'S RD
ST MARK'S RD

PH

Newport

17

EASTERLEY WAY

YARMOUTH ROAD

BARLEYCROFT
KINGS WAY

FERRIER
CT

CHURCH
FARM CR

BACK MARKET LANE

Newport
Farm

NEWPORT ROAD

ST MARK'S RD
FAKES RD
FAKES ROAD

6

Cross
(rems)

ORMESBY ROAD

YARMOUTH ROAD

Sundowner
Golf Course

Swimming
Pool

NR29

5

SEAGULL
RD

THE ESPLANADE

TERN RD

16

Carr
Farm

NORTH ROAD

Dowe Hill
Farm

Dowe
Hill

SANNE
RD
CALIFORNIA
AVENUE
PENGUIN RD
BEACH DRIVE

CLOSE
NIGH
TINGALE

THE PROMENADE

Sand
Cliffs

4

BECK AVE
DECOY ROAD

Mill
Farm

THOROUGHFARE LANE

Scratby
Hall

HEATHER
AVE

BEACH ROAD

Scratby

LITTLE SCRATBY
CRES
SCROBY CT
BEACH

WATER MDW CL

CHIMNEY SPRINGS

ORCHARD
CT

Ormesby
St Margaret

Scratby
Hall Farm

LADY
HAMILTON
LA

PO

SCROBY ROAD

ROTTENSTONE LA

SCRATBY
CRES
ROTTENSTONE LA

3

SPRUCE AVENUE
PRIVATE ROAD
FIRS AVE
PINE CL
COKER CL

MALLVIEW
Ormesby
Village
Jun Sch

BARTON WY
HICKLING WAY

FRITTON
CL
COLDHAM
CL

Gables
Farm

California

Ormesby
Village
Inf Sch

DENE AVE
WEST
RD
APPLETON CL

RANWORTH DR

THURNE WAY

LEATHWAY
LEATHWAY

Recreation
Ground

CALIFORNIA CRES
CALIFORNIA

15

MANOR WY
PIPPIN CL 3
OLD RSM
CHURCH
CLAYMORE GD
HILLSIDE CL

STATION ROAD

CALIFORNIA ROAD

CALIFORNIA
PH

2

PRIMROSE
CL
CROMER ROAD
PH
FILBY LANE
Old Hall
Farm
THE GREEN
STATION
RD

WAPPING

BRACECAMP CL
FOSTER CL
SNIPES
CL
ST
EDMONDS AVE

STATION ROAD

OLD COAST ROAD

California
Farm

Manship's
Plantation

Filby
Wood

Ormesby
Hall

Willow
Farm

YARMOUTH ROAD

Boarded
Barn Farm

FILBY LANE

A149

NOVA SCOTIA ROAD

Chapman's
Plantation

PH
Hotel

CAISTER
BY-PASS
ORMESBY
RD
YARMOUTH
RD

NR30

Pigeon
Wood

14

49 **A** **B** **50** **C** **D** **51** **E** **F**

A2
1 MANORFIELD CL
2 SPRUCE AVE
3 WORCESTER CL
4 CROSSWAYS

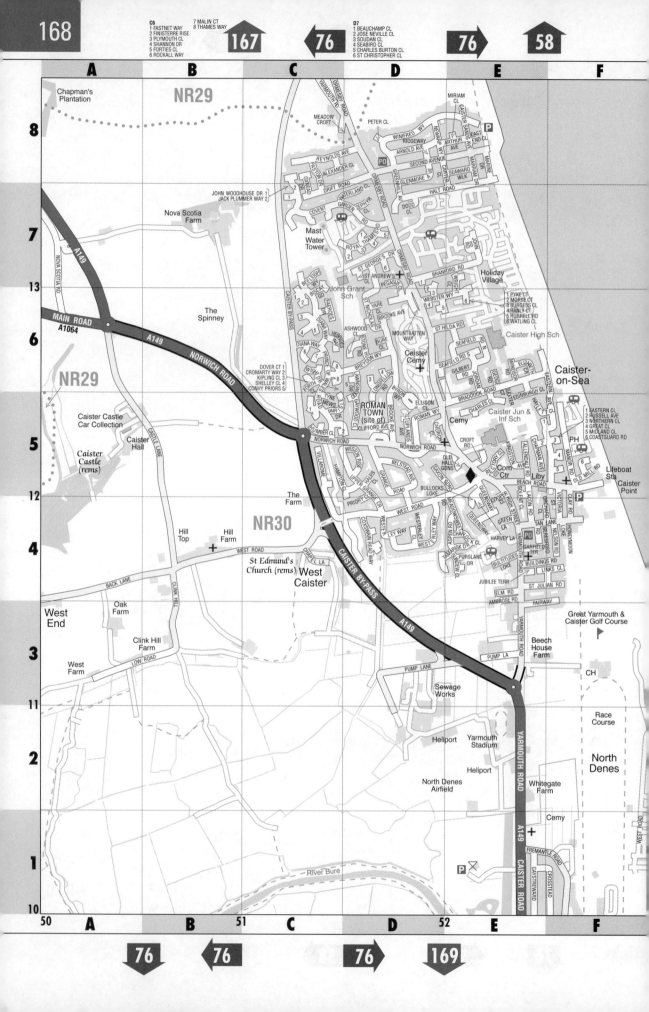

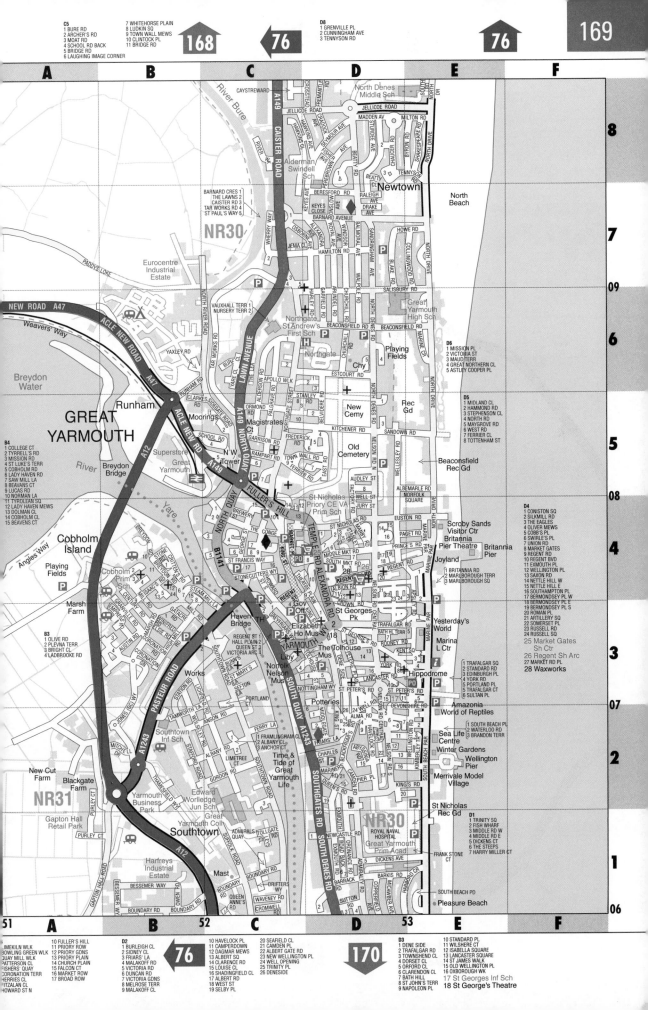

C5
1 BURE RD
2 ARCHER'S RD
3 MOAT RD
4 SCHOOL RD BACK
5 BRIDGE RD
6 LAUGHING IMAGE CORNER
7 WHITEHORSE PLAIN
8 LUDKIN SQ
9 TOWN WALL MEWS
10 CLINTOCK PL
11 BRIDGE RD

D8
1 GRENVILLE PL
2 CUNNINGHAM AVE
3 TENNYSON RD

BARNARD CRES 1
THE LAWNS 2
CAISTER RD 3
TAR WORKS RD 4
ST PAUL'S WAY 5

NR30

New Road A47

ACLE NEW ROAD

Eurocentre Industrial Estate

Breydon Water

GREAT YARMOUTH

Runham

B4
1 COLLEGE CT
2 TYRRELL'S RD
3 MISSION RD
4 ST LUKE'S TERR
5 COBHOLM RD
6 LADY HAVEN RD
7 SAW MILL LA
8 BEAVANS CT
9 LUCAS RD
10 NORMAN LA
11 TYROLEAN SQ
12 LADY HAVEN MEWS
13 DOLMAN CL
14 COBHOLM CL
15 BEAVANS CT

D6
1 MISSION PL
2 VICTORIA ST
3 MAUD TERR
4 GREAT NORTHERN CL
5 ASTLEY COOPER PL

D5
1 MIDLAND CL
2 HAMMOND RD
3 STEPHENSON CL
4 NORTH RD
5 MAYGROVE RD
6 WEST RD
7 FERRIER CL
8 TOTTENHAM ST

Cobholm Island

Marsh Farm

B3
1 OLIVE RD
2 PLEVNA TERR
3 BRIGHT CL
4 LADBROOKE RD

D4
1 CONISTON SQ
2 SILKMILL RD
3 THE EAGLES
4 OLIVER MEWS
5 COBB'S PL
6 SWIRLE'S PL
7 UNION RD
8 MARKET GATES
9 REGENT BVD
10 EXMOUTH PL
11 WELLINGTON PL
12 SAXON RD
13 SAXON RD
14 NETTLE HILL W
15 NETTLE HILL E
16 SOUTHAMPTON PL
17 BERMONDSEY PL E
18 BERMONDSEY PL W
19 BERMONDSEY PL S
20 ROMAN PL
21 ARTILLERY SQ
22 SOMERSET PL
23 RUSSELL RD
24 RUSSELL SQ
25 Market Gates Sh Ctr
26 Regent Sh Arc
27 MARKET RD PL
28 Waxworks

D1
1 TRINITY SQ
2 FISH WHARF
3 MIDDLE RD W
4 MIDDLE RD E
5 DICKENS CT
6 THE STEEPS
7 HARRY MILLER CT

Southtown

NR31

New Cut Farm

Gapton Hall Retail Park

Harfreys Industrial Estate

NR30

ROYAL NAVAL HOSPITAL
Great Yarmouth Prim Acad

South Beach PD
Pleasure Beach

LIMEKILN WLK
BOWLING GREEN WLK
QUAY MILL WLK
PATTERSON CL
FISHERS' QUAY
CORONATION TERR
TERRIES CL
FITZALAN CL
HOWARD ST N

10 FULLER'S HILL
11 PRIORY ROW
12 PRIORY GDNS
13 PRIORY PLAIN
14 CHURCH PLAIN
15 FALCON CT
16 MARKET ROW
17 BROAD ROW

D2
1 BURLEIGH CL
2 SIDNEY CL
3 FRIARS' LA
4 MALAKOFF RD
5 VICTORIA RD
6 DUNCAN RD
7 VICTORIA GDNS
8 MELROSE TERR
9 MALAKOFF CL

10 HAVELOCK PL
11 CAMPERDOWN
12 DAGMAR MEWS
13 ALBERT SQ
14 CLARENCE RD
15 LOUISE CL
16 SHADINGFIELD CL
17 ALBERT RD
18 WEST ST
19 SELBY PL

20 SEAFIELD CL
21 CAMDEN CL
22 ALBERT GATE RD
23 NEW WELLINGTON PL
24 WELL OPENING
25 TRINITY PL
26 DENESIDE

76

170

D3
1 DENE SIDE
2 TRAFALGAR RD
3 TOWNSHEND CL
4 DORSET CL
5 ORFORD CL
6 CLARENDON CL
7 BATH HILL
8 ST JOHN'S TERR
9 NAPOLEON PL

10 STANDARD PL
11 WILSHERE CT
12 ISABELLA SQUARE
13 LANCASTER RD
14 ST JAMES WALK
15 OLD WELLINGTON PL
16 OXBOROUGH WK
17 St Georges Inf Sch
18 St George's Theatre

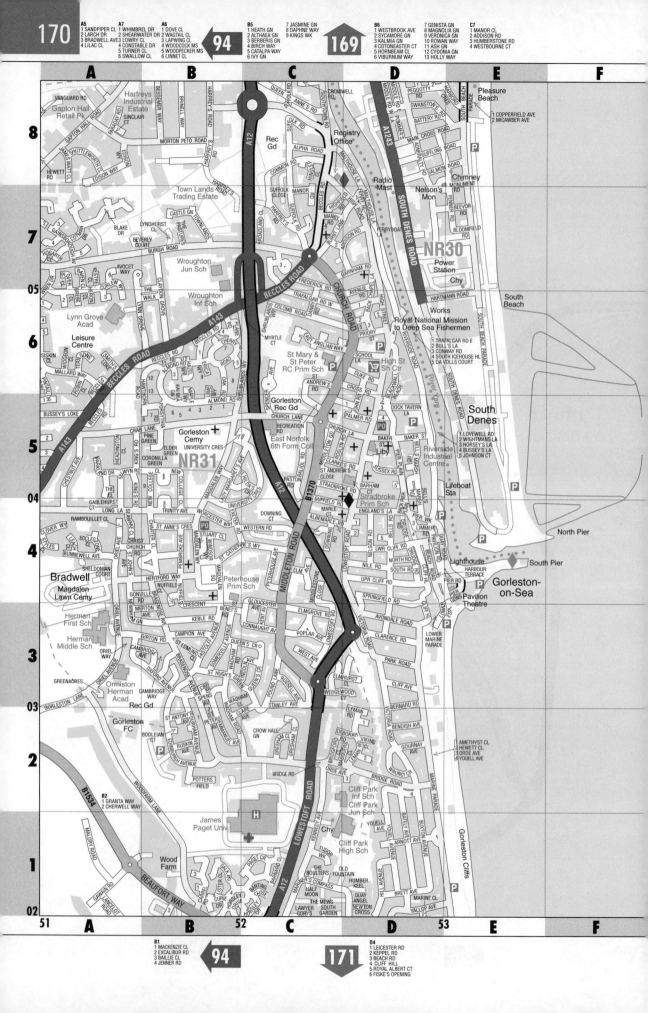

A   B   C   D   E   F

8
7
01
6
5
00
4
3
99
2
1
98

Hobland Plantation
Mast
The Bungalow
Hobland Farm
HOBLAND ROAD
Oakland Farm
SIDEGATE ROAD
LANCELOT RD
EXCALIBUR RD
HORSLEY DR
GALAHAD RD
CAMELOT RD
GUINEVERE RD
BEAUFORT WAY
Beacon Bsns Pk
Masons Farm
QUAY OSTEND
MARINER'S COMP
MARINER'S CL
YALLOP
MARINE CL
CLIFF LA
MARINE PARADE
LINKS ROAD
JOSHUA CL
THE FAIRWAY
MEADOW
LINKS RD
CH
WARREN ROAD
KENNEL LANE
Kennel Farm
Gorleston Golf Course
Long Belt
Corton Cliffs
LOWESTOFT ROAD
A12
Sidegate Farm
Valley Farm
NR31
D5
1 RANDALL CL
2 ST MARGARET'S WAY
3 ANGLIAN WAY
4 GROOMES CL
5 BISHOPS WK
6 ST CLARE CT
7 ST CLEMENT MEWS
8 HOPTON CT
Hopton on Sea
Reservoir
Sawmill
HALL ROAD
White House Farm
RACKHAM CL
FLOWERDAY CL
ROGER'S CL
KIEL
TEULON CL
LOWESTOFT ROAD
WALTERS
ANGLIAN WAY
HOPTON GDNS
MARINERS PARK CL
POTTERS
ST VINCENT WK
WARREN ROAD
Holiday Village
D4
1 CULLEY WY
2 NEWTON GAP CL
3 SAYERS GREEN
4 CUMBY WY
5 FREEMAN CL
6 JEX WY
7 ORMSBY CL
8 SPEEDWELL CL
9 GURNEY CL
10 BROTHERTON WY
11 SUFFOLK CL
12 WHITE CLOVER WY
13 KIDDS CL
14 LUSHERS MEADOW WY
Bloodman's Corner
Homeclose Shrubbery
DORKING ROAD
IMPERIAL MEWS
A12
HALL RD
PO
PH
THE LAURELS
JULIAN WAY
STATION ROAD
WARREN RD
PH
1 ST ANDREW CL
2 BARN CL
WATSONS
YARMOUTH ROAD
SEAFIELDS DR
SEAFIELDS DRIVE
IVES WAY
Hopton CE Prim Sch
OLD CHURCH RD
COAST RD
MANOR
GENEVA GDNS
MISBUL
MANOR GDNS
NAPLES
ZURICH CL
CADIZ WY
TURIN WY
PEBBLE VW WK
SEA VIEW RISE
BEACH ROAD
League Hole
Back LANE
Cuckoo Green
Cuckoo Green Farm
Elder Farm
DORKING ROAD
Home Farm
St Margaret's Church (rems)
Oak View Farm
LONGFULANS LANE
Holiday & Leisure Centre
COAST ROAD
Home Farm
JAY LANE
CHURCH LANE
Hall Farm
Elm Farm
Beehive Farm
Lothingland Middle Sch
Rector's Wood
Great Wood
Brickhill Wood
NR32
Red House Farm
MARKET LANE
YARMOUTH ROAD
A12
Fourways Farm
Mast
Woburn Farm
Corton Cliffs
COAST ROAD
CHURCH LA
STIRRUPS LANE
Suffolk STREET ATLAS A12 Lowestoft

Suffolk STREET ATLAS →

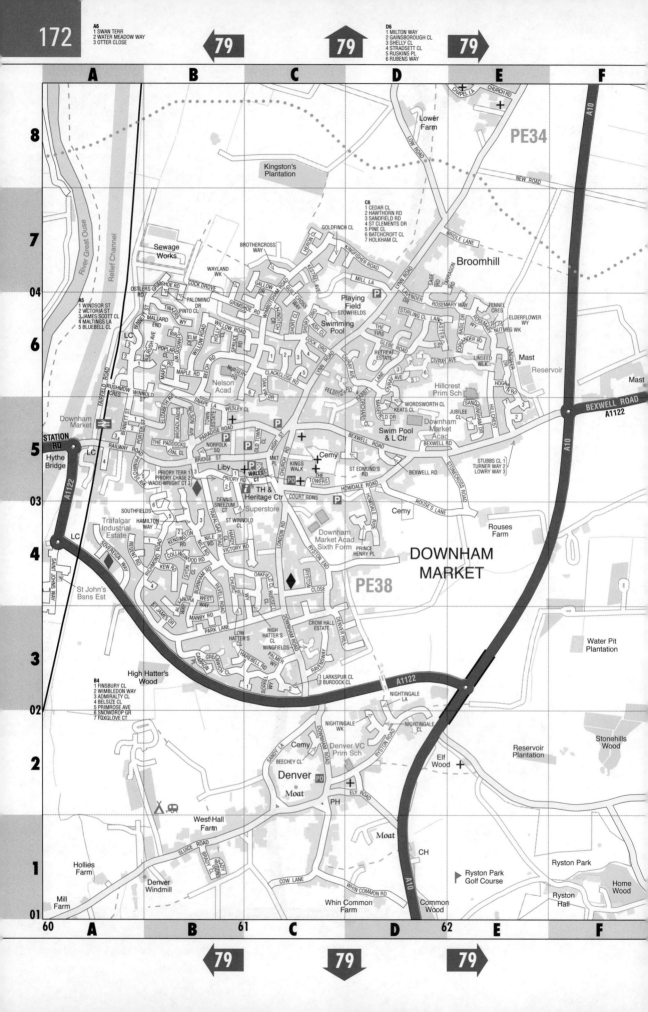

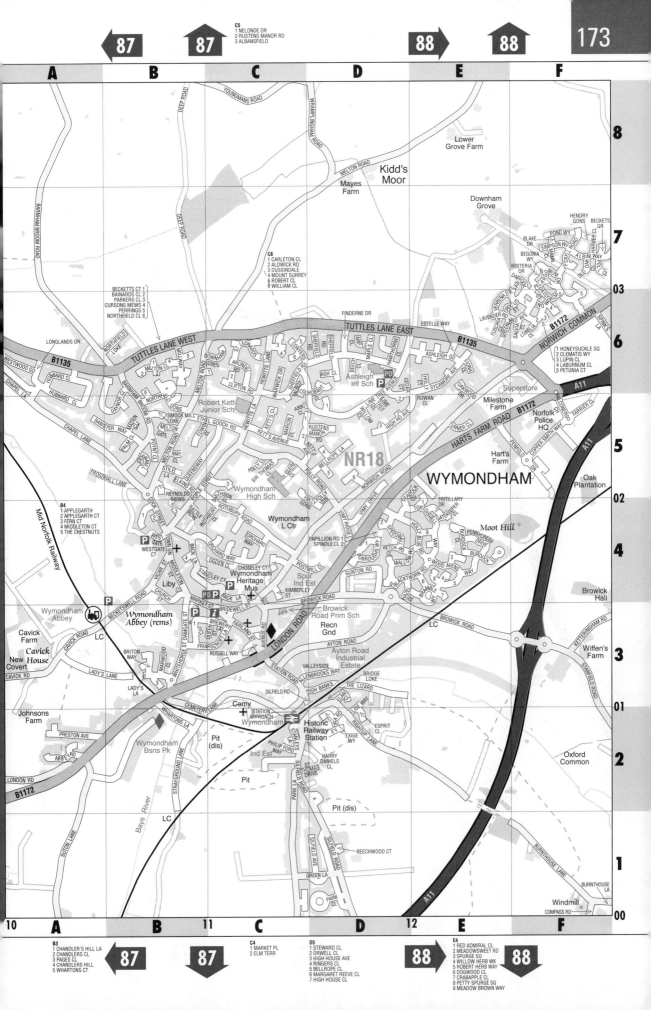

C5
1 NELONDE DR
2 RUSTENS MANOR RD
3 ALBANSFIELD

A **B** **C** **D** **E** **F**

Lower Grove Farm

Kidd's Moor

Mayes Farm

Downham Grove

C6
1 CARLETON CL
2 ALDWICK RD
3 DUSSINDALE
4 MOUNT SURREY
6 ROBERT CL
8 WILLIAM CL

HENDRY GDNS
BECKETS GR

BLAKE DR
POND WY
SIMPSON WY

BEGONIA WY
WISTERIA DR
DAFFODIL

BECKETTS CT 1
BAINARDS CL 2
PARKERS CL 3
CURSONS MEWS 4
PERRINGS 5
NORTHFIELD CL 6

TUTTLES LANE EAST
B1135

FINDERNE DR
ESTELLE WAY

NORWICH COMMON

03

06

LONGLANDS DR
NORTHFIELD LOKE

TUTTLES LANE WEST

B1135

LAVENDER CL

1 HONEYSUCKLE SQ
2 CLEMATIS WY
3 LUPIN CL
4 LABURNUM CL
5 PETUNIA CT

A11

WESTWOOD GD
HBBARD CL
HUBBARD CL

CHAPEL LA

MELTON CRES
NORTHFIE
NORTHK

DOWNHAM CRES

ST LEONARDS CL
HEWITTS LANE
WARWICK DR

SHEFFIELD RD
SHEFFIELD RD
COUNTESS

BEECH AV
MAPLE CL
HAWTHORNE CL
ASHLEIGH GD

Superstore

Milestone Farm

B1172

FALCONERS

FARRIER CL

BANISTER WAY

CLIFTON RD

ASH CL
HOBART CL

ASHLEIGH INF SCH

HOLLY
SYCAMORE AVE

OAKWOOD DR

Norfolk Police HQ

A11

CHAPEL LANE

Robert Kett Junior Sch

ETHEL GOOCH RD
KETT'S CL

ABBOT CL

LIME TREE AVE
CEDAR

ROWAN CL

WILLOW

TURNER RD

HARTS FARM ROAD

COPPER SMITH WAY

05

FROGSHALL LANE

SMOCK MILL LOKE
MELTON GATE

SIR THOMAS

MARION
KETT'S RD

RUSTENS MANOR RD

BELLROPE LA

HIGH HO AVE

Hart's Farm

NR18

WYMONDHAM

Oak Plantation

02

B4
1 APPLEGARTH
2 APPLEGARTH CT
3 FERN CT
4 MIDDLETON CT
5 THE CHESTNUTS

STILE LA
ELKINS QUEENSWAY

Wymondham High Sch

FOLLY CL
GLEN
FOLLY ROAD
FOLLY RD
FOLLY RD GDNS

NORWICH ROAD

VINY DRIVE

PEACOCK CL
FRITILLARY DR

TORT CASTLE
GATEKEEPER

Moot Hill

04

Mid Norfolk Railway

REYNOLDS MEWS

COOK STREET

Wymondham L Ctr

Wymondham Heritage Mus

ORCHARD WAY

PAPILLION RD 1
SPINDLE CL 2

POSTMILL CL

SPEEDWELL
HOLLY BLUE RD

PENNYCRESS DRIVE

BURDOCK CL
BURDOCK WAY

Browick Hall

03

WESTGATE CT

Liby

BACK ST

WYMONDHAM HERITAGE MUS

OGDEN CL
CHOSELEY CT
STANDLEY CT

Spur Ind Est
KIMBERLEY ST

GUNTON RD

BLACKTHORN RD

WOOD AVENS WAY

LC

BROWICK ROAD

01

Wymondham Abbey

LC

Wymondham Abbey (rems)

BECKETSWELL ROAD
CHURCH ST

MARKET ST
BRIDEWELL ST

Browick Road Prim Sch

Recn Gnd

Browick Road

Cavick Farm

Cavick New House Covert

CAVICK ROAD

BRITON WAY
MARWOOD RD
WHITEHORSE ST
DAMGATE ST

BREWERY LA
QUEEN ST
FAIRLAND ST

AVENUE RD

LONDON ROAD

AYTON ROAD

Ayton Road Industrial Estate

Wiffen's Farm

KETTERINGHAM RD
STANFIELD ROAD

01

CAVICK RD

LADY'S LANE

FRIARSCROFT LA
RUSSELL WAY

STATION ROAD

VALLEYSIDE
GLENBROOKS WAY

BRIDGE LOKE

THE LIZARD

Johnsons Farm

PRESTON AVE

ABBEY RD

LADY'S LA

SILFIELD RD

HIGH BANKS

ELSIE WAY
ESPRIT CL

Oxford Common

02

LONDON RD
B1172

Wymondham Bsns Pk

STRAYGROUND LANE

CEMETERY LANE

Cemy

STATION APPROACH

Wymondham

Historic Railway Station

PHILIP FORDS WAY

Ind Est

STANLEY'S LA

HARRY DANIELS CL

THOMAS DRIVE

PARK LA

SILFIELD ROAD

RIGHTUP LANE

EXIGE WY

01

Pit (dis)

Pit

Pit (dis)

Bays River

LC

GREEN LA

SILFIELD AVE

BEECHWOOD CT

PARK CL

Windmill

COMPASS RD

BURNTHOUSE LANE

BURNTHOUSE LA

A11

00

10 **A** **B** **11** **C** **D** **12** **E** **F**

B3
1 CHANDLER'S HILL LA
2 CHANDLERS CL
3 PAGES CL
4 CHANDLERS HILL
5 WHARTONS CT

◄ 87   ▼ 87

C4
1 MARKET PL
2 ELM TERR

D5
1 STEWARD CL
2 ORWELL CL
3 HIGH HOUSE AVE
4 RINGERS CL
5 BELLROPE CL
6 MARGARET REEVE CL
7 HIGH HOUSE CL

▲ 88

E4
1 RED ADMIRAL CL
2 MEADOWSWEET RD
3 SPURGE SQ
4 WILLOW HERB WK
5 ROBERT HERB WAY
6 DOGWOOD CL
7 CRABAPPLE CL
8 PETTY SPURGE SQ
9 MEADOW BROWN WAY

▲ 88

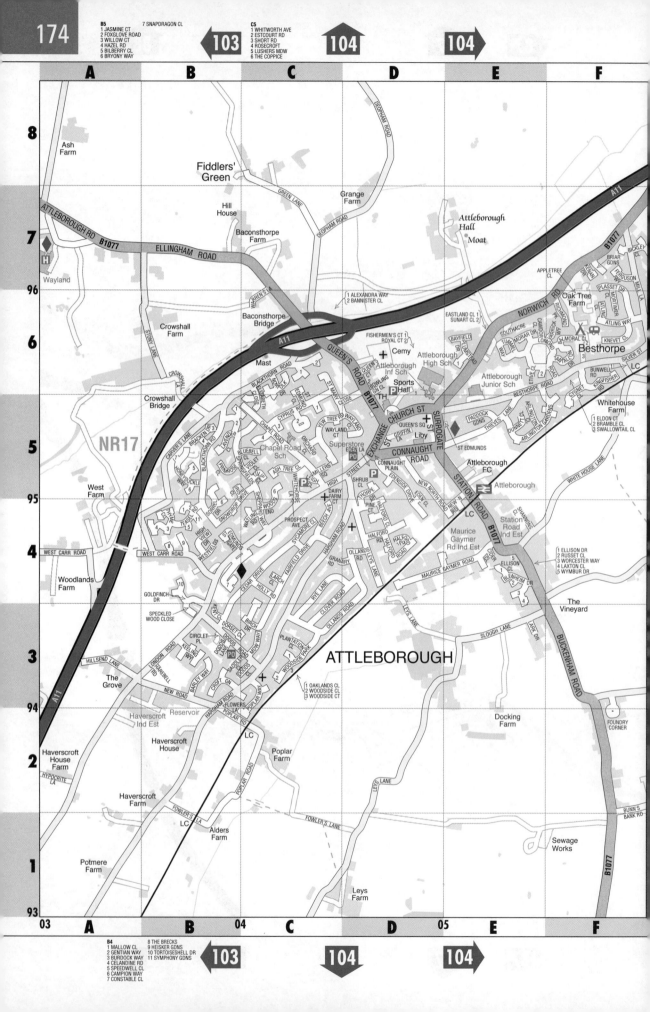

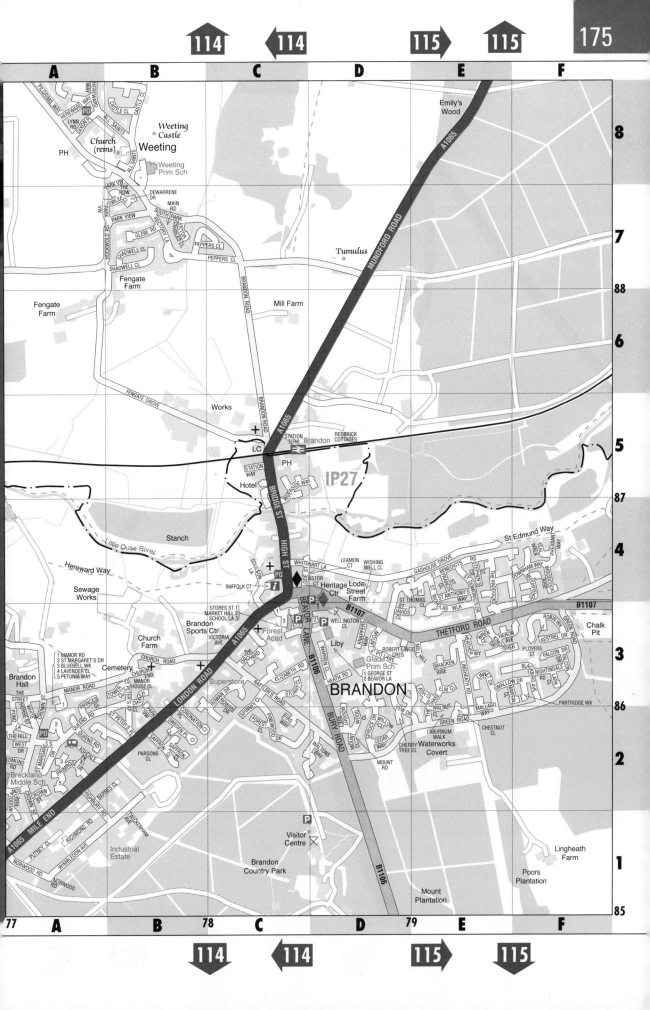

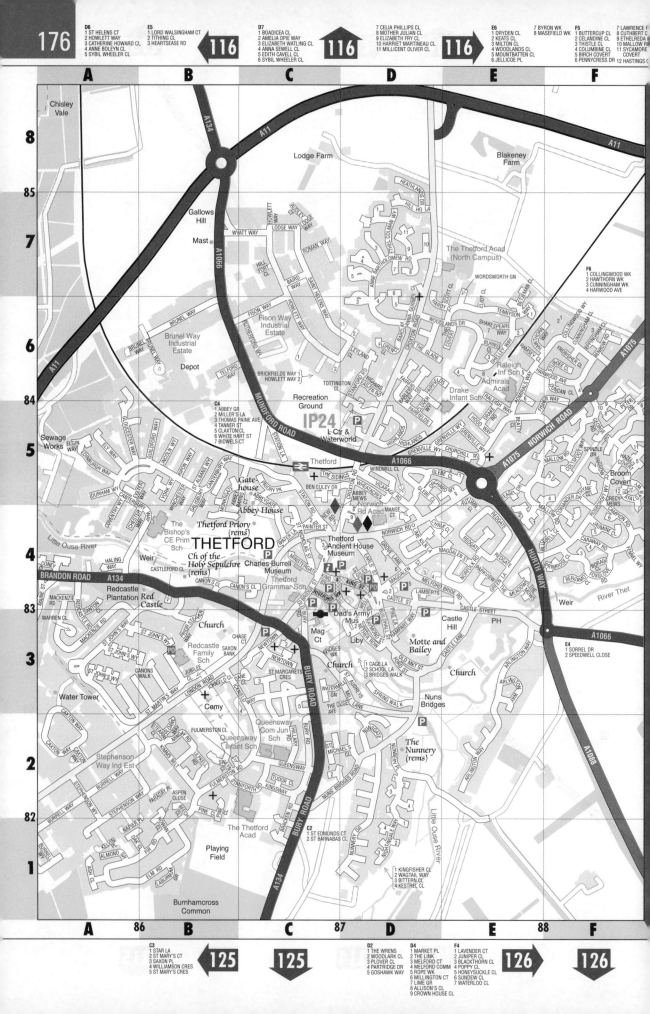

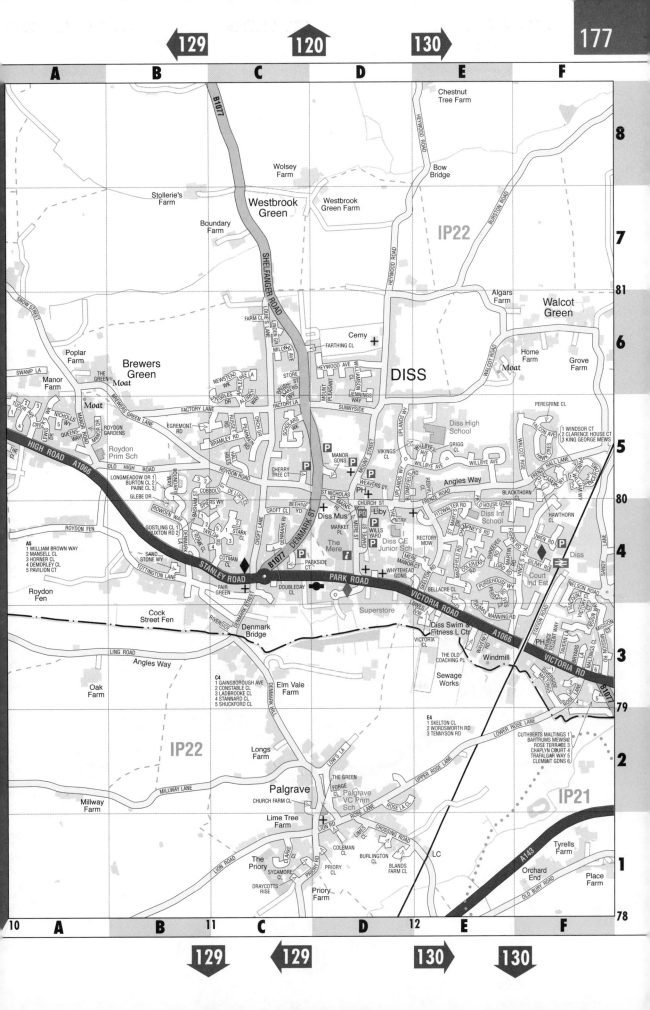

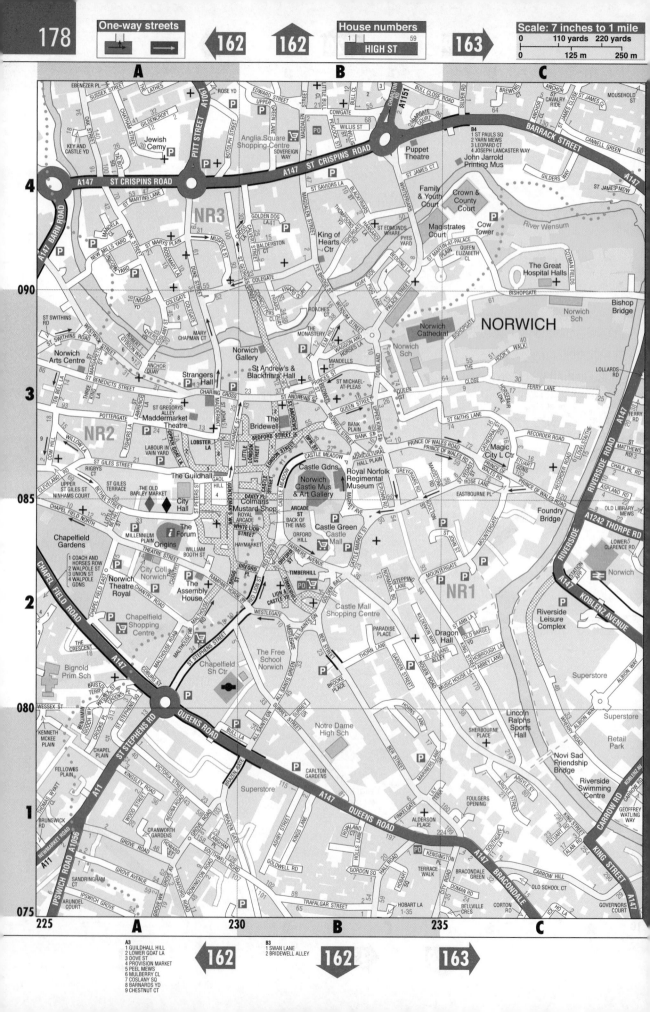

Index

Place name May be abbreviated on the map	**Church Rd 6** Beckenham BR2..........**53** C6

Location number Present when a number indicates the place's position in a crowded area of mapping

Locality, town or village Shown when more than one place has the same name

Postcode district District for the indexed place

Page and grid square Page number and grid reference for the standard mapping

Cities, towns and villages are listed in CAPITAL LETTERS

Public and commercial buildings are highlighted in **magenta**   **Places of interest** are highlighted in blue with a star★

Abbreviations used in the index

Acad	**Academy**	Comm	**Common**	Gd	**Ground**	L	**Leisure**	Prom	**Promenade**
App	**Approach**	Cott	**Cottage**	Gdn	**Garden**	La	**Lane**	Rd	**Road**
Arc	**Arcade**	Cres	**Crescent**	Gn	**Green**	Liby	**Library**	Recn	**Recreation**
Ave	**Avenue**	Cswy	**Causeway**	Gr	**Grove**	Mdw	**Meadow**	Ret	**Retail**
Bglw	**Bungalow**	Ct	**Court**	H	**Hall**	Meml	**Memorial**	Sh	**Shopping**
Bldg	**Building**	Ctr	**Centre**	Ho	**House**	Mkt	**Market**	Sq	**Square**
Bsns, Bus	**Business**	Ctry	**Country**	Hospl	**Hospital**	Mus	**Museum**	St	**Street**
Bvd	**Boulevard**	Cty	**County**	HQ	**Headquarters**	Orch	**Orchard**	Sta	**Station**
Cath	**Cathedral**	Dr	**Drive**	Hts	**Heights**	Pal	**Palace**	Terr	**Terrace**
Cir	**Circus**	Dro	**Drove**	Ind	**Industrial**	Par	**Parade**	TH	**Town Hall**
Cl	**Close**	Ed	**Education**	Inst	**Institute**	Pas	**Passage**	Univ	**University**
Cnr	**Corner**	Emb	**Embankment**	Int	**International**	Pk	**Park**	Wk, Wlk	**Walk**
Coll	**College**	Est	**Estate**	Intc	**Interchange**	Pl	**Place**	Wr	**Water**
Com	**Community**	Ex	**Exhibition**	Junc	**Junction**	Prec	**Precinct**	Yd	**Yard**

Index of towns, villages, streets, hospitals, industrial estates, railway stations, schools, shopping centres, universities and places of interest

100th Bomb Group Memorial
Mus, The★ IP21 ....131 A8

A

Abbey Barns Ct IP24 .....176 B5
Abbey Cl
  Horsham St Faith & Newton St
    Faith NR10 ....53 D1
  Sheringham NR26 ....138 D6
  Wendling NR19 ....66 F7
Abbeyfields PE32 ....29 D1
Abbeygate IP24 ....176 C5
Abbey Gn 1 IP24 ....176 C4
Abbey Hill IP21 ....131 A3
Abbey La
  Haveringland NR10 ......52 D6
  Norwich NR1 ....178 C2
Abbey Mews IP24 ....176 D5
Abbey Pk NR26 ....138 F5
Abbey Rd
  Flitcham with Appleton
    PE31 ....28 D3
  Flixton NR35 ....123 F4
  Great Massingham PE32...29 D1
  Horsham St Faith NR10 ...53 D1
  Old Buckenham NR17 ....104 D3
  Pentney PE32 ....63 B8
  Sheringham NR26 ....138 C6
  10 Watton IP25 ....84 E3
  Wymondham NR18 ......173 A2
Abbey St NR12 ....23 E4
Abbot Cl NR18 ....173 C5
  Norwich NR1 ....162 D2
Abbot Rd Horning NR12 ...55 E4
Abbot's Cl NR11 ....150 D7
Abbot's La NR10 ....90 B3
Abbots Way NR12 ....24 E4
Abels Cl NR10 ....155 C8
Aberdare Ct 6 NR1 ......163 B7
Aberdeen St PE30 ....146 F4
Abinger Way NR4 ....89 D8
Abington Gr 4 PE14 ......59 A1
Abraham Dr PE14 ....152 A3
Abram Ct NR20 ....49 D4
Abyssinia Rd NR30 ......169 D2
Acacia Ave Ashill IP25 ...84 A7
  East Dereham NR19 .....154 E1
  22 Martham NR29 ....57 D4
  Wisbech PE13 ....152 C8
Acacia Dr NR28 ....151 B5
Acacia Gr NR26 ....138 D4

Acacia Rd NR7...........163 E8
Access Rd NR21 ....15 D2
Acer Rd PE34 ....43 D4
Ackland Cl 7 NR29 ....58 B6
Acland Mews NR6 ....158 C4
ACLE NR13 ....166 B3
Acle High Sch NR13 .....166 B4
Acle New Rd NR30 ....169 B5
Acle Rd Beighton NR13 ...74 E2
  South Walsham NR13 .....74 C7
  Upton with Fishley NR13...166 A5
Acle St Edmund CE VC Prim
  Sch NR13 ....166 D4
Acle Sta NR13 ....166 B2
Aconite Rd PE30 ....147 B7
Acorn Cl 7 IP25 ....67 B2
Acorn Dr PE32 ....45 B6
Acorn Rd NR28 ....151 D6
Acorn Way NR19 ....154 D7
Acres Way NR8 ....155 E2
Ada Cole Ave NR16 ......103 D1
Ada Coxon Cl PE30 ......146 F8
Adam Cl PE30 ....147 C5
Adams La 4 NR11 ....19 F1
Adams Rd NR7 ....159 A5
Adastral Pl PE37 ....153 C5
Addey Cl NR6 ....158 F5
Addison Cl
  2 Coltishall NR12 ....54 C7
  Feltwell IP26 ....98 F1
Addison Rd 2 NR31 .....170 C7
Adeane Mdw IP26 ....100 A4
Adelaide Ave PE30 ......147 B7
Adelaide St 5 NR2 ......162 B7
Adey Cl NR11 ....150 B5
Adland Rd 25 IP25 ....84 F3
Admirals Acad IP24 .....176 E6
Admirals Cl PE30 ....147 D3
Admirals Ct PE37 ....153 C5
Admirals Dr PE13 ....152 D8
Admiral's Dr PE35 ......140 F1
Admirals Quay NR31 ....169 C1
Admirals Way
  Hethersett NR9 ....88 D8
  Thetford IP24 ....176 E5
Admirals Wlk 7 NR9 .....86 C5
Admiralty Cl 3 PE38 ....172 B4
Admiralty Rd NR30 ......169 D1
Admiral Wilson Wy PE37.153 C6
Adventurers' Dro PE33 ...81 B1
Aerodrome Cres NR7 ...163 D6
Afghan Pl NR3 ....158 E1

Agricultural Hall Plain
  NR1 ....178 B3
Ailmar Cl PE30............147 A4
Ainsworth Cl 7 NR20 .....50 B3
Airedale Cl 4 NR3.......158 C1
Airfield Rd PE33 ....83 C4
Airport Ind Est NR6.......158 C6
Airstation La IP21 ....121 E2
Akrotiri Sq IP25 ....84 F3
Alan Ave NR15 ....89 D1
Alan Jarvis Way PE34 ...144 D6
Alan Rd NR1 ....178 C1
Alban Rd PE30 ....148 C5
Albansfield 3 NR18......173 C5
Albany Cl NR31 ....169 C2
Albany Ct NR27 ....139 B7
Albany Rd
  Great Yarmouth NR31....169 C2
  Norwich NR3 ....162 D8
  Wisbech PE13 ....152 C6
Albemarle Rd
  Great Yarmouth NR30 ...169 D5
  Norwich NR2 ....162 B3
Albert Ct 18 PE13 ....152 C4
Albert Gate Rd 22 NR30 .169 D2
Albertine Cl NR3.........157 F1
Albert Myhill Cl 5 NR20 .154 E6
Albert Pl NR1............163 A6
Albert Rd 17 NR30 ......169 D2
Albert Shower Rd NR13 ...72 E8
Albert Sq 18 NR30 ......169 D2
Albert St Holt NR25 .....137 B6
  King's Lynn PE30 ....146 D5
Albert Terr NR2...........162 C4
Albini Wy Kidd's Moor NR18 86 B6
  Wymondham NR18 ....173 F7
Albion Dr Norwich NR7...159 A3
  Stalham NR12 ....89 D1
Albion Rd Bungay NR35 ...124 B8
  Great Yarmouth NR30.... 169 D4
  Mundesley NR11 ....143 A7
  Trunch NR28 ....22 E5
Albion Way Norwich NR1...178 C1
  Wroxham/Hoveton NR12 .164 D6
Alborough Loke 6 NR9 ...88 C7
ALBURGH IP20 ....122 F6
Alburgh Rd NR15 ....107 D4
Alburgh with Denton CE
  Prim Sch IP20...........123 A5
Alby Craft Ctr★ NR11 ....21 C3
ALBY HILL NR11 ....21 B5
ALDBOROUGH NR11 ......21 A5

Aldborough Prim Sch
  NR11....................21 B5
Aldborough Rd NR11.....21 A3
ALDEBY NR34 ....110 F4
Aldeby Rd NR34 ....110 F6
Alder Cl
  Great Yarmouth NR31....94 C7
  10 Mulbarton NR14.......89 B3
  North Walsham NR28 ....151 D7
  Poringland NR14 ....90 D4
Alder Covert IP24.........116 D2
Alderfen Wy NR12 ....164 E7
ALDERFORD NR9 ....52 A5
Alderman Peel High Sch
  NR23 ....136 D4
Alderman Swindell Sch
  NR30....................169 D8
Alderson Pl NR1..........178 B1
Alderson Rd NR30 ....169 C5
Alder Way NR8 ....155 E1
Aldis Ct NR19............154 D5
Aldis Rd NR13 ....166 B4
Aldiss Ave NR19 ....154 D3
Aldiss Cl PE37 ....153 D3
Aldiss Ct PE13 ....154 D6
Aldrich Way IP22 ....177 C5
Aldryche Rd NR1 ....163 B8
Aldwick Rd 2 NR18......173 C6
Alexander Cl
  Caister-on-Sea NR30.....168 C8
  18 Long Stratton NR15...106 E3
Alexander Rise NR11.....22 F8
Alexander Wy IP21 ......130 D5
Alexandra Ave NR30 ....169 D7
Alexandra Cl PE31 ......140 C4
Alexandra Rd
  Cromer NR27............139 B4
  Great Yarmouth NR30....169 D4
  Hunstanton PE36.........132 C3
  Mundesley NR11.........143 A8
  Norwich NR2 ....162 B6
  Sheringham NR26 ....138 D6
  Wisbech PE13 ....152 C5
Alexandra Way
  Attleborough NR17 ....174 C6
  Downham Market PE38....172 B3
Alex Moorhouse Way
  NR5....................156 A3
Alford Gr NR7 ....159 A3
Alfred Nicholls Ct NR3 ...158 D2
Alfred Rd NR27 ....139 A7
Alfric Cl 11 NR14..........91 F1

100–Alm

Algores Way PE13 ....152 B2
Alicante Wy NR5.........161 E6
Alice Fisher Cres PE30 ...146 F7
Alison Cl NR13............73 F3
Allanadale Rd NR4.......162 C1
Allenbrooks Way NR18...173 C3
Allenby's Chase 10 PE12 ..41 B8
Allen Cl PE34 ....61 B8
Allendale Rd NR30.......168 E5
Allen Meale Way 5 NR12 .39 B4
Allen's Ave NR7..........159 A4
Allens Cl 1 NR13.........73 D6
Allens La NR2 ....162 C4
Allen's La NR7...........159 A4
Allerton Cl NR7 ....159 B3
Allerton Rd NR7 ....159 B3
All Hallows' Hospl NR35 .109 B2
Allison's Cl 8 IP24 ....176 D4
Allison St NR10 ....36 A2
Allotment La NR25........9 B3
All Saints IP27............175 B8
All Saints Acad PE33......81 A2
All Saints CE Prim Sch
  NR21....................32 E7
All Saints CE VA Prim Sch
  IP22 ....120 B4
All Saints Cl
  Briston NR24............142 D4
  Runhall NR20............69 A5
  2 Weybourne NR25 ....8 F5
  Wicklewood NR18 ....87 B5
  1 Wisbech PE14 ....59 A1
All Saints Dr PE30 ......148 C4
All Saints Gn NR1........178 B1
All Saints La NR29 ....40 D2
All Saints Rd NR14 ......90 D5
All Saints Sch NR12......24 D3
ALL SAINTS SOUTH ELMHAM
  IP19....................124 B1
All Saints' St 15 PE30 ...146 D4
All Saints Way
  Beachamwell PE37 ....81 F8
  Mundesley NR11.........143 C6
All Saints Wlk 7 NR20 ...68 F6
Allthorpe Rd 12 IP20....122 D2
Allwood Ave NR19 ......154 C5
Alma Ave PE34 ....144 D6
Alma Chase PE34 ....144 D6

Alma Rd
Great Yarmouth NR30 . . . . . 169 D2
Snettisham PE31 . . . . 12 E5
Alma Terr NR3. . . . . .162 D8
Almond Cl 21 NR29 . . . . . .57 D4
Almond Dr NR4. . . . . .161 C1
Almond Gr IP24 . . . . .176 A1
Almond Rd NR31. . . . . .170 B6
Alpha Rd NR31. . . . . .170 C8
ALPINGTON NR14. . . . . .90 E4
Alpington & Bergh Apton CE
Prim Sch NR14 . . . . .90 F4
Alston Cl 3 NR14. . . . . . . .90 D5
Alston Rd NR6. . . . . .157 E2
Althaea Gn 2 NR31. . . . . .170 B5
Altongate 1 NR13 . . . . . . .72 D6
Amazona Zoo★ NR27 . . . . .139 B5
Amazonia World of
Reptiles★ NR30 . . . . .169 E2
Ambassador Way NR20. . . .154 F4
Ambleside
16 Hethersett NR9 . . . . . . .88 D8
5 Sculthorpe Airfield NR21 15 C2
Ambleside Cl NR5 . . . . . . .161 C6
Ambrose Cl 1 NR5 . . . . . .161 A7
Ambrose Rd NR30 . . . . . . .168 E3
Amderley Dr 6 NR4 . . . . . .89 C8
Amelia Opie Way 2
IP24. . . . . .176 D7
Ames Ct NR10 . . . . .35 B2
Amethyst Cl NR31. . . . . . . .170 D2
Amherst Cl 7 PE37. . . . . . .153 C3
Amhirst Cl 2 NR6. . . . . . . .158 F1
Amhurst Gdns NR31. . . . . . .94 A5
Amos Bacon Cl NR6. . . . . .158 F4
Ampthill St 6 NR1. . . . . . .162 C5
Amsterdam NR6 . . . . .158 B6
Amsterdam Way PE13. . . . .154 C2
Amys Cl IP25 . . . . .84 C4
Ancar Rd PE30. . . . . .148 D2
Anchorage View PE31. . . . . . .3 B6
Anchor Cl Norwich NR3 . . . .178 C4
Sheringham NR26 . . . . .138 E6
ANCHOR CORNER NR17 . . . . .86 A1
Anchor Cl NR31. . . . . .169 C2
Anchor Dro PE38 . . . . .112 B8
Anchor Pk PE31 . . . . .12 E4
Anchor Quay NR2. . . . . . . .178 A3
Anchor Rd
North Walsham NR28 . . . . .151 F5
Sutton Bridge PE34. . . . . . .41 F8
Anchor St Coltishall NR12. . .54 D6
5 Norwich NR3. . . . . .162 F8
Norwich NR3. . . . . .178 C4
Tunstead NR12 . . . . .38 B2
ANCHOR STREET NR12 . . . . .38 B3
Anchor Way 7 NR33. . . . . .111 F1
Anderson Cl
King's Lynn PE30 . . . . .146 E7
Wisbech PE13 . . . . .152 A7
Andrew Goodall Cl NR19 .154 C1
Andrew's Furlong NR16. . .119 E7
Andrews Pl IP36. . . . . .132 D2
Angela Cl 2 NR10 . . . . .53 B3
Angela Cres 3 NR10. . . . . . .53 B3
Angela Rd NR10 . . . . .53 B3
Angel Dr NR28. . . . . .151 B4
Angel Rd NR3 . . . . .158 D1
Angel Road Inf Sch NR3 158 D1
Angel Road Jun Sch
NR3. . . . . .158 D1
Angerstein Cl IP27. . . . . . .114 E8
Angle Rd PE14. . . . . .78 A7
Anglian Way 3 NR31. . . . . .171 D5
Anglia Sq NR3 . . . . .178 B4
Anglia Way PE13. . . . . .152 B2
Anglo-Saxon Cath & Bishops
Pal (remains of)★ NR20 .49 F8
Angus Mackay Ct NR6. . . .157 E4
ANMER PE31. . . . . .28 E8
Anmer Cl NR3 . . . . .158 F3
Anmer Rd PE31. . . . . .28 C5
Anna Gurney Cl IP24. . . . .176 D6
Anna Sewell Cl 4 IP24 . .176 D7
Anne Bartholomew Rd
IP24. . . . . .176 D7
Anne Boleyn Cl 4 IP24 .176 D6
Anne Cl NR7 . . . . .163 F8
Anne Rd PE12 . . . . .41 B8
Annes Cl PE30 . . . . .148 D1
Annes Dr PE36. . . . . .132 D1
Anne Stannard Way NR12 .23 F4
ANNIS HILL NR35 . . . . .124 C8
Annis Hill NR35 . . . . .124 C8
Annis Hill La 1 NR35 . . . .124 B8
Anson Cl
5 Hethersett NR9 . . . . .88 E8
Mundesley NR11. . . . . .143 A7
Anson Rd
Great Yarmouth NR31. . . . .169 C2
Norwich NR6. . . . . .158 B6
Anson's La NR15. . . . . .122 A8
Anson Wy 27 IP25 . . . . .84 F3
Ant Broads & Marshes
National Nature Reserve★
NR12. . . . . .55 B8
Anthony Curton CE Prim Sch
The PE14. . . . . .41 E4
Anthony Dr NR3 . . . . .158 F2
Anthony Nolan Rd PE30. .147 D3
ANTINGHAM NR28. . . . . .22 B4
Antingham Dr NR28. . . . . .151 D6
Antingham Hill NR28. . . . . .22 B3
Antingham Rd NR7 . . . . . . .159 D1

Antingham & Southrepps
Com Prim Sch NR11. . . . . .22 B5
Apeldoorn Wlk PE13 . . . . .152 D7
Apollo Wlk NR6. . . . . .169 C6
Appleacres NR6 . . . . .158 D5
Appledore Cl PE30 . . . . . . .148 C2
Appledore La 4 NR21. . . . .15 C2
Applegarth 1 NR18. . . . . . .173 B4
Applegarth Ct 2 NR18 . .173 B4
Appleton Dr NR29. . . . . . . .167 A3
Appleton Dro PE31. . . . . . . .27 F5
Appletree Cl
Besthorpe NR17. . . . . .174 F7
Heacham PE31 . . . . .133 C6
Appletree La IP22 . . . . . . .177 C5
Appleyard Cres NR3 . . . . . .158 A3
Apple Yd NR25. . . . . .137 B6
Apsley Ct NR5. . . . . .161 F6
Apsley Rd NR30. . . . . .169 E3
Arbor Ct NR27. . . . . .139 B6
Arbor Rd NR27. . . . . .139 B6
Arcade St NR1. . . . . .178 B2
Archbishop Sancroft High
Sch IP20 . . . . .122 D2
Archdale Cl PE33 . . . . .43 F3
Archdale St 3 PE30 . . . . . .146 E5
Archer Cl NR6 . . . . .159 A5
Archer La PE32 . . . . .46 F2
Archers' Ave 3 IP26. . . . . . .98 D1
Archer's Rd 2 NR30. . . . . .169 C5
Archibald Rd NR12. . . . . . . .24 A7
Arden Cl NR27. . . . . .11 A3
Arden Gr NR10. . . . . .157 E7
Arden Grove Inf Sch
NR10. . . . . .157 E7
Arderon Ct 2 NR2. . . . . . . .162 B7
Ardleigh Cl 3 PE13. . . . . . .152 E5
Ardney Rise NR3. . . . . .158 D3
Argyle St King's Lynn PE30 146 E3
Norwich NR1. . . . . .178 C1
Argyll Cres NR8. . . . . .156 E8
Arles Ave PE13 . . . . .152 E3
Arlington Cl NR17. . . . . . . .174 E5
Arlington Gdns NR17. . . . . .174 E5
Arlington La NR2 . . . . .162 C4
Arlington Pk Rd PE32 . . . . .44 C3
Arlington Way IP24 . . . . . .176 E3
Armada Cl PE13 . . . . .152 D8
Armes Cres NR2 . . . . .162 A8
Armes St NR2 . . . . .162 B7
ARMINGHALL NR14 . . . . .90 B7
Arminghall Cl NR3. . . . . . . .158 C3
Arminghall La NR14. . . . . . .89 F8
Armitage Cl NR4 . . . . .89 B8
Arms Pk Rd NR6. . . . . .158 B6
ARMS THE IP25 . . . . .83 F1
Armstrong Dr NR19. . . . . . .154 E7
Armstrong Rd NR7. . . . . . . .159 E2
Army Rd NR21. . . . . .15 C2
Arnfield La NR5. . . . . .161 B8
Arnold Ave NR30. . . . . .168 C8
Arnold Miller Rd NR1 . . . .162 F2
Arnold Pitcher Cl NR28 .151 D6
Arnott Ave NR31. . . . . .170 D1
Arnott Rd NR25. . . . . .137 D5
Arnside 22 NR9 . . . . .88 D8
Arthur Ave NR31. . . . . .168 E8
Arthur Rd NR21. . . . . .141 A6
Arthurton Rd NR10. . . . . . . .54 A1
Artillery Sq 21 NR30. . . . . .169 D4
Artillery St 12 PE13 . . . . . .152 C4
Arundel Cl NR20 . . . . .49 C4
Arundel Ct NR2. . . . . .178 A1
Arundel Dr PE30 . . . . .148 C1
Arundel Rd
Great Yarmouth NR30. . . . .169 D7
Wymondham NR18 . . . . . . .173 C6
Ascot Gdns NR19 . . . . .154 D3
Ashbey Rd PE30 . . . . .147 E8
Ashbourne Ind Est NR6. . .158 C4
Ashburton Cl NR31. . . . . . .136 C4
Ashburton Rd IP26 . . . . . . .100 C5
Ashby Rd
Ashby St Mary NR14. . . . . .91 C5
Repps with Bastwick NR29. .57 A3
Thurton NR14 . . . . .91 C4
ASHBY ST MARY NR14 . . . . .91 C5
Ashby St NR1. . . . . .178 B1
Ash Cl Brandon IP27 . . . . . .175 E3
Downham Market PE38. . . .172 C6
8 Etling Green NR20. . . . . .68 A8
10 Hethersett NR9 . . . . . . .88 D8
Reepham NR10 . . . . .149 D6
Swaffham PE37. . . . . .153 B5
Thetford IP24 . . . . .176 A1
Wymondham NR18 . . . . . . .173 D6
Ashcroft Cl NR4 . . . . .161 B1
Ashdale Pk
Old Hunstanton PE36 . . . .132 F8
Wisbech PE13 . . . . .152 A5
Ashdown Cl NR27. . . . . . . .139 C6
Ashdown Ct NR27. . . . . . . .139 C6
Ash Dr IP23 . . . . .130 C1
Ashes Farm La IP22. . . . . . .119 A2
Ashfield Ct PE34. . . . . .144 D6
Ashfield Hill PE30. . . . . . . .147 C4
Ashfield Rd NR28 . . . . .151 E6
Ashford Cl NR34. . . . . .110 C2
Ash Gn 11 NR31. . . . . .170 B6
Ash Gr King's Lynn PE30 . .148 D2
Norwich NR3. . . . . .158 E2
Sheringham NR26 . . . . .138 E5
4 West Winch PE33. . . . . . .43 E2
Ashgrove 5 NR8 . . . . .155 E2
ASHILL IP25 . . . . .84 A7
Ashill VC Prim Sch IP25 . .84 A7
Ash La NR16. . . . . .105 C2

Ashleigh Gdns NR18 . . . . .173 E6
Ashleigh Inf Sch NR18 . . .173 D6
Ashley Rd NR20. . . . . .49 D4
Ashley Wlk PE13. . . . . .154 D4
Ash Plough IP21. . . . . .131 E1
Ash Rd PE33 . . . . .63 B4
Ash Tree Cl NR17 . . . . .174 C5
Ash Tree Rd NR13. . . . . .74 D1
Ashwell Ct NR5. . . . . .160 F7
Ashtree Rd Norwich NR5 . .157 B2
25 Watton IP25. . . . . .84 E3
ASHWELLTHORPE NR16 . . . .105 F8
Ashwellthorpe Rd NR16. . .88 D1
ASHWICKEN PE32 . . . . .45 A6
Ashwicken CE Prim Sch
PE32. . . . . .44 F6
Ashwicken Rd PE32. . . . . . .45 A8
Ashwood Cl NR30. . . . . . . .168 D6
Ash Yd NR24. . . . . .18 D8
ASLACTON NR15. . . . . .106 A2
Aslacton Prim Sch NR15 106 A1
Aslack Way PE36. . . . . .2 A6
Aslacton Rd NR16. . . . . . . .106 B3
Aslake Cl NR7 . . . . .159 C5
Aspen Cl 28 Martham NR29 .57 D4
Thetford IP24 . . . . .176 B2
Aspen Rd NR30 . . . . .168 E4
Aspen Way NR4. . . . . .89 B8
Aspland Rd NR1 . . . . .178 C3
Assembly House The
NR2. . . . . .178 A2
Association Way 2 NR7 . .72 D4
Astell Rd NR1. . . . . .89 F8
Astley Cooper Pl
Brooke NR15 . . . . .90 E1
5 Great Yarmouth NR31 . .169 D6
Astley Cres PE36. . . . . .132 D6
Astley Prim Sch NR24. . . .142 C4
Astley Rd
Great & Little Plumstead
NR13. . . . . .73 B6
Little Plumstead NR13. . . . .165 A8
Norwich NR5. . . . . .160 F8
Astor Ct IP27 . . . . .175 D4
Atbara Terr PE30 . . . . .146 E4
Atcherley Sq PE31 . . . . .30 B3
Atkinson Cl NR5 . . . . .160 E8
Atlantic Ave NR7. . . . . .159 D5
Atling Cl NR17 . . . . .174 F6
Atling Way NR17. . . . . .174 F6
Atmere Cl 2 NR4. . . . . .161 F1
Atthill Rd NR2 . . . . .162 A7
ATTLEBOROUGH NR17 . . . . .174 D3
Attleborough High Sch
NR17. . . . . .174 D6
Attleborough Inf Sch
NR17. . . . . .174 D6
Attleborough Jun Sch
NR17. . . . . .174 E6
Attleborough Rd
Attleborough NR17. . . . . . .174 A7
Caston NR17 . . . . .102 F8
Deopham NR18. . . . . .86 E1
Great Ellingham NR17. . . . .103 F8
Little Ellingham NR17. . . . . .86 A2
Morley NR18 . . . . .87 A1
Attleborough Sta NR17 . .174 E5
ATTLEBRIDGE NR9. . . . . .52 B3
Attlee Way 4 NR19 . . . . . .154 C6
Attoe Wlk NR3. . . . . .158 D2
Aubrey Rix Cl NR20 . . . . . . .33 C3
Audax Rd NR6 . . . . .158 C6
Audley Cl IP22. . . . . .120 E2
Audley Ct IP24 . . . . .176 C7
Audley End IP21. . . . . .120 F1
Audley St NR30 . . . . .169 D5
Augusta Ct NR26. . . . . .138 D7
Augusta St NR26. . . . . .138 D7
Augustus Hare Dr 1
NR4. . . . . .161 C5
Aurania Ave NR1. . . . . .162 D3
Auster Cl NR6 . . . . .158 C4
Austin Fields PE30. . . . . . .146 E5
Austin Fields Ind Est
PE30. . . . . .146 E5
Austin Rd NR31. . . . . .169 B3
Austin St
Hunstanton PE36. . . . . . . .132 C5
King's Lynn PE30 . . . . .146 D5
Austin Wy NR6. . . . . .158 F7
Autumn Cl IP24. . . . . .176 E4
Autumn Dr NR5. . . . . .161 B8
Avebury Rd NR4 . . . . .162 B1
Aveling Way 6 NR33. . . . . .111 F1
Avenue Jun Sch NR2 . . . . .162 B5
Avenue Rd
Great Yarmouth NR31. . . . .170 D6
High Kelling NR25 . . . . .8 E2
Hunstanton PE36. . . . . . . .132 C4
King's Lynn PE30 . . . . .146 F4
North Walsham NR28 . . . . .151 C4
Norwich NR2. . . . . .162 B5
Wymondham NR18 . . . . . . .173 C3
Avenue S NR26 . . . . .138 E7
Avenues The
Langley with Hardley
NR14. . . . . .91 F4
Norwich NR4 . . . . .161 B4
Thurton NR14 . . . . .91 D3
Avenue The
Brome & Oakley IP23 . . . . .130 D3
Brookville IP26 . . . . .99 A7
Brumstead NR12. . . . . .24 A1
Dersingham PE35. . . . . . . .140 E1
Hemsby NR29 . . . . .167 A7

Avenue The continued
Holkham NR23. . . . . .5 A4
Horning NR12. . . . . .55 E4
Mundesley NR11. . . . . .143 C5
4 Necton PE37. . . . . .65 F4
New Holkham NR23 . . . . . . .5 A2
Northrepps NR27 . . . . .139 D3
Sheringham NR26 . . . . .138 E7
Snettisham PE31. . . . . .12 D4
Wiggenhall St Germans
PE34. . . . . .61 A8
Wroxham/Hoveton NR12 . .164 B4
Wymondham NR18 . . . . . . .87 D7
Avian Way NR7 . . . . .159 C2
Avocet Rise NR7. . . . . .159 E4
Avondale Cl NR13. . . . . .74 A2
Avondale Rd NR31. . . . . . . .170 D6
Avonmouth Rd 2 NR3. . . .158 C1
Avon Rd PE30. . . . . .148 C2
Awdry Dr PE13. . . . . .152 C3
Aylesbury Cl NR3. . . . . .158 D2
Aylmer Dr PE34. . . . . .60 C8
AYLMERTON NR11. . . . . .10 A3
AYLSHAM NR11 . . . . .150 B5
Aylsham Cres NR3 . . . . . . .158 C3
Aylsham High Sch NR11 150 D7
Aylsham Ind Est NR11. . . .150 E8
Aylsham Rd
Burgh & Tuttington NR11. . .36 E6
Cawston NR10. . . . . .35 B2
Felmingham NR28 . . . . .37 A8
North Walsham NR28 . . . . .22 C1
Norwich NR3. . . . . .158 C1
Oulton NR11 . . . . .35 E6
Swanton Abbott NR10. . . . .37 C4
Aylsham Rd Bsns Pk
NR6. . . . . .158 C2
Aylsham Sta NR11 . . . . . . .150 D5
Ayre Way PE30. . . . . .147 D8
Ayton Rd NR18. . . . . .173 D3
Ayton Rd Ind Est NR18 . .173 D3

B

BABINGLEY PE31 . . . . .27 D5
Babingley Cl 5 PE33. . . . . .61 D6
Babingley Pl PE33 . . . . .43 F4
Bachelor's La NR28 . . . . . . .23 E2
Back Chapel La NR31 . . . . .170 D6
Back Dro Upwell PE14. . . . . .77 D4
Welney PE14 . . . . .95 D4
Back Hills IP22 . . . . .128 E3
Back La Barford NR9 . . . . . .69 F2
Beeston with Bittering PE32 48 C2
Bircham PE31 . . . . .14 B3
Blakeney NR25 . . . . .7 C7
Burgh Castle NR31 . . . . .94 A8
Burnham Market PE31 . . . .135 D2
Burnham Thorpe PE31. . . . . .4 D4
Buxton with Lammas NR10. .35 E8
Castle Acre PE32. . . . . .46 F2
Catfield NR29 . . . . .56 C8
Cawston NR10. . . . . .35 B2
Dereham NR20 . . . . .68 A8
Diss IP22. . . . . .120 D3
East Rudham PE31 . . . . . . .30 B7
East Ruston NR12 . . . . .24 A3
Elsing NR20. . . . . .50 F3
Happisburgh NR12 . . . . .23 F2
Hempstead NR25 . . . . .19 E7
Hethersett NR9. . . . . .88 E8
Kenninghall NR16 . . . . .119 A5
Litcham PE32. . . . . .48 A4
Lound NR32. . . . . .94 C2
Lyng NR9 . . . . .51 A4
Lyng NR9 . . . . .51 A4
Marthan NR29 . . . . .57 D5
Mattishall NR20. . . . . .68 E6
Mileham NR32 . . . . .48 C6
North Elmham NR20 . . . . . .49 E7
Outwell PE14. . . . . .77 E7
Potter Heigham NR29 . . . . .56 E7
Quidenham NR16. . . . . . . .119 A8
Rackheath NR13 . . . . .54 D1
Ringland NR8. . . . . .52 C1
Rollesby NR29 . . . . .57 D3
Roughton NR11. . . . . .21 D8
Roydon PE32. . . . . .28 A1
Scole IP21. . . . . .121 A1
Scoulton NR9. . . . . .85 E3
South Creake NR21. . . . . . .15 E6
Stanfield NR20 . . . . .48 F8
St Mary, South Elmham
otherwise Homersfield
IP20. . . . . .123 B4
Upton with Fishley NR13. . .166 C8
Walsingham NR22. . . . . . . .16 F7
Wereham PE33 . . . . .80 E4
West Beckham NR25. . . . . . .9 B3
West Caister NR30 . . . . . . .168 A4
West Winch PE33 . . . . .43 E2
Wymondham NR18 . . . . . . .173 C4
Back Mkt La NR29 . . . . . . .167 B7
Back Mundesley Rd NR11 . 22 F8
Back of the Inns NR1. . . . .178 B2
Back Path 1 NR29. . . . . . . .58 B6
Back Pier Plain NR1. . . . . .178 B2
Back Rd Brockdish IP21 . . .131 B8
East Ruston NR12. . . . . . . .38 F6
Elm PE14. . . . . .77 A8
Pentney PE32 . . . . .63 C8
Somerton NR29 . . . . .57 E5
Wisbech PE14. . . . . .77 A7
Wood Dalling NR11. . . . . . . .34 D6
Yelverton NR14 . . . . .90 F5
Back St Binham NR21 . . . . . .6 E2
Fakenham NR21 . . . . .141 B3

Back St continued
Garboldisham IP22 . . . . . . .128 A8
Gayton PE32 . . . . .45 C5
Harpley PE31. . . . . .29 D5
Horsham St Faith NR10 . . . .53 D1
Lakenheath IP27 . . . . .113 E1
Litcham PE32. . . . . .48 A4
Mundesley NR11. . . . . .143 C5
Reepham NR10 . . . . .149 B4
South Creake NR21. . . . . . .15 D6
Tittleshall PE32. . . . . .48 B7
Trunch NR28 . . . . .22 E5
Back Terr PE37. . . . . .153 B5
Backwood La Howe NR15 . .90 C2
Shotesham NR15. . . . . .107 F8
Bacon Rd NR4. . . . . .161 F5
BACONSTHORPE NR25 . . . . .20 A8
Baconsthorpe Castle★
NR25. . . . . .9 A1
BACTON NR12. . . . . .23 E5
Bacton Cl PE30 . . . . .148 D3
BACTON GREEN NR12 . . . . .23 D5
Bacton Prim Sch NR12. . . .23 E4
Bacton Rd Bacton NR12 . . .23 D5
North Walsham NR28 . . . . .151 D6
Norwich NR3. . . . . .158 B2
Paston NR28 . . . . .143 E2
Witton NR28 . . . . .23 C1
Bader Cl PE30 . . . . .147 D4
Badger Cl NR14. . . . . .89 A2
Badger Rd NR5 . . . . .156 D1
Badgers Brook Rd NR8. . .155 F2
Bagge Rd PE30 . . . . .147 A5
BAGTHORPE PE31 . . . . .14 D3
Bagthorpe Rd NR8. . . . . . . .30 A7
Bahram Rd NR8. . . . . .156 A4
Bailey Cl
4 Hethersett NR9 . . . . .88 D7
6 Marthan NR29 . . . . .57 D5
Bailey La PE34. . . . . .145 E7
Bailey Rd NR27 . . . . .139 B5
Bailey St PE32 . . . . .46 F2
Bailiwick The 3 NR16 . . . .118 C5
Baillie Cl 3 NR31. . . . . .170 B1
Bainard Rise NR15. . . . . . . .107 C6
Bainards Cl NR18 . . . . .173 B6
Baines Rd 4 PE30 . . . . . . .146 D1
Baines Way 2 NR5. . . . . . . .160 E8
Baird Way IP24 . . . . .176 C7
Baker Cl King's Lynn PE30. .146 D1
North Walsham NR28 . . . . .151 D3
Baker La 3 PE30 . . . . .146 D4
Bakers La NR35. . . . . .109 A2
Bakers Rd NR3 . . . . .162 D8
Baker's Rd NR13. . . . . .75 A1
Baker St
Great Yarmouth NR31. . . . .170 D5
14 Stalham NR12 . . . . .39 B4
Bakers Yd NR23 . . . . .136 C6
Bakery Cl NR24 . . . . .142 E3
Bakery La NR9. . . . . .51 A5
Balderston Ct NR3. . . . . . . .178 B4
Baldock Cl 1 NR16. . . . . . .105 F5
Baldock Dr PE30. . . . . .147 B8
Baldric Rd NR8 . . . . .155 D1
Baldwin Cl 5 PE13 . . . . . . .152 D5
Baldwin Rd PE30. . . . . .147 C6
Baldwins Cl NR24. . . . . . . .142 D4
Baldwins Dro 4 PE14. . . . . .77 F6
BALE NR21. . . . . .18 B7
Bale Rd Brinton NR24 . . . . .18 C7
Hindringham NR21. . . . . . . .17 E7
Balfour Rd 4 NR27 . . . . . . .10 A5
Balfour St 4 NR3. . . . . .162 B8
Baliol Rd NR1. . . . . .170 C5
Ball's La NR21. . . . . .17 D5
Ballygate NR34 . . . . .110 C1
Balmoral Ave NR30 . . . . . . .169 D7
Balmoral Cl
Attleborough NR17. . . . . . .174 F6
Dersingham PE31. . . . . . . .140 D3
Balmoral Cres PE31. . . . . . .133 C5
Balmoral Rd PE30. . . . . . . .147 C7
Balmoral W PE31. . . . . .140 D3
Bambers La PE14 . . . . .59 C2
Bancroft Cl 7 NR14. . . . . . .89 F4
BANHAM NR16 . . . . .119 D7
Banham Barn Craft★
NR16. . . . . .119 C6
Banham Com Prim Sch
NR16. . . . . .119 D6
Banham Dr NR20 . . . . .50 B2
Banham Rd NR16. . . . . .119 B5
Banham's La NR35. . . . . . . .108 B2
Banham Zoo★ NR16. . . . . .119 C6
Banister Way NR18 . . . . . . .173 A5
Bank Dr PE13. . . . . .152 A7
Bank Loke 6 NR28 . . . . . . .151 C5
Bank Plain NR1. . . . . .178 B3
Bankside PE31. . . . . .133 B6
Bank Side PE34. . . . . .146 C5
Bank St Norwich NR2. . . . . .178 B3
Pulham Market IP21. . . . . .121 E5
BANNINGHAM NR11. . . . . . . .36 D8
Banningham Ct NR28. . . . .151 A4
Banningham Rd NR11. . . . .150 D8
Bannister Cl NR17 . . . . .174 C6
Bannister's Row PE13. . . . .152 B7
Banters La NR34 . . . . .124 F6
Banting Cl NR31. . . . . .170 C1
Banyard Ct PE13. . . . . .154 E5
Banyard Pl 6 NR19. . . . . . .154 D5
Banyards Pl PE33. . . . . .61 D4
Baptist Rd PE14. . . . . .77 D4
Barbastelle Cres NR9 . . . . . .88 C8
Barber Pl NR7 . . . . .163 E5
Barberry Cl 5 NR8 . . . . . . .155 B2

Barber's La
 Bedingham NR35.........108 B2
 Fakenham NR21........141 E4
Barbers Yd **1** NR17....104 D2
Barchams Yd **16** NR26...138 D7
Barclay Cl NR27.........139 A6
Barclay Gn NR7.........159 D1
Barclay Rd NR7.........159 E1
Bard Hill NR25............8 B6
Bardolph Pl PE34.........61 D1
Bardolphs Ct **1** NR8...155 D2
Bardolph's Way PE33....62 C6
Bar Dro PE14.............77 B8
Bardwell Rd
 Barningham IP31........127 C3
 Fakenham Magna IP24...126 D3
 Stanton IP31...........127 B1
Bardyke Bank PE14.......77 F4
BARFORD NR9............69 F2
Barford Prim Sch NR9...69 F2
Barford Rd
 Marlingford NR9.........69 E3
 Sheringham NR26........138 D7
 Topcroft NR35..........107 E2
Bargate Ct NR3.........178 B4
Barham Ct NR1..........170 D5
Barham's La NR16.......105 D4
Barker's Dro PE33........81 A3
Barkers Herne NR27.....139 A6
Barker's La Norwich NR7..159 A5
 Old Buckenham NR17.....104 B2
Barker St NR2..........162 C8
Barker Way **5** NR13....72 D6
Barkis Rd NR30.........169 D1
Barley Cl PE30.........148 D1
Barleycroft NR29.......167 B7
Barleyfield Rd **8** NR10..53 A3
Barleyview Cl **10** NR29..57 D2
Barley Way
 Attleborough NR17......174 B3
 Thetford IP24..........176 D6
BARMER PE31............14 F4
Barnaby Cl **5** NR19....154 C3
Barnard Ave NR30......169 D7
Barnard Cl
 Great Yarmouth NR31....170 C1
 5 Stoke Holy Cross NR14..89 F4
Barnard Cres NR30......169 C7
Barnard Rd NR5........160 E8
Barnards La PE33........61 D6
Barnards Rd NR28........38 A5
Barnards Yd **3** NR3...178 A3
Barnby Rd NR10.........37 B2
Barn Cl
 2 Hopton on Sea NR31..171 E5
 1 Lingwood NR13......74 A3
Barnes Cl Brandon IP27..175 A2
 Norwich NR7............159 D2
Barnesdale Rd **5** NR4..89 E8
Barnes' Rd IP21........121 C5
BARNEY NR21............17 F3
Barney Rd NR21.........17 F2
Barnfield Cl NR12.......39 E2
BARNHAM IP24..........125 F6
Barnham Broom Prim Sch
 NR9...................69 C2
Barnham Broom Rd
 East Tuddenham NR20....69 D5
 Wymondham NR18.......173 A7
Barnham CE Prim Sch
 IP24..................125 E5
Barnham Rd IP24.......126 B6
Barn Hill NR13..........73 E2
BARNINGHAM IP31.......127 C3
Barningham CE VC Prim Sch
 IP31..................127 C3
BARNINGHAM GREEN
 NR11..................20 A4
Barningham Pl NR11.....20 C5
Barningham Rd
 Gresham NR11..........20 D8
 Stanton IP31...........127 C1
Barn La Gressenhall NR19..49 B2
 Mautby NR29...........75 E6
Barn Mdw NR14........163 B2
Barn Piece Cl **9** NR13..55 A1
Barn Rd Docking PE31...134 C4
 Norwich NR2...........178 A4
Barns The NR16........105 C4
Barn Terr NR13.........165 C4
Barnwell Rd PE30......147 B6
Barondole La
 Alburgh IP20..........122 E8
 Topcroft NR35..........107 E2
Baron's Cl NR21........141 C4
Baron's Hall La NR21...141 D4
Barrack Rd
 Great Yarmouth NR30....169 D1
 Norwich NR1...........163 B7
Barrack St NR3.........178 C4
Barr Dr IP27...........113 E2
Barrett Cl PE30........147 B6
Barrett-Lennard Rd NR10..53 A4
Barrett Rd Holt NR25...137 D7
 Norwich NR1...........162 E1
Barri Cl NR14...........90 C3
Barroway Dro PE38......78 E6
Barrow Cl NR3.........157 F1
Barrow's Cnr IP24......125 A4
Barrows Hole La PE32...65 E7
Barsham Cl NR21........30 C4
Barsham Dr PE30.......148 E1
Barsham Rd NR21.......17 C3
Bartle Ct NR10.........37 B2
BARTON BENDISH PE33..81 A8
Barton Broad Nature
 Reserve★ NR12.........55 F7

Barton Cl
 North Walsham NR28....151 A4
 Swaffham PE37.........153 C2
Barton Ct PE30.........147 D5
Barton Dr NR12.........164 E6
Barton Rd
 Ashmanhaugh NR12......38 D1
 Coltishall NR10.........37 B2
 Wisbech PE13..........152 A4
Barton's La PE32........48 A8
BARTON TURF NR12......38 F1
Barton Way
 6 Norwich NR1......163 B5
 Ormesby St Margaret
 NR29.................167 B3
Bartrums Mews IP22....177 F3
Barwick Rd PE31........14 E6
Bases La NR23.........136 C6
Basey Rd NR13..........72 E8
Basham St IP22........177 B4
Basil Dr PE38..........172 E6
Basil Rd PE33..........80 A3
Bassingham Rd NR3....158 B2
BASTWICK NR29.........57 A4
Batchcroft Cl **6** PE38..172 C6
Batchelor Dr NR21......15 C2
Bately Ave NR31.......170 D1
Bateman Cl **3** NR5...160 F7
Bates Gn NR5..........161 C8
Bates La IP22..........119 D2
Bates's Dro CB6........95 D1
Bath Ave NR30.........154 F5
Bath Hill **7** NR30....169 D3
Bath Hills Rd NR35.....123 E8
Bath Hill Terr NR30.....169 D3
Bath Rd
 West Dereham PE33.....80 D5
 Wisbech PE13..........152 C7
Bathurst Rd **2** NR2...162 B5
Batterby Gn
 Fakenham NR21........141 A3
 Hempton NR21.........31 C8
Battery Rd NR30.......170 D8
BATTLESEA GREEN IP21..131 E2
Battlesea Hill IP21.....131 E2
BAWBURGH NR9........160 B6
Bawburgh Cl NR5......156 D1
Bawburgh La NR5......156 D1
Bawburgh Rd NR9......70 B5
Bawburgh Sch The NR9..160 B6
BAWDESWELL NR20.....50 E8
Bawdeswell Com Prim Sch
 NR20..................50 E7
Bawdeswell Rd NR20.....50 C7
BAWSEY PE32...........44 D6
Bawsey Ctry Pk★ PE32...44 D6
Baxter Cl **2** Hingham NR9..86 C5
 Long Stratton NR15.....106 E2
 3 Wisbech PE13.....152 E6
Baxter Ct
 Caister-On-Sea NR30....168 E6
 Norwich NR3...........158 B3
Baxter Rd NR9..........86 C5
Baxter Row NR19.......154 E4
Baxter's La NR15.......107 F8
Bayes Ct NR28.........151 B3
Bayes La NR16.........106 C6
Bayfield NR17..........174 E6
Bayfield Ave **3** NR19..154 C3
Bayfield Cl **1** Ixworth NR9..69 F2
 King's Lynn PE30.......147 D4
Baynard's La IP22......129 D7
Baynes Cl NR14.........90 C4
Bayse's La NR24........18 C5
Bayspole Rd **5** NR15...106 E3
Bazzy La NR25..........7 D4
BEACHAMWELL PE37.....81 E8
Beachamwell Rd PE33..81 B8
Beach Cl Hemsby NR29...167 E3
 Mundesley NR11.......143 C6
 Overstrand NR27.......11 A4
Beach Dr NR29.........167 E4
Beach La NR25..........8 E6
Beach Rd Bacton NR12..23 E5
 Caister-on-Sea NR30....168 E5
 Cley next the Sea NR25...7 E8
 Cromer NR27..........139 B7
 Eccles on Sea NR12.....24 E4
 3 Great Yarmouth NR31..170 D4
 Happisburgh NR12......24 C5
 Hemsby NR29..........167 C7
 Holme next the Sea PE36..1 F6
 Hopton on Sea NR31....171 E4
 Lessingham NR12.......24 E3
 Mundesley NR11.......143 C6
 Runton NR27..........10 C5
 Salthouse NR25........8 C6
 Sea Palling NR12.......40 A6
 Sheringham NR26.......138 E7
 Snettisham NR12.......12 A4
 Wells-next-the-Sea NR23..136 C7
 Winterton-on-Sea NR29...58 B6
Beach Terr Rd PE36....132 C4
Beacon Bsns Pk NR31...171 B8
Beaconsfield Rd
 Great Yarmouth NR30....169 D6
 Norwich NR3...........162 E8
Bears Cl **7** NR9.......86 C4
Bears La NR9..........86 C5
Bear's Dro PE37........153 B5
Bears Rd NR28.........143 D4
Beatrice Ave NR19.....154 D4
Beatrice Cl **6** NR28...151 C6

Beatrice Rd Norwich NR1..163 A6
 Wisbech PE13..........152 D7
Beatty Cl
 Great Yarmouth NR30....169 D8
 Thetford IP24..........176 E5
Beatty Rd
 Great Yarmouth NR30....169 D8
 Norwich NR4...........162 B1
Beauchamp Cl
 1 Caister-on-Sea NR30..168 D7
 Chedgrave NR14........91 F2
Beauchamp Rd **2** NR14..92 A2
Beaufort Cl NR6.......158 D6
Beaufort Way
 Great Yarmouth NR31....170 B1
 Hopton on Sea NR31....171 B8
Beaumont Pl **1** NR2...162 C4
Beaumont Rd NR5......157 B1
Beaumont Way PE30...147 C5
Beaupre Ave PE14......77 F7
Beaupré Com Prim Sch
 PE14..................77 F6
Beavans Ct **8** NR31...169 B4
Beavens Ct **15** NR31...169 B4
Beavor La IP27.........175 C4
BECCLES NR34.........110 D2
Becclesgate
 Beccles NR34..........110 D2
 East Dereham NR19.....154 D6
Beccles Mus★ NR34....110 C1
Beccles Rd Aldeby NR34..110 F4
 Aldeby, Wheatacre, Burgh St
 Peter NR34...........111 B4
 Belton with Browston NR31..94 A5
 Bungay NR35...........124 B8
 Carlton Colville NR33....111 F1
 Fritton & St Olaves NR31..93 E3
 Great Yarmouth NR31....170 A5
 Haddiscoe NR14.......110 E7
 Hales NR14............109 E7
 Loddon NR14..........92 A1
 Raveningham NR14....110 A7
 Thurlton NR14.........92 F1
Beccles Sta NR34......110 D1
BEESTON REGIS NR26...138 E7
BEESTON ST LAWRENCE
 NR12..................55 C8
BEETLEY NR20..........49 D4
Beetley Grange **1** NR20..49 D4
Beetley Mdws **9** NR20..49 D4
Beevor Rd NR30........170 E1
Begdale Rd PE14.......59 A1
Begonia Wy NR18......173 A7
BEIGHTON NR13.........74 C2
Beighton Rd NR13......166 A2
Bek Cl NR4............161 E2
BELAUGH NR12..........54 E5
BELAUGHTHE NR12.....160 A1
Beck Ave NR34.........124 F4
Becks Gn La NR34.....124 F4
Beckside NR10..........53 A2
Beck St IP22...........127 E3
Beck The Feltwell IP26...98 E1
 Kenninghall NR16......119 A5
Beck View **3** IP20....122 D2
Beck Way NR14........91 F1
Bedding La NR3........178 B4
Bede Cl PE30..........148 C4
Bedford Dr PE30.......148 B1
Bedford Mews NR26....138 C6
Bedford Row PE14......41 A4
Bedford St Norwich NR2..178 B3
 Wisbech PE13..........152 C6
Bedingfield Rd **6** NR20..50 B3
BEDINGHAM GREEN
 NR35..................108 B3
Beechamwell Rd PE33..81 B8
Beechan Dr PE30......147 D3
Beech Ave
 Attleborough NR17......174 C4
 King's Lynn PE30.......148 D2
 7 Marham PE33......63 D4
 Sheringham NR26.......138 D5
 Taverham NR8.........155 B1
Beechbank NR2.........162 B4
Beech Cl **6** NR13.....72 C6
Beech Cl **1** Gresham NR11..9 E1
 High Kelling NR25.......8 E2
 6 Loddon NR14......92 A1
 Scole IP21............130 C5
 Swaffham PE37........153 C4
 Thetford IP24..........176 B2
 Wymondham NR18......173 D6
Beech Cres **6** PE33....43 E2
Beechcroft NR5........156 F1
Beech Ct
 24 Long Stratton NR15...106 E3
 Swaffham PE13.........154 D5
 Taverham NR8.........155 A1
Beech Dr
 East Dereham NR19.....154 E1
 North Walsham NR28....151 B6
 Norwich NR1...........163 A8
 Norwich NR4...........162 B4
 Norwich NR6...........158 C4
 Strumpshaw NR13......73 F3
Beech Drift PE31.......140 D3
Beecheno Rd NR5......161 C8
Beeches Cl NR6........158 E4
Beeches La NR9.........86 E6
Beeches The **1** NR20...68 E6
Beechey PE38..........172 C2
Beechfields IP27.......175 F4
Beeching Cl **1** NR1...162 E1
Beeching Rd NR1......162 E2
Beech La NR29..........75 C8

Beechlands NR8.........155 B1
Beechlands Pk NR11....22 B7
Beech Rd Beetley NR20...49 D4
 Downham Market PE38...172 B6
 King's Lynn PE30.......146 E3
 Wroxham/Hoveton NR12..164 D3
Beech Rise **23** NR31...94 C7
Beech Tree Wy **10** NR35..123 F8
Beech Way Brundall NR13..165 C3
 Dickleburgh IP21.......121 C1
Beech Wlk NR14........90 D5
Beechwood Ave
 Aylmerton NR11........10 A3
 18 Watton IP25......84 D3
Beechwood Cl
 North Walsham NR28....151 D6
 Watlington PE33.......61 E5
Beechwood Ct NR18....173 D1
Beechwood Dr NR7.....159 E1
Beechwood Rd
 Hemsby NR29..........167 A8
 Wisbech PE13..........152 D6
Beechwoods NR6.......158 D5
Beehive Yd IP22.......177 C4
Beeleigh Way NR30....168 C7
Bee-Orchid Way NR14...91 C2
Beerlick's Loke NR14....73 B1
BEESTON PE32..........48 C2
Beeston Comm NR26...138 E6
Beeston Hall Sch NR27...9 F5
Beeston La
 Barton Turf NR12.......38 D1
 Beeston St Andrew NR12..159 B8
 Fransham NR19.........66 B8
Beeston Prim Sch PE32...48 C2
Beeston Rd
 Beeston with Bittering
 PE32.................48 D1
 Great Dunham PE32....66 A8
 Mileham PE32.........48 D5
 Sheringham NR26.......138 E7
BEESTON REGIS NR26...138 E7
BEESTON ST LAWRENCE
 NR12..................55 C8
BEETLEY NR20..........49 D4
Beetley Grange **1** NR20..49 D4
Beetley Mdws **9** NR20..49 D4
Beevor Rd NR30........170 E1
Begdale Rd PE14.......59 A1
Begonia Wy NR18......173 A7
BEIGHTON NR13.........74 C2
Beighton Rd NR13......166 A2
Bek Cl NR4............161 E2
BELAUGH NR12..........54 E5
Belaugh Gn La NR12...164 A8
Belaugh La NR12.......55 A7
Belaugh Rd NR12......164 C6
Beldorma Cl NR23.....136 D5
Belfry CE VA Prim Sch
 NR27..................11 A3
Belgrave Ave PE36.....132 C6
Belgrave Gdns NR19...154 E3
Bellacre Cl IP22........177 E4
Bellamy's La
 Burnham Norton PE31...135 C5
 West Walton PE14......59 A8
Bellamy Way NR14......90 C4
Bellands Way **4** NR23..130 C1
Bell Cl **13** Bawdeswell NR20..50 E2
 East Dereham NR19.....154 C5
 Little Snoring NR21.....17 B3
 Norwich NR6...........157 F6
 Taverham NR8.........156 E8
Bell La Rocklands NR17...103 B8
 Saham Toney IP25......84 C4
 Salhouse NR13........164 B1
Bell Mdw **1** Hingham NR9..86 C5
 9 Marthan NR29......57 D5
Bellmere Way IP25......84 C4
BELLMOUNT PE34.......144 A7
Bellomonte Cres NR8...156 F8
Bell Rd
 Barnham Broom NR9....69 B2
 Grimston PE32.........28 C1
 Norwich NR3...........158 E1
 Rocklands NR17........103 B8
Bellrope Cl **5** NR18....173 D5
Bellrope La Roydon IP22..129 D7
 Wymondham NR18......173 D5
Bell's Dro Littleport CB6...95 C2
 Runcton Holme PE33....61 C5
Bells La IP22...........128 C4
Bells Loke NR13........165 D3
Bell's Marsh Rd NR31...170 D5
Bell's Mdw **2** PE37....66 A4
Bells Rd NR31.........170 D4
Bell St IP26............98 E1
Bellview Cl NR24......142 B4
Bellville Cres NR4......178 C1
Belmore Cl NR7........159 E1
Belmore Rd NR7.......163 F8
Beloe Ave **4** NR5.....161 A7
Beloe Cres PE30.......146 D1
Belseybridge Rd NR35..108 F3
Belsize Cl **1** PE38....172 B4
Belsize Rd NR1........163 B7
Belstead Ave NR30....168 D5
BELTON NR31...........93 F6
Belt Rd NR13...........73 C7
Belvedere Pl **3** NR4...162 A3
Belvidere Rd NR30.....169 D5
Belvoir St NR2.........162 B6
Benbow Cl **6** NR9.....88 E8
Benbow Rd IP24........176 F4
Ben Culey Dr IP24......176 C5
Bendish Ave NR31.....170 D2
Bendish Way NR5......160 E2
Benedict Cl PE34......145 F5

Benedict Rd **10** NR12...55 E4
Benets View **3** NR28...151 E5
BENGATE NR28..........38 A6
Bengey's Rd **7** PE37...65 F4
Benjamin Ct NR27......139 B5
Benjamin Gooch Wy
 NR2..................178 A1
Bennett Cl
 Hunstanton PE36.......132 D2
 3 Watlington PE33...61 D5
Bennett Rd NR20........50 B2
Bennett St PE38........172 A5
Bennington's La
 Aylmerton NR11........138 F1
 East Beckham NR11.....9 D2
Benn's La PE34........144 C5
Ben's La PE33..........80 E4
Bensley Cl NR13.......166 C3
Bensley Rd
 1 Marthan NR29.....57 D5
 Norwich NR2...........162 A4
Bentinck Way **2** PE34..146 C5
Bentley Rd NR16.......105 F4
Bentley Way NR3......158 C4
Bentons Way NR10.....53 B8
Berberis La **3** NR31...170 B5
Beresford Rd
 Caister-on-Sea NR30....168 E4
 Great Yarmouth NR30....169 D7
 Holt NR25.............137 C5
Bergamot Cl IP24......176 F4
Bergen Way PE30......146 F8
BERGH APTON NR15.....91 A4
Bergh Apton Rd
 Alpington NR14........90 F4
 Mundham NR14........91 D1
Bermondsey Pl E **19**
 NR30.................169 D4
Bermondsey Pl S **18**
 NR30.................169 D4
Bermondsey Pl W **17**
 NR30.................169 D4
Bernard Cl High Kelling NR25..8 E2
 11 New Rackheath NR13..72 E7
Bernard Cres PE36.....132 D6
Bernard Rd Cromer NR27..139 A7
 Great Yarmouth NR30....170 D2
Berners Cl NR3........158 B1
Berners St NR3........158 B1
Berney Arms Sta NR30...93 D8
Berney Arms Windmill★
 NR30.................93 E7
Bernham Rd NR6.......157 E6
Berrington Rd NR6......157 F6
Berry Cl NR31..........93 F6
Berryfields NR13.......165 C5
Berry Hall Rd NR12.....38 E1
Berry's La NR9.........69 D6
Ber St NR1............178 B1
Bertie Rd NR3.........158 C1
Bertie Ward Way NR19..154 F2
Bertram Wy NR1.......163 A6
Berwick Cl NR24.......142 E4
Bessemer Rd NR4......162 D1
Bessemer Way NR31....169 B1
BESSINGHAM NR11......20 E7
Bessingham Rd NR25....20 E8
BESTHORPE NR17.......174 F6
Besthorpe Carr NR17...105 A6
Besthorpe Rd NR17.....174 E5
Bestthorpe Rd NR16....105 A5
Bethel St NR2..........178 A3
Betjeman Cl IP24.......176 E6
Betsy Cl NR5..........161 C6
Beulah St PE30........147 B6
Bevan Cl
 Carleton Rode NR16....105 C4
 Norwich NR5..........161 B6
Beveridge Way PE33....43 E4
Beverley Cl NR5.......161 E6
Beverley Rd
 Brundall NR13.........165 C3
 Norwich NR5..........161 E6
Beverley Way
 Clenchwarton PE34.....145 E5
 Taverham NR8.........156 F8
Beverly Ct NR31.......170 A7
Bevis Way PE30.......147 B7
Bewfield Rd **4** NR5...160 E8
Bewick Cl
 11 Great Yarmouth NR31...94 C8
 5 Snettisham PE31...12 E5
Bewit Rd NR7..........159 D4
Bexfield Rd NR20.......33 C4
BEXWELL PE38..........79 F6
Bexwell Rd Bexwell PE38..79 F6
 Downham Market PE38...172 D5
Bickley Cl NR21.......174 F7
Bide A Wee Cl IP26.....99 A7
Bidewell Cl NR8.......157 B7
Bidwell Rd NR13.......72 E8
Bidwels ct IP24........176 C4
Bier La IP22...........128 F5
Biffin Wy PE37.........153 C1
Big Back La **1** NR1....92 A2
Biggin Hill Way IP25....85 A3
Biggotts La NR15......108 E7
Biggs Rd PE14.........59 D4
Bignold Prim Sch NR2..178 A2
Bignold Rd NR3........158 A2
Bigod Rd **6** NR35....124 B8
Big Row NR14.........109 F2
Big Yard PE36..........2 A3
Big Yard The PE36.....132 E7
Bilberry Cl **5** NR17...174 B5

Bilbys NR14....110 B6
Billing Cl NR6....158 F5
BILLINGFORD
  Billingford NR20....50 B7
  Dickleburgh and Rushall IP21....130 E5
Billingford Rd
  1 Bawdeswell NR20....50 E7
  Bintree NR20....33 B1
BILLOCKBY NR29....75 A7
Bill Todd Way NR8....155 C2
Bilney La NR10....155 E8
Bilney Rd Beetley NR20....49 B4
  East Winch PE32....45 B1
  Pentney PE32....63 C8
Bingles Turn NR10....53 B7
BINHAM NR21....6 E2
Binham Rd
  Field Dalling NR25....7 A1
  Hindringham NR21....17 E8
  4 King's Lynn PE30....148 C3
  Langham NR25....7 A4
  Warham NR23....6 E8
Binsley Cl NR29....40 D2
BINTREE NR20....33 B2
Bintree Rd NR20....50 B8
Binyon Gdns NR8....156 D8
Birbeck Rd NR1....162 E2
BIRCHAM NEWTON PE31....14 C4
Bircham Rd Docking PE31....134 C4
  Reepham NR10....149 C5
  Snettisham PE31....13 A4
  Stanhoe PE31....14 E7
BIRCHAM TOFTS PE31....14 B3
Bircham Windmill★ PE31....14 A3
Birch Ave NR20....49 D4
Birch Cl
  East Dereham NR19....154 C4
  Little Melton NR9....160 D2
  North Walsham NR28....151 D6
  6 Snettisham PE31....12 E4
Birch Covert 1 IP24....176 F5
Birch Cres IP27....113 E2
Birch Ct Erpingham NR11....21 B2
  Norwich NR5....159 D4
Birch Dr
  Attleborough NR17....174 C3
  Roydon PE32....28 A2
Birches The PE30....148 D4
Birchfield Gdns NR14....89 B3
Birchfield La NR14....89 B3
Birchfield Rd PE38....78 E3
Birch Gr
  Sheringham NR26....138 D4
  West Winch PE33....43 E2
  Wisbech PE14....59 B1
Birchgrove Rd PE30....147 C4
Birch Rd Gayton PE32....45 C6
  11 Hethersett NR9....88 D8
Birch Tree Cl PE30....146 E4
Birch Way
  4 Great Yarmouth NR31....170 B5
  Mundham NR14....108 F4
Birchwood NR7....72 D3
Birchwood St 5 PE30....146 E6
Birchwood Way PE38....172 B6
Birdcage Wlk PE30....146 D3
Bird Cl PE34....146 C5
Birds Cnr IP25....67 E4
Birds Rd NR28....151 B3
Bird View Sq 1 IP26....98 E1
Birkbeck Cl
  King's Lynn PE30....148 B2
  Norwich NR18....162 E2
  Stoke Holy Cross NR14....90 B5
Birkbeck Way NR7....163 F7
Birkdale NR4....162 A2
Birkin Cl 3 NR16....105 F5
Birtles Way NR13....166 C3
Biscay Gdns NR30....168 C6
Bishop Bonner's Cottage Mus★ NR19....154 D5
Bishop Bridge Rd NR1....163 A6
Bishopgate NR1....178 C3
Bishop Herbert Cl NR30....69 B8
Bishop Rise 3 NR8....155 E2
Bishop's CE Prim Sch The IP24....176 B4
Bishop's Cl NR7....163 D5
Bishop's Rd
  Hunstanton PE36....132 C2
  King's Lynn PE30....147 B4
Bishops Wlk 5 NR31....171 C5
Bishy Barnebee Way NR5....160 F6
BITTERING NR19....48 F4
Bittering St
  4 Beetley NR20....49 C4
  2 Gressenhall NR20....49 C3
Bittern Ave NR7....159 E5
Bittern Cl Necton PE37....66 A3
  Thetford IP24....176 D1
Bittern Cres NR12....38 F1
Bittern Rd NR29....57 D3
Bittern St NR8....156 B5
Bixley Cl NR5....161 E6
Blackbarn Rd NR16....120 D8
Black Bear La PE13....152 F7
Blackberry Ct NR6....157 F2
Blackberry Gr NR27....10 C4
Blackberry Hall La NR11....11 D1
Blackbird Ave IP27....175 F3
Blackbird Cl 17 NR31....94 C8

Blackbird Wy 17 IP20....122 D1
BLACKBOROUGH END PE33....44 C1
Blackburn Rd NR6....158 C6
BLACK CARR NR17....105 A6
Blackdike Dro IP27....112 F5
Black Drif PE37....66 A4
Black Dro
  Downham West PE38....79 B6
  Feltwell PE38....97 F2
  Fincham PE33....80 D7
  Marshland St James PE14....60 D4
  Stow Bardolph PE34....78 E8
Blackdyke Cl 8 IP26....98 D1
Black Dyke Rd IP26....113 E7
Blackford PE30....147 D8
Blackfriars Rd
  King's Lynn PE30....146 E5
  8 Wisbech PE13....152 C5
Blackfriars' Rd NR30....169 D2
Blackfriars St
  King's Lynn PE30....146 D4
  Norwich NR3....178 B4
Blackhills Cnr NR13....73 C7
Blackhill Wood Ln NR8....156 A5
Blackhorse Cl 9 NR20....50 E7
Black Horse Dro CB6....96 E2
Blackhorse Mdw 10 NR9....50 E7
Black Horse Opening NR6....158 F2
Black Horse Rd
  Clenchwarton PE34....145 C4
  Runhall NR9....68 F1
Blackhorse St 11 NR2....162 C7
Blackhorse Yd NR3....136 C6
Black Mill La NR15....121 A7
Black Moor Rd IP25....67 D2
Blackmoor Row IP25....67 D1
Blacks Ave NR14....163 B2
Blackslough La NR16....119 D7
Blacksmith La IP24....125 E6
Blacksmiths La
  Ashwellthorpe NR16....106 B8
  Happisburgh NR12....24 B6
  Hindringham NR21....17 E7
Blacksmith's La
  Barton Bendish PE33....81 B8
  Morning Thorpe NR15....107 A2
Blacksmith's Loke NR32....94 C2
Blacksmith's Row 1 PE32....45 C6
Blacksmiths Way NR6....158 E5
Black St Hemsby NR29....58 B6
  Marthan NR29....57 D5
Blackthorn Ave NR25....137 C7
Blackthorn Cl Diss IP22....177 C5
  Norwich NR5....158 D4
  3 Thetford IP24....176 F5
Blackthorn Dr 3 NR19....154 C4
Blackthorn Rd
  Attleborough NR17....174 B5
  King's Lynn PE30....148 C3
  Wymondham NR18....173 D4
Blackthorn Way 16 NR14....90 C5
Blackwall Reach NR13....170 D5
BLACKWATER NR9....51 D6
Blackwater Cnr NR11....36 F5
Blackwater La
  Great Witchingham NR9....51 C6
  Heydon NR11....34 D8
Blackwell Ave NR7....159 A3
Bladewater Rd NR5....160 F5
Blake Cl PE32....28 A1
Blake Ct PE13....153 C2
Blake Dr
  Great Yarmouth NR31....170 A7
  Wymondham NR18....173 F7
BLAKENEY NR25....7 C6
Blakeney CE Prim Sch NR25....7 D6
Blakeney Cl NR4....161 E2
Blakeney Long La NR25....7 C4
Blakeney Point National Nature Reserve★ NR25....7 C8
Blakeney Short La NR25....7 C3
Blake Rd NR30....169 D7
Blakes Ct NR3....158 F3
Bland Rd NR5....161 B6
Blands Farm Cl IP22....177 D1
Blatchford Way PE31....133 B5
Blazey Dr NR18....88 B6
BLEACH GREEN IP21....131 F4
Blencowe Terr 23 PE13....152 C5
Blenheim Ave 4 NR29....57 D4
Blenheim Cl
  12 Long Stratton NR15....106 E3
  Norwich NR7....159 B5
Blenheim Cres
  Beeston with Bittering PE32....48 D2
  Griston IP25....85 A2
  Norwich NR7....159 B5
  Tittleshall PE32....48 A7
Blenheim Dr NR17....174 E4
BLENHEIM PARK NR21....15 C5
Blenheim Pk Prim Sch NR21....15 C3
Blenheim Rd
  King's Lynn PE30....147 C8
  Norwich NR7....159 B5
  Sculthorpe Airfield NR21....15 C3

Blenheim Way
  Emneth PE14....152 E2
  2 Roydon IP22....129 D7
  3 Watton IP25....84 C3
Blick Cl 5 PE33....43 F2
BLICKLING NR11....35 F7
Blickling Cl 1 PE30....148 F1
Blickling Hall★ NR11....35 F7
Blickling Rd
  Blickling NR11....150 A8
  Norwich NR6....158 C5
Blickling St NR21....30 C4
Bligh Cl NR14....90 D5
Blind Dick's La NR22....16 E7
Blind La Castle Acre PE32....46 F1
  Hockering NR9....51 A2
  Honingham NR9....69 F5
  Horsham St Faith NR10....53 D1
  Mattishall NR20....69 A7
Blithe Mdw Ct NR7....159 C3
Blithemeadow Dr NR7....159 C3
Blithewood Gdns NR7....159 C3
Blocka Rd NR32....93 F2
BLOFIELD NR13....165 F5
Blofield Cnr Rd NR13....73 B6
BLOFIELD CORNER NR13....73 C6
Blofield Heath NR13....73 B6
Blofield Loke NR12....164 E6
Blofield Prim Sch NR13....165 E7
Blofield Rd Brundall NR13....165 E3
  Lingwood & Burlingham NR13....73 F3
Blofields Loke NR11....150 C6
Blomefield Rd Diss IP22....177 D4
  Norwich NR3....158 B2
BLO' NORTON IP22....128 B6
Blo' Norton Rd IP22....128 C2
Bloodgate Hill NR11....15 D6
Bloodhills Rd NR29....57 F5
BLOODMAN'S CORNER NR32....171 A4
Bloodslat La NR12....23 D4
Bloomfield Rd NR30....170 E7
Bloomstile La NR25....8 B6
Bloomstiles NR25....8 B6
Blooms Turn NR28....22 E5
Blowlands La NR26....138 B5
Bluebell Cl
  Attleborough NR17....174 B5
  5 Downham Market PE38....172 A5
  4 East Dereham NR19....154 C4
  Thetford IP24....176 F4
Bluebell Cres NR4....161 D2
Bluebell Dr NR26....138 B6
Bluebell Gdns NR23....136 C5
Bluebell Prim Sch NR4....161 E4
Bluebell Rd
  Mulbarton NR14....89 B3
  North Walsham NR28....151 D6
  Norwich NR4....161 D3
Bluebell Way 19 NR31....94 C6
Bluebell Wlk
  Brandon IP27....175 A2
  Wiggenhall St Germans PE34....61 B8
Bluebell Woods NR27....139 E3
Blue Boar La NR7....159 D3
Blue Doors Loke NR31....94 C3
Blue Sky Cl NR31....94 C7
Bluestone Cres NR21....15 D6
Bluestone La NR21....15 D7
Bluestone Rd NR21....15 D6
Blundeston NR32....111 F8
Blundeville Manor 6 NR15....89 C1
Blunt's Cnr NR23....5 B2
Blyth Cres NR26....138 D6
Blythe Wy NR10....53 B4
Blyth Rd NR3....158 B2
Blyth's Wood Av 3 NR8....70 C7
BMI The Sandringham Hospl PE30....147 E6
Boadicea Cl 1 IP24....176 E7
Boal Quay PE30....146 D4
Boal St PE30....146 D4
Boardman Cl NR6....158 D3
Boat Dyke La NR13....166 D4
Boat Dyke Rd NR13....166 D4
Boathouse La NR32....111 F3
Boatmans Row NR23....136 C6
BOBBY HILL IP22....128 A1
Bob Carter Leisure Ctr NR8....157 A8
BODHAM NR25....9 A3
Bodleian Ct NR31....170 B2
BODNEY IP26....83 B1
Boileau Ave 6 NR16....105 F5
Boileau Cl 1 NR4....89 E8
Boleness Rd PE13....152 C2
Bolingbroke Rd NR3....158 B3
Boltons The PE30....148 C1
Bolts Cl NR23....136 D6
Bond Cl IP21....121 F4
Bonds Rd NR13....73 C7
Bond's Rd NR15....121 C4
Bond St 3 Cromer NR27....139 B7
  5 Hingham NR9....86 C5
  Norwich NR2....162 A7
Bone Rd NR8....157 B8
Bone's Dro NR23....4 F7
Boniface Cl NR4....162 C1
Bonnetts La PE14....60 B5
Boosey's Wlk 2 NR16....104 F1
Boot Binders Rd
  7 New Catton NR6....158 C1
  5 Norwich NR2....162 C8
Boot La IP22....120 D6
BOOTON NR10....149 E4

Booton Comm Nature Reserve★ NR10....149 E5
Booton Rd NR10....35 B2
Booty Rd NR7....159 F1
Borage Cl IP24....176 F4
Border La NR32....94 B2
Border Rd PE33....81 A2
Borley Cl IP31....126 D1
Borough Cl PE13....152 D3
Borrowdale Dr NR1....163 B8
Borton Rd 4 NR13....73 C6
Boscombe Rd IP25....85 A3
Bosgate Rise 6 NR29....57 C4
Boston Cl 4 NR19....154 C3
Boston End 6 IP24....116 A1
Boston Sq PE36....132 C5
Boston Sq Sensory Pk PE36....132 C5
Boston St NR3....158 D2
BOTESDALE IP22....128 F2
Botolph St NR3....178 A4
Boton Dr NR19....154 D7
Bottom Breck Cl NR5....156 F2
Botwright Dr 5 PE37....153 C3
Boudica's Way NR14....163 A1
Boughey Cl PE31....3 B6
BOUGHTON PE33....81 A5
Boughton Long Rd PE33....81 B7
Boughton Rd
  Fincham PE33....62 E1
  Stoke Ferry PE33....81 A3
Boulderside Cl 4 NR7....163 E7
Boulevard Rd 2 NR27....10 A5
Boulevard The
  Sheringham NR26....138 D7
  Thorpe End NR13....72 E6
Boulters The NR31....170 C1
Boulton Rd NR7....163 C7
Boulton St NR1....178 B2
Boundary Ave NR6....158 A4
Boundary Cl IP26....113 F7
Boundary La Norwich NR7....72 E3
  Paston NR28....23 B3
Boundary Rd
  Ashby with Oby NR29....56 E2
  Great Yarmouth NR31....169 B1
  1 Hockwold cum Wilton IP26....114 A7
  Marham PE33....63 C3
  Norton Subcourse NR14....92 D1
  Norwich NR6....157 F3
  Raveningham NR14....110 B8
Boundary Road East PE30....146 D6
Boundary Road West PE30....146 D6
Boundary Way 1 NR14....90 C5
Boundary Wy IP22....177 B5
Bourne Cl
  King's Lynn PE30....148 C2
  Long Stratton NR15....106 E3
BOWBECK IP31....127 A2
Bower Cl NR29....56 F6
Bowers Ave NR3....158 A2
Bowers Rd NR3....158 A2
Bow Hill NR9....70 A3
Bowlers Cl NR13....92 E7
Bowling Gn Cl
  Attleborough NR17....174 D6
  Crostwick NR12....54 B2
Bowling Gn The
  Raynham NR21....30 F4
  Wells-next-the-Sea NR23....136 D5
Bowling Gn Wlk 2 NR30....169 C4
Bowman Rd 4 NR4....89 E8
Bow St NR9....86 B1
BOWTHORPE NR5....160 F7
Bowthorpe Hall Gdns★ PE13....152 D5
Bowthorpe Hall Rd NR5....160 F7
Bowthorpe Rd
  Norwich NR5....161 D6
  Wisbech PE13....152 D5
Box's La PE37....153 D5
Boyces Rd PE13....152 E5
Boyd Ave 5 NR19....154 D1
Boylandhall La NR15....107 B4
Boyscott La Bungay NR35....124 A8
  Bungay NR35....124 A8
Brabazon Rd NR6....158 B5
Bracecamp Cl NR29....167 C2
Braces La NR35....109 E3
Bracey Ave NR6....158 F5
Bracken Ave
  3 Beetley NR20....49 D4
  Norwich NR6....158 A4
  Overstrand NR27....11 A3
Brackenbury Wall NR29....57 F8
Bracken Cl
  Fakenham NR21....141 F4
  Horsford NR10....53 B2
  Stratton Strawless NR10....53 A6
Bracken Dr NR17....174 B5
Bracken Rd
  King's Lynn PE30....148 C2
  Thetford IP24....176 C1
Bracken Rise
  Brandon IP27....175 E3
  Mundford IP26....100 A4
Bracken Way PE32....28 B1
Brackenwoods PE37....66 A4
BRACON ASH NR14....89 A2
Bracondale NR1....178 C1
Bracondale Cl 3 NR1....162 F3
Bracondale Gn NR1....178 C1
Bracondale Millgate NR14....163 A2

Bracon Rd NR31....93 F5
Bradcar Rd NR17....103 B2
Braddock Rd NR30....168 E5
Bradenham Way NR4....162 A1
BRADENHAM IP25....66 E4
Bradenham Hall Gdn & Arboretum★ IP25....66 E4
Bradenham La NR19....66 F6
Bradenham Rd IP25....67 A2
BRADFIELD NR28....22 C4
Bradfield Cl NR28....151 A6
Bradfield Dr 10 NR29....57 D5
Bradfield Pl 3 PE33....81 A3
Bradfield Rd
  Antingham NR11....22 C5
  North Walsham NR28....151 A6
  Swafield NR28....22 C3
Bradman's La NR18....87 D3
Bradmere La PE31....134 E5
Bradshaw Rd NR8....157 C7
BRADWELL Bradwell NR31....170 A4
  Great Yarmouth NR31....170 A4
Bradwell Ave 3 NR31....170 A5
Brady Cl PE38....172 B1
Brady Gdns PE38....172 B1
Braeburn Ave PE13....152 C8
Braeford Cl NR6....157 E2
Brailsford Cl NR20....68 A7
Braithwait Cl 1 NR5....161 A8
BRAKEFIELD GREEN NR19....68 D4
Brake La NR21....16 C4
Bramble Ave NR6....158 A6
Bramble Cl
  Besthorpe NR17....174 F6
  Mundesley NR11....143 D5
  Sculthorpe Airfield NR21....15 C2
  4 Taverham NR8....155 E2
Bramble Ct NR21....141 E4
Bramble Dr
  King's Lynn PE30....148 C2
  10 Sheringham NR26....138 B6
Bramble Gdns NR31....93 F5
Bramble La Outwell PE14....77 D7
  Swaffham PE37....153 F5
Brambles Cl 2 NR10....54 A1
Bramble Way
  11 Poringland NR14....90 D5
  Wymondham NR18....173 E4
Bramblewood NR12....39 B3
Brambling La
  5 Cringleford NR4....89 A8
  Cringleford NR4....161 B1
BRAMERTON NR14....90 F7
Bramerton La
  Framingham Pigot NR14....90 F7
  Rockland St Mary NR14....91 A7
Bramerton Rd NR14....91 A8
Bramfield Cl NR2....162 A7
Bramley Cl
  Wells-next-the-Sea NR23....136 D6
  West Lynn PE34....146 C4
Bramley Dr NR21....31 E5
Bramley Rd Dereham NR20....68 A8
  Diss IP22....177 C5
  Wisbech PE13....152 C7
BRAMPTON NR10....36 E3
Brampton Cl PE13....152 A4
Brampton Ct 12 NR5....161 A7
Brampton Sta NR10....36 E3
BRANCASTER PE31....3 B6
Brancaster CE Prim Sch PE31....3 B6
Brancaster Cl
  King's Lynn PE30....147 C8
  Taverham NR8....155 F3
Brancaster Rd PE31....134 E7
BRANCASTER STAITHE PE31....3 D7
Brancaster Way PE37....153 B2
Branch Rd NR13....75 B2
BRANDISTON NR10....52 B8
Brandiston Rd NR10....35 B2
BRANDON IP27....175 D3
BRANDON BANK PE38....112 B7
Brandon Cl Norwich NR6....157 E4
  3 Swaffham PE37....153 C3
BRANDON CREEK PE38....97 A2
Brandon Her Ctr★ IP27....175 D4
BRANDON PARVA NR9....69 B2
Brandon Rd
  Cockley Cley PE37....83 A8
  Methwold IP26....99 B4
  Saham Toney IP25....84 B3
  Swaffham PE37....65 A1
  Thetford IP24....176 A4
  Wangford IP27....114 C1
  Watton IP25....84 C3
  Weeting-with-Broomhill IP27....175 C5
Brandon Sports Ctr IP27....175 B3
Brandon Sta IP27....175 C5
Brandon Terr NR30....169 E2
Brand's La
  Felthorpe NR10....155 D6
  Tharston & Hapton NR15....106 C1
Brandvnvm (Roman Fort) (Branodunum)★ PE31....3 C6
Branford Rd
  Caister-on-Sea NR30....168 D7
  Norwich NR5....158 E1
Branksome Cl NR4....162 B2
Branksome Rd NR4....162 A2
Branodunum PE31....3 B7
Bransby Cl PE30....146 F4
Brasenose Ave NR31....170 B3

Brasier Rd NR3 . . . . .158 B2
Braydeston Ave NR13 . . . .165 D3
Braydeston Cres NR13 . . .165 D3
Braydeston Dr NR13 . . . . .165 F6
Braydeston Hall La NR13 . .73 E4
Brayfield Way NR6 . . . . . .158 F6
Braymeadow NR9. . . . . . . .160 C2
Braymeadow La NR9. . . . . .160 D2
Bray's La Guestwick NR20. . .34 A6
 Rocklands NR17 . . . . .103 A7
Brazen Gate NR1 . . . . . . .178 A1
Breck Farm Cl NR8 . . . . . .155 C2
Breck Farm La NR8 . . . . . .155 C2
Breckland Bsns Ctr
 NR19. . . . . .154 D5
Breckland Bsns Pk IP25 . .84 F3
Breckland Leisure Ctr &
 Waterworld IP24 . . . . . . .176 D5
Breckland Mid Sch IP27 .175 A2
Breckland Rd NR5 . . . . . . .157 A1
Brecklands
 Mundford IP26 . . . . .100 B4
 11 Stalham NR12 . . . . .39 B4
Brecklands Rd NR13 . . . . .165 E2
BRECKLES NR17. . . . . .102 E5
Breck Rd Norwich NR7 . . . .159 E2
 Weston Longville NR9. . . . . .51 E1
Brecks The 8 NR17. . . . . .174 B4
Brecon Rd NR15 . . . . .90 E2
Breeze Ave NR11 . . . . .150 B5
Brellows Hill PE34 . . . . . . .144 A5
Brenda Collison Cl PE31 .140 C4
Brenda James Cl 1 NR7 .163 E7
Brennewater Mews 4
 NR5 . . . . .161 A8
Brent Ave PE31 . . . . .12 E5
Brentwood Eaton NR4 . . . .162 A1
 1 Norwich NR5 . . . . .161 F1
Brereton Cl 1 NR5 . . . . . .161 C6
BRESSINGHAM 2 . . . . .129 C8
BRESSINGHAM COMMON
 IP22. . . . . .119 F1
Bressingham Prim Sch
 IP22. . . . . .129 B8
Bressingham Rd
 5 Gresham NR11. . . . . .9 E1
 Roydon IP22 . . . . .129 C8
Bressingham Steam Mus &
 Gdns* IP22. . . . . .129 C7
Breton Cl 10 NR19 . . . . . .154 D2
Brett Ave NR31 . . . . .170 D1
BRETTENHAM IP24 . . . . . .117 B2
Brettingham Ave NR4 . . . .89 B8
Brett Way PE30 . . . . .147 B8
Brewers Ct NR3 . . . . .178 C4
Brewers Gn La IP22 . . . . .177 B6
Brewery La NR18 . . . . .173 C3
Brewery Rd NR28 . . . . .22 D5
Brewery St NR30 . . . . .169 C4
Brewster Ct NR13 . . . . . . .165 D6
Brewsters 8 NR16 . . . . . .118 C5
Breydon Dr NR8 . . . . .156 C4
Breydon Dr N NR8 . . . . . . .156 C5
Breydon Junc NR30 . . . . . .76 C3
Breydon
 Great Yarmouth NR31 . . . . .169 B4
 King's Lynn PE30 . . . . .147 D5
 Norwich NR7 . . . . .159 A4
Breydon Way NR30 . . . . . .168 D6
Brian Ave NR1 . . . . .162 D3
Briar Ave NR31 . . . . .94 C7
Briar Cl 7 Dereham NR20 . .68 A8
 Grimston PE32 . . . . .28 B1
 King's Lynn PE30 . . . . .148 C3
 14 Lingwood NR13 . . . . . . .74 A3
 9 Necton PE37 . . . . .65 F4
Briar Gdns NR17 . . . . .174 F7
Briar La Edingthorpe NR28 . .23 B2
 Heckingham NR14. . . . . . . .109 F8
 Rickinghall Inferior IP22. . .128 D1
 Swainsthorpe NR14. . . . . . . .89 D3
Briar Rd
 39 Harleston IP20 . . . . . . .122 D2
 Hethersett NR9 . . . . .88 C8
Briars Ct NR5. . . . . .161 F7
Brickfield Cl NR3 . . . . .158 C4
Brickfield Loke NR8. . . . . .156 C5
Brickfields NR13 . . . . .73 F2
Brickfields Way IP24. . . . .176 C6
Brickkiln La
 Ashwellthorpe NR16 . . . . . .105 F7
 Mulbarton NR14 . . . . .89 C2
 South Lopham IP22 . . . . . . .128 F7
Brick Kiln La
 Bunwell NR16 . . . . .105 D2
 Gillingham NR34 . . . . .110 C5
 Long Stratton NR15. . . . . . .107 A5
 Shipdham IP25 . . . . .67 C2
Brick Kiln Rd
 Ellingham NR35. . . . . .109 C4
 Hevingham NR10. . . . . .53 A7
 North Walsham NR28 . . . . . .151 E6
 Thursford NR21. . . . . .17 F4
Brick Kilns Rd NR13. . . . . .73 B7
Brick La NR27 . . . . .10 B5
Brickle Loke NR14 . . . . . . .90 B5
Brickle Rd NR14 . . . . .90 B4
Brickley Cl PE31 . . . . .140 D7
Brickyard La PE31 . . . . .29 C4
Brickyard Rd NR28. . . . . . . .22 A2
Bridewell Alley 2 NR2 . . .178 B3
Bridewell La Acle NR13 . . .166 C4
 Botesdale IP22 . . . . .128 C2
Bridewell Mus The*
 NR2. . . . . .178 B3

Bridewell St
 1 Little Walsingham
 NR22. . . . . .16 F7
 Wymondham NR18 . . . . . . .173 C3
Bridge Broad Cl NR12. . . .164 C5
Bridge Cl Fakenham NR21 .141 C5
 16 Harleston IP20 . . . . . . .122 D2
 Heacham PE31 . . . . .133 C5
 Melton Constable NR24 . . . .142 B4
Bridgecourt NR29. . . . . .58 A4
Bridge Farm La NR4 . . . . .161 C6
Bridgefoot La NR25 . . . . . . .7 F5
Bridge Gdns NR19 . . . . . . .154 F1
BRIDGE GREEN IP22 . . . . .120 F2
Bridge Ind Est NR18. . . . . .173 C2
Bridge La IP25 . . . . .84 C6
Bridge Loke NR18. . . . . . . .173 D3
Bridge Mdw NR29 . . . . .58 A4
Bridge Rd
 Brome & Oakley IP21 . . . . . .130 C5
 Bunwell NR16 . . . . .105 F2
 Burston & Shimpling IP22. . .120 E3
 Colby NR11 . . . . .36 D8
 Downham West PE38 . . . . . . .79 B5
 5 Great Yarmouth NR30 . . .169 C5
 11 Great Yarmouth NR31 . .169 C6
 High Kelling NR25 . . . . .137 F8
 North Elmham NR20 . . . . . . .32 F3
 Potter Heigham NR29 . . . . . .56 F5
 Stoke Ferry PE33. . . . . .81 A2
 Sutton Bridge PE12. . . . . . . .41 A8
 Wymondham NR18 . . . . .88 B2
Bridge St Brandon IP27 . . .175 C4
 Carbrooke IP25 . . . . .85 A4
 Downham Market PE38. . . . .172 B5
 Fakenham NR21 . . . . .141 B3
 Gressenhall NR20 . . . . .49 C3
 Hilgay PE38 . . . . .79 E1
 14 King's Lynn PE30 . . . . . .146 D4
 Loddon NR14. . . . . .92 A2
 Stiffkey NR23. . . . . .6 C5
 Thetford IP24 . . . . .176 C4
 14 Wisbech PE13 . . . . .152 C5
Bridges Wlk
 Fakenham NR21 . . . . .141 A3
 Thetford IP24 . . . . .176 C3
 Thetford IP24 . . . . .176 C3
Bridgford Cl NR31 . . . . . . .170 C2
BRIDGHAM IP22 . . . . .117 F5
Bridgham La NR16 . . . . . . .117 F4
Bridle Cl PE14. . . . . .77 E6
Bridle La
 Downham Market PE38. . . . .172 D7
 Keswick NR4 . . . . .89 C4
Bridle Rd IP25 . . . . .84 C3
BRIGGATE NR28 . . . . .38 B6
Briggs Loke NR11. . . . . .36 D8
Brigg St NR1 . . . . .178 A2
Brigham Cl NR13 . . . . .165 C4
Bright Cl 3 NR13 . . . . .169 B3
Brighton Rd 1 NR15. . . . . .89 C1
Brightwell Rd NR13 . . . . . .158 D3
Brighty's Opening NR2. . .162 B7
Brig Sq NR23 . . . . .136 C6
Brigstock Rd PE13 . . . . . . .152 B7
Brimbelow Rd NR12. . . . . .164 D4
Brindle Dr 5 NR14 . . . . . . .89 B3
Brinell Way NR31 . . . . .170 B8
BRININGHAM NR24 . . . . . . .18 D4
BRINTON NR24 . . . . .18 D6
Brinton Rd NR24 . . . . .142 D8
Briscoe Way IP27 . . . . .113 E2
BRISLEY NR20. . . . . .49 A8
Brisley CE Prim Sch NR20 .32 A1
Bristol Cl NR5. . . . . .156 C1
Bristol Terr NR2 . . . . .178 A2
BRISTON NR24 . . . . .142 E4
Briston Rd Briston NR24. . .142 A5
 Corpusty NR11 . . . . .19 F1
 Edgefield NR24 . . . . .19 C5
 Wood Dalling NR11 . . . . .34 C6
Bristows Loke 18 NR12. . . .39 B4
Britannia Pier Theatre
 NR30. . . . . .169 E4
Britannia Rd
 Great Yarmouth NR30 . . . . .169 E4
 Norwich NR1 . . . . .163 A7
Britannia Way PE13 . . . . . .152 C2
Britannia Wy NR5. . . . . . . .156 C1
Britch La PE34. . . . . .42 B4
Briton's La
 Beeston Regis NR26 . . . . . . .138 F4
 Sheringham NR26 . . . . .9 F5
Briton's La Cl
 2 Beeston Regis NR27 . . . . .9 F5
 Sheringham NR26 . . . . .138 F5
Briton Way NR18 . . . . .173 B3
Britten Cl 9 PE33. . . . . . . .61 D6
Broadacres 4 NR13 . . . . . .74 B8
Broadcote NR15. . . . . .90 C6
Broad Dro Emneth PE14 . . .59 C1
 Grimston PE32 . . . . .45 C8
 Methwold IP26 . . . . .97 F6
 Upwell PE14 . . . . .77 D4
Broad End Ind Est PE14. . . .59 C4
Broad End La PE13. . . . . . .152 F4
Broad End Rd PE14 . . . . . .152 F4
Broaden La NR15 . . . . .107 C6
Broadfen Dro IP26. . . . . . . .98 B5
Broad Fen La NR28 . . . . . . .38 D4
Broadfields Way NR14 . . . .91 C7
Broadgate NR8. . . . . .155 B2
Broadgate NR27. . . . . .11 A2
Broadgate La
 Great Moulton NR15. . . . . . .121 B8
 Roydon PE32 . . . . .28 A2
Broadhurst Rd NR4 . . . . . .162 B1

Broad La Brancaster PE31 . . .3 A7
Great & Little Plumstead
 NR13. . . . . .72 F6
 South Walsham NR13 . . . . . .74 B8
 Swannington NR9 . . . . .52 B5
Broadland Cl
 Gorleston-On-Sea NR31 . . . .170 C7
 Reedham NR13 . . . . .93 A4
Broadland Dr NR13 . . . . . . .72 D6
Broadland High Sch
 NR12. . . . . .164 D6
Broadlands PE38 . . . . .172 B5
Broadlands Cl PE31. . . . . .140 C4
Broadland Sports Club
 NR29. . . . . .75 D8
Broadlands Rd NR12 . . . . . .39 C1
Broadland Way
 Acle NR13 . . . . .166 C3
 Postwick with Witton NR7. . .72 E3
Broadmead Gn NR13. . . . . .72 E6
Broadmoor Rd NR25. . . . . . .85 B4
Broad Rd Alburgh IP20 . . . .122 C8
 Fleggburgh NR29 . . . . .75 C8
Broad Reaches NR29. . . . . .56 C5
Broad Row NR30. . . . . .169 C4
Broadsman Cl NR1. . . . . . .163 A4
Broad St Bungay NR35 . . . .124 A8
 20 Harleston IP20 . . . . . . .122 D2
 King's Lynn PE30 . . . . .146 D5
Broad View 4 NR13 . . . . . .72 D6
Broadwater La PE32 . . . . . .45 B4
Broadwater Way 1 NR12 . .55 E4
Broad Way
 Dickleburgh & Rushall
 IP21 . . . . .130 D8
 Rocklands NR17 . . . . .103 A8
Broadway Cl 5 NR15 . . . . .107 C5
Broadway The
 Heacham NR31 . . . . .133 D5
 Honingham NR9. . . . . .69 E8
 Scarning NR19. . . . . .154 B2
Broadwood Cl NR11. . . . . . .11 C1
BROCKDISH IP21. . . . . .131 C6
Brockdish Prim Sch
 IP21 . . . . .131 D6
Brockley Gn 7 PE30 . . . . .147 C4
Brocks Rd PE37. . . . . .153 B6
Brockwell Ct NR3 . . . . .158 F2
BROME IP23 . . . . .130 B3
Brome Ave IP23 . . . . .130 C2
Bromedale Ave 19 NR14. . .89 B3
Brome Hall La IP21 . . . . . .130 D3
BROME STREET IP23. . . . . .130 D3
BROOKE NR15. . . . . .90 E2
Brooke Ave NR30 . . . . .168 D5
Brooke CE Prim Sch
 NR15. . . . . .90 E1
Brooke Rd Kirstead NR15. . .91 A1
 Mundham NR14. . . . . .108 F8
 Seething NR15. . . . . .91 C1
 Shotesham NR15. . . . . .107 F8
Brookes Dr NR28 . . . . .151 A4
Brookfield Cl NR15. . . . . . .106 F4
Brook Gr 8 NR19 . . . . .154 D3
Brook La Brookville NR26. . .99 A7
 Burgate IP22. . . . . .129 C3
 Needham NR20. . . . . .131 E8
 St Margaret, Ilketshall
 NR35. . . . . .124 C3
Brook Pl NR1. . . . . .178 B2
Brook Rd
 Dersingham PE31 . . . . .140 D2
 Norwich NR7 . . . . .72 E4
 Sheringham NR26 . . . . .138 E6
Brooks Dr NR19. . . . . .154 B4
Brookside NR20 . . . . .49 E8
Brooks Mdw NR14 . . . . .90 D5
Brooks Rd NR10 . . . . .53 B3
Brook St
 Buxton with Lammas
 NR10. . . . . .36 E1
 Cromer NR27. . . . . .139 C7
 Lamas NR10 . . . . .53 E8
BROOK THE IP22 . . . . .129 C3
BROOKVILLE IP26 . . . . .99 A6
Brookwell Springs 1
 PE32 . . . . .44 B3
Broom Ave Norwich NR6 . .158 A5
 Norwich NR7 . . . . .163 A8
Broom Cl 15 Martham NR29 .57 D4
 Norwich NR11 . . . . .162 F3
 Taverham NR8. . . . . .155 C3
BROOME NR35 . . . . .109 C2
Broomefield Rd NR14 . . . . .94 A5
Broome Gdns 2 NR31 . . . . .94 A5
Broom Gn Dr NR20. . . . . . . .32 E4
Broom Gn Rd NR20. . . . . . . .32 E2
BROOM GREEN NR20. . . . . .32 E2
BROOMHILL PE38. . . . . .172 E7
Broomhill 1 NR27 . . . . .10 B5
Broomhill La NR10 . . . . . . .149 B3
Broom Hill La IP24. . . . . . .126 C3
BROOMHOLM NR12 . . . . . . .23 E4
Broom La Easton NR9 . . . . .70 B5
 Witton NR28 . . . . .38 C8
Broom Rd
 Lakenheath IP27 . . . . .113 F1
 Wymondham NR18 . . . . . . .105 C6
BROOMSTHORPE PE31. . . . .30 C7
Broomsthorpe Rd PE31. . . .30 A7
Brothercross Way PE38 . . .172 C7
Brotherton Way 10 NR31 . .171 D4
Browick Rd NR18. . . . . . . .173 C5
Browick Road Prim Sch
 NR18. . . . . .173 C3
Brownes Gr 14 NR14 . . . . .92 A1

Browne St 5 NR2 . . . . . . .162 C7
Browning Pl PE30. . . . . . . .147 A8
Browns Acre IP23 . . . . . . .129 E1
Brownsfield NR11. . . . . .21 D8
Brownshill NR27 . . . . .139 B4
Brown's La
 Holme Hale IP25 . . . . .65 F2
 Mautby NR29 . . . . .76 B7
 Necton PE37 . . . . .65 F3
 Saxlingham Nethergate
 NR15. . . . . .107 B8
Brow of the Hill PE32 . . . . .44 E6
Browston Corner NR31. . . .94 C6
BROWSTON GREEN NR31. . .94 C6
Browston La NR32 . . . . .94 B3
Bruce Cl PE13 . . . . .152 C3
Brummel Cl 1 PE30 . . . . . .147 C5
Brumstead Rd
 Brumstead NR12. . . . . .24 A1
 Stalham NR12 . . . . .39 A4
BRUNDALL NR13 . . . . .165 D4
Brundall Gdns Sta NR13 .165 A3
Brundall Low Rd NR13 . . .72 F3
Brundall Prim Sch NR13 .165 D3
Brundall Rd NR13. . . . . . . .165 E4
Brundall Sta NR13 . . . . . . .165 D2
BRUNDISH NR14. . . . . .110 A6
Brundish Rd NR14 . . . . . . .110 A6
BRUNDISH NR14. . . . . .110 A6
Brunel Way IP24. . . . . .176 B6
Brunel Way Ind Est IP24 .176 B6
Brunswick Cl
 Dereham NR19 . . . . .154 C2
 North Walsham NR28 . . . . . .151 D6
Brunswick Rd NR2. . . . . . .178 A1
Brunswick Terr NR27 . . . .139 C7
Brush Hill NR20. . . . . .33 A6
Brushmakers Way IP22 . . .177 C6
Brush Mdw La PE34 . . . . . .42 B7
Brussels Cl NR19 . . . . .154 C2
Bryars La IP22. . . . . .177 F3
Bryggen Rd PE30 . . . . .146 F8
Bryony Cl 2 NR6 . . . . .158 D5
Bryony Cour NR25 . . . . . . .137 B7
Bryony Ct PE30 . . . . .148 C3
Bryony Way 6 NR17 . . . . .174 B5
Buccaneer Way 8 NR9 . . . .88 D8
Buck Courtney Cres NR6 .158 B2
BUCKENHAM NR13 . . . . . . .91 F8
Buckenham Cl
 1 Fakenham NR21. . . . . . . .141 C5
 Swaffham PE13 . . . . .153 B2
Buckenham Dr PE33 . . . . . .81 A2
Buckenham La NR13 . . . . . .73 F2
Buckenham Rd
 Attleborough NR17 . . . . . . .174 F3
 Aylsham NR11 . . . . .150 E6
 Lingwood & Burlingham
 NR13. . . . . .74 A2
 Strumpshaw NR13 . . . . .73 F2
Buckenham Sta NR13 . . . . .91 F8
Bucket Rd NR31 . . . . .15 D2
Buckingham Cl PE30 . . . . .148 C5
Buckingham Ct PE36. . . . .132 C5
Buckingham Dr 1 NR9 . . . .88 C7
Buckingham Rd NR4 . . . . .161 F3
Buckingham Wlk PE13 . . .152 D8
Buck La IP21 . . . . .130 C4
Buckland Rise 8 NR4. . . . .161 F1
Bucksholt Rd PE14. . . . . . . .59 B7
Buck's La NR18. . . . . .87 B3
Buckthorn Cl 3 NR8. . . . . .155 B2
Buck Yd NR7 . . . . .163 E5
Buddell's La NR23 . . . . .5 F2
Buggs Hole La IP22. . . . . . .128 A6
Bugg's Rd IP22 . . . . .129 B2
Buildings Rd NR30. . . . . . .168 E4
Bullacebush La NR13 . . . . .165 C5
Bullace Rd NR5 . . . . .156 F2
Bullard Rd NR1 . . . . .158 C3
Bull Cl
 East Tuddenham NR20. . . . . .69 C6
 4 Holt NR25. . . . . .137 B6
 Norwich NR3 . . . . .178 B4
Bull Cl La NR21 . . . . .17 B3
Bull Cl Rd NR3. . . . . .178 B4
Bullemer Cl 3 NR12 . . . . . .39 B4
Bullfinch Dr 15 IP20 . . . . .122 D1
Bullfinch Way 4 PE14 . . . . .77 A8
Bullies Way 3 NR13 . . . . . .73 D6
Bull La NR1. . . . . .178 A1
Bullman's Cross La NR20. .69 A6
Bullock Fair Cl 14 IP20. . .122 D2
Bullock Hill NR10 . . . . .53 E1
Bullock Rd PE34 . . . . .144 B1
Bullockshed La NR14 . . . . .91 A7
Bullocks Loke NR30. . . . . .168 E4
Bulls Gn La NR34 . . . . .110 D5
Bulls Gn Rd NR34 . . . . . . .110 C5
BULL'S GREEN NR14 . . . . .110 C5
Bull's La NR31 . . . . .170 D6
Bull's Row NR27 . . . . .11 A4
Bull St NR25 . . . . .137 B6
Bulmer La NR29 . . . . .58 B6
Bulmer Rd NR3 . . . . .158 A2
Bulrush Ave PE38. . . . . . . .172 A6
Bulrush Cl
 1 East Dereham NR19 . . . . .154 C4
 4 Horsford NR10. . . . . .53 A3
Bulstrode Ave 4 NR19 . . . .154 D2
Bultitudes Loke NR30. . . . .168 E4
Bulwer Rd
 East Dereham NR19 . . . . . .154 C4
 Lamas NR10 . . . . .36 E1
Bumstede Ct 5 NR5 . . . . .161 A8
BUMWELL HILL NR16. . . . .105 E2

Bungalow La NR7. . . . . .72 D3
BUNGAY NR35. . . . . .124 A8
Bungaygrave La IP20 . . . . .122 D6
Bungay High Sch NR35 . . .124 A7
Bungay Middle Sch
 NR35. . . . . .124 B8
Bungay Prim Sch NR35 . . .124 A8
Bungay Rd Bixley NR14. . . . .90 B8
 Dickleburgh & Rushall
 IP21. . . . . .130 E5
 Ellingham NR35. . . . . .109 C4
 Hempnall NR15 . . . . .107 D5
 Loddon NR14. . . . . .109 C7
 Poringland NR14 . . . . .90 D4
 Scole IP21 . . . . .130 D5
 Stockton NR34. . . . . .109 F4
 Thwaite NR35. . . . . .109 A5
Bunkel Rd NR13 . . . . .72 E8
BUNKER'S HILL
 Lound NR32. . . . . .94 C3
 Norwich NR5 . . . . .161 B7
Bunnett Ave PE30 . . . . . . .146 D2
Bunnewell Ave NR31. . . . .170 A4
Bunn's Bank Rd
 Attleborough NR17 . . . . . . .174 F2
 Old Buckenham NR17 . . . . .104 C4
Bunn's La
 Great Yarmouth NR31 . . . . .169 C3
 Starston IP20 . . . . .122 C2
Bunting's La IP26. . . . . .98 F5
Buntings The 15 NR31. . . . .94 C8
BUNWELL NR16 . . . . .105 D4
BUNWELL BOTTOM
 NR16. . . . . .105 C6
Bunwell Hill NR16 . . . . . . .105 D4
Bunwell Prim Sch NR16. . .105 D3
Bunwell Rd
 Aslacton NR16. . . . . .106 A2
 Attleborough NR17 . . . . . . .174 F6
 Besthorpe NR17 . . . . .104 C5
Bunwell St NR16. . . . . .105 B5
Bunyan Cl 3 NR13. . . . . . . .72 E3
Burch Cl PE30 . . . . .147 E4
Burcroft Rd PE13 . . . . .152 B6
Burdett Rd PE13 . . . . .152 B4
Burdock Cl
 Downham Market PE38. . . . .172 C3
 Wymondham NR18 . . . . . . .173 E4
Burdock La
 Hockwold cum Wilton
 IP26. . . . . .113 C7
 8 Wramplingham NR9. . . . . .69 F2
Burdock Way 3 NR17. . . . .174 B4
Bure Cl 9 Belton NR31. . . . .94 A6
 Caister-on-Sea NR30. . . . . .168 D6
 Great Yarmouth NR30 . . . . .169 C6
 4 King's Lynn PE30 . . . . . .147 E5
 1 Watlington PE33 . . . . .61 D6
 Wroxham/Hoveton NR12 . . .164 C5
Bure Marshes National
 Nature Reserve* NR13 . . . .55 E3
Bure Rd Briston NR24 . . . .142 D4
 1 Great Yarmouth NR30 . . .169 C5
Bure Valley La NR11 . . . . .150 E5
Bure Valley Sch NR11 . . . .150 C5
Bure Way NR11 . . . . .150 D5
BURGATE IP22 . . . . .129 C2
Burgate La NR14. . . . . .90 E5
Burgess Ct NR30 . . . . .168 D6
Burgess Rd NR3 . . . . .158 B2
Burgess Way 4 NR16 . . . . .90 E2
Burgh Beck Rd NR24 . . . . .142 B5
BURGH CASTLE NR31. . . . . .94 A7
BURGH COMMON NR17. . . .104 D5
Burgh Cty Prim Sch NR11 .36 D4
Burgh Hall Leisure Ctr
 NR31. . . . . .94 B7
Burgh La NR20. . . . . .68 F6
Burghley Rd PE30 . . . . . . .148 E1
BURGH NEXT AYLSHAM
 NR11. . . . . .36 D4
Burgh Rd Aylsham NR11. . .150 D6
 Burgh St Peter NR34. . . . . .111 C5
 Great Yarmouth NR31 . . . . .170 D7
BURGH ST MARGARET
 (FLEGGBURGH) NR29. . . . . .57 C1
BURGH ST PETER NR34. . . .111 C4
BURGH STUBBS NR24 . . . .142 B8
Burghwood Dr PE32 . . . . . .48 D6
Burgh Wood Rd NR29 . . . . .57 C1
Burhill Cl 3 NR4 . . . . .89 D8
Burkitt St PE30 . . . . .146 E6
Burleigh Cl 1 NR30. . . . . .169 D2
Burley Rd NR12. . . . . .38 A3
Burlingham Dr 2 NR33 . . .111 F1
BURLINGHAM GREEN
 NR13. . . . . .74 A5
Burlingham Rd NR13. . . . . .73 D6
Burlington Cl IP22. . . . . . . .177 D1
Burma Cl PE31. . . . . .140 C4
Burma Rd NR6. . . . . .158 E5
Burnet Rd
 Great Yarmouth NR31. . . . . .94 C6
 Norwich NR3 . . . . .157 F1
Burney Rd PE30 . . . . .146 D2
Burnham Ave PE30. . . . . . .147 C8
BURNHAM DEEPDALE
 PE31. . . . . .3 E6
BURNHAM MARKET
 PE31. . . . . .135 C3
Burnham Mkt Prim Sch
 PE31. . . . . .135 D4
BURNHAM NORTON
 PE31 . . . . .135 B6

BURNHAM OVERY STAITHE
PE31 . . . . .135 E6
BURNHAM OVERY TOWN
PE31 . . . . .135 E4
Burnham Rd
  Docking PE31 . . . . .134 E6
  Downham Market PE38. . .172 B4
  North Creake NR21. . . . . . .4 D2
  Ringstead PE36. . . . . .2 C3
  South Creake NR21. . . . . . .15 D7
BURNHAM THORPE PE31 . . .4 D4
Burns Cl
  East Dereham NR19 . . . . .154 C7
  Thetford IP24 . . . . .176 E6
  Yaxley IP23 . . . . .129 F1
Burnside 3 PE37 . . . . .66 A4
Burnt Fen Turnpike
  IP28. . . . . .112 D2
Burnt Fen Wy NR12 . . . . . .164 E6
Burnt Hill La NR33. . . . . . .111 F3
Burnt Hills NR27 . . . . .139 B4
Burnthouse Cres PE33 . . . .63 B4
Burnthouse Dro PE33 . . . . .63 C5
Burnthouse La
  Hethersett NR9 . . . . .160 C1
  Runhall NR20. . . . . .69 A4
  Scole IP20. . . . . .122 A1
  Toft Monks NR34. . . . . . .110 D5
  Wymondham NR18 . . . . .173 F1
Burnt House Rd NR13 . . . . .92 B6
Burnt La
  Great Yarmouth NR31 . . . .170 C4
  Wiggenhall St Mary Magdalen
  PE34. . . . . .61 A4
Burntoak La IP20 . . . . .122 E4
Burnt St NR23 . . . . .136 D5
Burntwood La NR12. . . . . . .54 C4
Burr Cl 14 IP25 . . . . .84 E3
Burrell Cl NR25. . . . . .137 D7
Burrell Way IP24 . . . . .176 A1
Burrettgate Rd PE13 . . . . .152 F5
Burrett Gdns PE13 . . . . . . .59 C5
Burrett Rd PE13 . . . . .59 C5
Burroughs Way NR18 . . . . .173 D4
Burrow Dr IP27. . . . . .113 C6
Burrows Gn NR34. . . . . . . .110 F5
BURSTON IP22 . . . . .120 F2
Burston Cl NR24 . . . . .142 B4
Burston Com Prim Sch
  IP22 . . . . .120 E2
Burston Rd
  Dickleburgh & Rushall
  IP21. . . . . .130 C8
  Diss IP22. . . . . .177 E7
  Gissing IP22 . . . . .120 F3
Burton Ave NR28 . . . . .151 B4
Burton Cl
  North Walsham NR28 . . . .151 B4
  Norwich NR6 . . . . .158 C5
  Roydon IP22 . . . . .177 B5
Burton Dr 9 NR13. . . . . . . .72 D4
Burton Rd NR6 . . . . .158 C5
Burtons Ct 16 NR13. . . . . . .146 D5
Burtontyne Ave NR19 . . . . .68 A7
Bury Bottom PE27 . . . . . . .115 A1
Bury End Botesdale IP22. . . .128 E3
  Brandon IP27 . . . . .175 D2
  Hepworth IP22 . . . . .127 F1
  Market Weston IP22. . . . .127 E4
  Rickinghall Inferior IP22. . .128 D1
  Thetford IP24 . . . . .176 C1
  Wortham IP22. . . . . .129 C4
Bury St NR2 . . . . .162 B4
Bush Cl PE31 . . . . .140 E3
Bush Dr NR12. . . . . .24 E4
Bush Est NR12. . . . . .24 D4
BUSH GREEN IP21 . . . . . . .122 A6
Bush La Dereham NR20. . . . .68 B8
  Wisbech PE13 . . . . .152 E5
Bush Rd Hemsby NR29 . . . . .58 B5
  Norwich NR6 . . . . .157 F7
BUSHY COMMON NR19. . . . .67 B8
Bussey Rd NR6 . . . . .158 D4
Bussey's La NR31 . . . . .170 D5
Bussey's Loke
  Great Yarmouth NR31. . . . .170 A5
  Hempnall NR15. . . . . . . .107 D5
BUSTARD'S GREEN
  NR16. . . . . .106 C3
Bustards' La PE14. . . . . . . .41 F3
Butchers La PE31 . . . . .3 B7
Butcher's La NR21 . . . . . . .141 B4
Buttercup Cl
  North Lynn PE30 . . . . . . .147 C7
  1 Thetford IP24 . . . . . . .176 F5
Buttercup Dr 14 NR31. . . . . .94 C6
Buttercup La PE34 . . . . . . .146 B4
Buttercup Way NR5. . . . . . .160 F6
Butter La NR14 . . . . .92 D1
Buttermere 1 NR29 . . . . . . .167 B7
Buttermere Rd 4 NR5 . . . . .161 C6
Butter's Hall La IP24. . . . . .102 C7
Butterwick 3 PE30. . . . . . .147 C5
Buttlands Cl NR21 . . . . .6 E2
Buttland's La PE33 . . . . . . .81 B8
Buttlands The
  Great Cressingham IP25. . . .83 D4
  Wells-next-the-Sea NR23 . .136 D5
Buttle's La NR15. . . . . .106 D3
Butts La NR26 . . . . .138 B5
Butts The NR5 . . . . .160 F8
BUXTON NR10. . . . . .36 E1
Buxton Ave NR31 . . . . .170 D1

Buxton Cl 4 Cromer NR27. . .10 B5
  Easton NR9 . . . . .70 B5
Buxton Prim Sch NR10. . . . . .36 F1
Buxton Rd Aylsham NR11. . .150 D5
  Cawston NR10. . . . . .35 D2
  Diss IP22. . . . . .177 B4
  Frettenham NR12 . . . . . . .53 F3
  Hainford NR10. . . . . .53 F5
  Horstead with Stanninghall
  NR12. . . . . .54 B6
  North Walsham NR28 . . . .151 B4
  Norwich NR3 . . . . .162 D8
  Spixworth NR10. . . . . . . .158 F8
Buxton Sta NR10 . . . . .36 F2
Byfield Ct 3 NR3. . . . . . . .158 C1
Bygone Cl NR29 . . . . .57 C1
Byron Ave PE13. . . . . .154 B7
Byron Rd
  Great Yarmouth NR30. . . .169 E8
  Taverham NR8. . . . . .156 D8
Byron Way NR30. . . . . . . .168 D6
Byron Wlk 7 IP24 . . . . . . .176 E6

C

Cabbell Rd NR27. . . . . . . .139 B7
Cabin Cl 11 NR33. . . . . . . .111 F1
Cabinet Cl NR19 . . . . .154 E4
Cadamys Yd NR23 . . . . . . .136 D5
Cadge Cl NR5. . . . . .161 D7
Cadge Rd NR5. . . . . .161 D6
Cadge's La NR9. . . . . .86 B3
Cadiz Way NR31. . . . . . . .171 E4
Cadman Way IP25 . . . . .84 D3
Cadogan Rd NR27. . . . . . . .139 B7
Caernarvon Rd NR2. . . . . . .162 B6
Cage La IP24 . . . . .176 D3
Cains The NR8. . . . . .155 C2
Cairns Ct NR4 . . . . .162 A1
Caister By-pass NR30. . . . .168 C4
Caister Castle Car
  Collection★
  NR30. . . . . .168 A5
Caister High Sch NR30. . . . .168 E6
Caister Jun & Inf Sch
  NR30. . . . . .168 E5
CAISTER-ON-SEA NR30 . . .168 F6
Caister Rd NR30 . . . . .169 C7
Caister Sands Ave NR29. . . .168 E4
Caistor La
  Caistor St Edmund NR14. . . .89 F6
  Poringland NR14. . . . . . . .90 B6
Caistor Roman Town★
  NR14. . . . . .89 F6
CAISTOR ST EDMUND
  NR14 . . . . .89 F6
Caius Cl PE31. . . . . .133 C5
Calamint Rd PE30. . . . . . . .147 A8
Caledonian Way 1 NR31. . . .94 A5
Caley Cl NR3 . . . . .157 F2
Caley St PE31. . . . . .133 D5
Calf La NR10. . . . . .53 E2
CALIFORNIA NR29. . . . . . .167 E3
California Ave NR29. . . . . .167 E4
California Cotts NR23 . . . . .136 E5
California Cres NR29. . . . . .167 F2
California Rd NR29. . . . . . .167 E2
Calkewood La IP22 . . . . . . .128 C1
CALTHORPE NR11 . . . . .21 A2
Calthorpe Cl Acle NR13. . . .166 B4
  2 Stalham NR12. . . . . . .39 B4
Calthorpe Rd
  Ingham NR12. . . . . .39 D4
  Norwich NR5. . . . . .161 B6
CALTHORPE STREET
  NR12 . . . . .39 D4
Calvert St NR3. . . . . .178 B4
Calves Well La
  Beeston Regis NR26. . . . . .138 F4
  Sheringham NR27. . . . . . .10 A5
Camargue Pl 4 PE13 . . . . .152 E3
Cambell Dr NR20 . . . . .50 B5
Camberley Rd NR4. . . . . . .162 A2
Cambers La PE31 . . . . .135 D2
Cambridge Ave NR31 . . . . .170 A3
Cambridge Dr PE13 . . . . . .152 A6
Cambridge Rd PE30. . . . . . .148 D5
Cambridge St
  Cromer NR27. . . . . .139 C7
  Norwich NR2 . . . . .162 C4
Cambridge Way NR31. . . . .170 B3
Camden Pl 21 NR30 . . . . . .169 D2
Camden Rd NR30 . . . . .169 D2
Camelia Cl NR9. . . . . .88 C8
Camelot Rd NR31 . . . . . . .171 B8
Cameron Cl PE31. . . . . . . .133 C4
Cameron Cres 4 PE31. . . . . .12 D4
Cameron Gn NR8 . . . . .156 E8
Camfrey 6 PE30. . . . . .147 B7
Campbell Cl PE36. . . . . . . .132 C4
Campbell Ct 1 NR3. . . . . . .162 F8
Camp Cl 2 IP26. . . . . .98 D1
Camperdown 11 NR30. . . . .169 D2
Camp Gr NR1. . . . . .163 A6
Camping Cl 8 NR20 . . . . . . .68 F6
Camping Field La NR12 . . . .39 B4
Campingland PE13. . . . . . . .153 C4
Camping Land PE37. . . . . . .153 C4
Campion Ave NR31 . . . . . . .170 B3
Campion Cl 4 NR28 . . . . . .151 E2
Campion Pl PE38 . . . . .172 B3
Campion Rd
  1 Dereham NR20 . . . . . . .68 A8
  Thetford IP24 . . . . .176 F4
Campion Way
  6 Attleborough NR17. . . . .174 B4

Campion Way *continued*
  3 Sheringham NR26. . . . . .138 B6
Campion Wy NR9. . . . . .88 C8
Camp La NR27. . . . . .10 A4
Camp Rd NR8. . . . . .155 C1
Campsey Rd PE38. . . . . .97 B6
Canada Cl 6 PE31. . . . . . . .12 E5
Canada Rd NR27 . . . . .139 B7
Canal Farm La NR28 . . . . . .38 C6
Canal St 6 PE13. . . . . .152 C5
Canaryfields NR1. . . . . . . .163 A4
Canary Way NR1. . . . . .163 A4
Canberra Rd IP25. . . . . .84 F3
Candlemaker Workshop★
  NR29. . . . . .75 A5
Candler's La 18 IP20 . . . . . .122 D2
Candle Stick NR5 . . . . .69 A3
Candlestick La PE32. . . . . . .45 C8
CANDLE STREET IP22 . . . . .128 D1
Canfor Rd NR13. . . . . .72 E7
CANGATE NR12. . . . . .55 C6
Cangate Rd NR12. . . . . .55 C6
Cannell Gn NR3. . . . . .178 C4
Cannell Rd 11 NR14. . . . . . .92 A1
Cannon Cl 6 IP25. . . . . .84 E3
Cannon St PE13. . . . . .152 C4
Cannon Terr 9 PE13. . . . . .152 C4
Cann's La NR9. . . . . .88 D7
Canon Cl 6 IP25 . . . . .84 E3
Canon Hoare Rd NR11. . . . .150 C4
Canon Pickering VC Jun Sch
  IP20 . . . . .122 D2
Canon Pott Cl PE31. . . . . . .133 D6
Canons Cl 2 IP19. . . . . . . .154 D2
Canon's Cl IP24 . . . . .176 B4
Canons Wlk IP24. . . . . . . .176 B3
Canon Wake Ct 4 NR29. . . . .56 C8
Canterbury Pl NR2. . . . . . .162 C7
Canterbury Way IP24 . . . . .176 B5
CANTLEY NR13 . . . . .92 B7
Cantley Cnr NR13. . . . . .74 B1
Cantley La Cringleford NR4. . .89 A8
  Ketteringham NR18. . . . . . .88 F6
Cantley Primary Sch
  NR13. . . . . .92 B7
Cantley Rd NR13. . . . . .92 D7
Cantley Sta NR13 . . . . .92 B6
Cants Cl 4 NR9 . . . . .69 F2
Capgrave Ave PE30. . . . . . .146 F8
Capps La IP19. . . . . .123 F1
Capstan Way 9 NR33. . . . . .111 F1
Captain Ford Wy NR19 . . . .154 E3
Captains Cl PE13. . . . . .153 D4
Caraway Dr 22 NR31. . . . . . .94 C6
Caraway Rd IP24 . . . . .176 F4
CARBROOKE IP25. . . . . . . .85 B5
Carbrooke Rd
  Caston NR17. . . . . .85 C1
  Griston IP25 . . . . .85 A2
Cardiff Rd NR2. . . . . .162 B5
Cardigan Pl NR2. . . . . .162 C7
Cardinal Cl NR9 . . . . .70 B5
Cardington Ct 1 NR13. . . . .166 D4
Cardington Rd IP25. . . . . . . .85 A3
Cardun Cl 3 NR13. . . . . .73 C6
Carey House Con Ctr
  PE37. . . . . .65 D1
CARGATE COMMON
  NR16. . . . . .105 E1
Cargate Comm Rd NR16. . . .105 E1
CARGATE GREEN NR13. . . .166 A8
Cargate La
  Saxlingham Nethergate
  NR15. . . . . .107 A8
  Upton with Fishley NR13. . .166 A8
Carl Cl 5 NR19. . . . . .154 D1
Carl Cres NR28 . . . . .22 E5
Carleton Cl 1 NR18. . . . . . .173 C6
CARLETON FOREHOE
  NR9 . . . . .87 C8
Carleton Rd NR7. . . . . .159 B3
CARLETON RODE NR16. . . .105 C3
Carleton Rode CE Prim Sch
  NR16. . . . . .105 C3
CARLETON ST PETER
  NR14 . . . . .91 E5
Carlton Cl NR19. . . . . .154 D4
Carlton Dr PE30 . . . . .148 D5
Carlton Gdns NR1. . . . . . . .178 B1
Carlton Marshes Nature
  Reserve★ NR33. . . . . . . .111 F3
Carlyle Rd NR1 . . . . .162 F3
Carmelite Terr 16 PE30. . . . .146 D4
Carmen's La NR28 . . . . .38 B3
Carn Cl NR13. . . . . .74 B2
Carnoustie NR4. . . . . .162 A1
Carnoustie Ct PE31. . . . . . . .41 C8
Carola Sutton Ct NR25 . . . .137 B5
Carol Cl NR4 . . . . .90 B5
Caroline Ct NR4 . . . . .161 F4
Carpenters Cotts NR25. . . . .137 B6
Carpenter's Wlk NR15. . . . .121 D7
Carrell Rd NR31 . . . . .170 B1
Carrington Rd NR27. . . . . . .139 D5
Carr La
  Great Moulton NR15. . . . . .106 B1
  Hoveton NR12. . . . . .164 F8
  Northrepps NR27 . . . . . . .139 C1
  Overstrand NR27. . . . . . . .11 A3
  Poringland NR14. . . . . . . .90 C4
  Wendling NR19 . . . . .66 F7
Carrow Abbey NR1. . . . . . . .163 A3
Carrow Cl NR1. . . . . .162 F3
Carrow Hill NR1. . . . . .178 C1
Carrow Rd NR1. . . . . .178 C1
Carrs Hill Cl NR8. . . . . .157 A4
Carrs Rd NR13 . . . . .92 A8
Carr Terr PE31. . . . . .134 E5

Carshalton Rd 2 NR1. . . . . .162 F3
Carter Cl
  Caister-on-Sea NR30. . . . .168 D8
  Swaffham PE37 . . . . .153 C2
Carterford Dr NR6 . . . . . . .158 E3
Carter Rd NR8. . . . . .157 A8
Carter's Cl PE30 . . . . .148 B1
Carter's La NR20. . . . . .50 A6
Carters Loke NR13. . . . . . .166 C2
Cart Gap Rd NR12. . . . . . . .24 C4
Cartledge Cl 1 NR19 . . . . . .154 D3
Cartmel 17 NR9. . . . . .88 D8
Carver's La NR17 . . . . .174 B5
Casaubon Cl 6 NR19 . . . . . .154 D3
Caslon Cl 3 NR21 . . . . .141 C5
Castelins Way 20 NR14. . . . .89 B3
Castell Cl IP21. . . . . .131 C1
Castell Rd NR19 . . . . .154 D7
CASTLE ACRE PE32 . . . . . . .46 F1
Castle Acre CE VC Prim Acad
  PE32. . . . . .46 F1
Castle Acre Castle★ PE32. . . .47 A2
Castle Acre Cl 2 PE30 . . . . .148 C3
Castleacre Rd
  Great Massingham PE32. . . .29 D1
  Swaffham PE37 . . . . .153 B8
Castle Acre Rd PE32 . . . . . .47 E1
Castle Cl 3 Gresham NR11 . . .9 E1
  King's Lynn PE30. . . . . . . .147 C8
  Weeting IP27 . . . . .175 B8
Castle Drift PE32 . . . . .48 D6
Castleford Cl IP24 . . . . . . .176 B4
Castle Gn NR31. . . . . .170 B7
Castle La Bungay NR35. . . . .124 A8
  Thetford IP24 . . . . .176 E3
  West Caister NR30. . . . . . .168 B5
Castle Mdw NR1. . . . . .178 B2
Castle Mkt St NR1 . . . . . . .178 B2
Castle Rd
  Mettingham NR35 . . . . . .124 D7
  Wormegay PE33 . . . . .62 C6
Castle Rise NR8. . . . . .155 E3
CASTLE RISING PE31. . . . . .27 C3
Castle Rising Castle★
  PE31. . . . . .27 C3
Castle Rising Rd PE30. . . . .148 D3
Castle Sq 16 PE13. . . . . . . .152 C5
Castle St Norwich NR2 . . . . .178 B3
  Thetford IP24 . . . . .176 D4
  Wroxham/Hoveton NR12. . .164 B3
Castleton Ave NR33. . . . . . .111 F1
Castleton Cl 1 NR5. . . . . . .160 F8
Castleton Way IP23 . . . . . . .130 A1
CASTON NR17. . . . . .102 E8
Caston CE VA Prim Sch
  NR17. . . . . .85 B1
Caston Cl 5 NR25 . . . . .137 B6
Caston Rd NR7 . . . . .163 F8
Catalpa Way 5 NR31 . . . . .170 B5
Catbridge La NR14. . . . . . . .89 A4
Catchpole Wlk NR21. . . . . .121 C1
CATFIELD NR29. . . . . .56 C8
Catfield CE Prim Sch
  NR29. . . . . .56 C8
Catfield Rd NR29. . . . . .56 D6
Cathedral Dr NR20. . . . . . . .49 E8
Cathedral St NR1 . . . . .178 C3
Catherine Howard Cl 3
  IP24. . . . . .176 D6
Catherine Wheel Opening 8
  NR3 . . . . .178 B3
Catling's La PE13. . . . . .41 A3
Catmere Herne NR14. . . . . . .89 A3
Cator Rd NR8. . . . . .155 F1
Catriona Ct NR25. . . . . .8 B6
Cats Cnr NR10. . . . . .37 B7
Cattle Mkt St 4 NR21 . . . . .141 C4
Catton Chase NR8. . . . . . . .158 D5
Catton Ct NR6 . . . . .158 E6
Catton Grove Prim Sch
  NR3. . . . . .158 C3
Catton Gr Rd NR3. . . . . . . .158 D2
Catton View Ct NR3. . . . . . .158 D3
Caudle Hill IP25. . . . . .83 E5
Caudwell Cl 2 NR14. . . . . . .89 F4
Causeway
  Brockdish IP21 . . . . .131 C6
  Norwich NR2. . . . . .162 C8
Causeway Dr 4 NR12. . . . . . .54 C6
Causeway The
  Heigham Bridge NR29. . . . .57 A5
  Hickling NR12. . . . . .39 F2
  Stow Bardolph PE34 . . . . .61 D1
Cavalier Cl 30 NR7. . . . . . . .72 D4
Cavell Cl NR14. . . . . .89 C5
Cavell Prim Sch NR1. . . . . .162 E1
Cavell Rd NR1 . . . . .162 E2
Cavendish Cl PE32. . . . . . . .44 C3
Cavenham Rd PE33. . . . . . . .80 E4
Cave's Cl PE34. . . . . .144 B5
Cavick Rd NR18. . . . . .173 A3
Cawdor Cl NR17. . . . . .174 E6
CAWSTON NR10. . . . . .35 B2
Cawston La
  Great Witchingham NR9 . . . .51 A7
  Little Witchingham NR9. . . .149 E1
Cawston Rd
  Aylsham NR11. . . . . .150 A5
  Reepham NR10 . . . . .149 D6
Cawstons Mdw 8 NR14. . . . .90 C6
Cawston VC Prim Sch
  NR10. . . . . .35 B2
Caxton Cl NR26 . . . . .138 F5
Caxton Ct PE30. . . . . .147 D4
Caxton Pk NR26 . . . . .138 F5
Caxton Rd NR34. . . . . .110 D1
Caxton Way IP24 . . . . .176 A2

Caystreward NR30. . . . . . . .168 E1
Cecil Cl 7 PE33. . . . . .61 D6
Cecil Gowing Ct NR7. . . . . .159 B4
Cecil Gowing Inf Sch
  NR7. . . . . .159 C3
Cecil Rd
  East Dereham NR20 . . . . .154 F5
  Norwich NR1 . . . . .162 D3
Cedar Ave 4 NR10. . . . . . . .54 A2
Cedar Cl
  1 Downham Market
  PE38. . . . . .172 C6
  12 Great Yarmouth NR31. . .94 C7
  19 Martham NR29. . . . . . .57 D4
  12 Mattishall NR20. . . . . . .68 E6
  North Elmham NR20 . . . . .49 E7
Cedar Ct
  North Walsham NR28 . . . .151 C5
  Taverham NR8. . . . . .155 C2
  Wymondham NR18 . . . . .173 D6
Cedar Dr
  Attleborough NR17. . . . . .174 C4
  10 Loddon NR14. . . . . . . .92 A1
Cedar Gr
  North Runcton PE33. . . . . .44 A3
  Sheringham NR26. . . . . . .138 D7
Cedar Rd Hethersett NR9. . . .88 C8
  Marham PE33 . . . . .63 B4
  Norwich NR1. . . . . .163 A5
Cedar Rise NR20. . . . . .68 E6
Cedar Row PE30. . . . . .147 B7
Cedar Springs PE31. . . . . . .133 B6
Cedars The Keswick N12. . . .23 F3
  Norwich NR2. . . . . .162 B4
  Shepherd's Port PE31. . . . .12 B4
Cedar Way Brandon IP27. . .175 D2
  Brundall NR13. . . . . .165 C3
  4 Gayton PE32 . . . . .45 C6
  King's Lynn PE34. . . . . . .146 C4
Cedarwood Cl NR4. . . . . . .161 C1
Cedar Wy 14 PE14. . . . . . . .59 A1
Celandine Cl 2 IP24. . . . . . .176 F5
Celandine La 6 NR26. . . . . .138 B6
Celandine Rd 4 NR17. . . . . .174 B4
Celia Phillips Cl 7 IP24. . . .176 D2
Cemetery La NR18 . . . . . . .173 B3
Cemetery Rd
  East Dereham NR19 . . . . .154 E7
  Lakenheath IP27. . . . . . . .113 C1
  Outwell PE14. . . . . .78 A6
Centenary Way PE12. . . . . . .41 C6
Central Ave NR7 . . . . .72 D3
Central Cl 1 NR9. . . . . .88 D7
Central Cres 2 NR9 . . . . . . .88 D7
Central Dr NR20 . . . . .50 A5
Central Rd Cromer NR27. . . .139 A7
  King's Lynn PE30. . . . . . .146 D6
Centre Cres PE31 . . . . .140 D3
Centre Point 6 PE30 . . . . . .147 D5
Centre Vale PE31. . . . . .140 D3
Centre Vale Rd PE31. . . . . .140 D3
Century Rd 6 Eye IP23. . . . .130 C1
  Great Yarmouth NR31. . . . .169 B3
Century Way NR8. . . . . . . .155 F3
Cere Rd NR7. . . . . .159 C4
CESS NR29. . . . . .57 C5
Cess Rd NR29. . . . . .57 C5
Chadwick Sq 2 PE30 . . . . .147 A7
Chaffinch Mews 18 IP20. . . .122 D1
Chalfont Wlk NR4. . . . . . . .161 E2
ChalGr Field 33 NR7. . . . . . .72 D4
Chalk Cl IP24. . . . . .176 D4
CHALKHILL IP25. . . . . .83 C4
Chalk Hill Rd NR1. . . . . . . .178 C3
Chalk La Culford IP31. . . . . .125 C1
  Narborough PE32. . . . . . . .63 E5
  North End NR16. . . . . . . .106 D2
  Sutton Bridge PE12. . . . . . .41 C7
Chalk Pit Cl 14 PE33 . . . . . .63 B4
Chalk Pit Rd PE31. . . . . .3 A6
Chalk Rd Brandon IP27. . . . .114 D5
  5 Walpole St Andrew PE14 .41 E4
Chalkrow La PE33. . . . . .81 F4
Chalk Wy IP26. . . . . .99 A5
Chamberlin Cl NR3 . . . . . . .158 E2
Chamberlin Ct NR13. . . . . . .165 E6
Chamberlin Rd NR3. . . . . . .158 D1
Chambers Rd NR3 . . . . .158 B3
Chameryhall La NR13. . . . . .73 F7
Champney's Rd IP22. . . . . .177 E4
Chancel Cl NR13. . . . . .165 C3
Chancellors Dr NR4. . . . . . .161 C4
Chandler Rd NR14 . . . . .89 F5
Chandlers Cl 2 NR18 . . . . . .173 B3
Chandlers Ct 8 NR4. . . . . . .89 C8
Chandlers Hill 4 NR18. . . . .173 B3
Chandler's Hill La 1
  NR18. . . . . .173 B3
Changi Rd 5 IP25. . . . . .84 F3
Chantry Cl 8 PE37. . . . . . . .65 F4
Chantry La PE37. . . . . .66 A4
Chantry Rd NR2 . . . . .178 A2
Chantry The NR2 . . . . .178 A2
Chapel Ave NR15 . . . . .106 E3
Chapel Bank PE36. . . . . . . .132 E6
Chapel Break Inf Sch
  NR5. . . . . .160 F8
Chapel Break Rd NR5. . . . . .160 E7
Chapel Cl
  Barnham Broom NR9 . . . . .69 C2
  Garboldisham IP22. . . . . .128 A8
  Pulham Market IP21. . . . . .121 C5
  Reepham NR10 . . . . .149 B5
  Tacolneston NR16. . . . . . .105 F4
  Winfarthing IP22. . . . . . . .120 B5
Chapel Cnr NR12. . . . . .55 D6
Chapel Ct Blofield NR13. . . .165 E6

Chapel Ct continued
Norwich NR6 . . . . .157 F5
CHAPEL FIELD NR12 . . . . . . .39 A3
Chapel Field NR13 . . . . .93 A4
Chapelfield Cl 🟦 NR29 . . . .56 C8
Chapel Field E 🟦 NR2 . . . . .178 A2
Chapel Field N NR2 . . . . . . .178 A2
Chapel Field Rd
Norwich NR2 . . . . .178 A2
Stalham NR12 . . . . .39 A3
Chapel Hill NR21 . . . . .141 B5
Chapel La Aldborough NR11 .21 A5
Ashby St Mary NR14 . . . . . . .91 D5
Barton Bendish PE33 . . . . . . .81 B8
Beeston with Bittering PE32 48 C2
Beetley NR20 . . . . .49 C4
Botesdale IP22 . . . . .128 E2
Burgate IP22 . . . . .129 C3
Coltishall NR12 . . . . .54 D7
East Dereham NR19 . . . . . .154 D2
Emneth PE14 . . . . .59 B2
Felthorpe NR10 . . . . .155 C8
Fincham PE33 . . . . .62 E1
Foulsham NR20 . . . . .33 D3
🟦 Great Yarmouth NR31 . . .94 C6
Hempstead NR25 . . . . .19 E8
Hockering NR20 . . . . .69 B8
Hunstanton PE36 . . . . .132 C4
Kirby Row NR35 . . . . .109 E3
Methwold IP26 . . . . .99 A5
Necton PE37 . . . . .66 A4
Norwich NR7 . . . . .163 E6
Potter Heigham NR29 . . . . . .56 F7
Ringstead PE36 . . . . .2 A3
Scarning NR19 . . . . .67 B7
Sculthorpe NR21 . . . . .16 B1
Shelton NR15 . . . . .107 B1
Shotesham NR15 . . . . .90 B2
Skeyton NR10 . . . . .37 B6
West Caister NR30 . . . . . . .168 C4
West Winch PE33 . . . . .43 E3
Wimbotsham PE34 . . . . . . .172 E8
Wiveton NR25 . . . . .7 E6
Wymondham NR18 . . . . . . .173 A5
Chapel Loke
Lessingham NR12 . . . . .24 C2
Salhouse NR13 . . . . .55 B1
🟦 Stoke Holy Cross NR14 . .89 F4
Surlingham NR14 . . . . .73 B1
Wymondham NR18 . . . . . .105 A8
Chapel Mdw NR35 . . . . . .109 E3
Chapel Rd
Alby with Thwaite NR11 . . . .21 B3
Ashby St Mary NR14 . . . . . . .91 D5
Attleborough NR17 . . . . . . .174 C5
Beighton NR13 . . . . .74 C2
Boughton PE33 . . . . .81 A4
Carleton Rode NR16 . . . . . .105 C3
Dersingham PE31 . . . . .140 D4
Dilham NR28 . . . . .38 B3
East Ruston NR12 . . . . .38 E6
Foxley NR20 . . . . .50 D8
Grimston PE32 . . . . .28 A1
Guestwick NR20 . . . . .33 F6
Hainford NR10 . . . . .53 E5
Halvergate NR13 . . . . .75 A2
Lingwood NR13 . . . . .73 F3
Longham NR19 . . . . .49 A2
Lowestoft NR33 . . . . .111 F1
Morley NR18 . . . . .87 B2
Neatishead NR12 . . . . .55 E6
Necton PE37 . . . . .66 B4
Norwich NR5 . . . . .157 A2
Paston NR28 . . . . .143 D1
Roughton NR11 . . . . .21 D8
Roydon PE32 . . . . .45 A8
Scole IP21 . . . . .121 B1
Sea Palling NR12 . . . . .40 A6
Southrepps NR11 . . . . .22 B6
St Andrew, Ilketshall NR34 124 F6
Swafield NR28 . . . . .22 D3
Terrington St Clement
PE34 . . . . .144 B5
Upton with Fishley NR13 . . .166 B8
Wisbech PE13 . . . . .152 B5
Wootton NR35 . . . . .108 C4
Wymondham NR18 . . . . . . .105 A8
Chapel Rd Sch NR17 . . . . .174 C5
Chapel Rise 🟦 PE33 . . . . . .63 B4
Chapel St Barford NR9 . . . . .70 A3
Cawston NR10 . . . . .35 B3
🟦 Cromer NR27 . . . . .139 B7
Diss IP22 . . . . .177 D4
🟦 Hingham NR9 . . . . .86 C5
Ixworth NR9 . . . . .69 F2
King's Lynn PE30 . . . . .146 D5
🟦 Old Buckenham NR16 . . .104 F1
Rocklands NR17 . . . . .103 B8
Shipdham IP25 . . . . .67 C2
Warham NR23 . . . . .6 A4
🟦 Wisbech PE13 . . . . .152 C4
Chapel Terr PE30 . . . . .148 B1
Chapel Wlk 🟦 NR19 . . . . . .154 E5
Chapel Yd Ashill IP25 . . . . .84 A7
Wells-next-the-Sea NR23 . .136 C6
Chaplyn Ct IP22 . . . . .177 F3
Chapman Ave NR30 . . . . . .168 E5
Chapmans Cl 🟦 NR26 . . . .138 D7
Chapnall Cl PE13 . . . . .152 F6
Chapnall Rd PE13 . . . . . . .152 F6
Chappshill Way 🟦 NR14 . . .89 B3
Chare Rd IP31 . . . . .127 B1
Charing Cross NR2 . . . . . .178 A3
Charles Ave Norwich NR7 .163 F8
Watton IP25 . . . . .84 D3
Charles Burrell Mus★
IP24 . . . . .176 C4

Charles Burton Cl 🟦
NR30 . . . . .168 D2
Charles Cl Acle NR13 . . . . .166 B4
Caister-on-Sea NR30 . . . . .168 E5
Cromer NR27 . . . . .10 C4
Dereham NR19 . . . . .154 C1
Wroxham/Hoveton NR12 . .164 C3
Charles Dewar Cl PE32 . . . . .29 D2
Charles Ewing Cl NR11 . . . .150 B5
Charles Jewson Ct NR6 . . . .158 B2
Charles Rash Cl NR28 . . . . .37 B8
Charles Rd
Fakenham NR21 . . . . .141 C6
Holt NR25 . . . . .137 C5
Hunstanton PE36 . . . . .132 C2
🟦 Sutton Bridge PE12 . . . . .41 B8
Charles Sq 🟦 NR2 . . . . . . .162 C6
Charles St
Great Yarmouth NR30 . . . . .169 D2
King's Lynn PE30 . . . . .146 E3
🟦 Wisbech PE13 . . . . .152 C4
Charles Watling Way 🟦
NR5 . . . . .160 E8
Charles Wood Rd NR19 . . .154 E8
Charlock PE30 . . . . .147 A8
Charlock Cl NR30 . . . . .168 E4
Charlock Dr 🟦 NR26 . . . . .138 B6
Charlotte's Cl 🟦 NR27 . . . . .9 F5
Charlton Rd NR3 . . . . .178 B4
Charmbeck Pk NR10 . . . . . .52 D8
Charolais Cl NR14 . . . . . . .163 B2
Charter Cl NR31 . . . . .170 B4
Chartwell Ct NR7 . . . . . . .158 F3
Chartwell Rd NR6 . . . . . . .158 D3
Chase Ave PE30 . . . . .146 E3
Chase Cl NR6 . . . . .158 D5
Chase Ct
East Dereham NR19 . . . . . .154 D6
Thetford IP24 . . . . .176 B3
Chase St PE13 . . . . .152 C6
Chase The Brandon IP27 . .175 E2
Brundall NR13 . . . . .165 F6
Stow Bardolph PE34 . . . . . .78 E7
Upwell PE14 . . . . .77 D3
Walpole St Andrew PE14 . . .41 A4
Wisbech PE13 . . . . .152 A7
Chatham St NR3 . . . . .178 A4
Chatsworth Rd PE36 . . . . .132 C3
Chaucer Cl 🟦 NR20 . . . . . .50 E7
Chaucer Rd NR30 . . . . . . .169 D8
Checker St PE30 . . . . .146 E3
CHEDGRAVE NR14 . . . . . . .92 A2
Cheese Hill 🟦 NR16 . . . . .118 C5
Chenery Dr NR7 . . . . .159 C5
Cheney Cres PE31 . . . . . . .133 D4
Cheney Hill PE31 . . . . .133 D4
Cheney's La NR16 . . . . . . .105 F5
Chepore La NR18 . . . . .87 C1
Chequers Cl Briston NR24 .142 E3
🟦 Long Stratton NR15 . . .106 D3
🟦 Roydon PE32 . . . . .28 A1
Chequers La
Bressingham IP22 . . . . .129 B3
Burston & Shimpling IP22 . .120 E4
Great Ellingham NR17 . . . . .103 E8
Gressenhall NR20 . . . . .49 B4
North Runcton PE33 . . . . . .44 A2
Saham Toney IP25 . . . . .84 C5
West Winch PE33 . . . . .43 F2
Chequer's La NR15 . . . . . . .107 D8
Chequers Rd Roydon PE32 . .28 A1
Tharston & Hapton NR15 . .106 D3
Wretton PE33 . . . . .80 E3
Chequers St
Docking PE31 . . . . .134 D4
East Ruston NR12 . . . . .38 F5
Gresham NR11 . . . . .9 E1
Cherry Cl
🟦 Great Yarmouth NR31 . . .94 C7
Marham PE33 . . . . .63 A4
Norwich NR1 . . . . .162 E3
Cherry Dr NR19 . . . . .154 F5
Cherry Drift NR19 . . . . . . .154 E6
Cherry La
Belton with Browston
NR31 . . . . .94 B4
Dereham NR20 . . . . .68 B7
Cherry Orch NR20 . . . . . . .154 F5
Cherry Rd
Great Yarmouth NR31 . . . . .170 B6
Wisbech PE13 . . . . .152 F6
Cherry Tree Acad Marham
Inf Sch PE33 . . . . .63 A4
Cherry Tree Ave 🟦 NR29 . .57 D4
Cherrytree Cl PE31 . . . . . . .133 D6
Cherry Tree Cl
Brandon IP27 . . . . .175 D2
Holt NR25 . . . . .137 B7
Mundford IP26 . . . . .100 A4
North Lopham IP22 . . . . . . .119 A2
Wortham IP22 . . . . .129 C4
Wretham IP24 . . . . .102 B1
Cherry Tree Ct IP22 . . . . . .177 C5
Cherry Tree Dr PE34 . . . . . .146 C4
Cherry Tree La NR28 . . . . .151 B5
Cherry Tree Rd
Carleton Rode NR16 . . . . . .105 A1
Plumstead NR11 . . . . .20 A6
Snettisham PE31 . . . . .12 E5
Tibenham NR16 . . . . .120 B7
Cherrywood
Alpington NR14 . . . . .90 F4
🟦 Redenhall with Harleston
IP20 . . . . .122 D1
Cherrywood Ave NR21 . . . . .15 C2
Chervil Wlk IP24 . . . . .116 D2
Cherwell Way 🟦 NR31 . . . .170 B2

Chesterfield Cotts 🟦
PE34 . . . . .139 B7
Chester Pl NR2 . . . . .162 C6
Chester St NR2 . . . . .162 C4
Chester Way IP24 . . . . .176 A4
Chestnut Ave
Great Yarmouth NR31 . . . . .170 A5
North Walsham NR28 . . . . .151 E4
Sculthorpe Airfield NR21 . . .15 C2
🟦 Spixworth NR10 . . . . . . .54 A2
Welney PE14 . . . . .95 D5
West Winch PE33 . . . . .43 E1
Chestnut Cl Brandon IP27 .175 E2
Dersingham PE31 . . . . .140 E3
East Dereham NR19 . . . . . .154 E1
Norwich NR5 . . . . .156 E2
🟦 Watlington PE33 . . . . . . .61 D5
Chestnut Ct 🟦 NR2 . . . . . .178 A3
Chestnut Gr NR26 . . . . . . .138 D4
Chestnut Hill 🟦 NR4 . . . . .161 F1
Chestnut Loke NR15 . . . . . .107 A6
Chestnut Pl NR4 . . . . .161 C1
Chestnut Rd
Dickleburgh IP21 . . . . .121 C1
East Dereham NR19 . . . . . .154 C5
Pulham St Mary IP21 . . . . .121 F4
🟦 Snettisham PE31 . . . . . . .12 E4
🟦 Tasburgh NR15 . . . . . . .106 F6
🟦 Watton IP25 . . . . .84 E3
🟦 Wisbech PE13 . . . . .152 C4
Chestnuts The
Rickinghall Inferior IP22 . . .128 E2
Wymondham NR18 . . . . . . .173 B4
Chestnut Terr PE12 . . . . . . .41 B8
Chestnut Wlk PE37 . . . . . . .81 F8
Chew Ct PE30 . . . . .147 E8
Cheyham Mount NR4 . . . . .161 F1
Cheyney Ave 🟦 NR13 . . . . .55 A1
CHICKERING IP21 . . . . .131 D3
Chickering Rd IP21 . . . . . . .131 B2
Childs Rd NR9 . . . . .88 C8
Childs Way NR26 . . . . .138 C5
Chiltern Cres PE36 . . . . . . .132 C3
Chilver House La PE32 . . . . .44 F2
Chilvers Pl PE31 . . . . .133 D5
Chimes Way NR10 . . . . . . .149 B4
Chimney Springs NR29 . . . .167 A3
Chimney St PE32 . . . . .46 F1
Chipperfield Rd NR7 . . . . . .159 E1
Chittock Cl 🟦 NR10 . . . . . .54 A1
Cholmondeley Way 🟦
PE33 . . . . .43 F2
Chopyngs Dole Cl NR7 . . . .159 C5
Choseley Ct NR18 . . . . .173 C4
Choseley Rd
Docking PE31 . . . . .134 C7
Thornham PE36 . . . . .2 D6
CHRISTCHURCH PE14 . . . . .95 A7
Christchurch Rd NR2 . . . . .162 A4
Christ Church Rd NR31 . . . .170 A4
Christie Cl 🟦 NR19 . . . . . .154 D1
Christine Ave NR13 . . . . . . .74 A2
Christine Rd 🟦 NR10 . . . . .54 A1
Christopher Cl
🟦 Newton Flotman NR15 . . .89 D1
🟦 Norwich NR1 . . . . .162 E2
Christopher Dr PE13 . . . . . .152 F6
Christophers Cl NR27 . . . . .139 D3
Church Alley NR13 . . . . . . .165 E6
Church Ave Croxton IP24 . .116 C5
Halvergate NR13 . . . . .74 F1
Little Ellingham NR17 . . . . . .86 A1
Norwich NR4 . . . . .162 B3
Church Ave E NR2 . . . . .162 B3
Church Bank
Marshland St James PE14 . . .60 C2
Terrington St Clement
PE34 . . . . .144 B6
Church Cl Antingham NR28 .22 B3
🟦 Bawdeswell NR20 . . . . . .50 E7
Beeston Regis NR27 . . . . . . .9 F5
Bixley NR14 . . . . .90 B7
Brandon IP27 . . . . .175 B3
Caister-on-Sea NR30 . . . . .168 D5
Cantley NR13 . . . . .92 C7
Colby NR11 . . . . .36 D8
🟦 Coltishall NR12 . . . . .54 C6
Grimston NR20 . . . . .45 B8
Hepworth IP22 . . . . .127 E1
🟦 Horstead with Stanninghall
NR12 . . . . .54 C6
King's Lynn PE34 . . . . .146 C4
Lamas NR10 . . . . .36 F1
🟦 Loddon NR14 . . . . .92 A2
🟦 Norwich NR2 . . . . .162 B8
Overstrand NR27 . . . . .11 A3
Pentney PE32 . . . . .63 C8
Poringland NR14 . . . . .90 C4
Pulham St Mary IP21 . . . . .122 A4
🟦 Roydon IP22 . . . . .129 D7
Sea Palling NR12 . . . . .40 B5
Shipdham IP25 . . . . .67 B2
South Walsham NR13 . . . . . .74 A8
Upper Sheringham NR26 . . .138 A4
Walpole St Andrew PE14 . . .41 E4
Whissonsett NR20 . . . . .31 D2
Wiggenhall St Mary Magdalen
PE34 . . . . .61 B6
Wortwell IP20 . . . . .122 F3
Church Cotts NR19 . . . . . . .48 E3
Church Crofts PE31 . . . . . . .27 C3
Church Dam NR13 . . . . .93 A5
Church Dro PE14 . . . . .77 F6
CHURCH END IP27 . . . . . . .175 B3
Church End IP27 . . . . .175 B3
Church Farm Cl
Palgrave IP22 . . . . .177 C2
🟦 Weybourne NR25 . . . . . . .8 F5

Church Farm Cres NR29. .167 B6
Church Farm La
East Dereham NR19 . . . . . .154 C5
Sparham NR9 . . . . .51 A6
Church Farm Rare Breeds
Ctr★ PE34 . . . . .79 F8
Church Farm Rd PE31 . . . .133 F7
Churchfarm Wlk PE33 . . . . .62 E1
Church Farm Wy IP27 . . . .113 E1
Church Field
Attlebridge NR9 . . . . .52 A4
🟦 Cringleford NR4 . . . . . . .89 B8
Churchfield Gn 🟦 NR7 . . .163 D8
Churchfield Rd 🟦 PE14 . . .77 F6
Churchfields NR9 . . . . .88 D8
Churchfields Rd NR15 . . . .106 F4
Church Gate 🟦 PE12 . . . . . .41 B8
Churchgate St 🟦 PE38 . . . .97 B5
Churchgate Way PE34 . . . .144 C5
Church Gdns IP31 . . . . . . .127 C3
Church Gn Norwich NR7 . . .159 B5
West Acre PE32 . . . . .46 B2
Church Gr PE14 . . . . .59 A2
Church Hill Banham NR16 .119 D7
Beighton NR13 . . . . .74 C3
Hoxne IP21 . . . . .131 A4
Reepham NR10 . . . . .149 C4
Saxlingham Nethergate
NR15 . . . . .107 D8
Starston IP20 . . . . .122 C3
Churchill Cl
Hevingham NR10 . . . . .53 B8
🟦 Watton IP25 . . . . .84 D3
Churchill Cres
Fincham PE33 . . . . .62 E1
Sheringham NR26 . . . . .138 B5
Churchill Pl NR15 . . . . .90 F2
Churchill Park Sch PO30 147 D4
Churchill Rd
Great Yarmouth NR30 . . . . .169 D6
Norwich NR3 . . . . .162 E8
Thetford IP24 . . . . .176 E5
Wisbech PE13 . . . . .152 D4
Churchill Way PE38 . . . . . .172 B4
Church La Aldeby NR34 . . . .110 F5
Aldby, Wheatacre, Burgh St
Peter NR34 . . . . .111 B5
Antingham NR28 . . . . .22 B3
Ashwellthorpe NR16 . . . . . .106 A7
Baconsthorpe NR25 . . . . . . .19 F7
Bacton NR28 . . . . .23 C3
Banham NR16 . . . . .119 D7
Barnham IP24 . . . . .125 F6
Barton Bendish PE33 . . . . . .81 B8
Belaugh NR12 . . . . .54 E4
Belton with Browston NR31 .94 A5
Billingford NR20 . . . . .50 B7
Bintree NR20 . . . . .33 B2
Bircham PE31 . . . . .14 B3
Blo' Norton IP22 . . . . .128 B6
Boughton PE33 . . . . .80 F5
Bracon Ash NR14 . . . . .88 F3
Bradenham IP25 . . . . .66 D4
Bressingham IP22 . . . . .129 B7
Briningham NR24 . . . . .18 D5
Briston NR24 . . . . .142 E4
Brockdish IP21 . . . . .131 C6
Broome NR35 . . . . .109 B3
Bunwell NR16 . . . . .105 D3
Burgh & Tuttington NR11. . .36 C4
Claxton NR14 . . . . .91 C5
Cley next the Sea NR25 . . . . .7 E6
Corton NR32 . . . . .171 F1
Cranworth IP25 . . . . .85 F7
Deopham NR18 . . . . .86 F4
Dersingham PE31 . . . . .140 E3
Ditchingham NR35 . . . . . . .108 F3
Easton NR9 . . . . .70 B6
East Tuddenham NR20 . . . . .69 C6
East Walton PE32 . . . . .45 E3
East Winch PE32 . . . . .44 F2
Felthorpe NR10 . . . . .155 D7
Filby NR29 . . . . .75 E8
Fleggburgh NR29 . . . . .57 A1
Frettenham NR12 . . . . .54 A5
Fritton & St Olaves NR31 . . .93 F3
Great Massingham PE32 . . . .29 D1
Great Yarmouth NR31 . . . . .170 C5
Gresham NR11 . . . . .9 E1
Gressenhall NR19 . . . . .49 C2
Guestwick NR20 . . . . .33 F6
Haddiscoe NR14 . . . . .110 E7
Hales NR14 . . . . .109 F7
Harpley PE31 . . . . .29 C5
Heacham PE31 . . . . .133 E6
Heckingham NR14 . . . . .92 C1
Heckingham NR14 . . . . .92 C1
Hemblington NR13 . . . . .73 F6
Hepworth IP22 . . . . .127 E1
Hevingham NR10 . . . . .36 B1
Hindolveston NR20 . . . . .33 C8
Hockwold cum Wilton
IP26 . . . . .114 A6
Holme Hale PE37 . . . . .65 F2
Ixworth NR9 . . . . .69 E6
Ketteringham NR18 . . . . . . .88 E5
King's Lynn PE30 . . . . .146 E4
Langley with Hardley NR14. .92 C3
Lessingham NR12 . . . . .24 C3
Leziate PE32 . . . . .44 F4
Little Ellingham NR17 . . . . . .86 A1
Little Massingham PE32 . . . .29 C2
Long Stratton NR15. . . . . . .106 F4
Lound NR32 . . . . .171 A3
Marham PE33 . . . . .63 A4
Marlingford NR9 . . . . .69 E4
Marsham NR10 . . . . .36 B2

Cha–Chu 185

Church La continued
Mattishall NR20. . . . . .68 F6
Mautby NR29. . . . . .75 D5
Morley NR18 . . . . .87 A3
Mundesley NR11 . . . . .143 C6
Mundford IP26 . . . . .100 B4
Neatishead NR12 . . . . .55 E6
North Elmham NR20 . . . . . .49 E8
Northwold PE33 . . . . .81 B2
Norwich NR4 . . . . .161 E1
Norwich NR7 . . . . .159 C5
Old Buckenham NR17 . . . . .104 D2
Oulton NR11 . . . . .35 C7
Potter Heigham NR29 . . . . . .56 F7
Redenhall with Harleston
IP20 . . . . .122 E3
Rickinghall Superior IP22 . .128 E1
Roydon PE32 . . . . .27 F2
Runcton Holme PE33 . . . . . .61 D4
Runhall NR9 . . . . .87 A8
Runhall NR20 . . . . .69 A6
Sheringham NR26 . . . . .138 F6
Shipdham IP25 . . . . .67 B2
Shouldham Thorpe PE33 . . . .62 B3
South Creake NR21 . . . . . . .14 D7
🟦 Southery PE38 . . . . .97 B5
Sparham NR9 . . . . .51 B6
Spixworth NR10 . . . . .53 F2
Sprowston NR7 . . . . .159 B5
Stanfield NR20 . . . . .48 F8
Stanhoe PE31 . . . . .14 E7
St Martin, South Elmham
otherwise Homersfield
IP20 . . . . .123 B4
Stuston IP21 . . . . .130 B4
Surlingham NR14. . . . . .73 A1
Sustead NR11 . . . . .21 B8
Swannington NR9 . . . . .52 B6
Swanton Abbott NR10 . . . . .37 C5
Terrington St John PE14 . . . .42 B2
Thelnetham IP22 . . . . .128 B5
Thompson IP24 . . . . .102 C7
Thwaite NR35 . . . . .109 A6
Tibenham NR16 . . . . .120 E8
Tilney All Saints PE34 . . . . . .42 E4
Tittleshall PE32 . . . . .48 B8
Tivetshall St Mary NR15 . . .121 B4
Tunstead NR12 . . . . .37 F1
Watlington PE33 . . . . .61 E6
Weasenham All Saints PE32 47 C8
Wicklewood NR18 . . . . .87 B5
Winfarthing IP22 . . . . .120 B1
Wood Dalling NR11 . . . . . . .34 B5
Wormegay PE33 . . . . .62 D6
Wroxham/Hoveton NR12 . .164 B3
Yaxham NR19 . . . . .68 A5
Church Lanes NR21 . . . . . .141 B5
Church Loke NR11 . . . . .21 D7
Churchman Rd NR7 . . . . . .159 C2
Church Marsh Nature
Reserve★ NR14. . . . . . . .73 A1
Church Mdw
Rickinghall Inferior IP22 . . .128 D2
Yelverton NR14 . . . . .90 E5
Church Mdw La NR14 . . . . .90 F4
Church Mews PE13 . . . . . .152 C5
Church of the Holy
Sepulchre (rems)★
IP24 . . . . .176 A4
Church Path PE33 . . . . .80 E2
Church Pl PE31 . . . . .134 D5
Church Plain
🟦 Great Yarmouth
NR30 . . . . .169 C4
Wells-next-the-Sea NR23 . .136 D5
Church Rd Alburgh IP20 . . .122 F6
Alpington NR14 . . . . .90 F4
Aslacton NR15 . . . . .106 A2
Aylmerton NR11 . . . . .10 A3
Bacton NR12 . . . . .23 D4
Barningham IP31 . . . . .127 C3
Barton Bendish PE33 . . . . . .81 B8
Barton Turf NR12 . . . . .55 E8
Beeston with Bittering PE32 48 B2
Beetley NR20 . . . . .49 B6
Bergh Apton NR15. . . . . . . .91 A3
Bintree NR20 . . . . .33 B2
Brandon IP27 . . . . .175 B3
Bridgham NR16 . . . . .118 C5
Brockdish IP21 . . . . .131 C6
Brundall NR13 . . . . .165 E6
Burgh Castle NR31 . . . . .93 F8
Cantley NR13 . . . . .92 D7
Carleton Rode NR16 . . . . . .105 C2
Catfield NR29 . . . . .56 C8
Christchurch PE14. . . . . . . .95 A7
Clenchwarton PE34 . . . . . .145 D5
Colby NR11 . . . . .36 D8
Colkirk NR21 . . . . .31 D5
Crimplesham PE33 . . . . .80 B6
Denham IP21. . . . . .131 A1
Deopham NR18 . . . . .86 E3
Dickleburgh & Rushall
IP21 . . . . .130 D8
Dilham NR28 . . . . .38 C4
Downham Market PE38. . . .172 C6
Earsham NR35. . . . . .123 F7
Ellingham NR35 . . . . .109 D3
Elm PE14 . . . . .78 B7
Elsing NR20 . . . . .50 F3
Felmingham NR28 . . . . .37 C7
Flitcham PE31 . . . . .28 C5
Flixton NR35 . . . . .123 E5
Fordham PE38 . . . . .79 B1
Freethorpe NR13. . . . . .92 F8

Church Rd continued
Frettenham NR10 . . . .**53** F4
Garboldisham IP22 . . . . . .**128** A8
Gillingham NR34 . . . .**110** C3
Great & Little Plumstead
  NR13. . . . .**73** A4
Great Yarmouth NR31 . . . .**170** C7
Griston IP25 . . . .**85** A1
Haddiscoe NR14 . . . .**110** E8
Hardingham NR9. . . . .**86** D7
Hedenham NR35. . . . .**108** E4
Hilgay PE38 . . . .**79** E1
Hoe NR20 . . . .**49** F6
Holme Hale IP25. . . . .**66** A2
Honington IP31 . . . .**126** D1
Horning NR12 . . . .**55** F3
Hunstanton PE36. . . . .**132** F7
Itteringham NR11 . . . .**20** C2
Ketteringham NR18. . . . . . .**88** D5
Kirby Cane NR35. . . . .**109** E4
Kirstead NR15. . . . .**90** F1
Leverington PE13 . . . .**152** F7
Lingwood & Burlingham
  NR13. . . . .**73** F3
Little Barningham NR11 . . .**20** C4
Market Weston IP22 . . . . .**127** E4
Marlingford NR9 . . . .**70** A3
Neatishead NR12 . . . .**55** E6
Newton Flotman NR15 . . . .**89** C1
North Lopham IP22. . . . . .**119** A1
Norton Subcourse NR14 . . .**92** E1
Ovington IP25 . . . .**84** E5
Postwick with Witton NR13. .**72** F3
Potter Heigham NR29. . . . .**56** F6
Quidenham NR16. . . . .**118** F8
Reedham NR13 . . . .**93** A5
Repps with Bastwick NR29. .**57** A4
Runhall NR9. . . . .**69** A1
Sea Palling NR12. . . . .**40** A5
Shelfanger IP22 . . . .**120** B2
Shouldham PE33 . . . .**62** E3
Shropham NR17 . . . .**103** B3
Sisland NR14. . . . .**91** D1
Snettisham PE31 . . . .**12** E5
Somerton NR29. . . . .**57** F6
South Lopham IP22. . . . . .**128** D8
Stockton NR34. . . . .**109** F5
Stoke Ferry PE33. . . . .**80** E2
Strumpshaw NR13. . . . .**91** F8
Sutton NR12 . . . .**39** C3
Swafield NR28. . . . .**22** C4
Swainsthorpe NR14. . . . . . .**89** D4
Tasburgh NR15. . . . .**106** F6
Terrington St John PE14. . . .**42** B1
Tharston & Hapton NR15 . **106** D5
Thompson IP24 . . . .**102** B7
Thurlton NR14. . . . .**92** F1
Thurne NR29. . . . .**56** E2
Tibenham NR16. . . . .**120** E8
Tilney All Saints PE34 . . . .**144** F1
Tilney St Lawrence PE34. . . .**42** D2
Toft Monks NR34. . . . .**110** D6
Topcroft NR35. . . . .**107** F3
Tunstead NR12 . . . .**55** B8
Upton with Fishley NR13. . .**166** A4
Wacton NR15. . . . .**106** C2
Walpole St Andrew PE14 . . .**41** E3
Walsingham NR22. . . . .**16** F8
Watlington PE34 . . . .**61** C6
Watton IP25 . . . .**84** E3
Wellingham PE32. . . . .**30** E1
Wereham PE33 . . . .**80** E4
West Beckham NR25. . . . . . .**9** C2
West Dereham PE33. . . . . . .**80** B4
Wheatacre NR34. . . . .**111** A5
Whinburgh & Westfield
  NR19. . . . .**68** A3
Wiggenhall St Germans
  PE34. . . . .**61** A8
Wimbotsham PE34 . . . . . .**172** E8
Wingfield IP21 . . . .**131** E3
Woodton NR35. . . . .**108** B5
Wortham IP22. . . . .**129** C5
Wreningham NR11. . . . .**88** E1
Wroxham/Hoveton NR12 . **164** D5
Yelverton NR14 . . . .**90** F5
Church Rd N IP21. . . . . . .**131** C7
Church St Ashill IP25. . . . . .**84** A7
Attleborough NR17 . . . . . .**174** D5
Bawburgh NR9 . . . .**160** A6
Bradenham IP25. . . . .**66** E3
Brisley NR20. . . . .**49** A8
Briston NR24. . . . .**142** E4
Carbrooke IP25. . . . .**85** A5
Coltishall NR12 . . . .**54** C6
Cromer NR27. . . . .**139** C6
Diss IP22. . . . .**177** D4
East Dereham NR19 . . . . .**154** D5
Elsing NR20. . . . .**50** F3
Gimingham NR11. . . . .**22** E7
Great Ellingham NR17. . . .**103** D7
23 Harleston IP20 . . . . . . **122** D2
Hingham NR9 . . . .**86** C5
Holt NR25 . . . .**137** C6
Horsford NR10. . . . .**53** B2
Hunstanton PE36. . . . .**132** C4
Kenninghall NR16 . . . .**119** B4
King's Lynn PE30. . . . .**146** D4
Litcham PE32. . . . .**48** A4
Little Walsingham NR22 . . . .**16** F1
New Buckenham NR16 . . .**104** F1
North Creake NR21. . . . . . .**15** D8
Northrepps NR27 . . . .**11** A2
11 North Walsham NR28 . **151** D5
Norwich NR6. . . . .**158** E5

Church St continued
Plumstead NR11 . . . .**20** A5
Reepham NR10 . . . .**149** C4
Sheringham NR26 . . . .**138** D7
Southrepps NR11 . . . .**22** B7
Stiffkey NR23. . . . .**6** D6
15 Sutton Bridge PE12 . . . .**41** B8
Thornham PE36. . . . .**2** D6
Trimingham NR11 . . . .**11** D1
Wells-next-the-Sea NR23 . **136** D5
Wymondham NR18 . . . . . .**173** B4
Church Terr
5 Outwell PE14 . . . .**77** F6
21 Wisbech PE13 . . . .**152** C5
Wroxham NR12 . . . .**164** B3
Church View
Harleston IP20 . . . .**122** E2
Marham PE33 . . . .**63** B4
Ormesby St Margaret
  NR29. . . . .**167** B2
Pentney PE37 . . . .**63** C8
Church View Cl
Norwich NR7. . . . .**159** B5
Reedham NR13 . . . .**93** A5
Church View Ct NR7. . . . .**159** B5
Churchway IP22. . . . .**128** F5
Church Wlk
Beachamwell PE37. . . . . . .**81** F8
Burnham Market PE31 . . .**135** B4
Great Yarmouth NR31 . . . .**94** C6
Shelfanger IP22 . . . .**120** B2
Churn Ct PE30. . . . .**147** C7
Cider Ct NR17 . . . .**174** E4
Cinder La NR34. . . . .**111** C6
Cintra Rd NR1 . . . .**163** B6
Circlet Pl NR17. . . . .**174** B3
Cirrus Way NR7. . . . .**159** C2
City Acad Norwich NR4. . **161** D5
City Coll Norwich NR2. . .**178** A2
City Ind Est NR2 . . . .**162** C8
City of Norwich Aviation
  Mus★ NR6. . . . .**53** D1
City of Norwich Sch NR4 **162** B2
City Rd NR1 . . . .**178** C1
City View Rd NR6. . . . . . .**158** A4
Civic Gdns NR3 . . . .**158** B3
Civray Ave PE38 . . . .**172** C6
Clabburn Cl **1** NR15. . . . .**89** C1
Clabon Fst Cl NR3 . . . . . .**158** F2
Clabon Rd NR3 . . . .**158** F2
Clabon Second Cl NR3 . . **158** F3
Clabon Third Cl NR3 . . . .**158** F3
Clackclose Rd PE38. . . . .**172** C6
Clancy Rd NR7. . . . .**159** C1
Clare Ave NR31 . . . .**170** B2
Clare Cl NR3. . . . .**158** E1
Claremont Rd
  Norwich NR4. . . . .**162** A2
  Wisbech PE13 . . . .**152** E5
Clarence Ct
  Hunstanton PE36. . . . . . .**132** C6
17 Watton IP25 . . . .**84** D3
Clarence House Ct IP22. .**177** F5
Clarence Rd
14 Great Yarmouth
  NR30. . . . .**169** D2
  Hunstanton PE36. . . . . . .**132** D6
  Norwich NR1 . . . .**163** A5
  Wisbech PE13 . . . .**152** D6
Clarendon Cl **6** NR30. . . .**169** D2
Clarendon Dr **10** NR29 . . .**57** D4
Clarendon Rd
  Norwich NR2. . . . .**162** C5
  Sculthorpe NR21. . . . . . .**141** A5
Clarendon Stps **1** NR2. .**162** B5
Clare Rd Cromer NR27 . . .**139** D5
  King's Lynn PE30. . . . . . .**148** C3
Clare Sch The NR4. . . . . .**162** A3
Clarke Cl IP27. . . . .**177** C1
Clarke Rd NR3. . . . .**162** D8
Clarke's Cl **2** NR2 . . . .**69** F2
Clarke's La Barsham NR34 **124** F7
  Gooderstone PE33 . . . . . .**82** A5
Clarkes Gdns NR30. . . . .**169** B5
Clarke's Rd NR31 . . . .**170** C5
Clark Rd NR35 . . . .**109** B2
Clark's La NR21. . . . .**17** E5
Clark's Loke **7** NR13. . . . .**73** D6
Clarkson Ave PE13. . . . . .**152** D5
Clarkson Ct PE13 . . . .**152** E6
Clarkson Inf Sch PE13 . . .**152** E6
Clarkson Rd
10 Lingwood NR13 . . . .**74** A3
  Norwich NR5. . . . .**161** C7
CLAXTON NR14. . . . .**91** D6
Claxton Cl Mileham PE32. .**48** D6
5 Thetford IP24. . . . .**176** C4
Claxton Cnr NR14. . . . . . .**91** C6
Claxtons Gdns NR29 . . . . .**57** C1
Claybrooke Pk PE14 . . . . .**59** C4
Claydon Gr NR31. . . . . . .**170** B7
Clay Hill PE32 . . . .**48** B7
Clay La Bacton NR28 . . . . .**23** B3
  Bradwell NR31. . . . .**94** C5
  Hepworth IP22 . . . .**127** F1
  Saxlingham Nethergate
    NR15. . . . .**107** A7
  Swannington NR9 . . . .**52** C7
Claymore Gdns NR29. . . .**167** B2
Claypit La NR21. . . . .**141** C5
Claypit Rd NR20 . . . .**33** D3
Clay Rd NR30 . . . .**168** F5
Clayton Cl
  Dersingham PE31 . . . . . .**140** D4
  Wisbech PE13 . . . .**152** F6
Clearview Dr NR14. . . . . . .**90** C5
Cleaves Dr NR22. . . . .**16** F8

Clematis Wy NR18 . . . . . .**173** F6
Clement Attlee Wy PE30 .**147** C3
Clement Gdns IP22 . . . . .**177** F3
Clements Cl IP21 . . . .**130** C5
Clement Scott Mews
  NR27. . . . .**139** D5
Clements Ct PE34. . . . . . .**144** B5
CLENCHWARTON PE34 . .**145** E5
Clenchwarton Prim Sch
  PE34. . . . .**145** E5
Clenchwarton Rd PE34. .**146** B4
Clere Cl NR18. . . . .**173** C5
Cleveland Rd NR2. . . . . . .**178** A3
Cleves Way NR8 . . . .**156** E4
Cley La IP25 . . . .**84** C4
Cley Marshes Nature
  Reserve★ NR25. . . . .**7** F7
CLEY NEXT THE SEA NR25 . . .**7** E6
Cley Rd Blakeney NR25 . . . . .**7** D6
  Bradwell NR31. . . . .**94** C7
  Cockley Cley PE37. . . . . . .**82** E8
  Holt NR25 . . . .**137** B8
  Swaffham PE37. . . . .**153** B2
Clickers Rd NR3 . . . .**162** C8
Cliff Ave Cromer NR27. . . .**139** C6
  Great Yarmouth NR31 . . .**170** D3
Cliff Cl NR13. . . . .**92** F4
Cliff Ct PE36. . . . .**132** C6
Cliff Dr NR27 . . . .**139** C7
Cliffe-en-Howe Rd PE32. .**44** F8
Cliff Hill **4** NR31 . . . .**170** D4
Cliff La Cromer NR27. . . . .**139** C6
  Great Yarmouth NR31 . . .**171** D8
Clifford Ave NR30. . . . . . .**168** D5
Clifford Burman Cl PE30 .**148** A1
Clifford Pye Cl NR10 . . . . .**35** B2
Cliff Par PE36. . . . .**132** C5
Cliff Pk High Sch NR31 . .**170** D1
Cliff Pk Inf Sch NR31 . . . .**170** D2
Cliff Pk Jun Sch NR31 . . .**170** D2
Cliff Rd Cromer NR27 . . . .**139** D5
  Overstrand NR27. . . . .**11** A3
  Sheringham NR26 . . . . . .**138** E7
Cliff Terr PE36. . . . .**132** C5
Clifton Cl **3** NR2 . . . .**162** C7
Clifton Pk NR27. . . . .**10** C5
Clifton Rd
  King's Lynn PE30. . . . . . .**148** B1
  Wymondham NR18 . . . . .**173** C6
Clifton St NR2 . . . .**162** B7
CLIFTONVILLE NR11. . . . .**143** B7
Clifton Way NR27. . . . .**11** B3
Clingos Wy IP26 . . . .**113** F7
Clink Hill NR30. . . . .**168** B4
Clink Rd NR12. . . . .**40** A6
Clintergate Rd IP20. . . . .**122** C6
CLINT GREEN NR19 . . . . . .**68** C6
Clint Hill IP31. . . . .**126** D2
Clintock Pl **10** NR30. . . . .**169** C5
Clint St NR29. . . . .**56** B5
Clipbush La
  Banham NR16. . . . .**119** C7
  Fakenham NR21. . . . .**141** E5
  Scoulton NR9. . . . .**85** C4
Clipped Hedge La NR11. . .**22** B7
CLIPPESBY NR29 . . . .**57** A1
CLIPPINGS GREEN NR20. . .**68** E7
Clipstreet La NR21. . . . . . .**18** B8
Close The Brancaster PE31 . .**3** D7
  Brundall NR13. . . . .**165** C4
  Docking PE31. . . . .**134** E4
  Great Yarmouth NR31 . . .**170** A5
  Hemsby NR29 . . . .**167** B7
  Holt NR25 . . . .**137** C5
  Little Melton NR9 . . . . . .**160** D2
  North Lopham IP22. . . . .**119** A2
  North Walsham NR28 . . .**151** D4
  Norwich NR1. . . . .**178** C3
  Rackheath NR13 . . . .**72** D8
  Roydon IP22 . . . .**177** A5
  Sheringham NR26 . . . . . .**138** D8
  Stow Bedon NR17. . . . . .**102** D7
Clough Dr **9** IP26 . . . .**98** E1
Clough La PE30. . . . .**146** D4
Clovelly Dr NR6. . . . .**157** E2
Clover Dr **7** NR26 . . . . . .**138** B6
Clover Hill Inf Sch NR5 . .**161** B8
Clover Hill Rd NR5. . . . . .**160** F8
Cloverland Dr **6** NR29 . .**167** B7
Clover Rd
  Attleborough NR17 . . . . .**174** C3
  Aylsham NR11 . . . .**150** D5
  Norwich NR7. . . . .**158** A4
Clover Way
  Fakenham NR21. . . . .**141** E4
  Great Yarmouth NR31 . . .**170** A4
  Thetford IP24 . . . .**176** D5
Clover Wlk PE34 . . . .**61** B8
Clowes Ct **1** NR34. . . . . . .**110** C1
Clubbs La NR23. . . . .**136** D6
Clunch Cl IP27 . . . .**113** E1
Clydesdale Dr NR29. . . . .**167** A7
Clydesdale Rise NR31. . . . .**94** C8
Clyffe Cotts NR1 . . . .**162** F3
Coach & Horses Row
  NR2. . . . .**178** A2
Coach House Ct **1** NR4 .**162** A3
Coach La NR19 . . . .**67** C6
Coachmans Ct NR7. . . . . .**158** F4
Coal Shed Gall, The★
  PE36. . . . .**132** C4
Coalwharf Rd PE13 . . . . .**152** B4
Coastguard Rd NR30. . . .**168** F5
Coast Rd Bacton NR12. . . .**23** F4
  Cley next the Sea NR25 . . . . .**7** F7
  Corton NR32. . . . .**171** F1
  Happisburgh NR12 . . . . . .**23** F3
  Hopton on Sea NR31. . . .**171** D4

Coast Rd continued
  Overstrand NR27. . . . .**11** B3
  Salthouse NR25. . . . .**8** A7
  Wiveton NR25 . . . .**7** D6
Coates Ct **5** PE14 . . . .**59** D2
COBBLER'S GREEN NR35 . **108** B2
Cobblers La PE14 . . . .**41** F2
Cobbleways The **9** NR29. .**58** B6
Cobbold St IP22 . . . .**177** B5
Cobbs Hill PE34. . . . .**144** B5
Cobb's Pl **5** NR30 . . . . . .**169** D4
Cob Cl **7** NR31. . . . .**94** C8
Cobham Way NR7. . . . . . .**159** C2
Cobholm Cl **14** NR31 . . . .**169** B4
COBHOLM ISLAND NR31. .**169** B4
Cobholm Prim Sch NR31 **169** B4
Cobholm Rd **5** NR31. . . . .**169** B4
Coblands **4** PE13 . . . .**152** D7
Coburg Cl **10** IP25 . . . .**84** D3
Coburg La IP25 . . . .**84** B6
Coburg St
9 King's Lynn PE30. . . . . .**146** E5
  Norwich NR2. . . . .**178** A2
Cochrane Cl IP25. . . . .**85** A3
Cock Dro PE38. . . . .**172** B7
Cocketts Dr PE13 . . . .**152** E5
Cock Fen Rd PE14 . . . .**95** D7
Cocklehole Rd PE34 . . . . .**41** F8
COCKLEY CLEY PE37. . . . . .**82** D7
Cock Rd NR14. . . . .**92** A3
Cockshoot Dr NR12. . . . .**164** E6
Cock St Ixworth NR9. . . . . .**69** E2
  Wymondham NR18 . . . . .**173** B5
COCKTHORPE NR23. . . . .**6** B5
Codling's La NR11. . . . . . .**150** A6
Coigncroft The NR13. . . .**165** E3
Coke Rd NR1. . . . .**162** E1
Coker's Hill NR22 . . . .**16** F7
COLBY NR11. . . . .**21** E2
Colby Dr NR31. . . . .**94** C5
Colby Prim Sch NR11 . . . .**36** E8
Coldershaw Rd NR6. . . . .**158** B4
Coldham Cl NR29 . . . .**167** B3
Coldham Hall Carnser
  NR14. . . . .**165** C1
Coldham Rd NR21. . . . .**17** D7
Coldham's La PE33 . . . .**80** A5
Cold Harbour Rd NR29. . . .**56** D4
Coldhorn Cres PE13. . . . .**152** D7
Coleburn Rd NR1. . . . .**89** E8
Colegate NR3. . . . .**178** A3
COLEGATE END IP21. . . . .**121** E6
Colegate End Rd IP21. . . .**121** E6
Coleman Cl
  Palgrave IP22 . . . .**177** D1
  Taverham NR8 . . . .**155** F2
Coleridge Cl NR8 . . . .**156** D8
Coleridge Rd IP22 . . . . . .**177** E4
Coles Way NR10. . . . .**149** C6
Colindeep La NR7. . . . . . .**159** C4
Colin Mclean Rd NR19 . .**154** C7
Colkett Dr NR6 . . . .**158** E3
COLKIRK NR21. . . . .**31** D5
Colkirk CE Prim Sch
  NR21. . . . .**31** D5
Collectors World of Eric St
  John Foti★ PE38. . . . . . .**79** B6
Colleen Cl Dereham NR19 . .**67** E5
  East Dereham NR19 . . . . **154** D1
College Cl IP22 . . . .**54** D7
College Dr PE31 . . . .**133** C4
College La Keswick NR4. . . .**89** C7
9 King's Lynn PE30. . . . . .**146** D4
  Runcton Holme PE33. . . . .**61** F3
College Rd
  Hockwold cum Wilton
    IP26 . . . .**113** F7
  Norwich NR2. . . . .**162** A5
  Thompson IP24 . . . .**102** C7
  Thurlton NR14. . . . .**110** D3
  Wereham PE33 . . . .**97** F8
Collen's Gn NR9 . . . .**51** B3
Collers Way NR10. . . . . . .**149** C6
Collett's Bridge La PE14. .**59** C1
Colley Hill Drift PE32. . . . .**48** D4
Collingwood Cl
  Heacham PE31 . . . .**133** D3
25 Hethersett NR9 . . . .**88** D7
  Poringland NR14. . . . .**90** C4
Collingwood Dr NR11. . . .**22** F8
Collingwood Rd
  Downham Market PE38. . .**172** B4
  Great Yarmouth NR30 . . .**169** E7
  Hunstanton PE36. . . . . . .**132** D3
Collingwood Way IP24. . .**176** F6
Collingwood Wlk **1**
  IP24. . . . .**176** F6
Collins Ct NR6. . . . .**158** D2
Collins La PE31. . . . .**133** D5
Collin's La PE33 . . . .**63** C5
Collis La NR29. . . . .**57** F5
Colman Ave **1** NR14. . . . .**89** F4
Colman Fst Sch NR4. . . . .**162** A3
Colman Hospl NR2. . . . . .**162** A4
Colman Jun Sch NR4 . . . .**161** F3
Colman Rd NR4. . . . .**161** F5
Colmans Mustard Shop★
  NR1. . . . .**178** B2
Colne Pl NR27. . . . .**139** B6
Colne Rd NR27 . . . .**139** B6

COLNEY NR4 . . . .**161** A4
Colney La Colney NR4. . . .**161** A3
  Hethersett NR9 . . . .**160** D1
Colney Rd PE30. . . . .**147** D5
Colomb Rd NR31. . . . .**170** C6
COLTISHALL NR12. . . . .**54** C6
Coltishall La NR10 . . . .**53** E2
Coltishall Prim Sch NR12 .**54** D7
Coltishall Rd
  Belaugh NR12 . . . .**164** A6
  Buxton with Lammas NR10. .**53** F8
Coltishall Sta NR12 . . . . . .**54** C7
COLTON NR9. . . . .**69** E4
Colton Rd NR9. . . . .**69** E6
Coltsfoot Rd NR10. . . . . . .**53** A7
Coltsfoot Way IP24 . . . . . .**176** F5
Columbia Way PE30. . . . .**146** F6
Columbine Cl **4** IP24. . . . .**176** F5
Columbine Dr **12** NR26 . .**138** B6
Columbine Rd NR10. . . . . .**53** B2
Columbine The NR5 . . . . .**160** E7
Colvile Rd PE13. . . . .**152** E5
Colville Rd NR24. . . . .**142** B5
Comber Cl IP21. . . . .**130** D6
Comet Rd **7** IP25. . . . .**84** F3
Comfrey Way IP24. . . . . . .**176** F5
Commercial Rd NR19 . . . .**154** E5
Common Drift NR20. . . . . .**49** C4
Common Dro
  Flitcham with Appleton
    PE31. . . . .**27** F5
  Southery PE38. . . . .**97** B5
Common End PE32. . . . . . .**47** D8
Common La
  Beccles NR34 . . . .**110** C1
  Beetley NR20. . . . .**49** E5
  Brancaster PE31 . . . .**3** D6
  Brockdish IP21 . . . .**131** D6
  Burgh & Tuttington NR11. .**36** E6
  East Walton PE32 . . . .**45** E3
  Field Dalling NR25. . . . .**7** B1
  Filby NR29. . . . .**75** E8
  Gayton PE32 . . . .**45** C4
  Great Witchingham NR9 . . .**51** E4
  King's Lynn PE30. . . . . . .**148** C2
  North Runcton PE33. . . . .**44** A2
  Norwich NR7. . . . .**163** F5
  Sheringham NR26 . . . . . .**138** E6
6 Southery PE38. . . . .**97** B5
  Thorpe Market NR11. . . . .**22** A6
Common La N **2** NR34. . .**110** C1
Common Loke NR14 . . . . .**92** A2
Common Pl **3** NR22 . . . . .**16** F7
Common Rd Aldeby NR34 .**111** B3
  Ashwellthorpe NR16 . . . .**105** E7
  Barton Turf NR12. . . . .**38** F1
  Botesdale IP22. . . . .**128** F1
  Bressingham IP22. . . . . . .**129** C8
  Brumstead NR12. . . . .**24** A1
  Burston & Shimpling IP22. .**120** E2
  Castle Acre PE32. . . . .**46** E1
  East Tuddenham NR20. . . .**69** B5
  Forncett NR16. . . . .**105** E5
  Foxley NR20. . . . .**33** D1
  Gissing NR15. . . . .**120** F5
  Great Yarmouth NR31. . . .**170** C8
  Hemsby NR29 . . . .**57** F4
  Hopton IP22 . . . .**127** F6
  Lessingham NR12 . . . .**24** E2
  Martham NR29 . . . .**57** B4
  Mundham NR14. . . . .**91** C1
  Neatishead NR12 . . . .**55** E6
  Pulham Market IP21. . . . .**121** E7
  Runcton Holme PE33. . . . .**61** D4
  Runhall NR20. . . . .**68** F4
  Scole IP21. . . . .**130** F8
  Shelfanger IP22 . . . .**119** F3
  Shelton NR15. . . . .**107** B1
  Skeyton NR10 . . . .**37** A6
  Snettisham PE31 . . . .**12** D4
  Somerton NR29. . . . .**57** E6
  Surlingham NR14. . . . . . .**165** B1
  Swafield NR28. . . . .**22** D4
  Thurne NR29. . . . .**56** E3
  Wacton NR15. . . . .**106** D2
  West Walton PE14. . . . . . .**59** D7
  Wiggenhall St Germans
    PE34. . . . .**60** F7
Commonside NR10 . . . . . .**35** A2
Common The
  Freethorpe NR13. . . . .**92** E7
  Hamrow NR20. . . . .**31** E2
1 Harleston IP20 . . . .**122** D1
  Lyng NR9 . . . .**51** A4
  Surlingham NR14. . . . . . .**165** A1
  Swardeston NR14. . . . .**89** B6
Commonwealth Way **12**
  NR7. . . . .**72** D4
Compass Rd NR18 . . . . . .**173** F1
Compit Hills NR27 . . . . . .**139** B3
Concorde Rd NR6. . . . . . .**158** C5
Conesford Dr NR1 . . . . . .**162** F3
CONEY WESTON IP31. . . .**127** B5
Coney Weston Rd
  Barningham IP31 . . . .**127** C4
  Sapiston IP31 . . . .**126** D2
Conference Way
  Colkirk NR21. . . . .**31** E5
  Wisbech PE13 . . . .**152** C8
Conge The NR30. . . . .**169** C4
CONGHAM PE32 . . . .**28** B2
Congham Rd PE32 . . . .**28** B1
Conifer Cl NR29 . . . .**167** A3
Coniston Cl
2 Hethersett NR9 . . . .**88** E8
  King's Lynn PE30. . . . . . .**148** F1
2 Norwich NR5. . . . .**161** C6
Coniston Rd NR15 . . . .**90** C1

Dark La Ashmanhaugh NR12 **38** C1
Dickleburgh & Rushall
IP21 . . . .**130** B6
Erpingham NR11 . . . .**21** A1
Kimberley NR18 . . . .**87** B7
Smallburgh NR12 . . . .**38** D3
Somerton NR29 . . . .**57** F6
Wretham IP24 . . . .**101** F2
Darlington Mews NR3 . . .**158** A4
Darrell Pl NR5 . . . .**161** D7
Darrow Gn Rd IP20 . . . . .**122** F8
DARROW GREEN IP20 . . .**122** E8
Darrow Wood* IP20 . . . . .**122** F8
Darrow Wood La IP22 . . .**120** A1
Darwin Cl 5 PE12 . . . .**41** B8
Darwin Wlk NR19 . . . .**154** D4
Daseley's Ct NR3 . . . .**148** A1
Dashwood Cl NR31 . . . .**93** F6
Dauber's La NR13 . . . .**74** C2
Davey Cl NR35 . . . .**124** C8
Davey Pl NR2 . . . .**178** B3
Davidson Cl NR7 . . . .**163** F7
Davidson Rd NR7 . . . .**163** F7
Da Volls Ct NR31 . . . .**170** D6
Davy Pl Heacham PE31 . . .**133** C5
7 Loddon NR14 . . . .**92** A1
Dawber Cl PE30 . . . .**147** B4
Dawes La 2 PE31 . . . .**12** E4
Dawnay Ave PE30 . . . .**148** B1
Dawsons Rd NR20 . . . .**33** C3
Day's La IP31 . . . .**127** C4
Day's Lode Rd PE14 . . . . . .**95** A4
Deacon Cl NR13 . . . .**165** D4
Deacon Dr 14 NR9 . . . .**88** D8
Deas Rd PE30 . . . .**148** D1
Deben Dr 14 NR31 . . . .**94** A6
Debenne Rd NR28 . . . .**151** C6
Debnam Cl 10 NR31 . . . . . .**94** A5
Deborah Rd NR31 . . . .**170** C2
De-Carle Smith Rd
NR13 . . . .**166** C4
De Caux Rd NR3 . . . .**158** E1
Decoy Rd
Lakenheath IP27 . . . .**112** F4
Ormesby St Margaret with
Scratby NR29 . . . .**167** A4
Ormesby St Michael NR29 . .**57** F2
Potter Heigham NR29 . . . . .**56** F7
Deepdale NR13 . . . .**165** D3
Deepdale Ave 1 NR29 . . . .**57** C4
Deep Rd NR18 . . . .**173** B6
Deer Row NR35 . . . .**109** D1
De Grey Cl NR5 . . . .**157** A1
De Grey Rd PE30 . . . .**147** B5
De Hague Rd NR4 . . . .**161** D4
De Havilland Rd
Dereham NR19 . . . .**154** C6
Wisbech PE13 . . . .**152** C6
Delane Rd NR8 . . . .**157** C7
Delft Way NR6 . . . .**158** A6
Delgate La PE31 . . . .**3** E7
Dell Cl NR15 . . . .**106** F8
Dell Cnr La NR13 . . . .**73** F5
Dell Cres NR5 . . . .**161** D7
Dell Loke NR14 . . . .**163** B2
Dell The Bodham NR25 . . . . .**9** A3
Hingham NR9 . . . .**86** B5
Mundesley NR11 . . . .**143** D5
Trowse Newton NR14 . . . . .**163** B2
Deloney Rd NR7 . . . .**159** C2
Delta Cl NR6 . . . .**158** C4
De Lucy Cl IP22 . . . .**177** C5
De Morley Cl 4 IP22 . . . . .**177** A5
De Morley Garth NR26 . . .**138** D6
De-Narde Rd NR19 . . . .**154** D7
Denbigh Rd NR2 . . . .**162** B5
Dene Ave NR29 . . . .**167** A3
Deneside 26 NR30 . . . .**169** D3
Dene Side 1 NR30 . . . .**169** D3
Denes The NR1 . . . .**163** C5
DENHAM IP21 . . . .**131** B1
Denham Low Rd IP21 . . . .**131** A1
Denham Rd IP21 . . . .**131** B2
Denmark Hill IP22 . . . .**177** C3
Denmark Opening NR3 . . .**158** E1
Denmark Rd
Beccles NR34 . . . .**110** D1
2 King's Lynn PE30 . . . . . .**147** B6
Norwich NR3 . . . .**158** E1
Denmark Rise IP22 . . . . . .**177** C3
Denmark St IP22 . . . .**177** C3
Denmead Cl 4 NR4 . . . . . .**89** D8
Dennis Rd NR6 . . . .**157** F7
Dennis Sneezum Ct
PE38 . . . .**172** B4
Denny Rd PE38 . . . .**147** A4
Denny's Hill IP20 . . . .**123** A2
Denny's Wlk PE32 . . . .**63** E7
DENTON IP20 . . . .**123** A4
Denton Rd Denton IP20 . . .**123** C6
Norwich NR3 . . . .**158** F2
DENVER PE38 . . . .**172** C2
Denver Hill PE38 . . . .**172** C3
Denver VC Prim Sch
PE38 . . . .**172** D2
Denver Windmill* PE38 .**172** B1
DEOPHAM NR18 . . . .**86** F3
DEOPHAM GREEN NR18 . .**86** E2
Deopham Rd
Attleborough NR17 . . . . . .**174** C7
Hingham NR9 . . . .**86** C4
Morley NR18 . . . .**87** A2
DEOPHAM STALLAND
NR9 . . . .**86** D2
Derby St NR2 . . . .**162** C7

DEREHAM NR20 . . . .**154** F4
Dereham 6th Form Coll
NR20 . . . .**154** F5
Dereham CE Inf Sch
NR19 . . . .**154** D5
Dereham CE Jun Acad
NR19 . . . .**154** D4
Dereham Hospl NR19 . . . .**154** E7
Dereham La NR19 . . . .**66** C8
Dereham Rd
5 Bawdeswell NR20 . . . . . .**50** E7
Beeston with Bittering PE32 **48** D2
Briningham NR24 . . . .**18** D5
Bylaugh NR20 . . . .**50** C5
Colkirk NR21 . . . .**31** E5
Costessey NR5 . . . .**156** D1
Dereham NR20 . . . .**50** B2
Easton NR9 . . . .**70** C5
Garvestone NR9 . . . .**68** C1
Gressenhall NR19 . . . .**49** C2
Hempton NR21 . . . .**141** B2
Hingham NR9 . . . .**86** B5
Honingham NR9 . . . .**69** D7
Kimberley NR18 . . . .**87** A7
Litcham PE32 . . . .**48** A4
Mattishall NR20 . . . .**68** D6
North Elmham NR20 . . . . . .**49** E6
1 Norwich NR5 . . . .**161** B8
Ovington IP25 . . . .**84** C5
Pudding Norton NR21 . . . .**141** B1
Reepham NR10 . . . .**149** A4
Scarning NR19 . . . .**154** A4
Shipdham IP25 . . . .**67** A1
25 Watton IP25 . . . .**84** D3
Whinburgh & Westfield
NR19 . . . .**67** F5
Whissonsett NR20 . . . .**31** E2
Yaxham NR19 . . . .**68** A5
DERSINGHAM PE31 . . . . .**140** D5
**Dersingham Bog National
Nature Reserve*** PE31 . . .**27** D7
Dersingham Inf Sch
PE31 . . . .**140** D4
Dersingham VA Prim Sch
PE31 . . . .**140** F3
Dersley Ct 1 NR5 . . . .**160** E7
Derwent Ave PE30 . . . . . .**148** F2
Desborough Way NR13 . . .**72** D4
Desmond Dr NR6 . . . .**158** F6
Devlin Dr 13 NR14 . . . .**90** C5
Devon Ave NR6 . . . .**157** E4
Devon Cres PE30 . . . .**148** D5
Devonshire Ct 1 PE30 . . . .**147** A7
Devonshire Rd NR30 . . . . .**169** D2
Devonshire St 4 NR2 . . . .**162** C7
Devon Way NR14 . . . .**163** C1
Dewarrene Dr IP27 . . . . . .**175** B7
De Warrenne Pl PE32 . . . . .**47** A2
Dewdrop Cl PE31 . . . .**133** D6
Dewing Rd NR13 . . . .**72** E8
Dexter Rd PE34 . . . .**79** A7
Dial Cl PE38 . . . .**172** B5
Diamond Cl IP22 . . . .**120** B5
Diamond Rd NR6 . . . .**158** B5
Diamond St PE30 . . . .**146** D2
Diamond Terr PE30 . . . . . .**146** D2
Diana Cl NR19 . . . .**154** C1
**Diana Princess of Wales
International Study Ctr The**
IP22 . . . .**127** C8
Dianas Dro PE36 . . . .**132** C2
Diana Way NR30 . . . .**168** C6
Dian Rd NR13 . . . .**165** E3
Dibden Rd NR3 . . . .**162** F8
Dickens Ave NR30 . . . .**169** D1
Dickens Ct 5 NR30 . . . . . .**169** D1
Dickfool's La NR16 . . . .**66** F8
DICKLEBURGH IP21 . . . . .**121** C1
DICKLEBURGH MOOR
IP21 . . . .**121** C2
Dickleburgh Prim Sch
IP21 . . . .**121** B1
Dickleburgh Rd IP21 . . . . .**121** A1
Dicks Mount NR34 . . . .**111** D3
Dicky Hill IP20 . . . .**122** D3
DIDLINGTON IP26 . . . .**99** E8
Digby Dr NR21 . . . .**141** B6
DILHAM NR28 . . . .**38** D4
Dilham Arts Ctr* NR28 . . .**38** C4
Dilham Dr NR12 . . . .**164** E7
Dilham Rd Honing NR28 . . .**38** C6
Worstead NR28 . . . .**38** A4
Dilldash La NR21 . . . .**17** A5
Dinosaur Adventure Pk*
NR9 . . . .**51** E4
Dirty La
North Tuddenham NR20 . . . .**50** E1
Pulham St Mary IP21 . . . . .**121** F3
Discovery Wlk PE13 . . . . .**152** E2
DISS IP22 . . . .**177** D6
Diss Bsns Ctr IP21 . . . .**130** B6
Diss CE Jun Sch IP22 . . . .**177** D4
Diss High Sch IP22 . . . .**177** E5
Diss Inf Sch IP22 . . . .**177** E4
Diss Mus* IP22 . . . .**177** D4
Diss Rd
Burston & Shimpling
IP22 . . . .**120** E1
Garboldisham IP22 . . . . . .**128** A8
Scole IP21 . . . .**130** C5
South Lopham IP22 . . . . . .**128** F8
Tibenham NR16 . . . .**120** C8
Wattisfield IP22 . . . .**128** B1
Diss Sta IP22 . . . .**177** F4
Diss Swimming & Fitness Ctr
IP22 . . . .**177** E3
Distillery Sq 5 NR2 . . . . . .**162** C6

DITCHINGHAM NR35 . . . .**109** A2
Ditchingham CE Prim Acad
NR35 . . . .**109** B2
Ditchingham Dam NR35 . .**109** A1
Dix Cl PE31 . . . .**133** E5
Dixon Rd Cromer NR27 . . .**139** B5
North Walsham NR28 . . . . .**151** D5
Norwich NR7 . . . .**159** A4
Dixon's Dro PE14 . . . .**59** C8
Dixon's Fold NR6 . . . .**158** F4
Dobbs' La NR13 . . . .**54** D2
Dobby Dr PE30 . . . .**146** D6
Dobson Way 3 NR34 . . . . .**110** D1
DOCKENEY NR34 . . . .**109** F2
DOCKING PE31 . . . .**134** C5
Docking CE Prim Sch
PE31 . . . .**134** D4
Docking Rd Ringstead PE36. . **2** B2
Sedgeford PE36 . . . .**13** B7
Stanhoe PE31 . . . .**14** D7
Syderstone PE31 . . . .**15** A3
Westgate PE31 . . . .**135** B2
Dock Tavern La NR31 . . . .**170** D5
Doctor's La IP21 . . . .**122** A2
Doctors Mdw 1 NR10 . . . .**53** D2
Doctors Rd NR13 . . . .**165** E6
Dodd Cl NR30 . . . .**168** D7
Dodderman Way NR5 . . . .**160** D8
Dodds Cl NR17 . . . .**174** B3
DODDSHILL PE31 . . . .**140** F3
Doddshill Rd PE31 . . . .**140** F3
Dodds La NR17 . . . .**174** B3
Dodds Rd NR17 . . . .**174** B3
Dodgers La NR15 . . . .**91** A3
Dodmans Cl PE30 . . . .**146** E5
Dodman's La NR19 . . . .**31** F2
Dodmans The NR19 . . . . . .**154** D4
Dodma Rd PE32 . . . .**47** C8
Dodson Dr
7 Beetley NR19 . . . .**49** C3
7 Gressenhall NR20 . . . . . .**49** C3
Doe La Banham NR16 . . . . .**119** E8
Old Buckenham NR17 . . . .**104** A1
Dog Cnr NR11 . . . .**35** A5
Dogger La NR23 . . . .**136** C6
Doggetts La NR12 . . . .**24** D4
Dog La Easton NR9 . . . .**70** B6
Horsford NR10 . . . .**155** F4
Shelfanger IP22 . . . .**120** A4
Dogs La NR34 . . . .**110** C3
Dogwood Cl 6 NR18 . . . . .**173** E4
Dogwood Rd NR6 . . . .**158** D4
Dohamero La 1 PE33 . . . . .**43** F2
Doit La IP22 . . . .**129** D7
Doit The IP22 . . . .**129** C6
Dolman Cl 13 NR31 . . . . . .**169** B4
Dolphin Gr NR2 . . . .**162** B8
Dolphin Rd NR5 . . . .**156** C1
Doman Rd NR1 . . . .**178** C1
Donchurch Cl 6 NR5 . . . . .**161** A7
Doran Dr IP25 . . . .**84** C4
Doris Barnes Ct 1 NR19 . .**154** E5
Doris Rd NR2 . . . .**162** B5
Dorking Rd NR31 . . . .**171** B4
Dorothea Dr 7 NR19 . . . . .**154** D3
Dorothy Ave NR31 . . . .**94** C7
Dorrs Dr IP25 . . . .**84** D4
Dorset Cl
Attleborough NR17 . . . . . .**174** B3
4 Great Yarmouth NR30 . .**169** D3
Doubleday Cl IP22 . . . .**177** C4
Doughty's Hospl NR3 . . . .**178** B4
Douglas Bader Cl NR28 . . .**151** C7
Douglas Cl Croxton IP24 . . .**116** C5
Norwich NR6 . . . .**158** D7
Douglas Haig Rd NR5 . . . .**161** D6
Doune Way 9 IP20 . . . .**122** D2
Douro Pl NR2 . . . .**162** C6
Dove Cl
1 Great Yarmouth
NR31 . . . .**170** A6
9 Harleston IP20 . . . .**122** D1
Dovecote Cl NR15 . . . .**90** F2
Dovecote Rd PE14 . . . .**77** D3
Dovedale Rd NR16 . . . .**105** F5
Dovedales Fold NR7 . . . . .**158** F4
Dovehouse La NR11 . . . . . .**21** B4
Dove House La 4 NR29 . . . .**56** F6
Dove La NR15 . . . .**90** C3
Dover Ct NR30 . . . .**168** C5
Dover St NR2 . . . .**162** B5
Dove St 3 NR2 . . . .**178** A3
Dovetail Cl PE34 . . . .**79** D8
Dow Cl NR5 . . . .**161** B8
Dowding Rd Norwich NR6 .**158** D4
3 Watton IP25 . . . .**84** F3
DOWE HILL NR29 . . . .**167** C5
Dow La NR12 . . . .**54** C3
Downham Cres NR18 . . . . .**173** B6
Downham Dro PE32 . . . .**63** F7
DOWNHAM MARKET
PE38 . . . .**172** D4
Downham Market Acad
PE38 . . . .**172** D5
Downham Market College
PE38 . . . .**172** C4
Downham Mkt Sta PE38 .**172** A5
Downham Prep Sch PE34 . .**79** E8
Downham Rd
Crimplesham PE33 . . . .**80** B7
Denver PE38 . . . .**172** C4
Fincham PE33 . . . .**62** E1
Nordelph PE38 . . . .**78** D3
Outwell PE14 . . . .**77** F6
Runcton Holme PE33 . . . . . .**61** D4
Stradsett PE33 . . . .**80** D8
Downham Way IP27 . . . . .**175** D4

Downing Ct NR31 . . . .**170** C4
Downing Mews NR5 . . . . .**160** D8
Downing Rd NR31 . . . .**170** C4
Down Mill Dr PE32 . . . .**65** C6
Downs Cl PE36 . . . .**132** C4
Downs Farm La IP20 . . . . .**123** B3
Downs Rd PE36 . . . .**132** C4
Dowsing Ct 5 NR13 . . . . . .**72** C5
Dowson Fst Sch NR3 . . . . .**158** A1
Dowson Rd NR3 . . . .**158** B1
DRABBLEGATE NR11 . . . .**150** D8
Drabblegate NR11 . . . .**150** D8
Drabbs La NR12 . . . .**38** E6
Dragonfly La
4 Cringleford NR4 . . . .**89** A8
Cringleford NR4 . . . .**161** B1
Dragon Hall* NR1 . . . .**178** C2
Dragoon Cl 27 NR7 . . . . . .**72** D4
Drake Ave NR30 . . . .**169** D7
Drake Cl 24 NR9 . . . .**88** D8
Drake Inf Sch IP24 . . . .**176** E6
Drake Rd IP24 . . . .**176** E5
Drakes Cl 5 NR16 . . . .**118** C5
Drakes Loke NR10 . . . .**36** F1
Drapers La NR35 . . . .**109** A3
Draper Way NR5 . . . .**160** D8
Draycote Cl PE30 . . . .**147** D8
Draycotts Rise IP22 . . . . . .**177** C1
DRAYTON NR8 . . . .**157** A8
Drayton CE Jun Sch NR8 .**156** F8
Drayton Com Inf Sch
NR8 . . . .**155** F1
Drayton Gr NR8 . . . .**156** F8
Draytonhall La NR19 . . . . .**154** B3
Drayton High Rd NR8 . . . .**157** A8
Drayton Ind Pk NR8 . . . . .**156** F7
Drayton La NR10 . . . .**53** B1
Drayton Lodge Pk NR8 . . .**157** B7
Drayton Rd NR3 . . . .**157** F3
Drayton Wood Rd NR6 . . .**157** D6
Dreibholz Ct NR20 . . . .**154** F5
Drewray Dr NR8 . . . .**155** E3
Dried Flower Ctr* NR12 . .**55** C7
Drifters Wy NR31 . . . .**169** C1
Drift Ind Est The NR21 . . .**141** D5
Drift La NR20 . . . .**49** C3
Driftlands NR21 . . . .**141** D5
Drift The
Caister-on-Sea NR30 . . . . .**168** C7
Lakenheath IP27 . . . .**113** E2
Norwich NR5 . . . .**161** B8
Trowse with Newton NR14 .**163** D1
Driftway PE30 . . . .**148** C1
Driftway The
1 Holt NR25 . . . .**137** C5
Sheringham NR26 . . . .**138** D8
Drill St NR21 . . . .**15** C3
Drinkwater Cl 9 NR9 . . . . .**86** C5
Drive The Acle NR13 . . . . . .**166** D4
East Winch PE34 . . . .**45** A2
Kidd's Moor NR18 . . . .**88** B6
Norwich NR5 . . . .**161** B8
Drout's La IP31 . . . .**127** C3
Drovers Rest NR15 . . . . . .**108** C8
Drove The Brandon IP27 . .**114** D4
Raynham NR21 . . . .**30** E4
Taverham NR8 . . . .**155** C2
Dr Torrens Wy NR5 . . . . . .**156** D2
Drudge Rd NR31 . . . .**170** D4
Druids La Litcham PE32 . . . .**48** A4
Shelfanger IP22 . . . .**120** B2
Druids' La IP22 . . . .**120** A3
Drunken Dro PE32 . . . .**46** C8
Drury Cl 10 NR5 . . . .**161** B8
Drury La
3 Castle Acre PE32 . . . . . .**46** F2
6 Loddon NR14 . . . .**91** F1
DRURYLANE IP25 . . . .**85** A4
Drusilla Wy NR19 . . . .**68** C6
Dryden Cl 1 IP24 . . . .**176** E6
Dryden Rd NR8 . . . .**156** D8
DRYMERE PE37 . . . .**64** C1
**Duchy of Lancaster
Methwold CE Prim Sch**
IP26 . . . .**99** A5
Duck Decoy Cl PE31 . . . . . .**140** C3
Duck Dro CB7 . . . .**112** A2
Duckett Cl 2 NR1 . . . .**162** E1
Duck's Foot Rd IP21 . . . . .**121** F6
Duffield Cres NR9 . . . .**51** A4
Duff Rd NR3 . . . .**158** D2
Dugard Ave NR1 . . . .**163** B8
Duke Rd NR31 . . . .**170** D6
Duke's La NR17 . . . .**102** E8
Duke's Rd NR35 . . . .**124** B7
Duke St Norwich NR3 . . . . .**178** A4
Wisbech PE13 . . . .**152** D4
Dukesway 1 NR35 . . . .**123** E8
Dulgate La PE37 . . . .**153** D2
Dulgate Rd NR35 . . . .**108** B3
Dull's Rd NR35 . . . .**109** C5
Dumbs La NR10 . . . .**53** E5
Dumplingbridge La IP27 .**113** C6
Dumpling Gn
Dereham NR19 . . . .**68** A6
East Dereham NR19 . . . . . .**154** F2
DUMPLING GREEN NR19 .**154** F3
Dunburgh Rd NR34 . . . . . .**110** A2
Duncan Cl IP24 . . . .**176** F6
Duncan Rd 6 NR30 . . . . . .**169** D2
Dun Cow Gdns PE34 . . . . .**144** E7

Dun Cow Rd NR34 . . . .**111** B4
Dunford La IP24 . . . .**102** A2
Dunham Rd Litcham PE32 . .**48** A4
Necton PE37 . . . .**65** F6
Dunhill La IP22 . . . .**127** F1
Dunkerley Ct 16 NR12 . . . .**39** B4
DUNKIRK NR11 . . . .**150** E8
Dunkirk NR11 . . . .**150** E8
Dunlin Dr NR4 . . . .**161** B1
Dunlop Rd NR19 . . . .**154** B6
Dunnett Cl NR17 . . . .**174** E5
Dunnetts Cl IP25 . . . .**84** A7
Dunning's La IP21 . . . .**121** E6
Dunnock Dr NR8 . . . .**156** A5
Dunns La NR21 . . . .**4** D1
DUNSTON NR14 . . . .**89** E5
Dunston Dro PE31 . . . .**133** B1
DUNTON NR21 . . . .**15** F1
Dunwood Dr NR6 . . . .**158** F7
Durbidge's Hill IP22 . . . . .**120** E1
Durham Ave NR31 . . . .**170** B2
Durham St NR2 . . . .**162** B4
Durham Way IP24 . . . .**176** A5
Dussindale 3 NR18 . . . . . .**173** C6
Dussindale Dr 13 NR7 . . . .**72** E4
DUSSINDALE PARK NR13 .**72** E4
Dussindale Prim Sch NR7 **72** D4
Duverlin Cl NR4 . . . .**162** A1
Dyball's La NR12 . . . .**38** F8
Dyers Yd NR3 . . . .**178** A3
Dye's Rd NR13 . . . .**73** C7
Dyes The NR20 . . . .**33** C5

E

Eade Rd NR3 . . . .**162** D8
Eagle Cl NR11 . . . .**21** B2
Eagle House NR16 . . . .**119** E7
Eagle Rd NR11 . . . .**21** B2
Eagles Ct NR23 . . . .**136** E6
Eagles The 3 NR30 . . . .**169** D4
Eagle Wlk 2 NR2 . . . .**162** C4
Earl Cl PE31 . . . .**140** C3
Earles Gdns NR4 . . . .**161** E6
EARLHAM NR4 . . . .**161** D5
Earlham Gn La NR5 . . . . . .**161** B7
Earlham Gr NR5 . . . .**161** D6
Earlham Rd NR4 . . . .**161** C5
Earlham W Ctr 5 NR5 . . . .**161** A5
Earl of Brandon Ave PE31 . .**30** B3
Earl Rd NR13 . . . .**72** E8
Earlsford Rd IP23 . . . .**129** C1
Earls' St IP24 . . . .**176** D4
Earl St 4 PE13 . . . .**152** D4
Earl Warren IP24 . . . .**116** C5
Earnshaw Ct NR1 . . . .**163** D5
EARSHAM NR35 . . . .**123** E8
Earsham CE VA Fst Sch
NR35 . . . .**123** F8
Earsham Dam NR35 . . . . . .**123** F8
Earsham Dr PE30 . . . .**147** D8
Earsham Rd NR35 . . . .**108** E2
EARSHAM STREET IP21 . .**131** F5
Earth La NR32 . . . .**94** C1
East Anglian Way NR31 . .**170** C6
East Anglia Transport Mus*
NR33 . . . .**111** F1
East Ave NR13 . . . .**165** E3
East Bank PE12 . . . .**41** C8
EAST BARSHAM NR21 . . . .**16** D4
EAST BILNEY NR20 . . . .**49** B6
East Bilney Hall NR20 . . . . .**49** A6
Eastbourne Pl NR1 . . . . . .**178** C3
EAST CARLETON NR14 . . . .**88** F4
East Carleton Rd NR14 . . . .**89** A4
East Cres NR30 . . . .**50** B5
East Dereham Sta NR20. .**154** F5
East End PE38 . . . .**79** E1
East End Cl NR30 . . . .**168** E8
Easterley Way NR29 . . . . .**167** A7
Eastern Ave
Caister-on-Sea NR30 . . . . .**168** E6
Norwich NR7 . . . .**72** D4
Eastern Cl
Caister-on-Sea NR30 . . . . .**168** E5
32 Norwich NR7 . . . .**72** D4
Eastern Cres NR7 . . . .**72** D4
Eastern Rd NR7 . . . .**72** D4
Eastern Yd PE30 . . . .**147** C7
East Farm NR10 . . . .**53** E3
Eastfen Dro IP26 . . . .**114** B6
Eastfield NR8 . . . .**156** D8
Eastfield Cl PE30 . . . .**147** A6
Eastfield Rd Hickling NR12. . **39** F2
Long Stratton NR15 . . . . . .**106** F4
1 Wisbech PE13 . . . .**152** E7
Eastfields
King's Lynn PE30 . . . .**147** C4
Narborough PE32 . . . .**63** C7
Eastfield Way PE13 . . . . . .**152** C6
EASTGATE NR10 . . . .**35** C2
Eastgate IP25 . . . .**67** D3
Eastgate Acad PE30 . . . . .**146** E5
Eastgate Dro
Congham PE31 . . . .**28** D2
Grimston PE32 . . . .**45** D8
Hillington PE31 . . . .**28** C3
Eastgate Rd PE36 . . . .**2** A6
Eastgate St
2 King's Lynn PE30 . . . . . .**146** E5
North Elmham NR20 . . . . . .**49** E7
Shouldham PE33 . . . .**62** D4
East Gn NR9 . . . .**68** F2
East Gr NR27 . . . .**139** C5
East Harbour Way PE31 . . .**35** C2
EAST HARLING NR16 . . . . .**118** C5

East Harling Prim Sch NR16......118 C5
East Harling Rd NR16...118 F4
EASTHAUGH NR9......51 C4
Easthaugh Rd NR9......51 D4
Easthill La NR14......90 E8
East Hills Rd NR5......156 E1
East La PE31......134 E4
Eastland Cl NR17......174 E6
Eastlands Bank PE14......41 E5
Eastleigh Gdns 6 NR9....69 F2
EAST LEXHAM PE32......47 D3
Eastmans La PE32......28 C1
Eastmoor Cl PE33......81 E4
Eastmoor Rd PE33......81 C7
East Norfolk 6th Form Coll NR31......170 C5
EASTON NR9......70 B5
Easton & Otley Coll (Easton Campus) NR9......70 B4
Easton Way NR10......35 C1
EAST RAYNHAM NR21......31 A4
East Rd
  Great Yarmouth NR30...169 D5
  Watton IP25......84 D3
EAST RUDHAM PE31......30 A7
EAST RUNTON NR27......10 B5
EAST RUSTON NR12......38 E6
East Ruston Area Inf Sch NR12......38 F7
East Ruston Old Vicarage Gdn* NR12......24 A3
East Ruston Rd NR28......38 D6
EAST SOMERTON NR29......58 A6
EAST TUDDENHAM NR20...69 C6
EAST WALTON PE32......45 E3
EAST WINCH PE32......44 F3
East Winch CE Prim Sch PE32......44 F3
East Winchcommon (Nature Reserve)* PE32......45 A2
East Winch Rd
  Leziate PE32......44 F5
  Middleton PE32......44 C2
Eastwood PE31......134 F3
EAST WRETHAM IP24......102 A1
EATON NR4......161 F2
Eaton Chase NR4......161 E2
Eaton Dro Sedgeford PE36...13 A7
  Snettisham PE31......12 F5
Eaton Gdns NR19......154 E3
Eaton Hall Sch NR4....161 F3
Eaton Rd NR4......162 B2
Eaton St Cringleford NR4...89 B8
  Norwich NR4......161 E1
EAU BRINK NR34......43 A3
Eau Brink Rd PE34......43 A2
Ebbisham Dr NR4......161 F1
Ebble Cl PE30......148 C2
Ebenezer Pl NR3......178 A4
ECCLES ON SEA NR12......24 E4
Eccles Rd NR25......137 C7
ECCLES ROAD NR16......103 E1
ECCLES ROAD Sta NR16...103 F1
Ecclestone Cl NR31......170 A4
Eckersley Dr NR21.....141 A6
Ecotech Ctr* PE37......153 B6
Ecton Gr PE14......59 A1
Ecton Wlk NR6......158 F5
Eddington Way NR9......70 B5
Eden Cl
  Bacton/Walcott NR12...23 E4
  Norwich NR7......163 C6
Edenhurst Cl NR4......161 F1
Eden La
  Attleborough NR17.....174 D5
  Attleborough NR17.....174 D5
Edenside Dr NR17......174 D5
Edge Bank PE14......77 F8
Edgebrook NR26......138 D6
EDGEFIELD NR24......19 D5
Edgefield Cl NR6......158 F7
Edgefield Hill NR25......137 C6
Edgefield Rd NR24......142 E5
EDGEFIELD STREET NR24...19 D4
EDGE GREEN NR16......119 B4
Edgehill 4 NR7......72 E4
Edges La 2 NR15......106 E3
Edge's La NR15......107 A3
Edgeworth Rd 6 NR5....161 C6
Edinburgh Ave
  Great Yarmouth NR31...170 B2
  King's Lynn PE30......147 C7
Edinburgh Cl
  6 Barnham IP24......125 F6
  Caister-on-Sea NR30....168 E5
  13 Watton IP25......84 D3
Edinburgh Ct 7 PE30...146 E5
Edinburgh Dr
  Fakenham NR21......141 C6
  Wisbech PE13......152 C8
Edinburgh Pl
  Great Yarmouth NR30...169 E3
  1 Wiggenhall St Germans PE34......43 B1
Edinburgh Rd Holt NR25...137 C5
  Norwich NR2......162 A6
Edinburgh Way
  Dersingham PE31......140 D3
  Thetford IP24......176 A5
EDINGTHORPE NR28......23 C3
EDINGTHORPE GREEN NR28......23 A2
Edison Way NR31......170 A8
Edith Cavell Cl 5 IP24...176 D7
Edma St PE30......146 E6
Edmondson Wlk NR21...141 D4

Edmund Bacon Ct 1 NR3......162 D8
Edmund de Moundeford Prim Sch IP26......98 E2
Edmund Moundford Rd 10 IP26......98 E1
Edmund Rd IP27......175 A2
Edrich Cl NR13......165 E6
Edrich Way NR5......160 E7
Edward Benefer Way
  King's Lynn PE30......146 D6
  North Wootton PE30....26 E1
Edward Gambling Ct 8 NR2......162 B8
Edward Rd NR29......58 B5
Edwards Cl NR20......50 B5
Edward Seago Pl NR15...90 E2
Edwards Rd NR7......159 A5
Edward St
  10 King's Lynn PE30...146 E3
  Norwich NR3......178 B4
Edward Worlledge Jun Sch NR31......169 C2
Edwin Cl NR18......173 B5
Eels Foot Rd NR29......57 E1
Eglinton Mews NR3.....158 C2
Egmere Medieval Village of* NR22......16 B8
Egmere Rd NR22......16 F8
Egremont Rd IP22......177 B5
Egyptian Goose Rd NR7...159 E5
Eighth Ave PE13......152 E4
El Alamein Way NR31....94 C8
Elan Cl NR18......173 D3
Elden's La PE26......98 F5
Elderberry Dr 5 NR20...68 A8
Elderberry Pl PE14......77 E6
Elderbush La NR29......56 C7
Elder Cl NR5......157 B2
Elderflower Mews NR5...160 F6
Elderflower Wy PE38....172 E6
Elder Gn NR31......170 B5
Elder La PE32......45 C8
Elders The IP27......113 F1
Elderton La NR28......22 B5
Eldon Ct NR17......174 F6
Eleanor Rd NR1......162 D3
Eleven Mile Rd NR18....87 C1
Elgin IP24......176 A5
Elgood's Brewery & Gdn* PE13......152 A4
Eliot Cl IP24......176 E6
Elise Way NR18......173 D2
Elizabethan House Mus* NR30......169 C3
Elizabeth Ave
  Downham Market PE38...172 B5
  Fakenham NR21......141 C6
  Norwich NR7......163 F7
Elizabeth Cl
  Attleborough NR17......174 C6
  East Dereham NR19.....154 D1
  Hunstanton PE36......132 C3
  Norwich NR7......159 A5
  Reepham NR10......149 B4
Elizabeth Cres
  Caister-on-Sea NR30....168 E6
  4 Holt NR25......137 C5
Elizabeth Dr PE37......65 F3
Elizabeth Fry Cl 9 IP24...176 D7
Elizabeth Fry Rd NR2...161 F4
Elizabeth Rd
  Brandon IP27......175 C3
  10 Poringland NR14......90 D5
Elizabeth Terr PE13......152 D4
Elizabeth Watling Cl 3 IP24......176 D7
Elizabeth Way 5 IP23...130 C1
Elizabeth Wlk 27 IP20...122 D2
Elkins Rd NR18......173 B5
Ellacar Rise 4 NR4......161 F1
Ellenhill NR27......139 D5
Ellerby Dr PE14......152 A3
Eller Dr PE33......43 E2
ELLINGHAM NR35......109 D3
Ellingham Prim Sch NR35......109 D3
Ellingham Rd
  Attleborough NR17......174 B7
  Scoulton NR9......85 E3
Ellington Rd
  2 Barnham IP24......125 F6
  Watton IP25......85 A3
Ellinor Rd NR28......151 D3
Elliott Cl NR25......137 C7
Ellis Cl 4 NR12......39 B4
Ellison Cl
  Attleborough NR17......174 E4
  Caister-On-Sea NR30....168 D5
Ellison Dr NR17......174 E4
ELM PE14......59 B1
Elm Ave NR11......59 B1
Elm CE Prim Sch PE14...59 B1
Elm Cl Acle NR13......166 C4
  Brandon IP27......175 C3
  Downham Market PE38...172 B6
  King's Lynn PE30......148 D2
  Lakenheath IP27......113 E2
  5 Lingwood NR13......74 A3
  Little Melton NR9......160 D2
  7 Loddon NR14......91 F1
  Mulbarton NR14......89 B3
  North Elmham NR20.....49 E8
  Norwich NR5......156 F2
  Yaxham NR19......68 A5
Elmdon Ct 9 NR1......163 A6
Elmer's La NR15......107 A8

Elmfield Dr PE14......152 E1
Elm Gr Garboldisham IP22...128 A8
  Sheringham NR26......138 E5
Elm Gr La NR3......158 B2
Elmgrove Rd NR31......170 C3
Elmham Rd Beetley NR20...49 D4
  North Elmham NR20.....50 A7
Elm High Rd PE14......152 E1
Elm Hill NR3......178 B3
Elmhurst Ave NR12......39 C2
Elmhurst Cl NR31......170 C3
Elmhurst Dr PE30......148 C2
Elm La NR31......30 D8
Elm Low Rd PE14......152 D2
Elm Pk NR19......154 E1
Elm Rd
  Caister-on-Sea NR30....168 E4
  Lingwood NR13......74 A3
  Marham PE33......63 B4
  Thetford IP24......176 B1
  Wisbech PE13......152 D3
Elm Rd Prim Sch PE13...152 E1
Elms Cl 6 NR35......123 F8
Elmside PE14......59 D1
Elms Rd NR34......110 E5
Elmstead Rd PE30......147 C4
Elms The
  Hindringham NR21......17 E6
  Norwich NR6......158 E6
Elm Terr 2 NR18......173 C4
Elmtree Gr PE33......43 E1
Elsden Cl 2 NR25......137 C5
Elsie Rd NR31......169 B3
ELSING NR20......50 F3
Elsing Dr PE30......148 D8
Elsing La Bawdeswell NR20...50 E6
  Dereham NR20......50 C1
Elsing Rd Lyng NR9......51 A5
  North Tuddenham NR20...50 E2
  Swanton Morley NR20....50 C4
Elstead Cl 11 NR4......89 C8
ELVEDEN IP24......125 A7
Elveden Cl NR4......161 F1
Elveden Rd IP24......125 D6
Elvina Rd 10 NR10......54 A2
Elvington PE30......147 D5
Elvin Rd NR14......154 D6
Elvin Way 3 NR3......157 F1
Elworthy Cl IP25......84 F3
Elwyn Rd 7 NR1......162 E2
Ely Pl 19 PE13......152 C5
Ely Row PE14......42 B1
Ely Sq NR2......162 C7
Ely Way PE14......176 A5
Embry Cl NR6......158 D6
Embry Cres NR6......158 C6
Emelson Cl NR19......154 D6
Emery Cl 5 NR26......138 C5
Emerys Cl NR27......11 A2
Emery's La NR11......21 B6
Emmanuel Ave NR31......170 B2
Emmas Way NR13......73 B6
Emmerich Ct 6 PE30...146 E5
Emms's La NR21......17 E7
EMNETH PE14......59 D2
EMNETH HUNGATE PE14...59 F2
Emneth Prim Sch PE14...59 D2
EMORSGATE PE34......42 B7
Emorsgate PE34......42 B7
Empire Ave PE30......147 B8
Empress Rd NR31......169 B3
Empsons Loke NR29......58 B6
End Lodge PE31......133 C5
Enfield Rd NR5......161 C6
Engine Rd Hilgay PE38...96 F7
  Sculthorpe Airfield NR21...15 C3
England's La NR31......170 D4
Englands Rd NR13......166 B4
English Rd NR6......158 A4
Ennerdale Dr PE30......148 F2
Ensign Wy IP22......177 F3
Enterprise Way
  Fakenham NR21......141 E5
  King's Lynn PE33......43 E4
  Wisbech PE13......152 A2
Entrance La NR15......90 E2
Entry The IP22......177 D4
Eppingham Cl IP24......176 F6
Epsom Gdns NR19......154 E3
Erica Way NR31......170 B6
Erins The 1 NR6......158 E1
Eriswell Dr IP27......113 E1
Ernest Dr NR6......158 F7
ERPINGHAM NR11......21 B2
Erpingham CE Prim Sch NR11......21 B2
Erpingham Ct PE36......132 E7
Esdelle St 9 NR3......162 D8
Esplanade NR27......139 B7
Esplanade The
  Hemsby NR29......167 E5
  Sheringham NR26......138 C7
Esprit Cl NR18......173 D2
Essex St NR2......162 C5
Estcourt Rd
  2 Attleborough NR17...174 C5
  Great Yarmouth NR30...169 D6
Estelle Way NR18......173 E6
Estuary Cl PE30......146 F2
Estuary Rd PE30......146 D7
Ethel Colman Way IP24...176 D7
Ethel Gooch Rd NR13...173 B5
Ethel Mann Rd NR35...124 B7
Ethel Rd NR1......163 A5
Ethel Terr 5 PE30......146 E3

Ethel Tipple Cl NR11...150 C4
Ethel Tipple Dr NR11...150 C4
ETLING GREEN NR20......68 B8
Eurocentre Ind Est NR30 169 B7
Europa Sq PE13......152 B2
Europa Way Norwich NR1...163 A2
  Wisbech PE13......152 B2
EUSTON IP24......126 B5
Euston Hall* IP24......126 B5
Euston Rd NR30......169 D4
Euston Way PE30......148 D1
Euximoor Dro PE14......77 B1
Eva Cl 4 IP25......67 B2
Evans Gdns PE36......132 D3
Evans Lombe Cl NR29...57 A4
Evans Way NR6......158 D6
Eve Rd NR13......72 E7
Evelyn Cl IP21......131 A3
Evelyn Way 4 NR21......147 A8
Eversley Rd NR6......158 B4
Everson Cl Norwich NR5...157 C1
  11 Tasburgh NR15......106 F6
Evora Rd NR18......173 D2
Ewing Cl NR10......149 B4
Excalibur Rd 2 NR31...170 B1
Exchange Cl NR8......155 D1
Exchange Rd 7 NR15...89 C1
Exchange Sq PE13......152 B5
Exchange St
  Attleborough NR17......174 D5
  32 Harleston IP20......122 D2
  Norwich NR2......178 A3
Exeter Cres PE30......148 D5
Exeter Rd NR31......170 B4
Exeter St NR2......162 C7
Exeter Way 9 IP24......176 F5
Exige Wy NR18......173 D2
Exmoor Gr NR18......88 D8
Exmouth Pl 11 NR30...169 D4
Exmouth Rd NR30......169 D1
Exton's Gdns PE30......146 F3
Exton's Pl PE30......147 A3
Exton's Rd PE30......146 F4
EYE IP23......130 C1
Eye Airfield Ind Est IP23 130 B2
Eye La PE31......30 B7
Eye Rd IP23......130 A1

F

Factory La IP22......177 B5
Factory Rd NR30......169 D5
Faeroes Dr NR30......168 C6
Fair Cl Beccles NR34......110 D1
  13 Feltwell IP26......98 E1
Fairfax Dr 6 Norwich NR7...72 D4
  3 Weeting IP27......114 E1
Fairfax Gall* PE31......135 C3
Fairfax Rd NR4......161 F4
Fairfield Cl
  Great & Little Plumstead NR13......73 B7
  Mundesley NR11......143 C6
Fairfield Dr NR17......174 C4
Fairfield Rd
  Downham Market PE38...172 A5
  5 Middleton PE32......44 B3
  Norwich NR2......162 C3
  4 Stoke Ferry PE33......81 A3
Fairfields Cawston NR10...35 B2
  Thetford IP24......176 D7
Fairfields Ind Est NR29...57 E5
Fairfields Way 11 IP26...98 E1
Fair Gn NR22......177 C4
FAIR GREEN PE32......44 B4
Fairhaven CE VA Prim Sch NR13......74 B8
Fairhaven Ct NR2......162 A6
Fairhaven Woodland & Water Gdn* NR13......74 A8
Fairhill Dro PE33......80 E2
Fairholme Cl IP25......84 A8
Fairholme Rd NR10......53 E4
Fairisle Dr NR30......168 C5
Fairland St NR18......173 C4
Fairmile Cl NR2......162 B3
FAIRSTEAD PE30......147 D4
Fairstead Cl
  North Walsham NR28.....151 A3
  Pulham Market IP21......121 E5
Fairstead Com Prim Sch PE30......147 D4
Fairstead Ct NR7......159 A3
Fairstead Dro PE33......62 D4
Fairstead La
  Hempnall NR15......107 A5
  Little Cressingham IP25...83 D3
Fairstead The
  Botesdale IP22......128 E3
  2 Cley next the Sea NR25...7 E6
  1 Holt NR25......137 B6
  Scottow NR10......37 D2
Fairview Cl NR8......157 A7
Fairview Dr 7 NR21......31 E5
Fairview Rd NR28......151 E4
Fairway
  Caister-on-Sea NR30....168 E3
  Costessey NR8......156 A5
  6 Costessey Park NR8...70 C7
Fairway Fst Sch NR4....162 A1
Fairway Mid Sch NR4...162 A1
Fairways Norwich NR6...157 D5
  Stuston IP21......130 B5
Fairway The NR31......171 D8

FAKENHAM NR21......141 D6
Fakenham Acad NR21...141 B6
Fakenham Coll NR21......141 B5
Fakenham Hill IP31......126 C2
Fakenham Ind Est NR21...141 E5
Fakenham Jun Sch NR21......141 C4
FAKENHAM MAGNA IP24......126 C3
Fakenham Mus* NR21...141 B3
Fakenham Race Course NR21......141 D2
Fakenham Rd
  Attlebridge NR9......52 C2
  Beetley NR20......49 C5
  Briston NR24......142 C5
  Docking PE31......134 E4
  East Rudham PE31......30 A7
  Foxley NR20......33 C1
  Great Snoring NR21......17 A5
  Ryburgh NR21......32 A6
  Sculthorpe NR21......141 A5
  South Creake NR21......15 E6
  Sparham NR9......51 A6
  Taverham NR8......155 B2
  Tittleshall PE32......48 A7
Fakenham View NR21......31 E5
Fakes Rd NR29......167 D6
Falcon Ave IP22......177 F5
Falcon Cl 15 NR30......169 C4
Falcon Dr IP27......175 F3
Falconers Chase NR18...173 F5
Falcon Jun Sch NR7......159 C3
Falcon La Bungay NR35...109 A1
  24 Wisbech PE13......152 C5
Falcon Mews NR7......159 C4
Falcon Rd 14 Feltwell IP26...98 E1
  Norwich NR7......159 C3
  Pulham Market IP21......121 E5
  7 Wisbech PE13......152 C5
Falcon Rd E NR7......159 C2
Falcon Rd W NR7......159 C4
Falgate NR10......35 C2
Falkland Cl NR6......157 D5
Falklands Dr PE13......152 E3
Falklands Rd PE12......41 A8
Falkland Way 13 NR31...94 C6
Fall Gn NR14......90 D4
Fallowfield
  4 Hemsby NR29......167 B7
  8 Poringland NR14......90 D5
Fallowfield Cl NR1......163 B8
Fallow Pipe Rd PE34......43 B2
Fallows The 3 NR8......155 D2
Faraday Pl IP24......176 B2
Faraday Rd NR31......170 A8
Fardell Rd 7 PE13......152 C4
Farebrother Way 2 NR19......154 C3
Farman Ave NR28......151 D5
Farman Cl 5 Belton NR31...94 A6
  Lyng NR9......51 A5
  7 Salhouse NR13......55 A1
Farm Cl Bungay NR35...124 B8
  Diss IP22......177 C6
  Lingwood NR13......74 A2
  11 Loddon NR14......92 A2
Farm Ct St IP20......123 A1
Farmers Ave NR1......178 B2
Farm La NR13......56 A1
Farmland Rd NR5......156 F1
Farm Rd Heckingham NR14...92 D1
  Worstead NR28......38 A7
Farm View NR28......151 E5
Farmway 7 NR19......154 E3
Farm Wlk Marham PE33...63 C5
  6 Necton PE37......65 F4
Farnborough Rd 9 IP25...84 F3
Farrier Cl NR18......173 F5
Farrier Rd 18 IP25......84 F3
Farrow Cl
  2 Great Moulton NR15...106 B1
  8 Mattishall NR20......68 E6
  2 Swanton Morley NR20...50 B3
Farthing Cl Diss IP22...177 D6
  Loddon NR14......109 D8
Farthing Dro
  Beck Row, Holywell Row & Kenny Hill IP27......112 E2
  Lakenheath IP27......113 A2
  Southery PE38......97 A2
Farthing Rd PE38......79 B5
Fastnet Way 1 NR30......168 C6
Fastolf Cl NR5......157 E5
Fastolff Ave NR31......170 B3
Fayers Terr PE30......147 A4
Fayregreen NR21......141 D4
Feale Abbey PE34......144 A1
Fearn's Cl NR27......139 D5
Featherstone Ct 5 NR19......154 D2
FELBRIGG NR11......10 C2
Felbrigg PE30......148 F1
Felbrigg Hall Garden & Park* NR11......10 B2
Felbrigg Rd
  Downham Market PE38...172 C6
  Roughton NR11......21 D8
Felbrigg Wlk NR11......30 C4
Fellowes Dr 2 NR31......94 C6
Fellowes Rd NR9......69 E6
Fellows Cl 7 Norwich NR5...161 C6
  Scole IP21......130 D5
Fell Way 3 NR31......94 C8

FELMINGHAM NR28 . . . . .37 A8
Felmingham Rd NR28 . . . . . .37 C7
Felsham Way NR8 . . . . .155 E2
Felsted Ave PE13 . . . . .152 E5
FELTHORPE NR10 . . . . .155 C8
Felthorpe Rd NR9 . . . . .52 B3
FELTWELL IP26 . . . . .98 D1
Feltwell Rd
  Hockwold cum Wilton
    IP26 . . . . .113 F7
  Methwold IP26 . . . . .98 E5
  Southery PE38 . . . . .97 D5
Fence Bank PE14 . . . . .42 A1
Fences Farm Rd PE34 . . . . .78 E8
Fen Cl PE13 . . . . .152 E6
Fen Dro PE33 . . . . .81 F3
Fendyke Rd PE14 . . . . .59 E1
Fen Folgate 6 IP25 . . . . . . .67 B2
FENGATE NR10 . . . . .150 C1
  Marsham NR10 . . . . .150 D1
Fengate Dro IP27 . . . . .175 B6
Fengate Rd PE14 . . . . .59 C5
Fen La Banham NR16 . . . . .119 B6
  Beccles NR34 . . . . .110 D2
  Ditchingham NR35 . . . . . .108 E3
  Garboldisham IP22 . . . . . .128 A7
  Grimston PE32 . . . . .45 A7
  Harling NR16 . . . . .118 C6
  Leziate PE32 . . . . .45 A6
  Marham PE33 . . . . .63 A5
  Rickinghall Inferior IP22 . .128 E2
  Roydon IP22 . . . . .129 C7
  Thelnetham IP22 . . . . . . .128 B5
Fenland Rd
  King's Lynn PE30 . . . . . . .147 C8
  Wisbech PE13 . . . . .152 E6
Fenland & W Norfolk
  Aviation Mus★ PE14 . . . . .59 C7
Fenn Cres NR3 . . . . .158 B1
Fennel Cres PE38 . . . . .172 E6
Fennel Way IP24 . . . . .176 F4
Fenner Rd NR30 . . . . .170 E7
Fen Rd Blo' Norton IP22 . . .128 B5
  Carleton Rode NR16 . . . . .105 C2
  Hinderclay IP22 . . . . .128 C5
  Marham PE33 . . . . .63 B4
  Scarning NR19 . . . . .154 B3
  Watlington PE33 . . . . .61 D5
FENSIDE NR29 . . . . .56 B8
Fenside PE31 . . . . .133 C4
Fen St Attleborough NR17 . .103 F3
  Old Buckenham NR17 . . . .104 C2
  Redgrave IP22 . . . . .128 F6
  Rocklands NR17 . . . . .103 B6
FEN STREET Hopton IP22 . .127 E6
  Redgrave IP22 . . . . .128 F6
Fen View
  Christchurch PE14 . . . . . . .95 A7
  East Dereham NR19 . . . . .154 C2
Fenway PE31 . . . . .133 B3
Fen Way 2 PE14 . . . . .59 A1
Ferguson Way NR17 . . . . . .174 F7
Fermoy Ave PE30 . . . . .146 E6
Fern Ct 3 NR18 . . . . .173 B4
Ferndale Cl NR6 . . . . .157 E4
Fern Dr 1 Cringleford NR4 . .89 A8
  North Walsham NR28 . . . .151 E5
Fern Gdns NR31 . . . . .93 F5
Fern Hill
  Dersingham PE31 . . . . . . .140 E4
  Norwich NR1 . . . . .163 B6
Fernlea Rd PE30 . . . . .147 C4
Fern Rd PE30 . . . . .147 B8
Ferrier Cl 7 NR30 . . . . .169 D5
Ferrier Ct NR29 . . . . .167 B6
Ferrier Rd NR30 . . . . .169 C5
Ferry Bank PE38 . . . . .97 A4
Ferryboat La NR31 . . . . .170 D7
Ferry Ct NR29 . . . . .75 A5
Ferrygate La NR29 . . . . .57 D5
Ferry Hill NR31 . . . . .170 D7
Ferry La
  Great Yarmouth NR31 . . . .169 C2
  17 King's Lynn PE30 . . . . .146 D5
  Norwich NR1 . . . . .178 C3
  Postwick with Witton NR13 .73 A2
  Stokesby with Herringby
    NR29 . . . . .75 B5
Ferry Rd
  Carleton St Peter NR14 . . . .91 E5
  Clenchwarton PE34 . . . . .145 F5
  Horning NR12 . . . . .55 E3
  King's Lynn PE34 . . . . . . .146 B6
  Norton Subcourse NR14 . . .92 D2
  Norwich NR1 . . . . .178 C3
  Oxborough PE33 . . . . .81 D3
  Reedham NR13 . . . . .92 E4
  Surlingham NR14 . . . . . . .165 A1
  Woodbastwick NR13 . . . . .55 D2
Ferry Sq PE34 . . . . .146 C5
Ferry St PE30 . . . . .146 D5
Ferry View Rd NR12 . . . . . . .55 E3
FERSFIELD IP22 . . . . .119 D2
Fersfield Rd
  Bressingham IP22 . . . . . . .129 B8
  Kenninghall NR16 . . . . . . .119 C4
  South Lopham IP22 . . . . . .128 F8
Festival Cl PE30 . . . . .148 B1
Festival Rd NR20 . . . . .50 B8
Festival Way CB6 . . . . .96 E2
Ffolkes Dr
  King's Lynn PE30 . . . . . . .148 C1
  Terrington St Clement
    PE34 . . . . .144 B5

Ffolkes Pl 1 PE33 . . . . .61 D3
FIDDLERS' GREEN NR17 . . .174 B8
Fiddle Wood Rd NR6 . . . . . .158 D4
Field Acre Way NR15 . . . . . .106 E4
Field Barn Cotts PE32 . . . . .46 E3
Fieldbarn Dro PE33 . . . . . . .82 A4
Field Barn La PE33 . . . . .61 F3
Fieldbarn Rd PE33 . . . . .81 B8
FIELD DALLING NR25 . . . . . . .7 B1
Field Dalling Rd
  Field Dalling NR25 . . . . .7 A3
  Gunthorpe NR21 . . . . .18 B8
Field End Cl PE30 . . . . .147 B6
Fieldfare Cl 6 NR12 . . . . . . .54 A1
Fieldfare Wy NR8 . . . . .156 A5
Field House Gdns IP22 . . . .177 E5
Field La Beetley NR20 . . . . . .49 C5
  Blofield NR13 . . . . .73 D6
  10 Blofield NR13 . . . . .73 D6
  Blofield NR13 . . . . .165 E8
  Fakenham NR21 . . . . .141 B6
  Hempnall NR15 . . . . .107 C4
  King's Lynn PE30 . . . . . . .147 B6
  Marsham NR10 . . . . .36 B2
  North Walsham NR28 . . . .151 E3
  Stody NR24 . . . . .142 F8
  Whinburgh & Westfield
    NR19 . . . . .67 F4
  Wretton PE33 . . . . .80 F3
Field Maple Rd IP25 . . . . . . .84 E3
Field Rd Brandon IP27 . . . .114 D4
  King's Lynn PE30 . . . . . . .147 B5
  Ringland NR8 . . . . .70 B8
  South Walsham NR13 . . . .74 B8
  Stalham NR12 . . . . .39 C3
Fields Rd NR34 . . . . .110 E6
Fields The Forncett NR16 . . .105 E5
  Hingham NR9 . . . . .86 C5
Fieldview NR5 . . . . .161 E6
Fiennes Rd 4 NR7 . . . . .72 D5
Fifers La NR6 . . . . .158 C6
Fifth Ave PE13 . . . . .152 E4
Fifty Dro CB6 . . . . .95 F3
Fifty Rd PE14 . . . . .95 A3
Filbert Rd NR14 . . . . .91 F1
Filberts PE30 . . . . .147 D5
FILBY NR29 . . . . .75 F8
Filby Cl Earlham NR5 . . . . . .161 E6
  Filby NR29 . . . . .75 F8
FILBY HEATH NR29 . . . . . . .76 B8
Filby La NR29 . . . . .167 A1
Filby Prim Sch NR29 . . . . . .75 E8
Filby Rd Coltishall NR10 . . . .37 B2
  Stokesby with Herringby
    NR29 . . . . .75 C6
  Swaffham PE37 . . . . .153 B2
FINCHAM PE33 . . . . .62 F1
Fincham Dro PE32 . . . . .64 B5
Fincham Rd
  Barton Bendish PE33 . . . . .81 A8
  Crimplesham PE33 . . . . . . .80 A8
  Fincham PE33 . . . . .63 A1
  Shouldham Thorpe PE33 . . .62 C2
  Stow Bardolph PE34 . . . . . .79 F8
  Wereham PE33 . . . . .80 F6
Finch Cl Cromer NR27 . . . . .139 C4
  Norwich NR3 . . . . .159 D2
Finchdale Cl 5 PE30 . . . . . .148 C4
Finchley Ct 4 NR2 . . . . . . .162 B7
Finch Way NR13 . . . . .165 C3
Finderne Dr NR18 . . . . .173 D6
Finishers Rd 8 NR6 . . . . . . .158 C1
Finisterre Rise 2 NR30 . . . .168 C6
Finkelgate NR1 . . . . .178 B1
Finningham Rd IP22 . . . . . .128 E1
Finsbury Cl 1 PE38 . . . . . . .172 B4
Fiona Cl NR18 . . . . .173 E6
Fir Cl Heacham PE31 . . . . . .133 C6
  Mundford IP26 . . . . .100 B4
Fir Covert Rd
  Carleton Rode NR16 . . . . .105 A1
  Taverham NR10 . . . . .155 B4
Firethorn Cl NR8 . . . . .155 B2
Fir Gr NR26 . . . . .138 D4
Fir La NR10 . . . . .34 A1
Firman Ct NR7 . . . . .163 F8
Fir Pk IP25 . . . . .84 A7
Fir Rd IP24 . . . . .176 B1
Firs Ave NR29 . . . . .167 A3
Firside Jun Sch NR6 . . . . . .158 A6
Firs La NR12 . . . . .39 C2
Firs Rd Hethersett NR9 . . . . .88 D7
  Norwich NR6 . . . . .157 F6
First Ave PE13 . . . . .152 D5
First Dro IP27 . . . . .113 C3
Firs The
  Downham Market PE38 . . .172 D6
  Lakenheath IP27 . . . . . . .113 F1
First Marsh Rd PE13 . . . . . . .59 A6
Firs Way IP27 . . . . .175 C2
Firtree Cl NR13 . . . . .165 B4
Fir Tree Cl NR29 . . . . .57 C1
Fir Tree Dr 7 PE33 . . . . .43 E2
Firtree Rd NR7 . . . . .159 E1
Firwood Cl NR1 . . . . .163 C8
Fisher Ave NR30 . . . . .169 D8
Fishergate NR3 . . . . .178 B4
Fisherman's Her Ctr★
  NR26 . . . . .138 D8
Fishermen's Ct NR17 . . . . . .174 D4
Fisher Rd Diss IP22 . . . . . . .177 E4
  Fakenham NR21 . . . . .141 B5
Fisher Row NR32 . . . . .111 F4
Fishers Cl NR5 . . . . .156 E1
Fishers End Cl 12 PE31 . . . .12 E5
Fishers La Beetley NR20 . . . .49 D6
  Norwich NR2 . . . . .178 A3
Fisher's La IP21 . . . . .131 A4
Fishers' Quay 5 NR30 . . . . .169 C4

Fisher Way IP24 . . . . .176 E5
FISHLEY NR13 . . . . .166 C6
Fishley View NR13 . . . . .166 B4
Fish Wharf 2 NR30 . . . . . . .169 D1
Fiskes Ct NR14 . . . . .89 F5
Fiske's Opening 6 NR31 170 D4
Fison Way IP24 . . . . .176 C6
Fison Way Ind Est IP24 . . . .176 C6
Fitton Rd PE34 . . . . .61 B8
Fitzalan St 3 NR30 . . . . . . .169 C4
Fitzgerald Rd
  Norwich NR1 . . . . .162 E1
  7 Poringland NR14 . . . . . .90 C5
Fitzhenry Mews 8 NR5 . . . .161 B8
Fitzwalter Rd IP22 . . . . .177 E4
Five Acre La NR35 . . . . .123 E7
Five Acres NR14 . . . . .89 F4
Five Alls Rd PE14 . . . . .41 F1
Five Crossways NR12 . . . . . .164 D8
Five Elms 4 PE30 . . . . .147 C4
Flag St NR21 . . . . .15 C2
FLAXLANDS NR16 . . . . .105 C4
Flaxlands NR16 . . . . .105 B4
Flaxlands Rd NR16 . . . . .105 C3
Fleet La NR13 . . . . .56 B1
Fleet Rd NR8 . . . . .156 B6
Fleetwood Dr 4 NR13 . . . . . .72 D4
Fleggburgh CE Prim Sch
  NR29 . . . . .75 C8
Fleggburgh Rd NR29 . . . . . . .57 C2
Flegg Gn PE33 . . . . .80 D4
Flegg High Sch NR29 . . . . . .57 E6
Fleming Ct 8 IP25 . . . . .84 D3
Fletcher Cl NR12 . . . . .55 A8
Fletcher Way Acle NR13 . . .166 D4
  Cromer NR27 . . . . .139 B5
  Norwich NR3 . . . . .158 C3
Flint Dr NR23 . . . . .136 D5
Flint Gate 17 PE12 . . . . .41 B8
Flint House Gdns 13 NR9 . . .88 C7
Flint House Rd PE14 . . . . . . .77 F1
Flint Way 2 PE14 . . . . .77 A8
FLITCHAM PE31 . . . . .28 C5
Flitcham Abbey PE31 . . . . . .28 D5
Flitcham Barns Ind Units
  PE31 . . . . .28 D5
Flitcham CE Prim Sch
  PE31 . . . . .28 C5
FLIXTON NR35 . . . . .123 D5
Flixton Marsh La NR32 . . . .111 F6
Flixton Rd Bungay NR35 . . .124 A7
  Flixton NR35 . . . . .123 E6
  Lound NR32 . . . . .94 C1
  Somerleyton, Ashby &
    Herringfleet NR32 . . . . .111 F8
  St Margaret, South Elmham
    IP20 . . . . .123 E3
Floral Loke NR32 . . . . .111 D8
FLORDON NR15 . . . . .106 D8
Flordon Rd
  Bracon Ash NR14 . . . . .88 F1
  Flordon NR15 . . . . .106 D8
Florence Barclay Cl
  IP24 . . . . .176 D6
Florence Rd NR1 . . . . .163 A6
Florence Wlk NR19 . . . . . . .154 C2
Florence Wy NR35 . . . . .109 D3
Florida Bvd NR21 . . . . .15 C2
Flowerday Cl NR31 . . . . . . .171 D5
Flowerdew Cl 12 NR9 . . . . .88 C7
Flowerdew's La NR13 . . . . . .74 B7
Flowerpot La NR15 . . . . . . .106 D3
Flowers La NR17 . . . . .174 B3
Fludge's La NR20 . . . . .49 B6
Flymore La NR17 . . . . .103 A8
Focus Sch (Swaffham
  Campus) PE37 . . . . .153 B6
Fodderfen Dro PE38 . . . . . .113 A7
FODDERSTONE GAP PE33 . .62 C4
Foldgate La PE34 . . . . .61 A5
Folgate NR16 . . . . .88 D1
Folgate Cl Costessey NR8 . .156 F5
  Thornham PE36 . . . . .2 D6
Folgate La Costessey NR8 . .156 F4
  Walpole PE14 . . . . .41 D3
Folgate Rd
  Heacham PE31 . . . . .133 C4
  North Walsham NR28 . . . .151 B6
Folland Ct 8 NR20 . . . . .50 E7
Follies The PE37 . . . . .65 F4
Folly Cl 9 PE30 . . . . .147 B7
Folly Cl Fakenham NR21 . . .141 D4
  King's Lynn PE30 . . . . . . .147 B7
  Mattishall NR20 . . . . .68 F6
Folly Gdns NR18 . . . . .173 C5
Folly La Beetley NR20 . . . . . .49 B6
  Bressingham IP22 . . . . . . .129 C8
  Claxton NR14 . . . . .91 D5
  3 Hingham NR9 . . . . .86 C5
  Old Buckenham NR17 . . . .104 F2
Folly Rd NR18 . . . . .173 C5
Folly View 5 PE37 . . . . .65 F4
Folly Yd PE32 . . . . .48 B7
Folwell Rd NR5 . . . . .156 E1
Footpath The 11 NR14 . . . . .90 C5
Ford Ave PE30 . . . . .148 D5
FORDHAM PE38 . . . . .79 D2
Ford St IP24 . . . . .176 D3
Foregate Cl 2 NR8 . . . . . . .155 D2
Foreman Cl PE31 . . . . .133 D3
Forester Cl 1 NR4 . . . . .162 C1
Forester's Ave PE38 . . . . . . .97 A8
Forest Gr PE37 . . . . .153 C1
Forest Mount NR31 . . . . . . .93 E3

Forest Ret Pk IP24 . . . . . . .125 D8
Forge Cl
  Old Buckenham NR17 . . . .104 D2
  Palgrave IP22 . . . . .177 D2
  Poringland NR14 . . . . .90 D4
Forge Gr NR14 . . . . .110 C2
Forge Orchards 1 NR14 . . .89 B3
Forge Rd NR14 . . . . .91 F3
Forge Way IP22 . . . . .128 A8
Forget-Me-Not Rd 3
  PE31 . . . . .12 D4
Forge Way IP22 . . . . .128 A8
Forman Cl 15 PE25 . . . . . . .84 E3
Forncett CE VA Prim Sch
  NR16 . . . . .106 B3
FORNCETT END NR16 . . . . .105 E4
Forncett Ind Steam Mus★
  NR16 . . . . .106 B5
Forncett Rd Bunwell NR16 105 E3
  Tharston & Hapton NR15 . 106 D4
FORNCETT ST MARY
  NR16 . . . . .106 B4
FORNCETT ST PETER
  NR16 . . . . .106 B4
Forster Cl 2 NR11 . . . . .150 D6
Forster Way NR11 . . . . .150 D6
Forsythia Rd NR31 . . . . .170 B5
Forth Cl NR30 . . . . .168 C5
Forties Cl 5 NR30 . . . . .168 C6
Fortress Rd 21 IP25 . . . . . . .84 F3
Fortune Gn NR14 . . . . .90 E4
Forum The★ NR2 . . . . .178 A2
Forwater Rd NR10 . . . . .34 B3
Foster Cl Brundall NR13 . . .165 B4
  Ormesby St Margaret
    NR29 . . . . .167 C2
Foster Rd NR3 . . . . .158 D3
FOUL ANCHOR PE13 . . . . . .41 A4
FOULDEN IP26 . . . . .82 A2
Foulgers Opening NR1 . . . .178 C1
FOULSHAM NR20 . . . . .33 D3
Foulsham Prim Sch NR20 . .33 D3
Foulsham Rd Bintree NR20 . .33 C2
  Guestwick NR20 . . . . .33 F4
  Guist NR20 . . . . .33 A4
  Hindolveston NR20 . . . . . .33 D7
  Wood Norton NR20 . . . . . .33 B6
Foundry Cl Bodham NR25 . . . .9 A3
  Foulsham NR20 . . . . .33 D3
  Northrepps NR27 . . . . .11 A2
  Sculthorpe NR21 . . . . .16 C2
Foundry Cnr NR17 . . . . .174 F2
Foundry La PE36 . . . . .2 A3
Foundry La PE36 . . . . .2 A3
Foundry Sq NR14 . . . . .154 D4
Fountaine Gr PE30 . . . . . . .148 C4
Fountains Rd NR4 . . . . .89 E8
Four Acres Est NR29 . . . . . .167 C8
Fourth Ave PE13 . . . . .152 E4
Fowell Cl NR5 . . . . .161 B6
Fowler's La NR17 . . . . .174 B2
Foxburrow Rd NR7 . . . . . . .159 A5
Foxcotte Cl NR6 . . . . .157 E7
Fox Covert 5 NR19 . . . . . . .154 C4
Foxes Loke 12 NR14 . . . . . .92 A1
Foxes Mdw 2 PE32 . . . . . . .46 F2
Foxglove Cl
  Fakenham NR21 . . . . .141 F4
  North Walsham NR28 . . . .151 E5
  Thurton NR14 . . . . .91 C4
Foxglove Ct 7 PE38 . . . . . .172 B4
Foxglove Dr 21 NR14 . . . . . .94 C6
Foxglove La NR26 . . . . .138 B6
Foxglove Rd
  2 Attleborough NR17 . . . .174 B5
  Thetford IP24 . . . . .176 F4
Foxglove Wlk PE34 . . . . .61 B8
Fox Gr 7 NR16 . . . . .118 C5
Fox Hill PE30 . . . . .123 C3
Fox Hill Rd NR12 . . . . .38 E7
FOXHOLE NR15 . . . . .107 A7
Foxhouse Rd 1 NR8 . . . . . . .70 C7
Fox La Brundall NR13 . . . . .165 B4
  Framingham Pigot NR14 . . .90 D6
  North Tuddenham NR20 . . .68 F8
FOXLEY NR20 . . . . .50 D8
Foxley Cl NR5 . . . . .161 D6
Foxley Rd
  Bawdeswell NR20 . . . . . . .50 D8
  Foulsham NR20 . . . . .33 C2
Foxley Wood National Nature
  Reserve★ NR10 . . . . .33 F1
Fox Rd Dereham NR19 . . . . .154 D4
  Framingham Pigot NR14 . . .90 D7
Fox's La PE34 . . . . .146 C6
Foxs Loke NR11 . . . . .150 B6
Foxwood 9 NR13 . . . . .73 D6
Foxwood Cl NR8 . . . . .155 E3
FRAMINGHAM EARL
  NR14 . . . . .90 D4
Framingham Earl High Sch
  NR14 . . . . .90 C6
Framingham Earl La
  NR14 . . . . .90 E5
Framingham La NR14 . . . . . .90 F7
FRAMINGHAM PIGOT
  NR14 . . . . .90 C6
Framingham Rd NR14 . . . . . .90 F7
Framlingham Cl NR31 . . . . .169 C2
FRAMINGHAM PIGOT
  NR14 . . . . .90 C6
Francis Cl NR27 . . . . .139 C5
Francis La NR13 . . . . .73 C6
Francis Rd NR15 . . . . .106 E3
Francis Stone Ct NR7 . . . . . .72 D3
Francis Way NR5 . . . . .160 E8
FRANKFORT NR12 . . . . .38 A3
Franklin Cl PE31 . . . . .12 D4
Frank Stone Ct NR30 . . . . .169 E1
FRANS GREEN NR20 . . . . . .51 D1
Fransham Forge★ NR19 . .66 D8

Fransham Rd PE32 . . . . .48 B1
Frazer Cres NR11 . . . . .143 A7
Fred Ackland Dr PE30 . . . . .147 C3
Fred Edge Cl PE32 . . . . .54 A4
Frederick Cl PE30 . . . . .148 D6
Frederick Rd NR30 . . . . . . .169 C5
Fred Nicholson Sch
  NR19 . . . . .154 E2
Fred Tuddenham Dr NR10 35 B3
Freebridge Haven PE33 . . . .43 F3
Freedom Bridge PE13 . . . . .152 B6
Free La NR35 . . . . .108 F2
Freeland Cl NR8 . . . . .155 E3
Freeland Cnr NR10 . . . . . . .155 C6
Freeman Cl
  5 Hopton On Sea NR31 . .171 D4
  Loddon NR14 . . . . .109 D8
Freeman Sq NR2 . . . . .162 C8
Freeman St NR23 . . . . .136 C6
Free School Norwich The
  NR1 . . . . .178 B2
Freestone Ct 7 PE30 . . . . .146 E4
FREETHORPE NR13 . . . . . . .92 E8
Freethorpe Com Prim Sch
  NR13 . . . . .92 F7
Freethorpe Rd
  Cantley NR13 . . . . .92 D6
  Freethorpe NR13 . . . . .74 F1
Freiston 2 PE30 . . . . .147 C5
Fremantle Rd NR30 . . . . . . .168 E1
Frenbury Ind Est NR6 . . . . .157 F3
French's Rd PE14 . . . . .41 C4
Frensham Rd NR3 . . . . .157 F2
FRENZE IP21 . . . . .130 B7
Frenze Hall La IP22 . . . . . . .177 F5
Frenze Rd IP22 . . . . .177 E4
Frere Cnr 6 IP22 . . . . .129 D7
Frere Rd
  30 Harleston IP20 . . . . . .122 D2
  Norwich NR7 . . . . .159 D1
Fresher Mews NR5 . . . . . . .160 F6
Freshfield Cl NR5 . . . . .161 C7
Freshgap La NR20 . . . . .33 G6
Freshwater Way NR8 . . . . . .155 F3
FRETTENHAM NR12 . . . . . . .54 A4
Frettenham Prim Sch
  NR12 . . . . .54 A4
Frettenham Rd
  Hainford NR10 . . . . .53 F5
  Horstead with Stanninghall
    NR12 . . . . .54 B5
Freyden Way NR12 . . . . .54 A4
Friarscroft La NR18 . . . . . . .173 B3
Friar's La PE31 . . . . .135 D4
Friars' La 3 NR30 . . . . .169 D2
Friars Quay NR3 . . . . .178 B3
Friars St PE30 . . . . .146 E3
Friars The 17 PE30 . . . . . . .146 D4
Friar Tuck Rd NR4 . . . . .162 C1
FRIDAY BRIDGE PE14 . . . . . .77 A7
Friday Bridge Prim Sch
  PE14 . . . . .77 A7
Fridaybridge Rd Elm PE14 . .77 A8
  Wisbech PE14 . . . . .59 A1
Friday Mkt 4 NR22 . . . . . . .16 F7
Friends Cl NR5 . . . . .161 D6
Friends Rd NR4 . . . . .161 C5
FRING IP31 . . . . .13 D5
Fring Rd Bircham PE31 . . . . .14 A3
  Snettisham PE31 . . . . .13 A5
Frinton Way 4 PE13 . . . . . .152 E5
Frith Way NR13 . . . . .106 B1
Fritillary Dr NR18 . . . . .173 E4
FRITTON
  Fritton and St Olaves
    NR31 . . . . .93 E3
  Ludham NR29 . . . . .56 B6
  Morning Thorpe NR15 . . . .107 B3
Fritton Cl NR29 . . . . .167 B3
Fritton La NR29 . . . . .56 B6
Fritton Lake Ctry World★
  NR31 . . . . .93 F2
Fritton Rd NR29 . . . . .56 E6
Frobisher Cl IP24 . . . . .176 F6
Frobisher Cres PE36 . . . . . .132 D3
Frogge La Coltishall NR12 . .54 C8
  Scottow NR12 . . . . .37 C1
FROGSHALL NR27 . . . . .11 B1
Frogshall La NR18 . . . . .173 A5
Frogs Hall La 3 NR1 . . . . . .163 B5
Frog's Hall La NR20 . . . . . . .50 C2
Frogs Hole Blofield NR13 . .165 D6
  Somerleyton, Ashby &
    Herringfleet NR32 . . . . .93 F1
Front Rd Tydd St Giles PE13 .41 A4
  Wood Dalling NR11 . . . . . .34 D6
Front St Binham NR21 . . . . . .6 E2
  Burnham Market PE31 . . . .135 C3
  Trunch NR28 . . . . .22 E5
Front Way PE30 . . . . .147 A7
Frost Cl Norwich NR7 . . . . .163 F8
  20 Watton IP25 . . . . .84 D3
FROST ROW NR9 . . . . .86 B4
Frost's La NR15 . . . . .106 B1
Fugill Rd NR7 . . . . .159 D1
Fulcher Ave NR27 . . . . .139 A7
Fulford Cl NR4 . . . . .162 A2
Fuller Cl
  2 Rackheath NR13 . . . . . .72 E7
  9 West Winch PE33 . . . . . .43 F2
Fuller Mews 5 NR5 . . . . . . .160 E8
Fuller Rd
  North Walsham NR28 . . . .151 B4
  Redenhall with Harleston
    IP20 . . . . .122 D1
Fuller's Cl NR34 . . . . .110 D5
Fuller's Hill 10 NR30 . . . . . .169 C4
Fullers Loke NR8 . . . . .155 F2

Fulmar Cl **9** NR31 . . . . . .94 C7
Fulmer La PE32 . . . . .46 E2
Fulmerston Cl IP24 . . . . . .176 B2
Fulmerston Rd IP24 . . . . .176 B2
FULMODESTON NR21 . . . . .17 F1
Fulmodeston Rd
　Fulmodeston NR21 . . . . . .18 B1
　Hindolveston NR20 . . . . . .33 C8
　Stibbard NR21 . . . . .32 E7
Fulton Cl NR4 . . . . .162 A1
FUNDENHALL NR16 . . . . . .106 A7
Fundenhall Rd NR15 . . . . .106 B7
Fundrey Rd PE13 . . . . . . .152 F6
Furlong Dro PE33 . . . . . . .81 A3
Furlong Rd **1** PE33 . . . . . .81 A3
Furness Rd PE30 . . . . . . .148 F1
Furthest Dro IP27 . . . . . . .113 C4
Furze Ave NR7 . . . . .163 E8
Furze Hill NR27 . . . . .139 C5
Furze Hill Dr NR28 . . . . . .151 E3
Furze La
　Great Witchingham NR9 . . .149 C2
　Guist NR20 . . . . .33 A6
Furze Rd NR7 . . . . .163 E8
Furze Way IP22 . . . . .129 B1
Fuschia Ct NR18 . . . . . . .173 E6
Fye Bridge St NR3 . . . . . .178 B4

G

Gablehurst Ct NR31 . . . . .170 A4
Gables Ave NR11 . . . . . . .22 B7
Gage Rd NR7 . . . . .159 C4
Gagman's La NR19 . . . . . .68 A5
Gainsborough Ave
　1 Diss IP22 . . . . .177 C4
　Great Yarmouth NR31 . . . .170 A7
Gainsborough Cl **2**
PE38 . . . . .172 D6
Galahad Rd NR31 . . . . . . .171 B8
Gale Cl NR14 . . . . .109 F8
Gales Ct NR23 . . . . .136 D6
Gales Rd NR23 . . . . .136 C6
Gallant's La NR16 . . . . . . .118 C5
Galley Cl **8** NR33 . . . . . .111 F1
Galley Hill NR3 . . . . .158 A2
Gallops The **16** IP25 . . . . .84 F3
Galloway Cl **6** NR20 . . . . .68 A8
Gallow Dr PE38 . . . . .172 C7
Gallowhill La NR24 . . . . . .18 C3
Gallow Hill (Tumulus)★
NR25 . . . . .8 B5
Gallow La PE33 . . . . .62 D2
Gallows La NR16 . . . . .103 E1
Gallus Cl NR27 . . . . .11 A2
Galyon Rd PE30 . . . . .147 B8
Gambling Cl NR6 . . . . . . .158 A7
Gamecock Cl NR16 . . . . . .158 C6
Gamewell Cl **6** NR1 . . . . .162 E2
Gangway The NR27 . . . . . .139 C7
Ganners Hill NR8 . . . . . . .155 E3
Gannet Rd NR29 . . . . .167 E4
Gant Cl **9** NR20 . . . . .68 F6
Gaol Hill NR2 . . . . .178 A3
Gaol St **13** PE13 . . . . . . .152 C4
Gapton Hall Ind Est
NR31 . . . . .170 A8
Gapton Hall Rd NR31 . . . . .170 A8
Gapton Hall Ret Pk
NR31 . . . . .169 A1
Garage La PE33 . . . . .61 E8
Garage Lane Ind Est PE33 .61 F8
GARBOLDISHAM IP22 . . . .128 A8
Garboldisham Church Prim
　Sch IP22 . . . . .128 A8
Garboldisham Rd
　Harling NR16 . . . . .118 C3
　Kenninghall NR16 . . . . . .118 F3
Garden Cl Briston NR24 . . .142 B4
　Bungay NR35 . . . . .124 B4
　North Walsham NR28 . . . .151 C6
　4 Watton IP25 . . . . . . .84 A6
Garden Ct
　King's Lynn PE30 . . . . . .147 A8
　1 Loddon NR14 . . . . . .92 A1
Gardeners Terr NR7 . . . . . .158 F4
Gardenhouse La IP22 . . . .128 E2
Garden La NR25 . . . . .8 A1
Garden Pl **2** NR3 . . . . . .162 E8
Garden Rd Brundall NR13 . .165 E6
　Hemsby NR29 . . . . .167 D7
　Sheringham NR26 . . . . . .138 D6
　3 Wiggenhall St Germans
　PE34 . . . . .43 B1
Garden Row PE30 . . . . . . .146 E3
Garden St Cromer NR27 . . .139 B7
　Norwich NR1 . . . . .178 B2
Gardyn Croft **5** NR8 . . . .155 D2
Garfield Rd PE30 . . . . . . .169 D7
Garfield Terr NR30 . . . . . .168 E4
Gargle Hill NR7 . . . . .163 F7
Gariannonum (Roman Fort)★
NR31 . . . . .93 D7
Garlic St IP21 . . . . .122 A2
GARLIC STREET IP21 . . . .122 A2
Garlondes **6** NR16 . . . . .118 C5
Garner's La PE34 . . . . .41 D8
Garnham Rd NR31 . . . . . .170 C7
Garrett Cl NR3 . . . . .158 F1
Garrick Gn NR6 . . . . .158 E5
Garrick Green Inf Sch
NR6 . . . . .158 E5
Garrison Rd NR30 . . . . . . .169 C5
Garrood Dr NR21 . . . . . . .141 E5
GARVESTONE NR9 . . . . . .68 C2
Garvestone Com Prim Sch
NR9 . . . . .68 C2

Garvestone Rd NR20 . . . . .68 E4
Garwood Cl PE30 . . . . . . .147 E4
Gas Hill NR1 . . . . .163 A6
Gashouse Dro IP27 . . . . . .175 E4
Gashouse Hill NR11 . . . . .150 D6
Gas House La PE12 . . . . . .41 B8
Gaskell Way PE30 . . . . . . .148 C1
GASTHORPE IP22 . . . . . . .127 D7
Gatacre Rd NR31 . . . . . . .169 B3
Gatehouse La PE30 . . . . . .148 C6
Gatekeeper Cl NR18 . . . . .173 E4
GATELEY NR20 . . . . .32 C3
Gateley Gdns NR3 . . . . . .158 B3
Gateley Rd NR20 . . . . .49 B8
Gaultree Sq PE14 . . . . . . .59 D2
Gavell St IP19 . . . . .124 D1
Gawain Rd NR31 . . . . . . .170 A1
Gawdy Cl **2** IP20 . . . . . .122 D2
Gawdy Rd NR1 . . . . .159 D1
Gaye Cres **1** IP23 . . . . . .130 C1
Gayford Rd NR10 . . . . .35 B3
Gaymer Cl NR16 . . . . .119 D7
Gaymer's Way NR28 . . . . .151 B6
Gaynor Cl NR18 . . . . .173 B5
GAYTON PE32 . . . . .45 C5
Gayton CE Prim Sch PE32 . .45 C5
Gayton Rd East Winch PE32 .45 A4
　Grimston PE32 . . . . .45 C8
　King's Lynn PE30 . . . . . .147 C5
Gayton Wlk NR6 . . . . .158 F6
GAYWOOD PE32 . . . . .147 B6
Gaywood Cl NR30 . . . . . . .168 D5
Gaywood Com Prim Sch
PE30 . . . . .147 C7
Gaywood Hall Dr PE30 . . . .147 B5
Gaywood Rd PE30 . . . . . . .146 F5
Geddes Way **5** NR20 . . . .68 F6
Gedge Rd NR30 . . . . .168 E6
GELDESTON NR34 . . . . . .109 F3
Geldeston Hill NR34 . . . . .109 F2
Geldeston Rd
　Ellingham NR35 . . . . . . .109 D2
　Geldeston NR34 . . . . . . .110 B2
Gelham Manor PE31 . . . . .140 C3
Generals Wlk **5** PE30 . . . .147 C5
Geneva Gdns NR31 . . . . . .171 E4
Genista Gn **7** NR31 . . . . .170 B6
Gentian Way **2** NR17 . . . .174 B4
Gentlemans Wlk NR14 . . . .92 A3
Gentleman's Wlk NR2 . . . .178 A3
Gentle Rise PE32 . . . . . . .113 E2
Gentry Pl NR1 . . . . .161 C8
Geoffrey Rd **4** NR1 . . . . .162 F3
Geoffrey Watling Wy
　Norwich NR1 . . . . .163 A4
　Norwich NR1 . . . . .178 C1
George Baldry Wy NR35 . . .124 B7
George Beck Rd **8** NR29 . .58 B6
George Borrow Rd
　2 East Dereham NR19 . . .154 F3
　Norwich NR1 . . . . .161 E5
George Cl NR8 . . . . .157 B8
George Cres **13** NR6 . . . . .118 C5
George Dance Pl NR5 . . . . .161 C7
George Dr NR8 . . . . .157 B7
George Edwards Rd
　NR21 . . . . .141 E5
George Eliot Way **6**
NR19 . . . . .154 D2
George Fox Way NR5 . . . . .161 B5
George Hill Norwich NR6 . . .158 E4
　Stanton IP31 . . . . .127 C1
George La Acle NR13 . . . . .166 B4
　2 Loddon NR14 . . . . . .92 A1
George Low Cl NR5 . . . . . .157 A1
George Pope Cl NR3 . . . . .158 C2
George Pope Rd NR3 . . . . .158 C2
George Raines Cl PE36 . . . .132 C3
George Rd IP24 . . . . .176 F5
Georges Rd NR19 . . . . . . .154 D5
George St Brandon IP27 . . .175 D3
　Great Yarmouth NR30 . . . .169 C4
　6 King's Lynn PE30 . . . .146 E6
　Sheringham NR26 . . . . . .138 D7
George Trollope Rd **15**
IP25 . . . . .84 D3
George Westwood Way
NR34 . . . . .110 D2
George White Jun Sch
NR3 . . . . .162 F8
George Winter Ct NR3 . . . .158 C2
Georgia Rd NR21 . . . . . . .15 C2
Gerald Cl NR1 . . . . .163 C8
Germander Ct **8** NR31 . . . .94 C6
German's La PE34 . . . . . . .42 A6
Gertrude Rd NR3 . . . . . . .158 F1
Ghost Hill Inf Sch NR8 . . . .156 D8
Gibbet La
　East Beckham NR11 . . . . .138 D2
　Wereham PE33 . . . . .80 C5
Gibbs Cl NR9 . . . . .160 B2
Gibson Rd **5** IP25 . . . . . .67 B2
Gidney Dr PE31 . . . . .133 C5
Gigli Cl NR28 . . . . .151 B3
Gilbard Rd NR5 . . . . .161 C7
Gilbert Rd NR14 . . . . .90 F4
Gilbert Rd NR30 . . . . .168 E6
Gilbert Way NR4 . . . . .161 B1
Gilchrist Cl **8** NR4 . . . . . .89 E8
Gildencroft NR3 . . . . .178 A4
Gildenswood NR16 . . . . . .105 F3
Gilders Wy NR3 . . . . .178 C4
Giles Rd NR10 . . . . .54 A1
GILLINGHAM NR34 . . . . . .110 C2
Gillingham Dam NR34 . . . .110 C2
Gillingham Rd NR34 . . . . .110 A2
Gillingham St Michaels CE
　Prim Acad NR34 . . . . . .110 B2

Gillingham Dam NR34 . . . .110 C2
Gilman Rd NR3 . . . . .158 F1
Gilpin's Ride NR19 . . . . . .154 D4
Gilray Rd IP22 . . . . .177 F4
GIMINGHAM NR11 . . . . . . .22 E7
Gimingham Rd
　Mundesley NR11 . . . . . . .143 A6
　Southrepps NR11 . . . . . . .22 C7
Gipsies La NR29 . . . . .56 D6
Gipsies' La NR25 . . . . .9 A3
Gipsy Cl NR5 . . . . .161 D6
Gipsy La NR5 . . . . .161 D6
　Watlington PE33 . . . . . . .61 D5
Girling Rd NR19 . . . . .154 C6
Girlings La NR7 . . . . .163 E5
Girton Rd
　Great Yarmouth NR31 . . . .170 A3
　Norwich NR2 . . . . .162 B4
GISSING IP22 . . . . .120 F4
Gissing Rd IP22 . . . . .120 F2
Glade Prim Sch IP27 . . . . .175 D3
Glade The Costessey NR8 . .156 F4
　Overstrand NR27 . . . . . . .11 A3
　Thetford IP24 . . . . .176 D6
Gladstone Rd
　Fakenham NR21 . . . . . . .141 B4
　4 King's Lynn PE30 . . . .146 E3
Gladstone St NR2 . . . . . . .162 B6
Glamis Ct **26** IP20 . . . . . .122 D2
GLANDFORD NR25 . . . . . . .7 E4
Glandford Rd NR25 . . . . . .7 E5
Glasbury Wlk PE13 . . . . . .153 C3
Glaven Cl NR25 . . . . .147 C5
Glaven Cl NR28 . . . . .151 D5
Glaven Hale Cl NR25 . . . . .137 C6
Glaven Rd NR25 . . . . .137 D5
Glebe Ave
　Hunstanton PE36 . . . . . .132 D5
　Watlington PE33 . . . . . . .61 D5
Glebe Cl Fransham NR19 . . .66 C7
　Hingham NR9 . . . . .86 B5
　19 Long Stratton NR15 . .106 E3
　Northwold IP26 . . . . .99 C8
　2 Potter Heigham NR29 . .56 F6
　Taverham NR8 . . . . .155 F1
　Thetford IP24 . . . . .176 D5
Glebe Ct NR28 . . . . .151 D6
Glebe Dr IP22 . . . . .177 B4
Glebe Est PE34 . . . . .144 F1
Glebe House Sch PE36 . . . .132 C3
Glebe La PE31 . . . . .135 F6
Glebeland Com Prim Sch
NR34 . . . . .110 E7
Glebe Mdw NR7 . . . . .103 E7
Glebe Rd Acle NR13 . . . . .166 C3
　Dersingham NR31 . . . . . .140 C4
　Downham Market PE38 . . .172 D6
　Gissing IP21 . . . . .121 A4
　Norwich NR2 . . . . .162 A4
　7 Watton IP25 . . . . . . .84 E3
　Weeting IP27 . . . . .175 B7
Glebes The **13** NR31 . . . . .94 A5
Glebe The
　2 Harling NR16 . . . . . .118 C5
　Hemsby NR29 . . . . .167 C8
　Honing NR28 . . . . .38 C6
　Postwick NR13 . . . . .72 F2
　Stibbard NR21 . . . . .32 E7
　Wells-next-the-Sea NR23 . .136 E4
Glebe Way **5** NR12 . . . . .54 C6
Glenalmond NR4 . . . . . . .162 A1
Glenburn Ave NR7 . . . . . . .159 A3
Glenburn Ct NR7 . . . . .159 A3
Glenda Cl NR5 . . . . .157 C1
Glenda Cres NR5 . . . . .157 B1
Glenda Ct NR5 . . . . .157 B1
Glenda Rd NR5 . . . . .157 C1
Glendenning Rd **4** NR1 . . .163 B5
Glendon Gdns PE13 . . . . . .152 A8
Glenfield Cl PE14 . . . . .78 A5
Glengarry Cl NR9 . . . . .88 C8
Glenham St **1** IP21 . . . . . .140 C4
Glenmore Ave NR30 . . . . . .168 D7
Glenmore Gdns NR3 . . . . .158 B2
Glenn Rd NR14 . . . . .90 C4
Globe La NR13 . . . . .165 C6
Globe Pl NR2 . . . . .162 C5
Globe St IP26 . . . . .99 A5
Glosthorpe Manor PE32 . . . .44 F5
Gloucester Ave NR31 . . . . .170 C4
Gloucester Ct PE13 . . . . . .152 D7
Gloucester Pl NR24 . . . . . .142 D4
Gloucester Rd PE30 . . . . . .147 B6
Gloucester St NR1 . . . . . . .162 B4
Gloucester Way IP24 . . . . .176 A5
Goat Willow Cl IP25 . . . . . .84 E3
Gobbett's Rd IP22 . . . . . . .128 C4
Goddard Cres **1** PE13 . . . .152 D7
Goddards Ct **14** IP25 . . . . .84 D3
Godfrey Rd **5** NR10 . . . . . .54 A2
Godric Pl NR2 . . . . .161 F6
Godwick Medieval Village
　of★ PE32 . . . . .31 C1
Godwin Rd PE13 . . . . .152 D7
Goffe Cl IP25 . . . . .84 D4
Goffins La PE14 . . . . .60 B6
Goggles La NR19 . . . . .66 C6
Gogg's Mill Rd NR21 . . . . .141 A3
Gogle Cl **8** NR20 . . . . . . .68 E6
Golden Ball St NR1 . . . . . .178 B2
Golden Dog La NR3 . . . . . .178 B4
Golden Gates NR23 . . . . . .136 B2
Golden Gates Dr NR23 . . . .136 A2
Golden Pightle **7** NR9 . . . .69 F2
Golden Sq **10** NR27 . . . . . .139 B7
Goldfinch Cl PE38 . . . . . . .172 C7
Goldfinch Dr NR17 . . . . . . .174 B4
Goldfinch Way **13** IP25 . . . .84 C3

Golding Pl Norwich NR2 . . .162 C6
　16 Wisbech PE13 . . . . . .152 C4
Goldsmith St NR2 . . . . . . .162 C7
Goldsmith Way IP21 . . . . .121 F4
Golds Pightle PE36 . . . . . . .2 B3
Goldwell Rd NR1 . . . . .178 B1
Golf Cl King's Lynn PE30 . . .148 D1
　Runton NR27 . . . . .10 A5
Golf Course Rd PE36 . . . . .132 E8
Golf La NR19 . . . . .154 D7
Golf Links Rd
　Brundall NR13 . . . . .165 D4
　Wymondham College
　NR18 . . . . .104 E8
Gong La PE31 . . . . .135 F6
Gonville Cl PE31 . . . . .133 C5
Gonville Rd NR31 . . . . . . .170 A4
Gooch Cl NR28 . . . . .151 C6
GOODERSTONE PE33 . . . . .82 A4
Gooderstone CE Prim Sch
　PE33 . . . . .82 A5
Gooderstone Rd **8** IP25 . . .83 F5
Gooderstone Water Gdns★
　PE33 . . . . .82 A5
Goodhale Rd **1** NR5 . . . . .161 B7
Goodman Sq **2** NR2 . . . . .162 C7
Goodminns PE36 . . . . .13 A7
Goodrick Pl PE13 . . . . . . .153 C4
Goodwin Rd NR11 . . . . . . .143 C6
Goodwins Rd PE30 . . . . . .146 E3
Goodwood Cl NR7 . . . . . . .159 E1
Goosander Cl **4** PE31 . . . .12 E5
Gooseacre La IP25 . . . . . . .67 D3
Gooseberry Hill NR20 . . . . .50 B3
Goose Gn
　8 Sutton Bridge PE12 . . .41 B8
　Winfarthing IP22 . . . . . . .120 C5
Goose Gn La IP22 . . . . . . .120 B6
Goose Gn Rd PE31 . . . . . . .12 E4
GOOSE GREEN IP22 . . . . .120 C5
Goose Green West **8**
NR34 . . . . .110 D1
Goose La
　Alby with Thwaite NR11 . . .21 B3
　Stalham NR12 . . . . .39 C4
Goose's La PE14 . . . . .41 D5
Gordon Ave NR7 . . . . .163 C7
Gordon Ct PE13 . . . . .152 B5
Gordon Fuller Cl IP26 . . . . .99 A7
Gordon Godfrey Way
　NR10 . . . . .53 A3
Gordon Rd Briston NR24 . . .142 A5
　3 East Dereham NR20 . . .154 E5
　Great Yarmouth NR31 . . . .169 C2
Gordon Sq NR1 . . . . .178 B1
Gordon Terr NR11 . . . . . . .143 B4
Gore La NR15 . . . . .121 C8
Gorgate Dr NR20 . . . . .49 D3
Gorgate Rd NR20 . . . . .49 E3
GORLESTON-ON-SEA
　NR31 . . . . .170 E4
Gormans La NR21 . . . . . . .31 D5
Gorse Ave NR6 . . . . .158 A5
Gorse Cl **1** Belton NR31 . . .94 A5
　Fakenham NR21 . . . . . . .141 F3
　Mundesley NR11 . . . . . . .143 B5
Gorse Ind Est IP24 . . . . . .125 C6
Gorse Rd NR7 . . . . .163 D8
Gorse View **4** NR20 . . . . .49 D4
Gorse Vw NR7 . . . . .159 E1
Goshawk Way **5** IP24 . . . .176 D2
Gosmoor La PE14 . . . . . . .59 B1
Gostling Cl IP22 . . . . .177 B4
Gothic Cl **2** IP20 . . . . . . .122 D1
Goulburn Rd NR7 . . . . . . .159 D1
Goulder Dr NR11 . . . . .150 B5
Gould Rd **1** NR2 . . . . . . .162 A4
Gournay Ave NR31 . . . . . .170 D2
Governors Ct NR1 . . . . . . .178 C1
Gower Cl PE36 . . . . .132 C4
Gowing Cl NR1 . . . . .157 F7
Gowing Ct NR3 . . . . .158 B3
Gowing Rd
　11 Mulbarton NR14 . . . . .89 B3
　Norwich NR6 . . . . .157 F6
Gowing Way NR15 . . . . . . .107 B5
Grace Edwards Cl NR8 . . . .155 F2
Grafton Cl PE30 . . . . .147 C8
Grafton Rd PE30 . . . . .147 C8
Graham Dr **2** PE32 . . . . . .44 B3
Graham Sq NR7 . . . . .159 D1
Graham St PE30 . . . . .146 E3
Grammar Sch Rd NR28 . . . .151 C4
Granary Cl Briston NR24 . . .142 F3
　Freethorpe NR13 . . . . . . .92 E7
　Hockering NR20 . . . . .69 B7
　9 Lingwood NR13 . . . . .74 A3
Granary Ct PE30 . . . . .146 D4
Granary Loke NR10 . . . . . .149 C4
Granary Rd NR17 . . . . . . .174 C4
Grand Cl NR19 . . . . .154 C4
Grange Ave NR27 . . . . . . .11 B3
Grange Cl Briston NR24 . . .142 B3
　Ludham NR29 . . . . .56 D5
　Norwich NR6 . . . . .158 E4
　10 Snettisham PE31 . . . .12 E4
　Wroxham/Hoveton NR12 . .164 E4
Grange Cres PE33 . . . . . . .63 C5
Grange Ct NR28 . . . . .151 C4
Grange Farm Cl NR29 . . . .75 F8
Grange La NR9 . . . . .69 F5
Grange Rd
　Caister-on-Sea NR30 . . . . .168 D5
　Cantley NR13 . . . . .92 C4
　Flixton NR35 . . . . .123 E4
　Hainford NR10 . . . . .53 F5
　Ludham NR29 . . . . .56 D5

Grange Rd continued
　Mundham NR14 . . . . . . .108 F7
　Norwich NR2 . . . . .162 A4
　Scarning NR19 . . . . .154 A4
　Sutton Bridge PE34 . . . . .41 E8
　Wendling NR19 . . . . .66 F8
　Wisbech PE13 . . . . .152 A7
GRANGE THE NR10 . . . . . .35 C1
Grange Wlk NR12 . . . . . . .164 C4
Granny Bard's La NR12 . . . .54 C3
Granta Way **1** NR31 . . . . .170 B2
Grantly Ct PE30 . . . . .147 D5
Grant Rd NR10 . . . . .54 A2
Grant St NR2 . . . . .162 A7
Granville Cl **8** NR12 . . . . . .39 B4
Granville Rd NR31 . . . . . . .169 B4
Granville Terr PE12 . . . . . .41 A8
Grapes Hill NR2 . . . . .162 C6
Grasmere **19** NR9 . . . . . . .88 D8
Grasmere Cl NR5 . . . . . . .161 C6
Grassgate La PE14 . . . . . .59 B7
Gravel Bank PE14 . . . . . . .60 D6
Gravel Dam NR32 . . . . . . .111 F4
Gravelfield Cl NR1 . . . . . . .163 B8
Gravel Hill NR14 . . . . .89 F4
Gravelhill La PE33 . . . . . . .43 F1
Gravelpit Hill NR17 . . . . . .102 F6
Gravel Pit La
　Haddiscoe NR14 . . . . . . .110 F8
　Holt NR25 . . . . .137 C5
Gray Dr NR20 . . . . .50 B4
Grays Fair NR5 . . . . .156 F1
Grays La PE14 . . . . .59 C2
Gray's La Barsham NR22 . . .16 E6
　Pulham Market IP21 . . . . .121 D5
Grays Rd NR34 . . . . .111 C3
Great Barn Rd NR23 . . . . . .5 A4
GREAT BARWICK PE31 . . . .14 E6
Great Barwick Medieval
　Village of★ PE31 . . . . . . .14 E6
GREAT BIRCHAM PE31 . . . .14 B3
Great Cl NR30 . . . . .168 F5
GREAT COMM La NR34 . . .124 D6
GREAT COMMON NR34 . . .124 D6
Great Comm La NR34 . . . .124 D6
GREAT CRESSINGHAM
　IP25 . . . . .83 D4
GREAT DUNHAM PE32 . . . .47 E1
Great Dunham Prim Sch
　PE32 . . . . .47 F1
Great Eastern Rd PE13 . . .152 B4
Great Eastern Way
　Fakenham NR21 . . . . . . .141 D4
　Wells-next-the-Sea NR23 . .136 E5
GREAT ELLINGHAM
　NR17 . . . . .103 E7
Great Ellingham Prim Sch
　NR17 . . . . .103 E7
GREAT FRANSHAM NR19 . . .66 B8
GREAT GREEN
　Burgate IP22 . . . . .129 B3
　Thrandeston IP21 . . . . . .130 A4
GREAT HAUTBOIS NR12 . . .54 C7
Great Hautbois Rd NR12 . . .54 C7
Greatheath Rd NR20 . . . . . .32 D1
GREAT HOCKHAM IP24 . . .102 E3
Great Hockham Prim Sch
　IP24 . . . . .102 E4
Great Hospl NR1 . . . . .178 C4
GREAT MASSINGHAM
　PE32 . . . . .29 D2
Great Massingham CE Prim
　Sch PE32 . . . . .29 E1
GREAT MELTON NR9 . . . . .70 B1
Great Melton Cl **29** NR9 . . .88 D8
Great Melton Rd
　Hethersett NR9 . . . . .88 C8
　Little Melton NR9 . . . . . .160 A2
GREAT MOULTON NR15 . . .106 B1
Great Northern Cl NR30 . . .169 D6
Great Palgrave Medieval
　Village of★ PE32 . . . . . . .65 B6
GREAT PLUMSTEAD NR13 . .72 F5
GREAT RYBURGH NR21 . . . .32 B6
GREAT SNORING NR21 . . . .17 A5
Great Snoring Rd NR21 . . . .17 D6
GREAT WALSINGHAM
　NR22 . . . . .17 A8
GREAT WITCHINGHAM
　NR9 . . . . .51 E7
Great Witchingham CE Prim
　Acad NR9 . . . . .51 E7
GREAT YARMOUTH
　NR30 . . . . .169 A5
Great Yarmouth Coll
　NR31 . . . . .169 C1
Great Yarmouth High Sch
　NR30 . . . . .169 E6
Great Yarmouth Prim Acad
　NR30 . . . . .169 E6
Great Yarmouth Race Course
　NR30 . . . . .168 F2
Great Yarmouth Sea Life
　Ctr★ NR30 . . . . .169 E2
Great Yarmouth Sta
　NR30 . . . . .169 B5
Grebe Cl
　Great Yarmouth NR31 . . . .170 A7
　7 Rollesby NR29 . . . . . .57 D2
Grebe Dr NR14 . . . . .91 F2
Greenacre Cl
　Brundall NR13 . . . . .165 C4
　King's Lynn PE30 . . . . . .148 B2
Green Acre Cl IP26 . . . . . .100 C5
Greenacre Rd NR9 . . . . . . .86 B5

Greenacres
Bradwell NR31 . . . .**170** A3
Little Melton NR9 . . . .**160** C2
Green Bank PE36 . . . .**2** A5
Greenborough Cl NR7. . . .**159** E2
Greenborough Rd NR7. . . .**159** E2
Green Cl Hempton NR21 . . . .**141** A2
Norwich NR5. . . . .**156** E1
Green Comm La PE14 . . . . . .**3** C6
Greencourts NR29 . . . .**58** B6
Green Ct Fakenham NR21. .**141** E4
Norwich NR7. . . . .**163** D7
Green Dragon La NR23. . .**136** D5
Green Dro PE14 . . . .**77** D6
Greenfield NR5. . . . .**156** D1
Greenfield Cl NR27 . . . . . .**139** C5
Greenfields NR16 . . . .**118** B5
Greenfields Rd NR20. . . .**154** F4
GREENGATE NR20 . . . .**50** B3
Greengate NR20 . . . .**50** B2
Greengate La
Bircham PE31 . . . .**13** F4
Great Massingham PE32. . .**29** C1
Green Gr PE33. . . . .**81** D8
Greenhill Ave NR30 . . . .**168** D8
Greenhill Rd PE32 . . . .**46** B2
Green Hills Cl NR8. . . . . .**156** F5
Green Hills Rd NR3. . . . . .**162** D8
Greenhoe Pl PE37 . . . .**153** B3
Green House La PE37 . . . .**153** E5
Green La Alpington NR14 . . .**90** F3
Attleborough NR17 . . . . . .**174** C7
Aylsham NR11 . . . .**150** A6
Bawburgh NR9 . . . .**160** C4
Beetley NR20. . . . .**49** D4
Billingford NR20. . . . .**49** F8
Burgh St Peter NR34. . . . .**111** C4
Burnham Thorpe PE31. . . . . .**4** D3
Caister-on-Sea NR30. . . . .**168** E4
Christchurch PE14. . . . .**95** A7
Coltishall NR12 . . . .**54** C6
Dereham NR19 . . . .**154** E8
Ditchingham NR35. . . . . . .**109** B2
Earsham NR35. . . . .**108** E2
5 Feltwell IP26 . . . .**98** C1
Filby NR29. . . . .**75** F8
Foulsham NR20. . . . .**33** E3
Great Ellingham NR17. . . .**103** E8
Great & Little Plumstead
NR13. . . . .**72** E5
Great Moulton NR15. . . . .**106** B1
Great Yarmouth NR31. . . . .**94** C6
Guist NR20 . . . .**33** A5
Hales NR14 . . . .**109** E8
Haveringland NR10. . . . .**52** E7
Horsford NR10 . . . .**53** B4
King's Lynn PE30. . . . .**148** E2
Little Ellingham NR17 . . . . .**86** A1
Methwold IP26 . . . .**99** A7
Mundford IP26 . . . .**100** B5
Park's Wood NR35. . . . . . .**108** E2
Postwick with Witton NR7. .**72** E4
Potter Heigham NR29. . . . . .**56** F6
Pudding Norton NR21. . . . .**141** A1
Redenhall with Harleston
IP20. . . . .**122** E2
Rocklands NR17 . . . .**103** C7
Saxlingham Nethergate
NR15. . . . .**107** B7
Shipdham IP25 . . . .**67** D4
Shipmeadow NR34 . . . . . .**109** F1
Somerleyton, Ashby &
Herringfleet NR32 . . . . .**111** E8
South Walsham NR13 . . . . .**74** B6
Starston IP20 . . . .**122** D4
Stow Bedon NR17. . . . . . .**103** B8
Syleham IP21 . . . .**131** C4
Thelnetham IP22. . . . .**128** A2
Thetford IP24 . . . .**176** E4
Thornham PE36. . . . .**2** D6
Thrandeston IP21. . . . . . .**129** F2
Tivetshall St Margaret
NR15. . . . .**121** B5
Toft Monks NR34. . . . . . .**110** C6
Tottenhill PE33 . . . .**61** F5
Troston IP31 . . . .**126** A1
Upwell PE14 . . . .**95** B6
Walsoken PE14. . . . .**152** F4
Wicklewood NR18. . . . .**87** C5
Wramplingham NR18. . . . . .**87** F7
Wymondham NR18 . . . . . .**173** D1
Yaxham NR19 . . . .**68** B6
Green La E NR13. . . . .**72** E7
Green La N NR13 . . . .**72** D5
Greenland Ave
King's Lynn PE30. . . . .**146** E8
Wymondham NR18 . . . . . .**173** E6
Wymondham NR18 . . . . . .**173** E6
Greenlands Way NR26 . .**138** C6
Greenlands Way W **2**
NR26. . . . .**138** B6
Green La W
Horsham St Faith NR13. . . .**53** D1
Rackheath NR13 . . . .**72** D8
Green Man La NR15. . . . . .**108** C8
Green Marsh Rd PE34. . . .**144** C7
Green Oak Rd **2** IP25. . . .**84** D3
Greenpark Ave PE30 . . . .**146** F6
Green Pk **42** IP20 . . . .**122** D2
Green Pk Rd NR10 . . . .**53** B3
Green Quay The **★** PE30 .**146** D4
Green Rd Brandon IP27 . . .**175** E2
Hales NR14. . . . .**109** E8

Green Rd continued
Upwell PE14 . . . .**77** E4
GREENSGATE NR9 . . . .**51** E2
Green's La NR27 . . . .**10** C4
Greens Rd
East Dereham NR20 . . . . . .**154** F3
North Walsham NR28 . . . . .**151** A5
Green's Road Ind Est
NR20. . . . .**154** F4
Green St IP21 . . . .**131** A4
GREEN THE NR18 . . . .**87** B4
Green The Ashill IP25. . . . . .**84** A7
Belton with Browston NR31 .**94** A5
Boughton PE33 . . . .**80** F4
Brisley NR20 . . . .**49** B8
Burnham Market PE31. . . .**135** C3
Deopham NR18 . . . .**86** E2
Dersingham PE31. . . . .**140** D4
Diss IP22. . . . .**177** A6
8 Earsham NR35. . . . .**123** F8
Fakenham NR21. . . . .**141** A3
Freethorpe NR13. . . . .**92** E8
Hickling NR12 . . . .**39** E2
Hockham IP24. . . . .**102** E3
Hunstanton PE36. . . . .**132** C4
Lound NR32. . . . .**94** C2
North Lopham IP22. . . . . .**119** A2
North Wootton PE30 . . . . .**148** C5
Norwich NR2. . . . .**178** D2
Ormesby St Margaret
NR29. . . . .**167** A2
Runhall NR9. . . . .**68** F2
Saxlingham Nethergate
NR15. . . . .**107** D7
Sculthorpe NR21. . . . .**16** C2
South Wootton PE30 . . . . .**149** C2
Surlingham NR14. . . . .**73** B1
Thornham PE36. . . . .**2** C6
Upton with Fishley NR13. .**166** B8
Wicklewood NR18. . . . .**87** B4
Green Way Barsham NR22 . .**16** C6
Stiffkey NR23. . . . .**6** C6
Swaffham PE37. . . . .**153** B6
Greenway Cl
Fakenham NR21. . . . .**141** C5
2 North Walsham NR28 . .**151** C5
Greenway La
Fakenham NR21. . . . .**141** C5
Tharston & Hapton NR15. .**106** D6
Greenway Pk NR21. . . . . .**141** C6
Greenways Bunwell NR16. .**105** D4
Flordon NR15 . . . .**106** E8
Holt NR25 . . . .**137** C7
Newton Flotman NR15 . . . .**89** C1
Norwich NR4. . . . .**161** F1
Greenways Cl NR15. . . . . .**106** E8
Greenways La
Bunwell NR16 . . . .**105** D4
Carleton Rode NR16 . . . . .**105** D4
Greenwich Cl
Dersingham PE31 . . . .**140** E3
Downham Market PE38. . . .**172** B3
Roydon PE32. . . . .**28** A1
Shotesham NR15. . . . .**90** B1
Green Wlk NR27 . . . .**139** E4
Greenwood Cl NR16 . . . . .**105** E8
Green Wood Dr NR19 . . . .**154** C5
Greenwood Rd NR4. . . . . .**162** C1
Greenwood Way
5 Shipdham IP25 . . . .**67** C2
Thorpe St Andrew NR7 . . .**159** F2
Greevegate PE36 . . . .**132** C4
Gregor Shanks Way **27**
IP25. . . . .**84** D3
Gregory Cl **1** PE30 . . . . . .**148** C5
Gregs Cl NR20. . . . .**68** F5
Grenville Cl **3** NR20 . . . . .**88** E8
Grenville Pl **1** NR30 . . . .**169** D8
Grenville Way IP24 . . . . .**176** D5
GRESHAM NR11 . . . .**9** E1
Gresham Cl
Great Yarmouth NR31. . . .**170** C2
King's Lynn PE30. . . . .**147** C8
Gresham Rd
Baconsthorpe NR25 . . . . . .**20** B8
Norwich NR3. . . . .**158** B2
Gresham's Prep Sch
NR25. . . . .**137** D7
Gresham's Sch NR25. . . .**137** C6
Gresham Village Sch NR11 .**9** E1
Gresley Cl NR20 . . . .**49** C4
GRESSENHALL NR20 . . . . . .**49** B3
**Gressenhall Farm &
Workhouse★** NR20 . . . . .**49** D4
Gressenhall Rd NR20. . . . . .**49** D4
Greyfriars Cl NR6. . . . .**158** E5
Greyfriars Prim Sch
PE30. . . . .**146** E4
Greyfriars Rd NR1 . . . .**178** B3
Greyfriars Way NR30. . . . .**169** C3
Greyhound La
Banham NR16 . . . .**119** D7
Hopton IP22 . . . .**127** C5
Greyhound Opening **7**
NR2. . . . .**162** C7
Greylag Cl
11 Salhouse NR13 . . . .**55** A1
8 Salhouse NR13. . . . .**55** A1
Grey Sedge PE30 . . . .**147** A7
Greys Manor NR16 . . . . . .**119** D6
Grice Cl **4** NR26. . . . .**138** C5
Griffin La
Attleborough NR17 . . . . . .**174** D5
Thorpe St Andrew NR7 . . . .**72** D3
Grigg Cl IP22. . . . .**177** E5
Grigsons Wood **1** NR16. .**118** C5
Grime's Graves★ IP27 . . .**115** C8
Grimmer La NR13. . . . .**92** B7
Grimmer's Rd **6** PE13 . . .**152** E7

Grimshoe Rd
Downham Market PE38. . . .**172** B6
Downham Market PE38. . . .**172** B7
GRIMSTON PE32. . . . .**28** B1
Grimston Pott Row Fst Sch
PE32. . . . .**45** A8
Grimston Rd Gayton PE32 . .**45** C6
King's Lynn PE30. . . . .**148** E1
Gristock Pl NR5. . . . .**161** C8
GRISTON IP25. . . . .**85** A2
Griston Ind Est IP25 . . . . . .**85** A1
Griston Rd
Thompson IP24 . . . .**102** B8
Watton IP25 . . . .**84** E3
Groomes Cl **4** NR31 . . . . .**171** D5
Grosvenor Rd
Norwich NR2. . . . .**162** B5
Wisbech PE13 . . . .**152** D7
Grouts La NR25 . . . .**8** B6
Grove Ave Norwich NR1 . . .**178** A1
Norwich NR5. . . . .**157** A1
Grovebury Cl NR13. . . . . . .**165** C4
Grove Cl
8 East Dereham NR19 . . . .**154** C4
Holt NR25 . . . .**137** D6
2 Newton Flotman NR15 . . .**89** C1
Grove Dale **3** NR15. . . . . . .**89** C1
Grovedale Cl NR5. . . . .**157** A1
Grove End IP21. . . . .**131** F1
Grove Gdns **10** Elm PE14 . . .**59** A1
7 Gayton PE32 . . . .**45** C6
Grove House Inf Com Sch
NR19. . . . .**154** D4
Grove La Booton NR10 . . . . .**52** A8
Fakenham NR21. . . . .**141** C6
Forncett NR16 . . . .**106** A3
Holt NR25 . . . .**137** D6
Sparham NR9 . . . .**51** B6
Tasburgh NR15 . . . .**106** F7
Thetford IP24 . . . .**176** D4
Grovelands PE31. . . . .**140** D8
Grove Rd Banham NR16 . . .**119** C6
Barsham NR21 . . . .**16** C4
Brockdish IP21 . . . .**131** C6
Cantley NR13. . . . .**92** D8
Cromer NR27. . . . .**139** D5
Gissing IP21 . . . .**121** A4
Hethersett NR9 . . . .**88** D8
Ingham NR12 . . . .**24** C1
4 Marthan NR29 . . . .**57** D5
Melton Constable NR24 . . .**142** A4
North Walsham NR28 . . . . .**151** D5
Norwich NR1. . . . .**178** A1
Repps with Bastwick NR29. .**57** A4
Starston IP20 . . . .**122** C2
Wells-next-the-Sea NR23 . .**136** E4
Groveside NR15. . . . .**30** A7
Grove The Coltishall NR12 . .**54** D6
East Dereham NR19 . . . . . .**154** D4
Fleggburgh NR29. . . . .**57** A1
2 Necton PE37 . . . .**65** F4
Roydon PE32. . . . .**28** A1
Shotesham NR15. . . . .**90** B2
Grove Way NR15. . . . .**89** C1
Grove Wlk NR1 . . . .**178** A1
Growle Abbey NR24. . . . . . .**19** B2
Grubb's La NR12. . . . .**24** C1
Grub La IP19 . . . .**124** E1
Grub St Happisburgh NR12. .**24** B4
Shotesham NR15. . . . .**90** B2
Guanock Pl **12** PE30. . . . . .**146** E3
Guanock Terr PE30 . . . . . .**146** E3
Guardian Rd NR5 . . . .**161** F7
Guardian Road Ind Est
NR5. . . . .**161** F7
Guelph Rd **2** NR1 . . . .**163** A6
Guernsey Rd NR3. . . . .**162** E8
GUESTWICK NR20 . . . .**34** A6
GUESTWICK GREEN NR20. . .**33** F5
Guestwick Rd
Foulsham NR20. . . . .**33** E4
Hindolveston NR20 . . . .**33** F7
Wood Norton NR20 . . . .**33** C6
Guildford Way IP24. . . . . .**176** B5
Guildhall Hill **1** NR2. . . .**178** A3
Guildhall La IP21 . . . .**121** E5
Guildhall St IP24 . . . .**176** D3
Guild Rd PE13 . . . .**152** E6
Guild St NR22. . . . .**16** F8
Guiler's La NR18. . . . .**105** B8
Guilt Cross Way PE38 . . . .**172** C6
Guinevere Rd NR31 . . . . . .**171** B8
GUIST NR20 . . . .**32** F4
Guist Bottom Rd NR21 . . . .**32** E6
Guist Rd NR20 . . . .**33** C4
Gulgate La NR11 . . . .**21** A1
Gull La NR14. . . . .**90** E6
Gullpit Dro PE34. . . . .**61** D1
Gunner Cl
Cliftonville NR11 . . . .**143** C6
3 Norwich NR7 . . . .**72** C5
Gunn Rd NR7. . . . .**159** D1
Gunn's Cnr NR12 . . . .**38** D2
Gunn St NR20. . . . .**33** C3
Gun St **7** NR26. . . . .**138** D7
GUNTHORPE NR24 . . . .**18** B5
Gunthorpe Rd PE14 . . . .**41** B5
Gunton La NR5. . . . .**157** B2
Gunton Rd Loddon NR14. . .**109** C8
Norwich NR2. . . . .**161** F5
Wymondham NR18 . . . . . .**173** D4
Gunton Sta NR11 . . . .**22** B6
Gurney Cl
9 Hopton On Sea NR31. .**171** D4
Norwich NR5. . . . .**161** B8
Gurney Ct NR5. . . . .**161** B8
Gurney Dr NR7 . . . .**159** D3
Gurney La NR4 . . . .**161** C2

Gurney Rd Norwich NR1 . . .**163** A7
Norwich NR5. . . . .**157** A1
Gwyn Cres NR21. . . . .**141** F5
Gymkhana Way PE31. . . . .**133** B5

H

Habgood Cl NR13. . . . .**166** C4
HACKFORD NR18 . . . .**87** A5
Hackford Rd
Hardingham NR9. . . . .**86** E6
Wicklewood NR18. . . . .**87** A5
Haconsfield **8** NR9. . . . . . .**88** D7
HADDISCOE NR14 . . . .**110** F8
Haddiscoe Dam NR14 . . . .**110** F8
Haddiscoe Rd NR14 . . . . . .**110** F6
Haddiscoe Sta NR31. . . . . .**93** D1
Hadfield Rd NR28. . . . .**151** B6
Hadley Cres PE31 . . . .**133** C5
Hadley Dr NR2. . . . .**161** F6
Hadley Rd NR26 . . . .**138** E6
Hagbech Hall Cl **2** PE14 . .**59** D2
Haggard's Cl IP25 . . . .**66** E3
Haig Cl NR19 . . . .**154** D3
HAINFORD NR10. . . . .**53** E5
Hainford Prim Sch NR10 . .**53** E6
Hainford Rd NR10. . . . .**53** E7
Halcombe Ct NR3. . . . .**158** E1
Halden Ave NR6 . . . .**157** F6
Hale Ct NR13 . . . .**73** A4
Hale Dro Littleport CB6. . . . .**96** B2
Welney PE14 . . . .**95** E6
Hale Fen Rd CB6. . . . .**96** B1
Hale Rd Ashill IP25 . . . .**84** A7
Bradenham IP25. . . . .**66** D3
Necton PE37 . . . .**65** F4
HALES NR14 . . . .**109** F8
Hales Cl NR30 . . . .**168** D5
Hales Ct NR25 . . . .**137** B6
HALES GREEN NR14. . . . . . .**109** E7
Hales St NR15 . . . .**121** B6
HALES STREET NR15 . . . . . .**121** A6
Halesworth Rd NR34 . . . . .**124** E4
Haley Cl **4** PE13 . . . .**152** C8
Half Acre Cl NR27. . . . .**10** A4
Half Mile Cl NR3 . . . .**158** B2
Half Mile Rd NR3 . . . .**158** B2
Half Moon NR31 . . . .**170** C1
Half Moon La IP22. . . . .**128** E4
Half Moon Way **1** NR2. . .**162** B8
Halford Cl NR17 . . . .**174** D4
Halford La IP22. . . . .**129** A7
Halford Pl NR17 . . . .**174** D4
Halford Rd NR17. . . . .**174** D4
Halfpenny La Beetley NR20 .**49** C5
Elm PE14 . . . .**59** A2
Wisbech PE14 . . . .**152** D1
Halfpenny Toll Rd PE14 . . .**95** B8
Half Year **7** NR27. . . . .**10** B5
Halifax Cres NR21. . . . .**15** C3
Haling Way IP24. . . . .**176** A4
Hallback La NR14 . . . .**90** A7
Hall Bridge Rd PE14. . . . . .**77** D5
Hall Cl
Burgh St Margaret
(Fleggburgh) NR29. . . . . .**57** C1
Fakenham NR21. . . . .**141** D4
Heacham PE31 . . . .**133** D7
4 Hemsby NR29 . . . .**167** A4
5 Hethersett NR9 . . . .**88** D7
3 Hingham NR9. . . . .**86** C4
3 Southery PE38 . . . .**97** B5
Hall Comm Rd NR29 . . . . . .**56** C4
Hall Cres PE33. . . . .**63** C5
Hall Dike PE14 . . . .**77** F7
Hall Dr Costessey NR5. . . . .**156** D2
16 Feltwell IP26 . . . .**98** E1
Honingham NR9. . . . .**69** E6
North Runcton PE33 . . . . . .**44** A3
Salhouse NR13 . . . .**55** A1
Santon Downham IP27 . . . .**115** C6
Hall Farm Cl NR13 . . . .**74** F1
Hall Farm Gdns PE32. . . . . .**44** F3
Hall Farm Pl NR9 . . . .**160** B6
Hallfield Rd NR29 . . . .**102** A7
Hallfields
Lakenheath IP27 . . . .**113** E2
Shouldham PE33 . . . .**62** D4
Hallgate **2** NR13 . . . .**72** D6
Hall Hills IP22 . . . .**177** C5
Hall La Baconsthorpe NR25 . .**19** F8
Bressingham IP22. . . . . . .**119** D1
Burston & Shimpling IP21. .**121** A2
Colkirk NR21 . . . .**31** E5
Deopham NR18 . . . .**86** F4
East Carleton NR14. . . . . . .**88** E4
East Dereham NR20 . . . . . .**154** F4
East Ruston NR12 . . . .**24** A4
East Tuddenham NR20. . . . .**69** B6
Felthorpe NR10. . . . .**52** E5
Frettenham NR12 . . . .**54** B3
Gunthorpe NR24 . . . .**18** A5
Hingham NR9 . . . .**86** C5
Horsford NR10 . . . .**53** B1
King's Lynn PE30. . . . .**148** B1
Knapton NR28 . . . .**143** B1
Long Stratton NR15. . . . . .**106** F3
Morley NR18 . . . .**87** B2
North Tuddenham NR20 . . . .**68** F8
North Walsham NR28 . . . . .**151** D5
Northwold IP26. . . . .**99** C7
Postwick with Witton NR13. .**72** F2
Redgrave IP22 . . . .**128** E4

Hall La continued
Ringstead PE36. . . . .**2** A3
Roydon IP22 . . . .**129** D7
Saxlingham Nethergate
NR15. . . . .**107** C7
Scole IP21 . . . .**130** F8
Shelfanger IP22 . . . .**120** B2
Shelton NR15. . . . .**122** A8
Taverham NR8. . . . .**157** B8
Tharston & Hapton NR15 . .**106** D5
Thompson IP24 . . . .**102** B7
Thornham PE36. . . . .**2** D6
Thursford NR21. . . . .**17** F5
Wacton NR15. . . . .**106** C1
West Winch PE33 . . . .**43** E2
Whissonsett NR20. . . . .**31** D2
Wiveton NR25 . . . .**7** D6
Wood Norton NR20 . . . .**33** B6
Hall Loke NR28 . . . .**38** C8
Hallmark Cl IP27 . . . .**113** E1
Hall Moor Rd NR9 . . . .**86** C4
Hall Orchards PE32. . . . . . .**44** C3
Hallowing Cres **3** NR15. .**106** B1
Hallowing La NR15. . . . . . .**121** B8
Hall Plain NR30. . . . .**169** C3
Hall Rd Alderford NR9 . . . . . .**52** A5
Barsham NR34 . . . .**124** F7
Barton Turf NR12. . . . .**55** E8
Bedingham NR35. . . . .**108** C3
Beetley NR20. . . . .**49** D5
Blofield NR13. . . . .**165** C6
Bracon Ash NR14 . . . .**88** E4
Brockdish IP21 . . . .**131** D7
Bunwell NR16 . . . .**105** E2
Burston & Shimpling IP22. .**120** E3
Cantley NR13. . . . .**92** C8
Carleton Rode NR16 . . . . .**105** B4
Catfield NR29 . . . .**56** B8
Clenchwarton PE34. . . . . .**145** D6
Cromer NR27. . . . .**139** B5
Earsham NR35. . . . .**123** E8
Easton NR9 . . . .**70** B5
Ellingham NR35. . . . .**109** C3
Elsing NR20. . . . .**50** D2
Felbrigg NR27. . . . .**139** A4
Fleggburgh NR29. . . . .**57** A1
Framingham Earl NR14. . . . .**90** D5
Gimingham NR11. . . . .**22** D7
Great Melton NR9 . . . .**88** B8
Great Witchingham NR9 . . .**51** F5
Hainford NR10. . . . .**53** E5
Hemsby NR29 . . . .**167** A7
Hoe NR20 . . . .**49** F3
Honing NR28 . . . .**38** D8
Hopton on Sea NR31. . . . .**171** B6
King's Lynn PE30. . . . .**148** C1
Ludham NR29. . . . .**56** B4
Marthan NR29 . . . .**57** D4
Mautby NR29. . . . .**76** A6
Northrepps NR27 . . . .**139** D2
Norwich NR1. . . . .**178** B1
Norwich NR5. . . . .**157** A2
Oulton NR11 . . . .**35** B7
Outwell PE14. . . . .**77** F7
Postwick with Witton
NR13. . . . .**165** A5
Pulham St Mary IP21 . . . .**122** A4
Reedham NR13 . . . .**92** F6
Roudham NR16 . . . .**117** E6
Runhall NR20. . . . .**69** A4
Smallburgh NR12 . . . .**38** D2
9 Snettisham PE31 . . . . . .**12** E5
Sutton NR12 . . . .**39** D3
Swafield NR28. . . . .**22** C5
Tacolneston NR16 . . . .**105** E6
Tharston & Hapton NR15 . .**106** E5
Thurton NR14 . . . .**91** C3
Tivetshall St Margaret
NR15. . . . .**121** B6
Toft Monks NR14. . . . .**110** D7
Walpole Highway PE14. . . . .**59** F8
Winfarthing IP22. . . . .**120** C5
Wood Dalling NR11 . . . . . .**34** C6
Hall Sch NR6 . . . .**158** D5
Halls Cnr NR10. . . . .**53** B8
Halls Cnr Rd NR10. . . . .**53** B8
Hall's Dr NR20. . . . .**49** C4
Halls Meadow Cl IP26. . . . .**99** A5
Hall St NR24. . . . .**142** E3
Hall Staithe NR21. . . . .**141** B4
Hall View Rd PE30 . . . .**147** B4
Hall Wlk NR9 . . . .**51** D5
Hallwong La IP20. . . . .**122** D3
Hall Wood Rd NR7 . . . .**159** D5
Halstead Cl **2** PE13. . . . . .**152** E5
Halton Rd **8** IP25 . . . .**84** F3
Halt Rd NR30 . . . .**168** D7
HALVERGATE NR14 . . . .**74** F1
Halvergate Rd
Beighton NR13 . . . .**74** E1
Reedham NR13 . . . .**93** A6
Hambling's Piece NR16. . .**118** C4
Hamburg Way PE30. . . . . .**147** A8
Hamilton Cl
North Walsham NR28 . . . . .**151** C5
South Walsham NR13 . . . . .**74** A8
Hamilton Ct **1** NR21 . . . . .**141** B4
Hamilton Dr PE37. . . . .**153** D3
Hamilton Rd
3 Cromer NR27. . . . .**139** B7
Great Yarmouth NR30 . . . .**169** D7
Old Hunstanton PE36 . . . .**132** E7
Hamilton Rd W PE36. . . . .**132** E7
Hamilton Wlk **9** NR29 . . . .**57** D4
Hamilton Wy NR35. . . . . . .**109** B2
Hamlet Cl NR28. . . . .**151** D7

Hamlin Way PE30 146 F1
Hammond Cl NR7 159 E3
Hammond Rd 2 NR30 169 D5
Hammond Way NR7 159 E3
Hamon Cl PE36 132 E7
Hamond Rd NR6 157 D5
Hampden Dr 19 NR7 72 D4
Hampden Rd 2 PE13 152 D5
Hampton Ave 3 NR14 92 F1
Hampton Cl NR30 168 C5
HAMROW NR20 31 D3
Hanbury Cl NR5 161 D5
Hancock Cl 3 NR12 54 C7
Hancock Ct 5 NR5 160 E7
Handel Dr NR19 154 F3
Handford Dr NR26 138 E6
Hand La Barsham NR21 16 C5
Hoveton NR12 164 C8
Hanginghill NR13 74 C6
Hankin Ct 3 NR4 161 C5
Hankinson's Est PE34 42 A5
Hanly Cl NR7 159 C2
Hanly Ct NR30 168 D6
Hannah Cl NR26 138 C6
Hannah Rd NR20 50 B4
Hannant Rd NR28 151 D6
Hanover Ct
Dersingham PE31 140 E3
King's Lynn PE30 147 D5
Hanover Gdns PE36 132 D3
Hanover Rd NR2 162 C4
Hanrae Cl NR26 138 F6
Hansa Rd PE30 146 F2
Hansard Cl NR3 158 B1
Hansard La NR3 178 B4
Hansard Rd NR3 158 B1
Hansell Rd NR7 163 F8
Hans Pl 4 NR27 139 B7
Hantons Loke NR13 74 B2
HANWORTH NR11 21 B6
Hanworth Cross NR11 21 D5
HAPPISBURGH NR12 24 C6
HAPPISBURGH COMMON
NR12 24 B4
Happisburgh Prim Sch
NR12 24 C5
Happisburgh Rd
East Ruston NR12 24 A3
Lessingham NR12 24 D4
North Walsham NR28 151 D4
Witton NR28 23 E2
HAPTON NR15 106 C7
Hapton CE Prim Sch
NR15 106 C7
Harbord Cl 4 NR28 151 C7
Harbord Cres NR30 170 D8
Harbord Rd Cromer NR27 139 C5
Norwich NR4 161 F5
Overstrand NR27 11 A3
Harbour La IP22 128 A7
Harbour Rd
1 Frettenham NR12 54 A4
Norwich NR1 163 A5
Harbour Terr NR31 170 E4
Harcourt Cl 3 NR3 162 F8
Hardesty Cl 9 NR14 90 D5
HARDINGHAM NR9 86 E6
Hardingham Dr 6 NR26 138 C5
Hardingham Rd NR9 86 D5
Hardingham St 4 NR9 86 C4
Hardings Wy PE30 146 D3
Hardley Cross★ NR14 92 E4
Hardley Hall La NR14 92 C3
Hardley Rd NR14 92 A2
Hardley St NR14 92 B3
HARDLEY STREET NR14 92 C4
HARDWICK
North Runcton PE30 147 B1
Shelton NR15 122 B8
Hardwick Cl 1 NR4 89 D8
Hardwick Ind Est PE30 147 A2
Hardwick Narrows PE33 43 F4
Hardwick Narrows Ind Est
PE30 146 F1
Hardwick Rd
King's Lynn PE30 146 E2
Pulham Market IP21 121 F7
Shelton NR15 122 C8
Hardy Cl
Downham Market PE38 172 B4
1 North Walsham NR28 151 C5
Thetford IP24 176 D6
Hardy Dr NR14 90 C4
Hardy Rd NR1 163 A4
Hardy's La PE32 46 C2
Harebell Rd
Attleborough NR17 174 B3
Downham Market PE38 172 B3
Hare Cl 2 NR14 89 B2
Harecroft Gdns PE30 146 E6
Harecroft Par 7 PE30 146 E6
Harecroft Rd PE13 152 B5
Harecroft Terr PE30 146 E6
Harefen La NR13 74 B7
Harefield Rd IP24 116 C5
Harefields PE31 134 D5
Hare Rd
Great & Little Plumstead
NR13 72 F5
West Lynn PE34 146 C5
Hares Cl NR21 17 C3
Harewood PE31 134 F4
Harewood Dr
9 King's Lynn PE30 146 E6
Taverham NR8 155 E3
Harewood Par 8 PE30 146 E6
Harford Manor Cl NR2 162 C2
Harford St NR1 162 E3
Harfreys Ind Est
Gorleston-on-Sea NR31 170 A8
Great Yarmouth NR31 169 B1
Harfrey's Rd NR31 170 B8
HARGATE NR16 105 D2
Hargate La PE34 42 B7
Hargham Cl 5 NR17 104 D2
Hargham Rd
Attleborough NR17 174 B2
Old Buckenham NR17 104 B2
Shropham NR17 103 C3
Harker Way 6 NR13 73 D6
HARLESTON IP20 122 D3
Harleston CE Prim Sch
IP20 122 E2
Harleston Mus★ IP20 122 D2
Harleston Rd
Pulham Market IP21 121 E4
Scole IP21 121 D1
Harley Rd NR30 169 D6
Harling Dro IP27 115 E7
Harling Rd
Garboldisham IP22 118 C2
Hockham IP24 102 E3
North Lopham IP22 119 A2
Harling Rd Sta NR16 118 A6
HARLING ROAD NR16 118 A7
Harlington Ave NR6 158 A4
Harlingwood La NR17 104 E1
Harman Cl 12 NR9 88 D8
Harman's La IP20 122 C1
Harmer Cl NR28 151 E5
Harmer Cres NR4 161 C1
Harmer La NR4 161 C1
Harmer Rd NR3 158 D3
Harmer's La NR11 21 A5
Harnser's Reach NR13 166 B8
Harp Cl NR21 141 B5
HARPER'S GREEN NR20 32 A1
Harper's La NR20 32 A1
HARPLEY PE31 29 D4
Harpley CE VC Prim Sch
PE31 29 C4
Harpsfield NR5 160 E8
Harp's Hall Rd PE14 59 E5
Harrier Cl 26 NR9 88 D8
Harriet Cl PE12 41 A8
Harriet Martineau Cl 10
IP24 176 D7
Harriott's Way NR11 150 B5
Harris Mews 2 NR5 161 A7
Harrisons Dr NR7 159 E3
Harris Rd
11 Swanton Morley NR20 50 B3
12 Watton IP25 84 F3
Harrold Cl
1 South Walsham NR13 74 B8
Taverham NR8 155 E2
Harrolds Cl PE13 59 C5
Harrow Cl PE34 146 C5
Harry Barber Cl 2 NR5 161 A8
Harry Blunt Way 10
NR19 154 C4
Harry Daniels Cl NR18 173 C2
Harry Miller Ct 7 NR30 169 D1
Harry Perry Cl NR4 162 C2
Harry's La IP21 121 E7
Harrys Way
Hunstanton PE36 132 D1
Wisbech PE13 152 C2
Harry Watson Ct NR6 158 C3
Harsnett Cl NR5 160 F8
Hartbee Rd NR6 158 C6
Hartford Manor Sch
NR4 162 C2
Hartington Rd NR27 139 D4
Hart La NR25 9 A2
Hartley Cl PE36 132 D4
Hartmann Rd NR30 170 E6
Harts Farm Rd NR18 173 E5
Harts La Cringleford NR4 161 C1
Wortham IP22 129 C4
Hart's La NR9 160 A7
Hartwell Rd NR12 164 C4
Harvard Rd 6 IP26 98 D1
Harvest Cl 1 NR10 53 E5
Harvest La NR21 17 D6
Harvey Cl
2 Hethersett NR9 88 C7
Norwich NR7 163 C7
Tasburgh NR15 106 E7
Wymondham NR18 173 F7
Harvey Dr NR28 151 C7
Harvey Est NR11 22 E7
Harvey Gn 10 NR14 91 F1
Harvey La
Caister-on-Sea NR30 168 E4
Dickleburgh IP21 121 C1
Norwich NR7 163 C6
Harvey's La NR15 108 D6
Harvey St 21 IP25 84 D3
Harwood Ave 4 IP24 176 E6
Harwood Rd NR1 162 E1
Hase's La NR9 51 C4
Haslips Cl 8 NR2 162 C7
Haspalls Rd PE37 153 B3
Hassett Cl 6 NR3 162 F8
HASSINGHAM NR13 92 B8
Hastings Ave NR6 158 A4
Hastings Cl Briston NR24 142 A5
6 Tasburgh NR15 106 F6
12 Thetford IP24 176 F5
Hastings Ct NR24 142 E4
Hastings Dr PE36 132 D6
Hastings La
15 Sheringham NR26 138 D7
Wiggenhall St Germans
PE34 61 C8
Hastings Rd 6 IP25 84 F3
Hastings Way NR12 39 C3
Hatherley Gdns PE33 81 B8
Hatton Rd NR1 162 E3
Haugh Cnr NR16 119 F7
Haugh Rd NR16 119 F8
Haughs End Rd NR12 164 F2
Hautbois Rd NR10 37 B2
Hauteyn Ct NR6 158 C2
Havaker The NR13 92 F5
Havant Cl NR4 161 E1
Havelock Pl 10 NR30 169 D2
Havelock Rd
Great Yarmouth NR30 169 D2
Norwich NR2 162 B6
Sheringham NR26 138 E5
Havergate 7 NR12 54 C6
Haveringland Rd NR10 52 E6
Haverscroft Cl NR8 155 D2
Haverscroft Ind Est
NR17 174 B2
Havers Rd NR3 158 B1
HAWES' GREEN NR15 89 F2
Hawk Cl 28 NR9 88 D8
Hawk Cres IP22 177 F5
Hawkes La NR14 89 A2
Hawkins Ave NR30 169 C8
Hawkins Cl NR30 169 C8
Hawkins Dr 1 PE13 152 E5
Hawthorn Ave 6 PE33 63 B4
Hawthorn Cl Diss IP22 177 F5
3 Spixworth NR10 54 A1
6 Watlington PE33 61 D5
Hawthorn Cotts PE31 140 D4
Hawthorn Cres NR31 94 C6
Hawthorn Dr
Dersingham PE31 140 D5
East Dereham NR19 154 B3
Hawthorne Ave
Grimston PE32 28 B1
Hellesdon NR6 158 A5
Wisbech PE13 152 C8
Hawthorne Cl
2 Loddon NR14 91 F1
Wymondham NR18 173 D6
Hawthorn Rd
2 Downham Market
PE38 172 C6
Emneth PE14 59 D1
6 Gayton PE32 45 C5
Great Yarmouth NR31 170 B6
Norwich NR5 157 A2
Hawthorn Rise NR11 143 B5
Hawthorns PE30 147 C4
Hawthorn Way IP24 176 E6
Hawthorn Wlk 2 IP24 176 F6
Haycroft 3 NR29 167 B7
Hayes La NR21 141 A5
Hayfield Rd PE30 148 C4
Haygate 2 IP23 130 C1
Hay Gn Rd PE34 144 A1
Hay Gn Rd N PE34 42 B6
Hay Gn Rd S PE34 42 A5
HAY GREEN PE34 144 A1
Haylett Cl NR30 168 E5
Haylock Cl NR16 105 D4
Haymarket NR2 178 B2
Haythill La IP26 98 D2
Hayward Cl 3 NR25 7 C6
Haywood End IP22 120 D6
Hazel Ave NR26 138 D4
Hazel Cl Grimston PE32 28 B1
5 King's Lynn PE30 148 C3
Taverham NR8 155 D1
West Winch PE33 43 E1
Wymondham NR18 173 D4
Hazel Covert IP24 176 F5
Hazel Cres 4 PE33 63 B4
Hazel Dr 27 NR29 57 D4
Hazel Gdns 1 PE13 152 D4
Hazel Gr NR19 154 F4
Hazell Rd NR28 151 C7
Hazel Rd
4 Attleborough NR17 174 B5
Norwich NR5 156 F1
Hazel Way NR31 170 B6
HEACHAM PE31 133 E4
Heacham Hall Ind Est
PE31 133 E7
Heacham Inf Sch PE31 133 D5
Heacham Jun Sch PE31 133 C4
Heacham Rd PE36 13 A7
Headington Cl NR31 170 A5
Headland Dro IP26 113 A5
Headley Dr NR28 151 C4
Hearne Ct 3 NR5 160 E8
Heartsease La NR7 159 B1
Heartsease Prim Acad
NR7 159 C1
Heartsease Rd 3 IP24 176 E5
Heartwell Rd NR27 139 C5
Heater La NR13 73 F4
Heath Cl 16 Horsford NR10 53 A3
Lenwade NR9 51 D5
Norwich NR6 158 A6
Heath Cres NR6 158 B5
Heath Dr NR25 137 D5
Heather Ave
Hemsby NR29 167 D4
Norwich NR6 158 A4
Heather Ave Inf Sch NR6 158 B4
Heather Barrow Ct NR21 141 D4
Heather Cl Hethersett NR9 88 C8
North Wootton PE30 148 D5
Heather Dr NR25 137 B7
Heather Gdns NR31 93 F6
Heather Rd 12 NR31 94 A6
Heather Way
Brandon IP27 175 E3
Great Moulton NR15 121 B8
Heatherwood Cl 7 NR13 72 D6
Heath Farm La NR11 36 E6
Heathfield Cl NR25 8 E3
Heathfield Rd NR25 8 E3
Heathgate NR3 163 A8
Heath Gn 1 NR31 170 B5
Heath La Fakenham NR21 141 F4
Gimingham NR11 22 D8
Great Witchingham NR9 51 E6
Gunthorpe NR24 18 B5
Lenwade NR9 51 D5
Mundesley NR11 143 B5
Roughton NR11 21 E8
Thursford NR21 17 E4
Tittleshall PE32 47 F7
Heathlands PE37 153 D2
Heathlands Dr IP24 176 D8
Heath Rd
Ashby with Oby NR29 57 B2
Banham NR16 119 E7
Brandon IP27 175 D3
Catfield NR29 56 D8
Corpusty NR11 19 D1
Dersingham PE31 140 D2
East Dereham NR19 154 C7
Felmingham NR28 37 B8
Fritton & St Olaves NR31 93 E1
Geldeston NR34 110 A3
Gunthorpe NR24 18 B5
Hevingham NR11 34 D8
Hickling NR12 39 E1
Hockering NR20 69 B8
Honing NR28 23 E1
Kenninghall NR16 119 A3
Lessingham NR12 24 F2
Lyng NR9 51 A4
Norwich NR3 162 D8
Quidenham NR16 118 E8
Rollesby NR29 57 E2
Sapiston IP31 126 E3
Sheringham NR26 138 D6
Shotesham NR15 107 F8
9 Thorpe End NR13 72 D6
Troston IP31 126 B1
Winfarthing IP22 120 A7
Heath Rise
Fakenham NR21 141 E4
Sculthorpe Airfield PE31 15 B3
Heathside Rd NR1 163 B5
HEATH THE
Fakenham NR21 141 F4
Hevingham NR10 53 A8
Stratton Strawless NR10 53 F8
Heath The NR10 52 F8
Heath Way Blofield NR13 73 C6
Fakenham NR21 141 F4
Hebrides Way NR30 168 C6
HECKFIELD GREEN IP21 131 B2
HECKINGHAM NR14 92 C1
Heckingham Holes NR14 92 B1
HEDENHAM NR35 108 E4
Hedgehog Wlk NR12 24 E4
Hedgelands 1 PE13 152 C8
Hedgemere 1 NR8 155 D2
Hedgerows The 8 NR5 161 A7
Hedley La NR33 111 F1
Heffer Cl NR19 154 D3
Heggatt Rd NR12 54 C5
Heidi Cl 7 NR19 154 D1
Heigham Gr NR2 162 C6
Heigham Rd NR2 162 B6
Heigham St NR2 162 B8
Heigham Watering 5
NR2 162 B8
Heights The NR1 163 B5
Heisker Gdns 9 NR17 174 B4
Helena Rd Norwich NR2 162 B6
Witton NR12 23 F3
Helen Ave 7 NR29 57 C4
Helford St 6 NR2 162 B8
HELHOUGHTON NR21 30 E5
HELLESDON NR6 157 F5
Hellesdon Cl NR5 161 D8
Hellesdon Hall Ind Est
NR6 157 E3
Hellesdon Hall Rd NR6 157 E1
Hellesdon High Sch NR6 157 E4
Hellesdon Hospl NR6 157 D4
Hellesdon Mill La NR6 157 D1
Hellesdon Pk Rd NR6 157 E3
Hellesdon Rd NR6 161 D8
Hellgate La NR11 20 F8
HELLINGTON NR14 91 B6
Hellington Cnr NR14 91 B5
Hellington Hill NR14 91 B6
Hellpit La NR24 19 B2
Helsinki Way NR19 154 C2
Helska Leisure Ctr NR12 55 E3
HEMBLINGTON NR13 73 E6
HEMBLINGTON CORNER
NR13 73 D6
Hemblington Hall Rd
NR13 73 E6
Hemblington Prim Sch
NR13 73 C6
Hemblington Rd NR13 73 E4
Hemington Cl PE30 147 D8
Hemlin Cl NR5 161 C6
Hemmant Way NR34 110 B3
Hemmings Cl 4 NR5 160 F7
Hemming Wy NR3 158 B1
HEMPNALL NR15 107 D5
HEMPNALL GREEN
NR15 107 D4
Hempnall Prim Sch
NR15 107 C5
Hempnall Rd NR35 108 A4
HEMPSTEAD
Hempstead NR25 19 E8
Lessingham NR12 24 E3
Hempstead Rd Holt NR25 137 D5
Lessingham NR12 24 D3
Hempsted Mews 4 NR5 160 E7
HEMPTON NR21 141 A3
Hempton Rd NR21 141 B3
HEMSBY NR29 167 A7
Hemsby Prim Sch NR29 167 A7
Hemsby Rd
13 Martham NR29 57 D4
Winterton-on-Sea NR29 58 B5
Henby Way NR7 163 D7
Henderson Green Prim Sch
NR5 161 E7
Henderson Rd NR4 161 F5
Hendon Ave 13 IP25 84 F3
Hendon Cl NR5 157 B1
Hendrie Rd NR25 137 C7
Hendry Gdns NR18 173 F7
HENGRAVE NR9 52 A6
Henley Rd NR2 162 A4
Hennessey's Loke NR28 23 A3
Henry Bell Cl PE30 147 A5
Henry Blogg Rd NR27 139 B5
Henry Cross Cl 1 IP25 67 C2
Henry Page Rd NR11 150 B5
Henry Preston Rd 1
NR15 106 F6
Henry's Ct 1 IP25 84 F3
Henry St PE13 152 C5
Henry Warby Ave 7 PE14 59 A1
Henry Ward Rd 1 IP20 122 D2
Henson Cl 3 PE13 152 C8
Henstead Rd NR9 88 D8
HEPWORTH IP22 127 E1
Hepworth Rd IP31 127 D3
Herbert Colman Cl NR13 73 E2
Herbert Dr IP26 98 F5
Herbert Nursey Cl NR8 157 C7
Herbert Ward Way PE34 144 D6
Hercules Cl NR6 157 F4
Hercules Rd NR6 157 F4
Hereford Way PE33 43 E4
Hereward Rd 1 PE13 152 D5
Hereward Way
5 Feltwell IP26 98 D1
Weeting IP27 175 A8
Weeting-with-Broomhill
IP27 114 E8
Herman Fst Sch NR31 170 A3
Herman Mid Sch NR31 170 A3
Hermanus Leisure Ctr
NR29 58 B6
Hermitage Cl 3 NR13 166 D4
Herne Cotts NR19 67 D5
Herne Dro PE14 95 D5
Herne La
Beeston with Bittering
PE32 48 C1
Shipdham NR19 67 D5
Herolf Way 11 IP20 122 D2
Heron Ave IP27 175 E3
Heron Cl
Downham Market PE38 172 C7
6 Fakenham NR21 141 E4
Great Yarmouth NR31 170 A7
10 Salhouse NR13 55 A1
Salhouse NR13 55 B1
Sprowston NR7 159 E5
Heron Gdns NR12 39 B3
Heron La PE30 146 E2
Heron Rd Costessey NR8 156 B5
Wisbech PE13 152 D2
Heron Way Hickling NR12 39 E1
12 Watton IP25 84 C3
Herrick Rd NR8 156 E8
Herries Cl 7 NR30 169 C4
HERRINGFLEET NR32 111 D8
Herringfleet Rd NR31 93 E2
Herring La NR9 69 A1
Herring's La PE31 135 C4
Hertford Way NR31 170 B4
HETHEL NR14 88 F3
Hethel Old Thorn Nature
Reserve★ NR14 88 E3
Hethel Rd NR16 88 D2
HETHERSETT NR9 88 C8
Hethersett Acad NR9 88 D8
Hethersett Jun Sch NR9 88 D7
Hethersett La NR4 160 F3
Hethersett Rd
East Carleton NR14 88 F5
Great Melton NR9 88 B8
Hethersett Woodside Inf Sch
NR9 88 D7
HEVINGHAM NR10 53 B7
Hevingham Prim Sch
NR10 53 B8
Hewett Acad The NR1 162 D2
Hewett Cl NR31 170 D2
Hewett Rd NR31 170 A8
Hewitt Cl 18 NR14 90 C5
Hewitts Cl NR24 142 E4
Hewitts La NR18 173 C5
Hextable Rd PE30 146 E6
HEYDON NR11 34 F6
Heydon Hall★ NR11 34 F6
Heydon La NR11 34 E7
Heydon Rd Aylsham NR11 150 A7
Corpusty NR11 34 F8

Heydon Rd continued
Wood Dalling NR11 . . . . **34** D6
Heyford Rd NR6 . . . . **158** C6
Heywood Ave IP22 . . . . . . **177** D6
Heywood Rd Diss IP22 . . . **177** E8
Shelfanger IP22 . . . . **120** C2
Tibenham NR16 . . . . **120** D6
Winfarthing IP22 . . . . **120** C5
Heywood The IP22 . . . . . . **120** E5
Hickathrift Field PE14 . . . . **61** A4
HICKLING NR12 . . . . **39** F3
Hickling Broad National
Nature Reserve ★ NR12 . . **57** A8
Hickling Broad Visitor Ctr ★
NR12 . . . . **40** A1
Hickling CE Inf Sch NR12 . **39** F2
Hickling Cl PE37 . . . . **153** C2
HICKLING GREEN NR12 . . . . **39** F2
HICKLING HEATH NR12 . . . . **39** E1
Hickling La NR14 . . . . **89** D4
Hickling Rd
Sea Palling NR12 . . . . **24** F1
Sutton NR12 . . . . **39** C2
Hickling Way NR29 . . . . . . **167** B3
Hickory Gdns 13 NR31 . . . . **94** C7
Hickory Rd PE30 . . . . **147** C5
Higdon Cl IP22 . . . . **120** E2
Higham Cl NR7 . . . . **159** A3
Higham Gn 3 PE30 . . . . . **147** C4
High Ash Rd NR18 . . . . **88** C5
High Banks NR18 . . . . **173** C3
Highbridge Gravel Dro
IP27 . . . . **113** D2
Highbridge Rd PE34 . . . . . . **78** F8
High Bridgham Rd NR16 . . **117** C5
High Bungay Rd NR14 . . . . **109** D8
Highbury Rd IP27 . . . . **175** A2
High Comm NR18 . . . . **87** D2
High Comm Rd IP22 . . . . . . **128** C8
High Cross NR20 . . . . **33** A2
High Ct IP20 . . . . **122** E2
High Fen Dro IP26 . . . . **98** D8
Highfield 3 Eye IP23 . . . . **130** C1
Field Dalling NR25 . . . . **7** B2
Great & Little Plumstead
NR13 . . . . **73** B7
King's Lynn PE30 . . . . **147** C5
Highfield Ave
Brundall NR13 . . . . **165** D3
Swaffham PE37 . . . . **153** A5
Highfield Cl
Foulsham NR20 . . . . **33** C4
1 Norwich NR7 . . . . **72** D3
Ryburgh NR21 . . . . **32** A6
Highfield La NR21 . . . . **32** A6
Highfield Rd
East Dereham NR19 . . . . . **154** D8
Fakenham NR21 . . . . **141** B5
Great Yarmouth NR31 . . . . **170** C2
Taverham NR8 . . . . **155** F1
Highfields
Felmingham NR28 . . . . **37** A8
Holly End PE14 . . . . **59** D1
Lakenheath IP27 . . . . **113** F1
Norwich NR5 . . . . **156** D1
Highfield Way 4 NR12 . . . **54** C7
Highgate PE30 . . . . **146** E5
Highgate Inf Sch PO30 . . . **146** F6
High Gn Brooke NR15 . . . . . **90** D1
Great Melton NR9 . . . . **88** B8
5 Great Moulton NR15 . . . **106** B1
Great Moulton NR15 . . . . . **121** B8
Norwich NR1 . . . . **163** B5
High Gn Gdns NR15 . . . . . . **90** D1
HIGH GREEN
Bradenham IP25 . . . . **66** E2
Fransham NR19 . . . . **48** E1
Great Melton NR9 . . . . **88** B8
Highgrove Ct NR14 . . . . **90** C6
High Hatter's Cl PE38 . . . . **172** C3
High Hill Rd NR12 . . . . **38** F6
High House Ave
7 Wymondham NR18 . . . . **173** D5
8 Wymondham NR18 . . . . **173** D5
High House Cotts PE32 . . . . **47** E5
High House La 8 NR13 . . . . **73** D6
High House Rd NR20 . . . . . . **49** C4
HIGH KELLING NR25 . . . . **8** E3
Highland NR14 . . . . **90** B6
Highland Ave NR2 . . . . **162** A4
Highland Cl NR13 . . . . **92** C6
Highland Cres NR14 . . . . . **163** B2
Highland Rd Norwich NR2 **162** A4
Taverham NR8 . . . . **155** D1
Highlands Costessey NR8 **156** F4
Thetford IP24 . . . . **176** D5
High Lodge Forest Ctr ★
IP27 . . . . **115** C3
High London La IP22 . . . . . **120** A4
Highlow Rd NR5 . . . . **157** A1
High Mill Rd NR31 . . . . **169** B3
Highmoor Dro IP26 . . . . **99** D8
High Noon La NR13 . . . . **73** E6
High Noon Rd NR11 . . . . **21** D2
HIGHOAK NR18 . . . . **87** B4
High Oak La NR18 . . . . **87** B4
High Oak Rd NR18 . . . . **87** B3
High Rd Beighton NR13 . . . . **74** A4
Bressingham IP22 . . . . **129** C8
Burgh Castle NR31 . . . . **94** B8
Cantley NR13 . . . . **92** B8
Forncett NR16 . . . . **106** B6
Great Yarmouth NR31 . . . . **170** D7

High Rd continued
Lessingham NR12 . . . . **24** C2
Needham IP20 . . . . **131** E7
Repps with Bastwick NR29 . **57** A4
Roydon IP22 . . . . **177** A5
Tilney St Lawrence PE34 . . . **60** F8
Wiggenhall St Germans
PE34 . . . . **42** F1
Wortwell IP20 . . . . **123** A3
High St
Attleborough NR17 . . . . . . **174** D5
Blakeney NR25 . . . . **7** C6
Brandon IP27 . . . . **175** C5
Caister-on-Sea NR30 . . . . . **168** E5
Castle Acre PE32 . . . . **46** F2
Cawston NR10 . . . . **35** B3
Cley next the Sea NR25 . . . . **7** E6
Coltishall NR12 . . . . **54** C7
Cromer NR27 . . . . **139** B7
Docking PE31 . . . . **134** E4
Downham Market PE38 . . . **172** C4
East Dereham NR19 . . . . . **154** D5
Feltwell IP26 . . . . **98** E1
Fincham PE33 . . . . **62** E1
Foulsham NR20 . . . . **33** D3
Great Yarmouth NR31 . . . . **170** D6
Heacham PE31 . . . . **133** D5
Hilgay PE38 . . . . **79** E1
Holt NR25 . . . . **137** B6
Hopton IP22 . . . . **127** F6
Hunstanton PE36 . . . . **132** C4
Ketteringham NR18 . . . . **88** D5
King's Lynn PE30 . . . . **146** D5
Lakenheath IP27 . . . . **113** E1
Loddon NR14 . . . . **92** A1
Ludham NR29 . . . . **56** C5
Marsham NR10 . . . . **150** C1
Methwold IP26 . . . . **99** A5
Mundesley NR11 . . . . **143** C5
North Elmham NR20 . . . . . . **49** E8
Northwold IP26 . . . . **99** C7
Overstrand NR27 . . . . **11** A3
Ringstead PE36 . . . . **2** A3
5 Sheringham NR26 . . . . . **138** D7
Shipdham IP25 . . . . **67** B2
Southrepps NR11 . . . . **22** B7
Stalham NR12 . . . . **39** B4
St Margaret, Ilketshall
NR35 . . . . **124** D3
Stoke Ferry PE33 . . . . **81** A2
Sutton Bridge PE12 . . . . **41** C8
Thelnetham IP22 . . . . **128** B4
Thornham PE36 . . . . **2** D6
Thursford NR21 . . . . **17** D5
Tittleshall PE32 . . . . **48** B8
Walsingham NR22 . . . . **16** F7
Watton IP25 . . . . **84** D3
Wells-next-the-Sea NR23 . **136** D5
Whissonsett NR20 . . . . **31** D2
Wicklewood NR18 . . . . **87** B5
Wighton NR23 . . . . **5** F2
Wisbech PE13 . . . . **152** C5
HIGH STREET NR35 . . . . . . **124** D3
Highview NR13 . . . . **165** E6
High View Dr NR17 . . . . . . **174** B4
Highview Pk NR27 . . . . **139** C4
High Way 15 NR13 . . . . **74** A3
High Wrong Cnr IP24 . . . . . **115** C1
Hilary Ave NR1 . . . . **163** B8
Hilary Cl 6 NR13 . . . . **74** A3
HILBOROUGH IP26 . . . . **83** A3
Hilda Brooks Wy NR5 . . . . **157** B2
Hilda Rd NR11 . . . . **143** C6
HILGAY PE38 . . . . **79** E1
Hilgay Rd Ryston PE38 . . . . **79** F3
West Dereham PE33 . . . . . . **80** A4
Hilgay Village Prim Sch
PE38 . . . . **79** E1
Hillary Rd IP24 . . . . **176** C2
Hill Ave NR13 . . . . **170** D1
Hillburn Rd PE13 . . . . **152** B4
Hill Cl NR27 . . . . **139** C4
Hill Comm NR12 . . . . **39** F1
HILL COMMON NR12 . . . . **39** F1
Hillcrest Acle NR13 . . . . . . **166** A3
Downham Market PE38 . . . **172** E5
Great Ryburgh NR21 . . . . . . **32** B6
7 Loddon NR14 . . . . **92** A2
Hillcrest Ave NR19 . . . . . . **154** C1
Hillcrest Prim Sch PE38 . . **172** E6
Hill Crest Rd NR7 . . . . **163** D7
Hillen Rd PE30 . . . . **146** D2
Hill Est The PE33 . . . . **62** B6
Hill Farm Rd NR15 . . . . . . **106** F3
Hillfield NR12 . . . . **38** D3
Hill Fields NR19 . . . . **154** C1
Hill Fort Cl IP24 . . . . **176** C7
Hillgate St PE34 . . . . **144** A4
Hill House La IP24 . . . . **176** D7
Hill House Rd
Bramerton NR14 . . . . **90** F8
Norwich NR1 . . . . **163** A5
Hillingdon Pk NR27 . . . . . . **11** A4
Hillings Way PE32 . . . . **28** A1
HILLINGTON PE31 . . . . **28** B4
Hillington Sq PE30 . . . . . . **146** E4
Hill La Runhall NR20 . . . . . . **69** A4
Sculthorpe Airfield NR21 . . **15** C2
Hillmead NR3 . . . . **158** D3
Hill Rd
Ingoldisthorpe PE31 . . . . . **140** C8
King's Lynn PE30 . . . . **147** B8
Middleton PE33 . . . . **44** B3
Morley NR18 . . . . **104** D8
Norwich NR5 . . . . **157** A2
Tibenham NR16 . . . . **120** F8
Wymondham NR18 . . . . . . **105** A7
Hill's Cl 3 Corpusty NR11 . . **19** F1

Hill's Cl continued
Sporle PE32 . . . . **65** C6
Hill's Ct PE38 . . . . **79** E1
Hillsend La NR17 . . . . **174** A3
Hillside
Barnham Broom NR9 . . . . . . **69** B2
Barsham NR21 . . . . **16** D5
Brandon IP27 . . . . **114** D4
Briston NR24 . . . . **142** B4
Cromer NR27 . . . . **139** C4
Loddon NR14 . . . . **92** A2
Marham PE33 . . . . **63** B5
Mundesley NR11 . . . . **143** D5
North Pickenham PE37 . . . . **65** E2
Poringland NR14 . . . . **90** C5
Roughton NR11 . . . . **10** D1
Sheringham NR26 . . . . **138** F7
Swaffham PE37 . . . . **153** D4
Hillside Animal Sanctuary ★
NR12 . . . . **54** B4
Hillside Ave NR7 . . . . **163** F6
Hillside Ave Prim Sch
NR7 . . . . **163** F6
Hillside Cl Norwich NR7 . . **163** F6
Ormesby St Margaret
NR29 . . . . **167** B2
Swardeston NR14 . . . . **89** C5
Hillside Cres NR18 . . . . **87** B5
Hillside Prim Sch NR31 . . . . **94** C7
Hillside Rd Horning NR12 . . **55** E3
Norwich NR7 . . . . **163** F6
Sheringham NR26 . . . . **138** F5
Hillside Rd E NR35 . . . . . . **124** B7
Hillside Rd W NR35 . . . . . . **124** A7
Hills Rd IP25 . . . . **84** C5
Hill St 19 Feltwell IP26 . . . . . **98** E1
Hunstanton PE36 . . . . **132** C4
Norwich NR2 . . . . **162** C4
5 Wisbech PE13 . . . . **152** C5
Hills The NR13 . . . . **92** F4
Hill The Brandon IP27 . . . . **175** A4
Coltishall NR12 . . . . **54** D7
Damgate NR13 . . . . **166** C2
Horsham St Faith NR10 . . . . **53** D1
Little Snoring NR21 . . . . **17** B3
Shipmeadow NR34 . . . . . . **124** F8
Westwick NR10 . . . . **37** D5
Woodbastwick NR13 . . . . . . **55** F1
Hill Top
Cley next the Sea NR25 . . . . **7** E7
Stanton IP31 . . . . **127** C1
Hill Top Dr NR8 . . . . **156** F3
Hilltop Way IP31 . . . . **127** C1
Hillview PE37 . . . . **65** E2
Hillview Dr NR29 . . . . **58** B6
Hill View Rd NR26 . . . . **138** E7
Hillvue Cl NR5 . . . . **157** A2
Hilly Cl IP31 . . . . **126** D1
Hilly Plantation NR7 . . . . . **163** E7
Hilton Cl PE37 . . . . **153** C4
Hilton Ct PE13 . . . . **153** D4
Hiltons La 5 PE34 . . . . **43** B1
Hinchingbrook Cl PE30 . . . **148** E1
HINDERCLAY IP22 . . . . **128** C3
Hinderclay La IP22 . . . . . . **128** B5
Hinderclay Rd
Redgrave IP22 . . . . **128** D5
Rickinghall Inferior IP22 . . **128** D3
Wattisfield IP22 . . . . **128** B1
HINDOLVESTON NR20 . . . . . **33** D8
Hindolveston Rd
Foulsham NR20 . . . . **33** D4
Fulmodeston NR21 . . . . **17** F1
Guestwick NR20 . . . . **33** F6
Thurning NR20 . . . . **34** A8
HINDRINGHAM NR21 . . . . . . **17** E7
Hindringham CE Prim Sch
NR21 . . . . **17** D7
Hindringham Rd
Binham NR21 . . . . **6** E2
Gunthorpe NR21 . . . . **18** A7
Hindringham NR21 . . . . **17** F7
Walsingham NR22 . . . . **17** A8
HINGHAM NR9 . . . . **86** C5
Hingham Prim Sch NR9 . . . **86** C5
Hingham Rd
Deopham NR18 . . . . **86** F5
Garvestone NR9 . . . . **86** C8
Great Ellingham NR17 . . . . **103** E8
Hardingham NR9 . . . . **86** E6
Little Ellingham NR17 . . . . . **86** A2
Hingley Cl NR31 . . . . **170** C8
Hinks Cl NR10 . . . . **155** C3
Hinshalwood Way NR8 . . . **156** E4
Hipkin Rd PE31 . . . . **140** C3
Hipperson Cl 2 NR28 . . . . **151** C7
Hippodrome ★ NR30 . . . . . **169** E3
Hobart Cl NR18 . . . . **173** C6
Hobart La NR1 . . . . **178** B1
Hobart Sq NR1 . . . . **178** B1
Hobb's La NR13 . . . . **92** D7
Hobbs's La NR15 . . . . **108** D7
Hobland Rd
Belton with Browston
NR31 . . . . **94** C4
Bradwell NR31 . . . . **171** A4
Hobrough La NR1 . . . . **178** C2
HOCKERING NR20 . . . . **69** B8
Hockering CE Prim Sch
NR20 . . . . **69** B8
HOCKERING HEATH NR20 . . **51** C1
Hockering La NR9 . . . . **160** B6
Hockham St PE30 . . . . **146** D2
HOCKWOLD CUM WILTON
IP26 . . . . **114** A7

Hockwold Prim Sch
IP26 . . . . **114** A6
Hockwold Rd IP27 . . . . **175** B7
Hodgson Rd NR4 . . . . **161** F5
HOE NR20 . . . . **49** F3
Hoe Hall NR20 . . . . **49** F3
Hoe Rd Hoe NR20 . . . . **49** F5
Longham NR19 . . . . **49** A3
Hoe Rd E NR20 . . . . **50** A1
Hoe Rd N NR20 . . . . **50** A3
Hoe Rd S NR20 . . . . **50** A2
Hoe Rough Nature Reserve ★
NR20 . . . . **49** E4
Hogarth Cl 18 NR31 . . . . . . **94** C8
Hogarth Rd PE38 . . . . **172** E6
Hog Bog La NR10 . . . . **53** F3
Hogg La NR35 . . . . **108** C1
Hogg's Dro PE33 . . . . **63** B5
Hogherd's La 9 PE13 . . . . **152** C5
Hog La NR34 . . . . **124** F2
Hogsty La IP21 . . . . **122** A1
Holbrigg La NR21 . . . . **17** C1
Holcombe Ave PE30 . . . . . **146** F3
Holders La IP26 . . . . **99** A7
Holgate Hill NR25 . . . . **8** D4
Holgate La 5 NR27 . . . . **10** B5
Holgate Rd
North Walsham NR28 . . . . . **151** F1
South Creake NR21 . . . . **15** C7
HOLKHAM NR23 . . . . **5** B6
Holkham Ave PE37 . . . . . . **153** B2
Holkham Cl 7 NR28 . . . . . . **172** C6
Holkham Gn NR21 . . . . **30** C4
Holkham Hall & Bygones
Mus ★ NR23 . . . . **5** A5
Holkham National Nature
Reserve ★ NR23 . . . . **5** B8
Holkham Rd NR23 . . . . **136** B6
Holland Ct 8 NR19 . . . . . . **154** D1
Holland's La NR35 . . . . **108** C3
Holley Wlk NR11 . . . . **150** C4
Hollies The
Clenchwarton PE34 . . . . . . **145** D5
5 North Walsham NR28 . . . **151** C5
Holl La Billingford NR20 . . . . **50** B7
Garvestone NR9 . . . . **68** B1
Holloway Rd NR14 . . . . **91** B8
Hollow Hill Rd NR35 . . . . . **109** A2
Hollow La
Barningham IP31 . . . . **127** D4
4 Langham NR25 . . . . **7** A4
Raynham NR21 . . . . **30** F3
Shotesham NR15 . . . . **89** F2
Hollow Way Hill NR34 . . . **110** D4
Holls La NR1 . . . . **178** B1
Hollway La NR20 . . . . **68** B8
Holly Ave 12 Elm PE14 . . . . **59** A1
Great Yarmouth NR31 . . . . . **94** C7
Holly Bank NR7 . . . . **159** A2
Holly Blue Mews NR8 . . . . **156** B6
Holly Blue Rd NR18 . . . . . . **173** E4
Hollybush Rd NR28 . . . . . . **151** F5
Holly Cl Dereham NR19 . . . **154** F4
Downham Market PE38 . . . **172** B6
Holt NR25 . . . . **137** D7
King's Lynn PE30 . . . . **148** D2
14 Marthan NR29 . . . . **57** D4
Mattishall NR20 . . . . **68** C6
Rougham PE32 . . . . **47** B7
1 North Walsham NR28 . . . **151** B4
Hollycroft Cl PE14 . . . . **59** C1
Hollycroft Rd PE14 . . . . **77** D8
Holly Ct
34 Harleston IP20 . . . . **122** D2
Swaffham PE13 . . . . **153** C4
Wymondham NR18 . . . . . . **173** E6
Holly Dr NR2 . . . . **162** A7
HOLLY END PE14 . . . . **59** D1
Holly Farm Rd NR13 . . . . . . **93** A4
Holly Gr NR26 . . . . **138** D5
Holly La Blofield NR13 . . . . **165** D7
Lackenheath IP27 . . . . **113** E1
9 Tharston & Hapton
NR15 . . . . **106** D3
Wood Dalling NR11 . . . . **34** D5
Holly Meadows Sch PE32 . **28** B1
Holly Rd NR17 . . . . **174** C4
Holly Way 13 NR31 . . . . . . **170** B6
Hollywell Gdns PE13 . . . . . **153** B4
Holman Cl NR11 . . . . **150** B7
Holman Rd NR11 . . . . **150** B6
Holman's Chase PE38 . . . . . **97** B6
Holme Cl Hopton IP22 . . . . **127** F6
Runcton Holme PE33 . . . . . . **61** D4
Holme Dunes National
Nature Reserve ★ PE36 . . . . **2** A8
HOLME HALE IP25 . . . . **66** B2
HOLME NEXT THE SEA
PE36 . . . . **2** A6
Holme Oak Gdns PE37 . . . **153** C3
Holme Rd PE36 . . . . **2** A4
Holmes Cl Acle NR13 . . . . . **166** B4
Norwich NR7 . . . . **163** D8
Holmesdale Rd NR13 . . . . **165** B4
Holmes Dr PE13 . . . . **152** E5
Holmes Rd
East Ruston NR12 . . . . **38** F5
Somerton NR29 . . . . **57** F7
Holmwood Rise NR7 . . . . . **163** C6
HOLT NR25 . . . . **137** D6
Holt Com Prim Sch
NR25 . . . . **137** B6
Holt Ct PE14 . . . . **41** E3
Holt Ctry Pk ★ NR25 . . . . . **137** C4
Holt House La PE32 . . . . **44** D5
Holt Rd Aylmerton NR11 . . . **10** B3
Briston NR24 . . . . **142** E5

Holt Rd continued
Cawston NR10 . . . . **35** D2
Cley next the Sea NR25 . . . . **7** E6
Cromer NR27 . . . . **139** A6
Fakenham NR21 . . . . **141** C4
Felthorpe NR10 . . . . **52** F6
Field Dalling NR25 . . . . **7** B2
Gresham NR11 . . . . **9** E1
Guist NR20 . . . . **32** F4
Hoe NR19 . . . . **154** C8
Langham NR25 . . . . **8** A1
Letheringsett with Glandford
NR25 . . . . **8** A1
Little Snoring NR21 . . . . **17** C3
Melton Constable NR24 . . . **142** A5
North Elmham NR20 . . . . . . **49** E7
Norwich NR10 . . . . **157** F8
Sheringham NR26 . . . . **138** B5
Thornage NR25 . . . . **18** F7
Upper Sheringham NR26 . . **138** C3
Walsingham NR22 . . . . **16** F1
Weybourne NR25 . . . . **8** E5
Holt's La PE38 . . . . **79** D1
Holt Sta NR25 . . . . **137** E8
Holway Cl NR27 . . . . **139** B3
Holway Rd NR26 . . . . **138** D5
Holway The NR29 . . . . **58** B6
Holworthy Rd NR5 . . . . . . **161** B8
Holy Rd NR24 . . . . **18** D5
Holyrood Dr PE31 . . . . **140** D3
Homebred La 1 NR14 . . . . . **91** F1
Home Cl
Great Ellingham NR17 . . . . **103** E8
Lyng NR9 . . . . **51** A4
5 Sheringham NR27 . . . . . . **10** A5
Homecroft NR9 . . . . **160** B2
Home Farm La NR18 . . . . . **104** B4
Home Farm Rd NR35 . . . . . **109** C3
Home Farm Rise NR25 . . . . . **8** A2
Homefield Ave NR31 . . . . . . **94** C7
Homefield Prim Sch
NR31 . . . . **94** C7
Homefields La PE36 . . . . . . **132** D4
Home La Hilborough IP25 . . **83** B4
Hindringham NR21 . . . . **17** E7
Homeland Rd 10 PE30 . . . . **146** E6
Homelea Cres 13 NR13 . . . . **74** A3
Home Piece IP22 . . . . **127** E4
Home Piece Rd NR23 . . . . **136** C5
HOMERSFIELD IP20 . . . . . . **123** B4
Homerton Ind Est NR16 . . **103** E1
Home St NR2 . . . . **162** C8
Homestead Cl 7 NR15 . . . . . **74** A3
Homestead Gdns NR29 . . . **167** B7
Honey Cl 2 NR11 . . . . **163** B7
Honeycombe Rd NR13 . . . . **73** B8
Honey Dro PE33 . . . . **80** B1
Honey Hill PE34 . . . . **79** D8
Honey Hills PE31 . . . . **14** A5
Honeymoon Loke NR30 . . **168** F4
Honeymoon Row NR23 . . . **136** D5
Honeypot Dro PE32 . . . . **46** C5
Honeypot La
Kirby Cane NR35 . . . . **109** C5
Longham NR19 . . . . **48** F2
Seething NR15 . . . . **108** E8
West Somerton NR29 . . . . . **57** F7
Honeypot Mdw NR35 . . . . **124** A8
Honeysuckle Cl
Cringleford NR4 . . . . **161** B1
North Walsham NR28 . . . . . **151** E4
5 Thetford IP24 . . . . **176** F4
Honeysuckle Dr NR20 . . . . **154** F4
Honeysuckle Sq NR18 . . . . **173** F6
Honeysuckle Way NR17 . . **174** B5
HONING NR28 . . . . **38** C6
HONINGHAM NR9 . . . . **69** E7
Honingham La NR8 . . . . **70** A8
Honingham Rd NR9 . . . . **69** C3
Honing Long La NR28 . . . . . **38** C7
Honing Rd NR28 . . . . **38** D5
Honing Row NR28 . . . . **38** A5
HONINGTON IP31 . . . . **126** D1
Honington Airfield IP31 . . . **126** A2
Honington CE VC Prim Sch
IP31 . . . . **126** D1
Honington Rise IP31 . . . . . **126** C1
Hood Way IP24 . . . . **176** E5
Hooker Rd NR7 . . . . **159** D1
Hooks Hill Rd NR26 . . . . . . **138** C6
Hook's Wlk NR1 . . . . **178** C3
Hookwood La NR18 . . . . . . **104** C8
Hooper La NR3 . . . . **158** F2
Hooton's Row PE38 . . . . **78** F6
Hope Ct PE30 . . . . **147** A8
Hope La PE14 . . . . **60** A4
HOPTON IP22 . . . . **127** F6
Hopton CE Prim Sch
NR31 . . . . **171** D4
Hopton CE VC Prim Sch
IP22 . . . . **127** F5
Hopton Cl 6 NR7 . . . . **72** C4
Hopton Ct 8 NR31 . . . . **171** D5
Hopton Gdns NR31 . . . . . . **171** D5
HOPTON ON SEA NR31 . . . . **171** D6
Hopton Rd
Barningham IP31 . . . . **127** D4
Garboldisham IP22 . . . . **128** A8
Thelnetham IP22 . . . . **128** A5
Horatio Ct 10 NR2 . . . . **162** B8
Horizon Views NR12 . . . . . . **24** C7
Hornbeam Cl
5 Great Yarmouth
NR31 . . . . **170** B6
Norwich NR7 . . . . **159** D4
Hornbeam Dr
9 Etling Green NR20 . . . . . . **68** A8
15 Poringland NR14 . . . . . . **90** C5

Hornbeam Rd NR28 151 C4
Horner Cl 3 IP22 177 A5
HORNING NR12 55 E4
Horning Cl NR5 161 D7
Horning Com Prim Sch NR12 55 F3
Horning Rd Hoveton NR12 164 E5
Neatishead NR12 55 D6
Woodbastwick NR13 55 D2
Horning Rd W NR12 164 C5
HORNINGTOFT NR20 31 F1
Hornor Cl NR2 162 C3
Horns La NR1 178 B2
Horns Row NR21 141 A3
Horsbeck Way NR10 53 A3
Horse Fair 2 PE13 152 C5
Horsefair Loke NR1 178 C3
Horsefen Rd NR29 56 D4
Horsehead Dro PE14 95 C8
Horse Rescue Ctr* NR16 103 C2
Horses Head NR13 166 B7
Horseshoe Cl NR5 156 E1
Horse Shoe Cl 17 IP25 84 F3
Horse-Shoe Cnr PE13 152 B7
Horseshoe Ct PE14 77 E6
Horseshoe La NR24 142 F4
Horse Shoe Rd NR20 69 A4
Horseshoe Terr PE13 152 B7
Horse Watering La NR35 109 E2
HORSEY NR29 40 D2
HORSEY CORNER NR29 40 D2
Horsey Rd NR29 57 E7
Horsey's La NR31 170 D5
Horsey Windpump* NR29 40 D1
HORSFORD NR10 53 B3
Horsford CE Inf Sch NR10 53 B3
Horsford CE VA Prim Sch NR10 53 B4
Horsford St 7 NR2 162 B8
HORSHAM ST FAITH NR10 53 D1
Horsley Dr
Great Yarmouth NR31 170 B1
Hopton on Sea NR31 171 D4
Horsley's Chase PE30 146 E2
Horsley's Ct 7 PE30 146 E3
Horsley's Field PE30 146 E2
Horsley's Fields Ind Est PE30 146 E2
HORSTEAD NR12 54 C6
Horton Rd PE30 147 D6
Hospital La
Hellesdon NR6 157 D3
Norwich NR1 162 E3
Hospital Rd
Great & Little Plumstead NR13 73 A5
Sutton Bridge PE12 41 E8
Wicklewood NR18 87 C4
Hospital Wlk PE30 146 E4
Hotblack Rd NR2 162 A8
Hotch La PE14 60 B8
Hotson Cl 5 NR15 106 D3
Houghton Ave PE30 148 D1
Houghton Cl 2 NR5 161 B8
Houghton Hall* PE31 29 C7
Houghton La PE37 65 E1
HOUGHTON ST GILES NR22 16 E6
House Gdns NR10 53 E5
Hovell's La IP26 99 C7
HOVETON NR12 164 D6
Hoveton Cl PE30 147 D5
Hoveton Dr PE37 153 C1
Hoveton Hall Gdns* NR12 55 B7
Hoveton Pl NR10 37 B2
Hoveton & Wroxham Sta NR12 164 C5
Howard Cl Harleston IP20 122 E2
Norwich NR7 163 D7
4 Swanton Morley NR20 50 B3
Terrington St Clement PE34 144 B4
Wortham IP22 129 C3
Howard Cres NR19 154 D4
Howard Inf Sch PE30 147 B4
Howard Mews NR3 158 E1
Howard St N 9 NR30 169 C4
Howard St S NR30 169 C4
Howards Cl PE36 132 E7
Howard's Hill NR27 139 A7
Howards Hill Cl NR27 10 C5
Howard's Hill Rd NR28 38 C7
Howards Hill W 1 NR27 139 A7
Howard St NR1 178 A1
Howards The PE30 148 D4
Howard's Way NR10 35 B2
Howard Way NR11 150 C5
Howdale Rd PE38 172 C5
Howdale Rise PE38 172 D5
HOWE NR15 90 D3
Howe Gn NR15 90 D2
Howe La NR15 90 D3
Howell Rd NR8 157 C6
Howe Rd NR30 169 D7
Howes Cl 10 NR9 88 D7
Howes La NR20 68 D6
Howes Yd 1 NR25 7 E6
HOW HILL NR29 56 B6
How Hill Nature Reserve* NR29 56 A6
How Hill Rd NR29 56 B6
Howland Cl NR21 141 B5
Howlett Cl
4 East Dereham NR19 154 D3
Howlett Cl *continued*
North Walsham NR28 151 A5
Howlett Dr NR5 161 A8
Howletts Hill PE13 152 C4
Howlett Way 2 IP24 176 D6
HOXNE IP21 131 A4
Hoxne Rd Denham IP21 131 B1
Eye IP23 130 E1
Syleham IP21 131 C4
Upper Weybread IP21 131 E6
Hubbard Cl
11 Long Stratton NR15 106 E3
Wymondham NR18 173 A6
Hubbard's Dro PE38 79 E1
Hubbards Loke NR9 51 D5
Hubbard's Loke 16 NR9 88 C7
Hudson Cl 1 IP24 116 A2
Hudson Leisure Ctr PE13 152 A5
Hudson Way NR5 160 E7
Hugh Cl PE30 148 C5
Hughenden Rd NR1 162 E3
Hughes Ct 13 NR9 88 D8
Hulton Rd PE30 147 A5
Hulver Rd NR13 73 E8
Hulver St NR19 66 F6
Humber Cl NR30 168 C5
Humber Keel NR31 170 D1
Humberstone Rd 3 NR31 170 C7
HUMBLETOFT NR19 154 C7
Humbletoft Rd NR19 154 C7
Humbleyard NR5 161 A7
Hungate La NR11 150 C4
Hungate Rd PE14 59 E2
Hungate St NR11 150 C5
Hungry Hill NR27 11 B2
HUNSTANTON PE36 132 D5
Hunstanton Commercial Pk PE36 132 D3
Hunstanton Inf Sch PE36 132 D4
Hunstanton Rd
Dersingham PE31 140 D5
Heacham PE31 132 D1
Hunstanton Sea Life Sanctuary* PE36 132 B3
Hunstead La NR15 90 F2
Hunt Cl Old Catton NR6 158 E7
5 Redenhall with Harleston IP20 122 D2
Hunter Ave NR20 68 F5
Hunter Dr 4 NR31 94 C8
Hunter Rd Norwich NR3 158 C3
Troston IP31 126 B1
Hunters Cl Brundall NR13 165 F5
Terrington St Clement PE34 144 F6
Hunter's Dro PE14 60 B6
Hunters Oak 2 IP25 84 E3
Hunters Rise PE33 43 F4
Hunters Rowe PE14 152 D2
Huntley Cres NR26 138 E6
HUNT'S CORNER NR16 119 C7
Hunts Gn NR16 105 B4
HUNWORTH NR24 19 A6
Hunworth Rd NR24 142 D8
Hurdle La NR25 7 E4
Hurd Rd NR4 161 E3
Hurn La NR16 106 A6
Hurn Rd Dereham NR20 68 A7
Taverham NR8 157 C7
Hurrell Rd NR30 168 D6
Hurricane Cl 22 IP25 84 F3
Hurricane Way NR6 158 C6
Hurst Rd 8 NR14 92 A2
Hurth Way IP24 176 E4
Husenbeth Cl NR8 156 E4
Hutchinson Rd NR5 161 D6
Huxley Cl NR1 162 F2
Huxley Rd NR1 162 F2
Hyde Cl PE31 14 D4
Hyde Ct NR13 72 E5
Hyde Rd NR19 154 D3
HYLTONS CROSSWAYS NR28 36 F8
Hypocrite La NR17 174 A2
Hyrn Cl NR29 57 D4
Hythe Rd Feltwell IP26 98 E3
Foulden IP26 82 A1
Methwold IP26 98 F5

I

Ice House Ct 17 NR15 106 E3
Ice House La NR1 178 C1
Iceni Acad (Methwold Site) IP26 99 A6
Iceni Dr PE37 153 D2
ICKBURGH IP26 100 B6
Icknield Cl IP24 176 B3
Icknield Way IP24 176 B3
Ickworth Cl PE30 148 E1
Ilex Ct NR7 159 D4
ILKETSHALL ST ANDREW NR34 124 E6
ILKETSHALL ST LAWRENCE NR34 124 F2
Ilketshall St Lawrence Sch NR34 124 F2
ILKETSHALL ST MARGARET NR35 124 B4
ILLINGTON IP24 117 D8
Illington Rd IP24 117 C8
ILPH Hall Farm* NR16 118 B7
Impala Cl NR6 159 A6
Imperial Mews NR31 171 C4
Impson Way IP26 100 A4
Incleborough Cl 2 NR27 10 B5
Independent Way 14 NR7 72 D4
Indigo Yd NR3 178 A3
INGHAM NR12 39 D4
Ingham Cnr NR12 24 D1
INGHAM CORNER NR12 24 D2
Ingham Rd
Lessingham NR12 24 D2
Stalham NR12 39 B4
INGLEBOROUGH PE14 41 B1
Ingleby Cl Heacham PE31 133 E6
King's Lynn PE30 147 B4
Ingle Rd PE14 59 B1
Ingloss La NR14 109 B7
Ingoldale PE31 140 C8
INGOLDISTHORPE PE31 140 D8
Ingoldisthorpe CE Prim Sch PE31 140 E8
Ingoldsby Ave PE31 140 C6
Ingolside PE31 12 D4
Ingram Ct NR1 162 E3
Ingram's Rd IP21 131 C7
INGWORTH NR11 36 B8
Inman Rd NR7 159 D4
INTWOOD NR4 89 B7
Intwood La
East Carleton NR14 89 A5
Swardeston NR14 89 C6
Intwood Rd NR4 89 B8
Invaders Ct NR23 136 D6
Ipswich Gr NR2 178 A1
Ipswich Rd Norwich NR2 178 A1
2 Norwich NR4 89 E8
Pulham Market NR15 121 E8
Saxlingham Nethergate NR15 107 A7
Scole IP21 130 D5
Yaxley IP23 130 A1
Ireton Cl 25 NR7 72 D4
Iris Cl NR17 174 B5
Irmingland Rd NR11 34 F8
Ironside Way NR9 86 D5
IRSTEAD NR12 56 A7
Irstead Rd
Barton Turf NR12 55 F7
Norwich NR5 161 E6
IRSTEAD STREET NR12 55 F6
Irving Rd NR4 162 C1
Irwin Cl NR10 149 C5
Isaac's Rd NR31 169 B4
Isabella Cl PE30 147 D3
Isabella Sq 12 NR30 169 D3
Isbets Dale NR8 155 D2
Isis Cl NR31 170 B3
Isle Bridge Rd PE14 77 E6
Isle Rd PE14 77 F7
ITTERINGHAM NR11 20 C1
ITTERINGHAM COMMON NR11 35 D8
Iveagh Cl PE31 140 E2
Ives Cl IP22 177 E4
Ives Rd NR6 158 D5
Ivory Rd NR4 161 E4
Ivy Gn 6 NR31 170 B5
Ivy Rd Earlham NR5 161 E7
3 Spixworth NR10 54 A2
IVY TODD PE37 66 B4
Ivy Todd Rd PE37 66 B4
Ivy Way NR20 68 E6
Ixworth Rd IP31 126 D1

J

Jack Plummer Way NR30 168 C7
Jaguar Rd 9 NR9 88 D8
James Cl PE30 148 B1
James Gn Cl 14 NR10 54 A2
James Jackson Rd PE31 140 C3
James Paget Univ Hospl NR31 170 B1
James Rd 7 NR12 55 E4
James Scott Cl 3 PE38 172 A5
James St PE36 132 D4
James Watt Cl NR31 170 A8
Jamieson Pl NR5 161 C8
Jamie Wright Cl NR26 138 C7
Jane Forby Cl PE33 80 E2
Jankin La PE34 144 A1
Jannys Cl NR11 150 B6
Jarrold Cl IP31 127 D3
Jarrold Way NR5 160 F8
Jarvie Cl PE36 13 A7
Jarvis Dr NR21 31 E5
Jarvis Rd PE30 146 E8
Jasmin Cl PE13 152 F7
Jasmine Cl Earlham NR4 161 E5
Thetford IP24 176 F4
Jasmine Ct 1 NR17 174 B5
Jasmine Gdns 7 NR31 94 C7
Jasmine Gn 7 NR31 170 B5
Jasmine Wk 3 NR4 89 A8
Javelin Rd NR6 158 C7
Jay Gdns NR5 160 E8
Jay La NR32 171 C3
Jay's Gn IP20 122 E2
Jeckyll Rd NR18 173 F7
Jefferey Ave 4 PE13 152 E7
Jeffery Cl PE30 146 E8
Jegon Cl NR11 150 D5
Jellicoe Pl 6 IP24 176 E5
Jellicoe Rd NR30 169 C8
Jema Cl NR31 169 C7
Jenkinsons Pightle NR35 108 B4
Jenner Cl NR35 124 B7
Jenner Rd 4 NR31 170 B1
Jennings Cl PE31 133 C5
Jennings Way IP22 177 D5
Jenny Lind Children's Hospl NR4 161 A2
Jenny Rd 8 NR10 54 A2
Jentique Cl NR19 154 E4
Jermyn Rd PE30 147 C6
Jermyn Way 1 NR15 106 D3
Jerningham Rd NR5 157 A1
Jessopp Cl Earlham NR2 161 F4
Norwich NR2 161 F4
Scarning NR19 67 B7
Jessopp Rd NR4 161 F4
Jetty Cl NR27 139 B7
Jetty Cliff NR27 139 C7
Jetty St 2 NR27 139 B7
Jewel Cl NR24 142 B4
Jews' La 10 NR31 94 C6
Jewson Rd NR3 158 C2
Jex Ave NR5 161 D8
Jex La NR5 161 D8
Jex Rd NR5 161 D8
Jex Wy 6 NR31 171 D4
Jickling Yd NR23 136 D6
Joan Short's La PE31 135 D3
Jobie Wood Cl NR7 159 D5
Jocelyn Cl IP21 121 E5
Joe Ellis Ct 6 NR5 161 B8
John Bates Cl 2 NR19 154 E5
John Chapman Cl 5 NR21 141 E4
John Childs Wy NR35 124 B7
John Davis Way PE33 61 D5
John Drewry Cl 2 NR14 90 D5
John F Kennedy Ct 2 PE13 152 D4
John Gale Ct NR8 155 E3
John Goshawk Rd NR19 154 E2
John Grant Sch NR30 168 C7
John Hill Cl 6 NR15 106 E3
John Hyrne Wy NR5 156 A3
John Jarrold Printing Mus* NR1 178 C4
John Kennedy Rd PE30 146 D6
John Morton Cres PE32 29 D1
John of Gaunt Inf Sch NR11 150 C5
John O'Gaunt Cl NR11 150 B6
John Rd
Caister-on-Sea NR30 168 E7
Great Yarmouth NR31 170 D5
Johnson Cl
7 East Dereham NR19 154 C3
New Costessey NR5 156 E1
Johnson Cres PE31 133 C4
Johnson Ct NR31 170 D5
Johnson Pl NR2 162 C5
JOHNSON STREET NR29 56 B4
John St 3 PE30 146 E3
John Stephenson Ct 1 NR6 158 F1
John Thompson Rd 3 PE13 152 D4
John Woodhouse Dr NR30 168 C7
Jolly Gardeners Ct 13 NR3 162 D8
Jolly Sailor Yd NR23 136 D6
Jolly's La NR13 166 A2
Jones (GC) Way NR31 169 B2
Jones's Dro PE14 95 E8
Jordan Cl Norwich NR5 161 B6
Taverham NR8 155 E4
JORDAN GREEN NR10 51 A8
Jordan La NR10 51 A8
Jordan Rd NR30 168 E6
Jose Neville Cl 2 NR30 168 D7
Josephine Cl NR1 162 D3
Joseph Lancaster Way 4 NR3 178 B4
Joshua Ct NR31 171 D8
Joy Ave 1 NR15 107 A8
Joyce La Heacham PE31 133 D5
Walpole PE14 41 F3
Joyce Rd NR35 124 B8
Joyce Way 9 NR7 72 D5
Joyland* NR30 169 E4
Jubilee Ave
4 East Dereham NR20 154 E6
East Harling NR16 118 C5
Fakenham NR21 141 C4
Heacham PE31 133 B5
Jubilee Bank Rd PE34 146 A5
Jubilee Cl Cawston NR10 35 B2
Downham Market PE38 172 E5
Erpingham NR11 21 B2
Hunstanton PE36 132 C3
Repps with Bastwick NR29 57 A4
Thetford IP24 176 B3
Weeting IP27 175 B7
Jubilee Ct 7 PE30 146 D4
Jubilee Dr
Dersingham PE31 140 C5
Sheringham NR26 138 E6
Jubilee Gdns 7 PE31 12 E4
Jubilee Hall La 2 PE32 45 C6
Jubilee La NR27 139 C4
Jubilee Rd Heacham PE31 133 A5
Holt NR25 137 B6
Lackenheath IP27 113 E2
Watton IP25 84 D3
Jubilee Rise PE33 61 D3
Jubilee Terr
Caister-on-Sea NR30 168 E4
Cromer NR27 139 D4
Norwich NR1 162 F3
Jubilee Way 11 PE37 65 F4
Jubilee Wlk
30 Martham NR29 57 D4
Wisbech PE13 152 D8
Judas La IP23 129 F1
Judges Dr NR4 161 F2
Judges Gdns NR8 155 E2
Judges Wlk NR4 161 F2
Juler Cl 4 NR28 151 C6
Julian Hospl NR2 161 F6
Julian Rd
King's Lynn PE30 148 C5
6 Spixworth NR10 54 A2
Julians Way IP21 121 E5
Julian Way NR31 171 D5
Junction Rd NR3 158 C1
Juniper Cl
Cringleford NR4 161 C1
2 Thetford IP24 176 F4
Juniper Dr 26 NR29 57 D4
Juniper Gr NR26 138 E5
Juniper Way NR8 155 B2
Jupiter Rd NR6 158 C4
Jury St NR30 169 D4

K

Kabin Rd NR5 157 B2
Kalmia Gn 3 NR31 170 B6
Karen Cl 15 Hethersett NR9 88 C7
Scole IP21 130 C5
Karoo Cl PE38 79 F6
Kate's La NR21 15 E8
Keable Cl 7 NR5 161 C6
Keats Cl
Downham Market PE38 172 D5
East Dereham NR19 154 C7
2 Thetford IP24 176 E6
Keats Rd NR8 156 D8
Keble Cl PE30 148 B4
Keble Rd NR31 170 B3
Kedleston Dr 10 NR4 89 B8
Keeble Ct PE30 146 D6
Keelan Cl NR6 158 B4
Keel Cl 12 NR33 111 F1
Keeling Hall La NR20 33 E3
Keeling Way NR17 174 B3
Keene Rd PE30 146 D1
Keepers Cl NR20 154 F5
Keepers Rd NR15 89 F1
Keepham Rd NR20 33 F2
Keep Rise NR35 124 A8
Keillers Cl PE13 152 A7
Keith Rd 9 NR20 50 B3
KELLING NR25 8 D5
Kelling Cl NR25 137 C7
Kelling Heath Pk Sta NR25 8 E4
Kelling Hospl NR25 137 F8
Kelling Prim Sch NR25 8 D6
Kelling Rd NR25 137 C7
Kell's Acres NR34 109 F3
Kell's Way NR34 109 F2
Kelsey Cl PE36 132 D7
Kelvin Pl IP24 176 A1
Kemp Dr NR19 154 C5
Kempe Cl NR7 159 C1
Kempe Rd PE34 146 C5
Kemp Rd NR28 151 C4
Kemp's Cl PE38 79 A4
Kemp's Rd IP21 122 A5
Kenan Dr NR17 174 F7
Kendal Cl 15 NR9 88 D8
Kendall Cl NR28 151 B6
Kendle Rd PE37 153 C1
Kendle Way PE30 147 E8
Kenhill Cl 2 PE31 12 E5
Kenlan Rd PE13 152 D6
Kennedy Ave NR31 170 C1
Kennedy Cl
East Dereham NR19 154 D1
Easton NR9 70 B5
Kennel Loke NR31 171 D8
Kenneth Mckee Plain NR2 178 A1
Kennett Cl NR4 161 F4
KENNINGHALL NR16 119 B5
Kenninghall Prim Sch NR16 119 A4
Kenninghall Rd
Banham NR16 119 B6
Harling NR16 118 E4
Kenninghall NR16 119 A3
Kenside Rd 1 PE31 12 E5
Kensington Cl NR15 107 C8
Kensington Pl NR1 178 B1
Kensington Rd
Downham Market PE38 172 B4
King's Lynn PE30 147 B6
Kent Ave NR31 170 C3
Kent Cl Attleborough NR17 174 B3
2 Sutton Bridge PE12 41 B8
Kentra Cl PE13 152 A8
Kent Rd PE30 147 B6
Kent Sq NR30 169 D3
Kenwood Rd PE31 133 D5
Kenwood Rd S PE31 133 D5
Kenwyn Cl NR25 137 C7
Kenyon Row NR34 110 C2
Keppel Cl PE32 48 A5
Keppel Rd 2 NR31 170 D4
KERDISTON NR10 34 C3
Kerdiston Rd
Reepham NR10 149 A6
Themelthorpe NR20 33 F2
Kered Cl NR6 157 F6

Kered Rd NR6 . . . . .157 F6
Kerkham Cl PE34 . . . . . .144 B4
Kerrich Cl PE31 . . . . .140 C3
Kerridge Ct NR25 . . . . . . .137 B6
Kerridges NR16 . . . . .118 C4
Kerridges The NR5. . . . . .156 F1
Kerridge Way
  Harleston IP20 . . . . . .122 D4
  Holt NR25 . . . . .137 B6
Kerrison Rd Bungay NR35 .124 B7
  Norwich NR1 . . . . .163 A4
Kerville St ❸ NR5 . . . . . .161 A7
Kestrel Ave
  Costessey NR8 . . . . .156 A5
  Downham Market PE38. . .172 C7
Kestrel Cl
  Burnham Market PE31 . .135 D1
  Great Yarmouth NR31 . . .170 A7
  Mulbarton NR14 . . . . .89 A3
  Swaffham PE37 . . . . .153 C2
  Thetford IP24 . . . . .176 D1
Kestrel Dr Brandon IP27 . .175 F3
  ❷ Great Yarmouth PE14 . . .152 D2
Kestrel Rd NR7 . . . . .159 C4
KESWICK Bacton NR12 . . . . .23 F4
  Keswick NR4 . . . . .89 C7
Keswick PE30. . . . . .147 D5
Keswick Cl NR4 . . . . .89 B8
Keswick Rd Bacton NR12 . . .23 F4
  Cringleford NR4 . . . . .89 B8
KETTERINGHAM NR18. . . . .88 E6
Ketteringham La NR9 . . . . .88 D6
Ketteringham Pk NR18. . . . .88 E6
Ketteringham Rd NR18 . . . .173 F3
KETTLESTONE NR21 . . . . . .17 C2
Kettlestone Rd NR21 . . . . . .17 B3
Kettlewell La ❶ PE30 . . . .146 E5
Kett's Ave NR18. . . . . .173 C5
Kett's Cl ❸ Hethersett NR9 .88 D7
  Wymondham NR18 . . . . . .173 C5
Ketts Hill PE37. . . . . .66 A4
Kett's Hill NR1. . . . . .163 A7
Kett's La NR9 . . . . .52 A6
Kett's Oak NR9 . . . . .88 C6
Ketts Rd NR28 . . . . .151 B4
Kevill Davis Dr NR13 . . . . . .73 A5
Kevin Wlk NR19 . . . . .154 D2
Kew Rd PE38 . . . . .172 B4
Key & Castle Yd NR3 . . . . .178 A4
Keyes Ave NR30 . . . . .169 D7
Keyes Cl ❺ NR1 . . . . .162 E2
Keyes Rd NR1 . . . . .162 E2
Keys Dr NR12. . . . . .164 B2
Keys Farm ❹ NR20 . . . . . .68 F6
Keys The NR15. . . . . .90 F2
Kidds Cl ❸ NR31. . . . . . . .171 D4
KIDD'S MOOR NR18. . . . . .173 B8
Kilderkin Cl PE14 . . . . .77 A7
Kilderkin Wy NR1. . . . . . . .178 B2
Kilham's Way
  King's Lynn PE30. . . . . . .146 E7
  North Wootton PE30 . . . . .26 E1
Kiln Cl NR4 . . . . .158 E7
Kiln Farm La IP22. . . . . . . .128 E1
Kiln La
  Dickleburgh & Rushall
  IP21. . . . . .130 F6
  Needham IP20. . . . . .131 D8
Kiln Rd ❺ NR10. . . . . .53 A3
Kilverstone Rd IP24. . . . . . .117 A2
KIMBERLEY NR18. . . . . .87 B6
Kimberley Pk Sta NR18 . . . .87 A6
Kimberley Rd NR28 . . . . . .151 D5
Kimberley St
  ❶ Norwich NR2 . . . . . . .162 C5
  Wymondham NR18 . . . . . .173 C4
Kimberley Terr NR30. . . . . .169 E2
Kimms Belt IP24. . . . . .176 B2
Kinderley Rd PE13 . . . . . . .152 C8
Kingcup PE30. . . . . .148 A1
King Edward VII Sch
  PE30. . . . . .147 A5
Kingfisher Cl
  ❻ Cringleford NR4. . . . . . .89 A8
  ❽ Fakenham NR21. . . . . .141 B4
  ❼ Fakenham NR21. . . . . .141 E4
  Great Yarmouth NR31. . . . .94 C7
  Thetford IP24 . . . . .176 D1
Kingfisher Dr
  Brandon IP27 . . . . .175 E3
  Necton PE37 . . . . .66 A3
  ❻ Wisbech PE14 . . . . . .152 D2
Kingfisher Rd
  Attleborough NR17 . . . . . .174 F6
  Downham Market PE38. . .172 C7
Kingfisher Way ❶❶ IP25 . . . .84 C3
King George Cl ❸ NR29. . . .57 D2
King George Mews IP22 . . .177 F5
King George Rd NR21 . . . . . .31 C7
King George's Ave ❷
  NR29. . . . . .57 D2
King George V Ave PE30 .146 F5
Kinghorn Rd NR1 . . . . .161 F4
King John Ave PE30. . . . . . .147 A5
King John Bank PE14 . . . . . .41 C5
King of Hearts Ctr★
  NR1. . . . . .178 B4
King's Arms St NR28 . . . . .151 C4
King's Ave Anmer PE31 . . . .28 C8
  King's Lynn PE30. . . . . . .147 A3
King's Cl NR28. . . . . .151 D5
Kings Croft PE31. . . . . .140 E4
Kings Ct NR27 . . . . .167 A8
Kingsdale ❶❻ NR13 . . . . . . .74 A3
King's Dam NR34. . . . . .110 B2

Kings Dr NR31. . . . . .94 C6
Kings Gn ❻ PE30 . . . . .147 C4
Kings Head La
  Deopham NR18 . . . . .87 A5
  North Lopham IP22. . . . . .119 A2
Kingshill IP24 . . . . .102 E3
Kings La NR1 . . . . .178 B1
Kingsleigh Cl NR28 . . . . . . .22 E5
Kingsley Ave PE13 . . . . . . .152 B4
Kingsley Rd NR1. . . . . .178 A1
Kings Loke NR29. . . . . .167 B8
KING'S LYNN PE30. . . . . . .147 A5
King's Lynn Arts Ctr
  (Guildhall)★ PE30 . . . . .146 D5
King's Lynn Rd PE36 . . . . .132 C4
King's Lynn Sports Ctr
  PE30. . . . . .146 F5
King's Lynn Sta PE30 . . . . .146 E5
King's Park Inf Sch NR19 .154 E6
Kings Rd Bungay NR35 . . . .124 B7
  East Dereham NR19 . . . . .154 E6
  Fakenham NR21 . . . . .141 A5
  Hunstanton PE36. . . . . . .132 D6
  Wisbech PE13 . . . . .152 C4
King's Rd
  Great Yarmouth NR30 . . .169 D2
  Holt NR25 . . . . .137 C5
  Topcroft NR35. . . . . .108 A4
Kings St NR14 . . . . .19 A6
King's Staithe La ❷
  PE30. . . . . .146 D4
King's Staithe Sq ❶
  PE30. . . . . .146 D4
King St East Harling NR16. .118 C5
  Great Yarmouth NR30 . . .169 C4
  King's Lynn PE30. . . . . . .146 D5
  Neatishead NR12 . . . . . . .55 E7
  Norwich NR1 . . . . .178 C1
  ❶❸ Sutton Bridge PE12 . . . .41 B8
  Swaffham PE37 . . . . .153 B4
  Thetford IP24 . . . . .176 C3
  Winterton-on-Sea NR29 . . .58 B6
  Wisbech PE13 . . . . .152 C5
Kingston Ave NR30 . . . . . .168 E5
Kingston Dr ❾ NR34. . . . . .110 D1
Kingston Rd NR19 . . . . . . .154 F3
Kingston Sq NR4. . . . . .162 A3
Kingsway ❼ Blakeney NR25 . .7 C6
  ❹ Earsham NR35. . . . . . . .123 F8
  King's Lynn PE30. . . . . . .146 E8
  Leverington PE13 . . . . . . .152 F7
  ❸ Newton Flotman NR15. .107 A8
  North Walsham NR28 . . . .151 A6
  Norwich NR2 . . . . .162 B4
  Thetford IP24 . . . . .176 C2
Kings Way NR29 . . . . .167 B7
King's Wk ❹ PE13 . . . . . . .152 C4
Kings Wlk
  Downham Market PE38. . .172 C5
  ❾ Great Yarmouth NR30 .170 B5
Kingswood Ave NR8 . . . . . .155 C2
Kingswood Cl
  Brooke NR15. . . . . .90 E1
  ❾ Norwich NR4 . . . . .89 C8
Kingswood Ct NR8. . . . . . . .155 D2
Kingswood Pk PE13. . . . . . .152 D3
King William Ct PE34. . . . .144 C5
Kinsale Ave NR6 . . . . .157 E5
Kinsale Inf & Jun Sch
  NR6. . . . . .157 E4
Kinver Cl NR4 . . . . .162 B3
Kipling Cl NR30 . . . . .168 D6
KIRBY BEDON NR14. . . . . . .90 E8
KIRBY CANE NR35. . . . . . . .109 E4
Kirby Cl ❺ NR29. . . . . .57 D5
KIRBY GREEN NR35. . . . . . .109 F5
  Norwich NR35. . . . . .163 C2
KIRBY ROW NR35. . . . . . . .109 E3
Kirby St PE30. . . . . .146 E5
Kirkgate La NR23 . . . . .6 A2
Kirkgate St
  Holme next the Sea PE36 . . . .2 A4
  Wisbech PE13 . . . . .152 E7
Kirkham's La PE14. . . . . .77 C8
Kirkhams Mdw NR19. . . . . .66 C7
Kirklands NR8 . . . . .156 E4
Kirklees ❻ NR4. . . . . .89 E8
Kirkpatrick Rd NR3. . . . . . .158 B2
Kirk Rd ❷ PE14. . . . . .41 D4
Kirkstead PE30 . . . . .147 D5
Kirstead Gn NR15. . . . . . . .108 C8
KIRSTEAD GREEN NR15. . .108 C8
Kirstead Ling NR15 . . . . . . .91 A1
Kirtons Cl ❸ PE14. . . . . .41 E4
Kitchener Cl IP27. . . . . .113 E2
Kitchener Rd
  Great Yarmouth NR30 . . .169 D5
  Melton Constable NR24 . . .142 B5
Kitchener St PE30 . . . . .146 D2
Kitlings Beck Rd NR28 . . . . .38 A7
Kittel Cl ❷❹ IP25 . . . . .84 D3
Kittens La NR15. . . . . .91 F1
Kittiwake Cl ❶❷ NR31. . . . . .94 C8
Kittles La NR10 . . . . .150 A1
Kittles Rd NR13 . . . . .74 D1
Knappers Way IP27 . . . . . . .175 D3
Knappers Wy ❸ NR8. . . . . . .70 C7
KNAPTON NR28. . . . . .143 B1
KNAPTON GREEN NR28. . . .22 F5
Knapton Rd Knapton NR28. .22 F3
  Mundesley NR11. . . . . . . .143 B4
  Trunch NR28 . . . . .22 E5
KNETTISHALL IP22 . . . . . . .127 C7
Knevet Cl NR17. . . . . .174 F6
Knights Gn NR26. . . . . .138 C5

Knight's La NR15 . . . . .89 E2
Knights Rd NR23 . . . . .158 B2
Knight St NR22 . . . . .16 F7
Knipe Cl ❷ NR16. . . . . .105 F5
Knitting Needle La NR23 . .136 E6
Knowland Gr NR5. . . . . . . .161 C8
Knowle Cres NR26 . . . . . . .138 E5
Knowle Rd NR26. . . . . .138 E6
Knowles' La NR12 . . . . .38 C2
Knowsley Rd NR3. . . . . .162 E8
Knox Ave NR1. . . . . .163 B8
Knox Cl NR1. . . . . .163 B8
Knox Rd NR1. . . . . .163 B7
Knudsen Cl ❹ NR15 . . . . . .107 C5
Knyvett Gn NR16. . . . . .105 F8
Koblenz Ave NR1 . . . . .178 C1
Kooreman Ave PE13 . . . . . .152 D7
Krons The NR15. . . . . .107 C5

L

Laburnham Rd NR28 . . . . . .151 B4
Laburnum Ave
  ❷ Marham PE33 . . . . .63 B4
  Taverham NR8. . . . . .155 B1
Laburnum Cl
  ❽ Great Yarmouth NR31 . . .94 C7
  ❾ Horsford NR10. . . . . . . .53 A3
  ❺ Wisbech PE13 . . . . . . .152 E7
  Wymondham NR18 . . . . . .173 F6
Laburnum Cres NR19 . . . . .154 E1
Laburnum Dr NR13 . . . . . . .165 F6
Laburnum Gr
  Reepham NR10 . . . . .149 C6
  Sheringham NR26 . . . . . .138 C4
  Thetford IP24 . . . . .176 B1
Laburnum Wlk IP27 . . . . . .175 E2
Lacey Cl ❻ PE33. . . . . .61 D6
Lacey Rd NR8. . . . . .155 D1
Lackford Cl NR13 . . . . .165 C4
Lacon Rd NR30 . . . . .168 E5
Ladbroke Pl NR1. . . . . .163 A4
Ladbrooke Cl ❸ IP22 . . . . .177 C4
Ladbrooke Rd ❹ NR31. . . .169 B3
Laddus Bank PE14. . . . . .77 A6
Laddus Dro PE14 . . . . .77 B6
Ladislaw Way ❶ NR19 . . . .154 C3
Lady Ann's Rd NR23. . . . . . . .5 B7
Lady Betty Rd NR1. . . . . . . .162 D3
Lady Dro PE38 . . . . .79 A6
Lady Hamilton La NR29 . . .167 C6
Lady Haven Mews ❶❷
  NR31. . . . . .169 C5
Lady Haven Rd ❻ NR31. . .169 B4
Lady Jane Grey Rd PE30. .146 F7
Lady La NR10 . . . . .53 E5
Lady Margaret's Ave
  NR31. . . . . .170 B4
Lady Mary Rd NR1 . . . . . . .162 D3
Lady's Dro ❶ PE14. . . . . . . .59 C2
Lady's La
  Bressingham IP22. . . . . . .119 F1
  Wymondham NR18 . . . . . .173 A3
Ladywood Cl ❾ PE33 . . . . . .63 B4
Ladywood Rd PE33. . . . . . . .63 B4
Lake Ave PE14. . . . . .95 C7
Lake Ct PE13 . . . . .152 D4
Lake Dro PE34. . . . . .61 C1
Lakeland ❸ IP26 . . . . .114 A7
Lakeland Cl NR13 . . . . .165 A8
Lakeland Way ❶ NR9 . . . . . .88 E8
Lakenfields NR1 . . . . .162 F2
LAKENHAM NR1. . . . . .162 F3
Lakenham Fst Sch NR1 . . .162 E3
Lakenham Prim Sch NR1 162 F3
Lakenham Rd NR4. . . . . . . .162 C2
Lakenham Way NR1. . . . . .162 E3
LAKENHEATH IP27. . . . . . .113 E2
Lakenheath Airfield
  IP27. . . . . .114 B1
Lakenheath Com Prim Sch
  IP27. . . . . .113 E1
Lakenheath Sta IP27. . . . . .113 F5
Lakes Ave NR14. . . . . .89 A3
LAKES END PE14 . . . . .95 C7
Lake View Cl NR9. . . . . .51 D5
Lake View Dr NR13 . . . . . . .165 B4
LAMAS NR10 . . . . .37 A2
Lambert Cl ❶ IP27. . . . . . . .114 E1
Lambert Rd NR7 . . . . .159 A3
Lamberts ❷❶ IP26 . . . . .98 E1
Lambert's La PE32. . . . . . . .30 D1
Lamb La NR21 . . . . .31 C7
Lammas Rd ❸ NR15 . . . . .106 F6
Lammas The IP26 . . . . .100 A4
Lamport Ct ❸ PE30. . . . . . .147 D6
Lamsey La PE31 . . . . .133 D3
Lancaster Ave NR21. . . . . .141 C5
Lancaster Cl
  Fakenham NR21. . . . . . . .141 C5
  Methwold IP26 . . . . .99 A5
  Norwich NR6. . . . . .158 D6
  ❼ Stalham NR12 . . . . .39 B4
Lancaster Cres PE38 . . . . . .172 D6
Lancaster Gdns NR11 . . . . .150 D5
Lancaster Pl ❶❶ PE31. . . . . . .12 E5
Lancaster Rd
  ❹ Feltwell IP26 . . . . .98 E1
  Great Yarmouth NR30 . . .169 D3
  King's Lynn PE30. . . . . . .147 B4
  Sculthorpe Airfield NR21. . .15 C3
Lancaster Rise 22 F8
Lancaster Sq ❶❸ NR30 . . . .169 D3
Lancaster Way PE32 . . . . . .44 F3
Lancelot Rd NR31. . . . . . . .170 A1
Lanchester Ct ❼ NR2 . . . . .162 B7
Landlow La NR9 . . . . .70 B1

Lane The Briston NR24. . . .142 D4
  Carleton St Peter NR14. . . .91 E5
  Little Barningham NR11 . . . .20 C4
  Winterton-on-Sea NR29 . . .58 B6
Lang Gate Way NR35. . . . .108 D2
LANGHAM NR25 . . . . .7 B3
Langham Ct
  Fakenham NR21. . . . . . . .141 D4
  Sheringham NR26 . . . . . .138 C7
Langham Glass & Rural
  Crafts★ NR25. . . . . .7 A4
Langham Gn NR13 . . . . . . .165 E4
Langham La NR25 . . . . .7 C3
Langham Pl NR1. . . . . .178 A1
Langham Rd Binham NR21. . .6 E2
  Blakeney NR25 . . . . .7 C6
  Field Dalling NR25. . . . . . . .7 A2
  Morston NR25 . . . . .7 A6
Langham St PE30 . . . . .146 D2
Langhorn's La PE14. . . . . . .78 A7
Langland NR25 . . . . .147 D6
Langley Cl ❻ NR4 . . . . .89 B8
Langley Gn NR14 . . . . .91 F6
Langley Prep Sch NR7. . . .163 D6
Langley Rd Cantley NR13 . . .92 C6
  Chedgrave NR14 . . . . .91 F3
  King's Lynn PE30. . . . . . .147 E8
  Loddon NR14. . . . . .92 A2
Langley Sch NR14 . . . . .91 F3
LANGLEY STREET NR14. . . .92 B4
Langley Wlk NR7 . . . . .92 A4
Langmere Rd Scole IP21 . .130 F8
  ❶ Watton IP25. . . . . .84 C3
Langton Cl ❺ NR5. . . . . . . .161 B7
LANGTON GREEN IP23 . . . .130 C1
Lansdowne Cl ❶❶ PE32 . . . . .45 C6
Lansdowne Rd NR6 . . . . . .158 B6
Lansdowne St ❹ PE30 . . . .146 E6
Lantern La NR12 . . . . .24 B5
Lapwing Cl ❸ NR31. . . . . .170 A6
Lapwing Dr NR8 . . . . .156 B5
Larch Cl
  Attleborough NR17 . . . . . .174 C4
  King's Lynn PE30 . . . . . . .148 D2
  Little Melton NR9 . . . . . . .160 D2
  Norwich NR7 . . . . .159 D4
Larch Cres NR25 . . . . .137 C7
Larch Dr
  ❶❽ Great Yarmouth NR31 . . .94 C7
  ❷ Great Yarmouth NR31 . . .170 A5
Larch Gr NR20 . . . . .49 E2
Larch Rd PE34 . . . . .43 D4
Lark Cl IP27 . . . . .175 F3
Lark Dr NR17 . . . . .174 E3
Larkey's La NR12 . . . . .38 F7
Larkman La NR5 . . . . .161 C7
Larkman Prim Sch NR5. . .161 D7
Lark Rd ❷ PE33 . . . . .61 D6
Lark Rise NR14 . . . . .89 A3
Larksfield PE13 . . . . .152 C3
Larks Pl NR20 . . . . .68 B8
Larkspur Cl PE38 . . . . .172 C3
Larkspur Ct ❽ NR19 . . . . .154 D2
Lark Way NR31 . . . . .94 C7
LARLING NR16 . . . . .118 B8
Larner's Drift NR19 . . . . . .154 D1
Larners Rd NR19. . . . . .154 D2
Larwood Cl ❶ PE37. . . . . . .66 A4
Larwood Way ❻ IP25. . . . . .67 C2
Larwood Wy NR10 . . . . .53 B4
Latchmoor La NR29. . . . . . .56 D5
Latchmoor Pk NR29. . . . . . .56 D5
Lathes The NR3. . . . . .178 A4
Latimer Rd NR1. . . . . .162 E1
Latimer Way PE37 . . . . .65 E1
Laud Cl ❷❹ NR7 . . . . .72 D4
Laughing Image Cnr ❻
  NR30. . . . . .169 C5
Launditch Cres PE38 . . . . .172 C6
Laundry Cl
  ❸ Norwich NR7 . . . . .163 E7
  Thorpe St Andrew NR7 . . .163 E7
Laundry La Blofield NR13 . . .73 B6
  Norwich NR7 . . . . .163 F7
Laundry Loke NR28 . . . . . .151 B6
Laurel Dr Brundall NR13 . . .165 D3
  Great Yarmouth NR31 . . . .94 C7
  Holt NR25 . . . . .137 D7
Laurel Gr Brundall NR13 . . .165 D3
  ❸ West Winch PE33. . . . . .43 E2
Laurel Rd NR7 . . . . .159 E1
Laurels Cres ❶ NR29 . . . . . .56 C5
Laurels Rd NR29 . . . . .56 D7
Laurels The NR31 . . . . .171 D5
Lavender Cl
  Attleborough NR17 . . . . . .174 B5
  Brandon IP27 . . . . .175 A2
  Heacham PE31. . . . . .133 E5
  Horsford NR10 . . . . .53 A4
Lavender Ct
  ❶❷ Hemsby NR29 . . . . .58 B6
  ❺ King's Lynn PE30 . . . . .147 B6
  ❶ Thetford IP24. . . . . . . .176 F4
Lavender Dr
  Cringleford NR4 . . . . .161 B1
  Downham Market PE38. . .172 C6
  ❾ Sheringham NR26 . . . . .138 C5
Lavender Gr NR19 . . . . . . .154 D2
Lavender Rd
  King's Lynn PE30. . . . . . .147 B6
  Wymondham NR18 . . . . . .173 E6
Lavengro Rd NR3 . . . . .163 A8
Lawn Ave NR30 . . . . .169 C6
Lawn Cl ❶❶ Horsford NR10 . . .53 B3

Lawn Cl continued
  Knapton NR28 . . . . .143 B1
Lawn Cres ❻ NR13 . . . . . .72 E6
Lawn's La
  Belton with Browston
  NR31. . . . . .94 A5
  Fleggburgh NR29. . . . . . . .57 B2
Lawns Loke
  Reepham NR10 . . . . .149 B3
  Stalham NR12 . . . . .39 A4
Lawns The
  Fakenham NR21 . . . . .141 C4
  Great Yarmouth NR30 . . .169 C7
  Wisbech PE13 . . . . .152 B6
Lawnswood Dr NR30 . . . . .168 D6
Lawrence Cl
  Fakenham NR21 . . . . .141 B5
  Harpley PE31. . . . . .29 D4
Lawrence Pl NR20 . . . . .50 D8
Lawrence Rd
  King's Lynn PE30. . . . . . .146 F2
  ❼ Thetford IP24. . . . . . . .176 F5
Lawrence's La PE38. . . . . . .79 E1
Lawrence Way PE37 . . . . . .153 A5
Lawson Rd Croxton IP24 . .116 C5
  Norwich NR3 . . . . .158 E1
Lawson Way NR26 . . . . . . .138 F7
Lawyer Corys NR31 . . . . . .170 C1
Laxfield Rd NR12 . . . . .39 C3
Laxton Cl NR17 . . . . .174 E4
Layer Cl ❺ Aylsham NR11 .150 D6
  Norwich NR5 . . . . .160 F7
Laylands Yd NR23. . . . . . . .136 C6
Layson Dr NR3. . . . . .158 E2
Layton Cl NR8 . . . . .157 B7
Leach Cl
  Great Yarmouth NR31. . . .170 A4
  Wisbech PE13 . . . . .152 C2
Leach's Turn NR14. . . . . . .165 B1
Leafield Rd PE30. . . . . .147 C3
Leafyoak La NR14. . . . . .90 C3
Leamon Ct IP27 . . . . .175 D4
Lea Rd ❷ NR29. . . . . .56 C8
Leaside PE31 . . . . .133 B6
Lea The NR30. . . . . .169 C6
Leatherpool La NR25. . . . . . .7 E6
Leathway NR29 . . . . .167 B2
Lea Way PE30 . . . . .147 B8
Lebanon Dr PE13 . . . . .152 F7
Leeder Hill NR13. . . . . .72 F2
Leeds Way ❺ NR12 . . . . . . .55 E4
Lees Yd NR25. . . . . .137 B6
Leete Way PE33 . . . . .43 E2
Lee Warner Ave NR21 . . . .141 D6
Lee Warner Rd ❶❶ PE13 . .153 C3
Leewood Cres NR5 . . . . . . .157 C1
Lefevre Way NR31 . . . . .94 C8
Lefroy Rd NR3. . . . . .158 A2
Legge-Bourke Ct PE13. . . .152 F6
Legge Pl ❼ PE34 . . . . .43 B1
Legrice Cres NR28 . . . . . . .151 C3
Leicester Ave PE30 . . . . . .147 B5
Leicester Rd ❶ NR31 . . . . .170 D4
Leicester St NR2. . . . . .162 C4
Leigh Cl NR17 . . . . .174 C5
Leman Cl ❽ NR14 . . . . .92 A1
Leman Gr ❾ NR14 . . . . . . .91 F1
Leman Rd NR31. . . . . .170 D2
Le Neve Rd NR10 . . . . .150 D1
Leng Cres NR4. . . . . .161 E2
Lenthall Cl ❶❽ NR7 . . . . . . .72 D4
LENWADE NR9 . . . . .51 D5
Leonard Cl ❹ PE30 . . . . . .147 B6
Leonard Medler Way
  NR10 . . . . .53 B8
Leonard's La IP26 . . . . .98 D1
Leonards St ❶❶ NR3 . . . . . .162 D8
Leopard Ct ❸ NR3 . . . . . . .178 B4
Leopold Cl ❷ NR4 . . . . . . .162 A3
Leopold Rd NR4 . . . . .162 A4
Lerowe Rd PE13 . . . . .152 E6
Les Baux Pl ❺ PE13. . . . . .152 E3
Lesley Wlk NR19 . . . . .154 D2
LESSINGHAM NR12 . . . . . . .24 D3
Lestrange PE36. . . . . .132 C4
Le Strange Ave PE30 . . . . .146 F7
Le Strange Cl NR2 . . . . . . .161 F5
LETHERINGSETT NR25 . . . . .8 A1
Letheringsett Rd NR25 . . . .18 F7
Letherington's La NR12. . . .55 D5
LETTON GREEN IP25 . . . . . .67 E1
Letton Rd IP25 . . . . .67 C2
Le Tunder Cl ❷ NR7 . . . . .163 E7
Leven Cl ❽ NR7 . . . . .72 D5
Leverington Rd PE13 . . . . .152 A6
Levers Cl PE30. . . . . .147 D8
Leveson Rd NR7 . . . . .159 B3
Levine Cl NR13 . . . . .165 A4
Levishaw Cl NR10 . . . . .36 E1
Lewis Cl Ashill IP25. . . . . . .84 A7
  Hopton IP22 . . . . .127 F6
Lewis Dr Roydon IP22 . . . . .177 A5
  Wiggenhall St Germans
  PE34. . . . . .61 A8
Lexham Rd
  Great Dunham PE32 . . . . . .47 A5
  King's Lynn PE30. . . . . . .147 E8
  Litcham PE32. . . . . .47 F4
Lexington Cl NR29 . . . . . . .167 A2
Leyland Cl IP24. . . . . .176 D6
Leys Cl NR31 . . . . .169 C1
Leys La
  Attleborough NR17. . . . . .174 D4
  Old Buckenham NR17 . . . .104 B3
  Yaxley IP23. . . . . .129 F1
Ley's La NR20. . . . . .51 C1
LEZIATE PE32 . . . . .44 D6
Leziate Dro Grimston PE32 . .45 A8

Leziate Dro *continued*
Leziate PE32 . . . .**44** F6
Leziate Heath Nature
Reserve★ PE32 . . . .**44** E6
Liberator CI
Rackheath NR13 . . . .**72** E8
23 Watton IP25 . . . .**84** F3
Liberator Cres 12 IP26 . .**98** D1
Liberator Rd NR6 . . . . . .**158** B6
Libra Ct NR7 . . . .**159** C4
Library CI NR13 . . . .**165** E6
Lichfield Rd NR31 . . . . . .**169** B3
Lichfield St NR21 . . . . . .**141** B4
Licking's Dro PE13 . . . . .**152** A2
Lifeboat Plain
18 Sheringham NR26 . . .**138** D7
6 Sheringham NR26 . . .**138** D7
Lighthouse CI
Happisburgh NR12 . . . .**24** C5
Hunstanton PE36 . . . .**132** D7
Lighthouse La PE36 . . . .**132** D6
Light La PE14 . . . .**59** D6
Lilac CI Brandon IP27 . . .**114** D4
9 East Dereham NR19 . . .**154** D2
20 Great Yarmouth NR31 . .**94** C7
4 Great Yarmouth NR31 . .**170** A5
1 Horsford NR10 . . . .**53** A3
Wisbech PE13 . . . .**152** F7
Lilac Dr Lackenheath IP27 .**113** E1
Lakenheath IP27 . . . .**113** E1
Lilac Gr NR26 . . . .**138** D4
Lilac Wood PE30 . . . . . .**147** B8
Lilburne Ave NR3 . . . . . .**158** C2
Lilian Ave NR6 . . . .**158** B4
Lilian Rd NR10 . . . .**54** A2
Lily Ave NR20 . . . .**69** B8
Lily La NR34 . . . .**111** A3
Lily Terr NR1 . . . .**178** B1
Limassol Rd NR19 . . . . .**154** C4
Lime Ave Stradsett PE33 . .**80** C8
Wisbech PE13 . . . .**152** C7
Lime CI 7 Harleston IP20 .**122** D1
Marham PE33 . . . .**63** A4
Lime Dr NR19 . . . .**154** D2
Lime Gr Gayton PE32 . . . . .**45** C6
Sheringham NR26 . . . . . .**138** D4
7 Thetford IP24 . . . .**176** D4
Lime Kiln CI
5 Cley next the Sea NR25. . .**7** E6
6 Newton Flotman NR15. . .**89** D1
Limekiln La
Houghton PE31 . . . .**29** D6
South End NR16 . . . .**106** C1
Upper Sheringham NR26. . .**138** A4
Lime Kiln La
2 Stoke Ferry PE33 . . . . .**81** A3
Thetford IP24 . . . .**176** D4
Lime Kiln Mews
9 New Catton NR6 . . . . .**158** C1
Norwich NR3 . . . .**162** C8
Lime Kiln Rd Gayton PE32 . .**45** C6
Sparham NR9 . . . .**50** F5
West Dereham PE33 . . . . . .**80** C5
Limekiln Wlk 1 NR30. . . .**169** C4
Limes Ave PE14 . . . .**59** A1
Limes CI IP22 . . . .**177** D1
Limes Rd 3 NR29 . . . .**56** C8
Lime St PE12 . . . .**41** C8
LIMES THE PE14 . . . .**59** C5
Limes The IP25 . . . .**84** A6
Lime Tree Ave
Costessey NR8 . . . .**156** F4
Long Stratton NR15 . . . . .**106** E2
Norwich NR7 . . . .**163** C7
Wymondham NR18 . . . . . .**173** D6
Lime Tree CI
Cromer NR27 . . . .**139** F4
2 East Dereham NR19 . . .**154** E6
9 Mattishall NR20 . . . . . .**68** E6
Wymondham NR18 . . . . . .**173** D5
Lime Tree Cres NR11 . . . .**66** C7
Limetree Ct
Great Yarmouth NR31 . . . .**169** C2
Taverham NR8 . . . .**155** B2
Lime Tree Rd
North Walsham NR28 . . . .**151** D5
Norwich NR2 . . . .**162** B3
Lime Tree Wlk IP25. . . . . .**84** D3
Lime Way NR31 . . . .**170** B5
Limmer Ave IP21 . . . . . .**121** C1
Limmer Rd NR31 . . . . . .**170** D4
LIMPENHOE NR13 . . . . . .**92** D6
Limpenhoe Rd
Cantley NR13 . . . .**92** C7
Reedham NR13 . . . .**92** E6
Linacre Ave NR7 . . . . . .**159** C4
Linacre CI NR7 . . . .**159** C3
Linalls Dr NR8 . . . .**156** C4
Lincoln Ave
Great Yarmouth NR31 . . . .**170** C3
Hingham NR9 . . . .**86** D5
Lincoln CI 12 NR20 . . . . . .**50** B3
Lincoln Ralphs Sports Hall
NR1 . . . .**178** C1
Lincoln Rd IP25 . . . .**84** F3
Lincoln Sq N PE36 . . . . .**132** C5
Lincoln Sq S PE36 . . . . .**132** C5
Lincoln St
Hunstanton PE36 . . . .**132** D5
Norwich NR2 . . . .**162** B5
Lincoln Way IP24 . . . . . .**176** B5
Linden CI NR18 . . . .**86** E3
Linden Gr Diss IP22 . . . . .**177** C6
Sheringham NR26 . . . . . .**138** D4
Linden Rd
Clenchwarton PE34. . . . . .**145** E5

Linden Rd *continued*
Norwich NR5 . . . .**157** C1
Linden Tree Gdns 15
NR31 . . . .**94** C7
Lindford Dr NR4 . . . .**89** C8
Lindley CI NR6 . . . .**158** E6
Lindley Rd 9 NR9 . . . . . .**88** C7
Lindley St NR21 . . . .**162** E3
Lindsay Rd NR7 . . . .**159** C4
Lineside NR19 . . . .**154** D3
Linford CI PE34 . . . .**145** D6
Linford Clapper La PE34 .**145** E6
Linford Est PE34 . . . .**145** E5
Ling CI 1 NR12 . . . .**54** C7
Ling Comm Rd PE30 . . . .**148** D6
Lingheath Rd IP27 . . . . .**175** E3
Ling House Rd PE31 . . . . . .**13** B1
Ling Rd IP22 . . . .**177** B3
Lings CI 5 NR10 . . . .**53** B3
Lings The NR9 . . . .**86** D8
LING THE NR15 . . . .**91** A1
Ling Way NR12 . . . .**54** C7
LINGWOOD NR13 . . . .**73** F3
Lingwood CI IP31 . . . . . .**127** D3
Lingwood Gdns 2 NR13 . .**74** A3
Lingwood Prim Acad
NR13 . . . .**73** F3
Lingwood Rd Blofield NR13 **73** E4
Brundall NR13 . . . .**165** F6
Lingwood Sta NR13 . . . . .**74** A3
Links Ave Brundall NR13 . .**165** F6
Cromer NR27 . . . .**139** D4
Norwich NR6 . . . .**157** F4
Links CI
Caister-on-Sea NR30 . . . .**168** E4
Norwich NR5 . . . .**157** D1
6 Thurlton NR14 . . . .**92** F1
Links Cres NR26 . . . .**138** C7
Links Rd
Great Yarmouth NR31 . . . .**171** D8
Mundesley NR11 . . . .**143** B6
Sheringham NR26 . . . . . .**138** C7
Links Way
Sheringham NR27 . . . .**10** A5
4 Thurlton NR14 . . . .**92** F1
Link The 2 IP24. . . . .**176** D4
Linmore Cres 3 IP25 . . . .**84** E3
Linmore CI IP25 . . . .**84** C3
Linn Chilvers Dr PE31 . . .**133** B5
Linnet CI 6 NR31 . . . . . .**170** A6
Linnet Cres IP27 . . . .**175** E3
Linnet Rd NR8 . . . .**156** A5
Linnets The NR5 . . . .**156** F1
Linseed Wlk PE38 . . . . . .**172** E6
Lintock Rd NR3 . . . .**158** D3
Linton CI NR7 . . . .**159** B3
Linton Cres NR7 . . . .**159** B4
Lion & Castle Yd NR1 . . .**178** B2
Lion CI NR5 . . . .**156** C1
Lion La NR14 . . . .**91** C3
Lion Rd
Buxton with Lammas
NR10 . . . .**36** E1
Palgrave IP22 . . . .**177** C1
Lion's Mouth NR11. . . . . .**10** A3
Lionwood Inf Sch NR1 . . .**163** B6
Lionwood Jun Sch NR1 . . .**163** B6
Lion Wood Rd NR1. . . . . .**163** B7
Lisbon Rd NR19 . . . .**154** C2
Lishman Rd NR7 . . . .**159** C2
Lisle Rd NR5 . . . .**160** F7
Lister CI NR31 . . . .**170** B1
Lister's Rd PE14 . . . .**77** E5
LITCHAM PE32 . . . .**48** A4
Litcham Hall PE32 . . . .**48** A4
Litcham High Sch PE32 . . .**48** A4
Litcham Prim Sch PE32. . . .**48** A5
Litcham Rd
Beeston with Bittering
PE32 . . . .**48** D4
Great Dunham PE32 . . . . . .**47** F2
Gressenhall PE32 . . . .**49** C3
Little Dunham PE32 . . . . . .**65** F8
Mileham PE32 . . . .**48** C5
Tittleshall PE32 . . . .**48** A6
Litcham Village Mus★
PE32 . . . .**48** A4
Litchmere Rd NR14 . . . . .**109** D6
Litester CI NR28 . . . .**151** D4
Little Armes St NR2. . . . .**162** A8
Little Barney La NR21 . . . .**17** F3
LITTLE BARNINGHAM
NR11 . . . .**20** C4
LITTLE BARWICK PE31 . . . .**14** E6
Littlebeck La NR15. . . . . .**108** B8
Little Bethel St NR2. . . . .**178** A2
**Little Bittering Medieval
Village of★** NR19 . . . . . .**48** F4
Little Bull CI NR3 . . . . . .**178** B4
Little Carr Rd PE30. . . . . .**148** D5
Little Church St PE13 . . . .**152** C5
LITTLE CRESSINGHAM
IP25 . . . .**83** E2
Little Dowgate PE13 . . . .**152** A7
LITTLE DUNHAM PE32 . . . .**65** E8
LITTLE ELLINGHAM NR17 . .**86** A2
Little Ellingham Rd NR9. . .**86** A3
Little Fendike La PE14 . . . .**77** E3
Littlefields NR19 . . . .**154** D5
LITTLE FRANSHAM NR19 . . .**66** B7
LITTLE GREEN IP22 . . . . .**129** B1
LITTLE HALE IP25 . . . .**67** A1
LITTLE HAUTBOIS NR12 . . .**54** B8
Little Hockham La PE14 . .**102** E2
Little Holme Rd PE34 . . . . .**41** F6
Little John Rd NR4 . . . . .**162** C1
Little La
1 Castle Acre PE32 . . . . .**46** F2

Little La *continued*
Docking PE31 . . . .**134** E4
9 Horsford NR10 . . . .**53** B3
Roydon PE32 . . . .**28** A1
Stoke Ferry PE33 . . . .**80** F3
LITTLE LONDON
Corpusty NR11 . . . .**19** E1
Marsham NR10 . . . .**36** A2
North Walsham NR28 . . . .**151** E7
Northwold IP26 . . . .**99** D7
Little London Rd
North Walsham NR28 . . . .**151** D8
Northwold IP26 . . . .**99** C7
Little London St NR2. . . . .**178** B3
Little Man's Way PE33 . . . .**81** A3
LITTLE MARSH NR25 . . . . . .**7** A1
LITTLE MASSINGHAM
PE32 . . . .**29** C3
LITTLE MELTON NR9 . . . .**160** C2
Little Melton Prim Sch
NR9 . . . .**160** C2
Little Melton Rd NR9 . . . .**160** B1
Little Money Rd NR13 . . . .**73** A8
Little Oulsham Dro IP26 . .**98** B2
LITTLE OUSE CB7 . . . . . .**112** A8
LITTLE PLUMSTEAD NR13 . .**73** B6
Little Plumstead CE Prim Sch
NR13 . . . .**73** A5
LITTLE RYBURGH NR21 . . . .**32** C7
Little Scratby Cres NR29 .**167** E4
LITTLE SNORING NR21 . . . .**17** B3
Little Snoring Prim Sch
NR21 . . . .**17** B3
Little Snoring Rd NR21 . . .**17** A5
LITTLE THORNAGE NR25. . . .**7** F1
LITTLE WALSINGHAM
NR22 . . . .**16** F7
Little Walsingham CI
PE30 . . . .**148** C3
Littlewood NR8 . . . .**155** F1
Littlewoods La NR12 . . . .**164** E5
Livingstone Rise NR11 . . . .**22** F8
Livingstone St NR2 . . . . .**162** A7
Lizard The NR18 . . . .**173** D3
Lloyd Ct NR25 . . . .**137** F8
Lloyd Rd Norwich NR1. . . .**163** B7
Taverham NR8 . . . .**155** B2
Loanin The NR1 . . . .**162** F3
Lobelia CI NR18. . . . .**173** F6
Lobelia La NR4 . . . .**89** B8
Lobelia St NR2 . . . .**178** A3
Loch La IP25 . . . .**84** D4
Lockerbie Flats 18 NR26. .**138** D7
Lockhart Rd NR35 . . . . . .**109** D3
Lock Rd NR28. . . . .**38** D6
Lock's La Dockeney NR34 . .**109** F2
Shipmeadow NR34 . . . . . .**109** F1
Locksley Rd NR4. . . . .**89** E8
Locksley Sch The NR4 . . . .**89** E8
LODDON NR14 . . . .**92** A1
Loddon NR14 . . . .**108** C7
Loddon Bsns Ctr NR14. . . .**92** A1
Loddon Cnr NR14. . . . . . .**108** C7
Loddon Ind Est NR14. . . . .**92** A1
Loddon Inf Sch 15 NR14 . .**92** A1
LODDON INGLOSS NR14. . .**109** B7
Loddon Jun Sch NR14 . . . .**91** F1
Loddon Rd
Ditchingham NR35. . . . . . .**109** B2
Gillingham NR34 . . . .**110** C2
Haddiscoe NR14 . . . .**110** D8
Heckingham NR14 . . . .**92** D1
Holverston NR14 . . . .**91** A5
Kirby Cane NR35 . . . .**109** E4
Norton Subcourse NR14 . . .**92** E1
Toft Monks NR34. . . . .**110** D7
Trowse with Newton NR14 .**163** C1
Yelverton NR14 . . . .**90** E6
Lode Ave NR14 . . . .**77** F5
Lode St IP27 . . . .**175** C4
Lodge Breck NR8 . . . .**157** A7
Lodge CI NR25 . . . .**137** B5
Lodge Dr IP22 . . . .**120** B5
Lodge Farm Dr NR6. . . . . .**158** D6
Lodge Farm Mdws NR20 . .**49** C4
Lodge Hill NR26 . . . .**138** A3
Lodge La Norwich NR6 . . .**158** E6
Riddlesworth IP22 . . . . . .**127** D7
Shelfanger IP22 . . . .**120** B1
13 Snettisham PE31 . . . . .**12** C4
Lodge Lane Inf Sch NR6 . .**158** E6
Lodge PI NR7 . . . .**163** E6
Lodge Rd Catfield NR29 . . .**56** B8
Feltwell IP26 . . . .**98** F2
Heacham PE31 . . . .**133** C5
Lingwood & Burlingham
NR13. . . . .**74** A3
St John, Ilketshall NR34 . . .**124** C6
Tivetshall St Margaret
NR15. . . . .**121** C6
Lodge Way IP24 . . . .**176** C7
Lodore Ave NR6 . . . .**158** A6
Loggers La IP22 . . . .**128** B5
Loke Rd PE30. . . . .**146** E6
Loke The
Belton with Browston
NR31. . . . .**93** F6
Briston NR24 . . . .**142** D4
Brumstead NR12. . . . .**24** A2
Cringleford NR4 . . . .**89** C8
Cromer NR27 . . . .**139** B6
East Beckham NR11. . . . .**9** D2
Felmingham NR28 . . . .**37** B8
Filby NR29 . . . .**75** E8
Freethorpe NR13 . . . .**92** E7
2 Gresham NR11. . . . .**9** E1

Loke The *continued*
Haddiscoe NR14 . . . .**110** F8
4 Hemsby NR29 . . . .**58** B6
Salhouse NR13 . . . .**55** B2
Strumpshaw NR13. . . . . . .**73** F2
Thorpe Market NR11. . . . . .**22** A7
Loke Wiffens 2 NR9. . . . . .**88** D8
Lollards Rd
1 Norwich NR1. . . . .**163** A6
Norwich NR1 . . . .**178** C3
Lolly Moor Nature Reserve★
NR19. . . . .**67** F5
Lomond Rd NR17 . . . . . .**174** F6
London La Mundford IP26 .**100** B4
South Creake NR21 . . . . . .**15** C5
London Rd
Attleborough NR17 . . . . . .**174** B3
Brandon IP27 . . . .**175** B3
Downham Market PE38. . . .**172** C4
East Dereham NR19 . . . . .**154** E4
Elveden IP24 . . . .**125** B7
Harleston IP20 . . . .**122** D1
King's Lynn PE30 . . . .**146** E4
Snetterton NR16 . . . .**103** D1
Thetford IP24 . . . .**176** B3
Wymondham NR18 . . . . . .**173** A2
London Road Ind Est
IP27 . . . .**175** B1
London St Brancaster PE31 . .**3** B7
Norwich NR2 . . . .**178** B3
Swaffham PE37 . . . .**153** C4
Whissonsett NR20. . . . .**31** D2
Londs The NR27 . . . .**11** A3
Lone Barn Rd NR7 . . . . . .**159** B2
Lonely Rd
Pulham St Mary IP21 . . . . .**122** B6
Scole IP21 . . . .**121** C2
Long Acre NR27 . . . .**10** A4
Long Barrow Dr NR28 . . . .**151** D3
Long Beach Est NR29 . . . .**167** C8
Longbow CI 3 NR4. . . . . .**162** C1
Longbrooke CI NR4. . . . . .**89** D4
Long Comm La NR10. . . . . .**37** D4
Long Dale NR8 . . . .**155** E2
Longdell Hills NR5. . . . . .**156** E2
Longdon CI 4 PE12. . . . . .**41** B8
Long Dro PE38 . . . .**97** D2
Longe Rd NR6 . . . .**158** F6
Longfellow Rd NR30 . . . .**168** D5
Longfield CI 4 NR14. . . . . .**91** F1
Longfield Gn 1 IP31. . . . .**126** B1
Longfields PE37 . . . .**153** C5
Longfields Rd NR7 . . . . . .**72** D5
Longfulans La NR31. . . . . .**171** D3
LONG GREEN IP22 . . . . . .**129** B4
LONGHAM NR19 . . . .**49** A2
Longham La NR20 . . . .**49** B3
Longham Rd NR19 . . . .**49** A2
Longhead La PE14 . . . .**59** A6
Long John Hill NR1 . . . . .**162** E2
LONG JOHN'S HILL NR1. . .**162** E2
Long La Baconsthorpe NR25 **20** A7
Bawburgh NR9 . . . .**160** B8
Burston & Shimpling IP22. .**120** E4
Catfield NR29 . . . .**56** D7
Feltwell IP26 . . . .**98** D1
Flordon NR15 . . . .**106** E8
Great Yarmouth NR31 . . . .**170** A4
Hoveton NR12 . . . .**164** F7
Mulbarton NR14 . . . .**89** B2
Saxlingham Nethergate
NR15. . . . .**107** B8
Southrepps NR11 . . . .**22** B8
Stoke Holy Cross NR14. . . .**89** F4
Strumpshaw NR13. . . . . . .**165** F2
Swaffham PE37 . . . .**153** E5
Tharston & Hapton NR15 . .**106** D6
West Winch PE33 . . . .**43** C2
Winfarthing IP22 . . . .**119** F7
Longlands Dr NR18. . . . . .**173** A6
Long Lots PE14 . . . .**59** F3
Longmead 4 NR1 . . . .**162** E2
Longmeadow NR13 . . . . .**165** B3
Longmeadow CI 5 NR5 . . . .**85** A1
Longmeadow Dr IP22. . . .**177** B5
Long Rd Barton Turf NR12. . .**55** F7
Poringland NR14 . . . .**90** C5
Saham Toney IP25. . . . .**84** F8
Terrington St Clement
PE34 . . . .**144** A8
Thurlton NR14 . . . .**93** A1
Wymondham NR18 . . . . . .**88** A1
Long Row Norwich NR3 . . .**158** D1
Tibenham NR16 . . . .**120** D6
Longs CI 4 NR15 . . . .**89** C1
Long's Cres NR13 . . . .**72** D7
Long St NR17 . . . .**103** E6
Long Straton Mill★
NR15. . . . .**106** F3
LONG STRATTON NR15 . . .**106** E3
Long Stratton High Sch
NR15. . . . .**106** E3
Long Stratton Ind Est
NR15. . . . .**106** D3
Long Stratton Leisure Ctr
NR15. . . . .**106** E4
Long Stratton Rd NR16. . .**105** F4
Longview 1 NR9 . . . .**88** D8
Longview CI 4 PE31. . . . . .**12** E4
Longwater La NR8 . . . . . .**156** D3
Longwater Ret Pk NR5. . .**156** A2
Lonsdale Cres NR9. . . . . . .**86** B5
Lonsdale Rd NR13 . . . .**72** E7
Lonsdale Terr PE13 . . . . .**152** C3
Loombe CI 3 NR20 . . . .**50** B3
Loop Rd NR11 . . . .**11** D1
Lopham Rd NR16 . . . .**118** D4
Lord Cres NR20 . . . .**50** B5

Lord Montgomery Wy 26
NR31 . . . .**94** C7
Lord Nelson CI PE32 . . . . .**48** C2
Lord Nelson Dr NR5. . . . .**156** C1
Lord Rd IP22 . . . .**177** E4
LORDSBRIDGE PE34 . . . . . .**60** E7
Lords Hill 7 NR8 . . . .**70** C7
Lord's La PE31 . . . .**133** D5
Lord's La NR31 . . . .**94** B7
Lord Walsingham Ct 1
IP24. . . . .**176** E5
Lorraine Gdns NR3. . . . . .**158** E3
Losinga Cres NR3 . . . .**158** B3
Losinga Rd PE30 . . . .**146** E7
Lothian St NR4 . . . .**162** C6
Lothingland Mid Sch
NR32. . . . .**171** A3
Louden Rd NR27 . . . .**139** B7
Louie's La IP22 . . . .**177** C6
Louis CI NR6. . . . .**158** D6
Louis Dahl Rd 3 NR31. . . . .**94** A6
Louise CI 15 NR30. . . . . . .**169** D2
LOUND NR32. . . . .**94** C1
Lound Dam NR14 . . . .**111** A7
Lound Rd
Belton with Browston
NR31. . . . .**94** B4
Norwich NR4, Ashby &
Herringfleet NR32 . . . . .**161** F5
Somerleyton, Ashby &
Herringfleet NR32 . . . . .**111** F8
Lovat CI IP20 . . . .**122** E2
Love La Fransham NR19 . . . .**66** D7
Sporle with Palgrave PE32 . .**65** C6
Wisbech PE13 . . . .**152** C4
Lovelace Rd NR4 . . . .**161** E4
Lovell Gdns IP25 . . . .**84** E3
Lovells The 6 PE14 . . . . . .**59** D2
Lovell Way PE34 . . . .**144** B4
Lovelstaithe NR1 . . . .**178** C3
Lovers' La NR29 . . . .**56** C4
Lovett CI NR5 . . . .**158** F6
Lovewell Rd NR31. . . . . . .**170** D5
Low Bungay Rd NR14 . . . .**92** A1
Low Comm
Aslacton NR16 . . . .**106** A2
Bunwell NR16 . . . .**105** E2
Deopham NR18 . . . .**86** A4
Hellington NR14 . . . .**91** B6
Reedham NR13 . . . .**93** A5
South Lopham IP22 . . . . . .**128** F7
Swardeston NR14 . . . .**89** B6
Low Comm La NR34. . . . . .**111** A5
LOW COMMON NR16 . . . . .**105** F3
Low Comm Rd
South Lopham IP22. . . . . .**128** E2
Thurton NR14 . . . .**91** D3
Low Ditch Rd IP20 . . . . . .**122** F4
LOWER BODHAM NR25. . . . .**9** A2
Lower Clarence Rd NR1. . .**178** C2
Lower Cliff Rd NR31 . . . . .**170** D4
LOWER DRAG WAY IP22. . .**128** D8
LOWER EAST CARLETON
NR14. . . . .**89** B6
Lower Espl NR31. . . . .**170** D3
Lower Globe La NR13 . . . .**165** E7
Lower Gn NR13 . . . .**92** E8
Lower Goat La 2 NR2. . . . .**178** A3
LOWER GRESHAM NR11 . . . .**9** F1
Lower Hall La NR24 . . . . . .**18** D7
Lower Hardley Rd NR14. . .**92** A2
Lower Kiln La NR15 . . . . . .**90** F3
Lower Lincoln St PE36 . . .**132** C5
Lower Marine Par NR31. . .**170** D3
Lower Oakley PE21. . . . . .**130** D4
Lower Rd Holme Hale IP25. .**66** B3
Rockland St Mary NR14. . . .**91** C7
Lower Rose La IP21. . . . . .**177** E2
Lower Spink's La NR11 . . . .**88** B4
Lower St Horning NR12. . . . .**55** E4
Salhouse NR13 . . . .**55** A1
LOWER STOW BEDON
NR17. . . . .**102** F5
LOWER STREET
Southrepps NR11 . . . .**22** C6
Wickmere NR11 . . . .**20** E5
LOWER TASBURGH
NR15. . . . .**106** E7
LOWER THURLTON NR14. . . .**93** A2
Lower Wells CI NR35. . . . .**109** A2
Lower Wood Nature
Reserve★ NR16. . . . .**105** E8
Lowes Ave NR25 . . . .**137** D5
Lowe's La PE31. . . . .**4** D4
Lowestoft Rd NR31 . . . . .**170** C1
Lowes View IP22 . . . .**177** E3
Low Farm Rd NR13. . . . . . .**75** A3
Lowfield PE30 . . . .**147** C4
Low Hatter's CI PE38. . . .**172** B3
Lowick CI 9 NR19 . . . .**154** D3
Low La Hevingham NR10. . . .**53** B8
Rocklands NR17 . . . .**103** B6
Terrington St Clement
PE34 . . . .**144** A5
Low Rd Alburgh IP20. . . . . .**122** F6
Bunwell NR16 . . . .**105** E1
Denton IP20 . . . .**123** B5
Dickleburgh & Rushall
IP21 . . . .**130** C5
Forncett NR16. . . . .**106** B5
Freethorpe NR13. . . . .**92** F7
Great & Little Plumstead
NR13. . . . .**72** B5
Grimston PE32 . . . .**28** B1
Haddiscoe NR14 . . . .**110** D7
Hedenham NR35 . . . .**108** D4

Low Rd continued
Hellesdon NR6. . . . .**157** C5
Hingham NR9 . . . .**86** B4
Keswick NR4 . . . .**89** C7
Kimberley NR9. . . . .**87** D8
King's Lynn PE30. . . . .**148** C1
Mautby NR29. . . . .**75** E5
Mettingham NR35 . . . .**109** D1
Narborough PE32 . . . .**63** F7
North Tuddenham NR20 . . . .**68** E8
Norton Subcourse NR14 . . . .**92** E2
Pentney PE32 . . . .**63** C8
Redenhall with Harleston
  IP20. . . . .**122** F1
Repps with Bastwick NR29. .**57** A4
Rollesby NR29. . . . .**57** D2
Roydon PE32 . . . .**28** A1
Scole IP21. . . . .**130** C5
Shelton NR15. . . . .**107** B1
Shropham NR17 . . . .**103** B3
Skeyton Corner NR10 . . . .**37** B6
South Walsham NR13 . . . .**74** B8
Starston IP20 . . . .**122** C3
St John, Ilketshall NR34 . . .**124** D6
St John's Fen End PE14 . . . . .**60** B6
Stoke Ferry PE33. . . . .**80** F2
Stow Bardolph PE34 . . . .**61** C2
Stow Bedon NR17. . . . .**102** E5
Strumpshaw NR13. . . . .**165** F1
Swaffham PE37. . . . .**153** A5
Tasburgh NR15 . . . .**106** E7
1 Thurlton NR14 . . . .**92** F1
Thurlton NR14 . . . .**93** B2
Tibenham NR16 . . . .**120** B8
Walpole Cross Keys PE34 . . .**42** A7
West Acre PE32 . . . .**46** C2
West Caister NR30 . . . .**168** A3
Wicklewood NR18 . . . .**87** C3
Wiggenhall St Germans
  PE34 . . . .**43** D3
Wimbotsham PE34 . . . .**172** D8
Winterton-on-Sea NR29 . . . .**58** B6
Wisbech PE14 . . . .**152** E1
Woodbastwick NR13. . . . .**55** C1
Wortham IP22. . . . .**129** A6
Wortwell IP20. . . . .**123** A3
Lowry Cl 3 NR31 . . . .**170** A7
Lowry Cole Rd NR6 . . . . . .**158** F5
Lowry Way PE38 . . . .**172** E5
Low Side PE14. . . . .**77** F6
Low's La IP22 . . . .**177** D2
Low St Hardingham NR9 . . .**86** E8
Hoxne IP21 . . . .**131** A4
Ketteringham NR18. . . . .**88** D6
Sloley NR12. . . . .**37** E3
Smallburgh NR12 . . . .**38** E3
St Margaret, Ilketshall
  NR35. . . . .**124** B4
Weasenham St Peter PE32. .**30** D2
Wicklewood NR18 . . . .**87** A5
LOW STREET NR9. . . . .**86** E8
LOW THARSTON NR15. . . . .**106** D6
Lowther Rd NR4 . . . .**162** B1
Low Wr La IP22. . . . .**129** D5
Loxwood NR6. . . . .**157** E6
Lubbock Cl NR2 . . . .**161** F5
Lubeck Rd PE30 . . . .**147** A8
Lucas Ct 2 NR7 . . . .**72** D5
Lucas La PE31 . . . .**135** E6
Lucas Rd 9 NR31. . . . .**169** B4
Lucerne Cl NR6 . . . .**158** F4
Lucerne Rd 9 NR31 . . . .**94** C6
Lucombe Dr PE13. . . . .**152** F7
Luddenham Rd NR20. . . . . .**50** B2
LUDHAM NR29 . . . .**56** D5
Ludham Airstrip NR29. . . . . . .**56** D6
Ludham Prim Sch NR29. . . .**56** C5
Potter Heigham NR29. . . . . . .**56** F5
Ludkin Sq 8 NR30. . . . .**169** C5
Lugger Yd NR23 . . . .**136** D6
Lug's La NR35. . . . .**109** B5
Luke Cl NR5. . . . .**156** F2
LUNDY GREEN NR15. . . . . . .**107** D3
Lupin Cl NR18 . . . .**173** F6
Luscombe Way 6 NR13. . . . .**72** E7
Lusher Cl 1 NR26 . . . .**138** C5
Lusher Rise NR5. . . . .**161** D8
Lusher's Loke NR7. . . . . . .**158** F4
Lushers Mdw 5 NR17. . . . .**174** C5
Lushers Meadow Wy 14
  NR31. . . . .**171** A4
Lushington Cl 9 NR5 . . . . .**161** B8
Luxembourg Way NR19 . . .**154** D3
Lydgate Cl NR19 . . . .**154** D3
Lyhart Rd NR4 . . . .**162** B1
Lynch Gn 6 NR9. . . . .**88** D8
Lyndford NR12 . . . .**39** B4
Lyndhurst NR31 . . . .**170** B7
Lyndhurst Ct PE36. . . . . . .**132** D3
Lynewood NR27. . . . .**139** D4
Lynewood Rd NR27 . . . . . .**139** D4
Lynfield Rd NR28 . . . .**151** C6
LYNFORD IP26 . . . .**100** D2
Lynford Rd IP26 . . . .**100** B5
LYNG NR9 . . . .**51** A4
LYNGATE
North Walsham NR28 . . . . .**151** A8
Worstead NR28. . . . .**38** A5
Lyngate Cl 8 NR9 . . . .**88** C7
Lyngate Ind Est NR28 . . . . .**151** A6
Lyngate Rd NR28 . . . .**151** B8
Lyng CE Prim Sch NR9. . . . . .**51** A4
Lyng Hall La NR20 . . . .**33** A7
Lyng Hall Rd NR20 . . . .**33** A7

Lyng La IP22 . . . .**118** F1
Lyng Rd NR9 . . . .**51** B5
Lynn Cl 7 NR7 . . . .**72** D5
Lynn Ct NR19 . . . .**154** E4
Lynn Gr NR31. . . . .**170** A6
Lynn Grove Acad NR31. . . . .**170** A6
Lynn La PE32 . . . .**29** D1
Lynn Mus* PE30 . . . .**146** E5
Lynn Rd
Castle Rising PE30 . . . .**148** F5
Clenchwarton PE34. . . . .**144** E5
Dersingham PE31 . . . .**140** C2
Downham Market PE38. . . . .**172** C6
East Rudham PE31 . . . .**30** A7
Gayton PE32 . . . .**45** C6
Grimston PE32 . . . .**28** B1
Heacham PE31 . . . .**133** E3
Ingoldisthorpe PE31 . . . . . .**140** C7
King's Lynn PE30. . . . .**147** A5
Littleport CB7 . . . .**96** E1
Middleton PE32 . . . .**44** D2
Roydon PE32 . . . .**28** A1
Runcton Holme PE33. . . . . . .**61** F4
Shouldham PE33 . . . .**62** D3
Shouldham Thorpe PE33 . . . .**62** B2
Southery PE38. . . . .**97** A6
Stow Bardolph PE34 . . . .**79** E8
Stradsett PE33 . . . .**80** C8
Swaffham PE37. . . . .**153** A5
Terrington St Clement PE34 .**42** A6
Tilney St Lawrence PE34. . . . .**42** D2
Walpole Cross Keys PE34. . . .**41** F6
Walsoken PE14. . . . .**59** B6
Watlington PE33 . . . .**61** E6
Weeting IP27 . . . .**175** A8
Wereham PE33 . . . .**80** D5
West Rudham PE31. . . . .**29** F6
West Walton PE14. . . . .**59** D8
West Winch PE33 . . . .**61** F8
Wiggenhall St Mary Magdalen
  PE34. . . . .**61** B6
Wisbech PE13 . . . .**152** C6
Wretton PE33 . . . .**80** F3
Lynn Rd Terr PE14 . . . .**59** D8
Lynn St PE37 . . . .**153** B4
Lynwood Terr 13 PE30 . . . .**146** E3
Lytton Rd NR8 . . . .**156** D8

M

MacArthur Dr 3 NR19 . . . .**154** C6
MacDonald Rd NR27 . . . . . .**139** A7
Mace Dr PE32 . . . .**48** D2
Mckee Dr NR16 . . . .**105** F5
MacKenzie Cl 1 NR31 . . . . .**170** B1
MacKenzie Rd IP24 . . . .**176** A3
Mackintosh Rd NR13 . . . . . .**72** E8
Mack's La NR8 . . . .**156** D7
Macks Loke NR24 . . . .**142** F2
Macmillan Way NR13 . . . . .**165** A8
Madden Ave NR30 . . . .**169** D8
Maddermarket Theatre
  NR2. . . . .**178** A3
Mad Dog La PE32 . . . .**29** C2
Maden Cl NR18 . . . .**173** B5
Magazine Cl PE13. . . . .**152** A4
Magazine La PE13 . . . .**152** A4
Magdalen Cl 3 NR3 . . . .**162** E8
Magdalen Gates Prim Sch
  NR3. . . . .**162** E8
Magdalen High Rd PE34. . . .**61** A6
Magdalen Rd
Norwich NR3 . . . .**162** E8
Tilney St Lawrence PE34. . . . .**60** D1
Wiggenhall St Germans
  PE34. . . . .**61** C7
Magdalen Sq NR31. . . . .**170** B4
Magdalen St
Norwich NR3 . . . .**178** B4
Thetford IP24 . . . .**176** D4
Magdalen Village Sch
  PE34. . . . .**61** B5
Magdalen Way NR31. . . . . .**170** B4
Magic City Leisure Ctr
  NR1. . . . .**178** C3
Magnay Rd NR8 . . . .**157** C7
Magnolia Cl
Fakenham NR21 . . . .**141** D4
Horsford NR10 . . . .**53** A4
Magnolia Dr IP27 . . . .**113** C5
Magnolia Gn 8 NR31 . . . . .**170** B6
Magnolia Wy NR8. . . . .**156** A4
Magpie Cl NR8 . . . .**156** A5
Magpie Ct 33 IP20 . . . .**122** D2
Magpie Hill IP22. . . . .**129** B5
Magpie La NR17 . . . .**103** B7
Magpie Rd NR3. . . . .**162** D8
Maida Vale 3 NR2. . . . .**162** B5
Maidens Cl 1 NR13. . . . .**72** E5
Maid Marian Rd NR4. . . . . .**162** C1
Maids Cross Hill IP27 . . . .**113** F1
Maidstone Rd NR1. . . . .**178** B3
Main Cross Rd NR30 . . . . . .**170** D8
Main Dereham Rd NR21. . . .**31** F4
Main Dr NR20. . . . .**32** E4
Maine St
  4 Thetford IP24 . . . .**116** A1
Thetford IP24 . . . .**176** A4
Main Rd
Clenchwarton PE34. . . . .**145** B5
Crimplesham PE33 . . . .**80** B6
Filby NR29. . . . .**76** A8
Fleggburgh NR13. . . . .**166** F6
Holme next the Sea PE36. . . . .**2** A5

Main Rd continued
Lingwood & Burlingham
  NR31. . . . .**74** A5
Methwold IP26 . . . .**99** A7
Narborough PE32 . . . .**63** E8
Rollesby NR29. . . . .**57** D2
Swardeston NR14 . . . .**89** C5
Tilney All Saints PE34. . . . . . .**42** E4
Upwell PE14 . . . .**77** E3
Walpole Highway PE14. . . . . .**59** E8
Weeting IP27 . . . .**175** B7
West Caister NR30 . . . .**168** A6
West Winch PE33 . . . .**61** F8
Wisbech PE14 . . . .**77** A7
Mainsail Yd NR23 . . . .**136** C6
Main St
Hockwold cum Wilton
  IP26. . . . .**113** F7
Honing NR28 . . . .**38** C6
Welney PE14. . . . .**95** D4
Malakoff Cl 9 NR30 . . . . . .**169** D2
Malakoff Rd 4 NR30. . . . . .**169** D2
Malborough Gn Cres
  NR29. . . . .**57** D4
Malbrook Rd NR5. . . . .**161** B7
Maldon Rd PE13 . . . .**152** E5
Malin Ct 7 NR30 . . . .**168** C6
Mallard Cl Brundall NR13 . .**165** E2
Chedgrave NR14 . . . .**91** F2
  7 Fakenham NR21. . . . . . .**141** E4
  9 Loddon NR14 . . . .**92** A3
  4 Salhouse NR13. . . . .**55** A1
  1 Snettisham NR31 . . . .**12** E4
Mallard End PE38. . . . .**172** B6
Mallard Rd 10 IP25 . . . .**84** C3
Mallard Way
Brandon IP27 . . . .**175** E2
Great Yarmouth NR31. . . . . .**170** A6
Hickling NR12 . . . .**39** F1
Mallard Wy NR7 . . . .**159** E5
Mallory Rd NR6. . . . .**158** D6
Mallow Cl 1 NR17. . . . .**174** B4
Mallow Rd 10 IP24. . . . . . .**176** F5
Mallow Way NR18 . . . .**173** D4
Malory Rd NR31 . . . .**170** A1
Malsters Cl IP26 . . . .**100** B5
Malt Dr PE13 . . . .**152** B3
Malthouse Cl 9 IP25 . . . . . .**84** D2
Malthouse Cres PE31 . . . . .**133** D5
Malthouse Croft PE37. . . . .**81** F8
Malthouse Ct
East Dereham NR20 . . . .**154** E5
  24 Redenhall with Harleston
  IP20. . . . .**122** D2
  8 Snettisham PE31 . . . .**12** E5
Thornham PE36. . . . .**2** D6
Malthouse Dr NR12 . . . . . .**164** E6
Malthouse La
Cantley NR13. . . . .**92** B6
Gissing IP22 . . . .**120** F4
Great Yarmouth NR31. . . . . .**170** C8
Guist NR20 . . . .**32** F4
Ludham NR29 . . . .**56** D5
Malthouse Pl NR23 . . . . . .**136** D6
Malthouse Rd
  4 Hethersett NR9 . . . .**88** C7
Norwich NR2 . . . .**178** A2
Malthouse Yd NR10 . . . . . .**149** C4
Malting Row IP31. . . . .**126** D1
Maltings Cl IP22 . . . .**177** F3
Maltings Dr 6 IP20. . . . . . .**122** D2
Maltings La 4 PE38. . . . . . .**172** A5
Maltings Way NR16 . . . . . .**119** B6
Maltmas Dro PE14 . . . .**77** A7
Malt's La IP26 . . . .**113** F7
Malvern Cl PE30 . . . .**148** D3
Malvern Rd 8 NR1 . . . .**163** A6
Manby Rd
Downham Market PE38. . . . .**172** B3
Great Yarmouth NR30. . . . . .**169** D4
Norwich NR7 . . . .**159** C1
Manchester Pl 3 NR2 . . . . .**162** C5
Mancroft Wlk 11 NR2 . . . . .**162** C7
Mandela Cl NR3. . . . .**178** A4
Mandells Ct NR3. . . . .**178** B3
Mangate St PE37 . . . .**153** C5
Mangreen NR14 . . . .**89** D6
Mangreen La NR14. . . . .**89** C5
Mann Cl NR18 . . . .**173** F7
Manning's La IP22. . . . . . .**128** B1
Mannington Hall* NR11 . .**20** C3
Mannington Pl PE30 . . . . . .**148** L1
Mann's La PE32 . . . .**50** B4
Manor Chase NR8 . . . .**156** E8
Manor Cl
  3 Aylsham NR11 . . . .**150** C6
  1 Great Yarmouth NR31 . .**170** C7
Hockering NR20 . . . .**69** B8
Horsham St Faith & Newton St
  Faith NR10 . . . .**53** D2
Ingoldisthorpe PE31 . . . . . .**140** D8
Lamas NR10 . . . .**36** E1
  4 Little Snoring NR21 . . . . .**17** B3
Tunstead NR12 . . . .**37** F1
Manor Cl Aylsham NR11. . .**150** C6
North Walsham NR28 . . . . .**151** E5
Manor Dr Litcham PE32 . . . .**48** A4
Roydon IP22 . . . .**177** A5
Terrington St John PE14. . . . .**42** B1
Manor Farm Cl NR8. . . . . .**157** A8
Manor Farm Dr NR23 . . . . .**136** D5
Manor Farm Rd
Denton IP20 . . . .**122** F8
Somerton NR29. . . . .**58** A6
St John, Ilketshall NR34. . . .**124** D7
Manorfield Cl 1 NR29 . . . .**167** A2
Manor Field Inf Sch
  NR15. . . . .**106** E3

Manor Gdns Diss IP22 . . . .**177** D5
Hopton on Sea NR31 . . . . . .**171** E4
  3 Lingwood NR13 . . . .**74** A3
Wisbech PE13 . . . .**152** A4
MANOR HOUSE PE32 . . . .**46** E2
Manor House Cl
Brandon IP27 . . . .**175** B3
Mautby NR29. . . . .**75** E6
Manor La PE31 . . . .**12** E5
Manor Pk Gdns 16 NR15. .**106** E3
Manor Rd Brandon IP27 . . .**175** A3
Caister-on-Sea NR30. . . . . .**168** F5
Cantley NR13. . . . .**92** B8
Dersingham PE31 . . . .**140** D2
Great Yarmouth NR31. . . . . .**170** C7
Griston IP25 . . . .**85** A2
Heacham PE31 . . . .**133** D8
Hilgay NR38 . . . .**79** D1
Hopton on Sea NR31 . . . . . .**171** D4
Horsham St Faith & Newton St
  Faith NR10 . . . .**53** D3
King's Lynn PE30. . . . .**148** C5
Long Stratton NR15 . . . .**106** E3
Mundesley NR11 . . . .**143** C6
Newton St Faith NR10. . . . . . .**53** D4
North Walsham NR28 . . . . .**151** E5
Roydon IP22 . . . .**177** A5
Scarning NR19. . . . .**154** A3
Stoke Ferry PE33. . . . .**80** F2
Terrington St Clement
  PE34. . . . .**144** B5
Manor Ridge NR13 . . . .**165** E6
Manorside PE31 . . . .**140** D2
Manor Way
Ormesby St Margaret
  NR29. . . . .**167** A2
Swaffham PE37. . . . .**153** C5
Manor Wlk NR25 . . . .**137** B6
Manse Ct IP24. . . . .**176** D4
Mansel Dr NR6 . . . .**158** E3
Mansell Cl 2 IP22. . . . .**177** A5
Mansell Rd PE13 . . . .**152** D3
Mansfield La NR1. . . . .**162** E1
MANSON GREEN NR9 . . . .**86** C6
Manthorpe Cl 5 NR1 . . . . .**162** E1
Mantle Cl NR7 . . . .**159** D4
Maple Ave PE13 . . . .**152** C7
Maple Cl 10 Beetley NR20 . .**49** D4
  10 Beetley NR20. . . . .**49** D4
  5 Gayton PE32 . . . .**45** C6
  20 Martham NR29. . . . .**57** D4
Wymondham NR18 . . . .**173** D6
Yaxley IP23 . . . .**129** F1
Maple Dr
King's Lynn PE30. . . . .**148** D3
Norwich NR2. . . . .**161** F7
Sculthorpe Airfield NR21. . . .**15** C3
Taverham NR8. . . . .**155** B1
Maple Gdns 17 NR31 . . . . . .**94** C7
Maple Rd
Downham Market PE38. . . . .**172** B6
  11 Elm PE14 . . . .**59** A1
King's Lynn PE34. . . . .**43** D4
Mapletree Cl 1 NR4 . . . . . .**161** C1
Great Yarmouth NR31. . . . . .**170** B6
Maple Wy 10 NR34. . . . . . .**110** D1
Mapplebeck Cl PE30 . . . . .**147** E4
Marauder Rd
Old Catton NR6 . . . .**158** D6
  24 Watton IP25. . . . .**84** F3
March La PE14. . . . .**59** E8
March Rd Elm PE14. . . . .**77** A7
Welney PE14. . . . .**95** C5
March Riverside PE14. . . . .**77** B4
Mardle Rd NR34 . . . .**110** D5
Mardle St NR5. . . . .**160** F5
Mardling Run NR13 . . . . . .**166** D3
Marea Mdws PE31 . . . .**133** D5
Margaret Cl
  3 East Dereham NR19 . . . .**154** D1
Norwich NR6. . . . .**157** D5
Margaret Cres NR7 . . . . . .**163** F7
Margaret Dewing Cl NR10 **54** B2
Margaret English Cl
  NR26. . . . .**138** C5
Margaret Lilly Way 1
  NR11. . . . .**21** A5
Margaret Paston Ave
  NR3 . . . .**158** A2
Margaret Rd NR5. . . . .**157** B2
Margaret Reeve Cl 6
  NR18. . . . .**173** D5
Margaret Rose Cl PE30. . . .**147** E4
Margarets Cl PE36. . . . .**132** D2
Margaretta Cl PE34. . . . . . .**145** F5
Margetson Ave NR7. . . . . .**163** C7
Marguerite Cl 11 NR31. . . . .**94** C6
MARHAM PE33 . . . .**63** C3
Marham Airfield PE33. . . . . . .**63** C3
Marham Cl PE34. . . . .**146** B5
Marham Rd PE33 . . . .**62** E2
Marie Cl NR13. . . . .**92** B6
Marigold Cl 6 NR1. . . . .**53** A3
Marina Leisure Ctr NR30 **169** E3
Marina Rd NR11 . . . .**143** C6
Marine Cl NR31. . . . .**170** D1
Marine Cres
Great Yarmouth NR30. . . . . .**169** E6
  5 Hemsby NR29. . . . .**58** B6
Marine Dr NR30 . . . .**168** E8
Marine Par NR31 . . . .**170** D2
Marine Rd NR31 . . . .**171** D8
Mariner's Compass
  NR31. . . . .**171** C8
Mariners La NR1. . . . .**178** B1
Mariners Pk Cl NR31 . . . . .**171** D5

Mariners' Rd NR30. . . . . . .**169** D2
Mariners Way PE30 . . . . . .**146** F8
Marion Cl NR18. . . . .**173** C5
Marion Rd NR1. . . . .**163** A6
Marionville Rd NR3 . . . . . .**158** E3
Marjoram Cl NR28 . . . .**151** E4
Marjoram Rd 24 NR31. . . . .**94** C6
Market Ave NR1 . . . .**178** B3
Market Cl NR12. . . . .**54** F8
Marketfield La NR10. . . . . . .**53** E2
Market Gates 3 NR30. . . . .**169** E4
Market Hill Brandon IP27. .**175** C3
Colkirk NR21 . . . .**31** D5
Diss IP22. . . . .**177** D4
Market La
Blundeston NR32. . . . .**171** D1
Brancaster PE31 . . . .**3** B6
Burston & Shimpling IP22 . .**120** E1
Crimplesham PE33 . . . .**80** A6
Filby NR29. . . . .**76** B7
Great Melton NR9 . . . .**70** C1
Great Moulton NR15 . . . . . .**106** C1
King's Lynn PE30. . . . .**146** D5
Little Melton NR9 . . . .**160** A2
Salthouse NR25. . . . .**8** B6
Shotesham NR15. . . . .**107** E8
Somerleyton, Ashby &
  Herringfleet NR32. . . . .**94** A1
Terrington St Clement PE34 . .**42** B6
Walpole Cross Keys PE14. . . .**41** F5
Wells-next-the-Sea NR23 . .**136** D4
Market Manor NR13 . . . . . .**166** C3
Market Mews PE13 . . . .**152** C5
Market Pl Aylsham NR11 . .**150** C6
Diss IP22. . . . .**177** D4
Downham Market PE38. . . . .**172** C5
  2 East Dereham NR19 . . . .**154** D5
Fakenham NR21 . . . .**141** B4
Great Yarmouth NR30 . . . . .**169** C4
  22 Harleston IP20 . . . .**122** D2
Holt NR25 . . . .**137** B6
  4 Loddon NR14 . . . .**92** A1
North Walsham NR28 . . . . .**151** C5
Reepham NR10 . . . .**149** B4
Swaffham PE13. . . . .**153** C4
  1 Thetford IP24. . . . .**176** D4
Westgate PE31 . . . .**135** C3
  14 Winterton-on-Sea NR39. .**58** B6
Wisbech PE13 . . . .**152** C5
  1 Wymondham NR18. . . . .**173** C4
Market Rd
Burgh Castle NR31 . . . .**94** B8
Potter Heigham NR29. . . . . . .**56** E6
Market Rd Pl 27 NR30. . . . .**169** C4
Market Row 16 NR30. . . . . .**169** C4
Market St
East Harling NR16 . . . .**118** C5
  15 King's Lynn PE30. . . . . .**146** E5
North Walsham NR28 . . . . .**151** C5
Shipdham IP25 . . . .**67** C2
Tunstead NR12 . . . .**37** F1
  18 Wisbech PE13 . . . .**152** C5
Wymondham NR18 . . . .**173** B4
MARKET WESTON IP22. . . . .**127** E4
Market Weston Rd IP22. . .**127** E3
Mark La IP27. . . . .**115** C6
Mark Lemmon Cl 2 NR4. . .**89** C8
Mark's Cl La NR9 . . . .**52** A7
Markshall Farm Rd NR14 . .**89** F7
Markshall La NR14. . . . .**89** F7
Marland Rd 4 NR8 . . . .**155** D2
Marlborough Ct PE13. . . . .**152** A4
Marlborough Rd NR3 . . . . .**162** E8
Marlborough Sq NR30 . . . .**169** E4
Marlborough Terr NR30. . .**169** E4
Marle Ct NR31. . . . .**170** C4
Marle Pit Cl NR16. . . . .**119** F7
Marl Hill Rd NR9. . . . .**51** F3
Marlinge Pl NR26. . . . .**138** F5
MARLINGFORD NR9. . . . .**70** A4
Marlingford Rd
Easton NR9 . . . .**160** A7
Marlingford NR9 . . . .**69** F4
Marlingford Sports Club
  NR9. . . . .**70** B4
Marlingford Way NR9 . . . . .**70** B5
Marlow Cl NR3 . . . .**158** F4
Marlpit La NR15 . . . .**106** F6
Marl Pit La NR5. . . . .**161** C8
Marlpit Rd
Hempstead NR25 . . . .**19** E7
Thompson IP24. . . . .**102** A7
Marram Dr NR30. . . . .**168** E8
Marrams Ave NR27. . . . . . .**139** C4
Marram Way PE31 . . . .**133** B6
Marriot Cl NR2 . . . .**162** C7
Marriott Chase NR8. . . . . .**155** E1
Marriotts Way 3 NR26. . . .**138** D7
Marriott Way NR24 . . . . . .**142** A5
Marryat Rd NR7 . . . .**159** C1
Marryats Loke 3 NR25. . . . . .**7** A4
Marshall Cl Norwich NR5. .**161** B8
  13 Spixworth NR10. . . . .**54** A2
Marshall Rd NR3. . . . .**158** B3
Marshall St 5 PE30. . . . . . .**146** E5
MARSHAM NR10. . . . .**150** D1
Marsham Prim Sch
  NR10. . . . .**150** C1
Marsh Cl 7 NR29. . . . .**57** D5
Marshgate NR28. . . . .**151** E6
Marsh La Aldeby NR34 . . . .**111** A6
Bracon Ash NR14 . . . .**89** A2
Burgh Castle NR31 . . . .**94** A8
Carlton Colville NR33 . . . . . .**111** F2
  3 Earsham NR35. . . . .**123** F4
King's Lynn PE30. . . . .**148** A1
  5 New Buckenham NR16 . .**104** F1

Marsh La *continued*
North Cove NR34. . . . .**111** B1
Somerleyton, Ashby &
  Herringfleet NR32 . . . . . .**111** C8
Tharston & Hapton NR15 . .**106** C8
Wells-next-the-Sea NR23 . **136** D5
Wiveton NR25 . . . .**7** E6
Worlingham NR34. . . . .**110** F1
Wortham IP22. . . . .**129** D4
Marshland High Sch PE14 **59** B8
MARSHLAND ST JAMES
  PE14. . . . .**60** A4
**Marshland St James VC Prim
  Sch** PE14. . . . .**60** A4
**Marshland Smeeth & Fen
  Mus**★ PE14. . . . .**60** C6
Marshland St PE34. . . . .**144** B5
Marsh Loke NR28. . . . .**23** D1
Marsh Rd Cantley NR13 . .**92** D6
Fleggburgh NR29. . . . .**75** C8
Fritton & St Olaves NR31 . . .**93** E3
Great Yarmouth NR31. . . . . .**169** B3
Halvergate NR13. . . . .**75** A1
North Wootton PE30 . . . . . .**148** A6
Outwell PE14. . . . .**77** F8
Potter Heigham NR29. . . . . . .**57** A6
Repps with Bastwick NR29. .**56** F4
South Walsham NR13 . . . . . .**74** B8
Terrington St Clement
  PE34. . . . .**144** F6
Thurne NR29. . . . .**56** E3
Upton with Fishley NR13. . .**166** B8
Walpole PE14 . . . .**41** C4
Wroxham/Hoveton NR12. .**164** D5
MARSH SIDE PE31. . . . .**3** C7
Marsh Side PE31. . . . .**3** B7
MARSH THE
  Thrandeston IP22. . . . .**129** F3
  Wortham IP22. . . . .**129** C4
Marsh The PE14 . . . .**41** C4
Marsh Wlk PE13 . . . .**152** D5
Marston La 10 NR4. . . . .**89** C8
Marston Moor 7 NR2. . . . . . .**72** D4
MARTHAM NR29. . . . .**57** D5
**Martham Broad National
  Nature Resrve**★ NR29. . .**57** D7
Martham Prim Sch NR29. .**57** D5
Martham Rd
  Martham NR29 . . . .**57** F4
  Rollesby NR29 . . . .**57** D3
  Somerton NR29. . . . .**57** E3
Martin Cl Brandon IP27 . .**175** E3
  5 Great Yarmouth NR31. .**94** C7
  Norwich NR7. . . . .**159** B4
  3 Weybourne NR25. . . . .**8** F5
Martineau La NR1. . . . .**162** F1
Martin Rd Diss IP22. . . . . . .**177** E4
  Harleston IP20. . . . .**122** E2
Marvell Gn 10 NR7. . . . .**72** D5
Marwood Cl NR18. . . . .**173** B3
Mary Chapman Cl 31 NR7 .**72** D4
Mary Chapman Ct NR3. . .**178** A3
Maryland NR23 . . . .**136** D5
Mary Unwin Rd NR19 . . . .**154** D4
Masefield Dr PE38 . . . .**172** D5
Masefield Mews NR19. . . . .**154** C7
Masefield Rd IP22. . . . .**177** E4
Masefield Wlk 8 IP24 . . . .**176** E4
Mashs Row NR11. . . . .**150** D8
Mason Gdns
  9 West Winch PE33. . . . . . .**43** E2
  11 West Winch PE33. . . . . .**43** F2
Mason Rd Norwich NR6 . .**158** B3
  5 Swanton Morley NR20. .**50** B3
Mason Road Ind Est NR6 **158** C4
Masons Dr PE37. . . . .**65** F4
Masquers Cl NR31. . . . .**170** C2
Massey Ct 2 NR21. . . . .**141** C3
Massingham Rd
  Castle Acre PE32. . . . .**46** F2
  Grimston PE31. . . . .**28** C1
  Norwich NR3. . . . .**158** B3
  Weasenham All Saints PE32 **30** B1
Mast Cl 13 NR33. . . . .**111** F1
Masters Ct NR28. . . . .**151** D5
Mather La IP20. . . . .**122** B1
MATLASKE NR11. . . . .**20** D5
Matlock Rd 1 NR1. . . . .**163** B5
Matsell Way NR19 . . . .**154** E5
Matthews Cl 4 NR15 . . . . .**106** F6
MATTISHALL NR20. . . . .**68** E5
MATTISHALL BURGH
  NR20. . . . .**68** F7
Mattishall La
  Hockering NR20. . . . .**69** A7
  Mattishall NR20. . . . .**68** F5
Mattishall Prim Sch NR20. **68** F5
Mattishall Rd
  Dereham NR20. . . . .**68** B8
  East Tuddenham NR20. . . . .**69** B6
  Garvestone NR9 . . . .**68** D2
  Honingham NR9. . . . .**69** D6
  Runhall NR9. . . . .**69** A3
Maud St NR2. . . . .**162** B6
Maud Terr NR30. . . . .**169** D6
MaureCt Dr NR13. . . . .**165** B5
Maurice Gaymer Rd
  NR17. . . . .**174** D4
**Maurice Gaymer Road Ind
  Est** NR17. . . . .**174** E4
Maurice Raes Cl 2 NR3. .**158** E1
MAUTBY NR29 . . . .**75** F7
Mautby La NR29. . . . .**75** F6
Mavish Cl NR15 . . . .**161** A6
Max Carter Cl NR28. . . . . . .**38** A4
Maybank NR28 . . . .**151** D7
May Cl NR18. . . . .**173** B5
Mayes Cl 7 NR5. . . . .**161** B4

Mayfair NR19. . . . .**67** B7
Mayfield Ave NR6. . . . .**158** B4
Mayfield Dr NR27. . . . .**139** B5
Mayfield Way NR28 . . . .**151** D7
Mayflower Ave PE30 . . . . .**146** F7
Mayflower Rd 1 PE13 . . . .**152** E3
Mayflower Way 14 IP20 . .**122** D1
Mayfly Rd PE37. . . . .**153** C2
Maygrove Rd 5 NR30. . . . .**169** D5
MAYPOLE GREEN NR34. . . . .**110** C6
Mayton Ave 2 NR12. . . . . . .**54** A4
Maze Ave 8 NR6 . . . .**70** C7
Mdws The 2 PE31. . . . .**12** D4
Mead Cl NR10. . . . .**36** E1
Meadon Way PE34. . . . .**146** A4
Meadowbrook Cl 5 NR1 **162** F3
Meadow Brown Way 9
  NR18. . . . .**173** E4
Meadow Cl
  2 Beetley NR20. . . . .**49** D4
  Cromer NR27. . . . .**139** A6
  3 Hemsby NR29. . . . .**167** A8
  Hethersett NR9 . . . .**88** C7
  Holt NR25 . . . .**137** D6
  3 King's Lynn PE30. . . . . . .**148** C5
  Mundesley NR11. . . . .**143** C5
  Narborough PE32. . . . .**63** E7
  North Walsham NR28 . . . . .**151** C6
  2 Norwich NR14. . . . .**163** B2
  Shipdham IP25. . . . .**67** D2
  5 Thurlton NR14. . . . .**92** F1
Meadow Cotts PE32. . . . . . .**48** B6
Meadowcroft NR29 . . . . . .**168** C8
Meadow Dr
  1 Beetley NR19. . . . .**49** C3
  6 East Dereham NR19 . . . .**154** C4
  1 Gressenhall NR20 . . . . . .**49** C3
  Lackenheath IP27. . . . .**113** E2
  Mundesley NR11. . . . .**143** C5
  Wroxham/Hoveton NR12. .**164** D4
Meadow Farm Dr NR4 . . . .**89** B7
Meadow Farm La NR10. . . .**53** E2
Meadowgate La PE14. . . . .**152** E3
Meadowgate Sch PE13. . . .**152** E3
Meadow Gdns NR6. . . . . . .**158** F4
Meadow Gr
  North Runcton PE33. . . . . . .**44** A2
  26 Watton IP25. . . . .**84** D3
Meadow La Briston NR24. .**142** B5
  Carbrooke IP25. . . . .**85** A5
  Kelling NR25. . . . .**8** D5
  North Lopham IP22. . . . . . .**119** A2
  North Pickenham PE37. . . . .**65** E1
  Norwich NR7. . . . .**163** F6
  5 Rollesby NR29 . . . .**57** A8
Meadowland Dr 17 NR31 . .**94** C6
Meadow Loke 2 NR20. . . . .**50** E7
Meadow Patch NR28. . . . . .**151** C6
Meadow Rd Bungay NR35 .**124** B8
  Cromer NR27. . . . .**139** B6
  Heacham PE31. . . . .**133** D5
  King's Lynn PE30. . . . .**148** C2
  Narborough PE32. . . . .**63** E7
  Norwich NR5. . . . .**157** A2
Meadowrise NR21 . . . .**15** E6
Meadow Rise NR29. . . . . . .**167** A8
Meadow Rise Ave NR2. . . .**162** A4
Meadow Rise Cl NR2. . . . . .**162** A4
Meadow Rise Rd NR2. . . . . .**162** A4
Meadows Dr NR14. . . . .**89** B2
Meadowside IP22. . . . .**128** B6
Meadows The
  Aylsham NR11. . . . .**150** C7
  17 Hethersett NR9 . . . .**88** C7
  6 Hingham NR9. . . . .**86** C4
  Shropham NR17 . . . .**103** B4
  South Wootton PE30. . . . . .**148** B2
  Thetford IP24. . . . .**176** E4
  Thurton NR14 . . . .**91** D4
Meadowsweet 13 NR10. . . .**53** A3
Meadowsweet Dr NR26 . .**138** C5
Meadowsweet Rd
  Caister-On-Sea NR30. . . . .**168** C4
  2 Wymondham NR18. . . . .**173** E4
Meadow Vale NR5 . . . .**157** A3
Meadowvale Gdns PE30. .**147** B7
Meadow View
  Brundall NR13 . . . .**165** D4
  Hockering NR20 . . . .**69** B7
Meadow View Terr NR11 **150** B5
Meadow Way
  Attleborough NR17 . . . . . .**174** C3
  East Carleton NR14. . . . . . .**88** F5
  Horsford NR10. . . . .**53** B3
  Norwich NR6. . . . .**157** F5
  Poringland NR14. . . . .**90** C4
  Sheringham NR26 . . . .**138** B6
Meadway 13 NR4. . . . .**89** B8
Mear Gdns NR1. . . . .**163** B6
Mears Cnr NR16. . . . .**105** B5
Medeswell 2 NR29. . . . . . .**167** B7
Medeswell Cl NR13. . . . . . .**165** C5
Medway Cl PE13. . . . .**152** E4
Meer Dyke La PE14. . . . .**59** D5
Meeting Hill Rd NR28. . . . .**38** A7
MEETING HOUSE HILL
  NR28. . . . .**38** B7
Meeting House Hill Rd
  NR28. . . . .**38** B6
Melbourne Rd
  North Walsham NR28 . . . .**151** D6
  4 Sheringham NR26 . . . . .**138** D7
Melford Bride Rd IP24. . . .**176** D4
Melford Cl PE30. . . . .**148** E1
Melford Comm 4 IP24 . . .**176** D4

Melford Ct 3 IP24. . . . .**176** D4
MELLIS IP23 . . . .**129** E1
Mellisash Rd IP23 . . . .**129** D1
Mellis CE VA Prim Sch
  IP23. . . . .**129** E1
Mellis Rd
  Thrandeston IP21. . . . .**129** F2
  Wortham IP22. . . . .**129** C3
  Yaxley IP23. . . . .**130** A1
Melrose Dr NR11. . . . .**10** A2
Melrose Rd NR4. . . . .**162** A3
Melrose Terr 8 NR30. . . . .**169** D2
Melton Cl NR14. . . . .**173** B6
MELTON CONSTABLE
  NR24. . . . .**142** B5
Melton Constable Hall★
  NR24. . . . .**18** D2
Melton Constable Ind Est
  NR24. . . . .**142** A4
Melton Cl NR31. . . . .**88** C8
Melton Dr
  Hunstanton PE36. . . . .**132** C3
  Taverham NR8. . . . .**155** F1
Melton Gate NR18. . . . .**173** B5
Melton Rd
  Hindolveston NR20. . . . .**33** D8
  Wymondham NR18 . . . . . .**173** B5
Melton St NR24. . . . .**142** A5
Melville Rd IP24 . . . .**116** C5
Memorial Rd NR10. . . . .**53** B4
Memorial Way
  Thorpe St Andrew NR7 . . .**72** C4
  Watton IP25. . . . .**84** D4
Memorial Wy 17 NR13. . . . .**74** A3
MENDHAM IP20. . . . .**123** A1
Mendham Cl
  36 Harleston IP20 . . . . . .**122** D2
  3 Norwich NR1. . . . .**162** E2
Mendham La
  38 Harleston IP20 . . . . . .**122** D2
  St Mary, South Elmham
    otherwise Homersfield
    IP20. . . . .**123** B3
Mendham Prim Sch
  IP20. . . . .**123** A4
Mercedes Ave PE36. . . . . .**132** D2
Merchants Ct NR27. . . . . . .**139** C7
Merchant Way NR6 . . . . . .**158** A4
Mere Cl IP25 . . . .**84** C4
Meredith Rd NR6. . . . .**157** E6
Mere Manor Ct IP22. . . . . .**177** D4
Mere Plot Dro PE33. . . . .**62** E5
Mere Rd Scoulton NR9. . . . .**85** E4
  Stow Bedon NR17. . . . .**102** E7
Mereside NR15 . . . .**90** F2
Mere St IP22 . . . .**177** D4
Mergate La NR14 . . . .**89** A2
Meridian Way NR7. . . . .**72** E3
Merlewood IP21. . . . .**121** C1
Merlin Ave NR7. . . . .**159** B4
Merlin Cl NR12. . . . .**164** D5
Merlin Mews NR7. . . . .**159** C4
Merriman Rd 5 NR29. . . . . .**57** C4
Merrivale Model Village★
  NR30. . . . .**169** E2
Merrow Gdns 7 NR4. . . . . . .**89** C8
Merryweather Cl 3
  NR15. . . . .**106** E3
Merryweather Rd 9
  PE13. . . . .**153** C3
MERTON IP25. . . . .**84** C1
Merton Ave NR31. . . . .**170** A3
Merton Rd Norwich NR2. .**162** A7
  Watton IP25. . . . .**84** D2
Mervyn King Cl NR21. . . . .**141** D4
Messenger Cl NR35. . . . . . .**124** A7
Metamec Dr NR19 . . . .**154** E3
Metcalf Ave NR3. . . . .**146** D2
Metcalf Cl 4 NR3. . . . .**157** F1
Meteor Cl NR6. . . . .**158** D7
Methuen Ave PE30. . . . . . .**147** A6
METHWOLD IP26. . . . .**99** A5
METHWOLD HYTHE IP26 . . .**98** E5
Methwold Rd
  Methwold IP26 . . . .**98** E5
  Northwold IP26. . . . .**99** C7
METTINGHAM NR35. . . . . . .**124** E8
METTON NR11 . . . .**21** C8
Metton Rd Felbrigg NR11 .**139** A2
  Roughton NR11. . . . .**21** D8
Mews Ct 7 IP25. . . . .**67** C2
Mews The
  Great Yarmouth NR31. . . .**170** C1
  4 Norwich NR2. . . . .**162** C4
Micawber Ave 2 NR30. . .**170** D8
Michaels Ct NR19. . . . .**154** C5
Midden Sta The NR23 . . . .**136** F4
Middlebrook Way
  Cromer NR27. . . . .**139** A6
  Runton NR27. . . . .**10** C4
Middle Dro Denver PE38 . . .**79** B4
  Marshland St James PE14. .**60** C2
  Stow Bardolph PE14. . . . . . .**78** D8
Middlegate NR30 . . . .**169** D2
MIDDLE HARLING NR16 . . .**118** B4
Middle Hill
  Alby with Thwaite NR11 . . .**21** A5
  Reedham NR13. . . . .**92** F4
Middle La NR34. . . . .**111** D4
Middlemarch Rd 5
  NR19. . . . .**154** D3
Middle Mkt Rd NR30. . . . .**169** D4
Middle Rd
  Blo' Norton IP22. . . . .**128** C6
  Docking PE31. . . . .**134** E4
  Earsham NR35. . . . .**123** C8

Middle Rd *continued*
  Great & Little Plumstead
    NR13. . . . .**72** F5
  Hardingham NR9. . . . .**86** E8
  Morning Thorpe NR15. . . .**107** B3
  Shouldham Thorpe PE33. . .**62** C2
  Terrington St Clement PE34 **42** B8
Middle Rd E 4 NR30. . . . . .**169** D1
Middle Rd W 3 NR30. . . . .**169** D1
Middlesex La NR13. . . . . . .**166** C3
Middle St NR11. . . . .**11** E1
Middlestone Cl NR31. . . . . .**170** C4
MIDDLETON PE32. . . . .**44** C3
Middleton Ave NR30. . . . . .**50** B4
Middleton CE Prim Acad
  PE32. . . . .**44** C2
Middleton Cl
  Norwich NR3. . . . .**158** C3
  2 Sheringham NR26 . . . . .**138** C5
Middleton Cres NR5 . . . . . .**156** E2
Middleton Ct 4 NR18. . . . .**173** B4
Middleton Gdns NR31. . . . .**170** C4
Middleton Rd NR31. . . . . . .**170** C4
Middleton's Ct NR6. . . . . . .**157** E4
Middleton's La NR6. . . . . . .**157** F5
Middleton St NR18. . . . .**173** B4
Middle Wall NR29. . . . .**57** A6
Middlewood 2 PE30. . . . . .**147** C4
Midland Cl
  Caister-on-Sea NR30. . . . .**168** F5
  1 Great Yarmouth NR30 .**169** D5
Midland Rd NR28 . . . .**151** C4
Midland St NR2. . . . .**162** C7
Midland Wlk NR2. . . . .**162** C7
Midmeadow 7 NR14. . . . . .**110** D1
Mid Norfolk Rly★ NR19 . .**154** E3
**Mid Yare National Nature
  Reserve**★ NR13. . . . . . .**165** D1
Mikanda Cl NR14. . . . .**152** C2
Mildenhall Rd CB7. . . . .**112** B3
MILE CROSS NR3. . . . .**158** A2
Mile Cross La NR3. . . . .**158** B1
Mile Cross Mid Sch NR3 **158** B1
Mile Cross Prim Sch
  NR3. . . . .**158** B2
Mile Cross Rd NR3. . . . .**162** B8
Mile End IP27. . . . .**175** A4
Mile End Cl NR4. . . . .**162** A3
Mile End Rd
  Littleport CB7. . . . .**112** A3
  Norwich NR4. . . . .**162** A3
MILEHAM PE32. . . . .**48** D6
Mileham Prim Sch PE32. .**48** D6
Mileham Rd
  Beeston with Bittering
    PE32. . . . .**48** C3
  Litcham PE32. . . . .**48** A4
Mile Rd
  Carleton Rode NR16 . . . . .**105** A5
  Garvestone NR9 . . . .**68** A1
Milestone Cl NR5. . . . .**156** F2
Milestone La NR18. . . . .**87** A4
Milford Rd 5 NR2. . . . .**162** B5
Millard Cl NR28. . . . .**151** A6
Mill Bank NR14 . . . .**59** F7
Mill Cl Aylsham NR11. . . . .**150** A6
  2 Blofield Heath NR13. . . .**73** D6
  Hempton NR21. . . . .**141** A3
  Hethersett NR9. . . . .**88** C7
  Hickling NR12 . . . .**39** F2
  Kirby Row NR35. . . . .**109** E3
  Mattishall NR20. . . . .**68** F5
  Norwich NR1. . . . .**162** E3
  Poringland NR14. . . . .**90** C5
  6 Salhouse NR13. . . . .**55** A1
  Thurton NR14 . . . .**91** C4
  Wisbech PE13. . . . .**152** C6
Mill Cnr NR9. . . . .**86** C4
Mill Comm NR14. . . . .**91** C4
MILL COMMON NR14. . . . . . .**91** C4
Mill Comm Rd NR28. . . . . . .**23** E2
Mill Cres NR13. . . . .**166** B4
Millcroft NR3. . . . .**158** E1
Mill Croft Cl NR5. . . . .**156** E1
Mill Ct Fakenham NR21. . .**141** B3
  Holt NR25 . . . .**137** B6
  Wells-next-the-Sea NR23 . **136** D5
Mill Drift
  Beeston with Bittering
    PE32. . . . .**48** C3
  Hockwold cum Wilton
    IP26. . . . .**114** A7
Mill Dro Goodestone PE33. .**81** F4
  Middleton PE32. . . . .**44** D2
  Southery PE38. . . . .**97** A5
Millennium Plain NR2. . . .**178** A2
Millennium Way PE34. . . .**146** A5
Miller Cl 7 NR19 . . . .**154** C4
Miller's Breck NR8. . . . . . .**155** D1
Millers Cl Bungay NR35 . .**124** B8
  4 Bungay NR35. . . . .**124** B8
Millers Dr IP21. . . . .**121** B1
Millers Gn 43 IP20. . . . . . .**122** D2
Millers La Harpley PE31 . . .**29** D4
  Norwich NR3. . . . .**158** D1
Miller's La
  2 Thetford IP24. . . . .**176** C4
  Wimbotsham PE34 . . . .**79** E8
Millers Rise IP27. . . . .**113** E2
Millers Sq NR17. . . . .**174** C5
Millers Way 1 NR10. . . . . . .**53** B3
Millers Wlk NR21. . . . .**141** C3
Mill Farm Nurseries
  PE37. . . . .**153** B2
Millfield Ashill IP25. . . . . . .**84** A8
  Eye IP23 . . . .**130** B1
Millfield Cl 5 NR13. . . . .**73** D6

Mill Field Cl PE14. . . . .**42** C1
Mill Field Ct 5 NR12. . . . . . .**54** A4
Millfield La PE33. . . . .**43** F3
Millfield Prim Sch NR28 .**151** B3
Millfield Rd
  Barningham IP31 . . . .**127** D3
  North Walsham NR28 . . . .**151** B4
Millfields 2 NR15 . . . .**107** C5
Millfleet 4 PE30. . . . .**146** E4
MILLGATE NR11. . . . .**150** D7
Millgate NR11. . . . .**150** D7
Millgate St IP26. . . . .**99** A5
Mill Gdns
  Bedingham NR35. . . . .**108** A3
  Horsford NR10. . . . .**53** B3
Mill Gn
  Burnham Market PE31 . . . .**135** D3
  Stoke Holy Cross NR14. . . . .**89** F4
MILL GREEN IP22. . . . .**120** E3
Mill Hill Bradenham IP25 . .**66** E3
  Bramerton NR14. . . . .**90** F8
  Brancaster PE31. . . . .**3** B6
  Brandon IP27 . . . .**175** E3
  2 Horning NR12. . . . .**55** E4
  Mettingham NR35. . . . .**109** D1
  Norwich NR3. . . . .**158** E2
  Roughton NR11. . . . .**139** A1
  Salhouse NR13. . . . .**55** B1
  Strumpshaw NR13. . . . .**73** F2
Millhill La NR18. . . . .**86** F2
Mill Hill Rd Boughton PE33. **80** F5
  Norwich NR2. . . . .**162** B5
Mill Houses PE30. . . . .**146** F6
Millicent Oliver Cl 11
  IP24. . . . .**176** D7
Millington Ct 6 IP24 . . . . .**176** D4
Mill La Acle NR13. . . . .**166** C3
  All Saints & St Nicholas, South
    Elmham IP20 . . . .**123** E1
  Aslacton NR15. . . . .**106** A1
  Attleborough NR17 . . . . . .**174** F7
  Aylsham NR11. . . . .**150** A6
  Bacton/Walcott NR12. . . . . .**23** E4
  Barnham IP24 . . . .**125** E6
  Bircham PE31. . . . .**13** F3
  Blackborough End PE32 . . . .**44** C1
  Briston NR24. . . . .**142** F3
  Brooke NR15. . . . .**108** A8
  Burnham Thorpe PE31. . . . . .**4** D4
  Carbrooke IP25. . . . .**85** B4
  Catfield NR29. . . . .**56** C7
  Claxton NR14. . . . .**91** E6
  Clenchwarton PE34. . . . . . .**145** F6
  Crimplesham PE33. . . . .**80** B7
  Cromer NR27. . . . .**10** B5
  Dereham NR19 . . . .**154** A8
  Docking PE31. . . . .**134** E4
  Downham Market PE38. . . .**172** D7
  Ellingham NR35. . . . .**109** E3
  Felthorpe NR10. . . . .**155** C8
  Fleggburgh NR29. . . . .**57** B1
  Foulsham NR20. . . . .**33** D4
  Garboldisham IP22. . . . . . .**128** A7
  Great Ellingham NR17. . . .**103** D7
  Great Massingham PE32. . . .**29** D2
  Great Yarmouth NR31. . . . .**94** C7
  Haddiscoe NR14 . . . .**110** D8
  Hindringham NR21. . . . .**17** E3
  Hockering NR20. . . . .**69** B7
  Hockwold cum Wilton
    IP26. . . . .**114** A7
  Hoe NR20 . . . .**49** D3
  Honingham NR9. . . . .**69** E6
  Hopton IP22 . . . .**127** F7
  Horsford NR10. . . . .**53** B3
  Horsham St Faith & Newton St
    Faith NR10. . . . .**53** E2
  Keswick NR4. . . . .**89** D7
  King's Lynn PE30. . . . .**147** B8
  Kirby Bedon NR14. . . . .**90** E7
  Long Stratton NR15. . . . . .**106** F3
  Morley NR18. . . . .**87** A3
  Newton Flotman NR15 . . . .**89** E2
  Norwich NR3. . . . .**162** E8
  Ormesby St Margaret with
    Scratby NR29 . . . .**58** A1
  Ovington IP25. . . . .**84** E5
  Postwick with Witton NR13. .**73** A3
  Pulham Market IP21. . . . . .**121** E5
  Redgrave IP22. . . . .**128** E5
  Repps with Bastwick NR29. .**57** B3
  Rickinghall Inferior IP22. . .**128** D2
  Rocklands NR17 . . . .**103** C7
  Seething NR15. . . . .**91** C1
  Shelton NR15. . . . .**122** B8
  1 Southery PE38. . . . .**97** B5
  St John, Ilketshall NR34. . .**124** E6
  14 Sutton Bridge PE12. . . . .**41** B8
  Swaffham PE37. . . . .**153** C3
  Syderstone PE31. . . . .**15** B3
  Thetford IP24. . . . .**176** D3
  Tilney St Lawrence PE34. . . .**42** C2
  Tunstead NR12 . . . .**38** A3
  Walpole Highway PE14. . . . .**59** F7
  Walsingham NR22. . . . .**16** F8
  West Walton PE14. . . . .**59** C8
  Weybread IP21. . . . .**131** F7
  Woodton NR35. . . . .**108** B4
  Wreningham NR16 . . . .**88** D1
  Yaxham NR19. . . . .**68** B5
Mill Loke 4 NR12. . . . .**55** E4
Millmarsh Dro IP27. . . . . . .**113** D2
Mill Orch IP21. . . . .**121** E5
Mill Pightle NR11. . . . .**150** B6
Mill Pool La NR35. . . . .**109** D2

Mill Rd Alburgh IP20 . . . .**122** E6
Aldborough NR11 . . . .**21** A6
All Saints South Elmham
IP19 . . . .**124** B1
Ashby St Mary NR14 . . . .**91** C4
Aylsham NR11 . . . .**150** C6
Bacton NR28 . . . .**23** A1
Banham NR16 . . . .**119** D7
Barnham Broom NR9 . . . .**69** B2
Barningham IP31 . . . .**127** C3
Barton Turf NR12 . . . .**38** E1
Bergh Apton NR14 . . . .**91** C4
Bintree NR20 . . . .**33** A2
Blofield Heath NR13 . . . .**73** D6
Botesdale IP22 . . . .**128** F2
Brancaster PE31 . . . .**3** B6
Briston NR24 . . . .**142** F3
Brockdish IP21 . . . .**131** B7
Burgh Castle NR31 . . . .**94** A7
Burgh St Peter NR34 . . . .**111** B4
Burnham Market PE31 . . . .**135** E4
Burston & Shimpling IP22 . . . .**120** E2
Carleton Rode NR16 . . . .**105** A4
Colby NR11 . . . .**36** F7
Coltishall NR12 . . . .**54** C6
Cromer NR27 . . . .**139** C5
Dersingham PE31 . . . .**140** F5
Dilham NR28 . . . .**38** D4
East Ruston NR12 . . . .**24** A4
Emneth PE14 . . . .**59** D2
Forncett NR16 . . . .**106** B3
Foxley NR20 . . . .**50** D8
Freethorpe NR13 . . . .**92** F8
Frettenham NR12 . . . .**54** A4
Great Yarmouth NR31 . . . .**169** B3
Gresham NR11 . . . .**9** D1
Halvergate NR13 . . . .**74** F1
Hardingham NR9 . . . .**86** E8
Harpley PE31 . . . .**29** D4
Hempnall NR15 . . . .**107** C5
Hemsby NR29 . . . .**58** A4
7 Hethersett NR9 . . . .**88** C7
Honington IP31 . . . .**126** D1
Kirby Bine NR35 . . . .**109** D3
Lakenheath IP27 . . . .**113** E1
Little Melton NR9 . . . .**160** B2
Loddon NR14 . . . .**92** A1
Long Stratton NR15 . . . .**107** A2
Marlingford NR9 . . . .**70** A3
Marsham NR10 . . . .**36** C2
Mattishall NR20 . . . .**68** E6
Mautby NR29 . . . .**75** D7
North Walsham NR28 . . . .**151** D3
Old Buckenham NR17 . . . .**104** C1
Potter Heigham NR29 . . . .**56** F5
Reedham NR13 . . . .**93** A5
Reepham NR10 . . . .**149** B2
Repps with Bastwick NR29 . . .**57** A4
Ryburgh NR21 . . . .**32** C6
Salhouse NR13 . . . .**55** A1
Shelton NR15 . . . .**122** B8
Shipdham IP25 . . . .**67** B2
Shouldham Thorpe PE33 . . . . .**62** C3
Stalham NR12 . . . .**39** A3
Stoke Holy Cross NR14 . . . . . .**89** F4
Stokesby with Herringby
NR29 . . . .**75** A6
Surlingham NR14 . . . .**91** B8
Sutton NR12 . . . .**39** C3
Terrington St John PE14 . . . . . .**42** B1
Thelnetham IP22 . . . .**128** B5
Thompson IP24 . . . .**102** A4
Thurlton NR14 . . . .**110** D8
Tibenham NR16 . . . .**120** D8
Tivetshall St Mary NR15 . . . . .**121** B5
Topcroft NR35 . . . .**107** F4
Walpole St Andrew PE14 . . . . .**41** E3
Watlington PE34 . . . .**61** D8
Watton IP25 . . . .**84** D3
Wells-next-the-Sea NR23 . . . .**136** B5
West Walton PE14 . . . .**59** B8
Weybread IP21 . . . .**131** F8
Whissonsett NR20 . . . .**31** D2
Wiggenhall St Germans
PE34 . . . .**43** C1
Wiggenhall St Mary Magdalen
PE34 . . . .**61** B5
Winfarthing IP22 . . . .**120** B4
Mill Rd S IP22 . . . .**128** F2
Mill Reach NR10 . . . .**36** F1
Mill Row NR11 . . . .**150** D7
Mills Cl NR8 . . . .**155** C1
Millside Hales NR14 . . . .**109** F8
Stalham NR12 . . . .**39** B3
Mill St Bradenham IP25 . . . . .**66** E3
Elsing NR20 . . . .**50** F4
Gimingham NR11 . . . .**22** E7
Holt NR25 . . . .**137** B6
Horsham St Faith NR10 . . . . . .**53** E2
Lamas NR10 . . . .**36** F1
Mattishall NR20 . . . .**68** F5
3 Necton PE37 . . . .**65** F4
Swanton Morley NR20 . . . .**50** E4
MILL STREET NR20 . . . .**50** E4
Millview NR29 . . . .**167** A3
Mill View
Barnham Broom NR9 . . . .**69** B2
Saham Toney IP25 . . . .**84** C5
Sedgeford PE36 . . . .**13** A7
Mill View Cl NR11 . . . .**143** D5
Millway NR18 . . . .**173** B6
Mill Way PE14 . . . .**77** B8
Millway Ave IP22 . . . .**177** C6
Millway La Palgrave IP22 . . .**177** B2
Wortham IP22 . . . .**129** D5

Milner Rd PE13 . . . .**152** C4
Milnes Way 3 NR33 . . . .**111** F1
Milton Ave PE30 . . . .**146** F5
Milton Cl
East Dereham NR19 . . . .**154** C7
Norwich NR1 . . . .**162** E3
3 Thetford IP24 . . . .**176** E6
Milton Dr NR14 . . . .**92** A1
Milton Rd
Great Yarmouth NR30 . . . .**169** D8
8 Swanton Morley NR20 . . . .**50** B3
Milton Way 1 PE38 . . . .**172** D6
Milverton Rd 1 NR1 . . . . . .**162** F3
Mindhams Yd NR23 . . . .**136** C6
Mingay Rd IP24 . . . .**176** B2
Minion Cl 8 NR7 . . . .**72** D4
Minns Cres 17 NR14 . . . .**90** C5
Minsmere Rd 7 NR31 . . . . . .**94** A6
Minster Cl PE30 . . . .**147** C5
Minstergate IP24 . . . .**176** C4
Miriam Cl NR29 . . . .**168** E8
Misburgh Way NR31 . . . . . .**171** E4
MISERY CORNER IP20 . . . . . .**122** F8
Mission Cl IP22 . . . .**177** F3
Mission La Docking PE31 . . . .**134** E4
Fakenham NR21 . . . .**141** E4
Mission Pl NR30 . . . .**169** D6
Mission Rd Diss IP22 . . . .**177** F3
Rackheath NR13 . . . .**72** E8
Mitchell Cl 10 IP26 . . . .**98** D1
Mitchell Ct 4 NR5 . . . .**160** F8
Mitchell Dr NR31 . . . .**169** B2
Mitre Ct NR3 . . . .**158** A3
Mitre Tavern Yd 4
NR28 . . . .**151** C5
Mitre Yd 9 NR28 . . . .**151** C5
Moat Rd
3 Great Yarmouth
NR30 . . . .**169** C5
Terrington St Clement
PE34 . . . .**144** B1
Modney Bridge Rd PE38 . . . .**96** F8
Mokyll Croft NR8 . . . .**155** D2
Moles La NR34 . . . .**124** D5
Molls Dro PE14 . . . .**77** C7
Monastery The NR3 . . . .**178** B3
Money Bank PE13 . . . .**152** E4
Moneyhill La NR9 . . . .**86** C3
Moneypot La IP22 . . . .**128** E5
Monkhams Dr 9 IP25 . . . . . .**84** E3
Monks Cl PE31 . . . .**14** D5
Monksgate IP24 . . . .**176** B4
Monkton Wy PE30 . . . .**147** C3
Mons Ave NR1 . . . .**163** A8
Montagu Cl PE30 . . . .**147** C3
Montagu Dr 4 IP27 . . . .**114** E1
Montague Rd NR26 . . . .**138** C7
Montcalm Rd NR1 . . . .**163** B6
Mont Cross 8 NR8 . . . .**155** D2
Montgomery Cl 2 NR5 . . . .**160** F7
Montgomery Way PE30 . . . .**147** D4
Montpelier Dr 1 IP24 . . . . .**116** A1
Montrose Ct 1 NR7 . . . .**72** D4
Monument Rd NR30 . . . .**170** E7
Moorditch La PE34 . . . .**42** E2
Moore Ave NR6 . . . .**158** F5
Moorend La NR21 . . . .**32** D7
Moorfield Rd 3 NR20 . . . . . .**68** E6
MOORGATE NR19 . . . .**154** D3
Moorgate Rd
East Dereham NR19 . . . .**154** D3
Hindringham NR21 . . . .**17** E8
Moorhen Cl NR7 . . . .**159** D5
Moorhouse Cl NR10 . . . .**149** C5
Moorings The PE33 . . . .**81** A2
Moor La Cranworth IP25 . . . . .**85** D7
Elsing NR20 . . . .**50** F3
Fransham NR19 . . . .**66** A7
Sculthorpe NR21 . . . .**16** B2
Stalham NR12 . . . .**39** C3
Moorland Cl NR7 . . . .**159** A2
Moorlands CE Prim Acad
NR31 . . . .**94** A5
Moorland Way 3 NR31 . . . . .**94** A5
Moor Rd
Burston & Shimpling
IP21 . . . .**121** B2
Stalham NR12 . . . .**39** C3
Moors The NR8 . . . .**155** C2
Moor The NR10 . . . .**149** E5
Morar Dr NR17 . . . .**174** E6
Morello Cl NR4 . . . .**161** E5
Morgans Way NR10 . . . .**53** C8
Morgan Way NR5 . . . .**160** F8
Morgrove La NR29 . . . .**167** D6
Morley CE Prim Sch NR18 **87** A2
Morleyfield La NR18 . . . .**87** A3
Morley Rd Beighton NR13 . . . .**74** D2
Deopham NR18 . . . .**86** E1
Sheringham NR26 . . . .**138** D6
Morley Rd N NR26 . . . .**138** D6
MORLEY ST BOTOLPH
NR18 . . . .**87** B2
Morleys Leet PE30 . . . .**146** D1
Morley St NR3 . . . .**162** F8
Mormor La IP21 . . . .**131** C8
MORNINGTHORPE NR15 . . .**107** A3
Mornington Rd NR2 . . . .**162** A4
Morris Cl 3 Norwich NR5 . .**161** B8
3 Stoke Holy Cross NR14 . .**89** F4
Morris Dr NR3 . . . .**165** A8
Morrison Cl NR28 . . . .**151** B5
Morris Rd NR28 . . . .**151** B4
Morris St NR26 . . . .**138** D7
Morse Ave NR1 . . . .**163** C7
Morse Cl Brundall NR13 . . . .**165** D3

Morse Cl continued
Great Witchingham NR9 . . . .**51** D5
Morse Ct NR30 . . . .**168** D6
Morse Rd NR1 . . . .**163** C7
MORSTON NR25 . . . .**7** B6
Morston Chase NR25. . . . .**6** F6
Morston Rd Blakeney NR25 . .**7** C6
Stiffkey NR23. . . . .**6** D6
Mortimer Cl NR17. . . . .**174** F6
MORTON NR9 . . . .**52** A4
Morton Cl 1 NR11. . . . .**150** D6
Morton Cres 22 NR31 . . . . . .**94** C7
Morton La NR9 . . . .**51** F3
Morton Peto Cl NR32 . . . . . .**111** D7
Morton Peto Rd NR31. . . . . .**170** B8
Morton Rd NR11. . . . .**150** D6
Mosely Ct NR5. . . . .**160** E8
Mosquito Cl 20 IP25 . . . .**84** F3
Mossfield Cl NR1. . . . .**163** B8
Mother Julian Cl 8
IP24. . . . .**176** D7
Mother Quy's IP24 . . . .**115** C1
Mottram Cl NR5 . . . .**161** D6
Motum Rd NR5 . . . .**161** C7
Moughton Ct 12 PE33 . . . . . .**43** F2
Moulton Rd
Halvergate NR13 . . . .**74** F1
Tivetshall St Margaret
NR15. . . . .**121** A7
MOULTON ST MARY
NR13. . . . .**74** D2
Mountain's Rd 2 NR11. . . . .**19** F1
Mountbatten Cl 5 IP24. . . .**176** E6
Mountbatten Dr
2 East Dereham NR19 . . . . . .**154** C6
Old Catton NR6 . . . .**159** A6
Wisbech PE13 . . . .**152** A7
Mountbatten Rd
Bungay NR35. . . . .**124** A7
Dersingham PE31 . . . .**140** C3
Mountbatten Way NR30 . . .**168** D6
Mount Cl Brandon IP27. . . . .**175** D2
Swaffham PE37 . . . .**153** A5
Mount Dr PE13 . . . .**152** E4
Mounteney Cl NR7. . . . .**159** A4
Mountergate NR1. . . . .**178** B2
Mountfield Ave
Hellesdon NR6. . . . .**157** F4
Norwich NR6. . . . .**158** A4
Mount Pk Cl PE32. . . . .**44** C3
MOUNT PLEASANT
NR17. . . . .**103** C5
Mount Pleasant
Diss IP22. . . . .**177** D5
Little Walsingham NR22 . . . . . .**16** F8
Norwich NR2. . . . .**162** B4
Mount Pleasant Dr 12
NR16 . . . .**118** C5
Mount Pleasant Rd PE13 . . .**152** C7
Mount Rd IP27 . . . .**175** D2
Mounts Pit La IP27 . . . .**175** D3
Mount St Cromer NR27. . . . .**139** B7
Diss IP22. . . . .**177** D5
King's Lynn PE30 . . . .**146** F4
Mount Surrey 4 NR18 . . . . .**173** C6
Mount Tumbledown Cl 7
PE12 . . . .**41** B8
Mousehold Ave NR3 . . . .**163** A8
Mousehold Inf Sch NR3 .**162** F8
Mousehold La NR7. . . . .**159** A3
Mousehold St NR3. . . . .**178** C4
Mowles Rd NR20. . . . .**68** C8
Moyse's Bank
Emneth Hungate PE14 . . . . . .**59** F2
Marshland St James PE14 . . . .**60** A2
Muck La NR13 . . . .**72** F8
Muckleburgh Collection
The★ NR25. . . . .**8** E6
MUCKLETON NR31. . . . .**3** F2
Mudd's Dro PE14 . . . .**77** F2
Mud Rd NR21. . . . .**15** D2
Muir La NR15. . . . .**106** B2
MULBARTON NR14. . . . .**89** B3
Mulbarton Jun Sch NR14 .**89** B3
Mulberry Cl
17 Feltwell IP26. . . . .**98** E1
6 Norwich NR3. . . . .**178** A3
Mulberry Ct 2 NR8. . . . .**155** B2
Mulberry Gr 4 NR31. . . . . . .**94** C6
Mulberry La NR15. . . . .**107** A3
Mulberry Rd PE30. . . . .**147** D4
Mulberry Tree Cl NR29. . . . .**75** F8
Mullicourt Rd PE14 . . . .**78** B6
Mumby's Dro PE14. . . . .**77** E1
MUNDESLEY NR11. . . . .**143** B5
Mundesley Hospl NR11 . .**22** F7
Mundesley Jun & Fst Sch
NR11. . . . .**143** B5
Mundesley Maritime Mus★
NR11. . . . .**143** C6
Mundesley Rd
Gimingham NR11. . . . .**22** E7
North Walsham NR28 . . . .**151** C5
Overstrand NR27. . . . .**11** A3
Paston NR28 . . . .**143** D3
Trimingham NR11 . . . .**11** E1
Trunch NR28 . . . .**22** F5
MUNDFORD IP26 . . . .**100** B4
Mundford CE Prim Acad
IP26 . . . .**100** B4
Mundford Rd
Thetford IP24 . . . .**176** C6
Weeting-with-Broomhill
IP27 . . . .**175** D7
MUNDHAM NR14. . . . .**91** C1
Mundham La NR14. . . . .**91** D2
Mundham Rd Loddon NR14 .**91** E1

Mundham Rd continued
Mundham NR14. . . . .**109** A8
Mundy's Rd IP20 . . . .**123** A1
Munhaven Cl NR11. . . . .**143** C5
Munnings Cl NR14. . . . .**89** D4
Munnings Rd NR7 . . . .**159** D5
Munson's La IP26. . . . .**98** E2
Munson's Pl IP26 . . . .**98** E2
Murgot's La PE33 . . . .**81** D7
Muriel Kenny Ct 10 NR9. . .**88** C7
Muriel Rd NR2. . . . .**162** A4
Muriel Way IP25. . . . .**85** B4
Murrayfield Rd NR6. . . . .**158** B5
Museum Sq PE13 . . . .**152** C5
Music House La NR1. . . . . . .**178** B2
Musketeer Way 29 NR7 . . .**72** D4
Mus of the Broads The★
NR12. . . . .**39** B3
Muspole St NR3 . . . .**178** A4
MUSTARD HYRN NR29. . . . . .**57** C5
Musticott Pl PE13. . . . .**152** F6
Mutford Gn IP27. . . . .**113** E2
Myles Way PE13 . . . .**152** C8
Myrtle Ave Costessey NR8 .**156** F3
East Dereham NR19 . . . .**154** E4
Myrtle Cl NR31 . . . .**170** C6
Myrtle Rd NR9 . . . .**88** C8

N

Naber Furlong 1 NR8. . . . . .**155** E2
Napier Cl PE30 . . . .**147** C5
Napier Pl Norwich NR2. . . . .**162** C7
Thetford IP24 . . . .**176** A1
Napier Wy NR19 . . . .**154** F3
Naples Cl NR31 . . . .**171** E4
Napoleon Pl 9 NR30. . . . . . .**169** D3
Napthans La NR34. . . . .**79** D8
NARBOROUGH PE32 . . . .**63** E7
Narborough CE Prim Sch
Narborough PE32 . . . .**63** E7
Winterton-on-Sea NR29 . . . . .**58** B6
Narborough Hill PE33. . . . . . .**63** E2
Narborough Rd PE32. . . . .**63** D8
Narford La PE32 . . . .**45** F3
Narford Rd PE32. . . . .**63** F7
NARROWGATE CORNER
NR29 . . . .**57** C2
Narrows Trading Est The
PE30. . . . .**147** A1
Naseby Way 23 NR7. . . . .**72** D4
Nash Rd NR10. . . . .**155** C8
Nash's La NR24 . . . .**23** E1
Nasmith Rd NR4. . . . .**161** E3
Natterers Rd NR9 . . . .**88** C8
Naylor Rd 1 NR3. . . . .**157** F1
Neale Cl NR11 . . . .**150** B6
Neatherd High Sch NR20 **154** F5
Neatherd Moor NR20 . . . . . .**154** F6
Neatherd Rd NR19 . . . .**154** E5
NEATISHEAD NR12. . . . .**55** C5
Neatishead CE Primary Sch
NR12. . . . .**55** D7
Neatishead Rd NR12 . . . .**55** C5
NEATON IP25 . . . .**84** E4
NECTON PE37 . . . .**65** F4
Necton CE Prim Sch PE37 **66** A4
Necton Rd PE32 . . . .**65** E7
NEEDHAM IP20. . . . .**131** D8
Needham Bank PE14. . . . .**77** C8
Needham Rd IP20 . . . .**122** C1
Neil Ave NR25 . . . .**137** B5
Neilsen Cl NR23. . . . .**136** C6
Nelonde Dr 1 NR18. . . . . . .**173** C5
Nelson Ave PE38. . . . .**172** B6
Nelson Bsns Ctr PE30. . . . . .**146** E8
Nelson Cl Bradenham IP25. . .**66** E3
Harleston IP20 . . . .**122** D3
4 Hethersett NR9 . . . .**88** E8
20 Poringland NR14 . . . .**90** C5
Nelson Cres PE37 . . . .**153** D3
Nelson Ct IP25 . . . .**84** D4
Nelson Dr
Hunstanton PE36. . . . .**132** D3
Plumstead Green NR13. . . . . .**165** A8
Nelson Gdns PE13 . . . .**152** D6
Nelson Hts NR27. . . . .**139** A7
Nelson Inf Sch NR2. . . . . .**162** B7
Nelson Pl 3 NR19 . . . .**154** D5
Nelson Rd
Caister-on-Sea NR30. . . . .**168** F4
Diss IP22. . . . .**177** F4
Fakenham NR21 . . . .**141** B4
Great Yarmouth NR31 . . . . . .**170** D4
North Walsham NR28 . . . .**151** D5
Sheringham NR26 . . . .**138** F7
Nelson Rd Central NR30. . . .**169** D3
Nelson Rd N NR30 . . . .**169** D5
Nelson Rd S NR30 . . . .**169** D2
Nelson's Loke NR17. . . . .**103** D6
Nelson St
King's Lynn PE30 . . . .**146** D4
Norwich NR2. . . . .**162** B7
Nelson Way
Hevingham NR10. . . . .**53** B8
Mundesley NR11 . . . .**143** A7
7 North Walsham NR28 . . . .**151** C5
Nene Cty Inf Sch PE13 . . . . .**152** D4
Nenelands PE12. . . . .**41** C8
Nene Mdws PE12 . . . .**41** C8
Nene Par PE13. . . . .**152** B6
Nene Quay PE13 . . . .**152** C5
Nene Rd Hunstanton PE36. . .**132** C4
4 Watlington PE33 . . . .**61** D6
Neptune Cl 25 NR31. . . . .**94** C4
Netherby Dr PE14. . . . .**152** F1

Nethergate St
Ditchingham NR35. . . . .**124** A8
Harpley PE31. . . . .**29** C4
Hopton IP22 . . . .**127** E6
Nether Row IP24 . . . .**176** D3
Netherwood Gn NR1. . . . . . .**162** F2
Nettle Hill E 15 NR30. . . . . .**169** D4
Nettle Hill W 15 NR30. . . . .**169** D4
Nettle Hill NR30. . . . .**169** D4
Neve's Cl NR13 . . . .**73** F3
Neville Cl
East Dereham NR19 . . . .**154** E1
Norwich NR7. . . . .**158** F3
Saham Toney IP25 . . . .**84** B5
Neville La PE31. . . . .**133** C6
Neville Rd Heacham PE31. . .**133** C6
Norwich NR7. . . . .**159** A3
Stalham NR12 . . . .**39** C3
Neville St NR2. . . . .**162** C5
Newall Rd 3 IP24 . . . .**125** F6
Newarch La NR14. . . . .**90** E7
Newark Cl 22 NR7. . . . .**72** D4
Newarp Way NR30. . . . .**168** D8
Newbegin Cl NR1 . . . .**163** C7
Newbegin Rd NR1. . . . .**163** B7
New Bridge La Elm PE14 . . . .**59** A1
Wisbech PE13 . . . .**152** A1
New Bridge Rd PE14. . . . .**77** D5
NEW BUCKENHAM NR16. . .**104** F8
Newbury Way 20 NR7 . . . . .**72** D4
Newby Rd 2 PE30 . . . .**147** D6
Newcastle Cl 3 NR7. . . . .**72** D4
Newcastle Rd NR30. . . . .**169** D1
NEW CATTON NR3 . . . .**158** D1
New Coll Cl NR31. . . . .**170** B5
Newcombe Cl PE14 . . . .**42** B1
Newcombe Dr 15 IP26 . . . . .**98** E3
New Comm Rd IP22 . . . .**127** F4
New Conduit St PE30. . . . . .**146** D5
NEW COSTESSEY NR5 . . . . .**157** A1
New Dro 3 PE13 . . . .**152** D2
New Eccles Hall Sch The
NR16. . . . .**118** F7
Newell Cresent NR27. . . . . . .**10** A6
New England Way 2
IP24. . . . .**116** A1
Newey's Way 2 IP22. . . . . . .**164** C5
New Fen Dro PE38 . . . .**97** A5
Newfen Gravel Dro IP27 .**113** D4
Newfields PE32 . . . .**65** C5
Newfound Dr NR4 . . . .**161** C1
NEWGATE NR25 . . . .**7** E5
Newgate NR35. . . . .**109** E3
NEWGATE CORNER NR29 . . .**75** C8
Newgate La
Kirby Cane NR35. . . . .**109** E3
Wells-next-the-Sea NR23 . . . .**136** D6
NEW HAINFORD NR10. . . . . .**53** D5
New Hampshire Way 5
IP24. . . . .**116** A1
Newhaven Cl NR27. . . . .**139** B6
Newhaven Ct NR27. . . . .**139** B6
NEW HOLKHAM NR23 . . . .**5** A2
NEW HOUGHTON PE31. . . . . .**29** D6
New Inn Hill NR14 . . . .**91** C7
New Inn La NR19 . . . .**154** B5
New La Banham NR16 . . . . . .**119** B8
Bradenham IP25 . . . .**66** F4
Hoveton NR12 . . . .**55** C4
Mattishall NR20. . . . .**68** F5
Newlands Ave PE30. . . . .**146** E7
Newlands 40 IP20 . . . .**122** D2
Newman Rd NR13. . . . .**72** D7
Newmarket Rd
2 Cringleford NR4. . . . .**89** B8
Norwich NR2. . . . .**178** A1
Newmarket St NR2. . . . .**162** C4
New Mills Yd NR3. . . . .**178** A4
Newnham Gn NR31 . . . .**170** A4
New N Rd NR17. . . . .**174** D5
New Par NR27 . . . .**139** C7
Newport NR29 . . . .**167** D6
Newport Rd
Hemsby NR29 . . . .**167** C6
South Walsham NR13 . . . .**74** A6
NEW RACKHEATH NR13 . . . .**72** E7
New Rd Acle NR13. . . . .**166** C3
Attleborough NR17. . . . .**174** B3
Aylsham NR11 . . . .**150** D7
Baconsthorpe NR25 . . . .**20** A8
Bawburgh NR9 . . . .**160** B6
Beccles NR34. . . . .**110** D2
Belton NR31 . . . .**94** A5
Blakeney NR25 . . . .**7** C6
Bodham NR25 . . . .**9** B1
Brettenham IP24 . . . .**117** B2
Brinton NR24. . . . .**18** D8
Burnham Overy Staithe
PE31. . . . .**135** E7
Catfield NR29 . . . .**56** C6
Crimplesham PE33 . . . .**80** A6
Dickleburgh & Rushall
IP21 . . . .**130** D8
Dunton NR21. . . . .**16** A2
Fritton & St Olaves NR31. . . . .**93** E3
Gissing IP22. . . . .**120** F4
Great Yarmouth NR30 . . . . . .**169** A6
Haddiscoe NR14 . . . .**110** F7
Halvergate NR13. . . . .**75** B4
Hethersett NR9. . . . .**88** C7
Hingham NR9 . . . .**86** C3
Itteringham NR11. . . . .**35** D8
King's Lynn PE30 . . . .**147** B6
12 Lingwood NR13. . . . .**74** A3
Longham NR19 . . . .**48** F2
Methwold IP26 . . . .**98** E5
Mettingham NR35. . . . .**124** C8
Morley NR18. . . . .**87** A3

New Rd *continued*
Northrepps NR27 . . . . **139** E1
North Runcton PE33 . . . . . . **44** A3
North Walsham NR28 . . . . **151** D5
Norton Subcourse NR14 . . . . **92** E1
Oulton NR11 . . . . **35** D7
Outwell PE14. . . . . **77** E5
Palgrave IP22 . . . . **129** F4
Reedham NR13 . . . . **92** F4
Reepham NR10 . . . . **149** C5
Saxlingham Nethergate
  NR15. . . . . **107** B8
Sculthorpe NR21. . . . . **16** A3
Sheringham NR26 . . . . **138** D7
Shipdham IP25 . . . . **67** B2
Shouldham PE33 . . . . **62** D4
Skeyton NR10 . . . . **37** A5
South Creake NR21. . . . . **15** D7
Stanfield NR20 . . . . **48** F7
St Cross, South Elmham
  IP20 . . . . **123** D1
Stokesby with Herringby
  NR29. . . . . **75** A6
Surlingham NR14. . . . . **73** B1
Sutton Bridge PE12. . . . . **41** B8
Sutton NR12 . . . . **39** D2
Tacolneston NR16 . . . . **105** E5
Thelnetham IP22. . . . . **127** F3
Thetford IP24 . . . . **176** C4
Thrandeston IP21 . . . . **130** A4
Tilney St Lawrence PE34. . . . **42** C1
Tivetshall St Mary NR15 . . **121** B4
Toft Monks NR34. . . . . **110** D6
Welney PE14. . . . . **95** D5
Whissonsett NR20. . . . . **31** D2
Wimbotsham PE34 . . . . **172** E8
Wiveton NR25 . . . . **7** E6
Wormegay PE33 . . . . **62** C8
New Roman Bank PE34 . . **144** B7
New Row PE31 . . . . **133** D6
New Sporle Rd PE37. . . . . **153** C5
NEW SPROWSTON NR3. . **158** E3
New St Cawston NR10. . . . . **35** B2
  Cromer NR27. . . . . **139** B7
  Holt NR25 . . . . **137** B6
  King's Lynn PE30. . . . . **147** B7
  Sheringham NR26 . . . . **138** D7
Newstead's La NR27 . . . . . . **10** C4
Newstead Wlk IP22. . . . . **177** C6
NEWTON PE32 . . . . **47** B2
Newton Cl
  Horsham St Faith & Newton St
    Faith NR10 . . . . **53** D4
  🔟 Newton Flotman NR15. . **89** D1
  Norwich NR4. . . . . **162** B1
Newton Cross NR31. . . . . **170** D1
NEWTON FLOTMAN NR15. . **89** C1
Newton Flotman CE Prim
  Sch NR15. . . . . **89** D1
Newton Gap Cl 🮥 NR31. . **171** D4
NEWTON GREENWAYS
  NR15. . . . . **89** D2
Newton Rd Hainford NR10 . . **53** E5
  Newton by Castle Acre
    PE32. . . . . **47** A2
  Sporle with Palgrave PE32 . . **65** C7
NEWTON ST FAITH NR10 . . **53** E4
Newton St NR10 . . . . **53** D4
NEWTOWN NR30. . . . . **169** D7
Newtown IP24. . . . . **176** C3
New Wellington Pl 🮳
  NR30 . . . . **169** D2
Neylond Cres NR6. . . . . . . **157** E6
Nicholas Ave PE34. . . . . . . **145** E6
Nicholas Hamond Acad The
  PE37. . . . . **153** C3
Nicholas Hamond Way 🮲
  PE37. . . . . **153** C3
Nicholas Mews 🮱 NR2. . **162** B7
Nicholls Way IP22. . . . . . . **177** A5
Nick's La IP23 . . . . **130** B2
Nicolson Ave NR30. . . . . . . **50** B5
Nidus Gdns NR19 . . . . **67** E5
Nightingale Cl
  Cromer NR27. . . . . **139** C4
  Denver PE38 . . . . **172** D2
  Fakenham NR21 . . . . **141** F4
  Hemsby NR29 . . . . **167** E4
  Mulbarton NR14 . . . . **89** A3
Nightingale Dr NR8. . . . . . **155** B1
Nightingale Inf Sch NR8 . **155** B1
Nightingale La
  Denver PE38 . . . . **172** D3
  🮸 Feltwell IP26. . . . . **98** E1
  🮷 Feltwell IP26. . . . . **98** E1
  Norwich NR3. . . . . **162** E8
Nightingale Rd IP27 . . . . . **175** F3
Nightingale Way NR1. . . . **176** D1
Nightingale Wlk PE38. . . . **172** C2
Nightmarsh La PE31. . . . . . **27** C4
Nile Rd
  Downham Market PE38. . . . **172** B4
  Great Yarmouth NR31. . . . . **170** D4
Nile St 🮹 NR2. . . . . **162** B7
Nimrod Cl 🮺 NR7. . . . . **88** D8
Nine Acre La NR24. . . . . **19** C4
Ninhams Ct NR2. . . . . **178** A3
Ninham St NR1. . . . . **162** E3
Nobbs' Cnr NR35. . . . . **108** A4
Nobb's Loke NR12 . . . . **38** F4
Nobel Cres NR12. . . . . **164** B4
Noble Cl NR7 . . . . **159** D1
Noel Cl NR31. . . . . **171** C5
NOGDAM END NR14. . . . . . **92** D3
Noot Alley 🮶 NR5. . . . . **161** B7
NORDELPH PE38 . . . . **78** D3
Nordelph Cnr NR9. . . . . **86** D6
NORDELPH CORNER NR9 . . **86** D6

Norfolk Arena PE34. . . . . **168** F2
Norfolk Dr NR17. . . . . **174** C6
Norfolk Lavender Visitor
  Ctr ✶ PE31. . . . . **133** E6
Norfolk Motor Cycle Mus✶
  NR28. . . . . **151** C4
Norfolk Nelson Mus✶
  NR30. . . . . **169** C3
Norfolk & Norwich Univ
  Hospl NR4 . . . . **161** A3
Norfolk Rd
  🮵 Honington IP31 . . . . **126** B1
  🔟 Marham PE33 . . . . **63** B4
  Norwich NR4. . . . . **161** B3
  Sheringham NR26 . . . . **138** D6
  Thetford IP24 . . . . **176** E4
Norfolk Record Office
  NR1. . . . . **162** F3
Norfolk Shire Horse Ctr✶
  NR27. . . . . **9** F5
Norfolk Sq
  Downham Market PE38. . . **172** B5
  Great Yarmouth NR30. . . . **169** E5
Norfolk St
  🮴 King's Lynn PE30. . . . . . **146** E5
  Norwich NR2. . . . . **162** C5
  Wisbech PE13. . . . . **152** C4
Norfolk & Suffolk Aviation
  Mus✶ NR35. . . . . **123** D6
Norfolk Wildlife Ctr &
  Country Pk✶ NR9 . . . . . . **51** C6
Norfolk Wildlife Hospl
  (RSPCA)✶ PE32 . . . . **44** F3
Norgate La IP21. . . . . **130** E6
Norgate Rd NR4. . . . . **161** E3
Norgate Way NR8. . . . . . . **156** E8
Norman CE Prim Sch The
  IP26 . . . . **99** C7
Norman Cl
  East Dereham NR19 . . . . . **154** C5
  Fakenham NR21 . . . . **141** B6
Norman Dr Northwold PE33 **81** B9
  Norwich NR6. . . . . **158** E7
Normandy Cl IP26 . . . . **99** C7
Normandy Dr NR19 . . . . . **154** D7
Norman La 🔟 NR31 . . . . . **169** B4
Norman Rd
  Flitcham with Appleton
    PE31. . . . . **28** E7
  Norwich NR3. . . . . **158** E1
Normans Bldgs NR1 . . . . **178** B2
Normans La NR21. . . . . **4** D1
Norman's Burrow Rd
  NR21. . . . . **31** B3
Norman Troller Ct 🮼
  NR27 . . . . **139** B7
Norman Way PE31 . . . . **15** B3
NORTHACRE NR17. . . . . **85** B1
NORTHALL GREEN
  Dereham NR20 . . . . **154** F8
  Hoe NR20 . . . . **49** F2
North Ave NR20. . . . . **50** B5
North Barningham Rd
  NR25 . . . . **20** D7
NORTH BARSHAM NR22 . . **16** D6
North Beach PE36 . . . . **132** B1
North Brink PE13 . . . . **152** A4
NORTH BURLINGHAM
  NR13. . . . . **74** A5
North Cambridgeshire Hospl
  PE13. . . . . **152** D5
NORTH COMMON IP22 . . . **127** D2
Northcote PE31. . . . . **134** D6
Northcote Rd 🮵 NR3. . . . . **162** E8
NORTH COURT IP27. . . . . . **114** C3
NORTH CREAKE NR21 . . . . . . **4** D1
NORTH DENES NR30 . . . . . **168** F2
North Denes Airfield
  NR30. . . . . **168** D2
North Denes Mid Sch
  NR30. . . . . **169** D8
North Denes Rd NR30. . . . **169** D6
North Dr Fakenham NR21. . **141** C5
  Great Yarmouth NR30. . . . **169** E4
NORTH ELMHAM NR20 . . . . **49** E8
North Elmham Chapel✶
  NR20. . . . . **49** F8
North Elmham Prim Sch
  NR20. . . . . **49** E8
NORTH END NR16 . . . . **103** C3
North End Haddiscoe NR14 . **93** B1
  Stoke Holy Cross NR14. . . . **89** E5
  Wisbech PE13 . . . . **152** B6
North End La NR16. . . . . . . **106** D3
Northern Cl NR30. . . . . **168** F5
North Everard St PE30 . . . **146** E3
Northfield Ave NR23 . . . . . **136** D6
Northfield Cl NR18. . . . . . . **173** B6
Northfield Cres NR23. . . . . **136** D6
Northfield Gdns NR18. . . . **173** B5
Northfield La
  Plumstead NR11 . . . . **20** B6
  Wells-next-the-Sea NR23 . . **136** C6
Northfield Loke NR18 . . . . **173** B6
Northfield Rd
  Forncett NR16. . . . . **106** A4
  Mundesley NR11. . . . . **143** C5
  North Walsham NR28 . . . . **151** B6
  Swaffham PE37. . . . . **153** C6
Northfields NR4 . . . . **161** E4
Northfields Way NR23. . . . **136** E6
North Gage Cl NR7. . . . . . **159** C8
Northgate Beccles NR34. . . **110** D1
  Dereham NR19 . . . . **154** C7
  🮺 Harleston IP20 . . . . **122** D1
  Hunstanton PE36. . . . . **132** C5
  Norwich NR6. . . . . **157** F5
  🮹 Thorpe End NR13. . . . . . **72** C6

Northgate High Sch
  NR19. . . . . **154** D6
Northgate Hospl NR30. . . **169** D6
Northgate Prec PE36. . . . . **132** C6
Northgate St Andrew's Fst
  Sch NR30. . . . . **169** C6
Northgate St NR30. . . . . . **169** C5
Northgate Way PE34. . . . . **144** D7
North Gn NR9 . . . . **68** B1
North Gn Rd IP21. . . . . . . **122** A4
NORTH GREEN
  Garvestone NR9 . . . . **68** C1
  Pulham St Mary IP21. . . . . **122** A7
North La NR21. . . . . **17** E5
North Lawn PE38 . . . . **97** B6
NORTH LOPHAM IP22 . . . . **119** A2
North Lopham Rd NR16 . . **119** A3
NORTH LYNN PE30. . . . . . **146** F7
North Lynn Bsns Village
  PE30. . . . . **148** A1
North Lynn Ind Est PE30 . **147** A8
North Mkt Rd
  🮻 Great Yarmouth
    NR30. . . . . **169** D4
  Winterton-on-Sea NR29 . . . **58** B6
North Norfolk Rly✶ NR26 . . **9** B6
Northolt Rd IP25 . . . . **85** A3
NORTH PICKENHAM PE37 . . **65** E1
North Pickenham Rd
  PE37. . . . . **153** D4
North Pk NR1. . . . . **141** B6
North Pk Ave NR4. . . . . . . **161** E4
North Pk Dr NR4. . . . . **161** F4
North Prom PE36 . . . . **132** C5
North Quay NR30 . . . . **169** C4
North Rd Bunwell NR16. . . **105** C4
  🮴 Great Yarmouth NR30 . **169** D5
  Great Yarmouth NR31. . . . **170** D4
  Hemsby NR29 . . . . **167** A7
  Ormesby St Margaret with
    Scratby NR29. . . . . **167** A4
  Watton IP25 . . . . **84** D3
NORTHREPPS NR27 . . . . . . **11** A2
Northrepps Prim Sch
  NR27. . . . . **11** A2
Northrepps Rd NR27 . . . . . **139** E3
North River Rd NR30. . . . . **169** C6
NORTH RUNCTON PE33. . . . **44** A2
Northside NR7. . . . . **72** E3
North St Brundall NR13. . . **165** E6
  Burnham Market PE31. . . . **135** C3
  🮶 Castle Acre PE32. . . . . . . **46** F2
  Great Dunham PE32 . . . . . . **47** E2
  King's Lynn PE30 . . . . **146** D6
  Langham NR25 . . . . **7** A4
  North Walsham NR28 . . . . **151** C5
  Sheringham NR26 . . . . **138** C7
  Wisbech PE13 . . . . **152** C5
NORTH TUDDENHAM
  NR20. . . . . **50** D1
Northumberland St NR2. . **162** B7
North View NR21 . . . . **17** F3
Northview Rd NR5. . . . . . . **157** C1
NORTH WALSHAM NR28 . . **151** E6
North Walsham & District
  War Memorial Hospl
  NR28. . . . . **151** C4
North Walsham Fst Sch
  NR28. . . . . **151** D5
North Walsham High Sch
  NR28. . . . . **151** D5
North Walsham Jun Sch
  NR28. . . . . **151** D5
North Walsham Rd
  Bacton NR28 . . . . **23** C3
  Coltishall NR12 . . . . **54** D7
  Crostwick NR12. . . . . **54** B2
  Felmingham NR28 . . . . **37** B8
  Happisburgh NR12 . . . . **23** F2
  Northrepps NR27 . . . . **10** E1
  Norwich NR6. . . . . **159** A5
  Paston NR28 . . . . **151** F7
  Sprowston NR6. . . . . **159** B6
  Swafield NR28. . . . . **22** E4
  Thorpe Market NR11. . . . . . **22** A7
  Witton NR28 . . . . **38** B8
North Walsham Sta
  NR28. . . . . **151** C4
North Way PE30 . . . . **147** A8
Northwell Pool Rd PE37. . **153** C5
North-West Twr✶ NR30 . . **169** C5
NORTHWOLD PE30. . . . . **99** C8
Northwold Rd IP26 . . . . **99** A6
NORTH WOOTTON PE30. . . **148** C5
North Wootton Com Sch
  PE30. . . . . **148** D4
NORTON CORNER NR11 . . . **34** C7
Norton Dr 🮴 Norwich NR4. . **89** D8
  Norwich NR4. . . . . **162** A1
Norton Hill NR13. . . . . **74** A8
Norton Rd NR14 . . . . **92** B1
Nortonsfield Cl NR25. . . . . **137** C7
NORTON SUBCOURSE
  NR14. . . . . **92** E1
Nortridge Rd NR5. . . . . . . **161** A7
Norvic Dr NR4. . . . . **161** E1
Norway Cl PE31. . . . . **133** C6
NORWICH NR2 . . . . **178** A3
Norwich Arts Ctr✶ NR2. . **178** A3
Norwich Bsns Pk NR4. . . **162** D1
Norwich Castle Mus & Art
  Gall✶ NR1 . . . . **178** B3
Norwich Cath✶ NR1 . . . . . **178** B3
Norwich City FC NR1 . . . . **163** A4
Norwich Cl 🮵 PE13 . . . . . **152** E6
Norwich Com Hospl NR2 . **161** F7
Norwich Comm NR18 . . . . **173** F6

Norwich Dr NR20 . . . . **32** E4
Norwich Gall✶ NR1. . . . . . **178** B3
Norwich Gates PE35 . . . . . **140** C1
Norwich High Sch for Girls
  NR2. . . . . **162** B3
Norwich Int Airport NR6 . **158** B7
Norwich La IP31. . . . . **127** A4
Norwich Puppet Theatre
  NR2. . . . . **178** B4
Norwich Rd Acle NR13. . . . **166** A3
  Ashmanhaugh NR12 . . . . . . **55** C7
  Attleborough NR17 . . . . . . **174** E6
  Aylsham NR11. . . . . **150** C6
  Barnham Broom NR9 . . . . . . **69** D2
  Bawdeswell NR20. . . . . **50** E7
  Bracon Ash NR14 . . . . **88** F2
  Briston NR24. . . . . **142** E5
  Brooke NR15. . . . . **90** E3
  Burgh & Tuttington NR11. . . **36** E6
  Caister-on-Sea NR30. . . . . **168** C5
  Cantley NR13. . . . . **92** D7
  Carbrooke IP25 . . . . **85** B3
  Cawston NR10. . . . . **35** B2
  Chedgrave NR14. . . . . **91** F2
  Cromer NR27. . . . . **139** C5
  Denton IP20 . . . . **123** B7
  Dickleburgh & Rushall
    IP21. . . . . **130** D6
  Ditchingham NR35. . . . . . . **109** A2
  Earsham NR35. . . . . **108** E1
  East Dereham NR20 . . . . . **154** F5
  East Tuddenham NR20. . . . . **69** C6
  Edgefield NR24 . . . . **19** D6
  Fakenham NR21 . . . . **141** C4
  Foxley NR20. . . . . **50** D8
  Gillingham NR34 . . . . **110** C2
  Great & Little Plumstead
    NR13. . . . . **73** A7
  Guist NR20 . . . . **33** A4
  Hardingham NR9 . . . . **86** E8
  🮭 Hethersett NR9 . . . . **88** D7
  Hingham NR9 . . . . **86** D5
  Holt NR25 . . . . **137** B5
  Horning NR12 . . . . **55** E4
  Horsham St Faith NR10 . . . . **53** D2
  Horstead with Stanninghall
    NR12. . . . . **54** C4
  Ingworth NR11 . . . . **36** B8
  Kimberley NR18. . . . . **87** B7
  Langley with Hardley NR14. . **91** F6
  Lingwood & Burlingham
    NR13. . . . . **74** A2
  🮭 Loddon NR14 . . . . **92** A2
  Long Stratton NR15. . . . . . **106** F5
  Ludham NR29 . . . . **56** C5
  Marlingford NR9 . . . . **69** F4
  Mattishall NR20. . . . . **68** F6
  Mulbarton NR14 . . . . **89** B4
  Neatishead NR12 . . . . **164** F8
  North Walsham NR28 . . . . **151** B3
  Norwich NR5. . . . . **157** B2
  Poringland NR14. . . . . **90** B6
  Pulham St Mary IP21 . . . . **121** F4
  Rackheath NR13. . . . . **72** F8
  Reepham NR10 . . . . **149** C5
  Roughton NR11. . . . . **21** D8
  Salhouse NR13 . . . . **55** B1
  Saxlingham Nethergate
    NR15. . . . . **107** B8
  Scole IP21. . . . . **121** B1
  Shotesham NR15. . . . . **89** F2
  Shouldham PE33 . . . . **62** A6
  Smallburgh NR12 . . . . **38** D2
  Stockton NR34. . . . . **109** F5
  Strumpshaw NR13. . . . . **73** F2
  Swaffham PE37 . . . . **153** D4
  Swanton Morley NR20. . . . . **50** B2
  🮴 Tacolneston NR16 . . . . . **105** F5
  Tacolneston NR16 . . . . **106** A6
  Tharston & Hapton NR15 . . **106** C7
  Thetford IP24 . . . . **176** D4
  Thurton NR14. . . . . **91** C3
  Tivetshall St Mary NR15 . . **121** D4
  West Caister NR30 . . . . . . **168** B6
  Weston Longville NR9 . . . . . **51** E5
  Woodton NR35 . . . . **108** C6
  Wroxham/Hoveton NR12 . . **164** B3
  Wymondham NR18 . . . . . . **173** D5
  Yaxham NR19 . . . . **68** B5
Norwich Research Pk
  NR4. . . . . **161** A4
Norwich Riverside NR1 . . **178** C2
Norwich Road Acad
  IP24 . . . . **176** D4
Norwich Sch
  Norwich NR1. . . . . **178** B3
  Norwich NR1. . . . . **178** C3
Norwich St
  East Dereham NR19 . . . . . **154** E5
  Fakenham NR21 . . . . **141** B4
  Hingham NR9 . . . . **86** C5
  Mundesley NR11. . . . . **143** A7
Norwich Sta NR1 . . . . **178** C2
Norwich Steiner Sch
  NR7. . . . . **161** E6
Norwich Theatre Royal
  NR2. . . . . **178** A2
Norwood Rd IP27. . . . . **175** A1
Notre Dame High Sch
  NR1. . . . . **178** B1
Notre Dame Prep Sch
  NR2. . . . . **162** B7
Nottingham Rd PE30 . . . . **146** E8
Nottingham Way NR30 . . . **169** C3
Notykin St NR5. . . . . **161** A8
Nourse Dr PE31. . . . . **133** E5

Nova Scotia Rd
  Filby NR30. . . . . **168** A7
  Ormesby St Margaret with
    Scratby NR29. . . . . **167** B1
Nowhere La PE33. . . . . **80** D4
Nuffield Cl NR31. . . . . **170** B4
Nuffield Cres NR31 . . . . . . **170** B4
Nunnery Dr IP24. . . . . **176** D1
Nunnery Pl IP24 . . . . **176** D2
Nunnery The✶ IP24. . . . . . **176** D2
Nunn's Way NR19 . . . . **154** D5
Nuns' Bridges Rd IP24. . . **176** C2
Nunsgate IP24. . . . . **176** D2
Nurseries Ave NR13. . . . . . **165** E4
Nursery Cl Acle NR13 . . . . **166** B4
  🮲 Beetley NR19. . . . . **49** C3
  🮹 Belton NR31. . . . . **94** A5
  🮲 Gressenhall NR20 . . . . . . **49** C3
  King's Lynn PE30. . . . . **148** C2
  🮭 Marthan NR29 . . . . **57** D5
  Norwich NR6. . . . . **157** E5
  🮲 Roydon PE32 . . . . **28** A1
Nursery Dr
  Hunstanton PE36. . . . . **132** D4
  North Walsham NR28 . . . . **151** B3
  Wisbech PE13 . . . . **152** E8
Nursery Gdns NR13 . . . . . **165** F6
Nursery La Brancaster PE31. . **3** E6
  Costessey NR8 . . . . **156** F3
  Hockwold cum Wilton
    IP26. . . . . **114** A6
  King's Lynn PE30 . . . . **148** C3
Nursery Rd PE38. . . . . **172** C6
Nursery Terr NR30. . . . . . **169** C6
Nursery Way PE32 . . . . **28** A1
Nursey Cl NR35. . . . . **109** D3
Nutfield Cl 🮷 NR4. . . . . . . **161** F1
Nuthall Cres PE30. . . . . . . **147** A8
Nut La NR27 . . . . **139** F3
Nutmeg Wlk PE38. . . . . . . **172** E6
Nuttele Cl NR15. . . . . **107** C6
Nuttery Vale IP23. . . . . . . **130** F2
Nutwood Cl NR8 . . . . **155** D2**

O

Oakapple Dr NR19 . . . . . . **154** D8
Oak Ave
  🮻 Great Yarmouth NR31. . . **94** C7
  King's Lynn PE30. . . . . **148** D2
  Marham PE33 . . . . **63** B4
  North Elmham NR20 . . . . . . **49** E2
  Norwich NR7. . . . . **163** F8
  🮭 Poringland NR14 . . . . **90** C5
  West Winch PE33 . . . . **43** F2
Oak Cl 🮴 Hethersett NR9 . . **88** D8
  Norwich NR5. . . . . **156** F2
  🮻 Tasburgh NR15. . . . . . . **106** F6
  Thetford IP24 . . . . **176** A1
Oak Cres IP23 . . . . **130** C1
Oakcroft Dr NR14. . . . . **90** C5
Oakdale Rd NR13 . . . . **165** D3
Oakdene NR21. . . . . **15** C2
Oak Dr Outwell PE14. . . . . . **77** F7
  Reepham NR10 . . . . **149** D6
Oakfield Cl PE38. . . . . **172** C4
Oakfield Dr 🮱 NR13 . . . . . **74** B8
Oakfield Rd
  Aylsham NR11. . . . . **150** C6
  Long Stratton NR15. . . . . . **106** F3
Oakfields NR14 . . . . **91** F2
Oakfields Cl 🮸 NR4. . . . . . **89** C8
Oakfields Rd NR4 . . . . **89** B8
Oak Gr 🮶 Horsford NR10 . . **53** B3
  Sheringham NR26 . . . . **138** D5
Oakhill NR13. . . . . **165** D3
Oak La East Ruston NR12. . . **38** E7
  🮲 Hingham NR9 . . . . **86** C4
  Norwich NR3. . . . . **158** D3
Oakland Dr 🮶 NR30. . . . . . **49** D4
Oaklands
  Little Snoring NR21. . . . . . . **17** C3
  🮴 Old Buckenham NR17 . . **104** D2
  Poringland NR14. . . . . **90** C6
  🮶 Taverham NR8 . . . . **155** B2
Oaklands Cl
  Attleborough NR17 . . . . . . **174** C3
  Halvergate NR13. . . . . **74** F2
Oaklands Dr
  Brandon IP27 . . . . **114** D4
  Cringleford NR4 . . . . **161** C1
  Walsoken PE13 . . . . **152** F7
Oaklands La 🮲 PE33. . . . . . **61** D3
Oaklands Pk NR28 . . . . . . **151** B6
Oaklands The PE37 . . . . . . **153** C3
Oakleigh Dr PE13 . . . . **153** A5
OAKLEY IP21. . . . . **130** E5
Oakley Church La IP21. . . **130** D4
Oakley Cl PE13 . . . . **152** E4
Oak Lodge NR7 . . . . **163** C5
Oak Meadow IP25 . . . . **67** B2
Oak Rd Dilham NR28 . . . . . . **38** D4
  Great Yarmouth NR31. . . . **170** B6
  North Walsham NR28 . . . . **151** B4
  Stoke Ferry PE33. . . . . **81** A2
Oakroyd Cres PE13 . . . . . . **152** C6
Oaks Cl PE37 . . . . **153** C3
Oaks Dr Necton PE37. . . . . . **65** F4
  Swaffham PE37 . . . . **153** C3
Oaks La NR34. . . . . **111** B5
Oak's La NR13. . . . . **72** F2
Oak St Fakenham NR21 . . . **141** B4
  Feltwell IP26. . . . . **98** E1
  Norwich NR3. . . . . **178** A4

Oaks The Ashill IP25......84 A7
🖪 Beetley NR19........49 C3
🆖 Elm PE14..........59 A1
🖪 Gressenhall NR20......49 C3
Mattishall NR20.........68 F5
Oak Tree Bsns Pk NR13...72 E8
Oak Tree Cl 🖪 NR29.....57 D5
Oaktree Dr NR7........159 B2
Oak Tree Way 🖪 IP20...122 D1
Oak View Dr PE38.....172 C6
Oak Wood NR13.......165 E5
Oakwood Cl NR19.....154 D8
Oakwood Dr NR18.....173 E6
Oakwood Rd NR19.....154 D8
Oasis Leisure Ctr PE36...132 C4
Oasis Sport & Leisure Club
NR7...................72 D5
Oasis Way PE36.......132 C2
Oatfield Chase NR14....89 B2
Oatfield Cl 🖪 NR10.....53 A3
Obelisk La NR28.......37 F5
Obelisk Plain NR25....137 A6
Occupation Rd 🖪 NR20...68 F6
Octagon Dr 🖪 PE13....152 A6
Octavia Cl PE13.......152 F6
Octavia Hill Birthplace Mus★
PE13.................152 C5
Oddfellows Field 🖪 NR25..7 C6
Oddfellows Row PE31...134 E4
Offley Ct 🖪 NR5......161 A8
Ogden Cl NR18........173 C4
Oil Mill La NR13......152 B5
Old Allotment Ct 🖪 NR3.162 F8
Old Bakery Ct PE31....133 C5
Old Barge Yd NR1.....178 C2
Old Barley Mkt The NR2..178 A3
Old Bear Ct NR28......151 C5
Old Becclesgate NR19...154 D5
OLD BEETLEY NR20......49 D5
Old Brandon Rd IP26....98 F1
Old Brewery Ct 🖪 NR30.146 E3
Old Brewery La NR10...149 C4
OLD BUCKENHAM NR17...104 D2
Old Buckenham Airfield★
NR17.................104 E4
Old Buckenham Com Prim
Sch NR17.............104 D3
Old Buckenham High Sch
NR17.................104 D2
Old Buckenham Rd
NR16................105 A4
Old Bungay Rd NR35....109 C4
Old Bury Rd
Palgrave IP22.........129 E4
Stuston IP21..........177 F1
Thetford IP24.........176 C4
Wortham IP22.........129 D4
OLD CATTON NR6.......158 E5
Old Catton CE Jun Sch
NR6..................158 E5
Old Chapel Rd
Cantley NR13...........92 E7
🖪 Hemsby NR29........58 B6
Old Chapel Way NR7....72 E3
Old Church Ct NR14....89 F6
Old Church Rd
Hainford NR10.........53 E6
Hopton on Sea NR31...171 D4
Snettisham PE31.......12 E5
Old Coaching Pl The
IP22.................177 E3
Old Coach Rd NR27....139 C6
Old Coal Yd The PE31...12 E4
Old Coast Rd NR29....167 E2
Old Fakenham Rd
Attlebridge NR9........52 B3
Foxley NR20...........50 D8
Old Farm La NR3......158 B1
Old Feltwell Rd IP26....99 A5
Oldfield Ave PE14......59 B1
Oldfield Ct 🖪 NR19....154 E6
Oldfield Dr PE34......144 B5
Oldfield La PE13.......152 B3
Old Forge Cl IP22......129 B4
Old Forge Ct Acle NR13.166 C4
Brockdish IP21.........131 D6
Old Fountain NR31.....170 C1
Old Friendship La NR10..35 C2
Old Grammar La 🖪
NR35................124 B8
Old Gr Ct NR3........158 D2
Old Hall Cl
Ashwellthorpe NR16....105 F8
🖪 Norwich NR14......163 B5
Saham Toney IP25......84 B5
Old Hall Dr PE31......140 E3
Old Hall Gdns Brooke NR15.90 F2
Buxton with Lammas NR10..37 E2
Old Hall Gdns NR30....168 E5
Oldhall La NR16.......118 C5
Old Hall La PE37.......81 F8
Oldhall Rd NR4........89 E8
Old Hall Rd
East Dereham NR19....154 D2
Mattishall NR20........68 D5
Witton NR28...........38 B8
OLD HALL STREET NR28..23 A4
Old Hall The PE31......27 C3
Old Harleston Rd NR35..123 E7
Old High Rd IP22......177 A5
Old Hithe Rd NR26....138 A6
OLD HUNSTANTON PE36..132 E8
Old Hunstanton Rd PE36.132 E7
Old Kiln 🔟 PE33......43 F2
Old La East Ruston NR12..24 A5

Old La continued
Happisburgh NR12......23 F1
Reepham NR10..........34 B1
Thelnetham IP22.......128 A2
Old Lakenham Hall Dr 🖪
NR1.................162 E1
Old Laundry Ct 🖪 NR2..162 B8
Old Laundry Mews NR1..163 A5
Old Liby Mews NR1.....178 C2
Old Lynn Rd PE13......152 E7
Old Maltings The PE13..153 B4
Old Manor Cl PE30.....148 C1
Oldmedow Rd PE30.....147 A2
Old Methwold Rd
Feltwell IP26...........98 E2
Northwold PE33........81 B2
Old Mill Dr IP21......121 F4
Old Mill Rd
Caister-on-Sea NR30....168 F5
🖪 Poringland NR14......90 C5
Roughton NR11........139 B1
Old Mill Terrace 🖪
NR34................110 D1
Old Mkt PE13.........152 C5
Old Mkt Cl NR13......166 C3
Old Mkt Gn 🖪 NR1.....92 A1
Old Mkt Pl 🗺 IP20....122 D2
Old Mkt St
🆖 King's Lynn PE30....146 E5
Thetford IP24.........176 D3
Old Mkt Way NR15....107 C5
Old Norwich Rd
Horsham St Faith & Newton St
Faith................53 D1
Yaxley IP23...........130 A1
Old Oak NR18.........173 F7
Old Orchard Cl 🔞 NR20...68 A8
Old Pal Rd NR2.......162 B7
Old Pools Dro CB6......95 F1
Old Post Office La NR35..109 E3
Old Post Office St
🖪 Fakenham NR21......141 B4
🖪 Shipdham IP25........67 B2
Old Post Rd NR24.....142 E4
Old Quarry Ct NR19....154 E6
Old Rd Acle NR13.......166 E5
🖪 Great Moulton NR15...106 B1
Old Rectory Cl
King's Lynn PE30.......148 D5
🖪 Mulbarton NR14.......89 B3
Norwich NR7..........163 B6
🖪 Roydon IP22.........129 D7
South Wootton PE30....148 B1
Old Rectory Rd NR12....24 A1
Old Reepham Rd 🖪 NR20..50 E7
Old Rly Rd IP20.......123 B5
Old Rly Yd PE31.......135 C2
Old Roman Bank PE14...144 A2
Old Sch Cl NR5.......161 E6
Old Sch Ct NR1.......178 C1
Old School Rd NR24....142 A4
Old Sch Rd
East Ruston NR12.......38 F8
Guestwick NR20........33 F5
Old Severalls Rd IP26....98 E6
Old South PE30.......147 C4
Old St 🖪 NR15.......107 A8
Old Sta La NR35.......109 C2
Old Sta Way 🖪 NR5...137 C5
Old Stoke Rd NR14.....89 F8
Oldsunway PE30.......146 D5
Old Town Way PE36....132 D6
Old Turnpike Rd NR11....21 D7
Old Vicarage Pk PE32....63 E7
Old Warren NR8.......155 D2
Oldwash La NR16......105 D3
Old Watton Rd NR4.....161 A5
Old Wellington Pl 🔞
NR30................169 D3
Old Wells Rd
Sculthorpe NR21........16 A2
Walsingham NR22.......16 E8
Old Woman's La NR25....7 F6
Old Yarmouth Rd NR12...39 C2
Olive Ave NR15........89 D1
Olive Cl NR5..........157 C1
Olive Cres NR10.......53 A4
Olive Fisher Ct NR21....141 B4
Oliver Ct 🖪 Cromer NR27.139 C6
🖪 Weeting IP27........114 E1
Olive Rd
Great Yarmouth NR31...169 B3
Norwich NR5..........157 C1
Oliver Mews 🖪 NR30....169 D4
Olivet Way NR21......141 C3
Olivia Cl NR21.......141 A5
Ollands Rd
Attleborough NR17.....174 C3
Reepham NR10.........149 C4
Ollard Ave PE13......152 D7
Olley Rd 🖪 NR27.......10 A5
Olney Rd NR19.......154 D5
Olympian Cl PE13......152 C2
Onedin Cl PE31.......140 C5
Onley St NR2.........162 B4
Onslow Ave NR30......169 D7
Onyx Ct 🔟 PE13......152 C4
Open Acad NR7.......159 C1
Opie St NR2..........178 B3
Opportune Rd PE13....152 C6
Orange Gr 🖪 PE13.....152 C4
ORANGE ROW PE34.....144 A6
Orange Row Rd NR34...144 A4
Orange Row Rd PE34...144 A6
Orchard Bank NR8.....156 E8
Orchard Cl Acle NR13...166 B4

Orchard Cl continued
Ashill IP25............84 A6
Attleborough NR17.....174 C5
Blofield Heath NR13.....73 C6
Brancaster Staithe PE31...3 D7
Briston NR24..........142 D4
Caister-on-Sea NR30....168 E4
Dersingham PE31.......140 D4
Downham Market PE38..172 D5
Fakenham NR21........141 D4
Holt NR25.............137 E7
🖪 Ixworth NR9.........69 F2
Mundesley NR11.......143 B7
North Elmham NR20.....49 E7
North Walsham NR28...151 C6
Norwich NR7..........163 C8
Roughton NR11.........21 D7
Sheringham NR26.......138 C6
Tacolneston NR16......105 F4
Watlington PE33........61 E5
🖪 Watton IP25..........84 D3
🖪 Wisbech PE14........59 A1
Orchard Cres 🖪 NR15...106 B1
Orchard Ct
King's Lynn PE30.......147 B6
Ormesby St Margaret
NR29................167 A3
Orchard Dr
Hellesdon NR6.........157 D3
🖪 Potter Heigham NR29..56 F6
West Walton PE14.......59 C8
Wisbech PE13.........152 E4
Orchard Gdns 🖪 PE30...147 B6
Orchard Gr Diss IP22....177 C5
Kettlestone NR21.......17 C2
King's Lynn PE34......146 C3
Orchard La Aylsham NR11.150 D4
Castle Acre PE32........46 F2
King's Lynn PE30......147 B5
Reepham NR10.........149 D5
Shouldham PE33........62 D4
Orchard Loke NR11......22 B7
Orchard Pl
Swaffham PE37........153 B4
Thompson IP24.........102 A4
Orchard Rd
🖪 Gayton PE32..........45 C6
Lingwood NR13.........73 F3
🖪 Mattishall NR20......68 C6
🖪 Spixworth NR10.......54 A2
🖪 Wiggenhall St Germans
PE34.................43 B1
Orchards CE Prim Sch
PE13.................152 D8
Orchard St NR2.......162 C7
Orchard The
🖪 Belton NR31..........94 A6
Brandon IP27..........175 C3
Orchard Way
Banham NR16..........119 D7
🖪 Burgh St Margaret
(Fleggburgh) NR29......57 C1
🖪 Hethersett NR9.......88 D8
🖪 Tasburgh NR15.......106 F6
Terrington St John PE14...42 B1
Thetford IP24.........176 D5
Wymondham NR18.....173 C4
Orchid Ave NR19......154 D1
Orchid Dr NR26.......138 B6
Orchids Cl NR35.......124 B7
Orde Ave NR31.......170 C2
Ordnance Rd NR30.....169 D1
Orford Cl 🖪 NR30.....169 D3
Orford Hill NR1.......178 B2
Orford Pl Norwich NR1..178 B2
🖪 West Winch PE33.....43 F2
Orford Rd PE37.......153 C6
Orford St NR1........178 B2
Orhard Gr PE33.......43 E2
Oriel Ave NR31........170 A3
Ormesby 🖪 PE30......147 D5
Ormesby La NR29.......76 A8
Ormesby Rd
Caister-on-Sea NR30....168 D7
Hemsby NR29.........167 A6
Ormesby St Margaret with
Scratby NR29..........168 C8
Scottow NR10...........37 B2
ORMESBY ST MARGARET
NR29................167 B3
ORMESBY ST MICHAEL
NR29.................58 A1
Ormesby Village Inf Sch
NR29................167 A2
Ormesby Village Jun Sch
NR29................167 A3
Ormiston Herman Acad
NR31................170 A3
Ormond Rd NR30......169 C5
Ormsby Cl 🖪 NR31.....171 D4
Orwell Cl
King's Lynn PE30.......147 D4
🖪 Wymondham NR18...173 D5
Orwell Cres NR31.......94 A6
Orwell Rd NR2........162 C3
Osbert Cl 🖪 NR1......162 E1
Osborne Ave NR30.....169 C7
Osborne Cl 🖪 NR28....151 C7
Osborne Ct NR4.......162 B3
Osborne Pk PE13......152 C7
Osborne Rd Norwich NR4..161 D2
Wisbech PE13.........152 B7
Osier Cl NR19........154 B4
Osier La NR25..........9 C1
Osprey Cl NR12.......164 D5
OSTEND NR12..........24 A7
Ostend Gap NR12.......24 A7

Ostend Pl NR12........24 A7
Ostend Rd NR12........24 A6
Ostlers Pl NR38.......172 B7
Ostrich La NR19.......49 A3
Ottaway Cl NR5.......157 A3
Otter Cl
🖪 Downham Market
PE38................172 A6
🆖 Salhouse NR13.......55 A1
Otter Dr 🗺 NR14......89 B3
Otter Rd PE37........153 C2
Otter Trust The★ NR35...123 E7
OULTON NR11..........35 B7
Oulton Cl PE37.......153 C2
Oulton Rd NR6........158 C5
OULTON STREET NR11....35 D6
Ouse Ave PE30.......146 D2
Ouse Ave The IP24.....176 C3
Ouse La NR12..........39 F1
Outney Rd NR35......124 A8
Out S Gates PE30.....146 E3
OUTWELL PE14..........77 F6
Outwell Rd Emneth PE14..59 B2
Stow Bardolph PE34.....78 E8
Oval Ave NR5.........161 C8
Oval Rd NR5.........157 C1
Oval The IP25.........84 B5
Overbury Rd NR6......158 A4
Over Cross NR16.......119 C8
Overstone Ct NR6......158 F5
OVERSTRAND NR27......11 A4
Overstrand Rd NR27....139 C6
Overstrand Sports Club
NR27.................11 A3
Overtons Way 🗺 NR14...90 C5
Overton Wy NR10......149 D6
Overwood La NR16.....106 A3
Overy Rd PE31........135 D3
OVINGTON IP25.........84 E5
Ovington Rd IP25......84 C4
Owen Rd Diss IP22.....177 F4
Great Yarmouth NR31...169 B1
Owen's Cl 🗺 NR15.....106 E3
Owl Dr 🖪 NR14........89 B3
OXBOROUGH PE33.......81 D4
Oxborough Dr PE30.....148 E1
Oxborough La NR21....141 C4
Oxborough Rd
Oxborough PE33........81 D3
Stoke Ferry PE33.......81 A2
Oxborough Wlk 🔞 NR31.169 D3
Oxburgh Cl 🖪 PE13....152 A7
Oxburgh Hall Gdns &
Estate★ PE33..........81 E4
Oxburgh Sq NR21.......30 C4
Oxcroft NR13.........166 C4
Oxford Ave NR31......170 B3
Oxford Pl PE34........144 F6
Oxford Rd 🖪 Feltwell IP26..98 E1
🖪 Feltwell IP26.........98 E1
Oxford St NR2........162 C5
Oxford Way 🔢 NR29....57 D4
OXNEAD NR10..........36 E2
Oxnead Dr NR30......168 C7
Oxnead La NR35.......107 F4
Oxnead Rd NR3........158 B2
OXWICK NR21..........31 D4

P

Pack La Briston NR24...142 F3
East Carleton NR14.....89 A6
Strumpshaw NR13.......73 F3
Packway The IP20.....123 A3
Paddock Cl Belton NR31..93 F6
🖪 Fakenham NR21.....141 E4
🗺 Watton IP25..........84 F3
Paddock Farm IP31.....127 B4
Paddock Farm Dr NR29..75 F8
Paddock Gdns NR17....174 E5
Paddock Rd 🔞 IP20....122 D2
Paddock St NR2.......162 C8
Paddocks The
Aylsham NR11.........150 C6
Bacton/Walcott NR12....23 D4
Beetley NR20..........49 D4
Brandon IP27..........175 E4
Griston IP25...........85 A1
Lakenheath IP27.......113 E1
Mileham PE32..........48 D6
Norwich NR6..........158 F6
Stradbroke IP21.......131 E1
Swaffham PE37........153 B3
Paddock The
🖪 Cromer NR27.........10 B5
Hemsby NR29.........167 A6
Trowse with Newton NR14.163 A2
Paddy's La NR9........51 E1
Paddys Loke NR30.....169 A7
Padgate NR13..........72 D6
Padgett's Rd PE14.......95 A6
Page Cl
🖪 North Walsham
NR28................151 C6
Poringland NR14.......90 C5
Page Rd Brundall NR13..165 C4
Norwich NR3..........157 F1
Pages Cl 🖪 NR18......173 B3
Pages La IP25..........84 B5
Page Stair La PE30.....146 D6
Paget Adams Dr 🖪 NR20..68 A8
Paget Cres NR31.......170 C1
Paget Rd NR30.......169 D4
Paige Cl 🖪 PE33........61 D5
Paiges Cl PE31........140 C4
Paine Cl IP22.........177 B5

Paine Rd NR7.........163 D8
Painter St IP24.......176 C4
Pakenham Dr PE31....140 C3
Palace St NR1........178 B3
Pales Gn 🖪 PE32.......46 F2
PALGRAVE IP22........177 C2
Palgrave Cl NR8......155 B1
Palgrave Rd
Great Dunham PE32.....47 E1
Great Yarmouth NR30...169 C5
Little Dunham PE32.....65 D8
Palgrave VC Prim Sch
IP22.................177 D2
Palling Rd NR12.......24 D1
Palm Cl NR18.........173 B5
Palmer Dr IP27.......113 E2
Palmer Rd
Great Yarmouth NR31...170 D5
🖪 New Rackheath NR13..72 E7
Norwich NR3..........158 C3
Palmers La NR12.......55 C5
Palmer's La
Aylsham NR11.........150 C5
Freethorpe NR13........92 F8
Palmer Way PE38......172 C3
Palomino Dr PE38.....172 B6
Pandora 🖪 PE30.......147 C4
Pansey Dr PE31.......140 C4
Panton Cl PE30........146 D2
PANXWORTH NR13......73 E7
Panxworth Church Rd
NR13.................73 E8
Panxworth Rd NR13.....73 F7
Paper St NR19.........68 C6
Papillion Rd NR18.....173 D4
Papplewick Cl 🖪 NR4...162 C1
Paradise La
🖪 Bawdeswell NR20.....50 E7
🖪 King's Lynn PE30.....146 D5
Paradise Par 🖪 PE30...146 D5
Paradise Pl NR1.......178 B2
Paradise Rd
🖪 Bawdeswell NR20.....50 E7
Downham Market PE38..172 B5
🖪 King's Lynn PE30.....146 D5
Paragon Pl 🖪 NR2.....162 C6
Parana Cl NR7.........159 C5
Parana Ct NR7........159 C5
Parana Rd NR7.......159 C5
Parish Rd NR10........53 D7
Park Ave 🖪 Barford NR9..69 F2
King's Lynn PE30......146 F4
North Walsham NR28...151 D5
Scottow NR10..........37 D2
Wisbech PE13.........152 C6
Park Cl Hethersett NR9...88 D7
Holt NR25.............137 D5
Norwich NR6..........158 E5
Thurton NR14...........91 C4
Wymondham NR18.....173 D1
Park Comm La NR16....119 B5
Park Cres PE34........61 B5
Park Ct Harling NR16...118 C5
North Walsham NR28...151 D5
Park Dr NR9...........88 C7
Parker Cl NR13.......165 B4
Parker Dr NR21.......141 D4
Parker Rd NR2........162 B5
Parker's CE Prim Sch
IP25..................84 C3
Parkers Cl
Saham Toney IP25......84 C5
Wymondham NR18.....173 B6
Parker's Cl NR9........70 C5
Parker's La NR15......106 F2
Parker's Rd 🔟 NR20....68 F6
Parkes La NR15.......106 D6
Park Est 🖪 IP25........67 B2
Park Farm La
Euston IP24...........126 C4
Hoxne IP21...........131 C2
Park Gn 🗺 NR9........88 D7
Park Highatt Dr 🖪 IP25...67 C2
Park High Sch PE30.....147 A4
Parkhill 🖪 PE32........44 B3
Park Hill PE31........140 D5
Parkington Wy IP22....128 B2
Park La Blofield NR13...165 B8
Cromer NR27.........139 D4
Deopham NR18........87 A4
Downham Market PE38..172 B3
Helhoughton NR21.......30 E5
Hockering NR20........69 C8
North Walsham NR28...151 C5
Norwich NR2..........162 B5
Reepham NR10........149 B4
Scarning NR19.........67 B6
Snettisham PE31........12 E4
Wymondham NR18.....173 C2
Parkland Cl 🖪 NR12.....55 E4
Parkland Cres
🖪 Horning NR12........55 E4
Norwich NR6..........158 F3
Parkland Dr NR31......170 A5
Parkland Est NR29.....167 A8
Parkland Rd NR6......158 F3
Parklands NR8........156 D4
Parklands Ave IP25......67 B2
Parklands Way 🗺 IP20..122 D2
Park Rd Cromer NR27...139 D5
Diss IP22.............177 D4
East Dereham NR19....154 E6
Great Yarmouth NR31...170 D3
Gressenhall NR20.......49 C3
Hunstanton PE36......132 C4
Spixworth NR10.........54 A1
St Cross, South Elmham
IP20.................123 C3

Park Rd *continued*
Upper Sheringham NR26...138 A4
Warham NR23..............6 A4
Wells-next-the-Sea NR23 .136 C6
Wisbech PE13 ....152 D5
Wroxham/Hoveton NR12 .164 B3
Parkside PE36 ....13 A7
Parkside Ct IP22.........177 C4
Parkside Dr NR6.........158 E5
Parkside Sch The NR2 ..162 A5
Park St PE13.............152 D5
Park The NR16...........118 B5
Parkview IP24............174 B4
Park View Botesdale IP22 .128 F3
Brandon IP27 ....175 B2
Horsford NR10 ....53 A3
Rollesby NR29 ....57 D3
Weeting IP27 ....175 A7
Park View Ave NR29.....57 D3
Parkway PE30 ....147 B4
Park Way NR6...........157 E5
Parliament Ct 5 NR7 ...72 D4
Parliament La IP24......102 A7
Parmenter Rd NR4.......161 F3
Parmeter Cl NR11........150 D6
Parrow La NR11..........21 C6
Parr Rd NR3.............158 A1
Parsons Cl IP27.........175 B2
Parsons La PE31.........14 D8
Parsons Mead NR4.......161 F1
Partridge Dr
Mulbarton NR14..........89 A3
4 Thetford IP24........176 D2
Partridge Gr PE37........153 D3
Partridge Rd NR11.......150 B6
Partridge Way NR6.......158 D4
Partridge Wlk IP27......175 F3
Parva NR11...............20 B4
Pasteur Rd NR31.........169 B2
PASTON NR28............143 D2
Paston Cl 4 NR11.........9 E1
Paston Coll NR28.........151 C5
Paston Dr NR30..........168 C8
Paston Great Barn ★
NR28...................143 E2
PASTON GREEN NR28....143 D1
Paston Rd
Great Yarmouth NR31....170 C5
Mundesley NR11 ....143 D5
Paston Way NR7.........159 C2
Pasture Cl PE31..........28 B4
Pastures The
5 Blakeney NR25........7 C6
Great Yarmouth NR31....170 B7
Hemsby NR29 ....167 A4
Little Snoring NR21......17 B3
Patricia Ave NR12.......54 C6
Patricia Rd NR1.........162 D3
Patrick Rd 4 NR15.......106 D3
Patten La NR15..........121 B3
Patterson Cl 4 NR30.....169 C4
Patteson Cl 8 NR4.......89 B8
Patteson Rd NR3.........162 D8
Paul Dr PE32..............29 D8
Paul Engelhard Wy NR10..35 B3
Pauls La NR27............11 A3
Pavilion Ct 5 IP22.......177 A5
Pavilion Rd NR31.........170 D4
Pavilion Theatre NR31 ..170 C4
Pavilion Wy NR20........154 F5
Paxman Rd PE30.........146 F2
Paxton Pl 3 NR2.........162 C4
Paxton Terr PE30.........146 E5
Payne Ave PE13..........152 D7
Paynes Hill IP20.........122 F6
Payne's La IP26..........98 C1
Peabody Rd NR11........150 A5
Peachman Way 5 NR7...72 D4
Peachtree St 6 NR21.....15 C2
Peacock Chase NR18.....173 D4
Peacock Gr NR8...........54 C6
Hockwold cum Wilton IP26 113 F6
Peacock Gr NR8..........158 C6
Peacock La Beetley NR20..49 E5
Holt NR25 ....137 B7
Peacock St NR3..........178 B4
Peacocks The NR25......137 C4
Peacock Way NR24......142 A4
Peakhall Rd PE32.........48 B8
Peakwell Cl NR8.........155 C2
Pearcefield NR3..........158 E2
Pearce Rd IP22...........177 E4
Pearce's Cl 2 IP26......114 A7
Pearmain Rd IP22........177 C5
Pearsons Cl
Freethorpe NR13..........92 E7
Holt NR25 ....137 C6
Pearson's Rd NR25.......137 C6
Peartree Ave 2 NR29....57 C4
Pear Tree Cl NR20........68 E6
Pear Tree Cnr NR21......31 C2
Peartree Way 9 PE14.....59 A1
PEASELAND GREEN NR20..50 F3
Peatlings La PE13........152 A7
Pebble Cl 3 PE12.........41 B8
Pebble View Wlk NR31...171 E4
Peck Cl NR5...............160 E8
Peckover Dr PE13.........152 B5
Peckover House ★ PE13 .152 B5
Peckover Prim Sch PE13 152 B6
Peckover Rd
Fakenham NR21..........141 A6
Norwich NR4 ....161 E3
Peckover Way PE30.......147 E8
Peddars Cl PE36..........132 D6
Peddars Dr PE36..........132 D6
Peddars' La NR34.........110 C6
Peddars Rise PE37........153 C4

Peddars Way NR8........155 D2
Peddars Way N PE36.......2 A4
Peddlars Turnpike NR20 ..33 F3
PEDHAM NR13..............73 D7
Pedham Rd NR13..........73 E7
Pedlars Croft 2 NR29....167 A8
Pedlar's Gr PE37..........153 C5
Pedlar's La NR21..........17 F1
Pedley La PE13...........152 A6
Peel Mews 5 NR3........178 A3
Peel St PE30.............146 F4
Pegasus Cl NR30.........168 D7
Pegg Cl NR9................70 B5
Peggotty Rd NR30.........170 D8
Pegg Rd NR26............138 C5
Pegg's La NR16...........105 E6
Pelargonium Dr NR18....173 F7
Peldon Dr PE13...........152 E5
Pelham Rd NR3...........158 D1
Pellew Rd NR21..........151 C6
Pell Pl 2 PE33............43 F2
Pell Rd PE13.............140 D4
Pemberton Rd 6 IP20...122 D1
Pembrey Cl NR3..........158 D3
Pembroke Ave NR31.......170 B4
Pembroke Rd NR2........162 B5
Pendlesham Rise NR8....155 E2
Pendula Rd PE13..........152 E7
Penfold Dr NR18..........173 E5
Penfold St NR11..........150 C6
Penguin Rd NR29.........167 D4
Penhill La NR17...........103 D7
Penn Cl NR8..............156 C6
Penn Gr NR3..............158 C1
Pennington Way PE31....140 A4
Penn Rd NR8.............156 D8
Pennycress Dr
6 Thetford IP24.........176 F5
Wymondham NR18......173 E4
Penny Croft 3 NR21......15 C2
Pennyfields NR35.........124 A7
PENNYGATE NR12.........38 E2
Pennygate La NR12........38 F1
Pennyroyal 1 NR6........158 D5
Penrose Cl PE30..........147 B8
Penrose Gdns PE13.......152 E4
Penrhyn Cl NR4...........161 E5
Penshurst Mews 5 NR4 .161 F1
Pensthorpe Nature Reserve
& Gdns ★ NR21..........32 B8
Pentney Abbey Leisure Ctr
PE32.....................63 A7
Pentney Dro PE33.........62 E6
Pentney La PE32..........63 D8
Pepper La PE38...........97 C8
Peppers IP27.............175 B7
Pepper's Gn PE30........148 B1
Percival Cl NR4...........161 A8
Percy Howes Cl 10 NR13 .72 D6
Perebrown Ave NR30.....169 D7
Pereers Cl NR25..........137 A7
Peregrine Cl Diss IP22...177 F5
Norwich NR7 ....159 C4
Peregrine Mews
8 Cringleford NR4.......89 A8
Norwich NR7 ....159 C4
Peregrine Rd NR7.........159 C4
Perkin Field PE34.........144 B4
Perrings NR18............173 B6
Perrys La NR10............35 C2
Persimmon PE30..........147 C5
Peter Ave NR13..........166 B3
Peter Beales Roses ★
NR17....................103 F3
Peter Cl NR29............168 D4
Peter Dr IP24.............176 F5
Peterhouse Ave NR31....170 C4
Peterhouse Prim Sch
NR31....................170 B4
Peterkin Rd 3 NR4.......89 B8
Peter Pulling Dr NR8.....156 A6
Peters Cl NR19...........154 C1
Peterscourt PE30.........147 D6
Peter's Dro PE34..........61 A7
Petersfield Cl NR15.......106 F4
Petersfield Dr 11 NR12...55 E4
Peterson Rd NR3.........158 A2
Peterson's La NR11.......150 B7
Peterspoint PE12..........41 A7
Peters Wy NR19...........68 C6
Peto Ct NR5..............161 C7
Peto's Cnr NR32..........111 F8
Petre Cl 3 NR28..........151 C7
Petticoat Dro PE32........64 E8
Petticoat La PE33.........62 D6
Pettingales 3 NR14......89 F4
Pettits La IP21...........130 C7
Petty Spurge Sq 8
NR18....................173 E4
Petts Cl 3 PE13..........152 E7
Pettus Rd NR4............161 E3
Peverell Rd NR5..........161 B7
Pheasant Cl NR14.........89 A3
Pheasants Wlk NR35.....123 E8
Pheasant Way IP27.......175 F4
Pheasant Wlk 2 NR13....74 B8
Phelps Rd NR7............163 F7
Philadelphia La NR3......158 D2
Philip Ford Way NR18....173 C2
Philip Nurse Rd PE31.....140 B3
Philip Pl NR19............154 D2
Philip Rudd Ct PE32......45 A8

Philips' Chase PE36......132 D2
Phillippo Cl 4 PE32......28 A1
Pickards Way PE13.......152 A6
Pickford Cl NR28.........151 E6
Picton Rd NR15..........106 D4
Pier Gdns NR31..........170 E4
Pier Pl NR30.............169 D2
Pier Plain NR31...........170 D5
Pier Rd NR31.............170 D4
Pier Wlk NR31............170 D4
Pigeon St PE14............41 D3
Pigg La NR3..............178 B4
Pightle Cl 21 NR14.......89 B3
Pightle The PE37.........153 C4
Pightle Way Lyng NR9....51 A4
Reepham NR10 ....149 C5
Pigot La NR14.............90 C6
Pike La IP24..............176 D3
Pikeman Pl NR13..........72 E5
Pikes Nursery 4 NR29....56 C5
Pilgrims Way
Little Cressingham IP25....83 F3
Weeting IP27 ....175 A8
Pilgrim's Way 1 IP20....122 D2
Pilling Pk Rd NR1........163 B7
Pilling Rd NR7............163 D7
Pilot St 2 PE30...........146 D5
PILSON GREEN NR13......74 B8
Pimpernel Rd NR10........53 B2
Pincushion Dro PE14.......78 B5
Pinder Cl NR3.............158 A1
Pinder Rd NR3............158 A1
Pine Ave Cockley Cley PE37..82 D7
Marham PE33 ....63 B4
Pine Cl
5 Downham Market
PE38..................172 C6
8 Eye IP23..............130 C1
4 Harleston IP20.........122 D1
Hunstanton PE36.........132 D4
17 Marham NR29.........57 D4
Norwich NR4 ....162 A5
Ormesby St Margaret
NR29..................167 A3
3 Snettisham PE31.......12 E4
Thetford IP24 ....176 B1
Pine Coombe 1 NR21.....15 C2
Pinecot Ave 7 NR31......94 C6
Pine Ct NR17.............174 D4
Pine Gn NR31............170 B5
Pine Gr
East Dereham NR19 .....154 D2
Sheringham NR26.........138 C6
Pineheath Rd NR25.........8 E3
Pinelodges The NR7.......163 C6
Pine Loke NR14............90 B5
Pine Mall PE31............133 C6
Pine Rd King's Lynn PE30 .148 D2
Norwich NR7 ....159 E1
Pines The NR4............161 B1
Pine Tree Chase PE33.....43 F1
Pine Tree Ct IP22.........127 F5
Pinetrees NR31............93 E3
Pine Trees Bsns Pk NR7. 159 D3
Pinetrees Rd NR7.........159 D3
Pine View NR7............139 F4
Pine Wlk 6 NR25..........8 F5
Pinewood Cl NR6.........157 F4
Pinewood Dr
Brandon IP27 ....175 C2
6 Horning NR12.........55 E4
Pinewood Leisure Ctr
NR25.....................9 B3
Pinfold La
Hindolveston NR20........33 D8
Northwold IP26...........99 B8
Pinfold Rd PE14...........77 E5
Pingle Rd PE14............78 A4
Pingles Rd PE30...........148 C4
Pinkney La NR24..........19 B5
Pintail Dr 2 Blakeney NR25. .7 C6
Great Yarmouth NR31....170 A6
Pinto Cl PE38.............172 B6
Pioneer Rd NR6...........159 A6
Piper Rd King's Lynn PE30 .146 F1
Norwich NR7 ....159 E1
Pipit's Mdw NR11.........21 A5
Pippin Cl Dereham NR19 .154 E3
Ormesby St Margaret
NR29..................167 A2
Pippin Gdns PE13.........152 F7
Pippin Gn NR4............161 E5
Pippin Pl PE13............152 E2
Pirnhow St NR35.........109 B1
Pishmire Cl NR5..........160 F6
Pitchford Rd NR5.........161 C6
Pit La PE37...............153 C4
Pit Rd
Aldeby, Wheatacre, Burgh St
Peter NR34............111 B4
Hemsby NR29 ....167 A4
Northrepps NR27 ....11 A1
Woodbastwick NR13......55 D1
Pit St NR10...............22 C6
Pitt Farm Gn NR8.........70 B8
Pitt's Hill NR15...........107 B8
Pitts Hill Cl NR15........107 B8
Pitt Sq NR9...............86 C4
Pitt St NR3...............178 A4
Pius Dro PE14.............77 E6
Plaford Rd NR7...........159 A2
Plane Rd NR31............170 B6
Plantation Cl NR17.......174 C3
Plantation Dr NR7........159 D3
Plantation Gdn The ★
NR2.....................162 C5
Plantation Rd
Aslacton NR15...........121 A7

Plantation Rd *continued*
Blofield NR13............165 F7
4 Fakenham NR21.......141 E4
North Walsham NR28....151 E5
Norwich NR6 ....157 E6
Plantation The NR2......162 B4
Plantsman Cl NR2........162 B3
Plasset Dr NR17..........174 F7
Platten's Cl 1 NR11......19 F1
Plattens Cl NR12.........164 B3
Playbarn The ★ NR15.....90 C3
Players Way NR6.........158 E6
Playing Field La 12 NR29..57 D4
Pleasance Cl PE30........147 A5
Pleasant Cl NR6..........157 D5
Pleasant Ct 1 PE30.......146 E3
Pleasant Pl PE31.........133 C6
Pleasant Row 1 PE37.....153 C3
Pleasure Beach ★ NR30 .169 E3
Plevna Terr NR31.........169 B3
Ploughboy La IP25.........84 C6
Plough La Hardingham NR9 .86 D6
Watlington PE33 ....61 E5
Ploughman Rd NR28......147 C4
Ploughman's Dro IP26.....98 B1
Ploughman's La NR21......17 C6
Ploughman's Piece PE36...2 E2
Plover Cl
Great Yarmouth NR31....170 A7
3 Thetford IP24.........176 D2
Plovers Ct IP27...........175 F3
Plovers Way IP26.........113 F7
Plowright Pl PE13.........153 B4
Plumbly Cl NR28.........151 D3
Plumb's Cl NR24..........142 E4
Plum La NR11.............20 C8
Plummers Hill NR23.......136 D5
Plummer's La NR15.......107 C7
Plump Rd NR15...........106 D5
Plumsgate Rd NR12........39 C1
Plumstead Dr NR17.......174 E6
PLUMSTEAD GREEN
Great and Little Plumstead
NR13...................73 B6
Plumstead NR11 ....20 B6
Plumstead Rd
Baconsthorpe NR25........20 A7
Edgefield NR24 ....19 E5
Great & Little Plumstead
NR13...................72 E6
4 Norwich NR1...........163 C8
Thorpe End NR13 ....72 E6
Woodbastwick NR13......73 D7
Plumstead Rd E NR13....163 D8
Plymouth Cl 3 NR30......168 C6
Pocahontas Way PE31.....133 E5
Pochard St NR8..........156 B5
POCKTHORPE
Sparham NR9 ....51 B5
Thompson IP24 ....102 A7
West Rudham PE31 ....29 F6
Pockthorpe Gate NR3....163 A7
Pockthorpe La IP24.......102 A7
Pockthorpe Loke
Barnham Broom NR9......69 D2
Hickling NR12 ....39 F2
Pockthorpe Rd NR9........88 A8
PODMORE NR19...........67 B7
Podmore La NR19..........67 C8
Poethlyn Dr NR8..........156 A5
Point Dr 2 PE37..........153 C3
Police Rd PE14............41 D4
Polka Rd NR23............136 D5
Pollard Rd NR10...........53 E6
POLLARD STREET NR12....23 D3
Poll Cl NR18..............173 F7
Pollywiggle Cl NR5.......161 A6
Pommer's La NR30........170 D8
Pond Cl 14 NR9...........88 C7
Pond Hills Rd NR25.......19 E7
Pond La Brandon IP27....175 A2
Knapton NR28 ....143 B2
Surlingham NR14.........73 B1
Taverham NR8 ....156 F8
Pond Rd Antingham NR28. .22 B4
East Dereham NR19 .....154 C2
3 Horsford NR10.........53 A3
Swafield NR28 ....22 C3
Ponds End La IP22........127 E4
Pond Wy NR18............173 F7
Pooley St IP22............128 F7
POOLEY STREET IP22......129 A8
Poorhouse La NR14........89 A2
Pope's La PE34............144 A4
Poplar Ave
Great Yarmouth NR31....170 C3
Heacham PE31 ....133 C5
King's Lynn PE34.........43 D4
5 Marham PE33..........63 B4
Norwich NR4 ....161 E1
Poplar Cl
Downham Market PE38....172 B6
2 Honington IP31........126 B1
12 Horsford NR10.........53 A3
Long Stratton NR15......106 F4
Norwich NR5 ....156 F2
Poplar Dr Filby NR29......75 F8
Happisburgh NR12 ....23 F3
King's Lynn PE30.........148 D2
Poplar Gr NR26...........138 E5
Poplar Pl 11 NR20.........68 A8
Poplar Rd
Attleborough NR17.......174 B2
West Winch PE33.........43 F1
Poplars The Hilgay PE38...96 F8
Spexhall IP19 ....124 F1
Swanton Abbott NR10.....37 C4
Tacolneston NR16........105 F4

Poplar Way NR17.........174 C2
Pople St NR18............173 B4
Poppy Cl Chedgrave NR14..91 F2
2 Cringleford NR4........89 A8
18 Lingwood NR13.......74 A3
North Walsham NR28....151 F5
4 Thetford IP24.........176 F4
Poppy Dr 5 NR26.........138 B6
Poppyfields
14 Horsford NR10.........53 A3
West Lynn PE34..........146 B4
Poppy Mews 6 PE13......152 E5
Poppy's La IP21...........121 F5
PORINGLAND NR14........90 C5
Poringland Prim Sch
NR14....................90 D5
Poringland Rd NR14.......90 B5
Porson Rd NR7............159 C1
Portal Ave IP25............84 F3
Portal Cl
4 Barnham IP24..........125 F6
7 Feltwell IP26..........98 D1
Portalfield 10 NR12.......39 B4
Porterbush Rd 18 NR14...89 B3
Porter Rd 8 NR15.........106 E3
Portersfield Rd NR2.......162 B5
Porter's La NR9............51 E5
Porter's Loke
1 Belton NR31............94 A6
Burgh Castle NR31 ....93 F6
Norwich NR7 ....159 A3
Porter's Rd Beighton NR13..74 E1
Freethorpe NR13..........92 E8
Porter St PE38............172 A5
Porthole Cl 10 NR33......111 F1
Portland Ct NR31.........169 C3
Portland Pl
Great Yarmouth NR30....169 E3
King's Lynn PE30 ....146 D2
3 Thetford IP24.........116 A1
Portland St
12 King's Lynn PE30.....146 E5
Norwich NR2 ....162 B5
Port Rd NR15.............122 B8
Port Row NR9.............51 B4
Portway Pl 6 NR2.........162 C7
Portway Sq 10 NR2.......162 C7
Portway The PE30.........146 D2
Postle Mews NR3.........158 A1
Post Mill PE30............147 C5
Postmill Cl NR18..........173 C4
Post Mill Cl NR7..........159 A3
Post Office Cl 8 NR13.....74 A3
Post Office La
Corpusty NR11 ....34 F8
Garvestone NR9 ....86 B8
Weston Longville NR9.....51 E7
12 Wisbech PE13.........152 C5
Post Office Rd
Dersingham PE31 ....140 D3
Frettenham NR12 ....54 A4
Great & Little Plumstead
NR13...................73 B7
Lingwood & Burlingham
NR13...................73 F3
Lingwood NR13 ....74 A3
Toft Monks NR34........110 E5
POSTWICK NR13...........72 F2
Postwick La NR13.........165 A4
Postwick Sta NR7..........72 F2
Potash La Bracon Ash NR16 .88 D2
Eye IP22 ....130 B2
Potato Dro PE14...........60 B4
Potspoon Hole
Coltishall NR12 ....54 D8
Tunstead NR12 ....37 D1
Pottergate NR2............178 A3
Pottergate St NR15.......106 A2
POTTERGATE STREET
NR15....................106 B2
POTTER HEIGHAM NR29...56 F6
Potter Heigham Rd NR29..56 D8
Potteries ★ NR30.........169 D2
Potters Cres NR15.........121 C8
Potters Dr NR31..........171 D5
Potter's La
Rickinghall Superior
IP22...................128 F1
Wymondham NR18......105 B6
Potters Vale IP22..........128 C3
Potters Wy 2 NR14........90 C5
POTTHORPE NR20..........49 A8
Pottles Alley 4 NR9.......86 C5
Pottle's La NR15...........92 F5
Poulter's Dro PE14........77 D1
Poultry Rd IP27...........113 A3
Pound Cl
4 Harleston IP20.........122 D2
Hevingham NR10.........53 C8
Pound Gn La IP25..........67 C2
Pound Hill IP25............84 B5
Pound La Aylsham NR11...150 B6
Brundall NR13 ....165 F5
Burgh St Margaret (Fleggburgh)
NR29..................75 C8
Ditchingham NR35........108 C2
Docking PE31 ....134 D5
Filby NR29 ....75 F8
Great Yarmouth NR31....170 C3
Heacham PE31 ....133 D6
Litcham PE32............48 A4
Loddon NR14............109 C8
North Tuddenham NR20...50 D2
Norwich NR7 ....72 D4
Runhall NR20............69 A4

Pound La continued
Sloley NR12 . . . .**37** F2
Toft Monks NR34 . . . . **110** D6
Pound Rd East Ruston NR12 . **38** F7
Hevingham NR10 . . . .**53** C8
Ludham NR29 . . . .**56** C5
North Walsham NR28 . . . . .**151** D5
Powell Ct 5 NR19 . . . .**154** C6
Power's Pl PE38 . . . .**79** D1
Poynt CI NR18 . . . .**173** B5
Pratts Hill NR14 . . . .**73** A1
Press La NR3 . . . .**158** C1
Preston Ave NR18 . . . .**173** A2
Preston CE Prim Sch
NR15 . . . .**106** F7
Preston Cl
Freethorpe NR13 . . . .**92** E7
Wroxham/Hoveton NR12 . .**164** B2
Preston La NR14 . . . . **109** F8
Preston Rd NR28 . . . .**151** D6
Pretoria Gr PE30 . . . .**148** D3
Pretty Dr IP21 . . . .**130** D6
Pride Way NR13 . . . .**72** E5
Primrose Ave
Downham Market PE38 . . . .**172** A5
5 Downham Market PE38 **172** B4
Primrose Cl
Attleborough NR17 . . . .**174** B5
East Dereham NR19 . . . .**154** B4
15 Mulbarton NR14 . . . .**89** B3
Mundesley NR11 . . . .**143** B5
Ormesby St Margaret
NR29 . . . .**167** A2
Thetford IP24 . . . .**176** F4
Trunch NR28 . . . .**22** E5
PRIMROSE CORNER NR13 . .**55** C1
Primrose Cres 2 NR7 . . . . .**72** D3
Primrose Ct 3 NR7 . . . .**72** D3
Primrose Dr IP27 . . . .**175** A2
PRIMROSE GREEN NR9 . . . . .**51** A3
Primrose Hill NR20 . . . .**50** B4
Primrose La
Crostwick NR12 . . . .**54** C3
Sheringham NR26 . . . .**138** B5
Swanton Morley NR20 . . . . . .**50** B4
Primrose Pl NR2 . . . .**162** B5
Primrose Rd Hingham NR9 . **86** B5
Norwich NR1 . . . .**163** A6
Primrose Sq NR20 . . . .**50** B4
Primrose Way
15 Great Yarmouth NR31 . .**94** C6
10 Horsford NR10 . . . .**53** A3
Primrose Wlk NR28 . . . .**151** E4
Primula Dr NR4 . . . .**161** D5
Prince Andrew Dr PE31 . . . .**140** D3
Prince Andrew's Cl
2 Aldborough NR11 . . . .**21** A5
Norwich NR6 . . . .**158** B5
Prince Andrew's Rd NR6 . .**158** B5
Prince Charles Cl PE31 . . . .**140** D3
Prince Edward Cl NR7 . . . .**163** F7
Prince Henry Pl PE38 . . . . .**172** D4
Prince of Wales Cl PE13 . .**152** D8
Prince of Wales Rd
Caister-on-Sea NR30 . . . . .**168** C6
Cromer NR27 . . . .**139** B7
Norwich NR1 . . . .**178** B3
Upton with Fishley NR13 . .**166** A8
Prince Regent Way IP22 . .**177** F3
Prince Rupert Way NR13 . .**72** D5
Princes Cl IP27 . . . .**175** A2
Prince's Rd PE13 . . . .**152** C4
Prince's Rd Bungay NR35 . .**124** A7
Great Yarmouth NR30 . . . . .**169** D4
Princess Beatrice Cl
NR6 . . . .**157** D2
Princess Cl 7 IP25 . . . .**84** D3
Princess Ct 6 NR25 . . . . . .**137** C5
Princess Dr PE36 . . . .**132** D2
Princess's Dr
Dersingham PE35 . . . .**140** C1
Sandringham PE35 . . . .**27** D7
Princes St
North Walsham NR28 . . . . .**151** A4
Norwich NR3 . . . .**178** B3
Swaffham PE37 . . . .**153** B4
Prince's St PE12 . . . .**41** B8
Princess Theatre PE36 . . . .**132** C4
Princess Way 5 NR35 . . . .**123** F8
Prince St PE13 . . . .**152** D5
Princes Way PE30 . . . .**146** F5
Prince William Cl PE36 . . .**132** C4
Prince William Wy IP22 . . .**177** F5
Pringle Way 5 PE38 . . . . . .**97** B5
Prins Ave PE13 . . . .**152** D7
Prins Ct 3 PE13 . . . .**152** D7
Printing Mus ★ NR34 . . . . .**110** D1
Prior Bank Orch 3
NR27 . . . .**139** C6
Prior Cl 5 NR15 . . . .**106** F6
Prior Rd NR7 . . . .**72** D5
Priors Dr NR6 . . . .**158** E6
Prior Stephen Way IP24 . .**176** B3
Priorswood NR8 . . . .**155** E3
Priory Chase
Downham Market PE38 . . . .**172** B5
Wormegay PE33 . . . .**61** F8
Priory Cl Acle NR13 . . . .**166** C3
Alpington NR14 . . . .**90** F5
Caister-on-Sea NR30 . . . . .**168** D4
2 Fritton & St Olaves
NR31 . . . .**93** D2
7 Hethersett NR9 . . . .**88** D7
Palgrave IP22 . . . .**177** D1
Sheringham NR26 . . . .**138** F5

Priory Cl continued
Sporle with Palgrave PE32 . .**65** D6
Priory Cres NR21 . . . .**6** E2
Priory Dro IP25 . . . .**83** D4
Priory Gdns
1 Fritton & St Olaves
NR31 . . . .**93** D2
12 Great Yarmouth NR30 . .**169** C4
Priory La Ingworth NR11 . . .**21** A1
12 Palgrave IP30 . . . .**146** D4
Shotesham NR15 . . . .**90** A2
Priory Maze & Gdns ★
NR26 . . . .**138** F6
Priory Pk IP24 . . . .**176** C5
Priory Pl PE32 . . . .**65** D6
Priory Plain 13 NR30 . . . . .**169** C4
Priory Rd Bacton NR12 . . . . .**23** E4
Castle Acre PE32 . . . .**46** F1
Downham Market PE38 . . . .**172** B5
Fritton & St Olaves NR31 . . .**93** D2
Great Cressingham IP25 . . . .**83** D5
Hethersett NR9 . . . .**88** D7
King's Lynn PE30 . . . .**148** C5
Palgrave IP22 . . . .**177** C1
Sheringham NR26 . . . .**138** E7
Watton IP25 . . . .**84** E3
Woodbastwick NR13 . . . .**55** F1
Priory Row 11 NR30 . . . . . .**169** C4
Priory St NR31 . . . .**170** D6
Priory Terr PE38 . . . .**172** B5
Priscilla Cl NR5 . . . .**161** D5
Pristow Gn La NR16 . . . . . .**120** E7
Private Rd Earsham NR35 . .**123** D8
Ormesby St Margaret
NR29 . . . .**167** A3
Procession La PE32 . . . . . .**153** F8
Proctor Ave 3 NR14 . . . . . .**92** A2
Proctor Cl 4 NR14 . . . .**92** A2
Proctor Rd
Chedgrave NR14 . . . .**91** F2
5 Loddon NR14 . . . .**92** A2
Norwich NR6 . . . .**158** F6
Proctors Cl PE30 . . . .**146** C2
Progress Way IP23 . . . .**130** B1
Promenade
Overstrand NR27 . . . .**11** A4
Sheringham NR26 . . . .**138** D7
Prom The NR29 . . . .**167** E4
Prophets Alley PE34 . . . . . .**61** B6
Prospect Cl NR13 . . . .**92** E7
Prospect Pl PE13 . . . .**152** C3
Proudfoot Way NR11 . . . . .**150** B5
Provan Cres 8 NR31 . . . . . .**94** A5
Provence Pl 2 PE13 . . . . . .**152** E3
Providence Pl
Briston NR24 . . . .**142** E5
8 Thorpe Hamlet NR1 . . .**163** A6
Providence St 5 PE30 . . . .**146** E4
Providence Terr PE13 . . . .**153** A5
Provision Mkt NR2 . . . .**178** A3
Provost Rd IP26 . . . .**98** D1
Puddingmoor NR34 . . . .**110** C1
PUDDING NORTON NR21 . .**141** B1
Pudding Norton Medieval
Village of ★ NR21 . . . .**31** E6
PUDDLEDOCK NR17 . . . . . .**104** C3
Pug St IP21 . . . .**121** B2
Pulham CE Prim Sch
IP21 . . . .**121** C5
PULHAM MARKET IP21 . . .**121** C5
PULHAM ST MARY IP21 . . .**121** F4
Pullover Rd PE34 . . . .**146** A1
Pump House Cl NR8 . . . .**70** C6
Pump La NR30 . . . .**168** D3
Punsfer Way PE34 . . . .**60** C8
Purbeck Cl PE13 . . . .**152** A4
Purdance Cl NR5 . . . .**160** D8
Purdy St NR25 . . . .**8** B6
Purdy Way NR11 . . . .**150** B6
Purfleet PE30 . . . .**146** D5
Purfleet St
11 King's Lynn PE30 . . . . .**146** D5
8 King's Lynn PE30 . . . . . .**146** D5
Purland Rd NR7 . . . .**159** D2
Purley Ct NR31 . . . .**169** A1
Pursehouse Way IP22 . . . .**177** E4
Purslane Dr NR30 . . . .**168** E4
Purtingay Cl NR4 . . . .**162** A4
Putney Cl IP27 . . . .**175** A1
Pyebush La NR13 . . . .**166** B5
Pyecroft Rd PE14 . . . .**41** E3
Pyehurn La NR10 . . . .**53** A3
Pyehurn Mews NR8 . . . . . .**155** E3
Pye La Cranworth IP25 . . . . .**86** A6
Deopham NR18 . . . .**86** E2
Pyes Cl 1 NR25 . . . .**7** C6
Pye's La Castle Acre PE32 . .**46** F2
Swanton Morley NR20 . . . . . .**50** C3
Pyes Mill Rd NR14 . . . .**92** A1
Pyes Yd NR3 . . . .**178** B4
Pyghtle The 4 NR16 . . . . .**118** C5
Pyke Ct NR30 . . . .**168** D7
Pyman Cl 1 NR29 . . . .**57** D5
Pymar's La 6 NR15 . . . . . .**107** C5
Pym Cl NR13 . . . .**72** E5
Pyrford Dr NR4 . . . .**161** F1

Q

Quaker Ct NR10 . . . .**52** E7
Quaker La
Fakenham NR21 . . . .**141** B4
Norwich NR6 . . . .**53** E1
8 Spixworth NR12 . . . .**54** A1
Tasburgh NR15 . . . .**106** F6
Wisbech PE13 . . . .**152** E3

Quarry La NR9 . . . .**51** A5
Quarry Rd NR8 . . . .**156** A5
Quaves La NR35 . . . .**124** A8
Quay Angel NR31 . . . .**170** D1
Quay La NR25 . . . .**7** A7
Quay Mill Wlk 3 NR30 . . .**169** C4
Quay Ostend NR31 . . . .**171** C8
Quay Rd NR31 . . . .**170** D4
Quay Side NR3 . . . .**178** B4
Quayside Ct IP27 . . . .**113** E2
Quay The Blakeney NR25 . . . .**7** C6
Wells-next-the-Sea NR23 . .**136** D6
Wiveton NR25 . . . .**7** E7
Quebec Cl 14 NR4 . . . .**89** B8
Quebec Rd
Dereham NR19 . . . .**154** D7
Norwich NR1 . . . .**163** A6
Quebec St NR19 . . . .**154** D5
Queen Anne's Rd NR31 . . .**170** C8
Queen Elizabeth Ave
PE30 . . . .**147** B7
Queen Elizabeth Cl NR3 . .**178** C4
Queen Elizabeth Dr
Dersingham PE31 . . . .**140** D3
Wisbech PE13 . . . .**152** D3
Queen Elizabeth Hospl
PE30 . . . .**147** E5
Queen Elizabeth Way
Bawsey PE30 . . . .**147** F6
Castle Rising PE30 . . . .**27** C1
Queen Mary Rd PE30 . . . . .**147** A5
Queens Ave PE30 . . . .**146** D2
Queens Cl 6 Blakeney NR25 . **7** C6
Norwich NR4 . . . .**162** A3
Queen's Cl PE33 . . . .**80** E4
Queen's Cres
Bircham PE31 . . . .**14** A3
Great Yarmouth NR31 . . . . .**170** B3
Queens Ct 1 NR15 . . . .**106** E3
Queen's Ct NR17 . . . .**174** D5
Queens Dr PE36 . . . .**132** C6
Queen's Dr PE14 . . . .**77** A7
Queens Gdns PE36 . . . .**132** D6
Queen's Hill Prim Sch
NR8 . . . .**156** A5
Queen's Pl 2 PE34 . . . .**43** B1
Queens Rd Brandon IP27 . .**175** A2
Cromer NR27 . . . .**139** D4
Norwich NR1 . . . .**178** A1
Wisbech PE13 . . . .**152** C4
Queen's Rd
Attleborough NR17 . . . .**174** C6
Clenchwarton PE34 . . . .**146** A5
Fakenham NR21 . . . .**141** C4
Great Yarmouth NR30 . . . . .**169** D2
Hethersett NR9 . . . .**88** D4
Holt NR25 . . . .**137** C5
Queen's Sq NR17 . . . .**174** D5
Queen St
Great Yarmouth NR30 . . . . .**169** C3
King's Lynn PE30 . . . .**146** D5
New Buckenham NR16 . . . .**104** F1
Norwich NR1 . . . .**178** B3
Stradbroke IP21 . . . .**131** E1
12 Sutton Bridge PE12 . . .**41** B8
Swaffham PE37 . . . .**153** B4
Wisbech PE13 . . . .**152** C4
Wymondham NR18 . . . .**173** C3
Queensway
Caister-on-Sea NR30 . . . . .**168** E4
7 Earsham NR35 . . . .**123** F8
King's Lynn PE30 . . . .**147** C6
North Walsham NR28 . . . . .**151** A5
Roydon IP22 . . . .**177** A5
Thetford IP24 . . . .**176** C2
Watton IP25 . . . .**84** D3
Wymondham NR18 . . . .**173** B5
Queensway Com Jun Sch
IP24 . . . .**176** C2
Queensway Inf Sch IP24 **176** C2
QUIDENHAM NR16 . . . .**118** F6
Quidenham Rd
Harling NR16 . . . .**118** D5
Kenninghall NR16 . . . .**119** A5
Quidenham NR16 . . . .**118** F8

R

Rabbit La
Downham Market PE38 . . . .**172** D6
Great Witchingham NR9 . . . .**51** E6
Raby Ave PE30 . . . .**146** E6
Racecourse Rd NR7 . . . . . .**159** E1
Raceys Cl 4 PE14 . . . .**59** D2
Rachel Cl 7 NR5 . . . .**161** C5
Rackham Cl NR31 . . . .**171** C5
Rackham Rd NR3 . . . .**158** D2
RACKHEATH NR13 . . . .**72** E8
Rackheath La NR12 . . . .**54** B2
Radcliffe Rd NR8 . . . .**155** E2
RAF Air Defence Radar
Mus ★ NR12 . . . .**55** E5
Recreation Road Inf Sch
NR2 . . . .**162** A5
Rafeman Cl 3 NR5 . . . .**160** E7
Raglan St 1 NR2 . . . .**162** C6
RAGMERE NR17 . . . .**104** D1
Ragmere Rd NR17 . . . .**104** D1
Railway App 2 NR26 . . . . .**138** D7
Railway Cl
Fakenham NR21 . . . .**141** D4
Melton Constable NR24 . . . .**142** C4
Railway Hill IP20 . . . .**122** C2
Railway La PE12 . . . .**41** B7
Railway Mus ★ NR18 . . . . .**173** D2
Railway Rd
Downham Market PE38 . . . .**172** A5
King's Lynn PE30 . . . .**146** E5
Wisbech PE13 . . . .**152** C3

Rainey Ct 37 IP20 . . . .**122** D2
Rainsborough Rise NR13 . .**72** D5
Rainsthorpe PE30 . . . .**147** D8
Rainthorpe Hall ★ NR15 . .**106** F8
Raleigh Ave NR30 . . . .**169** D7
Raleigh Inf Sch IP24 . . . . .**176** E6
Raleigh Rd PE30 . . . .**147** B4
Raleigh Way IP24 . . . .**176** E6
Ramblers The NR14 . . . .**90** B6
Rambouillet Cl NR31 . . . . .**170** A4
Ramillies Cl 6 NR19 . . . . .**154** E5
Ramirez Rd NR13 . . . .**72** E8
Ram La NR15 . . . .**121** C4
Ramms Ct NR23 . . . .**136** D6
Ramm's La PE37 . . . .**66** A4
Ramnoth Jun Sch PE13 . . .**152** C4
Ramnoth Rd PE13 . . . .**152** C4
Rampant Horse St NR2 . . .**178** A2
Rampart Rd NR30 . . . .**169** C5
Rampart Way IP24 . . . .**176** D3
Ramsay Gdns PE36 . . . .**132** D3
Ramsey Cl Norwich NR4 . . .**161** E3
Thetford IP24 . . . .**176** E6
Randall Cl 1 NR31 . . . .**171** D5
Randell Cl PE14 . . . .**151** D4
Randle Gn NR5 . . . .**161** C8
Randolf Rd NR1 . . . .**162** E2
Rands Rd PE14 . . . .**60** C5
Rangoon Cl NR7 . . . .**159** C4
Ransome Ave IP21 . . . .**130** D6
Ransome's Cl PE14 . . . .**77** E5
Ranson Rd NR1 . . . .**163** B5
RANWORTH NR13 . . . .**55** F1
Ranworth 5 PE30 . . . .**147** D5
Ranworth Cl
8 Belton NR31 . . . .**94** A6
Swaffham PE37 . . . .**153** B1
Ranworth Dr
Hoveton NR12 . . . .**164** E6
Ormesby St Margaret
NR29 . . . .**167** B2
Ranworth Rd
Blofield NR13 . . . .**165** F8
Norwich NR5 . . . .**161** D7
South Walsham NR13 . . . . . .**74** A8
Rash's Cres IP22 . . . .**129** C6
Rash's Gn NR19 . . . .**154** F2
Rash's Green Ind Est
NR19 . . . .**154** F2
Ratcliffe Rd NR21 . . . .**141** C4
RATTEN ROW PE14 . . . .**59** F8
Rattle Row Mileham PE32 . . .**48** C6
Wymondham NR18 . . . .**173** B4
Rattlerow Hill IP21 . . . .**131** F2
Rattler's Rd IP27 . . . .**175** C3
Raven Cl NR31 . . . .**170** A7
Raven Croft ★ NR27 . . . .**89** A8
RAVENINGHAM NR14 . . . . .**110** A7
Raveningham Gdns ★
NR14 . . . .**110** A7
Raveningham Rd
Gillingham NR34 . . . .**110** C4
Stockton NR34 . . . .**110** A5
Raven's La PE31 . . . .**29** D5
Ravensmere Inf Sch
NR34 . . . .**110** D1
Ravensway PE38 . . . .**172** C3
Ravine Rd NR31 . . . .**93** E1
Rawhall Rd NR20 . . . .**49** B5
Rawley Rd NR5 . . . .**161** B8
Rawlings Way 21 IP26 . . . .**98** E1
Rawlinsons La NR11 . . . . . .**150** C7
Ray Bond Way NR11 . . . . . .**150** C4
Raymond Cl NR6 . . . .**157** E7
Raymond Rd NR6 . . . .**157** F7
Raymond St
Thetford IP24 . . . .**176** D3
15 Wisbech PE13 . . . .**152** C4
Rayner's Cl 6 NR30 . . . .**68** E6
Rayner's La NR35 . . . .**109** D4
Rayner's Way NR20 . . . .**68** E6
Raynham Cl NR7 . . . .**147** B4
Raynham Rd Dunton NR21 . .**31** C6
Hempton NR21 . . . .**141** A2
Whissonsett NR20 . . . .**31** C2
Raynham Ride NR19 . . . . . .**154** D7
Raynham St NR2 . . . .**162** B7
Rayns Cl NR6 . . . .**158** F5
READING GREEN IP21 . . . . .**131** C1
Read's Cross NR14 . . . .**109** E8
Readscross La NR14 . . . . . .**109** E8
Recorder Rd NR1 . . . .**178** C3
Recreation Dr PE38 . . . .**97** A5
Recreation Gd Rd NR7 . . .**159** A4
Recreation Rd
East Dereham NR19 . . . .**154** C1
Great Yarmouth NR31 . . . . .**170** C5
Hethersett NR9 . . . .**88** C7
North Walsham NR28 . . . . .**151** B4
Norwich NR2 . . . .**162** A5
Stalham NR12 . . . .**39** A4
Recreation Road Inf Sch
NR2 . . . .**162** A5
Rectory Cl
Caister-on-Sea NR30 . . . . .**168** E5
Coltishall NR12 . . . .**54** D7
21 Long Stratton NR15 . .**106** E3
2 Newton Flotman NR15 . .**89** D1
Rollesby NR29 . . . .**57** C2
Roydon PE32 . . . .**27** F2
Rectory Ct NR3 . . . .**158** D2
Rectory Dr PE34 . . . .**145** E4
Rectory Gdns
Hingham NR9 . . . .**86** B5
Wisbech PE13 . . . .**152** E6
Rectory Hill IP22 . . . .**128** D2

Rectory La
Bracon Ash NR14 . . . .**88** E3
Bunwell NR16 . . . .**105** C4
Great Ellingham NR17 . . . . .**103** E8
Haddiscoe NR14 . . . .**110** F7
Hedenham NR35 . . . .**108** D4
Little Melton NR9 . . . .**160** A3
Loddon NR14 . . . .**92** A2
Mettingham NR35 . . . .**124** D8
Mulbarton NR14 . . . .**89** B3
North Runcton PE33 . . . .**44** A3
Poringland NR14 . . . .**90** D5
Scole IP21 . . . .**121** C1
Stuston IP21 . . . .**130** B4
Watlington PE33 . . . .**61** D5
Weeting IP27 . . . .**175** B7
West Winch PE33 . . . .**43** F3
Rectory Mdw Diss IP22 . . .**177** E4
Litcham PE32 . . . .**48** A4
Rectory Rd
Aldeby, Wheatacre, Burgh St
Peter NR34 . . . .**111** A4
Bacton NR28 . . . .**23** C3
Brome & Oakley IP23 . . . . . .**130** B3
Broome NR35 . . . .**109** B3
Burston & Shimpling IP22 . .**120** E2
2 Coltishall NR12 . . . .**54** C6
Dickleburgh IP21 . . . .**121** B1
East Carleton NR14 . . . .**89** A4
Edgefield NR24 . . . .**19** D5
Elsing NR20 . . . .**50** F4
Gillingham NR34 . . . .**110** B3
Gissing IP22 . . . .**120** F4
Haddiscoe NR14 . . . .**110** F7
Hockering NR20 . . . .**69** B8
Hoveton NR12 . . . .**55** A7
Lyng NR9 . . . .**51** B4
Northrepps NR27 . . . .**11** A1
Outwell PE14 . . . .**77** F6
Rocklands NR17 . . . .**103** B7
Shelfanger IP22 . . . .**120** B2
Sutton NR12 . . . .**39** C3
Swanton Morley NR20 . . . . . .**50** B4
Tivetshall St Mary NR15 . . .**121** C4
Topcroft NR35 . . . .**107** F4
Weston Longville NR9 . . . . . .**51** D2
Whissonsett NR20 . . . .**31** E2
Wood Norton NR20 . . . .**33** A7
Wortham IP22 . . . .**129** D6
Rectory Row NR21 . . . .**17** F3
Red Admiral Cl 1 NR18 . .**173** E4
Red Barn La NR11 . . . .**9** D1
Redbrick Cotts IP27 . . . . . .**175** D5
Red Bridge La NR5 . . . .**157** C2
Redcastle Family Sch
IP24 . . . .**176** B3
Redcastle Rd IP24 . . . .**176** A4
Redcliffe Way NR13 . . . . . .**165** B4
Red Cottage Cl NR3 . . . . . .**158** A2
Redell Cl 3 NR13 . . . .**55** A1
REDENHALL IP20 . . . .**122** D3
Redenhall Rd IP20 . . . .**122** D2
Redfern Cl
East Dereham NR19 . . . .**154** B4
King's Lynn PE30 . . . .**147** E8
Redfern Rd NR7 . . . .**159** D1
Redgate IP24 . . . .**176** E4
Redgate Hill PE36 . . . .**132** D5
Redgate Jun Sch PE36 . . . **132** D2
Redgate Rd PE13 . . . .**41** A4
REDGRAVE IP22 . . . .**128** E4
Redgrave & Lopham Fen
National Nature Reserve ★
IP22 . . . .**128** F6
Redgrave Rd
South Lopham IP22 . . . .**128** E7
Wortham IP22 . . . .**129** A5
Redhill Cl IP22 . . . .**177** E5
Redland Rd PE37 . . . .**153** C1
Red Lion Cl
Holme Hale IP25 . . . .**66** B2
Hoxne IP21 . . . .**131** A1
Red Lion St
3 Aylsham NR11 . . . .**150** C7
Norwich NR1 . . . .**178** B2
Red Lion Yd NR23 . . . .**136** D6
Redman Rd NR28 . . . .**151** D3
Redmere Cl 4 NR12 . . . .**54** A4
Redmere Dro CB7 . . . .**112** D5
RED PITS NR11 . . . .**34** D7
Redpoll Rd NR8 . . . .**156** B5
Red Robin Cl 9 NR15 . . . .**106** D3
Redwell St NR2 . . . .**178** B3
Redwing Dr
1 Great Yarmouth NR31 . .**94** C6
5 Wisbech PE14 . . . .**152** D2
Redwing Gdns 7 NR10 . . . .**54** A1
Redwings Horse Sanctuary
(Caldecott) ★ NR31 . . . .**93** F4
Reeder Cl NR19 . . . .**154** D3
Reeder's La NR14 . . . .**90** E4
REEDHAM NR13 . . . .**92** E5
Reedham Prim Sch NR13 . .**93** A4
Reedham Dr NR12 . . . .**164** E7
Reedham Rd Acle NR13 . . .**166** B1
Beighton NR13 . . . .**74** E1
Cantley NR13 . . . .**92** D6
Reedham Sta NR13 . . . .**92** F5
Reed La NR19 . . . .**48** F3
Reeds La NR31 . . . .**93** D2
Reeds Wy 13 NR14 . . . .**92** A1
Reed Way 3 PE14 . . . .**77** A8
REEPHAM NR10 . . . .**149** B5
Reepham High Sch & Coll
NR10 . . . .**149** B3
Reepham Prim Sch
NR10 . . . .**149** B4

Ree–St A 205

Reepham Rd
Bawdeswell NR20 50 F8
Briston NR24 142 E2
Felthorpe NR10 155 D5
Foulsham NR20 33 D3
Guestwick NR20 34 A5
Horsford NR10 157 D7
Norwich NR6 157 E2
Swannington NR9 52 B5
Thurning NR20 34 B8
Wood Dalling NR11 34 D5
Reeve Cl IP21 130 D6
Reeve Pl NR27 139 D4
Reeve's 3 NR35 124 B8
Reeves Ave PE30 147 B8
Reeves Cl NR20 50 E7
Reeves Ct NR28 151 C5
Reeves La IP26 114 A7
Reffley Com Sch PE30 147 D8
Reffley La PE30 147 D8
Regal Ct 23 IP25 84 D3
Regal Rd PE13 152 B2
Regency Ave PE30 147 C5
Regency Ct NR1 163 B7
Regent Bvd 10 NR30 169 D4
Regent Cl NR19 154 D1
Regent Pl 1 PE30 146 E4
Regent Rd
Downham Market PE38 172 A4
9 Great Yarmouth NR30 169 D4
Regents Cl NR25 137 B5
Regents Ct NR28 151 B5
Regents Pk PE30 147 C5
Regent St
Great Yarmouth NR30 169 C3
Wickmere NR11 20 E4
Regent Way 6 PE30 146 D4
Reg Houchen Rd PE31 140 C3
Regina Rd NR1 178 A1
Regis Ave 4 NR27 9 F5
Regis Pl NR26 138 E7
Reid Way PE30 147 A8
Renowood Cl PE32 48 B8
Renson Cl NR3 158 C4
Renwick Pk E NR27 10 A4
Renwick Pk W NR27 10 A4
REPPS NR29 56 F4
Repps Rd
Ashby with Oby NR29 57 B3
1 Martham NR29 57 D4
Thurne NR29 56 E3
Repton Ave NR6 158 D7
Repton Cl NR11 150 D5
Retreat Est PE38 172 D6
Reve Cres 5 NR13 73 C6
Revell Rd PE38 172 B4
Reydon Cl 10 NR5 161 A7
REYMERSTON NR9 68 C1
Reymerston Rd NR9 68 B2
Reynolds Ave NR30 168 C8
Reynolds La NR29 56 E7
Reynolds Mews NR18 173 B5
Reynolds Way PE31 140 C3
Rhombus Bsns Pk NR6 158 B5
Rhond The NR12 164 C5
Rhone Pl 3 PE13 152 E3
Rhoon Rd PE34 144 E8
Rice Way NR7 159 C2
Richard Easter Rd IP24 176 D6
Richard Haggard Cl 3 IP25 67 C2
Richard Hicks Dr 9 NR19 154 C4
Richardson Cres NR9 88 C8
Richards Rd NR21 15 D2
Richard Young Cl 2 PE13 152 C8
Richenda Cl 8 NR5 161 C5
Riches Cl 2 NR15 106 F6
Richmond Cl
Honingham NR9 69 E6
Lyng NR9 51 A5
Richmond Ct PE13 152 A4
Richmond Pk NR17 174 F6
Richmond Pl NR9 51 A4
Richmond Rd
Brandon IP27 175 A1
Downham Market PE38 172 B4
4 Long Stratton NR15 106 E3
Norwich NR5 156 E1
Saham Toney IP25 84 C4
Richmond Rise NR10 149 C5
RICKINGHALL IP22 128 E2
Rickinghall Rd IP22 128 C3
Rickwood Dr PE37 153 C1
Riddlesworth Hall Sch IP22 127 C8
Riddlings Ct NR3 158 D2
Rider Haggard Rd NR7 159 D1
Ridgeway
Caister-on-Sea NR30 168 D8
Cromer NR27 139 C4
Ridgeway The NR1 163 B8
Ridings The
5 Cringleford NR4 89 B8
Fakenham NR21 141 E4
Poringland NR14 90 C5
Ridland's Rd NR24 142 C1
RIDLINGTON NR28 23 E1
RIDLINGTON STREET NR28 23 E1
Rigby Cl 1 NR14 90 D5
Rigbys Ct NR2 178 A3
Rigg Cl 2 PE13 152 B3
Rightup Dro IP27 113 E5
Rightup La NR18 173 D2
Riley Cl NR7 159 D1
Rill Cl PE30 148 B4
Rimer Cl NR5 160 F6
Ringbank La NR11 21 A6
Ringers Cl 4 NR18 173 D5
Ringers La NR9 86 C5
RINGLAND NR8 70 B8
Ringland La
Costessey NR8 156 B6
Easton NR9 70 B5
Morton on the Hill NR9 52 A2
Weston Longville NR9 51 F3
Ringland Rd NR8 155 A1
Ringmere Cl 2 IP25 84 C3
Ringmere Rd 3 IP25 84 C3
Ringmore Rd PE38 97 B6
Ring Rd NR7 163 F7
Ringsfield Rd NR34 124 F5
RINGSTEAD PE36 2 A3
Ringstead Downs Nature Reserve* PE36 1 F2
Ringstead Rd
Burnham Market PE31 135 A2
Docking PE31 134 A6
Heacham PE31 133 E6
Ringstead PE36 2 A2
Sedgeford PE36 13 B8
Thornham PE36 2 D6
Ringwood Cl NR9 160 B2
Ripley Cl NR2 161 F5
Ripon Way IP24 176 B5
Rippingall Cl 6 NR11 150 D6
Rippingall Rd NR11 150 D6
Rise The 10 Loddon NR14 92 A2
Sheringham NR26 138 E6
Riseway Cl NR1 163 B8
Rising Way 3 NR29 57 C4
Rising Wy 9 NR29 57 C4
Risley Cl NR16 117 E5
River Cl PE32 63 E8
River Ct NR21 141 A3
Riverdale Ct NR13 165 D3
Riverdene Mews NR8 155 E3
River Dro PE33 80 F2
Rivergreen Ct NR1 163 E6
River La Cranworth IP25 85 F7
King's Lynn PE30 147 A6
Rivermead NR12 39 B3
River Rd West Acre PE32 46 B1
West Walton PE14 59 A8
Riverside
Cockley Cley PE37 82 D7
Diss IP22 177 B3
King's Lynn PE30 147 B7
Norwich NR1 178 C2
Reedham NR13 92 F4
Riverside Cl NR6 157 D2
Riverside Ctr NR12 164 C5
Riverside Est NR13 165 D1
Riverside Ind Ctr NR31 170 D5
Riverside Ind Est PE30 146 D7
Riverside Maltings IP22 177 F3
Riverside Rd
Great Yarmouth NR31 170 D6
Holt NR25 8 A1
Norwich NR1 178 C3
Wroxham/Hoveton NR12 164 C4
Riverside Swimming Ctr NR1 178 C1
Riverside Way
Brandon IP27 175 C5
1 Wisbech PE13 152 B3
Riverside Wlk IP24 176 C4
Riversway PE30 146 E7
River Terr PE13 152 A8
River View Beccles NR34 110 C2
7 Beetley NR20 49 D4
River View Cl NR21 141 E4
Riverview Dr NR13 166 B8
Riverview Wy PE30 147 C7
River Vw 7 NR20 49 D4
River Way NR31 93 F6
River Wlk
Great Yarmouth NR30 169 C8
King's Lynn PE34 146 C6
RNLI Henry Blogg Mus* NR27 139 B7
Roaches Ct NR3 178 B3
ROAD GREEN NR15 107 E4
Robberds Way NR5 160 E8
Robert Andrew Cl NR18 87 B2
Robert Balding Rd PE31 140 C3
Robert Cl Trunch NR28 22 E5
5 Wymondham NR18 173 C6
Robert Gybson Way NR2 178 A3
Robert Herb Way 5 NR18 173 E4
Robert Kett Jun Sch NR18 173 C5
Robert Key Dr 2 NR20 68 E6
Robert Linge Cres IP27 175 D3
Robert Norgate Cl NR12 54 C6
Roberts Cl 3 NR15 107 C5
Robertson Cl NR26 138 E6
Robert St 8 PE30 146 E3
Robin Ave 16 IP20 122 D1
Robin Cl Costessey NR8 156 A5
Great Yarmouth NR31 170 A5
Mulbarton NR14 89 A3
Robin Hill PE31 133 D8
Robin Hood Rd NR4 162 C1
Robin Kerkham Way PE34 145 E6
Robin Mews 4 PE14 152 D2
Robins La NR10 149 B4
Robinson Rd IP21 130 C5
Robinsons Cl IP23 129 D1
Robin Wlk IP27 175 F3
Robson Rd NR5 161 B6
Robyns Rd
3 Sheringham NR26 9 F5
Sheringham NR26 138 F5
Rocelin Cl NR3 158 E3
Rochford Rd 4 NR29 57 C4
Rochford Wlk 5 PE13 152 E5
Rockall Way 6 NR30 168 C6
Rockingham Rd NR5 161 C6
ROCKLAND ALL SAINTS NR17 103 B7
Rockland Cl PE13 153 B2
Rockland Dr NR7 163 C6
Rockland La NR17 85 F1
Rockland Rd NR14 90 F7
ROCKLAND ST MARY NR14 91 B7
Rockland St Mary Prim Sch NR14 91 B6
ROCKLAND ST PETER NR17 103 B8
Rocklands Com Prim Sch NR17 103 B7
Rocklands Rd NR17 103 B4
Rode La NR16 105 B3
Rodham Rd PE15 77 A1
Rodinghead 1 PE30 147 D5
Rodney Rd NR30 169 D3
Rodwell Cnr NR10 35 C1
Roedich Dr NR8 155 C1
Roe Dr NR5 161 E6
Roger Ride 3 NR19 154 D2
Rogers Cl 4 NR5 161 B7
Roger's Cl NR31 171 D5
Roger's La NR15 89 F1
Roland Dr NR15 107 D5
Rolfe Cres PE31 133 E5
ROLLESBY NR29 57 D2
Rollesby Ave PE13 153 B2
Rollesby Gdns 9 NR29 57 D2
Rollesby Pl NR10 37 B2
Rollesby Prim Sch NR29 57 D3
Rollesby Rd
Fleggburgh NR29 57 C1
King's Lynn PE30 147 A3
Martham NR29 57 D4
Swaffham PE37 153 B2
Rolleston Cl NR5 161 B7
Rollingpin La NR19 154 D4
Roman Cres PE37 153 D2
Roman Dr NR13 165 B3
Roman Pl 20 NR30 169 D4
Roman Way Brancaster PE31 3 B7
Caister-on-Sea NR30 168 D5
Thetford IP24 176 C7
Romany Cl 8 NR29 57 D2
Romany Rd NR3 158 F1
Romany Wlk 6 NR14 90 C5
Romer Dro PE33 81 B3
Romney Wlk NR19 154 D4
Ron Hill Rd NR8 156 A5
Rook Dr NR8 155 E2
Rookery Cl PE34 145 E5
Rookery Farm Rd NR28 23 F2
Rookery Hill NR14 91 B7
Rookery La NR35 107 F3
Rookery Rd PE34 145 E4
Rookery The IP27 114 D5
Rook's La 6 NR34 110 D1
Room La NR15 122 D8
Roosters Cl 13 PE31 12 E5
Ropemakers Row 5 NR3 158 C1
Ropes Hill NR12 55 D4
Ropes Hill Dyke NR12 55 D4
Ropes Wlk NR13 165 E6
Rope Wlk 5 IP24 176 D4
Rosa Cl NR12 54 B1
Rosalie Cl NR6 158 B4
Rosary Cl 8 NR14 89 B3
Rosary Rd NR1 163 A6
Rosa Vella Dr 3 NR20 68 A8
Roseacre Cl NR2 162 C2
Roseacre Est NR25 9 A2
Rose Ave Costessey NR8 156 A5
Roydon IP22 129 D7
Rosebay 1 PE30 148 C3
Rosebay Cl 5 NR6 158 D5
Roseberry Rd PE14 59 B1
Rosebery Ave
King's Lynn PE30 147 B6
7 Poringland NR14 90 D5
Rosebery Bsns Pk NR14 90 C4
Rosebery Rd
Cromer NR27 139 D5
Great & Little Plumstead NR13 73 A4
Norwich NR3 158 D1
3 Sheringham NR27 10 A5
Rose Cottage's NR19 66 D8
Rosecroft 4 NR17 174 C5
Rosecroft Way IP24 176 F4
Rosedale Cres 5 NR1 163 A6
Rosedale Gdns NR31 94 A5
Rose Dr Cringleford NR4 161 B1
8 Dereham NR20 68 A8
Rose Fair Cl PE13 152 D3
Rosefields NR13 165 E4
Rose Hall Gdns NR35 124 A8
Rose La Botesdale IP22 128 E3
Bungay NR35 124 A8
Diss IP22 177 F3
3 Elm PE14 59 A1
Norwich NR1 178 C3
Palgrave IP22 177 D1
Rose La Cl IP22 177 D2
Rosemary La
11 Gayton PE32 45 C6
2 New Buckenham NR16 104 F1
Rosemary La *continued*
Norwich NR3 178 A4
Rosemary Rd Blofield NR13 73 C6
Norwich NR7 159 B4
Rosemary Terr NR21 141 B5
Rosemary Way PE38 172 D6
Rosery The NR14 89 C3
Roses Ct NR23 136 D5
Rose Terrace IP22 177 F3
Rosetta Rd NR10 54 A2
Rose Valley 4 NR2 162 B5
Roseville Cl 2 NR1 163 B5
Rose Wlk Brundall NR13 165 C3
Sculthorpe Airfield NR21 15 C2
1 Wisbech PE13 152 A6
Rosewood NR28 151 E5
Rose Yd NR3 178 A4
Roslyn Rd NR31 170 C5
Rosslare NR4 162 A1
Rossons Rd NR8 155 C1
Rostwold Way NR3 158 D2
Rothbury Cl NR18 173 B4
Rothbury Rd NR18 173 C4
Rotten Marsh NR13 166 C2
Rottenstone La NR29 167 F3
Roudham Park Ind Est NR16 118 A6
Roudham Rd NR16 117 F6
Rouen Rd NR1 178 B2
ROUGHAM PE32 47 B7
Rougham Cnr IP26 99 F3
Rougham End PE32 47 C8
Rougham Hall PE32 47 A7
Rougham Rd PE32 29 E1
Roughlands IP27 113 E1
Rougholme Cl
6 Beetley NR19 49 C3
6 Gressenhall NR20 49 C3
Rought Ave IP27 175 D2
ROUGHTON NR11 21 E8
Roughton Rd
Roughton NR27 139 B2
Thorpe Market NR11 21 F7
Roughton Rd Sta NR27 139 B4
Roundabout La NR14 109 B8
Roundham Medieval Village of* NR16 117 E6
Roundhead Ct 26 NR7 72 D4
Round House Way NR4 161 B1
Roundtree Cl NR7 159 B2
Roundtree Way NR7 159 B2
Roundway Down 17 NR7 72 D4
Round Well Rd NR5 156 D1
Rouse's La PE38 172 D4
Rowan Cl
10 Great Yarmouth NR31 94 C7
Thetford IP24 176 B1
7 Watlington PE33 61 D5
Wisbech PE13 152 F7
Rowan Ct NR5 156 F1
Rowan Dr Brandon IP27 175 C3
Gayton PE32 45 C6
Rowan Rd King's Lynn PE34 43 D4
Martham NR29 57 D4
Rowan Way
Fakenham NR21 141 F4
10 Great Yarmouth NR31 170 B6
Holt NR25 137 B7
Rowden Way IP22 177 B4
Row Hill 6 PE33 43 F2
Rowington Rd NR1 178 A1
Rowland Ct NR1 178 B1
Rowley Cnr IP26 83 A5
Row's Mdw 1 NR15 107 C5
Row The Weeting IP27 175 A7
Wereham PE33 80 D3
West Dereham PE33 80 B4
Rowton Heath 16 NR7 72 D4
Roxley Cl NR7 163 F5
Royal Albert Ct 5 NR31 170 D4
Royal Arcade NR2 178 B2
Royal Ave NR30 169 D7
Royal Cl 11 PE12 41 B8
Royalist Dr 28 NR7 72 D4
Royal Norfolk Regimental Mus* NR1 178 B3
Royal Pl 2 PE13 152 C4
Royal Sovereign Cres 19 NR31 94 C8
Royal Thames Rd NR30 168 D7
Royden Way
3 Burgh St Margaret (Fleggburgh) NR29 57 C1
Roydon IP22 177 B4
ROYDON Roydon IP22 129 D7
Roydon PE32 28 A2
Roydon Comm National Nature Reserve* PE32 27 F1
Roydon Fen IP22 177 A4
Roydon Gdns IP22 177 A5
Roydon Prim Sch IP22 177 B5
Roydon Rd IP22 177 C5
Royston Gn NR28 151 D6
Rubens Way 6 PE38 172 D6
Rudd's Drift PE32 48 E5
Rudds La NR10 149 B3
Ruddy Duck La PE30 146 E2
Rudham CE Prim Sch PE31 30 A6
Rudham Rd
Great Massingham PE32 29 D2
Syderstone PE31 15 A3
Rudham Stile La NR21 141 B6
Rufus St NR8 156 A5
Rugge Dr NR4 161 E2
Rugg's La NR29 75 C8
Ruin Rd NR28 38 A5
Rumburgh La NR35 124 D2
Rump Cl 10 NR20 50 B3
Runcton Cl NR5 161 B7
RUNCTON HOLME PE33 61 D3
Runcton Holme CE VA Prim Sch PE33 61 E3
Runcton Rd PE33 61 F2
RUNHALL NR9 68 F2
Runhall Rd NR9 69 A2
RUNHAM
Great Yarmouth NR30 169 B5
Mautby NR29 75 E6
Runham Rd
Great Yarmouth NR30 169 B5
Stokesby NR29 75 B5
Run La NR14 91 B6
Runnel The NR5 160 F6
Runton House Cl NR27 10 A5
Runton Rd NR27 139 A7
Rupert St NR2 162 C4
RUSHALL IP21 121 F1
Rushall Rd IP20 122 B2
RUSHFORD IP24 126 E8
Rushford Rd
Coney Weston IP31 127 B5
Euston IP24 126 D7
RUSH GREEN NR9 69 B1
Rushmead Cl PE30 148 C3
Rushmeadow Cres PE38 172 A6
Rushmeadow Rd NR19 154 A5
Rushmer Way NR26 138 C5
Rushmore Rd NR7 159 A4
Ruskin Ave NR31 170 B2
Ruskin Cl PE31 133 E5
Ruskin Pl 5 PE38 172 D6
Ruskin Rd NR4 161 E4
Russell Ave
Caister-on-Sea NR30 168 E5
Great Yarmouth NR31 170 C3
Norwich NR7 159 B3
9 Spixworth NR10 54 A2
Russell Cl
Downham Market PE38 172 C4
Fairstead PE30 147 C3
Wells-next-the-Sea NR23 136 C6
Russell Ct NR23 136 D6
Russell Dr PE14 77 E6
Russell Rd NR30 169 D4
Russell Sq 24 NR30 169 D4
Russell St
King's Lynn PE30 146 F3
Norwich NR2 162 C7
Wisbech PE13 152 C6
Russell Terr
Mundesley NR11 143 C6
Trowse Newton NR14 163 B2
Russell Way NR18 173 C3
Russet Cl NR17 174 E4
Russet Gr NR4 161 E5
Russet Rd IP22 177 C5
Russets The PE14 77 E6
Russett Cl PE30 147 C8
Russet Way NR19 154 E3
Rustens Manor Rd 2 NR18 173 C5
Rustons Rd PE14 59 F3
Ruthen Pl 1 NR19 154 D5
Rutherford Way IP24 176 C6
Rutland St NR2 162 C4
Ryalla Drift PE30 148 B4
Ryburgh Dr NR20 32 D5
Rydal Cl NR5 161 C6
Ryders Way IP22 128 E2
Rye Ave NR3 158 B3
Rye Cl
North Walsham NR28 151 E6
Norwich NR3 158 B2
Rye La NR17 174 C4
Ryeland Rd 2 PE30 148 C4
Ryelands 5 NR29 167 B7
Ryelands Rd PE30 148 D4
Rye's Cl PE33 62 D3
Ryley Cl PE30 147 E8
Ryrie Ct NR4 161 E2
Ryston Cl PE38 172 C4
Ryston End PE38 172 C4
Ryston Pk PE38 172 F1
Ryston Rd Denver PE38 172 D2
West Dereham PE33 80 B4

S

Sackville Cl 4 NR30 169 C3
Sacred Heart School PE37 153 C5
Saddlebow Ind Est PE34 43 C4
Saddlebow Rd PE30 146 D1
Saddler Cl NR17 174 B3
Saddlers Dr 19 IP25 84 F3
Sadler Cl PE30 146 F7
Sadler Rd NR6 157 F7
Sadlers Ct 11 NR26 138 D7
Sadlers La NR26 138 C7
Sadlers Way NR28 151 E5
Saffron Cl IP27 175 B2
Saffron Sq NR6 158 C3
Sage Rd PE38 172 D7
SAHAM HILLS IP25 84 C6
Saham Rd IP25 84 C4
SAHAM TONEY IP25 84 C5
Sainsbury Ctr for the Visual Arts* NR4 161 C3
St Alban's Rd NR1 162 D3
St Albans Way IP24 176 B5

St Andrew Cl 1 NR31......171 E5
St Andrews Ave 5 NR7...72 D3
St Andrew's & Blackfriars
  Halls* NR1..........178 B3
St Andrew's CE Prim Sch
  PE37...............65 E1
St Andrews CE VA Prim Sch
  IP22..............119 A1
St Andrews Cl
  Barningham IP31.......127 C3
  Buxton with Lammas NR10..36 E1
  Framingham Earl NR14.....90 D5
  1 Hingham NR9........86 C4
  Long Stratton NR15.....106 E4
  Poringland NR14.......90 D5
  West Dereham PE33.....80 C4
  Worstead NR28.........38 A4
St Andrew's Cl
  Blofield NR13.........165 E5
  Caister-on-Sea NR30....168 D7
  Gorleston-on-Sea NR31...170 C5
  Holme Hale IP25........66 A2
  Holt NR25.............137 C6
  Northwold IP26.........99 C8
  3 Old Buckenham NR17...104 D2
St Andrews Dr
  3 Norwich NR4.........89 C8
  Quidenham NR16.........103 E1
St Andrews Drift 2 NR25...7 A4
St Andrews Hill NR2......178 B3
St Andrews La
  Necton PE37...........65 F5
  Roydon PE32...........28 A2
St Andrews Rd
  North Runcton PE30.....147 B3
  Norwich NR6...........157 D6
  Scole IP21............130 D5
St Andrew's Rd
  Great Yarmouth NR31....170 C6
  Lingwood NR13.........73 F3
  Sheringham NR26........138 D6
St Andrews St NR2........178 B3
St Andrews Way PE37.....65 F5
St Andrew's Way NR13....165 E5
St Andrews Wlk PE33......80 C5
St Anne's Cres
  Clenchwarton PE34......145 D6
  Great Yarmouth NR31....170 B4
St Annes Rd 4 NR14......90 D5
St Ann La NR1...........178 C2
St Anns Fort PE30.......146 D6
St Anthony's Way IP27...175 E4
St Antony's Ave NR31....170 B2
St Audreys Rd...........176 D3
St Augustines Gate 12
  NR3.................162 D8
St Augustine's RC Prim Sch
  NR8.................156 E3
St Augustines Rd PE13...152 C5
St Augustines St NR3....162 D8
St Augustines Way 3
  PE30................148 C4
St Austin's Gr NR26.....138 E7
St Barnabas Cl 2 IP24...176 C1
St Bartholomews Cl 4
  NR2.................162 B8
St Benedicts Cl NR34....110 D5
St Benedicts Rd IP27....175 E4
St Benedict's Rd 5
  NR34................110 D1
St Benedicts St NR2.....178 A3
St Benet's Abbey* NR12..56 C2
St Benets Ave NR28......151 E4
St Benet's Cl 9 NR12....39 B4
St Benets Gr PE30.......148 D3
St Benets Rd NR29.......56 C3
St Benet's Rd
  Great Yarmouth NR31....170 B3
  Stalham NR12..........39 B4
St Botolph's CE Prim Sch
  IP22................128 F3
St Botolph's Cl 3 PE30..148 C3
St Catherine's Ave 5
  NR29................56 C8
St Catherines Rd NR7....163 F8
St Catherine's Way NR31..170 B4
St Christopher Cl
  16 Belton NR31........94 A6
  6 Caister-on-Sea NR30..168 D7
St Christophers Cl NR15..108 C7
St Christophers Sch NR6..158 E4
St Clare Ct 6 NR31......171 D5
St Clement Cl 2 PE14....77 F6
St Clement Mews 7
  NR31................171 D5
St Clements Dr 4 PE38...172 C6
St Clement's High Sch
  PE34................144 C6
St Clements Hill NR3....158 E2
St Clements Way NR13....165 C4
St Crispins Rd NR3......178 A4
St Cross Rd IP20........123 B4
ST CROSS SOUTH ELMHAM
  IP20................123 D3
St Davids Cl
  Brandon IP27..........175 D3
  Long Stratton NR15.....106 E4
St David's Cl 17 NR31...94 A6
St Davids Dr 8 NR13.....72 D6
St David's Rd NR9.......88 C7
St Dominic Sq 8 PE30....146 D5
St Domonic's Dr IP27....175 E4
St Edmund Cl
  Attleborough NR17......174 C5

St Edmund Cl continued
  Great Yarmouth NR31....170 B3
  Poringland NR14........90 B6
St Edmund Rd IP27.......114 E8
St Edmunds Ave NR17.....174 E5
St Edmund's Ave PE36....132 D5
St Edmundsbury Rd
  PE30................146 E7
St Edmunds Cl
  Costessey NR8.........156 F5
  Norwich NR6...........157 E1
St Edmund's Com Foundation
  Sch PE30.............146 E8
St Edmunds Ct 1 IP24....176 C1
St Edmunds Dr PE14......59 D1
St Edmunds Gate
  Attleborough NR17......174 B4
  5 Honington IP31.......126 B1
St Edmund's Prim Sch
  IP21................131 A2
St Edmunds RC Prim Sch
  NR35................124 A8
St Edmunds Rd NR13......166 B3
St Edmund's Rd
  Downham Market PE38....172 D5
  Lingwood NR13.........73 F3
  Taverham NR8..........155 C1
St Edmund's Rise 2
  NR8.................155 C1
St Edmunds Sq 7 IP31....126 B1
St Edmund's Terr
  Hunstanton PE36........132 C4
  King's Lynn PE30.......146 C7
St Edmunds Wharf NR3....178 B4
St Ethelberts Cl PE31...135 C2
St Faith's CE Prim Sch
  NR10................53 E2
St Faith's Church* NR9...51 F7
St Faith's Dr PE30......147 A6
St Faiths La NR1........178 C3
St Faith's Rd NR6.......158 D6
St Francis Cl IP27......175 E4
St Francis Way NR30.....169 C4
St Furseys' Way 2 NR31..94 A6
St George's Cl
  Saham Toney IP25.......84 B5
  Thurton NR14..........91 C4
St Georges Ct PE36......2 D6
St George's Dr
  Caister-on-Sea NR30....168 D7
  East Dereham NR19......154 D1
St Georges Inf Sch 17
  NR30................169 D3
St Georges Mid Sch PE31..13 A1
St Georges Rd NR31......94 A6
St George's Rd NR30.....169 D3
St Georges St NR3.......178 A4
St George's Theatre 18
  NR30................169 D3
St Germans Prim Sch
  PE34................43 B1
St Giles Gr PE14........59 B1
St Giles' La IP24.......176 C4
St Giles Rd NR24........18 B2
St Giles St NR2.........178 A3
St Giles Terr NR2.......178 A3
St Gregorys Alley NR2...178 A3
St Guthlac Cl PE37......153 C6
St Helena Way NR10......53 A3
St Helens Cl 1 IP24.....176 D6
St Helens Rd NR12.......23 F3
St Helens Way IP24......176 C7
St Hilary Park Rd PE30..147 A1
St Hilda Cl NR19........154 C6
St Hilda Rd
  Caister-on-Sea NR30....168 D6
  East Dereham NR19......154 C6
St Hilda's Cres NR31....170 B5
St Hugh's Gn NR31.......170 B3
ST JAMES NR12...........54 E7
St James Cl NR3.........178 C4
St James Cres 18 NR31...94 A6
St James Ct NR3.........178 B4
St James Dr PE38........172 B4
St James Mdw NR3........178 C4
St James Rd IP19........124 A1
St James' Rd PE30.......146 E4
St James's Rd PE32......47 A2
St James St PE30........146 D4
St James Way NR15.......106 E4
St James Wlk 14 NR30....169 D3
St John Maddermarket
  NR2.................178 A3
St John's Ave NR3.......170 A4
St John's Bsns Est PE38..172 E4
St Johns Cl
  2 Norwich NR1........162 E2
  Swaffham PE37.........153 C4
St John's Cl
  Coltishall NR12........54 D7
  11 Hethersett NR9......88 D7
  Oxborough PE33........81 E4
St John's Com Prim Sch
  NR12................164 D5
St Johns Ct PE13........153 C4
ST JOHN'S FEN END PE14..60 B6
ST JOHN'S HIGHWAY
  PE14................42 B1
St Johns La NR14........109 A8
St John's RC Inf Sch
  NR2.................162 C6
St Johns Rd Belton NR31..93 F6
  Stalham NR12..........39 B4
St John's Rd
  Bungay NR35...........124 A8
  Terrington St John PE34..60 C8

St John St NR1..........178 C2
St John's Terr
  8 Great Yarmouth
  NR30................169 D3
  King's Lynn PE30.......146 E4
St Johns Way PE38.......172 A4
St John's Way 12 IP26...98 E1
St John the Baptist Cath*
  NR2.................162 C5
St Joseph's Rd NR26.....138 D6
St Julian Rd NR30.......168 E4
St Julians Alley NR1....178 B2
St Laurence Ave NR13....165 C4
St Lawrence Dr NR4......161 C4
St Lawrence La NR2......178 A3
St Leger NR15...........106 E3
St Leonards Cl
  Scole IP21............130 D5
  Wymondham NR18........173 C6
St Leonards Rd NR1......163 A6
St Leonards St IP26.....100 B4
St Leonards Terr 6 NR1..163 A6
St Luke's Terr 4 NR31...169 B4
St Magdalen Way NR13....153 C2
St Margarets Ave 8 PE33..63 B4
St Margarets Cl NR10....155 F3
St Margaret's Cl
  3 Coltishall NR12......54 C6
  Upton with Fishley NR13..166 B8
St Margaret's Cres IP24..176 C3
St Margarets Dr NR7.....159 C5
St Margaret's Dr IP27...175 A2
St Margarets Gdns NR12..164 D6
St Margarets La NR7.....159 B5
St Margaret's La
  1 Cromer NR27.........139 C6
  10 King's Lynn PE30....146 D4
St Margarets Mdw NR34...145 E5
ST MARGARET SOUTH
  ELMHAM IP20..........123 E2
St Margarets Pl NR12....40 A5
St Margarets Pl 11 PE30..146 D4
St Margaret's Rd
  Bungay NR35...........124 A6
  1 Cromer NR27.........139 C6
St Margarets St NR2.....178 A3
St Margaret's Way
  1 Burgh St Margaret
  (Fleggburgh) NR29......57 C1
  2 Hopton on Sea NR31...171 D5
St Marks Rd NR29........57 A4
St Martha's RC Prim Sch
  PE30................147 C2
St Martin-at-Palace Plain
  NR3.................178 B4
St Martins at Oak Wall La 7
  NR3.................162 D8
St Martins Cl 4 NR3.....162 D8
St Martin's Cl NR27.....139 C5
St Martin's Gdns 1
  NR16................104 F1
St Martins La NR3.......178 A4
St Martin's La IP24.....125 E6
St Martin's Rd
  2 Norwich NR3.........162 D8
  Wisbech PE13..........152 E7
St Martin's Way IP24....176 B2
St Mary Cl NR17.........174 C6
St Mary's 4 NR16........104 F1
St Mary & St Peter RC Prim
  Sch NR31.............170 C6
St Mary's CE VA Prim Sch
  NR11................21 E8
St Marys Cl NR13........73 A5
St Mary's Cl Alpington NR14..90 F5
  Flixton NR35..........123 E5
  Harleston IP20........122 E2
  Heacham PE31..........133 E6
  Hemsby NR29...........167 A7
  Horsham St Faith & Newton St
  Faith NR10...........53 E2
  King's Lynn PE30.......148 C2
  Newton Flotman NR15....89 C1
  12 Snettisham PE31.....12 E4
  South Walsham NR13.....74 A7
  1 Watton IP25.........84 E3
  Wroxham/Hoveton NR12..164 B4
St Mary's Com Prim Sch
  NR20................49 D4
St Mary's Cres 5 IP24...176 C3
St Mary's Ct 2 IP24.....176 C3
St Marys Dr NR16........103 E1
St Mary's Dr IP22.......177 E4
St Marys Gr NR7.........159 C5
St Mary's Jun Sch NR15..106 E4
St Marys La 1 NR25......7 A4
St Mary's La NR31.......169 C3
St Marys Mews IP27......113 E1
St Marys Plain NR3......178 A4
St Marys Rd
  Ashby St Mary NR14.....91 C4
  Hemsby NR29...........167 D6
  5 Norwich NR3.........162 D8
  12 Stalham NR12.......39 B4
St Mary's Rd Aldeby NR34..111 A3
  Cromer NR27...........139 B6
  20 Long Stratton NR15..106 E3
  Poringland NR14.......90 D5
  West Walton PE14......59 B8
St Mary's Way 3 NR31....151 C5
St Marys Wlk 5 NR15.....89 D1
St Matthew's Dr PE12....41 B8
St Matthews Rd NR1......178 C3
St Michael-at-Pleas
  NR3.................178 B3
St Michaels NR12........39 C2
St Michaels Ave NR11....150 A6

St Michael's Ave PE13...152 C7
St Michael's CE Acad
  NR30................146 D1
St Michael's CE Inf Sch
  NR11................150 C7
St Michaels Cl NR20.....69 B7
St Michael's Cl
  Aylsham NR11..........150 C7
  Ormesby St Michael NR29..58 A1
  Thetford IP24.........176 C2
St Michael's Cres IP25...83 D4
St Michael's Jun Sch
  NR5.................160 F8
ST MICHAEL SOUTH
  ELMHAM NR35..........124 A2
St Michael's Rd PE30....146 D1
St Michaels Way NR13....165 F2
St Michels Rd NR15......106 E4
St Mildreds Rd 3 NR5....161 B7
St Nicholas Cl
  Dersingham PE31.......140 E3
  8 Gayton PE32.........45 C6
  1 King's Lynn PE30.....146 D5
St Nicholas Ct
  1 Great Yarmouth NR31..94 C6
  10 North Walsham NR28..151 C5
St Nicholas Dr
  Caister-on-Sea NR30....168 D6
  Feltwell IP26.........98 E2
St Nicholas Gdns 6 NR31..94 C6
St Nicholas House Sch
  NR28................151 D4
St Nicholas Pl 1 NR26...138 D7
St Nicholas Priory CE VA
  Prim Sch NR30........169 C4
St Nicholas Rd
  Great Yarmouth NR30....169 D4
  North Walsham NR28....151 D5
St Nicholas Retail Park
  PE30................146 D6
St Nicholas's NR14......88 F3
ST NICHOLAS SOUTH
  ELMHAM IP20..........123 E2
St Nicholas St Diss IP22..177 D5
  East Dereham NR19.....154 D6
  3 King's Lynn PE30.....146 D5
  Thetford IP24.........176 C4
St Nicholas Wlk IP27....175 E4
ST OLAVES NR31..........93 D2
St Olaves Rd
  Herringfleet NR32......111 D8
  Norwich NR3...........162 E8
St Omer Cl NR14.........89 B4
St Pauls Cl NR6.........158 A5
St Paul's Cl
  Brockdish IP21........131 C6
  4 Horsford NR10.......53 B3
  6 Wisbech PE13........152 C4
St Paul's Rd N PE14.....59 D7
St Paul's Rd S PE14.....59 E7
St Pauls Sq 1 NR3.......178 B4
St Paul's Way NR30......169 C2
St Peter & St Paul Carbrooke
  IP25................85 A5
St Peter's App IP27.....175 B3
St Peters Ave NR31......170 B2
St Peter's CE Jun Sch
  PE13................152 E6
St Peter's CE Jun Sch
  NR9.................70 B5
St Peters Cl
  3 Cringleford NR4.....89 B8
  Knapton NR28.........143 B1
St Peter's Cl
  Brockdish IP21........131 C6
  King's Lynn PE34......146 B4
  Rockland St Peter NR17..103 B8
  Strumpshaw NR13.......73 F2
  Yaxham NR19..........68 A5
St Peters Dr NR9........70 B5
St Peters Hill NR18.....87 A2
St Peter's La NR12......164 E8
ST PETER SOUTH ELMHAM
  NR35................124 A3
St Peter's Pl IP27......175 B2
St Peters' Plain NR30...169 D3
St Peters Rd Outwell PE14..77 E5
  Watlington PE34.......61 C7
  Wiggenhall St Germans
  PE34................61 B8
St Peter's Rd Brooke NR15..90 F2
  Fakenham NR21........141 B6
  Great Yarmouth NR30....169 D3
  King's Lynn PE34......146 C5
  Lingwood NR13........73 F3
  9 Sheringham NR26.....138 D7
  6 Wisbech PE13........152 C4
St Peters St NR2........178 A2
St Peters Terr NR1......178 C4
St Peter's Way 12 NR10..54 A2
St Peter's Wlk PE26.....113 F7
St Philips Rd NR2.......162 B6
St Roberts Way 15 NR31..94 A6
St Saviors La NR3.......178 B4
St Stephen's Cres IP27..175 E4
St Stephens Rd NR1......178 A1
St Stephens Sq NR1......178 A1
St Stephens St NR1......178 A2
St Swithins Rd NR2......178 A3
St Thomas Cl IP27.......175 E4
St Thomas Dr NR18.......173 C2
St Thomas' La NR18......88 C4
St Thomas More RC Jun Sch
  NR2.................162 A4
St Thomas Rd NR2.......162 A6
St Thomas's La
  Ingoldisthorpe PE31....140 D8
  Snettisham PE31........12 F4

St Thomas's Rd NR29....167 C7
St Valery La PE30......146 D2
St Vedast St NR1.......178 C3
St Vincent Wlk NR31....171 E5
St Walstan's Cl
  Norwich NR5..........156 D1
  Taverham NR8.........156 D8
St Walstan's Rd NR8....156 D8
St Williams Prim Sch
  NR7................163 D8
St Williams Way NR7....163 C7
St Winnold Cl PE38.....172 B4
St Withburga La 8
  NR19...............154 D5
Saker Cl 11 NR7........72 D4
Salamanca Rd 7 NR15....106 D3
Salcott Dr PE13........152 E5
Sale Ct 5 NR14.........92 A1
Sale Rd NR7............159 D2
SALHOUSE NR13..........55 B1
Salhouse Bsns Pk NR7...159 D3
Salhouse Dr PE37.......153 B2
Salhouse Prim Sch NR13..55 B1
Salhouse Rd
  Dumpling Green NR19....154 F3
  Great & Little Plumstead
  NR13...............73 B6
  Hoveton NR12.........164 E7
  New Rackheath NR13....72 E7
  Norwich NR7..........159 C2
  Sprowston NR13.......72 D6
  Woodbastwick NR13....55 C1
  Wroxham NR12.........164 B2
Salhouse Road Ind Est
  NR7................159 C2
Salhouse Sta NR13......54 F1
Salisbury Rd
  Cromer NR27..........139 D4
  Great Yarmouth NR30....169 D6
  Norwich NR1..........163 B5
  Sheringham NR26.......138 E7
Salisbury Way IP24......176 B4
SALLE NR10.............149 E8
Sallow La
  Framingham Pigot NR14..90 E7
  Snetterton NR16.......118 B8
Salmond Dr 1 IP24......125 F6
Salmond Rd 11 IP25.....84 F3
Salmon Rd NR30.........170 D8
Salmon's Way NR21......141 F5
Salter Ave NR4.........161 E5
Salter's La PE32.......48 E4
SALTERS LODE PE38......79 A4
Salter's Rd PE30.......146 E2
Salters Way PE13.......152 A2
SALTHOUSE NR25.........8 B7
Salthouse Marshes Nature
  Reserve* NR25........8 B7
Saltings The PE34......144 A5
Salts Rd PE14..........59 C8
Salvia Cl NR18.........173 F6
Samphire 5 PE30........147 B2
Samphire Cl 8 NR25.....7 C6
Samphire Pl PE34.......146 C4
Sampson Rd NR28.......151 C3
Samson Rd NR6.........157 F4
Samson's La IP22.......129 C7
Samuel Rd 1 NR1.......163 B7
Sancroft Way IP20......123 A3
Sandale Rd PE30........147 C4
Sandall Rd PE13.......152 C3
Sandfield Rd 8 PE38....172 C6
Sandhole La NR13.......73 A7
Sandhole Rd NR13......74 F1
Sandholme Cl NR1.......163 B8
Sandover Cl 4 PE33.....43 F2
Sandown Rd
  Great Yarmouth NR30....169 D5
  Wisbech PE13.........152 A2
Sandpiper Cl 1 NR31....170 A5
Sandpiper Ct 13 NR39....58 B6
Sandpiper Wy PE30......146 E2
Sandpit La
  Gimingham NR11.......22 E8
  Saxlingham Nethergate
  NR15...............107 A8
  Thorpe Market NR11....21 F7
SANDRINGHAM PE35.......27 F7
Sandringham Ave
  Great Yarmouth NR30....169 D7
  12 Marham PE33........63 B4
  Wisbech PE13.........152 D6
Sandringham Cres
  King's Lynn PE30......148 D5
  West Raynham NR21.....30 C4
Sandringham Ct
  Norwich NR2..........178 A1
  6 Watton IP25........84 D3
Sandringham Ctry Pk*
  PE35...............27 E7
Sandringham Dr
  Downham Market PE38...172 E5
  Heacham PE31.........133 C4
Sandringham Gr PE36....132 C4
Sandringham House Mus &
  Gdns* PE35..........27 F7
Sandringham Rd
  Dersingham PE31.......140 E2
  Hunstanton PE36.......132 D4
  King's Lynn PE30......147 C2
  Norwich NR2..........162 B6
Sandringham Way PE37...153 C2
Sandringham & West Newton
  Prim Sch PE31........27 F6
Sands Cl NR31..........171 E4
Sand Stone Way IP22....177 B4
Sandy Cl PE31..........140 C7
Sandy Cres PE31........140 C7

Sandygate La PE34......144 F5
Sandy Hill La NR25........8 F4
Sandy La Aylsham NR11...150 B6
  Bacton NR12...........23 D3
  Barningham IP31......127 C4
  Beighton NR13.........74 D2
  Belton with Browston NR31.93 F5
  Blackborough End PE32...44 C2
  Bradwell NR31.........94 C8
  Buxton with Lammas NR10..53 F8
  Canadas NR11..........10 A3
  Cantley NR13..........92 E6
  Castle Acre PE32......47 A2
  Cromer NR27..........139 A6
  Denver PE38..........172 C2
  Dereham NR19.........154 C8
  Diss IP22............177 F4
  Docking PE31.........134 D6
  East Dereham NR19....154 C6
  East Tuddenham NR20...69 D8
  Fakenham NR21........141 A5
  Fleggburgh NR29........75 B8
  Great Massingham PE32..46 E8
  Grimston PE32.........44 C8
  Hardingham NR9........86 D7
  Hilgay PE38...........97 C8
  Hoveton NR12..........55 C4
  Ingoldisthorpe PE31...140 C7
  King's Lynn PE30......148 F1
  Loddon NR14...........92 B1
  Mundham NR14.........109 A7
  Norwich NR4..........162 D1
  Old Hunstanton PE36...132 E8
  Oulton NR11............35 B7
  Raveningham NR14.....110 B8
  Rocklands NR17........103 A6
  Runton NR27...........10 C4
  Sheringham NR27.......10 A5
  Somerton NR29.........57 E6
  Southrepps NR11........22 B7
  South Wootton PE30.....27 C1
  St Mary, South Elmham
    otherwise Homersfield
    IP20...............123 B3
  Taverham NR8.........156 C8
  Thurning NR20.........34 C8
  West Acre PE32.........46 B2
  Weston Longville NR9...51 D4
  Wisbech PE13.........152 F4
Sandy La E NR19.......154 C6
Sandyland PE13........152 B5
Sandy Way PE31........140 C7
Sankence La NR11.......35 E5
Santolina CI NR5......157 B1
Santon CI IP24........176 A3
SANTON DOWNHAM
  IP27.................115 C6
SAPISTON IP31.........126 D2
Sapiston Rd IP31......126 D1
Sapwell CI NR11.......150 A6
Saracen Rd NR6........157 F6
Sarahs Rd PE36........132 C2
Sarah W CI NR2........162 C4
Sarah Williman CI 2
  NR4.................161 C5
Sardis Way NR19.......154 D7
Saturday Mkt PI PE30..146 D4
Saunders Ct 7 NR1....163 A6
Savage CI PE30........147 D3
Savery CI NR5.........161 B6
Savory Rd PE13........152 B7
Sawmill CI Felthorpe NR10..52 F5
  Wymondham NR18......173 B5
Saw Mill La Brancaster PE31..3 B6
  7 Great Yarmouth NR31..169 B4
Sawston 1 PE30........147 B6
Sawyers CI NR5........156 E1
Sawyer's La NR13.......87 D2
SAXLINGHAM NR25........7 C2
SAXLINGHAM GREEN
  NR15................107 D7
Saxlingham La NR15...106 F7
SAXLINGHAM NETHERGATE
  NR15................107 C8
Saxlingham Nethergate CE
  Prim Sch NR15.......107 B7
Saxlingham Rd
  Blakeney NR25.........7 C5
  Saxlingham Nethergate
    NR15..............107 C8
  Shotesham NR15........89 F1
SAXLINGHAM THORPE
  NR15................107 A8
Saxon Bank PE30.......176 B3
Saxon CI 29 NR29......57 D4
Saxon Cres 3 IP31....126 B1
Saxon Ct PE37.........153 D2
Saxon Field PE31........3 B6
Saxonfields NR14.......90 C4
Saxon Gdns NR30......168 D5
Saxon PI Lakenheath IP27..113 E1
  3 Thetford IP24......176 C3
  Weeting IP27.........175 A8
Saxon Rd NR30.........169 D4
Saxon Way
  Dersingham PE31.....140 D4
  Wormegay PE33........62 C6
Saxon Wlk IP26........100 A4
SAXTHORPE NR11........19 F1
Sayer Cres NR27.......139 B5
Sayer Ct NR25...........9 A2
Sayers Gn 3 NR31.....171 D4
Sayers St 9 NR2......162 C7
Scama CI IP22.........129 A2
Scania Way PE30.......147 A1
Scarborough Rd NR22...17 A8
Scarfield La PE14......59 C2
Scarlet Rd NR4........162 D1

Scarnell Rd NR5.......161 C6
SCARNING NR19.........67 B7
Scarning Fen NR19....154 C2
Scarning VC Prim Sch
  NR19................154 A4
Scarrow Beck La NR11...21 A2
Sceptre CI NR6........158 A3
Scholars Wlk IP22....177 C5
School Ave NR7........163 F6
School CI Blofield NR13..165 E6
  Kenninghall NR16.....119 A4
  Knapton NR28.........143 A1
  Lakenheath IP27......113 E1
  3 Ludham NR29........56 C5
  Northrepps NR27.......11 A2
  4 Rollesby NR29.......57 D2
School Comm Rd NR12...24 C3
Schoolfield NR10......155 C8
School Hill Reedham NR13..93 A4
  Tasburgh NR15........106 E6
Schoolhouse La 1 NR11..150 C7
School La Brandon IP27..175 C3
  Cantley NR13..........92 B7
  Colney NR4...........160 E3
  East Dereham NR19....154 E1
  East Harling NR16....118 C5
  Gimingham NR11........22 E8
  Great Yarmouth NR31..170 D6
  17 Harleston IP20....122 D2
  Heckingham NR14......109 F8
  Little Dunham PE32....65 E7
  Little Melton NR9.....160 C2
  Neatishead NR12.......55 D7
  North Runcton PE33....44 A2
  Northwold IP26........99 C7
  Norwich NR7..........158 F3
  Rockland St Mary NR14..91 B7
  Runhall NR9...........68 F1
  Skeyton NR10..........37 A5
  Smallburgh NR12.......38 D3
  Stoke Ferry PE33......80 F2
  Surlingham NR14.......73 B1
  Thetford IP24.........176 D3
  Walpole St Andrew PE14..41 E3
  Wereham PE33..........80 E4
  Wiggenhall St Germans
    PE34................43 B1
  1 Wisbech PE13.......152 C5
  Wramplingham NR18....69 F1
  Wymondham NR18......105 A8
School Loke Bodham NR25..9 A2
  Hemsby NR29.........167 A7
School Pastures PE31....3 E7
School Plain NR19.....154 B5
School Rd Alburgh IP20..123 A5
  Aldborough NR11......21 A5
  Ashmanhaugh NR12.....55 B7
  Bacton NR12..........23 B4
  Barton Turf NR12......38 E1
  Bedingham NR35......108 B3
  Beetley NR20..........49 C5
  Blofield NR13........165 B8
  Bracon Ash NR14......89 A3
  Bradenham IP25........66 D3
  Bressingham IP22....129 B8
  Brisley NR20..........49 A8
  Catfield NR29.........56 C8
  Colkirk NR21..........31 D5
  Earsham NR35........123 F8
  East Ruston NR12......38 E7
  Erpingham NR11........21 B2
  Foulden IP26..........82 A1
  Freethorpe NR13.......92 F7
  Frettenham NR12.......54 A4
  8 Great Massingham PE32..29 D1
  Great Yarmouth NR30..169 B5
  Haveringland NR10.....52 D7
  Heacham PE31.........133 D5
  Hinderclay IP22......128 C3
  Holme Hale IP25.......66 A2
  Horning NR12..........55 F3
  Kirby Cane NR35......109 E4
  Lessingham NR12.......24 D3
  Lingwood NR13.........74 A3
  Little Cressingham IP25..83 F2
  Little Plumpstead NR13..73 B6
  Ludham NR29..........56 B5
  Marshland St James PE14..60 B4
  Mautby NR29...........75 E6
  Middleton PE32........44 C2
  Morning Thorpe NR15..107 B3
  Neatishead NR12.......55 E7
  1 Necton PE37.........65 F4
  Newton Flotman NR15...89 D1
  Outwell PE14..........77 D4
  Potter Heigham NR29...56 F6
  Reepham NR10.........149 B4
  Runcton Holme PE33....61 B4
  Sculthorpe Airfield NR21..15 C3
  Seething NR15........108 E8
  10 Snettisham PE31....12 E5
  South Walsham NR13...74 A8
  St Andrew, Ilketshall
    NR34...............124 E6
  Strumpshaw NR13.......73 F1
  Swannington NR9.......52 B5
  Taverham NR8.........155 F1
  Terrington St John PE14..60 B7
  Thompson IP24........102 B7
  Tilney All Saints PE14..42 E4
  Tilney St Lawrence PE34..60 C7
  Tivetshall St Mary NR15..121 B5
  Walpole Highway PE14...59 F8
  Walton Highway PE14...59 C8
  Watlington PE33.......61 C6
  Weasenham All Saints PE32..47 D8
  Weasenham St Peter PE32..30 D1
  West Rudham PE31......29 F6

School Rd continued
  West Walton PE14......59 B8
  Whissonsett NR20......31 E2
  Wiggenhall St Germans
    PE34................61 B8
  Worstead NR28.........38 A5
School Rd Back 4 NR30..169 C5
School Sq NR25........102 E3
School Terr 3 NR14...163 B2
School View NR34.....124 F1
SCOLE IP21............130 D6
Scole Comm IP21......130 C6
SCOLE COMMON IP21....130 C7
Scole Comm Rd IP21...130 D6
Scole Prim Sch IP21..130 D6
Scole Rd IP21.........131 D6
Scole St IP21.........130 C6
SCO RUSTON NR12.......54 E8
Scotch Hill Rd NR8...155 B1
Scotgate CI IP24......102 E3
Scott CI IP24.........176 E6
Scotter Rise 7 NR26..138 C5
Scottgate CI PE34....144 A5
SCOTTOW NR10..........37 D2
Scottow Rd NR10.......37 B2
Scott Rd NR1.........163 B5
Scott's Cnr NR16.....105 B4
Scott's Hill NR14.....89 A4
Scott's La IP26........99 A7
SCOULTON NR9..........85 E3
Scoulton Rd NR17......85 F2
SCRATBY NR29.........167 E4
Scratby Cres NR29....167 F3
Scratby Rd NR29......167 D3
Scrobie Sands Visitor Ctr★
  NR30................169 E4
Scroby Ct NR29.......167 E3
Scrumpy Way NR16....119 D7
SCULTHORPE NR21.......16 B2
Sculthorpe Airfield NR21..15 E2
Sculthorpe Ave PE34..146 B5
Sculthorpe Bvd 7 NR21..15 C2
Sculthorpe CE Prim Sch
  NR21................16 C2
Sculthorpe Eastgate
  NR21................141 A5
Sculthorpe Rd NR21...141 A5
Seabank Rd
  Heacham PE31........133 B6
  Wisbech PE13.........152 F6
Seabank Way PE30.....146 E2
Seabird 4 NR30.......168 D7
Seabrook Ct 9 NR5....161 A7
Sea CI PE31...........133 B6
Seacliff NR26.........138 E2
Seafield CI 20 NR30..169 D2
Seafield Rd N NR30...168 E6
Seafield Rd S NR30...168 B6
Seafields Dr NR31....171 D4
Seaforth Dr NR8......156 E8
Seagate PE36.........132 C3
Seagate Rd PE36......132 B3
Seagull Rd NR29......167 E5
Sea La NR36...........132 E7
Sea Lord CI PE37......153 C6
Seaman Dr PE30.......147 C3
Seamere Rd NR9........86 A4
SEA PALLING NR12......40 A4
Sea Palling Rd NR12...39 F3
Searle CI NR21.......141 F5
Sears CI NR11........150 C6
Seaside La NR12........24 E4
Seates The 6 NR8....155 D2
Seathwaite Rd PE30...147 D8
Seaview Cres NR26....138 D5
Sea View Rd
  Hemsby NR29.........167 D7
  Mundesley NR11......143 B7
Sea View Rise NR31...171 E4
Seawake CI NR31......170 A4
Seaward Cres NR11....143 B6
Seaward Wlk NR30.....168 E8
Seckar Dr NR15.......154 C4
Second Ave
  Caister-on-Sea NR30..168 D8
  Wisbech PE13........152 B4
Second Dro IP27......113 C3
Second Marsh Rd PE14..59 A7
Sedge CI NR21........141 E4
Sedge Dro PE38........96 C7
Sedgefen Dro PE38....112 E7
Sedgefen Rd IP27....112 F3
Sedge Fen Rd PE38....97 B3
SEDGEFORD PE36.......13 B7
Sedgeford La 5 PE30..146 D2
Sedgeford Prim Sch PE36 13 B7
Sedgeford Rd
  Docking PE31........134 B4
  Snettisham PE31......12 F5
Sedge Rd NR19.......154 B4
Seeche Abbey PE34.....43 D1
SEETHING NR14........108 F8
Seething Ling NR15...91 A1
Seething & Mumdham Prim
  Sch NR15...........108 E8
Seething Old Hall Pk
  NR15................91 B1
Seething Rd NR35.....108 D5
Seething St NR15.....108 E8
Seeview Cres NR12.....24 A7
Sefton Ave PE13......152 E6
Sefton La NR31.......169 C3
Sego Vale NR8........156 E8
Segrave Rd 6 PE30...147 A8
Selby PI 19 NR30.....169 D2
Self's La IP22........128 C7

Selwyn Ct IP21........121 E5
Selwyn Dr 9 NR31......94 A5
Selwyn Gdns IP21.....121 E5
Selwyn Rd NR31.......170 A5
Semere Gn La IP21....121 D2
Semere La IP21.......121 D4
Sendall Rd NR28......151 B3
Sennowe Rd NR20.......32 F4
Senter's Rd PE31.....140 D2
Seppings Rd NR31.....141 A6
Seppings Way NR13....72 E6
Serpentine La NR10....53 C6
SETCHEY PE33..........61 E8
Setch Rd Middleton PE33..44 A1
  West Winch PE33......43 F1
Seton Rd NR8.........155 E1
Setons Halt Sta NR23...5 F2
Seven Sisters CI PE30..146 D4
Seventh Ave PE13.....152 E4
Severalls Rd IP26......98 D5
Sewell Park Acad NR3..158 E2
Sewell Rd Lamas NR10...36 F1
  Norwich NR3.........158 E1
Sewells CI 5 NR15.....89 C1
Sewell's La NR15.......90 D3
Sexton Rd NR35.......108 C2
Seymour Ave
  Brandon IP27........114 D4
  Great Yarmouth NR30..169 D8
Shack La NR13........165 D6
Shadingfield CI 16 NR30..169 D2
SHADWELL IP24........117 C2
Shadwell CI IP27.....175 B7
Shakers' Rd Brandon IP27 115 A1
  Wangford IP27.......114 F1
Shakespeare Rd NR30..169 E8
Shakespeare Way
  Taverham NR8........156 B8
  Thetford IP24........176 E6
Shannock Ct 14 NR26..138 D7
Shannon Dr 4 NR30...168 C6
Shannons CI NR17....174 E4
Sharman Ave IP25......84 D4
Sharmans Loke NR31...93 F5
Sharon CI
  2 East Dereham NR19..154 D1
  Felmingham NR28......37 A8
Sharper's Cnr IP27...113 C2
Sharpes Corner IP27..113 C2
Sharpe Way NR29.....167 B2
Sharp St NR29.........56 C7
SHARP STREET NR29....56 C7
SHARRINGTON NR24.....18 D7
Sharrington Rd NR24...18 B5
Shawcross Rd NR27....10 A4
Shaw's Yd PE31........30 B7
Shearwater Dr 2 NR31..170 A7
Sheddick Ct NR19.....154 D6
Sheep Mdw CI NR5....156 E1
Sheffield Rd NR18....173 C5
Sheldonian Ct NR35...170 A4
Sheldrake CI NR21....141 F5
Sheldrick PI NR19....154 E2
Shelduck Dr 7 PE31...12 E5
SHELFANGER IP22......120 C2
Shelfanger Rd IP22...177 C7
Shelford Dr PE38.....147 B8
Shelley CI NR30.......168 D6
Shelley Dr NR8.......156 D8
Shelley Way IP24.....176 E6
Shell Mus The★ NR25...7 E4
Shelly CI 3 PE38.....172 D6
Shelterhouse Cnr IP24..125 A4
SHELTON NR15........107 B1
Shelton with Hardwick Com
  Sch NR15...........107 B1
Shepheard CI 1 NR28..151 C6
Shepheards CI NR11...150 E8
Shepherd CI
  Norwich NR4.........161 D5
  Sheringham NR26.....138 B6
Shepherds CI Cromer NR27 10 B5
  11 Horsford NR10.....53 A3
  Runton NR27..........10 B5
Shepherds Dr IP25.....84 C4
Shepherd's Fold PE37..153 D2
SHEPHERD'S GATE PE34..42 D4
Shepherdsgate Rd PE34..144 C1
Shepherds La
  Burgate IP22........129 B3
  Oulton NR11..........35 B6
Shepherd's La NR10....36 A2
Shepherds Pightle PE36..2 D6
SHEPHERD'S PORT PE31..12 B4
Shepherd Way NR8....155 E2
Shepley Cres 2 PE30..147 D5
Sheppard Way NR17...174 C5
Sherbourne PI NR1...178 C1
SHEREFORD NR21.......31 A4
Sheridan CI NR8......156 F8
Sheridan CI IP26.......99 A8
SHERINGHAM NR26.....138 C7
Sheringham Com Prim Sch
  NR26................138 C5
Sheringham High Sch
  NR26................138 D5
Sheringham Little Theatre
  NR26................138 D7
Sheringham Mus★
  NR26................138 D7
Sheringham Pk★ NR26...9 B6
Sheringham Pk Visitor Ctr★
  NR26................9 B7
Sheringham Rd
  West Beckham NR25....9 B3

Sheringham Rd continued
  Weybourne NR25.......8 F5
Sheringham Sta NR26..138 C7
Sheringham Woodfields Sch
  NR26................138 C5
SHERINGWOOD NR26....138 C5
Sheringwood NR26....138 E4
SHERNBORNE PE31......13 B3
Shernborne Rd PE31...140 E7
Sherwell Rd NR6......157 E6
Sherwood Ave PE13...152 D7
Sherwood Rd NR4.....162 C1
Sheval CI NR15.......121 A8
Shickle PI IP22.......127 F6
Shillgate Way NR8....155 B2
Shillito Rd NR13.....165 F6
SHIMPLING IP21.......121 A2
Shimpling Rd IP21....121 B1
SHINGHAM PE37.........82 A8
Shipden Ave NR27....139 A7
Shipden Ct NR27......139 A7
SHIPDHAM IP25.........67 B2
Shipdham Airfield IP25..67 E2
Shipdham Airfield Ind Est
  IP25.................67 F2
Shipdham Rd
  Carbrooke IP25.......85 A5
  East Dereham NR19...154 D1
  Scarning NR19........67 B6
  Shipdham NR19........67 E5
Shipfield NR3.........158 F2
Shipgate Rd PE31......29 B5
Ship La PE36...........2 C6
SHIPMEADOW NR34.....124 F8
Shippea Hill Sta CB7...112 C3
Shipstone Rd 11 NR3..162 D8
Shire Ave 5 NR31......94 C8
Shiregreen PE30......147 C4
Shire Horse Wy 15 IP25..84 F3
Shires The NR8.......155 F2
Shirley CI 3 NR12.....54 A4
Shoe Devil La NR35...124 C4
Shoemakers La PE37....64 E3
Shooters CI NR8......155 D1
Shop La Hethersett NR9..88 E8
  Tunstead NR12........38 A3
  Wells-next-the-Sea NR23 136 D6
Shop St NR19..........68 A3
Shorncliffe Ave NR19..158 C1
Shorncliffe CI 1 NR3..158 C1
Short Beck 18 PE26....98 E1
Short CI PE38.........172 C6
Short Dro PE38.......172 C6
Short Gn NR22........120 B5
SHORT GREEN IP22.....120 A5
Short La Billingford NR20..50 A8
  Feltwell IP26.........98 D1
  Happisburgh NR12.....24 B3
  Harpley PE31..........29 D4
  Mautby NR29..........75 E6
  Swardeston NR14......89 C5
Short Rd
  3 Attleborough NR17..174 C5
  Belton with Browston NR31..94 A4
Short St 8 NR15.......89 C1
Short-thorn Rd NR10...52 F5
SHOTESHAM NR15........90 A2
Shotesham La NR15...107 C8
Shotesham Rd Howe NR15..90 C2
  Poringland NR14......90 B3
  Woodton NR35........108 A6
Shotford Rd IP20.....122 D1
SHOULDHAM PE33........62 D4
Shouldham CI PE31....140 C3
Shouldham La PE37....153 A4
Shouldham Rd
  Marham PE33..........63 A3
  Shouldham Thorpe PE33..62 C2
SHOULDHAM THORPE
  PE33.................62 C3
Shreeves Rd IP22.....177 E4
SHROPHAM NR17.......103 B4
Shropham Rd IP24....102 E3
Shrub CI NR17........174 D5
Shrub Dro PE38.......112 E6
Shrub Hill PE38......112 F7
Shrublands The
  Horsford NR10........53 B4
  Norwich NR2.........162 B6
Shrublands Way NR31..170 B5
Shuckford CI 5 IP22..177 C4
Shuttleworth CI NR31..170 A8
Sidegate Rd
  Great Yarmouth NR30..169 C5
  Hopton on Sea NR31..171 B7
Sidell CI 11 NR4.......89 B8
SIDESTRAND NR27......11 C2
Sidestrand Hall Sch NR27 11 C2
Siding Rd NR34.......111 C1
Sidings The
  9 Earsham NR35......123 F8
  Thetford IP24........176 D3
  Thorpe Hamlet NR1...163 C6
Sidney CI
  2 Great Yarmouth
    ....169 D2
  8 Martham NR29......57 C4
Sidney Rd Costessey NR8..156 F4
  Ingham NR12..........39 C4
Sidney St PE30........146 F3
Sienna Mews 3 NR1...163 B7
Sigismund Rd NR1....162 D3
SILFIELD NR18.........88 A2
Silfield Ave NR18....173 D1
Silfield Gdn PE36....132 D4

208 Sil–Sta

Silfield Rd NR18 ....173 C2
Silfield Sch PE30 ....147 C6
Silfield St NR18 ....88 A2
Silkmill Rd 2 NR30 ......169 D4
Silt Rd Nordelph PE38 ....78 B2
  Runcton Holme PE33......61 C4
  Terrington St Clement PE34 .25 F3
  Upwell PE14 ....77 F1
Silver Birch Cl NR27 .....139 E4
Silver Cour NR27 ....11 A2
Silver Dr PE31...........140 C4
Silver Drift PE37 ....64 E5
Silver End NR10 ....149 B5
SILVERGATE NR11 ....35 F6
Silvergate La NR11.......35 F6
Silver Gdns 5 NR31 ......94 A5
SILVER GREEN NR15 ......107 E3
Silver Hill PE30 ....147 D6
Silver Rd NR3............178 C4
Silver St
  Attleborough NR17 .....174 F6
  Besthorpe NR17 ....104 F4
  Fleggburgh NR29.........75 C8
  Garvestone NR9 ....86 C8
  Norwich NR3............162 E8
  South Lopham IP22.....128 F7
  Wisbech PE13...........152 C6
Silvertree's Way PE33....43 E1
Silvo Rd NR8 ....156 A5
Simon Scotland Rd PE30 .146 F2
Simpson Cl NR28 ....151 B5
Simpson Wy NR18 ....173 F7
Sinclair Cl NR31.........170 A8
Sir Alfred Munnings Rd
  NR5....................156 A3
Sir Archdale Rd PE37 ....153 C6
Sir Douglas Bader Espl
  PE36...................132 C4
Sir Edward Stracey Rd
  NR13...................72 D8
Sir Lewis St PE30 ....146 E6
Sir Thomas Cl NR28 .....173 C5
Sir William's Cl NR11 ...150 D6
Sir William's La NR11...150 D7
Siskin Cl Costessey NR8 .156 A5
  Great Yarmouth NR31...170 A6
SISLAND NR14 ....91 E1
Sitka Cl PE31...........133 C4
Six Crossways NR14 .....91 D3
Sixteen Foot Bank PE14...77 D1
Sixth Ave PE13..........152 E4
Skedge Way 6 NR13......73 C6
Skelton Cl 1 IP22.......177 E4
Skelton Rd Diss IP22 ....177 B4
  Norwich NR7...........163 C8
Sketton View NR28 ......151 B3
SKEYTON NR10............37 A4
Skeyton Cnr NR10 ....37 B6
SKEYTON CORNER NR10...37 B6
Skeyton New Rd NR28 ...151 B5
Skeyton Rd Coltishall NR10 .37 B2
  North Walsham NR28 ...151 A4
Skinners La NR12........164 B2
Skinner's La IP20........122 B4
Skinners Mdw IP20......123 B8
Skipping Block Row NR18 88 B6
Skippon Way NR13.......72 D5
Skitfield Rd NR20 ....33 E6
Skoner Rd NR5 ....161 B8
Skoyles' La NR9 ....88 A8
Skye Cl NR5 ....161 A8
Skye Gdns IP26..........98 F1
Slade La
  Framingham Pigot NR14...90 C4
  Old Buckenham NR17 ...104 B1
  Wortham IP22..........129 B6
  Yelverton NR14 ....90 F6
Slade Rd NR21...........18 B7
Slad La NR20 ....50 C6
Sleaford Gn NR3.........158 C2
Sleigh La IP25...........84 E2
Sleights Dr PE14.........59 C5
Slessor Cl 2 IP25 ......84 F3
Slip Rd NR14 ....93 A1
Slipshoe La NR15 ....122 B7
Slip The PE36...........2 C3
Sloane Way IP24 ....176 B2
Sloe La NR13 ....72 D8
SLOLEY NR28 ....37 F4
Sloley Prim Sch NR12....37 F3
Sloley Rd NR28 ....38 A3
Slopers Rd NR18.........87 F7
Slough La
  Attleborough NR17 .....174 E3
  North Tuddenham NR20 ...68 E8
Slough Rd IP22..........129 A1
Slugs La NR32...........111 C8
Sluice Dro IP26.........113 E7
Sluice Rd Denver PE38...172 B1
  Wiggenhall St Germans
  PE34..................61 A8
Slutshole La
  Besthorpe NR17 ....104 D7
  Wymondham NR17 ......105 A7
SMALLBURGH NR12.........38 D3
Smallburgh Rd
  Barton Turf NR12.......55 E8
  Smallburgh NR12 ......38 D2
Smallholdings Rd PE34 ...145 D4
Small Lode PE14.........77 F5
SMALLWORTH IP22.........128 A4
Smallworth La IP22......128 B7
Smea The NR12...........39 E1
Smeat St 2 NR5.........161 B7
Smee La NR13............72 E4

Smee Rd NR13............72 F4
Smeeth Rd Emneth PE14 ...59 F2
  St John's Fen End PE14 ...60 A5
SMEETH THE PE14.........60 A5
Smith Ave PE30..........146 E6
Smithdale Rd NR5 ....157 B1
Smithdon High Sch
  PE31..................132 D4
Smithfield Rd NR1.......162 E3
Smiths Dr IP21..........121 B1
Smith's Dro PE38........112 C8
Smiths La NR21..........141 E5
Smith's Loke NR15.......170 A6
Smithson Cl NR18........173 C4
Smithson Dr NR20 ....68 F5
Smithson Loke NR19.....154 D1
Smithtyne Ave
  Dereham NR19..........68 A7
  3 East Dereham NR19...154 F3
Smithy Cl PE31..........133 D5
Smithy Rd PE31..........140 D8
Smock Mill Loke NR18...173 B5
Smugglers Cl PE36.......132 F8
Smugglers La PE36 ......132 F8
Smuggler's La NR10 .....149 B4
Smugglers' Rd IP26......100 F8
Snaefell Pk NR26 ....138 D6
Snake's La Lound NR32...94 C2
  Topcroft NR35..........108 A4
Snapdragon Cl 7 NR17 ...174 B5
Snape Hall Rd 14 NR15...166 E3
Snape Hill IP22..........128 C2
Snape La PE38...........172 B5
SNEATH COMMON NR15...121 A8
Sneath Rd NR15 ....121 A8
SNETTERTON NR16 ....103 D2
Snetterton Circuit NR16 118 D8
SNETTISHAM PE31.........12 E5
Snettisham Beach PE31...12 A3
Snettisham Nature Reserve*
  PE31..................12 A3
Snettisham Pk* PE31.....12 E4
Snettisham Prim Sch
  PE31..................12 E5
Snoring Rd NR11.........17 C3
Snowberry Cl 4 NR8 ....155 B2
Snowdrop Cl
  20 Bradwell NR31......94 C6
  West Lynn NR34........146 B4
Snowdrop Dr
  Attleborough NR17 .....174 B4
  11 Sheringham NR26...138 B6
Snowdrop Gr 6 PE38 ....172 B4
Snowdrop St NR18.......173 F6
Snowhill Dr NR19........154 D6
Snow's Hill 5 NR14......92 A2
Snow's La NR14 ....92 A2
Snow St IP22............177 A6
SNOW STREET IP22.......129 D8
Soame Cl NR11..........150 D5
Soames Pl NR19.........67 B7
Soanes Ct NR9...........51 A5
Softley Dr NR4..........161 C2
Soken Dr 5 Beetley NR19 .49 C3
  5 Gressenhall NR20 ...49 C3
Solace Cl NR35..........124 C8
Solario Rd NR8..........156 A5
Sole Cl 6 NR10..........53 B3
Soleme Rd NR3..........158 B1
Solent Cl NR30..........168 E5
Somerleyton Gdns NR2 .162 C5
Somerleyton Hall & Gdns*
  NR32..................111 E8
Somerleyton Prim Sch
  NR32..................111 D8
Somerleyton St 2 NR2 .162 C5
Somerleyton Sta NR32...111 C7
Somersby Cl 2 PE30.....147 A8
Somerset Pl 22 NR30....169 D4
Somerset Way NR8 ......155 A1
Somers Rd PE13.........152 B4
Somerton Rd
  Martham NR29..........57 D5
  Somerton NR29.........58 A6
Somerville Ave NR31.....170 B3
Somerville Rd 11 PE30 ..146 E3
Sorrel Ct PE30..........147 C8
Sorrel Dr
  Attleborough NR17 .....174 B4
  1 Thetford IP24........176 E4
Sorrel La NR20..........49 D5
Sorrel Rd 25 NR31......94 C6
Sorrel Way PE38.........172 C3
Sotherton Rd NR4 ....161 F3
Soudan Cl 3 NR30.......168 D7
SOUTH ACRE PE32........46 F1
Southacre NR17 ....174 E6
South Acre Hall PE32....46 E1
Southacre Rd PE32 ......65 C7
South Acre Rd PE32......46 F1
Southalls Wy NR3........158 F1
Southampton Pl 16
  NR30..................169 D4
South Ave Norwich NR7 .163 E5
  Swanton Morley Airfield
  NR20..................50 B5
South Beach PE31........133 A3
South Beach Par NR30...146 C6
South Beach Pl NR30 ...169 E2
South Beach Rd
  Heacham PE31..........133 A4
  Hunstanton PE36.......132 B3
SOUTHBURGH IP25........85 F7
Southburgh La NR9......86 A5
Southburgh Rd NR9......86 A7
SOUTH BURLINGHAM
  NR13..................74 B2

South Burlingham Rd
  NR13..................74 B3
South Cl NR25...........7 A6
South Cnr PE31..........3 B7
SOUTH CREAKE NR21......15 D6
South Creake Maize Maze*
  NR21..................15 E6
South Croft NR9.........88 C7
SOUTH DENES NR30.......170 E5
South Denes Rd NR30....169 D1
SOUTH END NR16.........103 C1
Southend Bradenham IP25..66 D3
  East Dereham NR19 ...154 D4
Southend Rd PE36 ....132 C3
Southern La IP22........128 D5
Southern Reach 7 NR14..89 B3
Southerwood NR6 ....158 D5
SOUTHERY PE38..........97 B5
Southery Prim Sch PE38 .97 A5
Southery Rd Feltwell IP26 ..98 B2
  Methwold IP26.........97 F3
South Everard St PE30 ..146 E3
Southfield PE32..........65 C5
Southfield Dr 8 PE31....43 F2
Southfield La PE13.......55 C1
Southfields
  Downham Market PE38...172 B4
  1 King's Lynn PE30....147 B6
Southfields Cl PE13......152 E8
South Gage Cl NR7......159 C4
SOUTHGATE
  Cawston NR10..........35 B3
  South Creake NR21.....15 E5
Southgate 12 IP20.......122 D1
Southgate Cl NR23.......136 C5
Southgate La
  Norwich NR1...........178 C1
  Snettisham PE31.......12 E4
Southgates Dr NR21.....141 B5
Southgates Rd NR30.....169 D2
Southgate St PE30.......146 E3
Southgate Wy NR24......142 E3
South Gdn NR31.........170 C1
South Gn
  East Dereham NR19 ...154 E3
  Terrington St Clement
  PE34..................144 B5
South Gn Gdns NR19....154 E3
SOUTH GREEN
  East Dereham NR19 ...154 E3
  Hoxne IP23............130 F1
  Mattishall NR20.......68 F5
  Pulham St Mary IP21...121 F2
  Terrington St Clement PE34 .42 B6
South Hill Cl NR7........163 F8
South Hill Rd NR7........163 F8
South Icehouse Hill
  NR31..................170 D6
Southlands PE37.........153 B2
SOUTH LOPHAM IP22.....128 D8
SOUTH LYNN PE30.......146 E2
South Lynn Plain PE30 ..146 E4
South Mkt Rd NR30......169 D4
South Moor Dr PE31.....133 D4
SOUTH PICKENHAM PE37 ..83 D6
South Pk IP27...........175 B7
South Pk Ave 2 NR4....162 A4
South Prom PE36........132 B3
South Quay
  Great Yarmouth NR30...169 C3
  8 King's Lynn PE30....146 D4
SOUTH RAYNHAM NR21...30 F3
South Rd
  Great Yarmouth NR30...169 E8
  Hemsby NR29...........167 D7
  Watton IP25...........84 D3
SOUTHREPPS NR11.......22 B7
Southrepps Rd
  Antingham NR28........22 B8
  Gimingham NR11.......22 E6
South Rise NR28.........151 B3
SOUTH RUNCTON PE33...61 F3
Southside PE34..........79 D8
South St
  Great Dunham PE32.....47 F1
  Hockwold cum Wilton IP26 113 F6
  2 King's Lynn PE30....146 E4
  Sheringham NR26.......138 C7
SOUTHTOWN NR31........169 B1
Southtown Infant Sch
  NR31..................169 B2
Southtown Rd NR31......169 C2
SOUTH WALSHAM NR13...74 A7
South Walsham Rd
  Acle NR13.............166 A5
  South Walsham NR13 ..74 B5
Southwell Rd
  5 Horsham St Faith & Newton
  St Faith NR10..........53 D2
  Norwich NR1...........178 A1
  Wisbech PE13..........152 C7
South Wlk NR13.........72 E5
SOUTHWOOD NR13.......92 D8
South Wood Dr NR14 ...90 B6
Southwood Rd
  Beighton NR13.........74 C1
  Cantley NR13..........92 C8
SOUTH WOOTTON PE30...148 D2
South Wootton Inf Sch
  PE30..................148 C2
South Wootton Jun Sch
  PE30..................148 B1
South Wootton La PE30 .148 C1
Sovereign Cl 2 PE13 ...152 A6
Sovereign Way PE38.....172 A4
Sowdlefield Wlk NR14 ...89 B2
Sow's Loke NR12........55 E6

SPA COMMON NR28.......23 A1
Spa La Aylsham NR11....150 B3
  Oulton NR11...........35 B8
Spalding's Chair Hill
  IP24..................126 E8
SPARHAM NR9 ....51 B6
SPARHAMHILL NR9 ....51 C5
Sparhawk Ave NR7 ......159 C4
Sparhawk Cl NR7 ....159 C4
Sparhawk Inf Sch NR7...159 C4
Spar Rd NR6............158 C5
Sparrow Cl 4 NR31......94 C7
Sparrowgate Rd PE14....59 C5
Speckled Wood Cl NR17..174 B3
Speedwell Cl
  5 Attleborough NR17 ...174 B4
  8 Hopton On Sea NR31..171 D4
  2 Thetford IP24........176 E4
Speedwell Rd NR18......173 D4
Speedwell Way
  Norwich NR5...........160 F5
  13 Redenhall with Harleston
  IP20..................122 D1
Speke St IP20...........162 A7
Spelman Rd NR2.........162 A4
Spencer Ave NR31.......170 C6
Spencer Cl
  Great & Little Plumstead
  NR13..................73 B7
  11 Lingwood NR13.....74 A3
  West Walton PE14......59 B8
Spencer Cres IP22.......177 F5
Spencer Ct 12 IP25......84 D3
Spencer Rd NR6.........158 C5
Spencers Cl NR20.......49 E7
Spencer St NR3.........162 E6
Spens Ave NR31.........170 B3
Spenser Ave NR28.......151 D4
Spenser Rd PE30........148 B1
Spice Chase PE34.......60 C7
Spicer's La NR16........106 B5
Spiers Way IP22.........177 B4
Spindle Cl NR18.........173 D4
Spindle Dr IP24.........176 F5
Spindle Rd NR6.........158 D4
Spindrift Cl 11 NR29....58 B6
Spinks La NR18.........88 B4
Spinks' La NR35.........108 D2
Spink's La NR18.........173 F6
Spinners Cl PE37 ....153 B5
Spinners La PE37 ....153 B5
Spinney Cl Beetley NR20 ..49 D4
  Brandon IP27..........175 C2
  King's Lynn PE30......148 B4
  9 Long Stratton NR15...106 E3
  Norwich NR7...........163 F8
Spinney Dr NR16........118 C4
Spinney Rd NR7.........163 E8
Spinney The NR7........110 B7
Spire Norwich Hospl
  NR5...................161 A5
Spirkett's La IP20.......122 D1
Spitalfields NR1.........163 A7
Spitfire Dr 28 IP25......84 F3
Spitfire Rd NR6.........158 C6
SPIXWORTH NR10........54 A2
Spixworth Inf Sch NR10...54 A2
Spixworth Rd
  Hainford NR10.........53 F4
  Horsham St Faith & Newton St
  Faith NR10............53 E5
  Norwich NR6...........158 E5
Splashes The PE37.......153 B7
Splash Leisure Complex
  NR26..................138 B7
Spong La
  Carleton St Peter NR14...91 D5
  East Carleton NR14....88 F4
  Shropham NR17........103 C4
SPOONER ROW NR18.....105 A8
Spooner Row Prim Sch
  NR18..................105 A8
Spooner Row Sta NR18...105 A8
SPORLE PE32............65 C6
Sporle Prim Acad PE32...65 D6
Sporle Rd
  Little Dunham PE32.....65 D7
  Swaffham PE37........153 C5
Springbank NR1.........162 E2
Spring Cl PE30..........148 C1
Spring Ct PE33..........80 D4
Springdale Cres NR13...165 B4
Springdale Rd NR13 ....165 B4
Springfield NR13........166 C3
Springfield Cl
  Crimplesham PE33 .....80 B6
  Hemsby NR29..........58 A4
  4 Weybourne NR25.....8 F5
Springfield N NR29 .....58 A4
Springfield Rd
  Great Yarmouth NR31...170 D4
  Hemsby NR29..........58 A4
  Norwich NR7...........159 D2
  Taverham NR8.........155 C1
  Walpole St Andrew PE14 ..41 D4
Springfields
  Attleborough NR17 .....174 B5
  12 Poringland NR14....90 C5
Springfield Way NR9....86 B5
Springfield Wlk IP21....121 E5
Spring Gr PE34..........144 B4
Spring La Forncett NR16..106 B5
  Hempnall NR15........107 E3
  King's Lynn PE30......147 C7
  North Barsham NR22...16 A7
  Shouldham PE33.......62 D4
  South Creake NR22.....16 A6
  Yaxham NR19...........68 B6

Springles The 6 NR27...10 B5
Spring Rd IP31..........127 A1
Spring Sedge 4 NR26....147 A8
Springvale 3 PE32......45 C6
Spring View 1 PE31.....12 D4
Springwell La NR9 ......51 F6
Springwell Rd NR20.....31 D2
Spring Wlk IP24.........176 B5
Springwood
  Taverham NR8.........155 E1
  Woodton NR35.........108 A6
Springwood High Sch
  PE30..................147 C6
SPROWSTON NR7.........159 B3
Sprowston High Sch
  NR7...................159 B3
Sprowston Inf & Jun Sch
  NR7...................159 A4
Sprowston Rd NR3.......158 F2
Sprowston Ret Pk NR7...159 C2
Spruce Ave 2 NR29.....167 A2
Spruce Cl PE31.........133 B6
Spruce Cres 4 NR14....90 C5
Spruce Dr IP27.........175 D2
Spruce Rd PE38.........172 B6
Spurdens Cres NR28 ....151 D3
Spurge Sq 3 NR18......173 E4
Spur La NR14...........90 C6
Spur Rd NR9............69 C2
Spynke Rd NR3.........158 B3
Squire's Dr PE14........77 E3
Squire's Dro PE14.......78 A3
Squires Hill PE33........63 B4
Squire's Rd NR13 ....75 A2
Stablefields IP26........99 C7
Stable Field Wy NR29...167 A7
Stables The 16 IP25.....84 E3
STACKSFORD NR17.......104 C1
Stacy Rd NR3...........162 E8
Staden Pk NR11.........11 D1
Stafford Ave NR5.......156 F1
Stafford Rd NR31.......169 B2
Stafford St NR2.........162 B6
Stag Pl PE30............147 A7
Stainsby Cl PE31........133 D4
Staithe Cl 3 NR12......55 E4
Staithe La PE36.........2 C7
Staithe Rd
  Barton Turf NR12......38 F1
  Burgh St Peter NR34...111 C3
  Catfield NR29.........56 D8
  Halvergate NR13.......166 F1
  Heacham PE31.........133 C5
  Hickling NR12.........56 C5
  Langley with Hardley NR14. .91 F4
  Ludham NR29..........56 C5
  Marthan NR29.........57 D5
  Repps with Bastwick NR29. .56 F4
  Somerton NR29........57 E6
  Stalham NR12.........39 B3
  Wisbech PE13..........152 E5
Staithe Stree NR23......136 D6
Staithe The NR11.......150 D8
Staitheway Rd NR12.....164 C4
STALHAM NR12...........39 B4
Stalham Acad NR12......39 B3
Stalham Com Inf Sch
  NR12..................39 B4
Stalham Firehouse Mus*
  NR12..................39 B3
STALHAM GREEN NR12...39 C3
Stalham High Sch NR12...39 B4
Stalham Rd
  Ashmanhaugh NR12.....55 C8
  Hickling NR12.........39 E2
  Sea Palling NR12......24 F1
  Wroxham/Hoveton NR12 164 D6
STALLAND COMMON
  NR17..................86 C1
Stalland La NR18........86 B6
Stalland The NR18.......86 B6
Stallett Way PE34.......60 C8
Standard Pl 10 NR30....169 D3
Standard Rd
  Great Yarmouth NR30...169 E3
  Wells-next-the-Sea NR23 .136 B6
Standley Ct NR18........173 B4
STANFIELD NR20 ....48 F7
Stanfield Rd Mileham PE32 .48 E6
  Tittleshall PE32........48 C7
  Wymondham NR18 .....173 F3
STANFORD IP24..........101 A5
Stanford Cres NR13......73 B7
Stanford Ct NR5.........161 E6
Stanford Rd IP24........176 D6
Stanford Tuck Rd NR28 .151 B7
STANHOE PE31...........14 E8
Stanhoe Rd PE31........134 E4
Staniforth Rd IP24......176 B2
Stanley Ave
  Great Yarmouth NR31...170 C3
  Neatishead NR12......55 E7
  Norwich NR7..........163 C5
Stanley Cl NR13.........92 B6
Stanley Dr
  11 East Harling NR16...118 C5
  Sutton Bridge PE12.....41 A8
Stanley Rd Diss IP22....177 B4
  Great Yarmouth NR30...169 C5
  North Walsham NR28 ..151 D6
Stanleys La NR18........173 C2
Stanley St 10 PE30......146 E5
Stanley Terr NR30.......169 D4
Stanmore Rd NR7.......163 E6
Stannard Cl 4 IP22......177 C4
Stannard Rd NR4........161 F5
Stanninghall Rd NR12...54 B4

Stan Petersen Cl NR1 .... 163 A6
STANTON CHARE IP31 .... 127 B1
Stanton Rd
Barningham IP31 .... 127 C2
Dersingham PE31 .... 140 C3
Star Farm Cl 21 NR31 .... 94 C6
Star Hill NR12 .... 24 C3
Stark Cl IP22 .... 177 C4
Star La
Long Stratton NR15 .... 106 E3
1 Thetford IP24 .... 176 C3
Tivetshall St Margaret
NR15 .... 121 C5
Starling Cl NR11 .... 150 C5
Starling Rd NR3 .... 162 D8
Starling Rise NR27 .... 11 B2
Starlings Wy NR9 .... 51 D5
Star Mdw NR21 .... 141 B4
STARSTON IP20 .... 122 C3
Starston La IP20 .... 122 C1
Statham Cl NR4 .... 162 B2
Station App Norwich NR1 .. 178 C2
12 Sheringham NR26 .... 138 D7
Wymondham NR18 .... 173 C2
Station Cl
East Dereham NR19 .... 154 D6
4 Lingwood NR13 .... 74 A3
6 Martham NR29 .... 57 D4
Sheringham NR27 .... 10 A5
Swainsthorpe NR14 .... 89 D4
Station Dr Fransham NR19 .. 66 A8
Reedham NR13 .... 92 F5
Wisbech PE13 .... 152 C4
Station Gdns PE13 .... 153 B5
Station Halt NR13 .... 165 B3
Station Hill IP20 .... 122 D2
Station La Garvestone NR9 .. 68 D1
Hethersett NR9 .... 88 E7
Thetford IP24 .... 176 C5
Thornham PE36 .... 2 C6
Station New Rd NR13 .... 165 D3
Station Rd Acle NR13 .... 166 B2
Alburgh IP20 .... 123 A5
Aldeby NR34 .... 110 F6
Attleborough NR17 .... 174 E5
Attlebridge NR9 .... 52 A4
Aylsham NR11 .... 150 D6
Barnham IP24 .... 125 E6
Beccles NR34 .... 110 D1
Brundall NR13 .... 165 D2
Burnham Market PE31 .... 135 C3
Burston & Shimpling IP21 .. 120 F2
Cantley NR13 .... 92 C6
Clenchwarton PE34 .... 145 B4
Coltishall NR12 .... 54 C7
Congham PE32 .... 27 F3
Corpusty NR11 .... 19 F1
Cromer NR27 .... 139 D5
Dersingham PE31 .... 140 B4
Diss IP22 .... 177 F3
Ditchingham NR35 .... 109 B2
Docking PE31 .... 134 D5
Downham Market PE38 .... 172 A5
2 Earsham NR35 .... 123 F8
East Dereham NR19 .... 154 E4
East Rudham PE31 .... 30 B5
East Winch PE32 .... 44 F3
Ellingham NR35 .... 109 D3
Flordon NR15 .... 106 E8
Forncett NR16 .... 106 C4
Foulsham NR20 .... 33 C3
Fransham NR19 .... 66 B7
Fulmodeston NR21 .... 17 F4
Geldeston NR34 .... 109 F2
Great Moulton NR15 .... 121 A7
Great Ryburgh NR21 .... 32 B6
Great Yarmouth NR31 .... 169 B3
Guestwick NR20 .... 33 F5
Haddiscoe NR31 .... 93 D1
Hardingham NR9 .... 86 E8
Harleston IP20 .... 122 D2
Heacham PE31 .... 133 D6
Hilgay PE38 .... 96 C6
Hindolveston NR20 .... 33 E8
Holme Hale IP25 .... 65 F2
Holt NR25 .... 137 C6
Honing NR28 .... 38 C6
Hopton on Sea NR31 .... 171 D4
Kimberley NR18 .... 87 A6
King's Lynn PE30 .... 148 B5
Lakenheath IP27 .... 112 E3
Lenwade NR9 .... 51 E5
Lingwood & Burlingham
NR13 .... 74 A3
Middleton PE32 .... 44 C4
Mundesley NR11 .... 143 B6
North Elmham NR20 .... 49 F7
North Walsham NR28 .... 151 B4
Ormesby St Margaret with
Scratby NR29 .... 167 B2
5 Potter Heigham NR29 .... 56 F6
Pulham Market IP21 .... 121 E4
Pulham St Mary IP21 .... 122 A4
Quidenham NR16 .... 118 E8
Rackheath/Salhouse NR13 .. 72 F8
Reedham NR13 .... 92 F5
Reepham NR10 .... 149 C5
Roydon PE32 .... 28 A2
Sheringham NR26 .... 138 D7
6 Sheringham NR27 .... 10 A5
Snettisham PE31 .... 12 D4
Somerleyton, Ashby &
Herringfleet NR32 .... 111 C7
South Wootton PE31 .... 149 C5
Stanhoe PE31 .... 14 E8
Strumpshaw NR13 .... 91 F8
Taverham NR8 .... 156 F8
Station Rd *continued*
Terrington St Clement
PE34 .... 144 C2
Thetford IP24 .... 176 C5
Thorpe Market NR11 .... 22 A6
Tilney All Saints PE34 .... 144 F2
Tivetshall St Margaret
NR15 .... 121 B7
Walsingham NR22 .... 16 F7
Walsoken PE14 .... 59 E4
Watlington PE33 .... 61 C6
Wells-next-the-Sea NR23 . 136 D5
Wendling NR19 .... 66 F7
West Dereham PE33 .... 80 B3
Weybourne NR25 .... 8 F5
Whinburgh & Westfield
NR19 .... 68 A5
Worstead NR28 .... 37 F3
Wroxham/Hoveton NR12 .. 164 C5
Wymondham NR18 .... 173 C3
Station Rd Ind Est NR17 . 174 E4
Station Rd N Belton NR31 .. 93 F6
Walpole Cross Keys PE14 ... 41 F5
Station Rd S Belton NR31 ... 93 F5
Walpole Cross Keys PE14 ... 41 F5
Station St PE37 .... 153 B5
Station Terr IP27 .... 175 C5
Station Way IP27 .... 175 C5
Station Yd PE13 .... 153 B5
Steam Mill La NR31 .... 169 B4
Stearne Cl IP24 .... 176 B2
Stebbings Cl 3 PE32 .... 28 A1
Steel's Dro PE38 .... 79 C1
Steepgreen Cl NR1 .... 163 C8
Steeple Chase NR8 .... 155 F2
Steeple La NR15 .... 106 A2
Steeple View
Swaffham PE13 .... 153 B4
Wisbech PE13 .... 152 E7
Steeps The 6 NR30 .... 169 D1
Steer Rd PE31 .... 27 B8
Steggles Dr IP22 .... 177 C5
Stegg's La NR19 .... 67 F4
Stephen Beaumont Way
NR19 .... 154 F2
Stephenson Cl
3 Great Yarmouth
NR30 .... 169 D5
West Raynham Airfield
PE31 .... 30 B3
Stephenson Way IP24 .... 176 A2
Stephenson Way Ind Est
IP24 .... 176 A2
Stepping La NR1 .... 178 B2
Steppings La NR15 .... 107 C3
Stepping Stone La NR12 .. 39 A4
Stepshort NR31 .... 94 A6
Stermyn St 22 PE13 .... 152 C5
Stevens Cl IP25 .... 84 D4
Steven's La
Ashwellthorpe NR16 .... 106 B8
Wreningham NR16 .... 88 E1
Stevenson Rd
Norwich NR5 .... 161 B7
Wroxham NR12 .... 164 B2
Stevens Rd Cromer NR27 .. 139 C4
2 Little Snoring NR21 .... 17 B3
Steward Cl
Saxlingham Nethergate
NR15 .... 107 B8
1 Wymondham NR18 .... 173 D5
Stewards Cl NR10 .... 149 C4
Steward St 4 NR3 .... 162 E8
Steward Way NR19 .... 154 C5
Stewks Hall Drift NR9 .... 51 B6
STIBBARD NR21 .... 32 E7
Stibbard Rd NR21 .... 17 F1
Stickfer La NR16 .... 106 A6
STIFFKEY NR23 .... 6 D5
Stiffkey Cl 8 PE33 .... 61 D6
Stiffkey Rd Warham NR23 ... 5 F5
Wells-next-the-Sea NR23 .. 136 F5
Stigand's Gate NR19 .... 154 D7
Stile Cl 12 NR14 .... 89 B3
Stile La NR18 .... 173 B5
Stileman Way 11 PE31 .... 12 E4
Stillington Cl NR7 .... 159 B3
Stilwell Dr NR19 .... 154 B6
Stirling Cl
Downham Market PE38 ... 172 D6
Taverham NR8 .... 155 F3
Stirling Rd
Old Catton NR6 .... 158 C6
Sculthorpe Airfield NR21 ... 15 C3
Stirrups La NR32 .... 171 E1
Stitch The PE14 .... 77 B8
Stockholm Way NR19 .... 154 C2
Stock Lea Rd 1 PE30 .... 148 C4
Stocks Hill NR9 .... 160 B5
Stocks La NR13 .... 165 E5
STOCKTON NR34 .... 109 F4
Stockton Rd NR34 .... 110 A3
Stockwell Rd NR8 .... 156 A5
STODY NR24 .... 18 F6
Stody Dr PE30 .... 148 E1
Stody Rd NR24 .... 18 D6
STOKE FERRY PE33 .... 80 F3
STOKE HOLY CROSS
NR14 .... 89 F4
Stoke Holy Cross Prim Sch
NR14 .... 89 F4
Stoke La NR14 .... 89 F5
Stoke Rd
Barton Bendish PE33 .... 81 C5
Bixley NR14 .... 162 F1
Boughton PE33 .... 81 A4
Caistor St Edmund NR14 ... 89 F7
Methwold IP26 .... 99 A6
Stoke Rd *continued*
Poringland NR14 .... 90 B5
Wereham PE33 .... 80 E4
Wormegay PE33 .... 62 A5
Stokes Ave IP25 .... 84 C3
STOKESBY NR29 .... 75 A5
Stokesby New Rd NR13 .. 166 F6
Stokesby Rd NR29 .... 75 D6
Stone Breck NR5 .... 156 E2
STONEBRIDGE IP24 .... 102 B1
Stonebridge Rd NR28 .... 23 D2
Stone Brigg NR18 .... 87 A7
Stone Cl 2 PE33 .... 61 D5
Stonecross Rd PE38 .... 172 D5
Stonecutters Way NR30 .. 169 C4
Stonefield Rd NR25 .... 20 A8
Stonegate Aylsham NR11 .. 150 A3
Morley NR18 .... 87 A3
Stonegate St PE30 .... 146 D4
Stone Hill Rd NR30 .... 168 D6
Stonehill Way NR27 .... 10 C4
Stonehill Way Ind Est
NR27 .... 10 C4
Stone House Cl NR6 .... 158 D2
Stonehouse Rd
Norwich NR7 .... 159 B4
Salhouse NR13 .... 54 F2
Upwell PE14 .... 77 E5
Stone La Bintree NR20 .... 33 B3
Bressingham IP22 .... 119 F2
5 Hingham NR9 .... 86 C4
Hoveton NR12 .... 164 D8
Runhall NR9 .... 68 F3
Stonemasons Ct NR13 .... 166 C3
Stone Rd 6 Beetley NR20 .. 49 D4
6 Beetley NR20 .... 49 D4
Briston NR24 .... 142 E2
East Dereham NR19 .... 154 C2
Great Yarmouth NR31 .... 169 B4
Halvergate NR13 .... 75 A1
Hockering NR20 .... 51 B1
Mattishall NR20 .... 68 C6
Norwich NR3 .... 158 C1
Strumpshaw NR13 .... 73 F1
Yaxham NR19 .... 68 B4
Stone St IP19 .... 124 F1
STONE STREET IP19 .... 124 F1
Stoney End 2 NR20 .... 68 F6
Stoney La Beetley NR20 .... 49 B4
Reepham NR10 .... 149 B6
Stoney Rd PE32 .... 27 F2
Stony Gr 2 NR8 .... 70 C7
Stony La
Attleborough NR17 .... 174 B6
Pulham Market IP21 .... 121 E7
Raveningham NR14 .... 110 B6
Tivetshall St Margaret
NR15 .... 121 B5
Wortwell IP20 .... 122 F4
Storbeck Rd 2 PE13 .... 152 D7
Stores St IP27 .... 175 C3
Storey's Loke NR27 .... 11 A2
Story's La NR16 .... 105 E5
STOW BARDOLPH PE34 .... 79 E8
Stow Barn Rd PE33 .... 80 A7
STOW BEDON NR17 .... 102 E7
Stow Bedon Rd IP24 .... 102 C7
STOWBRIDGE PE34 .... 61 B2
Stow Bridge Rd
Stow Bardolph PE34 .... 61 D1
Wimbotsham PE34 .... 79 E8
Stowfields PE38 .... 172 C6
Stow Gdns PE13 .... 152 E4
Stow La PE13 .... 152 E4
Stowlay La NR17 .... 103 B6
Stow Rd Outwell PE14 .... 78 A7
Runcton Holme PE33 .... 62 B3
Wiggenhall St Mary Magdalen
PE34 .... 61 B5
Wisbech PE13 .... 152 F5
Stow Windmill★ NR28 .. 143 D4
Stracey Rd Lamas NR10 .... 36 F1
Norwich NR1 .... 163 A5
Strachan Cl PE31 .... 133 E5
STRADBROKE IP21 .... 131 E1
Stradbroke CE Prim Sch
IP21 .... 131 E1
Stradbroke Prim Sch
NR31 .... 170 D5
Stradbroke Rd NR31 .... 170 C5
STRADSETT PE33 .... 80 D8
Stradsett Cl 4 PE38 .... 172 D6
Straight La 19 IP20 .... 122 D2
Strangers Hall★ NR2 .... 178 A3
Stranton Ave NR19 .... 68 A5
Strasbourg Way NR19 .... 154 B1
Stratford Cl
Dersingham PE31 .... 140 E3
Norwich NR1 .... 162 F2
Stratford Cres NR4 .... 161 C1
Stratford Dr NR1 .... 162 E3
Stratton Cl 6 PE37 .... 153 C3
Stratton Rd Hainford NR10 .. 53 E6
Stratton Strawless NR10 ... 53 E8
Wacton NR15 .... 106 D2
STRATTON ST MICHAEL
NR15 .... 106 F4
STRATTON STRAWLESS
NR10 .... 53 E7
Strawberry Cl 3 PE13 .... 152 A6
Strawberry Fields NR12 .. 39 B3
Straw Mus The★ NR11 .... 21 D3
Strayground La NR18 .... 173 B2
Street Hill NR12 .... 55 E7
Street The Acle NR13 .... 166 C3
Alburgh IP20 .... 122 F6
Aldborough NR11 .... 20 F5
Aldeby NR34 .... 110 F4
Street The *continued*
Ashby St Mary NR14 .... 91 C5
Ashwellthorpe NR16 .... 106 A8
Aslacton NR15 .... 106 A1
Aylmerton NR11 .... 10 A2
Baconsthorpe NR25 .... 19 F8
Bacton NR28 .... 23 B2
Barnham IP24 .... 125 E6
Barton Turf NR12 .... 55 E8
Bawdeswell NR20 .... 50 E7
Beachamwell PE37 .... 81 E8
Beeston with Bittering PE32 48 C2
Belaugh NR12 .... 164 A6
Bergh Apton NR15 .... 91 A3
Billingford NR20 .... 50 B7
Bintree NR20 .... 33 B2
Blo' Norton IP22 .... 128 B6
Booton NR10 .... 149 E4
Botesdale IP22 .... 128 E2
Bracon Ash NR14 .... 89 A3
Bramerton NR14 .... 90 F7
Brampton NR10 .... 36 E3
Brandon IP27 .... 175 A3
Bressingham IP22 .... 119 D2
Bridgham NR16 .... 117 E4
Brinton NR24 .... 18 D6
Brockdish IP21 .... 131 D6
Brome & Oakley IP23 .... 130 C3
Brooke NR15 .... 90 E2
Brundall NR13 .... 165 E5
Burgh & Tuttington NR11 .... 36 E4
Caston NR17 .... 102 E8
Catfield NR29 .... 56 C8
Claxton NR14 .... 91 D6
Coltishall NR12 .... 54 E7
Coney Weston IP31 .... 127 B4
Corpusty NR11 .... 19 F1
Costessey NR8 .... 156 E5
Croxton IP24 .... 116 C6
Dickleburgh IP21 .... 121 B1
Dilham NR28 .... 38 D4
Earsham NR35 .... 123 F8
East Tuddenham NR20 .... 69 C6
Erpingham NR11 .... 21 A2
Felthorpe NR10 .... 155 C8
Flixton NR35 .... 123 E6
Flordon NR15 .... 106 D8
Foxley NR20 .... 50 D8
Framingham Pigot NR14 .... 90 D6
Fulmodeston NR21 .... 17 F3
Garvestone NR9 .... 68 B1
Geldeston NR34 .... 109 F2
Gooderstone PE33 .... 81 F5
Great Cressingham IP25 .... 83 C4
Great Snoring NR21 .... 17 A5
Great Yarmouth NR30 .... 76 F5
Halvergate NR13 .... 74 F1
Hempnall NR15 .... 107 C5
Hemsby NR29 .... 167 A7
Hevingham NR10 .... 53 C8
Heydon NR11 .... 34 F6
Hickling NR12 .... 39 F2
Hinderclay IP22 .... 128 C3
Hindolveston NR20 .... 33 D8
Hindringham NR21 .... 17 E7
Hockering NR20 .... 69 B8
Honingham NR9 .... 69 E6
Horsey NR29 .... 40 E1
Kelling NR25 .... 8 C5
Ketteringham NR18 .... 88 E6
Kettlestone NR21 .... 17 C2
Knapton NR28 .... 143 B1
Lamas NR10 .... 37 A1
Lenwade NR9 .... 51 D5
Lessingham NR12 .... 24 D3
Little Barningham NR11 .... 20 B4
Little Snoring NR21 .... 17 B3
Long Stratton NR15 .... 106 E3
Lound NR32 .... 94 C2
Marham PE33 .... 63 B5
Market Weston IP22 .... 127 E4
Marlingford NR9 .... 69 E4
Mautby NR29 .... 75 E5
Melton Constable NR24 .... 142 A5
Mileham PE32 .... 48 D6
Morning Thorpe NR15 .... 107 C4
Morston NR25 .... 7 A6
Morton on the Hill NR9 .... 52 A3
North Lopham IP22 .... 119 A2
North Pickenham PE37 .... 65 E1
Norwich NR14 .... 163 B2
Ovington IP25 .... 84 E5
Poringland NR14 .... 90 C5
Pulham St Mary IP21 .... 122 A3
Redenhall with Harleston
IP20 .... 122 F1
Redgrave IP22 .... 128 E5
Reepham NR10 .... 149 C3
Riddlesworth IP22 .... 127 D7
Ringland NR8 .... 70 B8
Rockland St Mary NR14 .... 91 B7
Rocklands NR17 .... 103 C7
Rougham PE32 .... 47 B7
Ryburgh NR21 .... 32 C7
Salle NR10 .... 149 D8
Saxlingham Nethergate
NR15 .... 107 B8
Scoulton NR9 .... 85 D3
Sculthorpe Airfield PE31 .... 15 B3
Sculthorpe NR21 .... 16 B1
Sea Palling NR12 .... 40 A5
Shelton NR15 .... 122 B8
Shotesham NR15 .... 90 A2
Somerleyton, Ashby &
Herringfleet NR32 .... 111 D8
Somerton NR29 .... 57 F6
South Lopham IP22 .... 128 D8
South Pickenham PE37 .... 83 D7
Street The *continued*
South Walsham NR13 .... 74 A8
Sparham NR9 .... 51 B4
Sporle with Palgrave PE32 .. 65 C7
Starston IP20 .... 122 C3
St Margaret, South Elmham
IP20 .... 123 E2
St Michael South Elmham
IP19 .... 124 A2
Surlingham NR14 .... 165 B1
Sustead NR11 .... 20 E7
Swafield NR28 .... 151 D8
Swanton Abbott NR10 .... 37 C4
Swanton Novers NR24 .... 18 C2
Taverham NR8 .... 156 B8
Tharston & Hapton NR15 .. 106 C7
Themelthorpe NR20 .... 33 F2
Thornage NR25 .... 18 E6
Thurlton NR14 .... 92 F1
Thurne NR29 .... 56 E2
Thurton NR14 .... 91 C3
Tibenham NR16 .... 120 E8
Tivetshall St Mary NR15 ... 121 B5
Topcroft NR35 .... 107 F3
Warham NR23 .... 6 A4
Waterloo IP21 .... 130 C5
Wattisfield IP22 .... 128 A1
Wellingham PE32 .... 47 F8
West Beckham NR25 .... 9 B2
Weybourne NR25 .... 8 E5
Winfarthing IP22 .... 120 B4
Witton NR28 .... 23 E1
Wiveton NR25 .... 7 E6
Woodton NR35 .... 108 C5
Stretton Sch NR2 .... 162 C3
Strickland Ave 9 PE31 .... 12 E4
Strickland Cl 8 PE31 .... 12 E4
Stringers La NR20 .... 33 C3
Stringside Dro PE33 .... 81 B3
STRUMPSHAW NR13 .... 73 F2
Strumpshaw Rd NR13 .... 165 E3
Strumpshaw Steam Mus★
NR13 .... 73 E1
Stuart Cl Brandon IP27 .... 175 C3
Great Yarmouth NR31 .... 170 B4
7 Hethersett NR9 .... 88 D8
Stuart Dr 2 IP24 .... 116 A2
Stuart Gdns NR1 .... 178 C3
Stuart Rd Aylsham NR11 .. 150 C7
Norwich NR1 .... 178 C1
STUBB NR12 .... 39 F1
STUBBING'S GREEN
IP22 .... 129 A1
Stubb Rd NR12 .... 39 F2
Stubbs Cl PE38 .... 172 E5
Stubbs Gn La NR14 .... 109 C8
STUBBS GREEN NR14 .... 109 C8
Sturdee Ave NR30 .... 169 D8
Sturdee Cl IP24 .... 176 F6
Sturmy Cl 15 NR15 .... 106 E3
STUSTON IP21 .... 130 B5
Stuston La IP21 .... 130 B4
Stuston Rd IP21 .... 130 B5
Style Loke NR9 .... 69 F2
Styleman Rd PE36 .... 132 D4
Styles Cl NR31 .... 170 A4
Stylman Rd NR5 .... 161 A7
Suckling Ave NR3 .... 158 B3
Suckling Dro PE14 .... 78 C5
Suckling La
Framingham Pigot NR14 ... 90 D6
Hickling NR12 .... 39 F3
Suckling Pl NR35 .... 108 C5
SUFFIELD NR11 .... 21 F3
Suffield Cl
7 Cringleford NR4 .... 89 B8
3 Long Stratton NR15 .... 106 D3
North Walsham NR28 .... 151 A6
Suffield Ct NR6 .... 158 D2
Suffield Pk Inf Sch NR27 139 C5
Suffield Rd NR31 .... 170 C4
Suffield Way PE30 .... 147 B8
Suffling Rd NR30 .... 170 D8
Suffolk Ave IP31 .... 126 B1
Suffolk Cl
Great Yarmouth NR31 .... 170 C7
11 Hopton On Sea NR31 .. 171 D4
Suffolk Ct IP27 .... 175 C4
Suffolk Pl NR19 .... 154 C1
Suffolk Rd
Great Yarmouth NR31 .... 170 C8
King's Lynn PE30 .... 147 C6
Norwich NR4 .... 161 C3
Sheringham NR26 .... 138 D6
Suffolk Sq NR2 .... 162 C5
Suffolk Wlk NR4 .... 161 D3
Sugar La PE31 .... 140 E4
Sukey Way NR5 .... 160 F6
Sultan Pl NR31 .... 169 E3
Summer Cl
13 Framingham Earl
NR14 .... 90 D5
4 Walpole St Andrew PE14 41 E4
Summer Dr NR12 .... 164 D6
SUMMERFIELD PE31 .... 2 E1
Summerfield Cl PE13 .... 152 A6
Summerfield Rd NR29 .... 58 A4
SUMMERHILL PE31 .... 133 C3
Summerhouse Cl NR27 .... 139 A6
Summer La IP25 .... 85 A4
Sumpter Rd NR4 .... 161 E3
Sunart Cl NR17 .... 174 E6
Sun Barn Rd NR10 .... 149 B4
Sun Barn Wlk NR10 .... 149 B4
Suncroft NR1 .... 162 F2

Sunderland Cl NR6 . . . . .158 C6
Sundew Cl
  Caister-On-Sea NR30 . . . . . .168 E4
  6 Thetford IP24 . . . . .176 F4
Sunk Rd NR22 . . . . .16 F7
Sun La
  Great Yarmouth NR31 . . . . . .94 C6
  Norwich NR3 . . . . .158 D1
Sunley Cl NR35 . . . . .109 C2
Sunningdale NR4 . . . . .162 A2
Sunninghill Cl
  18 Bradwell NR31 . . . . .94 C8
  14 Great Yarmouth NR31 . . .94 C8
Sunny Cl NR5 . . . . .157 B1
Sunny Cnr NR28 . . . . .151 B4
Sunny Gr NR5 . . . . .161 B8
Sunny Hill NR1 . . . . .162 E2
Sunnyside
  Bedingham NR35 . . . . .108 C4
  Diss IP22 . . . . .177 D5
  Heacham PE31 . . . . .133 D5
Sunnyside Ave 10 NR14 . . . .90 C5
Sunnyside Cl PE31 . . . . .133 D5
Sunnyside Rd PE32 . . . . .29 D2
Sun Rd NR35 . . . . .109 B2
Sunsalve Ride NR19 . . . . . . .154 C1
Sunset Gdns PE13 . . . . .152 E2
Sunset Wlk NR12 . . . . .24 E4
Supple Cl NR1 . . . . .163 C7
SURLINGHAM NR14 . . . . . . .73 B1
Surlingham Com Prim Sch
  NR14 . . . . .73 B1
Surlingham Dr PE37 . . . . . . .153 B1
Surlingham La
  Bramerton NR14 . . . . .90 F8
  Rockland St Mary NR14 . . . .91 B8
Surrey Cl NR7 . . . . .159 C5
Surrey Gr NR1 . . . . .178 B1
Surrey St Cromer NR27 . . . .139 C7
  6 King's Lynn PE30 . . . . . .146 D5
  Norwich NR1 . . . . .178 B2
  6 Wiggenhall St Germans
  PE34 . . . . .43 B1
Surrogate St NR17 . . . . .174 D5
Sursham Ave NR6 . . . . .158 F4
Sussex Rd NR31 . . . . .170 D5
Sussex St NR3 . . . . .178 A4
SUSTEAD NR11 . . . . .21 A7
Sustead La NR11 . . . . .20 F8
Sustead Rd NR11 . . . . .9 F1
Suters Dr NR8 . . . . .155 E2
Sutherland Ave NR6 . . . . . . .158 A4
Sutherland Ct Gdns
  NR27 . . . . .139 C6
SUTON NR18 . . . . .87 D2
Suton La NR18 . . . . .173 A1
SUTTON NR12 . . . . .39 C3
SUTTON BRIDGE PE12 . . . .41 B7
Sutton Bridge Westmere
  Comm Prim Sch PE12 . . .41 B8
Sutton Cres NR13 . . . . .92 F8
Sutton Est PE31 . . . . .135 C2
Sutton Fst Sch NR12 . . . . . .39 C2
Sutton Lea PE31 . . . . .135 C2
Sutton Mdws PE13 . . . . .152 A8
Sutton Rd Catfield NR29 . . . .39 C1
  Great Yarmouth NR30 . . . . .169 D1
  Hickling NR12 . . . . .39 A4
  Swaffham PE37 . . . . .153 B1
  Terrington St Clement
  PE34 . . . . .144 A4
  Walpole Cross Keys PE34 . . .42 A7
  Wisbech PE13 . . . . .152 A7
Suttons Cl 1 PE14 . . . . .77 F6
Sutton Windmill & Broads
  Mus★ NR12 . . . . .39 D2
SWAFFHAM PE37 . . . . .153 D4
Swaffham CE Inf Sch
  PE37 . . . . .153 C4
Swaffham CE Jun Sch
  PE37 . . . . .153 B2
Swaffham Com Hospl
  PE37 . . . . .153 C5
Swaffham Gap PE38 . . . . . . .82 C1
Swaffham Leisure Ctr
  PE37 . . . . .153 C2
Swaffham Mus★ PE37 . .153 B4
Swaffham Raceway PE37 . . .64 C4
Swaffham Rd Ashill IP25 . . . .84 A7
  Barton Bendish PE33 . . . . . .63 C2
  Cockley Cley PE37 . . . . .82 D7
  East Dereham NR19 . . . . . .154 D6
  Mundford IP26 . . . . .100 B4
  Narborough PE32 . . . . .63 F7
  Oxborough PE33 . . . . .81 E4
  Raynham NR21 . . . . .30 F2
  Swaffham PE37 . . . . .64 A4
  Watton IP25 . . . . .84 C4
SWAFIELD NR28 . . . . .22 E3
Swafield Rise NR28 . . . . . . .151 D7
Swafield St NR5 . . . . .160 F7
SWAINSTHORPE NR14 . . . .89 D3
Swale The NR5 . . . . .160 F6
Swallow Cl 6 NR31 . . . . . . .170 A7
Swallow Dr IP27 . . . . .175 E3
Swallowfield Rd PE30 . . . . . .147 C4
Swallowtail Cl
  Besthorpe NR17 . . . . .174 F6
  Bowthorpe NR5 . . . . .160 F5
Swamp La
  Great Ellingham NR17 . . . . .103 F7
  Roydon IP22 . . . . .177 A6
Swan Cl Aylsham NR11 . . . . .150 C6
  Swannington NR9 . . . . .52 B5
Swan Cotts PE32 . . . . .47 D5

Swan Dr NR20 . . . . .49 C3
Swan Entry 2 NR22 . . . . . . .16 F7
Swangey La NR17 . . . . .103 D4
Swan La
  Coney Weston IP31 . . . . . . .127 B4
  Fincham PE33 . . . . .62 C1
  King's Lynn PE30 . . . . .147 A6
  1 Norwich NR2 . . . . .178 B3
  Redenhall with Harleston
  IP20 . . . . .122 D2
  Shipdham IP25 . . . . .67 C3
  Tharston & Hapton NR15 . . .106 E4
Swan Loke NR28 . . . . .151 C5
Swann Gr NR25 . . . . .137 C6
SWANNINGTON NR9 . . . . . .52 B6
Swanns Yd NR28 . . . . .38 A4
Swan Rd NR19 . . . . .154 E4
Swans Cl NR25 . . . . .7 B3
Swansea Rd NR2 . . . . .162 B5
Swansgate NR6 . . . . .158 E6
Swan St Fakenham NR21 . . .141 B3
  Horsham St Faith NR10 . . . .53 D2
Swanston's Rd NR30 . . . . . .170 D8
Swan Terr 1 NR29 . . . . .172 A6
Swanton Abbot Rd NR10 . . .37 A5
SWANTON ABBOTT NR10 . .37 C4
Swanton Abbott Com Prim
  Sch NR10 . . . . .37 B5
Swanton Ave NR19 . . . . . . .154 E7
Swanton Cl NR19 . . . . .154 E7
Swanton Dr NR20 . . . . .154 E6
Swanton Gr NR19 . . . . .154 E6
SWANTON HILL NR10 . . . . .37 C5
SWANTON MORLEY NR20 . .50 B3
Swanton Morley Prim Sch
  NR20 . . . . .50 B4
Swanton Morley Rd
  Hoe NR20 . . . . .50 A6
  North Elmham NR20 . . . . . .49 F6
SWANTON NOVERS NR24 . .18 B3
Swanton Rd
  Dereham NR20 . . . . .50 A1
  East Dereham NR19 . . . . . .154 E6
  Gunthorpe NR24 . . . . .18 B5
  Norwich NR3 . . . . .162 B8
SWARDESTON NR14 . . . . . .89 C5
Swardeston La NR14 . . . . . .89 B6
Swargate La NR15 . . . . .108 E8
Swash La NR13 . . . . .54 D2
Sweden Pl IP27 . . . . .175 B2
Sweetacres 7 NR29 . . . . . . .167 B6
Sweetbriar Gdns NR20 . . . . .49 C4
Sweetbriar La
  Edgefield NR24 . . . . .19 D5
  Sheringham NR26 . . . . .138 C7
Sweet Briar Rd
  7 Long Stratton NR15 . . . .106 E3
  Norwich NR6 . . . . .161 F8
Sweet Briar Rd Ind Est
  NR3 . . . . .157 F1
Sweyn Cl IP24 . . . . .176 B2
Swim Rd NR29 . . . . .75 F6
Swinbourne Cl NR6 . . . . . . .158 E3
Swindells Cl NR5 . . . . .157 A2
Swingy La NR18 . . . . .87 A3
Swirle's Pl 6 NR30 . . . . . . .169 D4
Swiss Terr PE30 . . . . .146 F5
Sybil Rd PE13 . . . . .152 C6
Sybil Wheeler Cl 5
  IP24 . . . . .176 D6
Sycamore Ave
  16 Great Yarmouth NR31 . .94 C7
  23 Martham NR29 . . . . .57 D4
  Wymondham NR18 . . . . . . .173 E6
Sycamore Cl
  Attleborough NR17 . . . . . . .174 C4
  King's Lynn PE30 . . . . .148 D2
  8 Loddon NR14 . . . . .91 F1
  North Walsham NR28 . . . . .151 D6
  Palgrave IP22 . . . . .177 C1
  Thompson IP24 . . . . .102 A7
Sycamore Covert
  Thetford IP24 . . . . .116 D2
  11 Thetford IP24 . . . . .176 F5
Sycamore Cres NR21 . . . . . .161 F7
Sycamore Ct 2 NR4 . . . . . . .161 C1
Sycamore Gn 2 NR31 . . . . .170 B6
Sycamore Gr NR26 . . . . .138 D5
Sycamores The NR19 . . . . . .154 E3
Sycamore Way IP27 . . . . . . .177 F5
Sydenham Cl NR13 . . . . . . .166 B4
SYDERSTONE PE31 . . . . . . .15 B3
Syderstone Comm Nature
  Reserve★ PE31 . . . . .15 A3
Syderstone Rd NR21 . . . . . .15 B3
Sydney Dye Ct PE32 . . . . . . .65 C5
Sydney Rd 11 NR10 . . . . . . .54 A2
Sydney Terr 2 PE30 . . . . . .146 D1
Syers La PE32 . . . . .48 D2
SYLEHAM IP21 . . . . .131 D5
Syleham Hall La IP21 . . . . . .131 F5
Syleham Rd IP21 . . . . .131 B4
Sylvan Cl NR6 . . . . .157 E6
Sylvan Way
  2 Blofield Heath NR13 . . . .73 C6
  Taverham NR8 . . . . .156 E8
Sylvden Dr PE13 . . . . .152 F6
Symonds Ave NR29 . . . . . . .167 E2
Symphony Gdns 11 NR17 . .174 B4
Syon Cl PE38 . . . . .172 B4
Sywell Cl NR6 . . . . .158 F6
Sywell Gr 5 PE14 . . . . .59 A1

T

Tabernacle La NR16 . . . . . .105 F4
TACOLNESTON NR16 . . . . . .105 F5
Tacolneston CE Prim Sch
  NR16 . . . . .105 F6
Tagg Way 3 NR13 . . . . .72 E7
Talbot Cl NR18 . . . . .173 C5
Talbots Mdw IP21 . . . . .130 B5
Talbot Sq NR3 . . . . .178 A4
Tales of the Old Gaol
  House★ PE30 . . . . .146 D4
Taleworth Cl 11 NR5 . . . . . .161 A7
Tallon St IP26 . . . . .82 A2
Tamarind Mews NR4 . . . . . . .161 E1
Tamarisk PE30 . . . . .148 B1
Tamarisk Dr NR30 . . . . .168 E4
Tamworth La NR31 . . . . .169 B2
Tanager Cl NR3 . . . . .158 D3
Tan La NR30 . . . . .168 E4
Tanners Gn NR9 . . . . .68 C3
Tanner St 4 IP24 . . . . .176 C4
Tanning La 7 NR16 . . . . . . .104 F1
Tanns La IP22 . . . . .119 A2
Tansy Cl NR6 . . . . .158 D4
Tantallon Dr NR17 . . . . .174 F6
Target Hill IP20 . . . . .123 B2
Tarragon Cl 16 NR31 . . . . . .94 C6
Tarragon Rd PE38 . . . . .172 D7
Tar Works Rd NR30 . . . . . . .169 C6
TASBURGH NR15 . . . . .106 F7
Tasburgh Cl PE30 . . . . .147 D3
Tasburgh Rd NR15 . . . . .106 F8
Tasman Dr NR11 . . . . .22 F8
Tas Valley Vineyard★
  NR16 . . . . .106 A3
Tate Loke NR12 . . . . .39 F1
TATTERFORD NR21 . . . . . . .30 E7
Tatterford Dr PE31 . . . . .30 E7
TATTERSETT PE31 . . . . .15 C1
Tattersett Pk Bsns Ctr
  NR21 . . . . .15 C1
Tattersett Rd PE31 . . . . .15 B2
Tattlepot Rd IP21 . . . . .121 E5
TAVERHAM NR8 . . . . .155 C1
Taverham Chase NR8 . . . . . .156 D8
Taverham Hall Sch NR8 . . . .156 A8
Taverham High Sch NR8 . . .155 B2
Taverham Jun Sch NR8 . . . .156 C8
Taverham La NR8 . . . . .156 C6
Taverham Rd
  Felthorpe NR10 . . . . .155 C7
  Honingham NR9 . . . . .69 F6
  Taverham NR8 . . . . .156 D8
Tavern Cl NR20 . . . . .49 D4
Tavern La Diss IP22 . . . . . . .177 F3
  East Dereham NR19 . . . . . .154 C4
Tavistock Rd PE13 . . . . .152 D5
Tawny Sedge 3 PE30 . . . . .147 A8
Taylor Ave 9 NR4 . . . . .89 B8
Taylor Drift NR16 . . . . .118 D4
Taylor Rd Diss IP22 . . . . . . .177 B4
  Norwich NR5 . . . . .161 C6
Taylor's La
  Gressenhall NR20 . . . . .49 C3
  Norwich NR6 . . . . .158 D6
  Trimingham NR11 . . . . .11 E1
Taylors Loke
  3 Cley next the Sea NR25 . .7 E6
  1 Hemsby NR29 . . . . .167 A8
Taylor Wy NR13 . . . . .165 A8
Taymor Pl IP14 . . . . .95 D4
Teal Cl 3 PE31 . . . . .12 E5
Teal Dr NR8 . . . . .156 B5
Teal Wlk Brandon IP27 . . . . .175 F4
  16 Great Yarmouth NR31 . .94 C8
Teasel Cl NR20 . . . . .68 A8
Teasel Dr NR29 . . . . .176 C5
Teasel Rd NR17 . . . . .174 B4
Teasel Rise 4 NR26 . . . . . .138 B6
Tebbutt Ave 6 NR19 . . . . . .154 C3
Tedder Cl
  5 Barnham IP24 . . . . .125 F6
  13 Watton IP25 . . . . .84 E3
Ted Ellis Nature Reserve★
  NR14 . . . . .91 D8
Tee Cl 1 NR14 . . . . .89 B2
Telegraph La E NR1 . . . . . . .163 B6
Telegraph La W 4 NR1 . . . .163 A6
Telford Cl
  King's Lynn PE30 . . . . .147 D4
  2 Norwich NR3 . . . . .157 F1
Telford Way IP24 . . . . .176 B6
Temple Cl NR25 . . . . .8 F6
Temple Dr NR25 . . . . .8 F6
Templemere NR3 . . . . .159 A2
Temple Rd
  Great Yarmouth NR30 . . . . .169 D4
  King's Lynn PE30 . . . . .148 D1
  Norwich NR3 . . . . .158 D1
Templewood La NR25 . . . . . .137 F8
Ten Bell La NR2 . . . . .178 A3
TEN MILE BANK PE38 . . . . .96 E7
Ten Mile Bank Hilgay PE38 . .96 F6
  Littleport CB6 . . . . .96 E1
Ten Mile Bank Prim Sch
  PE38 . . . . .96 F7
Tennyson Ave PE30 . . . . . . .146 F4
Tennyson Rd
  3 Diss IP22 . . . . .177 E4
  3 Great Yarmouth NR30 . .169 D8
  King's Lynn PE30 . . . . .146 F4
Tennyson Way IP24 . . . . . . .176 E6
Tensing St NR35 . . . . .108 C5
Terence Airey Ct 25
  IP20 . . . . .122 D2
Terence Ave NR7 . . . . .159 A4

Teresa Rd 6 NR12 . . . . .39 B4
Tern Cl 9 IP25 . . . . .84 C3
Tern Gdns NR31 . . . . .170 A6
Tern Rd NR29 . . . . .167 E5
Terrace Wlk NR1 . . . . .178 B1
Terrington Cl 3 PE14 . . . . . .59 D2
TERRINGTON ST CLEMENT
  PE34 . . . . .144 B4
Terrington St Clement Com
  Sch PE34 . . . . .144 C6
TERRINGTON ST JOHN
  PE34 . . . . .42 C2
Terrington St John Cty Prim
  Sch PE14 . . . . .60 B8
Terr The 12 NR28 . . . . .151 C5
Tesmonde Cl NR5 . . . . .160 E7
Testerton Cotts NR21 . . . . . .32 A6
Teulon Cl NR31 . . . . .171 C5
Texas Ave NR21 . . . . .15 C2
Texel Way NR11 . . . . .143 A7
Thacker Way NR5 . . . . .160 F6
Thain's La NR27 . . . . .10 B5
Thamesfield Way NR31 . . . . .169 B2
Thames Way 8 NR30 . . . . . .168 C6
THARSTON NR15 . . . . .106 E5
Thatchwood Ave PE14 . . . . .59 C2
Theatre Plain NR30 . . . . . . .169 C4
Theatre Rd NR23 . . . . .136 C6
Theatre St
  East Dereham NR19 . . . . . .154 D6
  Norwich NR2 . . . . .178 A2
  Swaffham PE37 . . . . .153 B4
THELNETHAM IP22 . . . . . . .128 B5
Thelnetham Rd
  Blo' Norton IP22 . . . . .128 B6
  Hopton IP22 . . . . .127 F5
THELVETON IP21 . . . . .130 D8
THEMELTHORPE NR20 . . . .33 F2
Themelthorpe Rd NR20 . . . .33 E1
Theobald Rd NR1 . . . . .89 E8
THETFORD IP24 . . . . .176 B4
Thetford Acad (North
  Campus) The IP24 . . . . . .176 E7
Thetford Acad The IP24 . .176 C1
Thetford Ancient House
  Mus★ IP24 . . . . .176 C4
Thetford Gram Sch IP24 . . .176 C4
Thetford L Ctr & Waterworld
  IP24 . . . . .176 D5
Thetford Priory★ IP24 . .176 C4
Thetford Rd
  Brandon IP27 . . . . .175 E3
  Coney Weston IP31 . . . . . . .127 B4
  Euston IP24 . . . . .126 B6
  Garboldisham IP22 . . . . . . .127 F8
  Northwold IP26 . . . . .99 B8
  Santon Downham IP27 . . . .115 B5
  Watton IP25 . . . . .84 D3
  Wretham IP24 . . . . .117 A7
Thetford Sta IP24 . . . . .176 C5
Thetford Warren Lodge★
  IP24 . . . . .115 E3
Thetford Way PE30 . . . . . . .148 C3
Thicket The 6 NR8 . . . . . . .155 E2
Thiefgate La PE34 . . . . .43 D2
Thieves' Bridge Rd PE33 . . .61 E5
Thieves La NR13 . . . . .55 A1
Thieves' La
  Attleborough NR17 . . . . . . .174 C5
  Burgh & Tuttington NR11 . . .36 E6
  Little Ellingham NR17 . . . . .103 C8
Third Ave PE13 . . . . .152 E5
Third Marsh Rd PE14 . . . . . .59 A7
Thirlby Rd NR28 . . . . .151 D3
Thirlmere 18 NR9 . . . . .88 D8
Thistle Cl Norwich NR5 . . . .160 F5
  3 Thetford IP24 . . . . .176 F5
Thistledown Rd NR10 . . . . . .53 B2
Thomas Bardwell Dr
  NR35 . . . . .124 B7
Thomas Bole Cl IP22 . . . . . .128 A8
Thomas Bullock Prim Sch
  IP25 . . . . .67 C2
Thomas Cl 4 PE33 . . . . . . .61 D5
Thomas Clarkson Acad
  PE13 . . . . .152 D3
Thomas Dix Ct NR28 . . . . . .151 D5
Thomas Drew Cl PE31 . . . . .140 C3
Thomas Glover Ct NR6 . . . .158 C2
Thomas Manning Rd
  IP22 . . . . .177 E4
Thomas Paine Ave 3
  IP24 . . . . .176 C4
Thomas St PE30 . . . . .146 E3
Thomas Vere Rd NR7 . . . . . .163 F7
Thomas Way NR30 . . . . .168 C6
Thomas Wy NR10 . . . . .53 B4
Thomas Wyatt Cl NR2 . . . . .178 A1
THOMPSON IP24 . . . . .102 A8
Thompson Ave 7 NR25 . . . .137 C5
Thompson Cl NR20 . . . . .50 B4
Thompson Prim Sch
  IP24 . . . . .102 B7
Thompson Rd Griston IP25 . .85 A1
  Norwich NR7 . . . . .163 F8
Thompson's La PE33 . . . . . .81 A2
Thompsons Yd NR3 . . . . . . .178 A4
Thor Cl NR7 . . . . .163 E2
Thoresby Ave PE30 . . . . . . .147 B4
Thoresby Coll PE30 . . . . . . .146 D4
Thor Loke NR7 . . . . .163 E2
THORNAGE NR25 . . . . .18 F7
Thornage Rd NR25 . . . . .137 A5
Thornham Cl NR7 . . . . .159 B2
Thornham Cnr PE36 . . . . . . .2 E2
Thornham Rd
  Methwold IP26 . . . . .99 A6

Thornham Rd continued
  Norwich NR7 . . . . .159 B2
Thorn La NR1 . . . . .178 B2
Thorn Rd Catfield NR29 . . . .56 C8
  Fakenham NR21 . . . . .141 D4
Thornton Cl NR24 . . . . .142 E4
Thornycroft Gdns 1
  NR33 . . . . .111 F1
Thoroughfare La NR29 . . . . .167 B4
Thoroughfare The IP20 . . . . .122 D2
Thorp Ct NR19 . . . . .154 D4
THORPE NR14 . . . . .93 B1
Thorpe Abbots Rd IP21 . . . .131 A8
THORPE ABBOTTS IP21 . . . .131 B6
Thorpe Ave NR7 . . . . .163 E8
Thorpe Cl NR7 . . . . .163 F7
Thorpe Dr NR17 . . . . .174 D4
THORPE END NR13 . . . . . . .72 D6
Thorpe Hall Cl NR7 . . . . . . .163 C5
THORPE HAMLET NR1 . . . . .163 B6
Thorpeland Cl 4 PE33 . . . . .61 D3
Thorpeland La 3 PE33 . . . . .61 D3
THORPE MARKET NR11 . . . .22 A6
THORPE MARRIOTT NR8 . . .155 F2
Thorpe Mews NR7 . . . . .163 F6
Thorpe Mkt Rd NR11 . . . . . .21 E7
Thorpe Rd
  Haddiscoe NR14 . . . . .110 F8
  Norwich NR7 . . . . .178 C2
  Southrepps NR11 . . . . .22 A7
THORPE ROW IP25 . . . . . . .67 C4
THORPE ST ANDREW
  NR7 . . . . .163 F8
Thorpe St Andrew Sch
  NR7 . . . . .72 D4
THORPLAND PE33 . . . . .61 D3
Thorpland Rd NR21 . . . . . . .141 E6
Thor Rd NR7 . . . . .163 E7
THRANDESTON IP21 . . . . . .129 F3
Threadneedle St NR15 . . . . .91 A4
Three Acre Cl NR12 . . . . . . .164 C6
Three Cnr Dr NR6 . . . . .158 F6
THREE COCKED HAT
  NR34 . . . . .110 D7
THREEHAMMER COMMON
  NR12 . . . . .55 E6
THREE HOLES PE14 . . . . . . .77 E3
Three King La NR2 . . . . .178 A3
Three Mile La NR5 . . . . .156 F1
Three Oaks 6 PE30 . . . . . . .147 C5
Three Post Rd 5 IP25 . . . . .84 C3
Three Score Rd
  Colney NR5 . . . . .161 A5
  Norwich NR5 . . . . .160 F5
Threxton Rd IP25 . . . . .84 C3
Threxton Road Ind Est
  IP25 . . . . .84 C3
THRIGBY NR29 . . . . .75 D7
Thrigby Hall Wildlife Gdns★
  NR29 . . . . .75 E7
Thrigby Rd NR29 . . . . .75 D8
Throckmorton Yd 5
  NR3 . . . . .162 E8
Thrush Cl 2 NR14 . . . . .89 B3
Thumb La NR20 . . . . .31 F2
Thunder La NR7 . . . . .163 E7
THURGARTON NR11 . . . . . . .20 F5
Thurgarton Rd NR11 . . . . . . .21 A5
Thurland's Dro PE14 . . . . . . .77 D5
Thurlby Rd NR5 . . . . .160 E8
Thurling Loke NR7 . . . . .159 E1
Thurling Plain NR7 . . . . .159 E1
Thurlin Rd PE30 . . . . .147 B4
Thurloe Cl PE13 . . . . .152 C2
Thurlow Cl NR5 . . . . .160 E8
THURLTON NR14 . . . . .92 F1
Thurlton Prim Sch NR14 . . .92 F1
Thurlton Rd NR14 . . . . .110 B7
THURNE NR29 . . . . .56 E3
Thurne Rd NR29 . . . . .57 A2
Thurne Rise 2 NR29 . . . . . .57 D5
Thurne Way NR29 . . . . .167 B3
THURNING NR11 . . . . .34 C7
Thurning Rd NR20 . . . . .33 E8
THURSFORD NR21 . . . . .17 E4
Thursford Collection★
  NR21 . . . . .17 D5
THURSFORD GREEN
  NR21 . . . . .17 D5
Thursford Rd
  Great Snoring NR21 . . . . . .17 A5
  Hindringham NR21 . . . . . . .17 E6
  1 Little Snoring NR21 . . . .17 B3
Thursford Wood Nature
  Reserve★ NR21 . . . . .17 D4
Thurston Cl 3 NR5 . . . . . . .160 F8
Thurst Rd NR27 . . . . .11 A3
THURTON NR14 . . . . .91 D4
Thurton Prim Sch NR14 . . . .91 D4
THUXTON NR9 . . . . .68 D2
Thuxton Sta NR9 . . . . .68 C2
Thwaite Rd NR35 . . . . .109 A2
THWAITE ST MARY
  NR35 . . . . .109 A5
Thwaites Oak Cl NR15 . . . . .121 B5
Thyme Cl
  Attleborough NR17 . . . . . . .174 B4
  Thetford IP24 . . . . .176 F5
Thynne's La NR20 . . . . .68 E5
TIBENHAM NR16 . . . . .120 E8
Tibenham Rd NR15 . . . . . . .121 A8
Tiercel Ave NR7 . . . . .159 C4
Tillett Cl NR29 . . . . .167 C2
Tillett Rd NR3 . . . . .158 E2
Tills Cl NR6 . . . . .158 F4
Tills Rd NR6 . . . . .159 A5
TILNEY ALL SAINTS
  PE34 . . . . .144 F1

Tilney All Saints CE Prim Sch
PE34 . . . . **42** E4
TILNEY CUM ISLINGTON
PE34 . . . . **60** F8
TILNEY FEN END PE34 . . . . . . **60** C6
TILNEY HIGH END PE34 . . . . **42** D4
Tilney Rd NR20 . . . . **69** C6
TILNEY ST LAWRENCE
PE34 . . . . **60** D8
Tilney St Lawrence Com
Prim Sch PE34 . . . . **60** C8
Timberhill NR1 . . . . **178** B2
Timber Rd NR16 . . . . **118** C5
Time & Tide Mus of Great
Yarmouth ★ NR30 . . . . . . **169** D2
Timothy CI NR1 . . . . **163** B8
Timperley Est NR21 . . . . **31** D5
Tindall CI PE13 . . . . **152** C8
Tinker's Dro PE13 . . . . **1** D1
Tinkers' La Garvestone NR9 **68** C1
Strumpshaw NR13 . . . . **73** D1
Tinker's La NR15 . . . . **121** C4
Tinkers Wy PE38 . . . . **172** B6
Tintern Gr **4** PE30 . . . . **148** C4
Tippett CI NR5 . . . . **160** F6
TIPPS END PE14 . . . . **95** C6
Tipton CI NR19 . . . . **154** D2
TITCHWELL PE31 . . . . **2** F7
Titchwell Marsh Nature
Reserve ★ PE31 . . . . **2** F7
Tithe Barn CI IP26 . . . . **100** C5
Tithebarn La Marham PE33 **63** D6
2 Thurlton NR14 . . . . **92** F1
Tithe Barn La NR24 . . . . . . **142** F3
Tithing CI **2** IP24 . . . . **176** E5
Titlow Rd **28** IP20 . . . . **122** D2
TITTLESHALL PE32 . . . . **48** B8
Tittleshall Rd
Litcham PE32 . . . . **48** A5
Mileham NR20 . . . . **48** E8
Tittleshall PE32 . . . . **48** C6
Tivetshall Prim Sch
NR15 . . . . **121** B5
Tivetshall Rd IP21 . . . . **121** D5
TIVETSHALL ST MARGARET
NR15 . . . . **121** B5
TIVETSHALL ST MARY
NR15 . . . . **121** B5
Toad Hole Cottage Mus ★
NR29 . . . . **56** A6
Toad La Ditchingham NR35 **108** F5
Great & Little Plumstead
NR13 . . . . **72** F5
Thwaite NR35 . . . . **109** A5
Todhunter Ave NR34 . . . . . **110** C2
Todkill's La PE12 . . . . **41** C8
Toftes PI **4** NR5 . . . . **161** B8
Toftmead CI NR19 . . . . **154** E3
TOFT MONKS NR34 . . . . **110** D5
TOFTREES NR21 . . . . **31** B6
Toftrees Rd NR21 . . . . **31** B7
TOFTWOOD NR19 . . . . **154** E4
Toftwood Inf Sch NR19 . . **154** E2
Toftwood Jun Sch NR19 . . **154** E1
Tolhouse Mus ★ NR30 . . . . **169** C3
Tolhouse St NR30 . . . . **169** C3
Toll Bar NR21 . . . . **141** A6
Tollgate Rd NR31 . . . . **169** C1
Tollgate Way NR5 . . . . **161** A5
Tollhouse Rd NR5 . . . . **161** E7
Tolwin Wlk **3** NR6 . . . . **158** F1
Tolye Rd NR5 . . . . **160** F7
Tombland NR1 . . . . **178** B3
Tooks Comm La NR34 . . . . **124** F5
Topcliffe Ave **2** NR13 . . . . **55** A1
TOPCROFT NR35 . . . . **107** F3
TOPCROFT STREET
NR35 . . . . **107** F2
Top Driftway NR20 . . . . **117** C8
Top Rd Belaugh NR12 . . . . **164** A6
St Andrew, Ilketshall
NR34 . . . . **124** E5
Wicklewood NR18 . . . . **87** B4
Wingfield IP21 . . . . **131** E3
TOPROW NR16 . . . . **88** E1
Topshill Rd NR11 . . . . **21** E6
Torrey CI PE31 . . . . **133** E5
Tortoiseshell Dr **10**
NR17 . . . . **174** B4
Tortoishell Way NR18 . . . . **173** E4
Tottenham St **8** NR30 . . . **169** D5
TOTTENHILL PE33 . . . . **62** A5
TOTTENHILL ROW PE33 . . . **61** E7
Tottenhill Row PE33 . . . . . . **61** E1
TOTTINGTON IP24 . . . . **101** E6
Tottington CI
6 Norwich NR5 . . . . **160** F8
Thetford IP24 . . . . **176** D6
Tottington La IP22 . . . . . . **177** B4
Tottington Rd
Little Cressingham IP25 . . **101** C8
Thompson IP24 . . . . **102** A7
Tottington IP24 . . . . **101** F7
Tower CI Brandon IP27 . . . **175** B3
Costessey NR8 . . . . **156** C4
TOWER END PE32 . . . . **44** C4
Tower Hill Costessey NR8 **156** C4
Norwich NR7 . . . . **163** D6
Tower Hill Pk NR8 . . . . **156** C4
Tower La Middleton PE32 . . **44** B4
Sidestrand NR27 . . . . **11** B3
Tower Mdws PE31 . . . . **133** C5
Tower Mill Rd NR35 . . . . . . **124** A8
Tower PI **13** PE30 . . . . **146** D4
Tower Rd
Burgh St Margaret
(Fleggburgh) NR29 . . . . . . **57** C1
Burnham Overy PE31 . . . . **135** E7

Tower Rd continued
Canadas NR11 . . . . **10** A4
Elm PE14 . . . . **77** A7
Hilgay PE38 . . . . **97** A8
Repps with Bastwick NR29 . **57** A5
Terrington St Clement
PE34 . . . . **144** C7
Tower St PE30 . . . . **146** D4
Town Bridge **25** PE13 . . . . **152** B5
Town CI Corpusty NR11 . . . . **19** E1
East Winch PE32 . . . . **44** F3
Holt NR25 . . . . **137** B6
Town CI House Prep Sch
NR2 . . . . **162** C3
Town CI Rd NR2 . . . . **162** C3
Town Cnr NR10 . . . . **53** C8
Town End NR11 . . . . **143** C6
Town Gn NR18 . . . . **173** B4
Town Gn Rd IP25 . . . . **84** E3
TOWN GREEN
Alby with Thwaite NR11 . . . **21** C4
South Walsham NR13 . . . . . **74** A7
Town House Dr NR8 . . . . . **156** C4
Town House Drift PE32 . . . . **48** D2
Town House La IP22 . . . . . **128** B2
Town House Mus ★ PE30 **146** D4
Town House Rd NR8 . . . . . **156** F4
Town La Aylsham NR11 . . . **150** C7
Brancaster Staithe PE31 . . . . **3** D7
Castle Acre PE32 . . . . **46** F2
Garvestone NR9 . . . . **68** C2
Townlands NR31 . . . . **170** B7
Town Lands Trading Est
NR31 . . . . **170** B7
Townley CI PE14 . . . . **77** E5
Townley Prim Sch PE14 . . . **95** A7
Town Rd
Burgh St Margaret
(Fleggburgh) NR29 . . . . . . **57** C1
Ingham NR12 . . . . **39** C4
Townsend Gn N NR21 . . . . **141** F5
Townsend Rd
Norwich NR4 . . . . **162** C1
Upwell PE14 . . . . **77** E3
Townshend CI **3** NR30 . . . **169** D3
Townsend Gn E NR21 . . . . **141** F5
Townsend Gn W NR21 . . . . **141** F5
Townshend PI **4** IP25 . . . . **67** C2
Townshend Rd
Dereham NR20 . . . . **154** D7
Wisbech PE13 . . . . **152** D6
Townshend Terr **2**
PE30 . . . . **146** E6
Town St Outwell PE14 . . . . **77** D5
Swanton Morley NR20 . . . . **50** B4
Town Wall Mews **9**
NR30 . . . . **169** C5
Town Wall Rd NR30 . . . . . . **169** C5
Town Yd **4** NR25 . . . . **7** E6
Tracey Rd NR7 . . . . **159** E1
Trafalgar Ct
Cliftonville NR11 . . . . **143** C7
Great Yarmouth NR30 . . . . **169** E3
Trafalgar Ind Est PE38 . . . **172** A4
Trafalgar Rd
Downham Market PE38 . . . **172** B4
2 Great Yarmouth NR30 . **169** D3
Trafalgar Rd E NR31 . . . . . **170** D6
Trafalgar Rd W NR31 . . . . . **170** C6
Trafalgar Sq
Great Yarmouth NR30 . . . . **169** E3
Poringland NR14 . . . . **90** C4
Trafalgar St NR1 . . . . **178** B1
Trafalgar Wy Diss IP22 . . . **177** F3
Thetford IP24 . . . . **176** F5
Trafalgar Yd NR11 . . . . **150** C2
Trafford Est PE14 . . . . **59** C8
Trafford Pk **1** PE13 . . . . . **152** E6
Trafford Rd Norwich NR1 . **178** A1
Wisbech PE13 . . . . **152** D5
Trafford Wlk NR12 . . . . . . **164** B2
Trafford Wy NR10 . . . . **54** B2
Traice Rd NR16 . . . . **105** D7
Transport La NR14 . . . . . . **109** D7
Trap La NR21 . . . . **141** B6
Trelawny Rd **5** NR29 . . . . **57** D4
Tremaine CI NR6 . . . . **157** E1
Trenchard Cres **4** IP25 . . **84** F3
Trenchard Sq IP26 . . . . **98** D1
Trendall Rd NR7 . . . . **159** C4
Trenowaths PI **1** PE30 . . **146** D5
Trent V C CI IP26 . . . . **99** A5
Tretts La NR29 . . . . **57** C1
Trident Dr NR1 . . . . **163** A7
TRIMINGHAM NR11 . . . . **11** D2
Trimingham Rd
Gimingham NR11 . . . . **22** E8
Trimingham NR11 . . . . **11** E1
Trimming Wlk NR8 . . . . . . **156** E8
Trinity Ave NR31 . . . . **170** B4
Trinity CI
East Dereham NR19 . . . . . . **154** D6
Norwich NR13 . . . . **72** D8
Trinity Gdns NR35 . . . . . . **124** A8
Trinity Hospl (Bede House) ★
PE31 . . . . **27** C1
Trinity PI **25** NR30 . . . . . . **169** D2
Trinity Rd Fakenham NR21 **141** E6
Walpole Highway PE14 . . . . **59** F8
Wisbech PE13 . . . . **152** E6
Trinity Sq **1** NR30 . . . . . . **169** D1
Trinity St NR2 . . . . **162** C5
Triple Plea La NR35 . . . . . **108** B4
Triple Plea Rd NR35 . . . . . **108** B4
Trix Rd NR2 . . . . **162** C4
Tropical Butterfly World ★
NR17 . . . . **103** F5
Trory St NR2 . . . . **162** C5

Troston Rd IP31 . . . . **126** C1
Troutbeck **21** NR9 . . . . **88** D8
TROWSE NEWTON NR14 . . . **163** B3
Trowse Prim Sch NR14 . . . **163** B2
True's Yd Fishing Heritage
Mus ★ PE30 . . . . **146** D6
Truman CI
9 Norwich NR4 . . . . **161** C5
Rackheath/Salhouse NR13 . **72** F8
Trumpery La NR14 . . . . **90** C8
TRUNCH NR28 . . . . **22** E5
Trunch Hill IP20 . . . . **122** E5
Trunch Rd Denton IP20 . . . **123** B6
Mundesley NR11 . . . . **143** B4
Swafield NR28 . . . . **22** E4
Trust CI NR29 . . . . **57** C1
Tubby Dr NR14 . . . . **90** C5
Tucker St NR27 . . . . **139** B7
Tucks Rd NR28 . . . . **38** A5
Tuckswood Com Prim Sch
NR4 . . . . **162** D1
Tuckswood Ctr **2** NR4 . . . **162** C1
Tuckswood La NR4 . . . . . . **162** D1
Tuddenham Rd NR11 . . . . . **150** B6
Tud La IP22 . . . . **69** E6
Tudor Ave IP22 . . . . **177** A5
Tudor CI IP24 . . . . **176** C2
Tudor Cres PE36 . . . . **132** D2
Tudor Rose Wy **45** IP20 . . **122** D2
Tudor Way
Dersingham PE31 . . . . **140** D4
6 Mulbarton NR14 . . . . . . **89** B3
Tudor Wlk
Great Yarmouth NR31 . . . . **170** C1
6 Honington IP31 . . . . . . **126** B1
Tuesday Mkt PI **5** PE30 . . **146** D5
Tuffen La IP22 . . . . **128** B4
Tulip CI NR17 . . . . **174** C5
Tulip Gdns NR4 . . . . **89** B8
Tulip Tree Dr **5** NR14 . . . . **90** C5
Tumbler Hill PE37 . . . . **153** C6
Tumbleyhill Rd PE32 . . . . . **46** C3
Tumbril La IP21 . . . . **131** D7
Tummel Way NR17 . . . . **174** E6
Tunbeck CI IP20 . . . . **123** A3
Tunbeck Rd IP20 . . . . **123** A4
TUNGATE NR28 . . . . **37** C8
Tungate Cres NR4 . . . . **89** B8
Tungate Rd NR28 . . . . **151** A5
Tungate Way **6** NR12 . . . . **54** C6
Tunneys La NR35 . . . . **109** B2
Tunn St **4** NR21 . . . . **141** B4
Tunns Yd NR23 . . . . **136** D6
Tuns Rd PE37 . . . . **65** F4
TUNSTALL CI **5** NR5 . . . . . **161** A7
Tunstall Rd NR13 . . . . **74** F2
TUNSTEAD NR12 . . . . **37** F1
Tunstead La NR12 . . . . **164** D6
Tunstead Prim Sch NR12 . **37** F1
Tunstead Rd
Tunstead NR12 . . . . **37** E1
1 Wroxham/Hoveton
NR12 . . . . **164** C5
Turbine Way PE37 . . . . **153** B6
Turbo Rd NR21 . . . . **15** C2
Turbus Rd PE30 . . . . **146** E7
Turf Fen La NR29 . . . . **56** B5
Turf Lot Dro PE14 . . . . **95** B5
Turf Moor Rd NR21 . . . . **16** C1
Turin Way NR31 . . . . **171** E4
Turkey La NR4 . . . . **19** D6
Turnberry NR4 . . . . **162** A1
Turner CI
Ditchingham NR35 . . . . . . **109** B2
5 Great Yarmouth NR31 . **170** A7
Wymondham NR18 . . . . **173** E5
Turner Rd NR2 . . . . **162** A7
Turner's CI PE34 . . . . **79** E8
Turner Way PE38 . . . . **172** E5
Turnham Gn **10** NR7 . . . . . **72** D4
Turnpike CI Foxley NR20 . . **50** D8
2 Wisbech PE13 . . . . **152** E6
Turnpike The
Ashwellthorpe NR16 . . . . . **106** A7
Carleton Rode NR16 . . . . . **105** D2
Turn The NR10 . . . . **53** A8
Tusser Rd NR8 . . . . **156** E8
Tusting CI NR7 . . . . **158** F4
TUTTINGTON NR11 . . . . **36** E6
Tuttington Rd NR11 . . . . . . **150** F8
Tuttles La E NR18 . . . . **173** D6
Tuttles La W NR18 . . . . . . **173** B6
Tuxhill Chase PE34 . . . . . . **42** B4
Tuxhill Rd PE34 . . . . **42** B5
Twelveacre NR4 . . . . **161** F4
Twickenham Ave IP27 . . . . **175** B1
Twickenham Rd NR6 . . . . . **158** B5
Twiss CI **8** IP22 . . . . **129** D7
Two Acres **6** PE32 . . . . **44** B3
Two Fields Way **11** NR20 . . **50** E7
Two Furlong Hill NR23 . . . **136** C5
Two Saints CI NR12 . . . . . **164** D7
Two Sisters CI **6** PE12 . . . . **41** B8
Twrs The PE38 . . . . **172** C5
TWYFORD NR20 . . . . **33** B3
Twyford La NR20 . . . . **33** C3
Twyford Rd NR20 . . . . **33** A6
TYBY NR11 . . . . **34** B6
Tyndale PE30 . . . . **148** C5
Tyne Mews NR30 . . . . **168** C5
Tyrell Cres PE30 . . . . **148** D1
Tyrolean Sq NR31 . . . . **169** B4
Tyrrell's Rd **2** NR31 . . . . . **169** B4

U

UEA Sportspark NR4 . . . . **161** D4
Ulfkell Rd IP24 . . . . **176** B2
Ullswater Ave
Castle Rising PE30 . . . . **27** C1
King's Lynn PE30 . . . . **148** F1
Ullswater Dr **20** NR9 . . . . . **88** D8
Ulph PI PE31 . . . . **135** D3
Uncle's La IP19 . . . . **124** B2
Unicorn Yd
2 Aylsham NR11 . . . . **150** C6
Norwich NR3 . . . . **178** A4
Union Drift NR20 . . . . **68** A8
Union La
4 King's Lynn PE30 . . . . **146** D4
Wortham IP22 . . . . **129** D5
Union PI **17** PE13 . . . . **152** C5
Union Rd
7 Great Yarmouth
NR30 . . . . **169** D4
Smallburgh NR12 . . . . **38** C3
Union St Norwich NR2 . . . . **178** A2
University Cres NR31 . . . . **170** B4
University Dr NR4 . . . . **161** C5
University of E Anglia
Norwich NR4 . . . . **161** C3
Norwich NR4 . . . . **157** A4
Unthank Rd NR4 . . . . **161** F2
Upcher CI **28** IP26 . . . . **98** E1
UPGATE NR9 . . . . **52** C5
Upgate NR14 . . . . **90** D5
Upgate Rd NR15 . . . . **108** E7
Upgate St
Carleton Rode NR16 . . . . . **105** A4
Southery PE38 . . . . **97** B5
UPGATE STREET
Bedingham NR35 . . . . **108** B2
Old Buckenham NR16 . . . . **105** A3
Uphalle NR18 . . . . **155** D1
Uplands Ave NR30 . . . . . . **168** D5
Uplands Pk NR26 . . . . **138** C6
Uplands Way IP22 . . . . **177** D5
UPPER BRANDON PARVA
NR9 . . . . **68** E3
Upper Breckland Rd
NR5 . . . . **156** F1
Upper Brook La IP20 . . . . **131** E8
Upper Burnthouse La
IP20 . . . . **131** E8
Upper Cliff Rd NR31 . . . . . **170** D4
Upper Goat La NR2 . . . . . . **178** A3
Upper Grange Cres
NR30 . . . . **168** D5
Upper Green La NR3 . . . . . **178** B4
UPPER GUIST NR20 . . . . **33** A5
Upper Hall La NR24 . . . . . . **18** D8
Upper Harmans La IP20 . . **122** B1
UPPER HELLESDON NR3 . . **158** C3
Upper Kiln La NR15 . . . . . . **90** F4
Upper King St NR1 . . . . . . **178** B3
Upper Mkt **3** NR21 . . . . . **141** B4
Upper Oakley IP21 . . . . . . **130** E4
Upper Olland St NR35 . . . **124** A8
Upper Rose La IP22 . . . . . **177** E2
Upper St Giles St NR2 . . . **178** A3
UPPER SHERINGHAM
NR26 . . . . **138** A5
Upper St Gissing IP22 . . . **120** F4
Salhouse NR13 . . . . **55** D3
Upper Stafford Ave NR5 . **156** F1
Upper Staithe Rd **18** NR12 **38** B4
UPPER STOKE NR14 . . . . **90** B5
UPPER STREET
Dickleburgh and Rushall
IP21 . . . . **130** F4
Horning NR12 . . . . **55** F4
Hoveton NR12 . . . . **55** C5
Southrepps NR11 . . . . **22** B7
Tunstead NR12 . . . . **38** A3
Upper Tumbril La
Brockdish IP20 . . . . **131** D8
Needham IP20 . . . . **122** A1
Scole IP20 . . . . **131** D8
UPPER WEYBREAD IP21 . . **131** E6
UPTON NR13 . . . . **166** A8
Upton Broad Nature
Reserve ★ NR13 . . . . **74** C8
Upton CI NR4 . . . . **162** A3
Upton Dr PE37 . . . . **153** B2
UPTON GREEN NR13 . . . . . **166** B8
Upton Rd Norwich NR4 . . **162** A3
South Walsham NR13 . . . . . **74** B8
Uptons Way IP26 . . . . **82** A2
Upton Way NR12 . . . . **24** C5
UPWELL PE14 . . . . **77** F5
Upwell Com Prim Sch
PE14 . . . . **77** D4
Upwell Rd PE14 . . . . **95** A7
Utopia Way NR12 . . . . **39** B3
Utting CI **19** NR14 . . . . **90** C5

V

Vale CI **8** NR10 . . . . **53** B3
Vale Ct **5** IP27 . . . . **114** E1
Vale Gn NR6 . . . . **158** B1
Valentine Ct PE36 . . . . . . **132** D5
Valentine Rd PE36 . . . . . . **132** D4
Valentine St **3** NR2 . . . . . **162** C6
Vale Rd High Kelling NR25 . **8** F3
Mundesley NR11 . . . . **143** A8
Thurton NR14 . . . . **91** C3
Valerian Rise IP24 . . . . . . **116** D2
Valinger's PI **6** PE30 . . . . **146** E4

Valingers Rd PE30 . . . . **146** E3
Valley CI **1** NR35 . . . . **123** F7
Valley Dr The NR1 . . . . **163** B8
Valley Gdns **1** NR28 . . . . **151** E5
Valley La NR25 . . . . **137** B5
Valley Prim Sch NR5 . . . . . **161** C8
Valley Rd Norwich NR5 . . . **157** C1
9 Tasburgh NR15 . . . . . . **106** F6
Valley Rise **140** C4
Valleyside NR18 . . . . **173** C4
Valley Side Rd **1** NR1 . . . **163** C8
Valley View NR19 . . . . **154** C6
Valley View Cres NR5 . . . . **157** A1
Valley Way NR21 . . . . **141** E4
Valpy Ave NR3 . . . . **158** A1
Vancouver Ave PE30 . . . . . **146** E3
Vancouver Ct
15 King's Lynn PE30 . . . . **146** D5
North Lynn PE30 . . . . **147** C7
Vancouver Rd **3** NR7 . . . . **163** C8
Vane CI NR7 . . . . **72** D4
Vanguard Chase NR5 . . . . **156** C1
Vanguard Rd
2 Great Yarmouth NR31 . **94** C8
Great Yarmouth NR31 . . . . **170** A8
Varsity Rd IP25 . . . . **84** F3
Varvel Ave NR7 . . . . **159** C4
Vassar Ct **6** NR20 . . . . **68** F6
Vaunces La IP21 . . . . **131** B8
Vaunce's La IP21 . . . . **131** B8
Vauxhall St NR2 . . . . **162** C5
Vauxhall Terr NR30 . . . . . . **169** C6
Vawdrey Rd NR8 . . . . **155** F1
Veltshaw CI PE31 . . . . **133** B4
Venables CI NR1 . . . . **163** B7
Venta Icenorum (Roman
Town) ★ NR14 . . . . **89** E6
Ventura CI IP26 . . . . **98** F5
Vera CI **10** PE13 . . . . **72** E7
Vera Rd
New Rackheath NR13 . . . . . **72** E7
Norwich NR6 . . . . **158** B4
Verbena Dr NR18 . . . . **173** E6
Verbena Rd NR4 . . . . **161** B1
Verdon's La NR18 . . . . **87** F2
Verdun Rd PE13 . . . . **152** D5
Veronica Gn **9** NR31 . . . . **170** B6
Vervain CI **23** NR31 . . . . . . **94** C6
Vetch CI NR1 . . . . **173** D4
Viburnum Way **6** NR31 . . **170** B6
Vicarage CI
Costessey NR8 . . . . **156** F5
Foulden PE26 . . . . **82** A1
1 Potter Heigham NR29 . . **56** F6
Vicarage La Bungay NR35 **124** C8
Hoveton NR12 . . . . **164** E5
Vicarage Mdws NR19 . . . . **154** D4
Vicarage Rd
Cromer NR27 . . . . **139** B6
Deopham NR18 . . . . **86** D3
East Ruston NR12 . . . . **24** A3
Foulden IP26 . . . . **82** A2
Hockham IP24 . . . . **102** D3
Norwich NR3 . . . . **158** C1
Paston NR28 . . . . **143** D2
Salhouse NR13 . . . . **55** A2
Sheringham NR26 . . . . **138** C6
Thetford IP24 . . . . **176** D5
Wingfield IP21 . . . . **131** E3
Worstead NR28 . . . . **38** A5
Vicarage St NR28 . . . . **151** C5
Vicarage Wlk **11** IP25 . . . . **84** E3
Vicar St NR18 . . . . **173** B4
Viceroy CI PE31 . . . . **140** C4
Victor Charles CI IP27 . . . **175** B7
Victoria Arc NR30 . . . . **169** C3
Victoria Ave
Brandon IP27 . . . . **175** C3
Hunstanton PE36 . . . . **132** D5
Victoria CI Diss IP22 . . . . . **177** E3
Heacham PE31 . . . . **133** E6
Taverham NR8 . . . . **156** C8
Victoria Cotts PE31 . . . . . **133** D6
Victoria Ct
Sheringham NR26 . . . . **138** E7
22 Watton IP25 . . . . **84** D3
Victoria Gdns **7** NR30 . . . **169** D2
Victoria Hill IP23 . . . . **130** C1
Victoria La Deopham NR18 . **86** F3
Fakenham NR21 . . . . **141** E4
Victoria PI **17** PE13 . . . . . **152** C5
Victoria Rd Diss IP22 . . . . **177** D4
5 Great Yarmouth NR30 . **169** D2
Great Yarmouth NR31 . . . . **170** D3
Mundesley NR11 . . . . **143** C6
3 Taverham NR8 . . . . . . **155** C1
Taverham NR8 . . . . **156** C8
Terrington St John PE34 . . **42** C2
Wisbech PE13 . . . . **152** C4
Victoria St
Caister-on-Sea NR30 . . . . **168** F4
2 Downham Market PE38 **172** A5
Great Yarmouth NR30 . . . . **169** D6
Norwich NR1 . . . . **178** A4
Sheringham NR26 . . . . **138** D7
Victoria Terr PE34 . . . . . . **146** C4
Victoria Way NR5 . . . . **157** B2
Victory CI IP22 . . . . **177** F3
Victory Gr NR5 . . . . **156** C1
Victory La PE34 . . . . **60** C8
Victory Rd
Downham Market PE38 . . . **172** B4
Wisbech PE13 . . . . **152** B3
Vienna Wlk NR19 . . . . **154** C1

Viking Cl
Great Yarmouth NR31 . . . . 170 D2
Swaffham PE37 . . . . 153 D2
Viking Rd ▋ NR31 . . . . 94 C8
Vikings Cl IP22 . . . . 177 D5
Village Cl ▋ NR4 . . . . 161 C5
Villarome NR30 . . . . 168 C5
Villebois Rd PE33 . . . . 63 B4
Vimy Dr NR18 . . . . 173 D4
Vimy Ridge NR18 . . . . 173 D4
Vincent Cl ▋ IP26 . . . . 98 E1
Vincent Pl ▋ PE33 . . . . 84 D3
Vincent Rd Norwich NR1 . . 163 A7
Sheringham NR26 . . . . 138 E7
Vincents Rd NR9 . . . . 69 A4
Vince's Rd IP22 . . . . 177 F4
Vine Cl
Coney Weston IP31 . . . . 127 B5
Hemsby NR29 . . . . 167 B8
Vine Ct NR21 . . . . 141 B4
Vinegar La IP20 . . . . 122 F6
Vine Hill PE34 . . . . 61 C2
Vinery Cl ▋ PE34 . . . . 146 C5
Viola Cl NR4 . . . . 89 B8
Violet Cl
Attleborough NR17 . . . . . . 174 C5
▋ Great Yarmouth NR31 . . 94 C6
Violet Dr NR26 . . . . 138 B6
Violet Elvin Cl NR5 . . . . . . 161 F5
Violet Rd NR3 . . . . 158 F1
Violet Way NR19 . . . . 154 C4
Virginia Cl NR7 . . . . 159 C4
Viscount Cl IP22 . . . . 177 F4
Vole Ct PE30 . . . . 147 C7
Vong La Grimston PE32 . . . . 28 B1
Roydon PE32 . . . . 45 A8
Vulcan Rd N NR6 . . . . 158 C5
Vulcan Rd S NR6 . . . . 158 C4

W

WACTON NR15 . . . . 106 C2
Waddington Ct ▋ NR2 . . 162 B7
Waddington St NR2 . . . . . . 162 B7
Waddling La NR32 . . . . 111 F7
Wade Cl NR11 . . . . 150 C5
Wadehall La NR34 . . . . 111 B1
Wades Way NR28 . . . . 22 E5
Wadham Cl NR31 . . . . 170 B3
Wadham Rd NR31 . . . . 170 B3
Waggon & Horses La
NR3 . . . . 178 B3
Wagtail Cl ▋ NR31 . . . . . . 170 A6
Wagtail Way IP24 . . . . 176 D1
WAINFORD NR35 . . . . 109 B1
Wainford Mills Rd
Bungay NR35 . . . . 124 C8
Wainford NR35 . . . . 109 C1
Wainford Rd NR35 . . . . 124 C8
Wakefield Rd NR5 . . . . 161 C5
Wakehurst Cl ▋ NR4 . . . . 161 F1
Wakes La NR19 . . . . 154 D5
Walcot Cl NR5 . . . . 161 A7
WALCOT GREEN IP22 . . . . 177 F6
Walcot Rd IP22 . . . . 177 E6
Walcot Rise IP22 . . . . 177 F5
WALCOTT N12 . . . . 24 A7
Walcott Road N12 . . . . 23 E4
Waldeck Rd NR4 . . . . 162 A3
Waldegrave ▋ NR5 . . . . . . 161 A8
Waldemar Ave NR6 . . . . . . 158 B5
Waldemar Pk NR6 . . . . 158 B5
Wales Bank PE14 . . . . 59 A1
Wales Ct PE38 . . . . 172 C5
Walkers Cl PE31 . . . . 135 D2
Walker St ▋ PE30 . . . . 146 E6
Walkers Wy NR35 . . . . 124 B8
Walks The NR34 . . . . 111 A4
Walk The
Great Yarmouth NR31 . . . . 170 B6
Hickling NR12 . . . . 39 F3
Oulton NR11 . . . . 35 A8
Walkway The NR12 . . . . 24 A7
Wallace Cl Dereham NR19 154 B6
King's Lynn PE30 . . . . 147 D4
Wallace Twite Way PE31 140 C3
Waller Cl NR13 . . . . 72 D5
Wallers La NR20 . . . . 33 C3
Wallflower La PE34 . . . . . . 146 B4
Wallgate La NR21 . . . . 17 D5
Wall La PE31 . . . . 29 C4
Wall Rd Erpingham NR11 . . . 20 F3
Norwich NR3 . . . . 158 A4
Wall's La NR25 . . . . 7 F3
Walnut Ave ▋ PE33 . . . . . 43 E2
Walnut Ave N ▋ PE33 . . . . 43 E2
Walnut Cl Brandon IP27 . . 175 E2
Foulden IP26 . . . . 82 A2
Hopton IP22 . . . . 127 F5
Taverham NR8 . . . . 155 D2
Walnut Dr IP26 . . . . 83 A3
Walnut Gr
▋ Fakenham NR21 . . . . . . 141 E4
Watton IP25 . . . . 84 D4
Walnut Hill NR14 . . . . 73 A1
Walnut Pl PE33 . . . . 82 A5
Walnut Rd PE14 . . . . 41 E3
Walnuts The
Grimston PE32 . . . . 28 B1
Norwich NR4 . . . . 162 A2
Walnut Tree Ave ▋ NR29 . 57 D4
Walnut Wlk PE33 . . . . 63 B4

Walnut Wy NR19 . . . . 154 E4
Walpole Bank PE14 . . . . . . 41 C3
Walpole Rd NR35 . . . . 109 B2
WALPOLE CROSS KEYS
PE34 . . . . 41 F7
Walpole Cross Keys Prim Sch
PE34 . . . . 42 A6
Walpole Gdns NR2 . . . . 178 A2
WALPOLE HIGHWAY PE14 . 59 F8
Walpole Highway Prim Sch
PE14 . . . . 59 F8
Walpole La PE14 . . . . 41 F4
WALPOLE MARSH PE14 . . . 41 C4
Walpole Rd
Great Yarmouth NR30 . . . . 169 D7
King's Lynn PE30 . . . . 146 E7
WALPOLE ST ANDREW
PE14 . . . . 41 D4
WALPOLE ST PETER PE14 . . 41 E3
Walpole St NR2 . . . . 178 A2
Walpole Wy ▋ PE33 . . . . . 43 E2
Walpole Wr Gdns★ PE14 . 41 E3
Walpole Wy NR13 . . . . 92 E7
Walsham Cl ▋ PE30 . . . . . 147 D5
Walsingham Abbey Grounds
& Shirehall Mus★ NR22 . 16 F7
Walsingham Ct ▋ PE13 . . 152 A7
Walsingham Dr NR8 . . . . . . 155 E3
Walsingham Prim Sch
NR22 . . . . 16 F8
Walsingham Rd
Binham NR21 . . . . 6 C1
Burnham Thorpe PE31 . . . . 135 F2
Grear Balsingham NR22 . . . 17 B8
WALSOKEN PE13 . . . . 152 F6
Walsoken Rd PE14 . . . . 59 D3
Walter Howes Cres NR4 . . . 44 C3
Walter Rd NR19 . . . . 154 E1
Walters Cl NR31 . . . . 171 D5
Walters Rd NR8 . . . . 156 C8
Walton Cl PE30 . . . . 148 C4
WALTON HIGHWAY PE14 . . 59 E8
Walton Rd Norwich NR1 . . 162 E3
St John's Fen End PE14 . . . 60 A3
West Walton PE14 . . . . 59 F5
Wisbech PE13 . . . . 152 E7
Waltons Way IP27 . . . . 175 D2
WALTON WARREN PE32 . . . 45 E2
WANGFORD IP27 . . . . 114 C2
Wangford Rd IP27 . . . . 113 F3
Wansbrough Rd ▋ NR15 106 E3
Wanton La PE34 . . . . 144 A5
Waples Way NR19 . . . . 154 D3
Wapping NR29 . . . . 167 A2
Warbler Cl ▋ NR31 . . . . . . 94 C7
Wardley Hill Rd NR35 . . . . 109 D4
Ward Rd NR13 . . . . 55 B1
Ward's Chase PE34 . . . . 79 B8
WARHAM NR23 . . . . 6 A4
Warham Rd Binham NR21 . . . 6 E2
Wells-next-the-Sea NR23 . . 136 E4
Warham St Mary's Halt Sta
NR23 . . . . 5 F4
Waring Rd NR5 . . . . 161 B6
Warman's Cl NR9 . . . . 160 B6
Warner Ave NR19 . . . . 154 E7
Warners End NR9 . . . . 85 E3
Warner Rd Cl ▋ NR27 . . . . 139 C6
Warnett Rd NR7 . . . . 159 D1
Warren Ave
Fakenham NR21 . . . . 141 F4
Norwich NR6 . . . . 158 A5
Warren Cl Brandon IP27 . . 175 D3
High Kelling NR25 . . . . 8 E3
▋ Horsford NR10 . . . . 53 A3
Thetford IP24 . . . . 176 A3
Watlington PE33 . . . . 61 D5
Warren Ct ▋ NR27 . . . . . . 139 C6
Warren Dr NR11 . . . . 143 B5
Warren Gn NR13 . . . . 72 F8
Warren Loke NR31 . . . . 93 E3
Warren Pl ▋ NR19 . . . . . . 154 D1
Warren Rd
Great Yarmouth NR31 . . . . 171 D8
High Kelling NR25 . . . . 8 E3
Hopton on Sea NR31 . . . . . 171 D5
Shouldham PE33 . . . . 62 D4
Southrepps NR11 . . . . 22 C6
Warren's La NR17 . . . . 174 C6
Warren's Rd PE34 . . . . 145 D6
Warren's Way ▋ NR16 . . . 105 F5
Warrens Yd NR23 . . . . 136 C5
Warren The Cromer NR27 . . 139 C6
Horsham St Faith & Newton St
Faith NR10 . . . . 53 D2
Little Snoring NR21 . . . . 17 C3
Norwich NR6 . . . . 158 E4
Warren View NR12 . . . . 109 D8
Warstade Way PE37 . . . . . . 153 B4
Warwick Dr NR18 . . . . 173 C5
Warwick St NR2 . . . . 162 B5
Washbridge ▋ NR19 . . . . . 154 D5
Wash La Alburgh IP20 . . . . . 122 E7
Aslacton NR15 . . . . 106 A1
Banham NR16 . . . . 119 D6
Burgh St Peter NR34 . . . . . 111 C4
Clenchwarton PE34 . . . . . . 145 E6
Gissing IP22 . . . . 120 E5
Hales NR14 . . . . 109 E6
Hinderclay IP22 . . . . 128 C4
Howe NR15 . . . . 90 C2
Redgrave IP22 . . . . 129 A5
Saxlingham Nethergate
NR15 . . . . 107 D8
Shelfanger IP22 . . . . 120 B2
Shotesham NR15 . . . . 89 F1
South End NR16 . . . . 103 B1

Wash La continued
St Peter, South Elmham
NR35 . . . . 123 F3
Topcroft NR35 . . . . 108 A4
Wacton NR15 . . . . 106 B2
Whissonsett NR20 . . . . 31 E2
Wash National Nature
Reserve The★ PE30 . . . . . 26 B5
Washpit Dro
South Acre PE32 . . . . 64 D8
Swaffham PE37 . . . . 153 C8
West Rudham PE31 . . . . . . 29 F6
Wash Rd PE14 . . . . 95 E4
Watch House Hill NR35 . . . 124 C8
Watch House La NR12 . . . . . 23 E4
Waterbank Rd ▋ NR26 . . . 138 D7
Watercress La NR20 . . . . . . 68 E6
Waterden Cl ▋ PE30 . . . . 147 A8
Water End La PE32 . . . . 48 D2
Waterfield Ave NR21 . . . . . 141 D5
Waterfield Cl ▋ NR21 . . . . 141 C5
Waterfield Mdws NR28 . . . 151 E5
Water Gdns The PE13 . . . . . 152 A5
WATERHEATH NR34 . . . . . . 110 E5
Waterheath Rd NR34 . . . . . 110 E5
Watering La PE33 . . . . 43 E2
Watering Piece La NR29 . . . 56 C7
Wateringpit La NR12 . . . . . . 55 A8
Watering Rd IP21 . . . . 131 B1
Watering The ▋ NR31 . . . . 162 D8
Water La Barnham IP24 . . . . 125 E6
Barsham NR21 . . . . 16 F4
Botesdale IP22 . . . . 128 D1
Cringleford NR4 . . . . 161 D1
Garboldisham IP22 . . . . . . 128 A8
Great & Little Plumstead
NR13 . . . . 73 A5
Ingham NR12 . . . . 24 D2
▋ King's Lynn PE30 . . . . . 146 D5
Letheringsett with Glandford
NR25 . . . . 8 A2
Middleton PE32 . . . . 44 C1
Mundesley NR11 . . . . 143 C4
Neatishead NR12 . . . . 55 E7
Runton NR27 . . . . 10 A5
Thelnetham IP22 . . . . 128 B5
Thetford IP24 . . . . 176 C4
Waterland Cl NR30 . . . . 168 C7
Waterlees Rd
Walsoken PE13 . . . . 59 A6
▋ Wisbech PE13 . . . . 152 E7
WATERLOO Aldeby NR34 . . 110 E4
Dickleburgh and Rushall
IP21 . . . . 130 C6
Hainford NR10 . . . . 53 E6
Waterloo Ave ▋ IP22 . . . . 129 D7
Waterloo Cl
▋ Horsham St Faith
NR10 . . . . 53 D2
▋ Thetford IP24 . . . . 176 F4
Waterloo Pk Ave NR3 . . . . . 158 C1
Waterloo Pk Cl ▋ NR3 . . . 158 C1
Waterloo Rd
Great Yarmouth NR30 . . . . 169 E2
Hainford NR10 . . . . 53 D6
Horsham St Faith NR10 . . . 53 E2
Norwich NR3 . . . . 162 D8
Waterloo St ▋ PE30 . . . . . 146 E5
Waterlow Rd PE34 . . . . 42 C4
Waterman Rd NR2 . . . . 161 F7
Waterman's La PE38 . . . . . . 79 D1
Waterman's Way PE38 . . . . 79 A4
Water Mdw Cl NR29 . . . . . . 167 A3
Water Mdw Way ▋
PE38 . . . . 172 A6
Watermeadow Cl ▋ NR14. 91 F1
Watermill Cl NR11 . . . . 9 F1
Watermill Gn NR20 . . . . . . 176 C3
Watermill La PE37 . . . . 82 A6
Water Mill La IP21 . . . . 131 A4
Water Moor La NR21 . . . . . 141 C6
Watersfield Way NR19 . . . . 154 D2
Waterside PE30 . . . . 146 F7
Waterside Dr NR35 . . . . 109 B1
Waterside The NR6 . . . . 157 D3
Waters La NR29 . . . . 167 A7
Water Sports Ctr PE34 . . . . 43 C3
Water Twr Rd NR14 . . . . . . 88 E4
Waterworks Rd
Norwich NR2 . . . . 162 A7
Old Hunstanton PE36 . . . . . 132 F7
Watery La
Beeston with Bittering
PE32 . . . . 48 B3
Grimston PE32 . . . . 45 B8
Guist NR20 . . . . 33 A4
Matlask NR11 . . . . 20 D5
Necton PE37 . . . . 66 B4
Scarning NR19 . . . . 154 A1
Shipdham IP25 . . . . 67 C2
Wathen Way NR10 . . . . 150 C1
Watkin Rd NR4 . . . . 89 E8
Watling Cl NR30 . . . . 168 E6
Watling Rd
Attleborough NR17 . . . . . . 174 F6
Norwich NR7 . . . . 159 D1
Watlings Ct ▋ NR2 . . . . . . 162 C6
Watlings The NR19 . . . . 67 B6
WATLINGTON PE33 . . . . . . 61 E5
Watlington Com Prim Sch
PE33 . . . . 61 D5
Watlington Rd PE33 . . . . . . 61 F6
Watlington Sta PE33 . . . . . . 61 D5
Watson Gr ▋ NR2 . . . . 162 B8
Watsons Cl NR31 . . . . 171 E4
Watson-Watt Gdns
NR11 . . . . 143 A7
WATTISFIELD IP22 . . . . 128 B1

WATTLEFIELD NR18 . . . . . . 105 C7
Wattlefield Rd
Tacolneston NR16 . . . . 105 C6
Wymondham NR18 . . . . . . 88 A1
WATTON IP25 . . . . 84 E3
WATTON GREEN IP25 . . . . 84 E4
Watton Jun Sch IP25 . . . . . 84 D3
Watton Rd Ashill IP25 . . . . . 84 A6
Barford NR9 . . . . 69 E2
Colney NR4 . . . . 160 F4
Great Cressingham IP25 . . . 83 D4
Great Ellingham NR17 . . . . 103 D8
Great Melton NR9 . . . . 70 B2
Griston IP25 . . . . 85 A2
Hingham NR9 . . . . 86 B5
Hockham IP24 . . . . 102 E4
Larling NR16 . . . . 118 A4
Little Cressingham IP25 . . . 83 F2
Little Melton NR9 . . . . 160 B4
North Pickenham PE37 . . . . 83 C8
Shipdham IP25 . . . . 67 B1
Shropham NR17 . . . . 103 A4
Stow Bedon NR17 . . . . 102 D7
Swaffham PE37 . . . . 153 D7
Thompson IP25 . . . . 102 A8
Waunci Cres NR31 . . . . 170 D2
Wavell Rd NR19 . . . . 154 C7
Waveney CE First Sch
NR31 . . . . 94 A5
Waveney Cl
Hoveton NR12 . . . . 164 E6
Hunstanton PE36 . . . . 132 D3
Wells-next-the-Sea NR23 . . 136 D4
Waveney Cres ▋ NR35 . . 123 F7
Waveney Dr
▋ Belton NR31 . . . . 94 A6
Wroxham/Hoveton NR12 . 164 D5
Waveney Hill NR32 . . . . 111 F3
Waveney Hts IP21 . . . . 131 C6
Waveney Rd
Bungay NR35 . . . . 124 B8
Diss IP22 . . . . 177 E3
Ditchingham NR35 . . . . . . 109 C1
Great Yarmouth NR31 . . . . 169 C1
Hunstanton PE36 . . . . 132 C3
King's Lynn PE30 . . . . 147 D5
Waveney Valley Swimming
Pool NR35 . . . . 124 B7
Waverley Rd NR4 . . . . 162 A2
WAXHAM NR12 . . . . 40 C5
Waxham Cl NR12 . . . . 40 A5
Waxham Rd NR12 . . . . 40 B5
Waxwing Wy NR8 . . . . 156 B5
Waxworks ▋ NR30 . . . . . . 169 D4
Wayford Rd NR12 . . . . 38 F4
Wayland Ave ▋ IP25 . . . . . 84 C3
Wayland Cl NR17 . . . . 174 D5
Wayland Com High Sch
IP25 . . . . 84 D3
Wayland Ct NR17 . . . . 174 A7
Wayland Hospl NR17 . . . . . 174 A7
Wayland Rd NR17 . . . . 103 C8
Wayland Way NR16 . . . . . . 119 D7
Wayland Wlk PE38 . . . . 172 B7
WEASENHAM ALL SAINTS
PE32 . . . . 47 C8
Weasenham CE Prim Sch
PE32 . . . . 47 D8
Weasenham La ▋ PE13 . . 152 C5
Weasenham Rd
Great Massingham PE32 . . . 29 E1
Litcham PE32 . . . . 47 E7
WEASENHAM ST PETER
PE32 . . . . 30 D1
Weatherby Rd NR5 . . . . 160 D8
Weavers Cl
▋ Horsham St Faith
NR10 . . . . 53 D2
North Walsham NR28 . . . . 151 B4
Weavers Croft ▋ IP20 . . . . 122 D2
Weavers Ct IP22 . . . . 177 D5
Weavers View NR12 . . . . . . 37 F1
Webb Dr ▋ NR13 . . . . 72 E7
Webbs Cl ▋ NR28 . . . . 151 E5
Webdell Ct ▋ NR1 . . . . 162 E1
Webster Cl
▋ Norwich NR5 . . . . 161 B8
▋ Stoke Holy Cross NR14. 89 F4
Webster Way NR30 . . . . 168 D6
Wedgewood Ct NR31 . . . . . 170 C3
Wedgwood Dr PE13 . . . . . . 152 D5
Weedon Way PE30 . . . . 147 D4
WEETING IP27 . . . . 175 B8
Weeting Castle★ IP27 . . . . 114 E8
Weeting Heath National
Nature Reserve★ IP27 . . 114 C7
Weeting VC Prim Sch
IP27 . . . . 175 B8
Welbeck Ave ▋ NR29 . . . . 57 D4
Welbeck Rd PE13 . . . . 152 E4
WELBORNE NR20 . . . . 69 A4
Welborne Rd NR20 . . . . 68 F5
WELBOURNE COMMON
NR20 . . . . 68 F4
Welden Rd NR19 . . . . 154 B4
Welgate Cl ▋ NR20 . . . . . . 68 E6
Welgate Rd NR20 . . . . 68 E5
Welholme's Cl ▋ NR15 . . 106 E3
Wellbeck NR15 . . . . 90 F2
Wellbeck Rd NR15 . . . . 91 A2
Well Cl NR9 . . . . 51 A6
Well Creek Rd PE14 . . . . . . 77 F6
Well End PE14 . . . . 77 A7
Wellesley Ave NR1 . . . . 163 B7
Wellesley Ave N ▋ NR1 . . 163 B7
Wellesley Ave S NR1 . . . . . 163 B6
Wellesley Rd
Great Yarmouth NR30 . . . . 169 D5

Wellesley Rd continued
▋ Long Stratton NR15 . . . 106 D3
Wellesley St ▋ PE30 . . . . 146 E5
Well Hall La PE32 . . . . 45 A6
Well Hill NR19 . . . . 68 C5
WELLINGHAM PE32 . . . . . . 30 F1
Wellingham Rd
Litcham PE32 . . . . 47 F6
Tittleshall PE32 . . . . 48 A3
Wellington Cl
Brandon IP27 . . . . 175 D3
Gimingham NR11 . . . . 22 C6
Wellington Cres NR21 . . . . 15 C3
Wellington Gn ▋ NR2 . . . . 162 C6
Wellington La NR2 . . . . 162 C6
Wellington Pl ▋ NR30 . . . 169 D4
Wellington Rd
Briston NR24 . . . . 142 B4
East Dereham NR19 . . . . . 154 D5
▋ Feltwell IP26 . . . . 98 E1
Great Yarmouth NR30 . . . . 169 E2
▋ Long Stratton NR15 . . . 106 D3
Norwich NR2 . . . . 162 C6
Wellington Terr ▋ PE13 . 152 C4
Well La NR9 . . . . 51 A6
Well Loke NR3 . . . . 158 B3
Well Medieval Village of★
PE32 . . . . 45 B7
Well Opening ▋ NR30 . . . 169 D2
Well Rd Cantley NR13 . . . . . 92 D6
Great Yarmouth NR30 . . . . 169 D2
Wells Ave NR28 . . . . 151 A3
Wells Cl ▋ NR10 . . . . 53 E5
Wells' La IP20 . . . . 122 D1
Wells Maritime Mus★
NR23 . . . . 136 D6
WELLS-NEXT-THE-SEA 136 C5
Wells next the Sea Prim Sch
NR23 . . . . 136 E5
Wells next the Sea Sta
NR23 . . . . 136 F4
Wellspring Rd NR11 . . . . . . 22 C8
Wells Rd
Burnham Overy Staithe
PE31 . . . . 135 E7
Fakenham NR21 . . . . 141 B4
Hindringham NR21 . . . . . . 17 D6
Needham IP20 . . . . 122 C1
North Creake NR21 . . . . . . 4 D1
Stiffkey NR23 . . . . 6 C6
Walsingham NR22 . . . . 16 F8
Wighton NR23 . . . . 5 F3
Well St Docking PE31 . . . . . 134 C5
Great Yarmouth NR30 . . . . 169 D4
Thetford IP24 . . . . 176 D3
Witton NR28 . . . . 23 D3
WELNEY PE14 . . . . 95 D4
Welney Wildfowl Refuge★
PE14 . . . . 95 F6
Welsford Rd
▋ Norwich NR4 . . . . 89 D8
Norwich NR4 . . . . 162 B1
Weltons Loke NR9 . . . . 52 A6
Wendene NR5 . . . . 160 F7
WENDLING NR19 . . . . 66 F8
Wendling Rd NR19 . . . . 48 F2
Wendover Rd NR13 . . . . . . 72 D8
Wenman Ct ▋ NR5 . . . . . . 160 F8
Wensom Cl ▋ PE33 . . . . . . 61 D6
Wensum Cres NR6 . . . . 157 D3
Wensum Ct NR21 . . . . 32 C6
Wensum Dr NR20 . . . . 49 F7
Wensum Gdns ▋ NR20 . . . 50 B3
Wensum Jun Sch NR2 . . . . 162 A7
Wensum Mdws Mental
Health Hospl NR6 . . . . . . 157 D4
Wensum Rd NR9 . . . . 51 A4
Wensum St NR3 . . . . 178 B3
Wensum Valley Cl NR6 . . . 157 D4
Wensum Way
▋ Belton NR31 . . . . 94 A6
▋ Fakenham NR21 . . . . . 141 E4
Wensum Wlk NR8 . . . . 155 F3
Wentworth Cl ▋ IP27 . . . . 114 E1
Wentworth Gn NR4 . . . . . . 161 F2
WEREHAM PE33 . . . . 80 E4
Wereham Row PE33 . . . . . . 80 D3
Wesley Ave NR34 . . . . 144 B5
Wesley Cl
Downham Market PE38 . . . 172 B5
▋ Mattishall NR20 . . . . . . 68 E6
Mundesley NR11 . . . . 143 D5
Terrington St Clement
PE34 . . . . 144 B5
Wesley Rd
King's Lynn PE30 . . . . 148 C5
Terrington St Clement
PE34 . . . . 144 B5
Wessex St NR2 . . . . 178 A1
WEST ACRE PE32 . . . . 46 B2
West Acre Gdns★ PE32 . . . 46 B4
West Acre Rd PE37 . . . . 153 A6
West Ave
Great Yarmouth NR31 . . . . 170 C3
Ormesby St Margaret
NR29 . . . . 167 A3
WEST BARSHAM NR21 . . . . 16 C4
WEST BECKHAM NR25 . . . . 9 C2
WEST BILNEY PE32 . . . . . . 45 B2
Westbourne Ct ▋ NR31 . . 170 C7
Westbourne Rd NR12 . . . . . 54 D7
Westbriggs Dro PE33 . . . . . 62 B5
Westbrook Ave ▋ NR31 . . 170 B6
WESTBROOK GREEN
IP22 . . . . 177 C7
WEST CAISTER NR30 . . . . . 168 C4

West Carr Rd NR17 . . . . . .174 A4
West Church St NR16 . . .119 A5
West Cl NR5 . . . . .157 A2
West Cliff Cromer NR27 . . .139 B7
  Sheringham NR26 . . . . . .138 D7
Westcliff Ave NR27 . . . . .139 A7
West Cres NR20 . . . . .50 A5
West Croft NR9 . . . . .88 C7
WEST DEREHAM PE33 . . . .80 B4
West Dereham Rd PE33 . .80 D3
West Dro N PE14 . . . . .59 D8
  ■ Friday Bridge PE14 . . . . .77 A8
West Dro S PE14. . . . . . . .59 D8
West Earlham Inf & Jun Sch
  NR5. . . . . .161 D6
WEST END Necton IP25 . . . .66 C4
  West Caister NR30 . . . . . . .76 B6
West End Briston NR24 . . .142 F5
  Costessey NR8 . . . . .156 C4
  Hilgay PE38. . . . . .79 D1
  Northwold IP26 . . . . .99 B8
West End Ave
  Brundall NR13. . . . . . . .165 A4
  Costessey NR8 . . . . .156 C5
West End Ct ■ IP25 . . . . . .84 C3
West End St NR2. . . . . . .162 B7
Westerley Cl NR30 . . . . . .168 D4
Westerley Way NR30 . . . .168 D4
Western Ave NR7 . . . . . .163 E6
Western Bypass 150 B5
Western Cl ■ IP26 . . . . . . .98 D1
Western Rd NR31 . . . . . .170 C4
WESTFIELD NR19 . . . . . . .67 F4
Westfield Ave NR23 . . . .136 C6
Westfield Cl ■ NR29. . . . . .57 C1
Westfield Inf Sch IP25 . . . .84 B2
Westfield La NR19 . . . . . .154 F1
Westfield Rd
  Brundall NR13 . . . . .165 D4
  East Dereham NR19 . . . .154 E2
  Swaffham PE37 . . . . . . .153 B4
  Wisbech PE13 . . . . .152 E7
Westfields
  Attleborough NR17 . . . . .174 B4
  King's Lynn PE30 . . . . . .147 C4
  Narborough PE32 . . . . . . .63 E7
Westfields Cl
  Terrington St John PE14 . . .60 C8
  Tilney St Lawrence PE34. . .42 C1
WESTGATE Binham NR21. . . .6 B3
  Burrnham PE31 . . . . . . .135 B3
Westgate Hevingham NR10. .53 A8
  Hunstanton PE36. . . . . . .132 C4
  Norwich NR6 . . . . .157 F5
  Shropham NR17 . . . . . . .103 B4
  Walsingham NR22. . . . . . .16 F8
West Gate NR18 . . . . . . .173 B4
Westgate Cl NR2. . . . . . .162 A4
Westgate Ct NR18 . . . . . .173 B4
Westgate Gn NR10. . . . . . .53 B8
Westgate Rd PE36 . . . . .1 F6
Westgate St
  Hevingham NR10. . . . . . . .52 B8
  Hilborough PE37 . . . . .83 A3
  Holme next the Sea PE36 . . .2 A6
  Shouldham PE33 . . . . .62 D4
  Southery PE38. . . . . .97 A5
WESTGATE STREET NR10. .53 B8
Westhall IP21 . . . . .131 F1
West Hall Rd
  Dersingham PE31 . . . . . .140 D3
  Mundford IP26 . . . . .100 B4
WEST HARLING NR16 . . . .118 A3
West Harling Rd NR16 . . .118 B4
WEST HEAD PE34. . . . . . . .78 E4
West Head Rd PE34 . . . . . .78 F8
West Herne La IP22. . . . . .128 D5
Westhorpe Cl ■ PE30. . . .147 A8
West La NR10. . . . . .53 D1
Westland Chase PE33 . . . . .43 F1
Westlegate NR1 . . . . .178 B2
WEST LEXHAM PE32 . . . . . .47 C4
West Lexham Hall PE32 . . .47 C4
WEST LYNN PE34. . . . . . .146 C5
West Lynn Prim Sch
  PE34. . . . . .146 C5
Westmark PE30. . . . . . . .147 C4
Westmead Ave PE13 . . . .152 E2
Westmead Rd NR21 . . . . .141 C4
WEST NEWTON PE31 . . . . .27 F6
Weston Cl ■ NR13. . . . . . .73 C6
Weston Ct NR6 . . . . .158 F6
WESTON GREEN NR9. . . . . .51 E1
WESTON LONGVILLE NR9. . .51 E3
Weston Miller Dr PE13 . . .152 C7
Weston Rd Easton NR9. . . . .70 A7
  Norwich NR3. . . . . .158 C3
  ■ Wisbech PE13 . . . . . .152 C4
Weston Rise NR30 . . . . . .168 D5
Weston Sq ■ NR25 . . . . .137 B6
Weston Terr NR26 . . . . . .138 E7
Weston Wood Cl NR7. . . .163 E7
Weston Wood Rd NR7. . . .163 D7
West Parade
  Norwich NR2. . . . . .162 B6
  Wisbech PE13 . . . . .152 C5
WEST PORINGLAND NR14 . .90 B4
West Pottergate NR2 . . . .162 B6
WEST RAYNHAM NR21 . . . .30 E4
West Raynham Prim Acad
  NR21. . . . . .30 F4
West Raynham Rd NR21. . .30 F4
West Rd
  Caister-on-Sea NR30. . . . .168 D4
  Dersingham PE31 . . . . . .140 D3
  Great Yarmouth NR30 . . .168 F1
  Norwich NR5. . . . . .157 A2

West Rd continued
  Ormesby St Margaret
  NR29. . . . . .167 A2
  Shouldham Thorpe PE33 . . .62 C2
  Tacolneston NR16. . . . . .105 F4
  Watton IP25 . . . . .84 D3
  West Caister NR30 . . . . . .168 B4
WEST RUDHAM PE31. . . . . .29 F7
WEST RUNTON NR27. . . . . .10 A5
West Runton Sta NR27. . . . .10 A5
Westry PE13 . . . . .59 C5
WEST SOMERTON NR29. . . .57 E6
West Stree ■ NR30. . . . . .169 D2
WEST TOFTS IP26 . . . . . . .100 F4
West Tofts Rd IP26 . . . . . .100 D3
West View Dereham NR19 .154 E1
  South Pickenham PE37. . . . .83 D7
West View Dr NR13 . . . . . .74 A2
West View Rd NR13 . . . . .165 E6
WEST WALTON PE14 . . . . . .59 B8
West Walton Com Prim Sch
  PE14. . . . . .59 C8
West Walton Ct PE14 . . . . .59 E6
West Way
  Downham Market PE38. . . .172 B4
  Stow Bardolph PE34 . . . . .61 D1
  Tacolneston NR16. . . . . .105 E5
  Wimbotsham PE34 . . . . . .79 D8
WESTWICK NR10 . . . . .37 D6
Westwick Dr PE34 . . . . . .151 A4
Westwick Rd NR28 . . . . . .37 F5
Westwick St NR2 . . . . . . .178 A3
WEST WINCH PE33 . . . . . . .43 E3
West Winch Prim Sch
  PE33. . . . . .43 E2
West Winch Rd PE33. . . . . .43 F4
West Wood Cotts NR21. . . . .32 B5
Westwood Dr NR6. . . . . . .157 D6
Westwood Gdns NR18. . . .173 A6
Westwood La NR21 . . . . . .32 B5
WEYBOURNE NR25 . . . . .8 F5
Weybourne Rd
  Bodham NR25 . . . . .9 A3
  Sheringham NR26 . . . . . .138 B7
Weybourne Sta NR25 . . . . . .8 F5
Weynor Gdns NR25 . . . . . . .8 E5
Whalers Farrow PE30 . . . .146 E2
Wharf St PE12 . . . . .41 B8
Wharton Dr NR28 . . . . . . .151 E7
Whartons La ■ NR18 . . . .173 B3
WHEATACRE NR34 . . . . . . .111 B5
Wheatacre Cl ■ NR10 . . . . .53 A3
Wheatacres IP24 . . . . . . .176 D5
Wheatcroft Way NR20. . . . .68 A8
Wheatfield Rd ■ NR4. . . . .89 B3
Wheatfields
  Hillington PE31 . . . . .28 B4
  Rickinghall Superior IP22 . .128 E2
  Wheat Fields NR8. . . . . .155 F2
Wheatfield Way NR15 . . . .106 F4
Wheatley Bank PE14 . . . . .59 C5
Wheatley Dr PE30. . . . . . .148 B4
Wheatley Rd NR7 . . . . . . .161 F7
Wheelbarrow La IP20. . . . .123 F1
Wheeler Cres NR9 . . . . . . .70 B5
Wheeler Rd NR3. . . . . . . .158 A1
Wheelers La NR15 . . . . . .108 E8
Wheel Rd NR14. . . . . .90 E4
Wheelwright Rd PE30 . . . .147 C5
Wheelwrights Cl NR13 . . . .92 E8
Wherry Cl NR28. . . . . . . .151 E7
Wherry Rd Bungay NR35 . .124 C8
  Norwich NR1. . . . . .178 C1
Wherry Reach ■ NR13. . . .166 D4
Wherry Way NR30 . . . . . .169 C7
Whetstone Wy PE14 . . . . . .77 E6
Whiffler Rd NR3 . . . . .157 F2
Whiffler Road Trad Est
  NR3. . . . . .158 A2
Whiley La ■ NR12 . . . . . . .39 B4
Whimbrel Dr
  ■ Great Yarmouth NR31 . . .94 C8
  ■ Great Yarmouth NR31 . . .170 A7
WHIMPWELL GREEN
  NR12. . . . . .24 C4
Whimpwell St NR12. . . . . . .24 C4
WHINBURGH NR19 . . . . . . .68 A3
Whinburgh Rd NR19 . . . . . .67 F3
Whinchat Way ■ NR31 . . . .94 C7
Whin Comm Rd
  Denver PE38 . . . . .172 D1
  Tottenhill PE33 . . . . .61 F6
Whinmere Rd NR12 . . . . . .39 E3
Whipp's La NR16. . . . . . . .105 F7
Whisson Cl ■ PE30. . . . . .147 A8
WHISSONSETT NR20 . . . . . .31 D2
Whissonsett Rd NR20 . . . . .48 E8
Whistle Dro IP28 . . . . . . .112 D1
Whistlefish Ct NR5. . . . . .161 E7
Whitby St ■ PE13 . . . . . .152 C5
Whitebeam Cres IP25. . . . . .84 E3
White City Rd PE14 . . . . . .78 D6
White Clover Rd ■ NR31. . .94 C6
White Clover Wy ■
  NR31. . . . . .171 D4
White Cross
  Burgh & Tuttington NR11. . .36 E4
  Hardingham NR9. . . . . . . .86 D4
Whitecross La PE34. . . . . .144 E4
White Cross Rd PE37. . . . .153 C4
Whitedike Dro IP26. . . . . .113 B8
White Farm La NR7 . . . . . .163 C6
Whitefriars NR3 . . . . .178 B4
Whitefriars CE Prim Acad
  PE30. . . . . .146 D3
Whitefriars Rd PE30 . . . . .146 D3

Whitefriars Terr PE30. . . .146 D3
White Gate La NR11. . . . . .11 D2
White Gates NR5 . . . . . . .156 E1
Whitegates Cl ■ NR9 . . . . .88 D7
Whitegates Rd NR11 . . . . . .22 B7
White Hall Dr PE34 . . . . . .146 C4
Whitehall Rd NR2. . . . . . .162 B5
Whitehall Yd ■ NR26 . . . .138 D7
Whitehart La IP27 . . . . . .175 C4
Whitehart St ■ IP27 . . . . .176 C4
White Hart St
  ■ Aylsham NR11 . . . . . . .150 C7
  East Harling NR16. . . . . .118 C5
  Foulden IP26. . . . . .82 A2
White Heath Rd NR15 . . . . .91 B3
White Horse Dr PE31. . . . .140 C4
Whitehorse La NR17 . . . . .174 C5
White Horse La
  Bixley NR14 . . . . .89 F8
  Trowse with Newton NR14 .163 A1
  Worstead NR28 . . . . .38 B6
Whitehorse Plain ■
  NR30. . . . . .169 C5
Whitehorse St
  ■ Fakenham NR21 . . . . . .141 C3
  Wymondham NR18 . . . . .173 B3
White Horse St IP27 . . . . .175 A2
White House Cl NR3 . . . . .158 B3
White House Dr ■ NR15 . .106 C3
White House Est NR27 . . . . .9 E4
White House Farm La
  IP21. . . . . .122 B2
White House Gdns ■
  NR14. . . . . .90 D5
Whitehouse La
  Earsham NR35. . . . . . . .108 C1
  Wicklewood NR18 . . . . . .87 C4
White House La NR17. . . . .174 F5
White House Rd CB7. . . . .112 A7
White La PE33 . . . . .63 A3
Whitelands NR21 . . . . . . .141 D5
White Lion Ct ■ PE30. . . .146 D5
White Lion Rd
  Coltishall NR12 . . . . .54 D6
  Wheatacre NR34. . . . . . .111 B4
White Lion St ■ Holt NR25 .137 B6
  Norwich NR2. . . . . .178 A2
White Lodge Bsns Est
  NR4. . . . . .89 E8
White Oaks PE37 . . . . .65 E2
Whiteplot Rd IP26 . . . . . . .98 D5
White Post Rd NR11 . . . . . .21 D5
White Rd
  Barton Bendish PE33 . . . . .63 D1
  Methwold IP26 . . . . .99 A5
White Rose Cl NR5. . . . . .161 D8
White Sedge PE30 . . . . . .147 A8
White St NR29 . . . . .57 D5
Whitethorn Cl ■ NR6. . . . .158 D5
Whiteway Rd NR1. . . . . . .135 B3
White Woman La NR6. . . . .159 A6
White Woman La Sch
  NR6. . . . . .158 F6
Whiting Rd NR4 . . . . .162 D1
Whiting's La NR17 . . . . . .103 A6
Whitley Cl ■ Feltwell IP26 . .98 E1
  Old Catton NR6 . . . . . . .158 C6
Whitlingham Ctry Pk★
  NR7. . . . . .163 E4
Whitlingham La NR14. . . . .163 C4
Whitsands Rd PE37 . . . . . .153 A5
WHITTINGTON PE33 . . . . . .81 B2
Whittington Hill PE33 . . . . .81 B2
Whittome Mill PE38. . . . . . .79 D1
Whitwell Rd Norwich NR1 .163 A7
  Reepham NR10. . . . . . . .149 A2
  Sparham NR9 . . . . .51 B6
Whitwell St NR10. . . . . . .149 C3
WHITWELL STREET
  NR10. . . . . .149 C3
Whitworth Ave ■ NR17 . . .174 C5
Whytehead Gdns IP22 . . . .177 D4
WICKEN GREEN VILLAGE
  NR21. . . . . .15 D2
Wick Farm Cl ■ IP25 . . . . .84 D3
WICKHAMPTON NR13 . . . . .93 A8
Wickhampton Rd NR13. . . . .93 A8
Wick La NR29. . . . . .57 D2
Wicklewood Prim Sch
  NR18. . . . . .87 B5
Wicklewood Rd NR18 . . . . .87 B6
WICKMERE NR11 . . . . .20 F4
Wickmere Rd NR11 . . . . . .20 C5
Wicks Sq ■ NR19. . . . . . .154 D5
Wiclewood Way PE31. . . . .140 C3
Widgeon Cl NR31 . . . . . . .170 A6
Wier Ave NR29. . . . . .68 F6
Wiggenhall Rd PE34 . . . . . .42 E3
WIGGENHALL ST GERMANS
  PE34. . . . . .43 C1
WIGGENHALL ST MARY
  MAGDALEN PE34. . . . . . . .61 B6
WIGGENHALL ST MARY THE
  VIRGIN PE34. . . . . .61 A8
WIGGENHALL ST PETER
  PE34. . . . . .61 C8
Wiggets La NR11 . . . . .34 D7
Wigg Rd NR21 . . . . .141 B6
Wiggs Rd NR14 . . . . .110 F7
Wight Dr NR30. . . . . .168 C6
Wightmans La NR31 . . . . .170 D5
WIGHTON NR23 . . . . .6 A2
Wighton Halt Sta NR23 . . . . .5 F3
Wigwam Hill IP22 . . . . . . .129 C5
Wilberforce Rd
  Norwich NR5. . . . . .161 B6
  Wisbech PE13 . . . . .152 D5

WILBY NR16 . . . . .119 A8
Wilby Rd Norwich NR1 . . . .162 E1
  Quidenham NR16. . . . . . .118 F6
Wildbriar Cl PE33 . . . . . . .43 E1
Wild Cherry Cl IP25 . . . . . .84 E3
Wilde Rd ■ NR13. . . . . . . .72 E7
Wilderness Cl ■ IP20. . . . .122 D1
Wilderness La IP20 . . . . . .122 D2
Wilderness Rd NR8 . . . . . .156 A5
Wildfields Cl PE34. . . . . . .145 D5
Wildfields Rd PE34. . . . . .145 C6
Wild Flower Ctr★ NR25 . . . .7 E3
Wildflower Way NR35. . . . .109 A2
Wild Radish Cl ■ NR14 . . . .89 B3
Wild Rd NR3. . . . . .158 D1
Wilkins Ct NR5 . . . . .161 C7
Wilkinson Rd NR13 . . . . . .72 E7
Wilkinson Way NR28. . . . .151 D4
Wilkins Rd PE14 . . . . .59 D3
Wilks Farm Dr NR7 . . . . . .159 A5
Willbye Ave IP22 . . . . . . .177 E5
William Booth Rd PE30. . . .147 D5
William Booth St NR2. . . . .178 A2
William Brown Way ■
  IP22. . . . . .177 A5
William Bush Cl NR10 . . . . .35 B2
William Childerhouse Way ■
  NR5. . . . . .160 E7
William Cl ■ Watton IP25. .84 D3
  ■ Wymondham NR18. . . . .173 C6
William Cowper Cl NR19 . .154 E1
William Frost Wy NR5. . . . .156 B3
William Kett Cl NR1. . . . . .163 A6
William Marriot Mus★
  NR25. . . . . .137 E8
William Mear Gdns NR1. . .163 B6
William O'Callaghan Pl ■
  NR19 . . . . .154 D5
William Paston Rd NR28 . .151 D6
William Peck Rd ■ NR10. . .54 A2
William Rd
  Fakenham NR21 . . . . . . .141 F5
  Wisbech PE13 . . . . .152 C5
Williams Loke NR7. . . . . . .163 D8
Williamson Cl Diss IP22 . . .177 D6
  Norwich NR3. . . . . .159 C2
Williamson Cres ■ IP24 . . .176 C2
William St ■ PE30. . . . . . .146 E3
Williams Way
  ■ Holt NR25 . . . . .137 C5
  ■ North Walsham NR28 . . .151 C6
  Old Catton NR19 . . . . . .154 C1
Willman Cl PE31 . . . . .133 D6
Willis St NR3 . . . . .178 B4
Willoughby Way ■ NR13. . .72 E7
Willow Ave NR31 . . . . .94 C7
Willowbrook Cl ■ NR33. . .111 F1
Willow Cl Brandon IP27 . . .175 D2
  Lingwood NR13. . . . . .74 A2
  Long Stratton NR15. . . . . .106 E2
  ■ Mattishall NR20 . . . . . .68 E6
  Middleton PE32. . . . . . . .44 B4
  North Walsham NR28 . . . .151 D7
  Wortwell IP20. . . . . .123 A4
  Wymondham NR18 . . . . .173 D5
Willow Cres ■ PE33 . . . . . .63 B4
Willowcroft Wy NR4. . . . . .89 B8
Willow Ct
  ■ Attleborough NR17 . . . .174 D4
  Beetley NR20. . . . . .49 D4
Willow Dr
  Clenchwarton PE34 . . . . .145 E5
  Dersingham PE31 . . . . . .140 D3
  King's Lynn PE33 . . . . . . .43 F4
  Tilney All Saints PE34 . . . . .42 E4
  West Winch PE33 . . . . . . .43 F1
Willow Gr
  East Dereham NR19 . . . .154 D2
  Sheringham NR26 . . . . . .138 E5
  Willow Heath Rd PE33 . . . .80 B7
Willow Herb Wlk ■
  NR18. . . . . .173 E4
Willow La
  Bedingham NR35. . . . . . .108 B3
  Broome NR35 . . . . .109 C3
  Carbrooke IP25. . . . . . . .85 B5
  Norwich NR2. . . . . .178 A3
Willow Pk PE33 . . . . .147 C8
Willow Pl PE33 . . . . .62 A5
Willow Rd
  Downham Market PE38. . . .172 B6
  East Dereham NR19 . . . .154 B4
  Hunstanton PE36. . . . . . .132 C3
  King's Lynn PE30 . . . . . .148 D2
Willows Ct ■ NR29. . . . . . .57 D4
Willow Tree Cl PE34 . . . . .146 D5
Willow Way
  ■ Ludham NR29. . . . . . . .56 C5
  ■ Marthan NR29 . . . . . . .57 D4
  Wisbech PE13 . . . . .152 D3
Willow Wlk ■ IP20 . . . . . .122 D1
WILNEY GREEN IP22. . . . . .129 A8
Wilshere Ct ■ NR30. . . . . .169 D3
Wilson Dr PE33 . . . . .44 F3
Wilson Rd ■ NR1. . . . . . . .163 B5
Wilson's Dro PE32 . . . . . . .45 E3
Wilson's Way NR25 . . . . . . .7 D6
Wilton Cres ■ PE30 . . . . .148 C5
Wilton Rd Feltwell IP26 . . . .98 E1
  Heacham PE31 . . . . .133 C6
Wilton View NR28. . . . . . .151 D5
Wimbledon Ave IP27 . . . . .175 A1
Wimbledon Way ■ PE38 . . .172 B4
WIMBOTSHAM PE34. . . . . . .79 D8
Wimbotsham Rd PE38. . . . .172 C6
Wimbotsham & Stow Com
  Sch PE34. . . . . .79 D8

Wimpole Dr PE30 . . . . . . .148 E1
Winceby Cl
  ■ Norwich NR7 . . . . .72 D4
  Wisbech PE14 . . . . .152 A3
Winchcomb Rd NR2 . . . . . .161 F7
Winchester Twr NR2 . . . . .162 C5
Winchester Way IP24 . . . .176 B5
Winch Rd PE32 . . . . .45 C5
Wincliff Dr NR25. . . . . .8 E3
Windermere Cl NR15. . . . . .90 E3
Windermere Rd PE30 . . . .148 F2
Windle The NR13 . . . . .74 C5
Windmill Ave NR20 . . . . . .68 A8
Windmill Cl
  Poringland NR14. . . . . . . .90 C4
  Thetford IP24 . . . . .176 D5
Windmill Ct ■ PE30 . . . . .147 C5
Windmill Hill PE31 . . . . . . .14 A3
Windmill La
  Costessey NR8 . . . . .157 A4
  Syleham IP21 . . . . .131 D5
  Wretham IP24 . . . . .102 B1
Windmill Rd
  Gimingham NR11. . . . . . .22 F8
  ■ Marham PE33 . . . . . . .63 B4
  Norwich NR3. . . . . .158 F2
  Worstead NR28 . . . . .38 A6
  Wortwell IP20. . . . . .123 A3
Windsor Ave NR30 . . . . . .169 D7
Windsor Chase NR5 . . . . .155 D1
Windsor Cl ■ IP24 . . . . . .125 F6
Windsor Cres PE31 . . . . . .133 C5
Windsor Ct Diss IP22 . . . . .177 F5
  ■ Watton IP25. . . . . .84 D3
Windsor Dr
  Dersingham PE31 . . . . . .140 D3
  Wisbech PE13 . . . . .152 D8
Windsor Pk
  East Dereham NR19 . . . .154 D8
  ■ King's Lynn PE30 . . . . .146 E3
Windsor Pk Gdns PE6. . . . .159 A6
Windsor Rd
  Caister-on-Sea NR30. . . . .168 E6
  Cantley NR13. . . . . .92 C6
  King's Lynn PE30 . . . . . .146 E3
  Norwich NR6. . . . . .158 A5
Windsor Rise PE36. . . . . . .132 C2
Windsor St ■ PE38 . . . . . .172 A5
Windsor Terr NR30. . . . . . .146 E3
Windsor Way NR31 . . . . . .170 B4
Windy Cres PE33. . . . . . . .63 B3
Windy La NR15 . . . . .107 B8
Windy Ridge PE33 . . . . . . .63 B3
WINFARTHING IP22. . . . . . .120 B4
Winfarthing Ave PE30. . . . .146 D3
Winfarthing Rd
  Banham NR16 . . . . .119 D6
  Shelfanger IP22 . . . . . . .120 B2
Wingate Way NR2. . . . . . .162 C7
WINGFIELD IP21. . . . . .131 E4
Wingfield PE30 . . . . .147 D5
WINGFIELD GREEN IP21. . .131 D4
Wingfield Rd
  Lakenheath IP27 . . . . . . .113 E2
  Norwich NR3. . . . . .162 D8
  Syleham IP21 . . . . .131 D5
  Weybread IP21 . . . . . . .131 F6
Wingfields PE38 . . . . .172 C3
Wing's La NR20. . . . . .33 B7
Wings Rd IP27. . . . . .113 E1
Winifred Ct NR26 . . . . . . .138 E7
Winifred Rd NR31. . . . . . .169 B3
Winifred Way NR20 . . . . . .168 D8
Winmer Ave ■ NR29. . . . . .58 B6
Winners Wlk NR8. . . . . . .155 E3
Winnold St PE38 . . . . . . .172 A6
Winn's Cl NR25 . . . . .137 A7
Winsford Way NR5. . . . . . .157 C1
Winstanley Rd ■ NR7 . . . . .72 D4
Winston Churchill Dr
  PE30. . . . . .147 C4
Winston Dr NR21 . . . . .15 E6
Winter Gdns★ NR30 . . . . .169 E2
Winter Rd NR2 . . . . .162 A6
Winterton Dures National
  Nature Reserve★ NR29 . . .58 B7
WINTERTON-ON-SEA
  NR29. . . . . .58 C6
Winterton Rd
  Hemsby NR29 . . . . .167 B8
  Somerton NR29. . . . . . . .57 F6
WISBECH PE13 . . . . .152 A6
Wisbech Castle★ PE13. . . .152 C4
Wisbech & Fenland Mus★
  PE13. . . . . .152 C4
Wisbech Gram Sch PE13. . .152 B5
Wisbech Rd
  King's Lynn PE30. . . . . . .146 D2
  Manea PE15. . . . . .95 A2
  Nordelph PE38 . . . . .78 D4
  Outwell PE14. . . . . .77 F7
  Walpole PE14 . . . . .41 D4
  Walsoken PE13. . . . . . . .152 E8
  Welney PE14 . . . . .95 D5
Wishing Well Cl IP27 . . . . .175 D4
Wissey View IP26. . . . . . .100 B4
Wistaria Rd PE13 . . . . . . .152 F7
Wisteria Cl NR20 . . . . . . .154 E3
Wisteria Dr NR18 . . . . . . .173 F7
Witard Cl NR7. . . . . .159 D1
Witard Rd NR7 . . . . .163 D6
Witchcraft Wy NR13. . . . . .72 E8
WITHERGATE NR28 . . . . . . .38 A6
Withersdale Rd IP20. . . . . .123 A1
Withington St ■ PE12 . . . . .41 B8

Withy Way NR8 ....155 E1
WITTON NR13 ....165 A6
WITTON BRIDGE NR28.... 23 E2
Witton Cl Heacham PE31 .133 C5
  Reedham NR13 ....92 F5
Witton Gn NR13 ....92 F5
Witton La NR13 ....165 A8
Wittons La IP21 ....131 A3
WIVETON NR25 ....7 E6
Wiveton Rd NR25 ....7 D6
Woburn St NR2 ....162 C5
Wodehouse Cl **1** NR12 ...39 B4
Wodehouse Ct **11** IP25...84 D3
Wodehouse Rd
  Bacton NR12 ....23 D4
  Old Hunstanton PE36 ...132 E7
Wodehouse St NR3 ....162 E8
Wolfe Rd NR1 ....163 B7
WOLFERD GREEN NR15...90 B2
WOLFERTON PE31 ....27 B7
Wolferton Dr PE37 ....153 B2
Wollaston Ave NR19 .....154 D7
Wolseley Rd NR31 ....169 B2
WOLTERTON NR11 ....20 E2
Wolterton Pk* NR11......20 E2
Wolterton Rd NR11 ....20 C2
Womersley Cl **5** NR1 ...163 B7
Womersley Rd NR1 ....163 B7
Wood Avens Way NR18..173 E4
WOODBASTWICK NR13....55 D2
Woodbastwick Rd
  Blofield Heath NR13 .....73 C6
  Blofield NR13.....165 E7
  Woodbastwick NR13......55 E1
Woodbine Cl
  North Walsham NR28 ....151 F5
  Potter Heigham NR29 ....56 F7
Woodbridge Way PE30..147 D4
Wood Cl Brandon IP27 ...175 D2
  Kenninghall NR16 ....119 A4
Woodcock Cl NR3 ....158 D3
Woodcock Hill **4** NR8...70 C7
Woodcock La PE34 ....61 B7
Woodcock Mews **4**
  NR31 ....170 A6
Woodcock Rd
  Cromer NR27...........139 B5
  Norwich NR3 ....158 C3
  Stonebridge IP24...........102 B2
Woodcock Rise IP27...175 F4
Woodcock's La NR9......88 A8
Woodcote Pk PE13...........152 A4
Woodcroft Cl NR7 ....159 E2
Woodcutters Wy IP27...113 E2
WOOD DALLING NR11....34 D6
Wood Dalling Rd
  Guestwick NR20 ....34 A6
  Reepham NR10 ....149 C6
Wood Dr **11** Beetley
  NR20 ....49 D4
  11 Beetley NR20...........49 D4
Wood End Cl NR14...........109 F8
Woodend Rd PE31 ....133 E5
Woodfarm La NR31...........170 A2
Woodfield Briston NR24...142 C4
  1 East Dereham NR19 ...154 D1
Woodfield Rd NR25...........137 C7
Woodforde Rd NR7 ....159 D2
Woodfordes Brewery &
  Visitors Ctr* NR13.....55 C2
WOODGATE NR20...........50 C3
Woodgate **12** NR4...........89 B8
Woodgate La NR20...........50 B3
Woodgate Rd NR20...........50 A2
Woodgate Way PE31...134 F4
Woodgate Wy NR11...150 A5
Wood Gn NR13 ....72 F8
WOOD GREEN NR15...106 F2
Woodhall Rd PE38 ....97 B8
Woodham Leas NR6 ...158 E6
Wood Hill NR8...........156 D8
Woodhill Rise NR5...........161 C8
Woodhouse Cl **1** NR26 ..138 B6

Wood La Aldeby NR34.....110 E5
  Bedingham NR35...........108 C2
  Bradenham IP25...........66 D4
  Bressingham IP22...........119 E2
  Bunwell NR16 ....105 D3
  Burgh & Tuttington NR11...36 D5
  Dickleburgh & Rushall
    IP21 ....130 F6
  Great Ellingham NR17...103 D8
  Hepworth IP22 ....127 E2
  Holme Hale IP25...........66 B1
  Honingham NR9...........69 E8
  Kelling NR25 ....8 C5
  Little Ellingham NR17.....86 B1
  Long Stratton NR15...........107 A2
  Morley NR18 ....87 A1
  Pulham Market IP21...121 E8
  Scole IP21...........130 F8
  Starston IP20 ....122 C5
  Strumpshaw NR13...........73 F2
  Swardeston NR14...........89 C5
  Thelnetham IP22...........128 A2
  Watton IP25 ....84 E3
  Wicklewood NR18...........87 B4
Woodland Dr
  Bungay NR35...........124 A7
  Ellingham NR35...........109 E3
  Norwich NR6 ....158 E6
  Thorpe End NR13...........72 D5
Woodland Farm Ind Units
  NR10...........53 A6
Woodland Gdns PE30 ...148 D5
Woodland La NR24...........142 F2
Woodland Rd NR6 ....157 E6
Woodland Rise
  Cromer NR27...........139 E4
  Sheringham NR26...........138 E5
  12 Tasburgh NR15...........106 F6
Woodland Rise W NR26..138 D4
Woodlands
  35 Harleston IP20...........122 D2
  7 Thorpe Marriott NR8...155 B2
Woodlands Cl Holt NR25..137 D7
  4 Thetford IP24...........176 E6
Woodlands Cres **1** NR7...72 D5
Woodlands Ct PE13...........152 F7
Woodlands Dr IP24...........176 D6
Woodlands Mid Sch
  NR31...........94 C6
Woodlands Rd NR5...........157 A2
Woodlands Rise IP27...175 A2
Woodlands The IP25...........84 A7
Woodlands Way Rd NR12..55 D4
Woodland View Jun Sch
  NR10...........54 A2
Woodland View Mobile
  Home Pk NR10...........53 D6
Woodlark Cl **2** IP24...........176 D2
WOOD NORTON NR20...33 A7
Wood Norton Rd
  Foulsham NR20 ....33 C5
  Stibbard NR21...........32 E7
Woodpecker Dr **8** IP25..84 C3
Woodpecker La NR4...........161 B1
Woodpecker Mews **5**
  NR31...........170 A6
Woodpecker Wy NR8...156 B5
WOODRISING NR9...........85 E6
Woodrising Rd NR9...........85 D4
Wood Rising Rd NR9...........86 A5
Woodrow Ave NR25...........137 B5
Woodrow La NR15...........121 A8
Woodrow Pl NR1 ....163 B6
Woodruff Cl **3** NR6...........158 D5
Wood St Rd NR29...........56 B8
Woods Cl
  Ditchingham NR35...........109 A2
  3 Hethersett NR9...........88 C7
Woods End NR17...........174 C4
Woodside
  Burnham Market PE31 ...135 A2
  5 King's Lynn PE30...147 C4
  North Walsham NR28 ....151 E4
Woodside Ave
  Dersingham PE31 ....140 C5
  Heacham PE31 ....133 D4

Woodside Cl
  Attleborough NR17...........174 C3
  Dersingham PE31 ....140 C5
  1 Taverham NR8...........155 C1
Woodside Ct NR17...........174 C3
Woodside Pk NR17...........174 C3
Woodside Rd NR7 ....159 E1
Wood's La NR20 ....49 B8
Wood St Norwich NR1...178 A1
  Wisbech PE13...........152 B6
Woodstock La NR15...........120 F8
Woodstock Way **3** NR29...57 D4
WOODTON NR35...........108 C4
Woodton Prim Sch
  NR35...........108 C5
Woodton Rd NR35...........108 A7
Woodview NR28...........38 A4
Wood View NR28...........151 A4
Wood View Cl IP25...........84 C4
Wood View Ct NR5...........157 A2
Woodview Rd NR9...........70 B5
Wood View Rd NR6...........157 E5
Woodward Ave
  12 Necton PE37...........65 F4
  6 Necton PE37...........66 A4
Woodward Cl PE33...........62 D4
Woodward Rd NR3...........158 B2
Woodwark Ave **3** PE30 ...146 E6
Woodyard **14** NR16...........118 C5
Woodyard Cl **9** NR14...........89 B3
Woodyard Sq The NR35 ..108 C5
Wooll Dr NR8...........151 D7
Woolner's La NR14 ....90 E7
Woolstencroft Ave PE30..146 F7
Worcester Rd PE30...........147 B7
Worcester St **3** NR29...167 A2
Worcester Rd
  New Costessey NR5...........156 C1
  Wisbech PE13...........152 C7
Worcester Way
  Attleborough NR17...........174 E4
  Great Yarmouth NR31...170 B4
Wordsworth Cl PE38 ...172 D5
Wordsworth Gn IP24...176 E7
Wordsworth Rd
  2 Diss IP22...........177 E4
  Norwich NR5...........161 C6
Workhouse La
  Foulsham NR20 ....33 D4
  Lundy Green NR15 ...... 107 D3
  Tilney St Lawrence NR34...42 C1
  Upwell PE14 ....77 D4
Workhouse Rd NR12...........38 C3
Worlds End NR13...........74 C1
WORMEGAY PE33...........62 C7
Wormegay CE Prim Sch
  PE33...........62 A6
Wormegay Rd
  Blackborough End PE32 ...44 C1
  Wormegay PE32...........62 D8
WORSTEAD NR28...........38 A5
Worstead CE Prim Sch
  NR28...........38 A5
Worstead Rd NR28...........38 A4
Worstead Sta NR28...........37 F4
WORTHAM IP22...........129 B4
Wortham Cl **3** NR5...........161 A8
Wortham Prim Sch IP22..129 C4
WORTHING NR20...........49 F6
Worthing Rd
  North Elmham NR20 ....49 F7
  Swanton Morley NR20...........50 B6
WORTWELL IP20...........123 B4
WRAMPLINGHAM NR9......69 E1
Wramplingham Rd NR18..173 D8
Wrench Cl **4** NR11...........150 D6
Wrench Rd NR5...........161 D6
Wren Cl Brandon IP27...175 E3
  Necton PE37...........66 A3
  Norwich NR4...........161 B2
Wren Dr
  2 Great Yarmouth NR31..94 C7
  Great Yarmouth NR31...170 A6
WRENINGHAM NR16...........88 D1
Wreningham Prim Sch
  NR16...........88 D1

Wrens The **1** IP24......176 D2
Wretham Rd IP24...........102 E3
WRETTON PE33...........80 E3
Wretton Fen Dro PE33...80 D1
Wretton Rd PE33...........80 F2
Wretton Row PE33...........80 E3
Wright Ave NR19...........154 D1
Wright Cl NR30...........168 E7
Wright Dr NR19...........154 C4
Wrights Cl NR11...........150 C7
Wright's Cl Holt NR25....137 C7
  North Walsham NR28 ....151 B4
Wright's La PE12...........41 B8
Wright's Loke NR28...........22 E5
Wright's Wlk **12** NR19...154 D5
Wroe The PE14...........59 C1
Wroo Rd NR17...........103 F5
Wroughton Infant Sch
  NR31...........170 B6
Wroughton Jun Sch
  NR31...........170 B7
WROXHAM NR12...........164 D3
Wroxham Ave PE37...153 C2
Wroxham Rd
  Coltishall NR12...........54 E6
  Rackheath NR13...........72 D8
  Salhouse NR13...........54 E2
  Sprowston NR7...........159 C5
Wroxham Sta NR12...........164 C6
Wyatt St PE31...........146 E5
Wyatt Way IP24...........176 B7
Wycliffe Rd NR4...........161 D3
Wylde Croft NR8...........155 D2
Wymans Way NR21...........141 E5
Wymbur Dr NR17...........174 E4
Wymer Dr NR11...........150 C4
Wymers La NR13...........74 B8
Wymer St NR2...........162 B6
WYMONDHAM NR18...173 E5
Wymondham Abbey (rems)*
  NR18...........173 B3
Wymondham Abbey Sta
  NR18...........173 A3
Wymondham Bsns Pk
  NR18...........173 B2
Wymondham Coll NR18...87 B1
Wymondham Heritage Mus*
  NR18...........173 C4
Wymondham High Sch
  NR18...........173 C5
Wymondham Hist Rly Sta*
  NR18...........173 D2
Wymondham Leisure Ctr
  NR18...........173 C4
Wymondham Rd
  Bracon Ash NR14...........88 E2
  Bunwell NR16...........105 B5
  East Carleton NR14...........88 F4
  Flordon NR15...........106 C8
  Kimberley NR18...........87 B6
  Morley NR18...........87 A3
  Wreningham NR16...........88 B2
  Wymondham NR18...........105 A8
Wymondham Sta NR18..173 C2
Wyndfields **10** PE37...65 F4
Wyndham Pk NR27...........10 C5
Wyndham St NR26...........138 D7
Wyngates NR13...........165 F6
Wynne's La PE34...........145 C4

Y

Yallop Ave NR31...........171 D8
Yare Cl
  Caister-on-Sea NR30.....168 D6
  Great Yarmouth NR30...169 C6
Yare Rd NR31...........94 A6
Yare Valley Dr NR4...........161 C2
Yare Valley Rise NR13...165 C3
Yare View Cl NR13...........92 F4
Yarmouth Bsns Pk NR31.169 B2
Yarmouth Rd
  Blofield NR13...........165 F6
  Broome NR35...........110 C2
  Brundall NR13...........165 C5

Yarmouth Rd continued
  Caister-on-Sea NR30......168 E2
  Corton NR32...........171 D1
  Dilham NR28...........38 C4
  Geldeston NR34...........110 A3
  Hales NR14...........109 F8
  Hemsby NR29...........167 A6
  Kirby Cane NR35...........109 E3
  Lound NR32...........94 B3
  Ludham NR29...........56 C5
  North Walsham NR28 ....151 C4
  Norwich NR7...........163 E5
  Ormesby St Margaret
    NR29...........167 C1
  Postwick with Witton
    NR13...........165 A5
  Raveningham NR14...........110 B8
  Stalham NR12...........39 B3
  Thurlton NR14...........93 A1
  Toft Monks NR34...........110 C6
  Worstead NR28...........38 A6
Yarmouth Stadium NR30 168 E2
Yarmouth Way NR30...169 C3
Yarn Mews **2** NR3...........178 B4
Yarrington Way NR5...160 E8
Yarrow Cl IP24...........176 F5
Yarrow Rd Bintree NR20...33 B2
  2 Dereham NR20...........68 A8
YAXHAM NR19...........68 A5
Yaxham CE Prim Sch
  NR19...........68 C6
Yaxham Rd
  East Dereham NR19...........154 E4
  Mattishall NR20...........68 C8
Yaxham Sta NR19...........68 A4
YAXLEY IP23...........130 A1
Yaxley's La NR11...........150 C6
Yaxley's Rd NR30...........169 B6
Yaxley Way NR5...........161 A8
Yeats Way NR19...........154 B6
YELVERTON NR14...........90 E5
Yelverton Cl NR6...........157 D5
Yelverton Rd NR14...........90 E5
Yeoman's Cl **2** NR35 ...124 B8
Yesmere **16** NR14...........89 B3
Yesterday's World*
  NR30...........169 E3
Yew Ct NR7...........159 D4
Yew Dr IP27...........175 D2
Yew Tree Cl **24** NR31...94 C7
Yew Tree Ct NR20...........69 B7
Yew Tree Hollow **25**
  NR15...........106 E3
Yew Tree Rd NR17...........174 C5
Yew Tree Wy **12** NR20...68 A8
York Ave PE36...........132 D5
York Gdns PE13...........152 D6
York La **13** NR12...........39 B4
York Rd **4** Cromer NR27...139 D5
  Great Yarmouth NR30 ...169 D3
  King's Lynn PE30...........146 E3
  Wisbech PE13...........152 D6
York Row PE13...........152 C5
York St NR2...........162 B4
York Terr Cromer NR27 ...139 D5
  Wisbech PE13...........152 C6
York Villa Cl NR29...........75 E8
York Way IP24...........176 B5
Youell Ave NR31...........170 D1
Youngmans Cl NR28...........151 D3
Youngmans La NR12...........38 E6
Youngman's La NR10...........37 C5
Youngmans Rd NR18...........173 C8
Young's Cres NR13...........92 E7
Young's Row PE12...........41 A8

Z

Zara Way NR19...........154 C1
Zephyr Cl NR30...........168 D7
Zig-Zag La NR15...........108 C8
Zobel Cl NR3...........157 F2
Zurich Cl NR31...........171 E4